ARVIND V. PHATAK

TEMPLE UNIVERSITY

INTERNATIONAL MANAGEMENT

CONCEPTS & CASES

SOUTH-WESTERN College Publishing

An International Thomson Publishing Company

Editor-in-Chief: Valerie A. Ashton
Acquisitions Editor: Randy G. Haubner
Production Editor: Shelley Brewer
Production House: Cover to Cover
Cover Design: Tin Box Studio/Sandy Weinstein
Cover Photos: Images provided by © 1994 Photo Disc
Marketing Manager: Stephen E. Momper

Library of Congress Cataloging-in-Publication Data

Phatak, Arvind V.
    International management : concepts and cases / Arvind V. Phatak.
      p.   cm.
    Includes bibliographical references and index.
    ISBN 0-538-85415-4
    1. International business enterprises--Management. 2. Industrial
management. 3. Competition, International. I. Title.
    HD62.4.P523   1996
    658'.049--dc20
                                              96-35066
                                             CIP

1 2 3 4 5 6 7 8 9 MT 4 3 2 1 0 9 8 7 6
Printed in the United States of America

I(T)P
International Thomson Publishing
South-Western College Publishing is an ITP Company.
The ITP trademark is used under license.

Preface

The world was quite different when I wrote my first book, *Evolution of World Enterprises*, some 25 years ago. There was no North American Free Trade Agreement (NAFTA), the European Union was in its infancy, the Soviet Union was a dominant global power, the Pacific Basin countries were still in the developing stage economically, Japan was starting to impose its financial and industrial muscle in the global economic arena, and India, China, Mexico, and Brazil were economically poor and underdeveloped. Politically the world was divided into three blocs— the Western bloc led by the United States, the Eastern bloc led by the Soviet Union, and a third bloc comprising the so-called non-aligned countries.

How things have changed. Now we have NAFTA linking the economies of Canada, the United States, and Mexico. The European Union has mushroomed to include fifteen countries that are linked to form a unified common market; the Soviet Union no longer exists and in its place we have several independent countries that are committed to deregulation and market-driven economies; the countries of the Pacific Basin have emerged as dominant economic powers on the world economic scene; and Brazil, China, Mexico, and India—having abandoned state-controlled economic systems—have embraced free trade and economic liberalization, placed out the welcome mat to foreign companies and investments, and braced themselves to become the emerging economic giants of the next century.

More than ever before, we live in a world of interdependent nation-states. The worldwide drive towards free trade, coupled with the considerable ease with which labor, capital, knowledge, raw materials, managerial capabilities, and intermediate and finished goods and services can be transferred and traded among countries, have given companies that primarily served the home markets the incentive to reach out and serve foreign markets as well. The opening up of markets that were once closed to foreign companies has brought foreign competition within the once-protected borders of such countries. In most, if not all, industries survival of companies requires competition in key foreign markets. Consequently, companies that are no longer protected from foreign competitors are themselves propelled into establishing operations in foreign markets in order to make a dent into the competitive armor of their foreign competitors. The numerous manufacturing plants and marketing organizations established by European, Korean, Japanese, German, Swedish, and American car companies in each others' markets are examples of companies counterattacking competitors in order to exploit foreign market opportunities and to protect their respective domestic and world market shares.

International companies are the beneficiaries of, as well as the reason for, the growing interdependence among nations. Countries and companies can raise capital in the many financial centers of the world, such as New York, London, Paris, Zurich, Singapore, Hong Kong, and Tokyo. Comparative advantage of countries is often the factor that decides where certain components and finished products produced are manufactured, and where they are eventually marketed. For example, Levi Strauss has jeans and other apparel made by contractors in Bangladesh that are then sold in markets throughout the world. IBM, Microsoft, and other U.S.-based computer software companies have their software written by Indian software developers based in India as well as in the United States. Such activities involving the transfer by international companies of capital, knowledge, people, resources, and products from one country to another is a consequence of, as well as the promoter of, the interdependence among nation-states of the world.

The Focus of the Book

This book is about the challenges, tasks, processes, and practices that managers in international companies are involved in all the time. The basic premise of this book is that managing an international company brings forth managerial dilemmas and challenges that are not only different in nature but far more complex than those normally encountered by managers in a largely domestically oriented company. As such, the emphasis of this book is upon the managerial processes, tasks, and issues that managers in an international company must handle effectively in a dynamic global economic, political, legal, and cultural environment of international business.

Why I Wrote This Book

Some years ago I wrote *International Dimensions of Management*, which is now in its 4th edition. That book is primarily aimed as a supplementary text to be used in conjunction with a main text in courses that need to incorporate the international dimensions in the course contents. Several colleagues urged me to write a full-length book on international management, including text and mini-cases, which could be used as a principal text in a free-standing international management course. I succumbed to the encouragement offered by my colleagues and wrote this book for them and for their students. As such I have built this book on the foundation provided by *International Dimensions of Management*.

What Sets This Book Apart

I have found that students like real examples from the business press of concepts discussed in the classroom. Contemporary business examples make the subject real and "alive." I ask my students to bring to each class clippings from business magazines such as *Fortune, Business Week, The Wall Street Journal,* and *The Economist,* and other places such as the business sections of *The New York Times* and local newspapers. We spend several minutes discussing what has been read in the business press. I have transposed this practice into this book in the form of *practical insights*. Numerous practical insights sprinkled throughout the book illustrate key concepts with contemporary examples of events and phenomenon from the business world. Students should be able to relate the concepts presented in the book to the realities of the business world, and practical insights are meant to do this.

Many teachers like the opportunity to discuss mini-cases as well as comprehensive cases to illustrate and apply the key ideas developed in the book chapters. To that end, one or more mini-cases are included after each chapter, and several comprehensive cases are included at the end of the book. Typically a mini-case could be discussed in 20 to 30 minutes of class time. Analyses and discussion of the comprehensive cases at the end of the book might consume anywhere from one to one and one-half hours.

How the Chapters Are Organized

The organization of the book follows the following structure:

Part 1. Introduction to International Management and International Companies
Part 2. The International Business Environment
Part 3. Management in the International Context

Part 1 serves as an introduction to international business, international management, and international companies. Throughout the book the terms international, multinational, global, and transnational are used synonymously and the reasons for doing so are explained in this section.

Chapter 1 includes topics such as the definition of international management, the evolution of international companies, and the generic objectives and sources of competitive advantage of international/global companies.

Part 2 includes an examination of the dynamic external environment in which international companies have to function. Chapters 2 and 3 focus on the international economic environment, and Chapters 4, 5, and 6 cover the international legal, political, and cultural environments, respectively.

Part 3 is mainly about the management functions in an international company. Chapter 7 deals with the subject of international business negotiations. Chapters 8, 9, 10, and 11 examine strategic planning, international functional dispersion and integration strategies, modes of entry into foreign markets, and strategies for competitive superiority, respectively. Chapter 12 describes the basic organizational design patterns in international companies. Chapter 13 focuses on international human resources management, and Chapter 14 is an examination of the process of controlling foreign subsidiaries. Chapter 15 discusses the ethical and moral dilemmas facing international managers as they perform the managerial functions in a diversified international business environment.

Different Formats for Using the Text

The contents of this book can be organized in a variety of ways. Instructors may choose to have students read the five chapters on the environment of international business on their own if there is a course specifically designed to cover this subject in the curriculum. In such cases instructors should cover Chapter 1 and than proceed directly to Chapter 7. However, in a course dedicated to the subject of international management, every attempt should be made to render comprehensive in-class coverage of Chapters 7 through 15. Nevertheless, students must be made to appreciate the challenges and problems that the international business environment bestows upon international managers.

The mini-cases after each chapter could be discussed immediately after the completion of a chapter, alternatively, several mini-cases could be discussed as a group after the completion of several chapters in Part 2, and again after Part 3. I suggest that several sessions be reserved after all chapters have been discussed in class for the discussion of the comprehensive cases at the end of the book.

Supplements

Instructor's Manual and Test Bank   A comprehensive instructor's manual designed to help in the instructor's classroom teaching responsibilities is available. The manual contains a detailed outline of the key concepts in each chapter presented in a format suitable for use as teaching notes by the instructor. A large multiple-choice test bank is available as well. The instructor's manual includes a listing of cases that are available from a variety of sources, as well as a list of videos, which can be used in conjunction with this book.

Acknowledgments

I would like to thank the many people who made this book possible. My students at Temple University who sharpened my thinking by their challenging questions and observations deserve my gratitude.

I am grateful to the following reviewers for their constructive critiques and suggestions. I sincerely believe that their comments were invaluable in improving the quality of this book:

Refik Culpan, Penn State Harrisburg
Peter J. Dowling, University of Tasmania
Rakesh B. Sambnarya, Rutgers University—Camden
Ryh-Song Yeh, The Chinese University of Hong Kong

I thank Sri Beldona for obtaining permissions for all copyrighted materials, and for obtaining information and statistics without much notice. Harsh Mishra and Shoba Annavarjula were most helpful in developing the instructor's manual. I could not have finished this book on schedule without the tireless work of John Volkmar. John was instrumental in managing the entire book project—keeping track of various deadlines, drawing the graphs and charts on PowerPoint, writing and calling case contributors for updates and permissions, more than once going through the entire manuscript to check for inconsistencies and misplacement of references, and keeping in constant contact with my publisher. Thank you very much John for your help and support.

I am grateful to the Marketing/Management Team at South-Western College Publishing for their sincere interest and help in ensuring that this book was published on schedule. They include Randy Haubner, Acquisitions Editor; Shelley Brewer, Production Editor; Steve Momper, Marketing Manager; and Sue Disselkamp, Manufacturing Coordinator. Others who contributed include Debbie Kokoruda, Art Director; Julie Batsch, Promotions Project Manager; and at Cover to Cover Publishing, Sandra Thomson.

I must thank my wife Rhoda and my children for being my cheerleaders. There were times when I was ready to give up on this book, but their cheerful encouragement kept me going. Rhoda typed almost all practical insights borrowed from magazines and newspapers, photocopied countless newspaper columns, and provided me with the administrative support I needed when I did my work at home. Thanks Rhoda!

When I signed my book contract with South-Western in June 1993, I made a pledge to my brother, Anil, that I would complete this book and that I would dedicate it to him. Anil passed away on January 31, 1994.

To the everlasting memory of my dear brother, Anil (August 7, 1939–January 31, 1994).

. . . But the good they die young,
I looked around and he's gone.

Contents

Contents

Contents

Contents

Contents

Contents

Contents

An Introduction to International Companies and International Management

LEARNING OBJECTIVES

After completing this chapter, you will be able to:

- Define international management, international companies, and international business.
- Discuss the stages of development of an international company.
- Explain the sources of competitive advantage for an international firm and three strategic objectives it may pursue to attain that advantage.

This book is about the challenge of managing the international activities of international companies. As such, it is about the unique opportunities and problems that confront managers in international companies as they navigate through the extremely complex and ever-changing economic, political, legal, and cultural environment of a world of increasingly interdependent nation-states. The choices that international managers make—regarding plant location, products and services marketed in different countries or regions of the world, the mode used to penetrate foreign markets, the hiring of personnel to manage foreign operations, and so on—must take into account the limits imposed on such choices by the external environment, as well as the imperative to simultaneously adapt to local conditions and to function efficiently on a global scale.

The need for international management in a firm becomes critical when a company becomes involved in foreign direct investment. Foreign direct investment (FDI) is a long-term equity investment in a foreign affiliate or subsidiary; it gives the parent company (the investor) varying degrees of managerial control over the foreign operation, depending upon the percentage of ownership by the parent company. The more FDI that a company makes in a foreign affiliate, the greater the managerial control that it would have over that foreign affiliate. FDI involves the establishment of facilities, buildings, plants, and equipment for the production of goods and/or services in a foreign country. FDI is accompanied by the need to manage, market, and finance the foreign production. Enterprise functions such as marketing, production, and finance are managed by people. Managing the various enterprise functions abroad requires that managers in the parent company, as well as in every foreign affiliate, have the necessary skills and experience to manage the affairs of affiliates in countries whose political, cultural, economic, and financial environments may be very different from one another. It therefore follows that the greater a company's FDI, the greater its need for skilled international managers.

International management activities in a firm begin when the firm's managers either initiate the establishment of a foreign affiliate from scratch or buy an existing firm, and they continue as long as there are one or more functioning foreign affiliates owned by the parent company.

Throughout this book, when we consider the elements of international management, our subject will always be the international, multinational, global, or transnational firm. *Many scholars of international business make a distinction among international, multinational, global, and transnational companies; however, the rationale for using the terms interchangeably will be explained in detail in Chapter 9. Also used synonymously are the terms affiliate and subsidiary; in addition, we make no distinction among the terms company, corporation, enterprise, and firm.*

WHAT IS INTERNATIONAL BUSINESS?

International companies are simultaneously involved in several international business activities such as export, import, countertrade, licensing, and foreign direct investment. Therefore, we should at this juncture understand what international business is. There are many different definitions of international business. First let us see what some of them are, and then we shall arrive at our own definition.

John D. Daniels and Lee H. Radebaugh define international business as "all business transactions that involve two or more countries."[1] The business relationships may be private or governmental. In the case of private firms the transactions are for profit.

Government-sponsored activities in international business may or may not have a profit orientation. Donald A. Ball and Wendell H. McCullough, Jr. say that international business is "business whose activities involve the crossing of national boundaries."[2] To Betty Jane Punett and David A. Ricks, it is "any commercial, industrial, or professional endeavor involving two or more nations."[3]

There are many such definitions of international business. We shall define *international business* as *those business activities of private or public enterprises that involve the movement across national boundaries of resources, goods, services, knowledge, or skills.* The resources that may be involved in the transfer are raw materials, capital, and people; goods transferred may include semifinished and finished assemblies and products; services transferred include functions such as accounting, legal counsel, and banking activities; knowledge includes technology and organizational learning; and skills sent from one country to another include managerial and technical skills.

INTERNATIONAL MANAGEMENT DEFINED

In very general terms, international management is the management of a firm's activities on an international scale. Before we define international management, let us define the term management.

Management is the process aimed at accomplishing organizational objectives by (1) effectively coordinating the procurement, allocation, and utilization of the human, financial, intellectual, and physical resources of the organization and (2) maintaining the organization in a state of satisfactory, dynamic equilibrium with the environment. There are two basic premises in this definition of management. First, management is needed to coordinate the human, financial, intellectual, and physical resources, and to integrate them into a unified whole. Without such coordination the resources would remain unrelated and disorganized and, therefore, inefficiently used. The second premise in the definition is that an organization lives in a dynamic environment that constantly affects its operations. Thus, one managerial task is to forecast the environmental forces that are likely to have a significant impact on the firm in the immediate and distant future, and to determine the probable impact. Also, managers must respond to the environmental forecasts by designing appropriate strategies to ensure the survival and growth of the organization as it interacts with its dynamic environment.

On the basis of the preceding definition of management, we can now define international management as *a process of accomplishing the global objectives of a firm by (1) effectively coordinating the procurement, allocation, and utilization of the human, financial, intellectual, and physical resources of the firm within and across national boundaries and (2) effectively charting the path toward the desired organizational goals by navigating the firm through a global environment that is not only dynamic but often very hostile to the firm's very survival.*

INTERNATIONAL MANAGEMENT AND INTERNATIONAL COMPANIES

Any firm that has one or more foreign affiliates is involved in international management; it does not have to be a billion-dollar corporation. Even small- and medium-sized firms can and do have international operations in several countries. Many international companies do not qualify for the Fortune 500 or the Business Week Global 1000 list of the largest international corporations. Even though they do not come close to Ford and General Motors in terms of total sales, gross profits, total assets, and other similar measures of company size, they are still multinational companies. Many firms in Europe and Japan have also developed a multinational structure; and, in the last ten years or so, we have seen many government-owned enterprises that have become multinational. The 1960s laid the foundations for the massive growth of international companies. The growth of that decade far exceeded any achieved earlier by the United States or other industrialized countries of the world.

Although international enterprises are dissimilar in many respects (size of sales and profits, markets served, and location of affiliates abroad) they all have some common features. To begin, *an international company is an enterprise that has operations in two or more countries. If it has operations in several countries then it may have a network of wholly or partially (jointly with one or more foreign partners) owned producing and marketing foreign affiliates or subsidiaries. The foreign affiliates may be linked with the parent company and with each other by ties of common ownership and by a common global strategy to which each affiliate is responsive and committed. The parent company may control the foreign affiliates via resources that it allocates to each affiliate—capital, technology, trademarks, patents, and manpower—and through the right to approve each affiliate's long- and short-range plans and budgets.*

As pointed out earlier, there are many small- and medium-sized multinational companies. However, generally we are talking about a large corporation whose revenues, profits, and assets typically run into hundreds of millions of dollars. For example, sales of Japan's Mitsubishi Corporation, ranked number one in the world on the basis of total sales in *The Business Week Global 1000*, were reported to be $206.3 billion. In that same year the profits of the Royal Dutch/ Shell Group, the largest in the world in terms of profitability, were reported to be $6.43 billion.[4] The top 100 international companies in the world had about $3.4 trillion in assets in 1992, of which approximately $1.3 trillion were held outside their respective home countries.[5] The economic power of these companies is evident in the fact that they are estimated to account for about one-third of the combined outward FDI of their home countries. Because the largest international companies control such a large pool of assets, they exercise considerable influence over the home and host countries' output, economic policies, trade and technology flows, and employment and labor practices.

Another characteristic of multinational companies is that they own a large number of foreign affiliates. During the early 1990s, there were about 37,000 international companies, of which 26,000 were based in fourteen developed home countries. The total number of foreign affiliates stands at about 206,000,[6] a dramatic increase over the 3,500 manufacturing affiliates established between 1946-1961.[7] These developments have resulted in the sales of foreign affiliates exceeding exports as the principle means of bringing goods and services to foreign markets.[8]

International companies tend to gravitate toward certain types of business activities. The assets of large multinational companies are deployed in motor vehicle manufacture, electronics, mining and petroleum, trading, and chemical and pharmaceutical industries.[9]

A large proportion of the total business activities of multinational companies is located in the developed countries of Western Europe, Canada, Japan, and the United States. It is estimated that about two-thirds of the world's direct investments are in the developed countries.

THE ENVIRONMENT OF INTERNATIONAL MANAGEMENT

A manager in an international company performs her or his managerial functions in an environment that is far more complex than that of her or his counterpart in a domestic company (see Figure 1-1). The international environment is the total world environment. However, it is also the sum total of the environments of every nation in which the company has its foreign affiliates. The environment within each nation consists of four dimensions: economic, legal, political, and cultural. Exhibit 1-1 lists the factors typically found in each element of the environment. We shall examine the economic dimension in Chapters 2 and 3, and will take up the remaining three dimensions in Chapters 4, 5, and 6, respectively.

DIFFERENT TYPES OF INTERNATIONAL BUSINESS

An international company can achieve its international business aims via different forms of foreign market entry modes such as

- Exporting
- Countertrade
- Contract manufacturing
- Licensing
- Franchising
- Turnkey projects
- Equity-based ventures: wholly owned/joint ventures

We shall examine these entry modes in detail in Chapter 10.

EVOLUTION OF A GLOBAL ENTERPRISE

As a uninational (domestic) company evolves into a full-fledged global enterprise, it goes through several distinct but overlapping evolutionary stages. Some companies go through these stages rapidly—in a few years—whereas others may take many years to evolve into truly global firms. All companies do not systematically proceed from one evolutionary stage to another; some skip one or several of the stages. The following applies mainly to manufacturing firms. The evolutionary pattern in service firms is covered following this section.

FIGURE 1-1
The International Environment

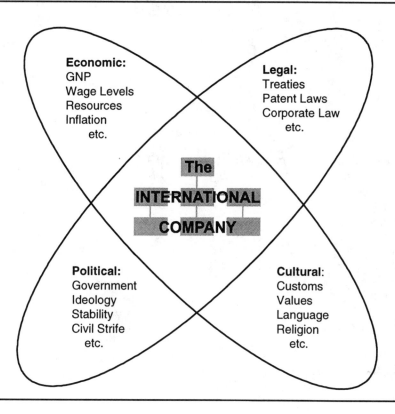

Stage 1: Foreign Inquiry

Stage 1 begins when a company receives an inquiry about one of its products directly from a foreign businessperson or from an independent domestic exporter and importer. The company may ignore the inquiry, in which case there is no further evolutionary development. However, if the company responds positively and has its product sold in the foreign market at a profit, then the stage is set for more sales of its products abroad; and the company executives probably become favorably disposed toward the export of their products. Other inquiries from foreign buyers are received more enthusiastically, and the company sells its products abroad through a domestic export middleperson. The middleperson could be an export merchant, an export commission house, a resident buyer (a buyer who is domiciled in the exporting company's home market and represents all types of private or governmental foreign buyers), a broker, a combination export manager (an exporter who serves as the exclusive export department of several noncompeting manufacturers), or a manufacturer's agent. (Unlike the combination export managers, who make sales in the name of each company they represent, the manufacturer's agents retain their identifies by operating in their own names.)

EXHIBIT 1-1
The International Environment

Economic Environment
Level of economic development
Population
Gross national product
Per capita income
Literacy level
Social infrastructure
Natural resources
Climate
Membership in regional economic blocs (EU; NAFTA; LAFTA)
Monetary and fiscal policies
Wage and salary levels
Nature of competition
Currency convertability
Inflation
Taxation system
Interest rates

Legal Environment
Legal tradition
Effectiveness of legal system
Treaties with foreign nations
Patent trademark laws
Laws affecting business firms

Political System
Form of government
Political ideology
Stability of government
Strength of opposition parties and groups
Social unrest
Political strife and insurgency
Governmental attitude towards foreign firms
Foreign policy

Cultural Environment
Customs, norms, values, beliefs
Language
Attitudes
Motivations
Social institutions
Status symbols
Religious beliefs

Stage 2: Export Manager

As the company's exports continue to expand and the executives decide that the time is ripe to take export management into their own hands and no longer rely on unsolicited inquiries from abroad, a decision is made to assume a proactive rather than a reactive posture towards exports. Hence, an export manager with a small staff is appointed to actively search for foreign markets for the company's products.

Stage 3: Export Department and Direct Sales

As export sales continue their upward surge, the company has difficulty operating with only an export manager and his or her small staff. A full-fledged export department or division is established at the same level as the domestic sales department. The company then drops the domestic export middleperson and begins to sell directly to importers or buyers located in foreign markets.

Stage 4: Sales Branches and Subsidiaries

Further growth of export sales requires the establishment of sales branches abroad to handle sales and promotional work. A sales branch manager is directly responsible to the home office, and the branch sells directly to middlepersons in the foreign markets. A sales branch gradually evolves into a sales subsidiary, which is incorporated and domiciled in the foreign country, and which enjoys greater autonomy than it had as a sales branch.

Stage 5: Assembly Abroad

Assembly abroad occurs for three major reasons: cheaper shipping costs for unassembled products, lower tariffs, and cheaper labor. The company may begin assembly operation in one or more of the foreign markets if it is more profitable to export the disassembled product abroad rather than the whole product. Often tariffs and transportation costs are lower on unassembled parts and components than on the assembled, finished product. For example, the parts of an unassembled TV set can be packed in a smaller box than can a fully assembled set. Because surface freight is charged on volume, unassembled parts in a smaller box are cheaper to ship than is a fully assembled set in a much larger box. Also, tariffs in the form of customs duties on imports are often less on the unassembled product (because of the smaller amount of value added in an unassembled product) than on the finished product. A large number of Japanese TV sets are assembled in India for these reasons.

Companies often establish assembly operations abroad for a third reason—to take advantage of the foreign country's pool of cheap labor. For this purpose, many American, European, and Japanese companies have established assembly operations in Mexico, Singapore, India, Sri Lanka, Mauritius, and the Dominican Republic. Products assembled in these countries are primarily meant to serve the American and third-country (neither home nor host) markets of Europe and Japan. For example, Westinghouse Electric Corporation has built four plants in the Dominican Republic to assemble a wide variety of electromechanical and electronic products that are then shipped to its plants in Puerto Rico or the United States for finishing and testing. Carter-Galvis, a Greensboro, North Carolina, apparel firm also has a plant in the Dominican Republic where shirts, pants, and jeans are sewn from fabric cut in the United States. Factory wages in the Dominican Republic average about 60 cents an hour, including fringe benefits. Even at higher skill levels, wages are much lower than those in the United States, with experienced mechanics and electricians earning approximately $310 a month.

Stage 6: Production Abroad

After the previous stages have been accomplished, the next step is the establishment of production abroad. At this time the company has a well-developed export program supported by country market studies, by promotion and distribution programs tailored to the needs of each country market, and by research into the identification of new foreign markets. The company's executives may now begin to experience difficulties in increasing the total sales volume and profit in foreign markets in which they currently have a foothold; or they may find it impossible to enter other potentially lucrative markets via exports. These difficulties often occur when the local governments impose high tariffs or quotas on the import of certain products, or when they ban their import totally if the products are being produced locally by a domestic company. In such cases the company executives decide to penetrate the foreign market by producing the product right in the foreign market itself.

After establishing a manufacturing facility in a foreign market, the company now manages its total business in a foreign country. It must, therefore, perform the many business functions abroad—purchasing, finance, human resource planning and management, manufacturing, marketing, and so on. The company is also obligated to make significant commitments of technical, management, and financial resources to the new foreign entity.

The company learns from its experience with the first foreign manufacturing venture, and this knowledge paves the way for the establishment of other foreign manufacturing plants abroad. At the same time, the company continues to export its products and to license its technology to foreign businesses and, increasingly, to its own foreign affiliates.

In maturing as an international exporter, licensor, and producer of products, the company meets the global demand for its products with exports from several of its foreign production affiliates, as well as with exports from the parent company and with the products of the foreign licensing arrangements. As the complexity of managing the geographically far-flung operations in several countries increases, the parent company managers recognize the benefits of integrating and tightening the company's global operations and of managing the entire company as one global organizational system. The motivation to use the systems approach in managing the company as one unit, with each foreign and domestic affiliate functioning as a subunit of the whole company, arises when several questions emerge to confront the company:

1 Which of the several foreign affiliates should export to a third-country market?

2. Different affiliates operate in countries with differing inflation rates and corporate tax structures, so how should the financial resources of each affiliate be managed with the objective of maximizing the total global earnings of the entire company?

3. Can promotional expenditures be lowered by standardizing advertising internationally?

Questions such as these make the parent company management perceive the company as one global enterprise system and not merely as an aggregation of several autonomous domestic and foreign affiliates. When the parent company's management begins to see the advantages of making strategic decisions—in various functional areas such as purchasing, finance, production, marketing, personnel, and research and development—from the perspective of the company as one integrated system, the stage is set for the company's evolution to a multinational enterprise.

Stage 7: Integration of Foreign Affiliates

As the parent company managers decide to integrate the various foreign affiliates into one multinational enterprise system, the affiliates lose considerable autonomy, as strategic decisions are now made by top management at the company headquarters. The company's management begins to view the entire world as its theater of operations; it plans, organizes, staffs, and controls its international operations from a global perspective. Strategic decisions are made after a careful analysis of their worldwide implications: In what country should we build our next production facility? Throughout the world, where are our markets, and from which production center should they be served? From which sources in the world should we borrow capital to finance our current and future operations? Where should our research and development laboratories be located? From which countries should we recruit people? When the management of the company starts thinking and operating in global terms, then it has evolved into a true global enterprise. (See Figure 1-2.)

Not all companies go through each of the seven stages described in the preceding sections. Some companies stop short of complete integration of their domestic and foreign operations, preferring instead to manage their domestic and foreign operations in a decentralized manner, without an overall global strategy. Others may choose to coordinate the operations of affiliates in a certain region of the world, such as Europe, and keep the affiliates in other regions unattached and semiautonomous. Still other companies may decide to think globally with respect to only

FIGURE 1-2
The Evolution of a Multinational Enterprise

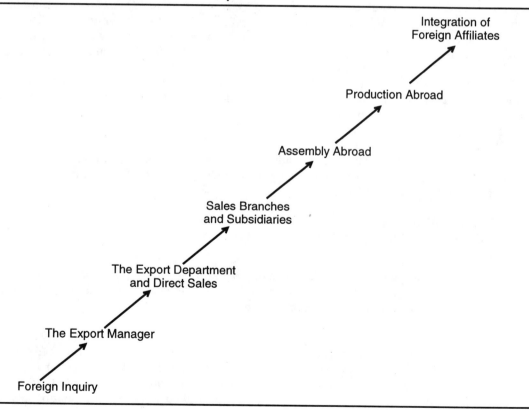

Integration of
Foreign Affiliates

Production Abroad

Assembly Abroad

Sales Branches
and Subsidiaries

The Export Department
and Direct Sales

The Export Manager

Foreign Inquiry

a few, but not all, of the enterprise functions. For instance, managers may think in worldwide terms where financial and production issues are concerned, but not for marketing, personnel, purchasing, and research and development. Thus there are different degrees of globalization of operations. Some firms may progress further along the multinational path and become true global enterprises, whereas others may choose to end their journey along the path at various milestones along the way. (We shall examine this issue in detail in Chapter 9.)

Many changes in management practices and organizational structure occur as a firm evolves into a multinational company. Some of these changes involve a radical reorientation in the attitudes and values of the managers with respect to both the role of the company in the world economy and the allegiance of the company to the home country. Another significant arena for change is the managers' perceptions of people of different nationalities, cultures, and races.

Evolution of Service Firms into Global Enterprises

We have examined the typical stages in the evolution of mainly manufacturing firms into global enterprises. However, we must note that not all international companies are in the manufacturing sector. In fact, some of the largest global companies are in the services sector. The ones that readily come to mind are firms in the banking industry such as Citicorp, Sumitomo, Sanwa, Fuji, and Lloyds; firms in the hotel industry such as Marriott, Hilton, and Holiday Inns; firms in the fast-food industry such as Pizza Hut, KFC, and McDonald's; and rental car firms such as Hertz and Avis.

Unlike firms in the manufacturing sector, service firms in the hotel, fast-food, and rental car businesses do not go through the various evolutionary stages as they evolve from the purely domestic stage to the more mature international and global stage. After establishing franchise systems at home, service firms enter foreign markets by establishing franchises in foreign countries. Some of the foreign franchises may be wholly owned by the parent company, whereas others may be jointly owned with host country entrepreneurs, and yet still others may be wholly owned by host country franchisees. A franchisee does business in the host country under the franchisor's trade name and follows the policies, procedures, and operational systems established and imposed by the franchisor. In exchange, the franchisee gives fees, royalties, and other compensation to the franchisor.

Firms in the banking industry expand their operations abroad mainly through wholly owned foreign subsidiaries and branches. Franchising as a mode of foreign market entry is practically unknown in the banking industry.

WHY INTERNATIONAL COMPANIES ENGAGE IN INTERNATIONAL OPERATIONS

An international company may have several motivations for establishing foreign operations. Some of them have been alluded to in the preceding paragraphs on the evolution of multinational enterprises. Let us examine some of the other motivations for foreign operations, grouped into three categories: market motives, strategic motives, and economic motives.

Market Motives

To protect and maintain a market position abroad, many companies have been forced to establish production facilities in foreign markets that once were served through exports but later were threatened with the imposition of high tariffs or quotas. The voluntary restrictions in 1980 of exports to the United States of Japanese automobiles prompted Japanese auto companies such as Toyota and Nissan to build car manufacturing plants in the United States. Similarly, many U.S. companies have established plants in the European Union—commonly known as the European Common Market—to jump over the common tariff and non-tariff barriers raised by member countries against imports from non-EU countries.

The expectation of immense business opportunities in an integrated and unified market of the fifteen-nation European Union (Great Britain, Ireland, France, Germany, the Netherlands, Belgium, Luxembourg, Italy, Greece, Spain, Denmark, Portugal, Austria, Sweden, and Finland) has brought an upsurge of Japanese direct investment in Europe. Japanese banks and companies in the manufacturing sector have been investing, buying European companies, setting up manufacturing subsidiaries, and boosting sales forces all over Europe. They are investing now, believing that Europe will be a good market, and also because they fear that, unlike the United States, Europe will resist mass imports of Japanese goods when most internal European trade barriers fall, as expected by the year 2000.

Japan's business activities in Europe intensified in 1990 when Japanese companies decided Europe was serious about market unification after 1992. Now Japanese companies want a foothold in Europe before protectionism keeps them out. The existence of huge European trade imbalances with Japan has prompted a number of European countries to adopt measures such as import quotas and anti-dumping tariffs. Japanese companies have responded by building new manufacturing plants and buying existing manufacturing capacity inside what could become a European fortress.

The small size of the domestic market is the reason given by European companies that have developed multinational structures. Companies based in Switzerland (e.g., Hoffman La-Roche, Sandoz, and Ciba-Geigy) a nation whose population is only about six million, could not have survived in their industry had they limited their business horizons to only the Swiss market. These companies, and others like them, were forced to seek markets abroad, which eventually led to the creation of foreign manufacturing facilities in their major markets.

Strategic Motives

Rapid expansion of a foreign market for the company's product, along with the desire to obtain a large market share in it before a major competitor can get in, are other strong driving forces for companies to engage in foreign production. There are many distinct advantages that a firm can enjoy by producing a product in a foreign market, even if there are not import barriers— for example, the ability to meet the demand for the product quickly, good public relations with customers and the host government, and improved service. Moreover, local production often allows the company to take advantage of incentives that the host government may be offering to foreign companies that make direct investments in the country—reduced taxes for several years, free land, low-interest loans, and a guarantee of no labor strife.

The need for vertical integration is another reason for the multinationalization of operations. Companies are pushed into making direct investment abroad so that they can capture a source of supply or new markets for their products. For example, a company in the oil exploration and drilling business may integrate "downstream" by acquiring or building an oil refinery in a foreign country that has a market for its refined products. Conversely, a company that has strong distribution channels (e.g., gas stations) in a country but needs a steady source of supply of gasoline at predictable prices may integrate "upstream" and acquire an oil producer and refiner in another country.

Yet another reason for establishing foreign operations is to follow the company's major customers abroad. When the Japanese automakers—Honda, Toyota, Nissan, Mazda, Subaru, and

Isuzu—established car manufacturing plants in the United States, their Japanese suppliers followed and set up their own plants in the United States. There are today approximately 270 Japanese-owned parts suppliers in the United States, representing an investment of $5.5 billion and employing more than 30,000 workers. Most of these supplier-firms provide glass, brake systems, seats, air conditioners, heaters, filters, fuel pumps, and other components directly to the production plants.[10] AT&T has made a big push overseas, mainly to satisfy the telecommunications needs of its large global customers who had themselves made their own push into overseas markets. Fearing that its major customers—the global companies—would turn to rival companies such as IBM and Japan's NEC if it did not operate advanced voice and data networks around the world, the company formed several joint ventures and strategic alliances around the globe. Employment abroad for AT&T has jumped from a mere 50 people in 1983 to 21,000 in more than forty countries.[11] Like AT&T, Federal Express followed the lead of its customers who increasingly wanted packages sent to Asia and Europe. Accordingly, with the aim of "keeping it purple"—the color of Federal's planes and vans—the company set out to duplicate its business abroad.[12]

A large number of companies have established operations abroad to exploit the strong brand name of their products. Realizing that they could not fully exploit their advantage by way of exports, they have set up plants in their major foreign markets. Examples of companies that have used this strategy are Coca-Cola, Heinz, Corn Products, and Del Monte.

A global company may decide to locate its manufacturing plant in a country that is of strategic importance for the company's exports to a third country. For instance, Japanese companies have strictly observed the Arab boycott of Israel and therefore cannot export to Israel directly from Japan. However, Japanese plants in the United States can export their U.S.-made products to Israel, and this is exactly what the Japanese auto company, Honda Motor Company, is doing. It is exporting Honda Civic sedans to Israel from its plant in Ohio. In the same vein, Northern Telecom Ltd., the Canadian telecommunications giant, has moved many of its manufacturing operations to the United States in order to gain the competitive edge that an American company can obtain in securing Japanese contracts. Northern Telecom made this strategic move to the United States knowing that the Japanese would favor U.S. companies because of Japan's huge trade surplus with the United States.[13]

Firms have been known to move their operations to ecologically and environmentally friendly countries. It has been alleged that companies have moved their environmentally harmful operations to countries in Africa, Asia, and Latin America, which do not have strict laws for environmental protection as does the United States. Companies do not necessarily have to migrate to developing countries to avoid environmental risks. A case in point is Germany's BASF, which moved its biotechnology research laboratory focusing on cancer and immune-system research from Germany—where it faced legal and political challenges from the environmentally conscious Green movement—to Cambridge, Massachusetts, which, according to BASF's director of biotechnology research, had more or less settled any controversies involving safety, animal rights, and the environment.[14]

Recognizing that scientific talent and brain power are not the monopoly of any one country or group of countries, global companies are establishing technological research and development centers around the world. Companies like IBM have established such centers in Japan to tap into the Japanese "innovation culture." Several global companies in a variety of knowledge-based industries such as biotechnology, pharmaceuticals, and electronics have set up such centers in the countries of the so-called Triad, comprising Europe, the Pacific Basin (including Japan), and the United States. This strategy has paid rich dividends for Xerox, which has introduced eighty different office-copier models in the United States that were engineered and built by its Japanese joint venture, Fuji-Xerox Company. And Banglore, India, has become the global center for software development for major computer and software companies.

Economic Motives

Another reason companies set up foreign plants is to eliminate or reduce high transportation costs, particularly if the ratio of the per-unit transportation expenditures to the per-unit selling price of the product is very high. For instance, if the product costs $10 to ship but it can be marketed for no more than $25 in the foreign market, all other things being nearly equal, the company may decide to produce it in the market in order to improve its competitiveness and profit margin.

Cheap labor is often the strongest incentive for companies to establish foreign operations. For example, over the past two decades over 2,000 maquiladoras have sprung up near the United States–Mexico border. These plants take advantage of cheap labor to assemble American-made components for re-export to the United States. Farther inside Mexico, in Mexico City, Chrysler assembles the Ram Charger for shipment to the U.S. market.[15] The economics of assembly in Mexico are favorable because jobs that fetch $12 an hour, fully "burdened" with benefits, Social Security, and so on can be had in Mexico for between $1.50 and $2 an hour.[16] In the 1950s and 1960s, many American companies had established not just assembly plants, but fully integrated manufacturing plants in countries in Southeast Asia such as Taiwan, Singapore, and Hong Kong. As wages in these countries have risen, companies are now shifting their investment sights and moving to Malaysia and Thailand.

Companies in pharmaceutical and high-technology industries that must spend large sums of money on research and development for new products and processes are compelled to look for ways to improve their sales volume in order to support their laboratories. If the domestic sales volume and exports do not raise the necessary cash flow, then strategically located manufacturing and sales affiliates are established abroad with the objective of attaining higher levels of sales volume and cash flow.

A factor that companies take into account in locating production plants is the comparative production costs in their major country markets. For example, a company that has major market positions in Japan, Germany, and the United States would be concerned about how costs are affected by the cross-exchange rates between the Japanese yen, the German mark, and the U.S. dollar. If the yen were to rise significantly in value against the U.S. dollar and the German mark, then exports to the United States and Germany of the company's Japanese-produced products could become relatively noncompetitive because of the rise of the yen-denominated Japanese wage rates and exports, especially if labor costs added significantly to the total product value. In such an event, the economics of production and distribution permitting, the company would gain if it could shift its production to either the United States or Germany. In fact, in 1990 and 1991, when the yen appreciated against the U.S. dollar, Japanese auto companies used their U.S. plants to ship cars to Europe and even back to Japan! In 1993, BMW and Mercedes, two of the major luxury automakers of Germany, decided to commence manufacture of some models in the United States because of the highly noncompetitive labor rates in Germany largely due to the high value of the German mark. Global companies invest in favor of operational flexibility and in the ability to shift the sourcing of products and components from country to country. Global companies are therefore motivated to make major investments in operations and supply sites in their major country markets.

In the preceding few pages, we have introduced some of the many reasons why a firm may choose to "go international." However, it is important to remember that each company's decision should be based on a careful assessment of its own distinctive strengths (and weaknesses) and the potential for it to strengthen its overall competitive position by making the international move. In the next section, we look at one proposed framework for assessing such potential benefits.

INTERNATIONAL/GLOBAL COMPANIES: OBJECTIVES AND SOURCES OF COMPETITIVE ADVANTAGE

Sumantra Ghoshal, in his seminal article "Global Strategy: An Organizing Framework,"[17] has offered an excellent framework that explains the broad categories of objectives of a global firm and the sources for developing an international/global firm's competitive advantage. The framework is presented in Exhibit 1-2.

As shown in Exhibit 1-2, there are three categories of objectives pursued by a global firm: (1) achieving efficiency, (2) managing risks, and (3) innovating, learning, and adapting. The key

EXHIBIT 1-2

Global Strategy: An Organizing Framework

Strategic Objectives	*Sources of Competitive Advantage*		
	National Differences	*Scale Economies*	*Scope Economies*
Achieving efficiency in current operations.	Benefiting from differences in factor costs—wages and cost of capital.	Expanding and exploiting potential scale economies in each activity.	Sharing investments and costs across products, markets, and businesses.
Managing risks.	Managing different kinds of risks arising from market- or policy-induced changes in comparative advantage of different countries.	Balancing scale with strategic and operational flexibility.	Portfolio diversification of risks and creation of options and side-bets.
Innovation, learning, and adapting.	Learning from societal differences in organizational and managerial processes and systems.	Benefiting from experience—cost reduction and innovation.	Sharing learning across organizational components in different products, markets, or businesses.

Source: Sumantra Ghoshal, "Global Strategy: An Organizing Framework," *Strategic Management Journal*, Vol. 8, 1987, p. 428.

is to create a firm's competitive advantage by developing and implementing strategies that optimize the firm's achievement of these three categories of objectives. This may require trade-offs to be made between the objectives because on occasion they may conflict with each other. For example, the objective of achieving efficiency through economies of scale in production may conflict with the objective of minimizing risks emanating from economic or political conditions in a country where the plant may be located. Ghoshal identifies three sources through which a global firm may derive its competitive advantage: (1) national differences, (2) scale economies, and (3) scope economies. According to Ghoshal, "The strategic task of managing globally is to use all three sources of competitive advantage to optimize efficiency, risk, and learning simultaneously in a worldwide business. The key to a successful global strategy is to manage the interactions between these different goals and means."[18]

Achieving Efficiency

If a firm is viewed as an input-output system, its overall efficiency is defined as a ratio of the value of all its outputs to the costs of all its inputs. A firm obtains the surplus resources needed to grow and prosper by maximizing this ratio. It may enhance the value of its products or services (outputs) by making them of higher quality than those of its competitors, and at the same time may lower the costs of inputs by obtaining low-cost factors of production, such as labor and raw materials. Different business functions, such as production, research and development, marketing, etc., have different factor intensities. A firm could exploit national differences by locating a function in that country which has a comparative advantage in providing the factors required to perform it, such as locating labor-intensive production in low-wage countries such as Malaysia or Mexico, and locating research and development activities in countries that have capable scientists who can do the work but who do not have to be paid high salaries. As an example, many American companies such as Hewlett-Packard, Oracle, Novell, Motorola, Texas Instruments, and Digital have established centers for software development work in India, where qualified personnel to write innovative software are plentiful and can be employed for as little as $300 a month.[19]

A firm could enjoy the benefits of scale economies such as lower costs and higher quality resulting from specialization by designating one plant to serve as the sole producer of a component for use in the final assembly of a product. For example, a plant in the Philippines may make transmissions, another in Malaysia the steering mechanisms, and one in Thailand the engines. Each country would then do the final assembly of the complete automobile. Toyota is rapidly moving in this direction.

The concept of scope economies is based upon the notion that savings and cost reductions will accrue when two or more products can share the same asset, such as a production plant, distribution channel, brand name, or staff services such as legal, public relations, etc. A global company such as Coca-Cola enjoys a competitive advantage because it is in a position to produce two or more products in one plant rather than two separate plants, market its products through common distribution channels, and share its world-famous brand name across a wide range of products.

Managing Risks

A global company faces a number of different types of risks—economic, legal, political, and competitive. The nature and severity of such risks are not the same for all countries. A global company is in a position to manage such risks effectively by planning and implementing strategies aimed at diffusing risk. For example, in a country that has high levels of unemployment, a global company could deflect restrictive and unfriendly governmental policies by sourcing products for world markets in that country, thus increasing much-needed employment opportunities for the local populace. An example of such a strategy is the transfer of significant amounts of car production to the United States by Japanese automakers such as Toyota, Honda, and Nissan. One of the principal motivations behind this strategy was to minimize the growing anti-Japanese sentiment in the U.S. due to the alleged job losses caused by Japanese imports.

The benefits of scale economies must be weighed against their risks. A plant located in a country because of its low wages could lose its locational advantage if the wage rates in the country rise significantly because of economic development or appreciation of the country's currency. Global companies manage such risks by distributing production in more than one country even at the expense of benefits due to lower scale economies. Japanese car companies have managed currency and wage-rate risks, caused by rising wage rates in Japan and the much stronger Japanese yen vis-à-vis the U.S. dollar, by exporting cars made in U.S.-based plants back to Japan. The flexibility afforded to Japanese car companies by having plants both in the United States and Japan was responsible for their effective management of risk.

Innovation and Learning

A global company has a distinct advantage over its purely domestic competitor because of the multiple environments in which the global company operates. A company that has operations in many countries is exposed to a diversity of experiences and stimuli. Being in many countries allows it to develop a variety of capabilities. It provides a global company with opportunities to learn skills and acquire knowledge of a country that can be transferred and applied in many other countries where it has operations. For example, a company that has operations in Japan can learn about the very best aspects of the Japanese management system and adapt and use those that are most useful in its American or European operations. General Electric is marketing in India an ultrasound unit designed by Indian engineers, the technology of which was developed in GE's Japanese operations.

Hewlett-Packard has continued pouring resources into the Asian region, opening a laboratory in Japan and new manufacturing facilities in Japan and Malaysia, while simultaneously beefing up its engineering, project management, and design capacity in Singapore. Such investments provide not only increased sales in the region but also skills and expertise in how to improve the production process, something that it lacks in the United States. According to a Hewlett-Packard spokesman, "In the U.S., all great engineers want to work on product innovation; in Asia, the best guys want to work on improving the production process."[20] Hewlett-Packard can learn process-improvement techniques from its Asian operations and transfer the knowledge not only to its U.S. operations but to operations worldwide.

Eli Lilly & Company, USA, a global research-based pharmaceutical corporation and Ranbaxy Laboratories Limited, India's largest pharmaceutical company, have formed a path-breaking alliance to set up joint ventures in India and the United States. In the first phase, a state-of-the-art research, development, and manufacturing facility is being set up in India to develop products for the U.S. market. This will be on par with international research laboratories and will undertake chemical, pharmaceutical, and analytical research, utilizing the most modern equipment and scientific instrumentation.[21] In this example, Eli Lilly's strategy apparently is to tap into the research capabilities of Indian scientists, and thereby to learn and develop innovative new products and processes.

Ford, Toyota, and Honda have embarked upon the ambitious project of building a "world car." *Practical Insight 1-1* shows how Toyota and Honda are taking advantage of national differences, economies of scale, and economies of scope, with the intent of achieving greater efficiency, spreading risk, and learning from worldwide operations.

The framework we have discussed in this chapter is very useful in identifying possible sources of competitive advantage for an international company. However, it still remains to translate the suggested strategies into operating decisions that can realize the broader goals. We explore this topic in depth in Chapter 9, The Nature and Scope of International Integration Strategies, using the concept of the value chain to illustrate how an international firm establishes the optimum mix of functional and geographic integration to achieve its strategic objectives. But before we take up the issue of strategy, we turn in the next section of the book to a discussion of the environmental context within which the international firm must operate. In the next chapter, we set the stage with an overview of the current global economic environment, high-lighting some trends that are important for international managers.

PRACTICAL INSIGHT 1-1
Want To Be More Efficient, Spread Risk, and Learn and Innovate at the Same Time? — Try Building a "World Car."

Japanese car companies such as Toyota and the Honda Motor Company are pioneering the auto industry's truly global manufacturing system. The companies' aim is to perfect a car's design and production in one place and then churn out thousands of "world" cars each year that can be made in one place and sold worldwide. In an industry where the cost of tailoring car models to different markets can run into billions of dollars, the "world car" approach of Toyota and Honda—and one which Ford is hoping to emulate—is targeted at sharply curtailing development costs, maximizing the use of assembly plants, and preserving the assembly-line efficiencies that are a hallmark of the Japanese "lean" production system.

As for Honda, the goal is to create a "global base of complementary supply," says Roger Lambert, Honda's manager of corporate communications. "Japan can supply North America and Europe, North America can supply Japan and Europe, and Europe can supply Japan and the United States. So far, the first two are true. This means that you can more profitably utilize your production bases and talents."

The strategy of shipping components and fully assembled products from the U.S. to Europe and Japan couldn't have come at a more opportune time for the Japanese car companies, especially when political pressures are intense to reduce the Japanese trade surplus with the United States. The task was made easier due to the strength of the Japanese yen, which has risen about 50 percent against the U.S. dollar. That has made production of cars in the United States cheaper, by some estimates, by $2,500 to $3000 per car. That saving more than compensates for the transportation costs for a car overseas.

For the first time, Toyota is creating a system that will give it the capability to manage the car production levels in Japan and the United States. It is moving toward a global manufacturing system that will enable it to enhance manufacturing efficiency by fine-tuning global production levels on a quarterly basis in response to economic conditions in different markets.

Source: Adapted from Paul Ingrassia, "Ford to Export Parts to Europe For a New Car," *The Wall Street Journal*, September 29, 1992, p. A5; Jane Perlez, "Toyota and Honda Create Global Production System," *The New York Times*, March 26, 1993, pp. A1 and D2.

SUMMARY

The purpose of this chapter was to provide an introduction to international management and to the world of the international company. The nature of international business was explained first, and we saw that the need for international management and managers arises when companies begin to export goods or services.

Although there are scores of small international companies, generally when one speaks about them the reference is to the large multinationals. Increasingly, people are referring to these giant companies with operations throughout the world not as international, but as global, companies. International management and global companies are more or less like Siamese twins or the two sides of a coin. The growth of global companies has resulted from the astute management of these enterprises by international managers. And the management of multinational corporations epitomizes what international management is all about.

We saw something of the dimensions and drastic growth of multinational companies during the 1960s. Next we looked at the different international business activities of multinational companies, then examined the typical stages in the evolution of multinational companies. After this, we studied how global companies exploit economies of scale, economies of scope, and national differences to achieve their three generic objectives: (1) efficiency in current operations, (2) managing risks, and (3) innovation, learning, and adaptation.

QUESTIONS FOR THOUGHT AND DISCUSSION

1. What is international business? How does it differ from international management?

2. Discuss the characteristics of multinational companies. What forces have contributed to their development and growth?

3. How does a domestic company typically evolve into one that is multinational? How and why does change occur in the relationship between the parent company and foreign affiliates as the company becomes multinational?

4. Identify and explain the three categories of broad objectives of global companies. What strategic actions can a global company take in order to develop competitive advantage against its competitors?

5. Discuss the key differences between economies of scale and economies of scope.

6. Discuss how national differences can serve as a source of competitive advantage for a global company.

Notes

1 John D. Daniels and Lee H. Radebaugh, *International Business: Environment and Operations*, 6th. ed., Addison-Wesley, Reading, Mass, 1992, p. 8.

2 Donald A. Ball and Wendell H. McCulloch, Jr., *International Business: Introduction and Essentials*, 4th. ed., BPI/Irwin Homewood, Illinois, 1990, p. 17.

3 Betty Jane Punett and David A. Ricks, *International Business*, (Boston: PWS/Kent Publishing Company, 1992), p. 7.

4 "The Business Week Global 1000," *Business Week*, July 10, 1995, p. 62.

5   United Nations Conference on Trade and Development, *World Investment Report 1994*, New York: United Nations, 1994, pp. 5-8.

6   Ibid., p. 131.

7   John H. Dunning, "Changes in the level and structure of international production: the last one hundred years," in Mark Casson (ed.), *The Growth of International Business*, Allen and Irwin, London, 1983, pp. 84-139.

8   United Nations Conference on Trade and Development, *World Investment Report 1994*, New York: United Nations, 1994, p. 131.

9   Ibid., p. 9.

10 Martin Kenney and Richard Florida, "How the Japanese Industry is Rebuilding the Rust Belt," *Technology Review*, February-March 1991, p. 28.

11 Dinah Lee, Jonathan Levine, and Peter Coy, "ATT Slowly Gets Its Global Wires Uncrossed," *Business Week*, February 11, 1991, p. 82.

12 Daniel Pearl, "Federal Express Finds Its pioneering Formula Falls Flat Overseas," *The Wall Street Journal*, April 15, 1991, p. A8.

13 William J. Holstein, Stanley Reed, Jonathan Kapstein, Todd Vogel, and Joseph Weber, "The Stateless Corporation," *Business Week*, May 14, 1990, p. 99.

14 Ibid., p. 100.

15 Paul Magnusson, Stephen Baker, David Beach, Gail DeGeorge, and William C. Symonda, "The Mexico Pact: Worth the Price?" *Business Week*, May 27, 1991, pp. 33-34.

16 Kevin McDermott, "Border Crossing Ahead," *D & B Reports*, January-February 1991, p. 24.

17 Sumantra Ghoshal, "Global Strategy: An Organizing Framework," *Strategic Management Journal*, Vol. 8, 1987, pp. 425-440.

18 Ibid., p. 427.

19 Michael Zielenziger, "India's star rises in technology race," *San Jose Mercury News*, July 4, 1995, pp. 1A & 22A.

20 Paul Blustein, "Hewlett-Packard's Role in Asia Marks the Growth Area for U.S.," *Philadelphia Inquirer*, November 26, 1993, p. C4.

21 From an advertisement placed by Ranbaxy Laboratories Limited in *India Abroad*, May 5, 1995, p. 11.

Further Reading

Bible, Geoffrey C., "Global Competition: Getting Ahead, Staying Ahead," *Executive Speeches*, Vol. 7, No. 2, October/November 1992, pp. 1-6.

Daniels, John D., and Lee H. Radebaugh, *International Business: Environments and Operations*, 5th ed., Addison-Wesley, Reading, Mass., 1989.

Farmer, Richard N., and Barry B. Richman, *International Business: An Operational Theory*. Richard D. Irwin, Homewood, Ill., 1966.

Lei, David, and John W. Slocum, Jr., Global Strategy, Competence-Building and Strategic Alliances, *California Management Review*, Vol. 35, (1), Fall 1992, pp. 81-97.

Phatak, Arvind V., *Evolution of World Enterprises*, American Management Association, New York, 1971.

——*Managing Multinational Corporations*, Praeger Publishers, New York, 1974.

Vernon, Raymond, and Louis T. Wells, Jr., *Manager in the International Economy*, 4th ed., Prentice-Hall, Englewood Cliffs, N.J., 1981.

Walle, A.H., "International Business and Raging Tigers: Operationalizing the Global Paradigm," *Management Decision*, Vol. 30, No. 2, 1992, pp. 35-39.

Weigand, Robert E., "International Trade Without Money," *Harvard Business Review*, November-December, 1977.

Global Economic
Developments and Trends

LEARNING OBJECTIVES

After completing this chapter, you will be able to:

- Discuss the importance and scope of international trade in the world economy and the role of international companies in conducting that trade.
- Understand the implications of differences in labor, living, and product costs among different countries for the international firm.
- Describe six important trends in the contemporary international business environment that are shaping the ways in which international companies must act to remain competitive.

The global environment of business is changing at all times. Some of these changes are being brought on by international companies. There are environmental changes that international companies have an influence upon but which they cannot control. And there are environmental changes that international companies can neither influence nor control. In this chapter, we shall examine changes in the global economic environment that fall under each of these categories.

First we shall review historical and comparative statistics in areas such as foreign direct investments, international trade, the wealth of nations as measured in terms of gross domestic product, and comparative labor costs in selected countries, and look at the largest international companies in the world. We shall also take an overview of the living costs and prices of selected goods and services in a variety of countries.

Later in the chapter we shall examine economic trends that have been evolving since the recent past, are still in progress, and which should continue to unfold in the years ahead. The trends chosen for study are those that we believe will have a major impact on international firms in particular and international business at large.

FOREIGN DIRECT INVESTMENT AND TRADE

Foreign direct investment (FDI) is investment in foreign countries in plant, equipment, facilities, and buildings for the production of goods and/or services. As long as FDI flows remain positive, they signify the expansion of international companies in foreign markets, even though there might be a drop in the amounts during some years. FDI inflows indicate the countries and regions that are attractive markets for international companies, and FDI outflows represent the role played by the investor countries in international trade and commerce. FDI numbers also signify the relative importance of international companies in the production of goods and services in foreign countries. Because knowledge and technology is often embedded in the plant and equipment shipped abroad, FDI also is indicative of the part played by international companies in the transfer of technology to foreign countries.

FDI inflows for developed countries (rich countries of the world), developing countries, and Central and Eastern Europe are presented in Exhibit 2-1. The most significant data in this exhibit is the massive increase in FDI inflows in developing countries from $31 billion in 1991 to $80 billion in 1993, an increase of 158 percent. In contrast, FDI inflows in developed countries declined significantly from $121 billion in 1991 to $109 billion, a decline of 10 percent. The share of the developing countries of global FDI inflows increased from 24 percent in 1991 to 41 percent in 1993, whereas for the same period that of the developed countries declined from 74 percent to 56 percent (Exhibit 2-2).

The outflows of FDI are insignificant for developing countries, more than 95 percent of which are sourced in the developed countries (Exhibits 2-3 and 2-4, pages 23 and 24, respectively). The FDI data in the exhibits reveal that the developing countries as a group were the big magnets attracting FDI from developed countries. Of the developing countries, the vibrant economies of South, East, and Southeast Asia absorbed 57 percent of total inflows to developing countries.[1]

EXHIBIT 2-1

Inflows of Foreign Direct Investment (Billions of Dollars)

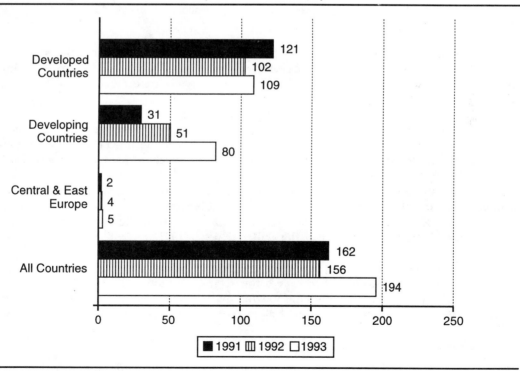

Source: UNCTAD, *World Investment Report 1994*, United Nations, New York, 1994, p. 12.

EXHIBIT 2-2
Inflows of Foreign Direct Investment [Share in Total (percentage)]

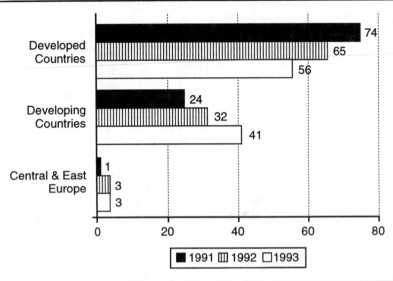

Source: UNCTAD, *World Investment Report 1994*, United Nations, New York, 1994, p. 12.

The world's ten largest recipients of FDI inflows in the 1990s are identified in Exhibit 2-5, page 25, which shows that only three developing countries—Argentina, Mexico, and China—are in this exclusive club. However the chart shows the growing importance of China as a recipient of FDI.

The five major countries making FDIs are shown in Exhibit 2-6 on page 26. As we can see, the biggest FDI outflows are from the United States. Except for the United States and the United Kingdom, FDI outflows from France, Germany, and Japan have declined considerably since 1990. Notwithstanding the decline, these countries continued to account for two-thirds of worldwide outflows.

The total share of five major countries (Exhibit 2-7, page 27) in the world shows that the United States and the United Kingdom have had the largest and second largest shares, respectively, and increasing stakes in global foreign direct investments; however, those of Japan and France, which were almost as large as the United States in 1991 and 1992, respectively, have since declined precipitously.[2]

The worldwide FDI stock—a proxy for the productive capacity of international companies outside their home countries—reached an estimated $2.1 trillion in 1993, with the United States holding total FDI stock of $539 billion, followed by the United Kingdom with $247 billion, and Japan, Germany, and France with $264 billion, $196 billion, and $182 billion respectively.[3]

LARGEST EXPORTERS IN THE WORLD

The five largest foreign direct investors—United States, United Kingdom, France, Germany, and Japan—are also the five largest exporting countries in the world (Exhibits 2-8 and 2-9, pages 28

EXHIBIT 2-3
Outflows of Foreign Direct Investment (Billions of Dollars)

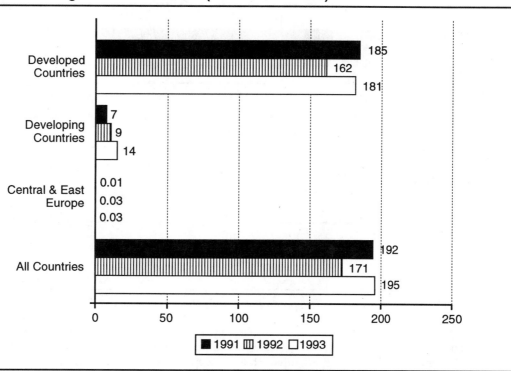

Source: UNCTAD, *World Investment Report 1994*, United Nations, New York, 1994, p. 12.

and 29, respectively). Thus, the data on foreign direct investments and export performance of countries shows that dominant roles in global direct investments and global trade are played by the same five countries.

COMPARATIVE GROSS DOMESTIC PRODUCT

The same five countries that dominate in shares of total global direct investments and exports are also ranked in the top six of the ten largest economies of the world (Exhibit 2-10, page 30). The GDP and GNP per capita ranking of the top ten countries in U.S. dollars adjusted for purchasing power parity shows that six—United States, Canada, Germany, Japan, Belgium, Australia—of the ten largest economies appear in the ranking (Exhibit 2-11, page 31). However, we should be careful in how we interpret these figures. High per capita incomes adjusted for purchasing power parity do not necessarily reflect the size of a country's market, because market size depends upon the proportion of the population that has the per capita income (market size = per capita income × number of people in the per capita income group). For example, United Arab Emirates tops the list in Exhibit 2-11, but it is a very tiny country with a population of only

23

EXHIBIT 2-4
Outflows of Foreign Direct Investment [Share in Total (percentage)]

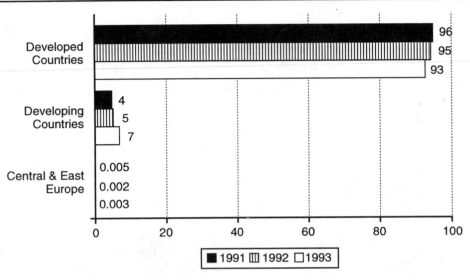

Source: UNCTAD, *World Investment Report 1994*, United Nations, New York, 1994, p. 12.

1.6 million. And Luxembourg is a city/state with a population of only 385 thousand people. In comparison, the population of the United States is approximately 253 million and that of Japan is 124 million. Therefore, in order to obtain a rough sketch of market size, population figures, gross domestic product, and per capita income figures should be used in conjunction with each other.

COMPARATIVE LABOR COSTS

As we shall see in subsequent chapters, labor costs play a very important role in the comparative advantage of countries as labor-intensive production sites. All other things being equal, international companies have a propensity to locate labor-intensive activities in countries where the labor costs for such activities are low. Labor costs per hour in manufacturing for several countries (see Exhibit 2-12, page 32) show that the developing countries have a distinct advantage in labor costs. The figures in this exhibit are in U.S. dollars and therefore the rankings reflect the exchange rates of the U.S. dollar vis-à-vis other currencies. If the U.S. dollar were to appreciate significantly vis-à-vis other currencies, then the relative rankings of labor costs in U.S. dollars would be altered. The high per-hour labor costs in Germany and Japan are largely due to the appreciation of the Japanese yen and the German mark against the U.S. dollar during the past several years. The surge of Japanese, American, and European production facilities Asian countries, and of American production in Mexico, was primarily because of the low labor costs in those countries.

Wage levels are low in developing countries, but not just in the low-skilled group. Workers in emerging nations are doing more sophisticated high-tech jobs and for a lot less than their counterparts in the rich countries. For example, "at a Silicon Graphics, Inc. joint venture in

EXHIBIT 2-5

World's Ten Largest Recipients of FDI Inflows in the 1990s (Billions of Dollars)

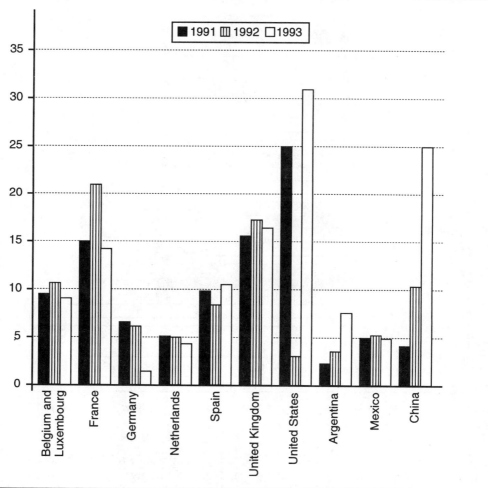

Source: UNCTAD, *World Investment Report 1994*, United Nations, New York, 1994, p. 69.

Bangalore, India, software designers earning $300 a month are developing programs to produce three-dimensional images for diagnosing brain disorders."[4]   On average, an engineer earns $51,000 annually in Tokyo, $36,600 in Chicago, $17,900 in Bangkok, Thailand, but only $4,200 in Budapest, Hungary, and a paltry $2,100 in Bombay. An experienced circuit-board designer can command an annual salary of up to $100,000; an equally good engineer in Taiwan can be hired for about $25,000. In India and China one can hire a talented PhD for less than $10,000 a year.[5]

Rapid advances in telecommunications are bringing inexpensive high-tech workers within easy reach of international companies. Just as it became easy to shift manufacturing to virtually

EXHIBIT 2-6
Outflows of FDI from Five Major Countries (Billions of Dollars)

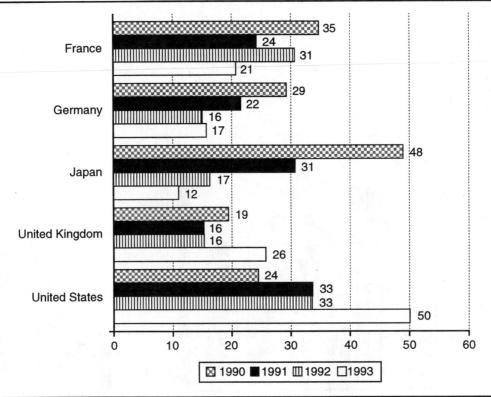

Source: UNCTAD, *World Investment Report 1994*, United Nations, New York, 1994, p. 17.

any part of the world in the 1970s and 1980s, today it is possible to shift knowledge-based work to distant locations. Cities such as Singapore, Taipei, Edinburgh, and Penang (Malaysia) have emerged as hubs for worldwide product development. Citibank uses skilled employees in India, Hong Kong, Singapore, and Australia to develop products for its global financial services and to manage data. M.W. Kellogg farms out to its Mexican partner architectural-engineering work for power and chemical plants that it builds around the world.[6] By now it must be clear that the competitive edge of developing countries is not limited to cheap, low-skilled labor. Developing countries now have a competitive edge in high-tech, knowledge-based jobs as well.

WORLD'S LARGEST INTERNATIONAL COMPANIES

International companies are the principal carriers of direct investment, products, services, and technology across national boundaries. It was estimated that the 100 largest international companies (not including those in banking and finance) had about $3.4 trillion in global assets in 1992, of which about $1.3 trillion were held outside their respective home countries. These firms

EXHIBIT 2-7

Outflows of FDI from Five Major Countries (As Percentage of World Share)

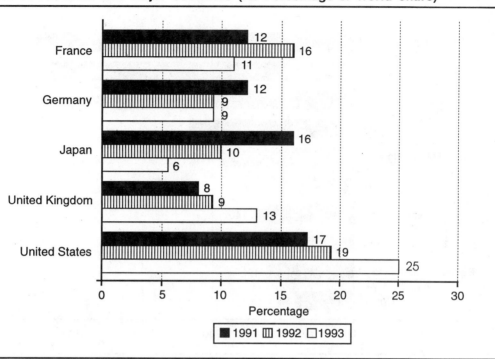

Source: UNCTAD, *World Investment Report 1994*, United Nations, New York, 1994, p. 17.

are estimated to account for about one-third of the combined outward FDI of their countries of origin.[7] Because they control such a large pool of assets and stock of investment, large international companies are capable of exercising considerable influence over a home and host country's gross domestic product, jobs creation, technological infusion and transfers, trade patterns, and macroeconomic policies.

If the ten largest international companies in the world are ranked by sales, six of the top ten companies are Japanese keiretsu (group of companies characterized by a network of interlocking equity structure among the member companies). The Japanese keiretsu are involved in a number of industries and businesses worldwide such as automobiles, electronics, banking, and international trade. As such they wield great power and influence on the global business arena. Three companies in the ranking are American—General Motors, Ford, and Exxon—and Royal Dutch/ Shell is Anglo-Dutch. All ten companies have combined sales of $1,568 billion, a total which is larger than the gross domestic product of several countries, including France ($1,014 billion), and almost as large as the GDP of Germany ($1,608 billion).[8]

If the ten largest companies in the world are ranked by profits, all but the largest and the smallest are American companies. Royal Dutch Shell, the largest, is Anglo-Dutch, and HSBC Holdings, the smallest, is British. The combined profits of the ten companies amount to $48.69 billion.[9]

EXHIBIT 2-8
Top Ten Exporting Countries (Value of Exports in Billions of Dollars for 1992)

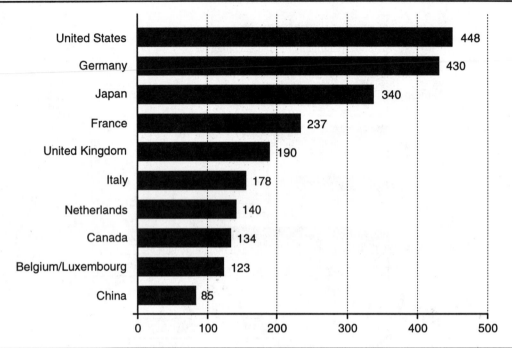

Source: *Nouvelle Economiste*, December 10, 1993, p. 23, from GATT, OECD.

These data manifest the colossal power that international companies, especially the large ones, can wield on the global business and economic arena, and because of the close inter-dependence between the international economic and political system, on the global political arena as well. (We shall examine in detail the interdependence between these two systems in Chapter 5, The Political Environment of International Business.)

Similarly of the ten largest banks in the world, the top eight are Japanese. If merger talks between Mitsubishi Bank and the Bank of Tokyo are successful, Tokyo Mitsubishi will be the largest bank in the world with combined assets of over $700 billion. It would make Tokyo Mitsubishi 40 percent larger than the second largest bank and twice the size of its largest foreign competitor, France's Crédit Lyonnais. Not a single bank in the top ten list is American. This is evidence of the considerable financial clout in the world financial markets exercised by Japanese banks, which, in conjunction with the Japanese companies, create a mammoth global Japanese industrial-financial complex that is a force to be reckoned with by non-Japanese international companies.[10]

COMPARATIVE LIVING AND PRODUCT COSTS

As businesspeople travel, reside, or open subsidiaries in foreign countries, they face a variety of unfamiliar conditions and situations. We shall discuss this topic in the next few chapters. For

EXHIBIT 2-9

Top Ten Exporting Countries [Export Share as a Percentage of the Total Group (1992)]

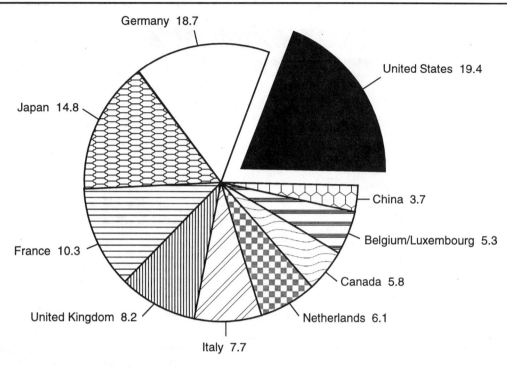

Source: Nouvelle Economiste, December 10, 1993, p. 23, from GATT, OECD.

now, let us present an overview of some of the differences in living costs and product prices that may pleasantly or unpleasantly surprise the businessperson as he or she travels abroad.

The living costs in selected cities are shown in Exhibit 2-13 on page 33. Living in Tokyo can be more than twice as expensive as living in London, New York, Rome, or Chicago. And living costs are 37 percent cheaper in Mexico City than in New York City. International managers would be advised to take into account cost-of-living differentials in negotiations on salaries and cost-of-living allowances before accepting a foreign assignment.

International managers are obliged to entertain clients and business associates. Business entertainment is an essential international business activity. Entertaining prospective business partners is important in all countries but it is especially critical to the success of business negotiations in countries such as Japan, Mexico, and most Latin American countries. In these countries building a relationship based upon trust and goodwill must precede business-related conversation and transactions. If you were to take a client for dinner, in Tokyo the cost would be approximately $70 per person—twice as much as the same dinner would cost in New York City—as compared to $21 in Mexico City or $15 in San Paulo, Brazil.

One of the paradoxes businesspeople experience abroad is that office rents are higher in some developing countries than in the rich countries. For example, rents for offices and living quarters

EXHIBIT 2-10

Comparative Ranking of Top 10 Countries ... GDP [In Billions of U.S. Dollars (1991)]

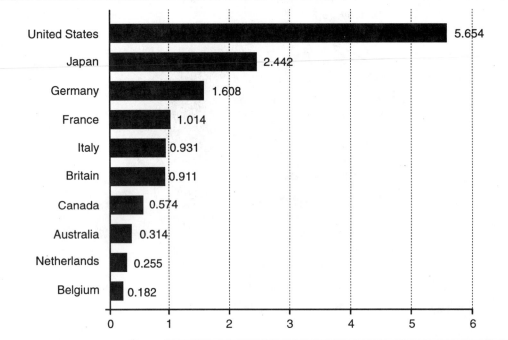

Source: Adapted from "The Global Economy: How They Stack Up," *Fortune*, July 25, 1994, p. 119.

are higher in Bombay than in Tokyo. It is less than one-half as expensive to rent in mid-town New York City than it is in Bombay, Beijing or Shanghai. This may come as a surprise to most international businesspeople planning to open offices in the newly emerging markets of China and India. Newly arrived executives in Bombay might pay $10,000 a month for a one-bedroom flat. Businesspeople should realize that within a country rents are higher in some cities than in others. For example, in India it is less than one-half as expensive to rent office and living space in New Delhi as in Bombay; therefore many companies have opened offices in New Delhi instead.

A cup of coffee costs $13.03 in Hong Kong, a bottle of Coke costs $1.89 in Tokyo, and Kodak film costs $7.72 in Paris (Exhibit 2-14, page 34). Businesspeople will find that there are some items that will cost much more in one country than another. The differences in price are due to differences in sales tax, import duties, and overhead expenses.

CURRENT TRENDS IN THE INTERNATIONAL ECONOMY

Thus far in the chapter, we have reviewed historical, comparative data on foreign direct investment and trade, leading exporting countries, gross domestic product of countries, comparative labor costs, and the largest international companies in the world. This should give one a broad picture of countries and companies that are significant players in the global business arena and

EXHIBIT 2-11

**Comparative Ranking of Top 10 Countries . . . Per Capita GDP/GNP
[For 1991 in U.S. Dollars (adjusted for purchasing power parity)]**

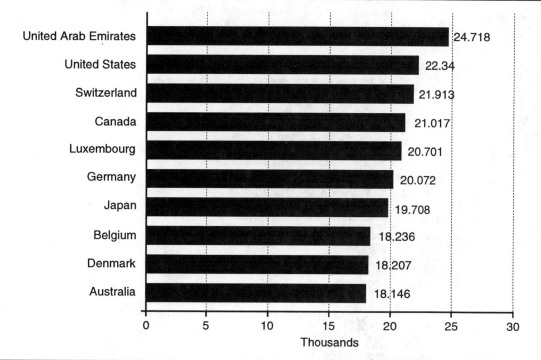

Source: Adapted from "The Global Economy: How They Stack Up," *Fortune,* July 25, 1994, p. 119.

which are likely to remain in somewhat the same positions for the forseeable future. We concluded this section of the chapter with an overview of the living costs and prices of products in several countries. In the following sections we shall review general economic trends that began evolving during the recent past and which are still unfolding worldwide. The trends discussed are those with critical impacts on international companies in particular and international business at large. We shall cover the following developments that are still in progress:

- The global thrust for a market economy
- Privatization
- The burgeoning middle class
- The global information technology revolution
- The emergence of the East Asian economies
- The movement toward free trade and trade blocs (examined in detail in Chapter 3)

31

EXHIBIT 2-12
Invasion of the Job Snatchers
Labor Costs* in the Manufacturing Sector

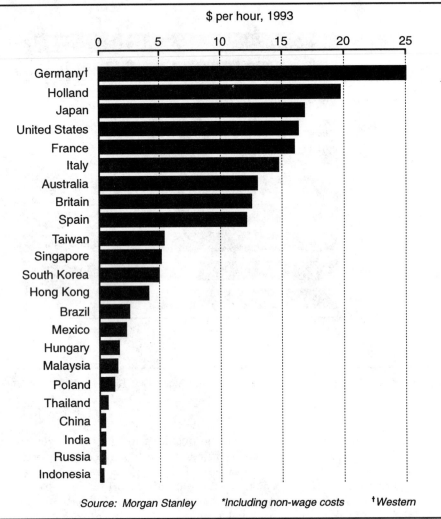

$ per hour, 1993

Source: Morgan Stanley   *Including non-wage costs   †Western

The Global Thrust for a Market Economy

The collapse of the former Soviet Union conveyed a powerful message to governments of countries, especially to those of the former Soviet bloc countries and other Socialist countries: that communism and state-controlled economic planning does not work. The superiority of capitalism and private enterprise was evident in the far-superior economic performance of Western

EXHIBIT 2-13

Living Costs in Selected Cities

A study of 125 cities worldwide. The survey
is based on New York's score of 100 points.
Philadelphia was not surveyed.

Rank/City		Points
	Most expensive	
1	Tokyo	220
2	Osaka, Japan	208
3	Zurich, Switzerland	143
4	Geneva	141
5	Oslo, Norway	137
	Other selected cities	
17	Paris	123
20	Berlin	122
38	London	110
53	Madrid/New York	100
72	Chicago	94
80	Miami/San Francisco	92
87	Washington	92
92	Boston/Houston	90
110	Atlanta/Toronto	81
125	Mexico City	63

Source: Corporate Resource Group

Source: Adapted from "Most Expensive Cities? Try Tokyo and Osaka," *The Philadelphia Inquirer,* June 8,
1995, p. C1.

European countries vis-à-vis those of the Soviet bloc countries in Eastern Europe. The contrast
was most dramatic between the economic performance of West and East Germany before the fall
of the Berlin Wall. Communist countries, former communist countries, and third-world countries
that had adopted the model of centralized planning for economic development have abandoned
it in favor of free markets and liberalization of various segments of their economies. Countries
such as China (which is still officially communist), India, Brazil, Argentina, Chile, and all countries
of Eastern Europe have turned away from centralized government planners and toward freer
markets.

Free markets and industry deregulation have opened up markets in countries that were at
one time closed to foreign companies. China and India alone have a combined total population
of almost two billion people, who are craving for a greater variety of quality products, better
infrastructure such as roads and electricity, and quality of life enhancing products and services.
For example, India is desperately short of energy—electricity supply is chronically short (only 10
percent of demand) and per-capita power consumption is only 3 percent that of the United States.
The power sector in India has attracted some of the biggest names: Enron, AES, and Cogentrix
Energy of the U.S., and South Korea's Daewoo. This is just one example of the opportunities for
international companies resulting from the embrace of the free-market concept and industry

EXHIBIT 2-14
Costs of Consumer Goods Around the World (U.S. $)

	Bangkok	Frankfurt	Hong Kong	London	Mexico	New York	Paris	Singapore	Sydney	Taipei	Tokyo	Toronto
Rolex watch	4,814	4,123	3,626	4,473	6,505	5,304	4,900	4,120	5,721	3,824	8,589	6,322
Bally shoes	370	412	257	176	152	304	190	248	264	333	709	331
Automatic camera	804	673	730	759	1,435	682	856	535	974	478	1,159	748
CD player	491	733	271	492	382*	262	467	287	508	742	428	460
Celine handbag	1,089	550	977	905	n/a	913	832	909	1,152	822	1,675	1,205
Chanel perfume	137	123	96	103	177	135	108	61	150	126	206	133
Coffee	4.60	5.18	13.03	5.29	2.96	5.29	7.71	9.10	4.68	20.7	14.58	5.31
Coke bottle	1.16	1.03	0.80	0.91	0.88	0.81	1.77	0.89	0.84	1.16	1.89	1.58
Discman	645	549	340	547	350*	239	488	401	644	220	471	513
Eye-glass frames	191	458	228	317	366	277	299	205	303	220	653	309
Gold necklace	269	106	186	259	841	522	389	166	394	194	859	321
Kodak film	3.78	5.32	4.01	6.48	5.56	6.39	7.72	3.66	6.64	4.19	6.51	5.95
Mineral water	2.12	1.25	1.95	1.14	1.97	2.28	0.92	1.94	1.41	3.54	4.58	1.73
Petrol	3.78	0.93	1.02	0.86	1.31	0.36	0.95	0.71	0.49	0.73	1.31	0.50
Ralph Lauren shirt	126	100	45	72	40	49	101	66	56	61	137	46
Video camera	1,405	1,603	988	1,440	1,512*	1,132	1,524	904	1,238	1,204	1,302	1,663

*Comparable model

Sources: 1993 EIU Cost of Living Survey, EIU Custom Publishing (Mexican prices as of November 1993).

Source: "Toasting the Good Life," Crossborder, Winter 1994, p. 44.

deregulation by countries worldwide. Similar opportunities have opened up in Russia, Poland, and Hungary.

The fervor of economic liberalization and deregulation is not limited to the developing countries and to countries of the former Soviet Bloc. Capitalist countries such as England and the United States have moved dramatically in removing restrictive regulations on industries such as air transportation, telecommunications, banking, and insurance. The political climate in the United States favors less centralized federal government and greater delegation of governmental authority to the state and local levels. For example, government regulations governing itineraries, routes, airfares, and new entrants into the industry have been abolished in the airline industry. Deregulation has removed the boundaries between the computer, long-distance and local telephone, and direct broadcast and cable television industries, and created an integrated telecommunications industry. Deregulation of banking and insurance industries has created a unified financial services industry.

The advent of deregulation of the airline, telecommunications, and financial services industries is a global phenomenon. These developments have spawned numerous cross-industry and cross-national alliances, mergers, and acquisitions (this subject matter will be covered in detail in Chapter 11).

When markets are large and laws do not prevent people from building companies and keeping their profits, large numbers of citizens become wealth-builders and entrepreneurs. Large numbers of third-world countries are developing much faster than would have been possible under centralized planning. Already there are signs that free enterprise is working in countries that are new converts to the free-market idea. China's gross domestic product grew 10 percent in 1994, and that of Malaysia and Thailand at 8.5 percent and 8.1 percent, respectively, far faster than the sluggish rate of less than 3.5 percent in most countries of Europe and North America. The growth rate for developing countries in Asia averaged a lofty 7.8 percent. According to the economic consulting firm DRI/McGraw-Hill, by the end of the decade one-tenth of everything produced in the world will be sourced in Asia.[11] The economies of Latin America, which had been stagnant for most of the 1970s and 1980s, grew at the rate of 3 percent in 1994, with better-than-average growth rates achieved in Argentina and Chile of almost 5 percent. The countries of Eastern Europe are expected to grow at the rate of 4 to 6 percent during the next several years.[12]

Privatization

Burdensome public-sector debts, continued poor performance of many state-owned enterprises, the adoption of market-driven economic policies, and the desire to attract foreign direct investments have led to the implementation of privatization programs allowing international companies to participate in many parts of the world. Privatization is the transfer of ownership or control of an enterprise from the government/public sector to the private sector. In other words, it is the transfer of ownership, the sale of an enterprise, to the private sector, be it the general public, private corporations, or private investors. With broader acceptance of the term, its meaning has broadened to include the economic and political setting in which privatization occurs, since the environment in which the private enterprises are required to operate and market reforms are implemented is an essential element in successful privatization.

Privatization of state-owned enterprises is in vogue in developed and developing countries alike. The primary motives for privatization are both economic and political and they vary from country to country. For example, the privatization of British Telecom, British Air, and British Rail by the British government headed by Prime Minister Margaret Thatcher was in response to a political ideology that preached that the State had no business getting itself involved in any sector of the economy that private enterprise was capable of handling on its own. On the other hand, the privatization programs of China, India, and Mexico have had more to do with the growing needs of the population that cannot be met by the government due to budgetary pressures. These countries have turned over infrastructure projects in fields such as electricity generation and telecommunications to private-sector companies from home and abroad. For instance, India needs to raise about $200 billion to meet its goal of adding 142,000 megawatts of power capacity by the year 2010, an expense that it cannot afford. It has therefore turned to companies such as Enron, Bechtel, and Mission Energy to fulfill this need.

The World Bank estimates that one billion people lack clean water, electric power has yet to reach two billion people, and the demand for modern telecommunications networks far outstrips supply. The number of privatized enterprises has grown by leaps and bounds in recent years. From 1988 to 1992, the value of privatization in all countries totaled $185 billion. Although developed countries started privatization much earlier than other countries, the privatization rush since the late 1980s has concentrated in the developing countries and in the transitional economies of central and eastern Europe. The privatization of over 400 medium-sized and large state-owned enterprises in developing countries from 1988-1992 has raised over $49 billion. Future privatization of state-owned enterprises in western Europe alone could amount to $150 billion by 1998. More privatizations in developed countries are scheduled in the future in industries such as air transport, telecommunications, oil, and utilities, all considered to be of strategic importance to the national interests of a number of countries.[13]

The trend towards privatization of state-owned enterprises gives international firms and international investors an opportunity to enter potentially lucrative markets that were once closed to private enterprise. It also provides international companies an opportunity to capitalize on the comparative advantage of countries that have opened their doors to foreign companies. Several European and American companies have either purchased part or total shares of various state-owned firms in eastern Europe to benefit from the competitive advantage to be gained when state-of-the-art technology is combined with a workforce that is not only cheap but skilled as well. Others have bought into state-owned enterprises in order to enter the local market, or to use it as an export base to third-country markets.

Privatization of state-owned enterprises is expected to foster greater competition in domestic industry, resulting in greater efficiency and higher profitability in the privatized firms, all of which are likely to have a favorable impact on the investment climate in the country for international companies.

The Burgeoning Middle Class

Economic development in the developing countries of Latin America and Asia and in the transitional economies of eastern and central Europe is creating a flourishing middle class that has massive purchasing power to buy VCRs, CDs, TV sets, camcorders, computers, automobiles, and washing machines, as well as personal consumer products such as toothpaste, soap, and cereals. Asia is growing a huge crop of consumers. Hundreds of millions will enter or approach the middle class before the end of the decade. Eastern Europe's 300 million consumers, freed from the communist yoke, need almost all conceivable consumer durable and nondurable products. South America, long shackled with burdensome inflation, is finally getting its economic house in order, and consumers in countries such as Brazil, Argentina, and Chile are ready for international brand products.

But just what is the middle class in these countries? In India, households earning more than $1,400 annually are placed in the upper middle-class category, and there are 100 million that fall in this grouping. The lower middle class consists of households earning $700 to $1,400 per year, and there are 200 million people in this group.[14] In China the middle class means household incomes of more than $1,000 per annum. In Poland, middle-class income is $3,000 annually.[15] Incomes are difficult to estimate because people often underreport income in household surveys. Therefore shopping bills and electricity bills are often used to make estimates of household consumption, and from it the household incomes. Based upon such estimates, in Indonesia middle class is a family with shopping bills of more than $140 a month.[16]

How can one place a household that earns less than $1,500 annually in the middle class? In the United States and in most western European countries such low incomes would place a household at or below the poverty level. The answer lies in the fact that money generally goes further in developing countries. In developing Asia, a person earning $250 annually can afford Gillette razors and Palmolive shaving cream, and at $1,000 a person can afford to buy a Hitachi television set. A study by the Whirlpool Corporation revealed that a household in an eastern European country making $1,000 a year can afford a refrigerator and one earning $2,000 a year can afford an automatic washer.[17] This is because the buying patterns of people in different countries are not the same. Consumers show incredible ingenuity in using their disposable incomes to buy what really matters to them. For instance, "the poorest slums of Calcutta are home to 70,000 VCRs. In Mexico, homes with color televisions outnumber those with running water. . . . In China, where per capita income is less than $600, the Swiss company Rado is selling thousands of its $1,000 watches."[18]

"Says Peter Kennedy, a director of the Futures Group: 'Companies are always astonished by the levels of consumption these incomes support.' His company, like many others, emphasizes per capita incomes based on their relative purchasing power to give a more realistic picture of disposal income. The Futures Group estimates that the number of middle-class workers earning between $10,000 and $40,000, based on purchasing power parity (the typical market basket of goods and services that a country's currency would buy in the home market) is 83 million in China, 17 million in Brazil, and 6 million in South Africa."[19]

The size of the middle class and its purchasing power in developing countries and in the transitional countries of eastern and central Europe makes it imperative that international companies not ignore the vast business opportunities that it offers. International companies should not be blinded by the false impression that countries that are poor in relation to their counterparts in Europe and North America do not have large enough markets worth pursuing, when in fact the middle-class market in countries such as India and China has a purchasing power that is larger than many countries of western Europe!

The Global Information Technology Revolution

Countries and companies around the world are becoming linked together by networks of computers, wireless services such as cellular phones and the Internet, the worldwide network of computers linked by digital phone lines. CNN in India, fax machines in Brazil, cellular phones in the tropical forests of Sri Lanka, satellite dishes in Pakistan, and videophones in London, Paris, and New York are all part of a telecommunications revolution that is changing the way people live and work the world over. High-capacity fiber optics cables, digital switches, and satellites are making it possible for international companies in Germany, as well as tiny textile mills in Thailand, to conduct business anywhere, anytime, and to work with customers, bankers, and suppliers anywhere in the world. Digital phone and TV signals that can be bounced off satellites to be picked up by small dish antennas is making communications with a supplier company in a village in China or Vietnam inexpensive and easy.

Picture the following scene at IBM's PC Direct Operation in Research Triangle Park, North Carolina:

> Rows of sales reps answer calls from customers—about 5000 a day—and take orders for various models of IBM PCs. As they talk, the sales reps enter the particulars of the order on-screen—the new PC will incorporate, say, a 486 DX2 66 chip, 16 megabytes of RAM, a built-in fax modem, and so on—and check to make sure the parts are available. Finished orders are zapped to a nearby assembly plant where computers check them every ten minutes.
>
> Those same computers automatically set production in motion. From a small control room, they send a radio signal to workers called "kitters" on the floor below, like Ron Robinson. He receives the data on his hand-held bar-code reader and then walks from one bar-coded location to another, picking up a hard disk from a bin here, a memory board from a bin there. When he has gathered the complete kit that will become a PC, Robinson takes it to an assembly station.
>
> There assembler Tisha Hyman scans the bar code on each part as she builds the machine, and checks her assembly-control screen to make sure the factory system has subtracted each part from inventory. Soon the new PC travels down the line to be automatically tested and packaged—for delivery to the customer the next day by Airborne Express, if the customer so requests.[20]

Similar linkages between the customer and the production center via telephone, computers, and video equipment have been utilized in other industries, including apparel and consumer electronics.

"Virtual banking" has arrived in the banking industry. The industry is being transformed into a grand electronic net that transcends national boundaries. Automated teller machines (ATMs) allow customers to withdraw cash from their bank accounts in the local currency almost anywhere in the world. Citibank's sophisticated electronic system in Singapore allows a banker in any Asian branch to check all of a customer's account information. The system includes notes of all previous conversations with the customer, so when a customer goes to a Malaysian branch of Citibank, a representative there can start where his colleague in Hong Kong left off. And Chase Manhattan Corporation processes millions of dollars worth of transactions involving currency, global securities services, and dividend payments input from a satellite network that connects its offices in New York, Hong Kong, Luxembourg, and Tokyo.[21]

In the automobile industry, high speed videoconferencing is being used in conjunction with computer-aided design (CAD) to bring together design engineers based in research centers in different continents to work as a team in designing the shape of a new automobile. For example, in designing the "world car" at the Ford Motor Company, "an elaborate system using videoconferencing and shared computer-aided design allowed staffers in Germany, Britain, and the U.S. to work on the project together."[22]

These described scenarios at IBM and Ford are possible because companies, in increasing numbers, are creating local area networks (LAN) that link computers and peripheral devices within a company, building, or a limited area, allowing them to share information and programs. LANs are the central nervous systems of companies. They carry everything from E-mail to desktop videoconferencing. LANs can be connected with each other to form a wide area network (WAN)—an enterprise-wide communications network that allows signals to be transmitted from a LAN via public or private line to other LANs in distant locations.

A networked corporation can do business anywhere in the world, anytime. For instance, L.M. Ericsson has 17,000 engineers in 40 research centers located in 20 countries all over the world, all linked into one network. Development teams in Australia and England work together on the same design, then zip off the final blueprint to a factory in China.[23]

What does the global information technology revolution mean to the world economies, and to international companies in particular? For one thing, it means that the world is getting smaller—the concepts of space and distance as measured in miles and kilometers are becoming less relevant. Instead, the measurement of distance in terms of time taken to get to someplace or to reach someone is becoming far more relevant and important. Whereas it might take about 30 hours to fly from Philadelphia to Beijing, China; or 24 hours for a document to reach any place on earth by Federal Express or DHL; with the technology that is available today, one can "travel" to, or "reach" someone, just about anywhere in the world instantaneously through one or more of the following: telephone, E-mail, computer networking, and videoconferencing. For international companies these developments mean that they must incorporate the latest technological advances in their communications and management systems, or face the risk of falling behind competitors that do.

The Emergence of the East Asian Economies

The big story of the last quarter of the 20th century is the emergence of the economic power of countries in East Asia, and particularly of those in the Pacific Basin. (See the map of east Asia in Exhibit 2-15.) *The Economist* in its survey of the global economy had this to say:

> Over the next 25 years, the world will see the biggest shift in economic strength for more than a century. Today the so-called industrial economies dominate the globe, as they have for the past 150 years or so. Yet within a generation several are to be dwarfed by newly emerging economic giants. History suggests, alas, that such shifts in economic power are rarely smooth. A growing number of people in the rich industrial world are already urging their governments to prepare for battle against the upstarts.[24]

The economic giants and "upstarts" that this quotation is referring to are the countries in East Asia and particularly those in the Pacific Rim. The forecast of the economic dominance of the Asian countries are based upon the forecasts of the real gross domestic product growth rates made by The World Bank, which indicate that for the period 1994-2003 the countries in the Pacific Basin and South Asia are expected to grow at the rate of 5.3 percent and 7.6 percent annually respectively, versus a puny rate of 2.7 percent for the same period for the rich industrial countries.[25]

The dominance of the rich industrialized countries in the world economy is far smaller than is generally recognized. Measuring each country's output by valuing its goods and services in dollars at international exchange rates produces the ranking shown in Exhibit 2-16 on page 41. However, if a nation's output is measured in terms of the purchasing power of its own currency at home, rather than the currency's value on international exchanges, i.e., on the basis of purchasing power parity, the picture looks quite different, as seen in Exhibit 2-17 on page 42. In Exhibit 2-17(a), five of the top fifteen countries ranked by their economic size are Asian: Japan, China, India, Indonesia, and South Korea. And if the GDP for developed and developing countries continues to grow at the rate forecast by The World Bank for this next decade, by the year 2020

EXHIBIT 2-15
Countries of East Asia

the rich countries' share of global output may shrink to less than two-fifths, as shown in Exhibit 2-17(b), and the ranking of the fifteen largest economies would change dramatically as shown in Exhibit 2-17(c), as China will overtake the United States as the world's largest economy and as many as eight of the fifteen countries will belong to the East Asian region.

It is true that the GDP forecasts shown in Exhibit 2-17 are just extrapolations of current trends, and therefore it is very likely that the Asian economies will slow down as they become richer and grow to resemble today's rich countries. However, the trends do point to the growing economic power of Asian economies, and historically giant economic leaps by countries are not unprecedented.

The competitiveness of an economy is indicative of its future prospects for growth. A recent IMD Executive Opinion Survey of leading business executives shows that they expect the United States and Japan to remain as the most competitive economies in 2030. However, the survey also reveals that executives expect seven of the ten most competitive economies to be Asian. (See Exhibit 2-18 on page 43.)

The growth of the economic power of Asian economies is also manifested in data that indicate that there is a definite trend towards greater intra-Asian trade. Asian manufacturers no longer

EXHIBIT 2-16

13 Largest Economies, Based on GDP, 1992 (GDP in $US Trillion)

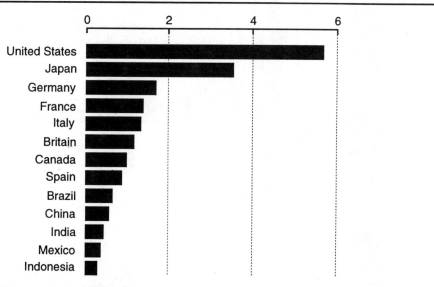

Source: OECD, World Bank International Monetary Fund.

need customers in European and North American countries as much now as they once did. Since 1986, intra-Asian exports and imports have increased from 31 percent to 50 percent in 1992.[26] Exhibit 2-19 on page 44, shows the breakdown of Asian trade. Trade in Asia is dominated by Asian countries with North America and western Europe playing the second biggest role. A similar picture emerges regarding the pattern of foreign direct investment (FDI) in Asia. FDI in Asia (not including Japanese investment) is mostly intraregional, and if one were to include Japanese investments into the region, then the FDI that is intra-Asian amounts to 69 percent of the total.

There is growing competition for Asian markets between the two economic superpowers— the United States and Japan. The Japanese have a much bigger lead over the United States in exports to Asia, and the gap seems to be widening. Moreover, the United States' FDI in Asia, although growing fast, still lags that of Japan in cumulative amounts. As of 1992, the total cumulative FDI for the United States amounted to just over $31 billion, as opposed to Japan's nearly $60 billion. A fact that accounts for the larger Japanese exports than from the United States is that Japan's foreign aid has "stressed infrastructure and industrial projects—an emphasis that builds ties between industrialists and local elites. . . and Japanese companies have concentrated on factories and distribution, whereas more than half of U.S. investment has been in petroleum, a depletable resource. The upshot is that Japan's exports to Asia are exceeding America's exports to the region by an ever-widening margin."[27]

Nevertheless, the importance of the Asian markets for American companies is growing, in that Asians have a growing appetite for American goods. But more importantly it shows that the Asian region has surpassed Europe as America's export destination. It is anticipated that East Asian economies will create an increasing demand for American products. The Office of the U.S. Trade

EXHIBIT 2-17
Largest Economies, Based on Purchasing Power Parity

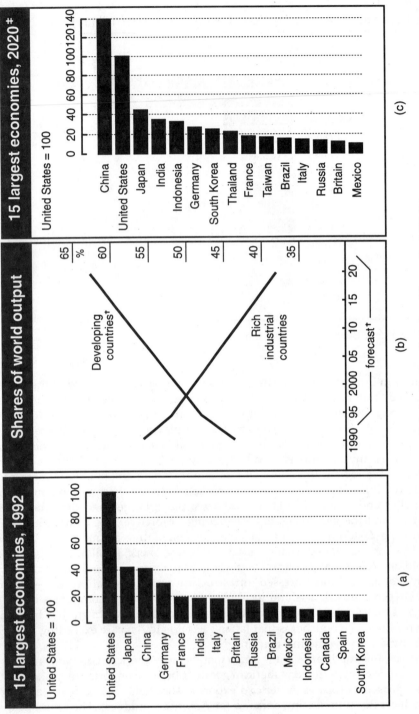

2020 vision GDPs at PPP*

15 largest economies, 1992

United States = 100

United States
Japan
China
Germany
France
India
Italy
Britain
Russia
Brazil
Mexico
Indonesia
Canada
Spain
South Korea

(a)

Shares of world output

%
65
60
55
50
45
40
35

Developing countries†

Rich industrial countries

1990 95 2000 05 10 15 20
—— forecast† ——

(b)

15 largest economies, 2020‡

United States = 100

0 20 40 60 80 100 120 140

China
United States
Japan
India
Indonesia
Germany
South Korea
Thailand
France
Taiwan
Brazil
Italy
Russia
Britain
Mexico

(c)

Source: World Bank   *Purchasing-power parity   †including Eastern Europe and former Soviet Union
‡Forecasts assume countries continue to grow at regional rates projected in the World Bank's Global Economic Prospects

Source: "The Global Economy," *The Economist,* October 1, 1994, p. 4. © 1994, The Economist Newspaper, Ltd.   Reprinted by permission. All rights reserved.

EXHIBIT 2-18

Economic Competitiveness in 2030 (Business leaders' rankings*)

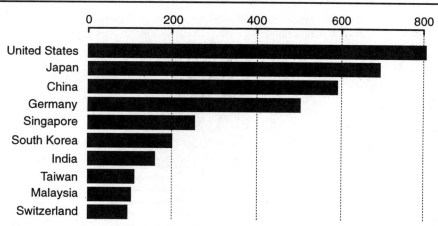

Source: IMD Executive Opinion Survey
*Based on number of responses

Representative estimates that by the year 2010, United States' exports in 1994 dollars to East Asia (excluding Japan) will increase to $248 billion from the 1994 total of approximately $94 billion. Similar projections for the European Union estimate total exports of $128 billion by 2010, an increase of only $33 billion from the 1994 figures of $95 billion.[28]

The previous discussion of the emergence of the East Asian economies strongly suggests that the future competitive battles for market shares will be fought in the East Asian markets, because that area is where the markets are growing. Future prosperity of countries and companies depends more on expanding trade with the booming economies of East Asia than in the mature markets of Europe. International companies have no choice but to get actively involved in the Asian markets, because if they do not, they will lose their competitive positions to those companies that do.

The Movement Toward Free Trade and Trade Blocs

A dominant trend of the last quarter of the 20th century has been the movement of countries toward the promotion of free trade, and the tendency of countries to form trade blocs that favor free trade amongst member countries at the expense of nonmembers. The World Trade Organization has succeeded the General Agreement on Tariff and Trade, we have witnessed the maturing of the European Union, the creation of NAFTA, and the movement toward the formation of trade blocs in South America and in Asia. These important changes in the global trading system will be covered in the next chapter.

The six trends that we have briefly discussed are by no means all of the important factors in today's international business arena, but each does represent a significant issue, an understanding of which is vital to the ability of the international manager to find a profitable niche in the

EXHIBIT 2-19
Asia's Trading Partners

In 1992, more than half of import and export trade
in Asia was among the Asian countries themselves.

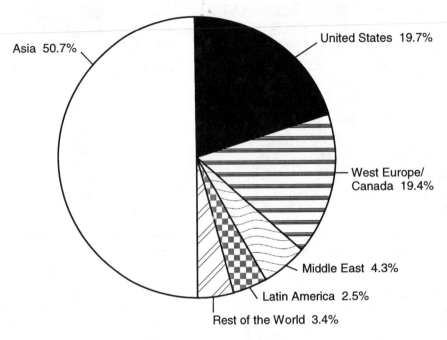

Asia 50.7%

United States 19.7%

West Europe/
Canada 19.4%

Middle East 4.3%

Latin America 2.5%

Rest of the World 3.4%

Source: International Monetary Fund

Source: Laurence Zuckerman, "Defying Gravity: Trade Will Help Most Asian Nations Soar in 1994," *The Wall Street Journal Classroom Edition*, February 1994, pp. 12-13.

international marketplace for the firm. While trends change over time, it is imperative that the international manager be able to identify at any time the underlying directions in which the marketplace and competitive environment is moving. This allows the manager to take advantage of new opportunities, while remaining sensitive to the limitations of the business environment. In the next chapter we take a more detailed look at the challenges and opportunities offered by the last of the trends introduced here—the movement towards free trade and regional trade blocs.

SUMMARY

International trade and foreign direct investment (FDI) bind the countries of the world together through the transfer of resources, capital, and products between and among them. International firms are essential to both trade and FDI, regardless of whether they are primarily exporters of finished goods and services, or actively involved in investment and production in other countries.

FDI flows can be used as indicators of firm expansion, market attractiveness, technology transfer, and the relative importance of international companies in domestic economies.

Because of the large pools of assets and investment stock controlled by major international companies, they can wield significant influence over national economic conditions and policies. In smaller, less-developed countries, large international companies may be the principal supplier of jobs, technology, and gross domestic product. Even in large, developed countries, the large internationals' control of huge assets afford them a high degree of economic and political power.

An important factor in assessing the attractiveness of a potential foreign investment by an international company is the comparative cost structure of the target location being considered. Costs for skilled and unskilled labor, real estate and office space, and living and entertainment expenses are properly evaluated in terms of their absolute cost in terms of the company's home currency. However, consumer market potential is more appropriately assessed in terms of the relative buying power of the consumers.

An understanding of the current trends underlying the global business environment is essential to the international manager. Six important trends present today include the global thrust for a market economy; the move toward privatization of previously state-owned enterprises; the tremendous increase, worldwide, in the numbers of middle-class consumers; the revolution in global communications and information technology; the emergence of economic power in East Asia; and the movement toward regional trade blocs and overall freer international trade.

QUESTIONS FOR THOUGHT AND DISCUSSION

1. Pick one company from the lists of the largest international companies provided in the chapter and obtain a recent annual report or other printed company data source (e.g., Moody's) about it. In how many different countries does the firm do business? Do you think its revenues come mostly from exports or from FDI? Based on the information you have, write a short paragraph explaining how this company contributes to international trade.

2. Find an article in the current business press that illustrates a strategic decision made by an international firm to capitalize on a comparative advantage in labor or other costs in another country. Discuss the implications of this decision on the company, the home country, and the new host country.

3. In the text, we identified six trends that characterize today's global business environment. Can you think of any others that are important today? What emerging trends can you foresee in the future that might have a great effect on the international company? Discuss.

4. Explain the importance of FDI inflows and FDI outflows to a country. What do they signify? Which is better—inflow or outflow? Why?

5. What factors can you think of that might account for the strong showing of the East Asian economies in recent years? Do you think they can sustain their rate of development? Why or why not?

MINI-CASE
G.E. Finds Tough Going in Hungary

Budapest, July 23—Five years ago (1989), amid handshakes and grins, the General Electric Company agreed to acquire Tungsram, a maker of lighting products and one of Hungary's industrial gems, in a deal that many believed would show other leading Western corporations how to turn Communist-run enterprises into money makers.

Almost immediately, other ambitious American companies took notice of General Electric's investment in eastern Europe, and it became a beacon of hope for Hungary's workers and government leaders.

But as losses mounted, General Electric soon faced the reality of what happens when grand expectations collide with the grim realities of an embedded culture of waste, inefficiency, and indifference about customers and quality.

The Americans huffed that the Hungarians were lackadaisical; the Hungarians thought the Americans pushy. The company's aggressive management system depends on communication between workers and managers; the Communist system had forbidden it.

The Americans wanted sales, marketing, and pampering of customers; the Hungarians believed these things took care of themselves. Hungarians expected General Electric to deliver lush Western-style wages. But the company came to Hungary to pay lower wages for making and exporting light bulbs, auto headlights and other products to western Europe. After a series of raises Tungsram workers now average $2 an hour.

"Human engineering was much more difficult than product engineering," said Charles P. Pieper, the General Electric executive brought in 19 months ago by John F. Welch, Jr., chairman and chief executive, to rescue G.E.'s investment. Now the company says it has turned the corner at Tungsram and the operation has been profitable for a year.

Getting there meant laying off half of Tungsram's nearly 20,000 workers, including three of every four managers. The company began weekly huddles between Tungsram and American managers linked by conference call and it created a system of worker team meetings to devise ways to work more efficiently.

It also invested in new equipment to increase productivity and reduce waste. When General Electric arrived, half of what the workers made was scrapped because of defects. Now, the company says it has raised productivity by 50 percent.

Timing Not Understood

Outside analysts who have studied General Electric's acquisition say it will turn out to be a wise investment in the long term. "But once they made the strategic decision of buying a Communist-run company in eastern Europe, General Electric didn't understand how long it would take to bring things up to par," said Paul Marer, professor of international business at Indiana University.

A former employee, Istvan Kosa, 49, a financial analyst, said he understood General Electric's strategy but that emotionally it was draining.

"For those who lived through it, it seemed cruel," he said. "We were forced into a situation where we had to sit down two or three times a year and decide how we were going to reduce the number of employees and reorganize the cost. When I started in that accounting unit in 1991 there were 36 of us, when I left there were only 8."

General Electric has long been considered by business leaders as one of America's most admired companies. It has never had an annual loss, and until a scandal at its brokerage firm subsidiary this year it had a string of 73 quarters in which it had recorded rising profits. Its chief, Mr. Welsh, is a fierce competitor who wants to dominate each of General Electric's 12 businesses.

Toiling for Capitalism

Mr. Welsh's ambitions have reached the most remote Tungsram plant, where his drive for productivity raised some unusual parallels. "In Hungary many of us had to attend the Marx-Engels-

Lenin University and learn slogans," said Janos Szlivka, the leader of the Independent Trade Union of Tungsram Employees at the Kisvarda factory in eastern Hungary. Instead of "Work, work, work for the Worker's Brigade," Tungsram employees were told to toil so General Electric could "become the most productive company on earth."

Mr. Szlivka pulled out a copy of a General Electric book given to him at a motivational seminar and thumbed through the pages. "Welch's slogans," he said, "'If we're not No. 1 or No. 2 in a business, improve it, close it or sell it.' The workers don't like it."

General Electric says that in ordering layoffs it was careful to first edge out those near retirement. Employees received nine months of wages, well above what Hungarian law requires, and were given counseling for other opportunities. But many women on Hungary's generous three-year maternity leave have not been rehired. And as General Electric bore down on productivity goals in 1992 and 1993, many workers were dismissed because the company no longer believed that they were needed.

Machines, Not People

Those who stayed were told to work harder. The company adapted its American system of "action workouts" at Tungsram to wring more efficiencies out of the workers. These "workouts," or teams of workers tackling specific problems, reflect Mr. Welch's belief in a "boundary-less" culture in which employees remove obstacles to work more efficiently. The goal, General Electric assured skeptical Tungsram workers, was to make quality lights to improve sales which in turn would increase orders to the plants.

But workouts resulted in more machines and fewer people, making them a hard sell on the factory floor.

Mr. Szlivka, the union official, said these efficiencies had gone as far as humanly possible. "I don't know if the workers can be squeezed any more," he said.

If General Electric methods were demanding for the workers, they were an ordeal for the managers.

"For the first year, it was very difficult to know whether I could live up to the expectations or not. Not only for me but for the other managers," said Miklos Horvath, 54, the manager of the Tungsram plant in Nagykanisza, in southwest Hungary.

Classes in English

Mr. Horvath, like most of the survivors, had to attend English classes, a daunting undertaking at his age. He knew if he could not perform smoothly in weekly conference calls with his American peers he would not last.

Many did not. "A lot of people who were not driven and who couldn't stomach it left," said Ivan Volgyes, a G.E. consultant.

General Electric agreed to pay $150 million for 50.1 percent of Tungsram in 1989, but in less than four years it announced that it had "lost the equity value of the company" and pumped in another $195 million of fresh capital. Still more money followed and all told, General Electric has invested $550 million in Tungsram and now virtually owns it.

Tungsram, which accounted for 3 percent of Hungary's gross national product, was a low-cost way for General Electric to enter the western European market where it had never been much of a force in the lighting business. Tungsram had 7 percent of the western European market in 1989, and Mercedes-Benz was a big customer of its headlights. Tungsram's share was better than General Electric's 2 percent slice of the market. General Electric also believed that Tungsram would be the vehicle for taking on Philips, the big Dutch electronics company, and the Osram unit of Siemens of Germany.

Hard-Headed Guidelines

But a year into the deal, General Electric discovered outdated equipment, poor distribution and sales, and arcane accounting procedures that had disguised losses.

To cut costs, Mr. Pieper issued hard-headed guidelines for layoffs: "I said, 'If we have ten people in an area, look at the requirements for the next ten years. If we need six, consider not laying off four but laying off six and adding two later.'"

Company officials now say the combination of General Electric's productivity drive and Hungarian scientific ability is bringing results. With Tungsram and a British subsidiary, the former lighting business of Thorn EMI P.L.C., General Electric now has 16 percent of the market, company officials said.

"I hope now you're looking at a winning culture," said Mr. Pieper, who is based in London. "Our yields today are equal to the best we have in the world."

Better Productivity Cited

Mr. Pieper attributed much of the improved picture to better productivity. "This is where the workouts are important," he said.

For example, a war room plastered with productivity goals was opened at the Nagykanisza plant so adjusters could move from the factory floor to a conference table and figure out how to rejigger machines to save time and improve quality.

In one instance, the time it took to reset a machine from making one kind of lamp to making another kind was reduced from 955 minutes in March 1993 to 480 minutes to 200 minutes three months later.

In May, General Electric persuaded the Hungarian government to grant another five-year tax holiday on profits, arguing that a similar break in the first five years had meant little because there were no profits.

Higher Wages Sought

So as the operation turns profitable and some assembly-line workers are being rehired at the Tungsram plants in Kisvarda and Nagykanisza, the question of higher wages looms. Mr. Szlivka, the union leader, says the workers feel cheated because they were told in 1990 that with fewer workers wages would rise.

But pay has failed to keep up with inflation. Last year, Hungary's inflation was 28 percent but Tungsram wages rose only 6 percent. This year, with inflation at 22 percent, the union won a 16 percent increase.

A national survey by the union last year showed that 36 percent of Tungsram workers lived in families that were on the Hungarian poverty line, a far higher number than in 1988.

General Electric says that Tungsram wages, which average $320 a month, are in the top 25 percent in each of the eight plant towns.

"Labor is so cheap here," Mr. Szlivka said. "In England, people who work in this industry make 10 pounds an hour. They make 1 pound an hour here. The past four years have really meant that people have had to work more and the money that they make doesn't even come near the inflation level. So it shouldn't be any surprise they are not crazy about General Electric."

But General Electric's experience has not translated into a ground swell against foreign takeovers.

"I don't think General Electric has made people against foreign investment," Mr. Szlivka said. "The workers are not against development but at the same time they want to be able to make a living. The workers don't understand why they make less money if the products they produce are as good as Philips's. Why is there such a difference in wages? Since the Iron Curtain was removed, people can see what is happening elsewhere."

Source: Jane Perlez, *The New York Times*, Monday, July 25, 1994, p. D1. Copyright © 1994 by The New York Times Company. Reprinted by permission.

Discussion Questions for Mini-Case

1. What strategic reasons induced GE to buy Tungsram?
2. Should GE have anticipated the problems that were experienced in managing Tungsram? Explain why.
3. How can GE justify the lower-than-inflation wage increases given to Tungsram employees?
4. Is GE's acquisition of Tungsram a success or failure (a) from GE's perspective, (b) from the Hungarian government's perspective, and (c) from the workers' perspective?
5. Explain the economic, political, cultural, and other factors that might explain why there was almost no opposition from the union and workers to the massive layoffs engineered by GE at Tungsram.
6. What lessons can other international companies and GE learn from GE's acquisition of a state-owned enterprise? Could the lessons learned be equally applicable in all circumstances involving the acquisition of a state-owned enterprise?

Notes

1 United Nations Conference on Trade and Development, *World Investment Report 1994*, United Nations, New York, 1994, p. 13 and table II.10, p. 59.
2 Ibid., Table I.6, p. 17.
3 Ibid., Table I.8, p. 19.
4 Pete Engardio, Rob Hof, Elizabeth Malkin, Neil Gross, and Karen Lowry Miller, "High Tech Jobs all over the World," *Business Week*, 21st Century Capitalism, Special 1994 Bonus Issue, November 18, 1994, pp. 112-119.
5 Ibid.
6 Ibid.
7 United Nations Conference on Trade and Development, *World Investment Report 1994*, United Nations, New York, 1994, p. 5.
8 *Business Week,* "The Business Week 1000," July 10, 1995, p. 62.
9 Ibid., p. 62.
10 "Japanese Banking: The Big One," *The Economist,* April 1, 1995, p. 61.
11 Christopher Farell, "The Triple Revolution," *Business Week*, Special 1994 Bonus Issue, November 18, 1994, p. 17.
12 Ibid.
13 "Selling the State," *The Economist,* August 21, 1993.

14 Rahul Jacob, "India is Open for Business," *Fortune*, November 16, 1992, p. 128.

15 Rahul Jacob, "The Big Rise: Middle Classes Explode Around the Globe, Bringing New Markets and Prosperity," *Fortune*, May 30, 1994, pp. 74-90.

16 Ibid.

17 Bill Saporito, "Where the Global Action Is," *Fortune*, Autumn/Winter 1993, pp. 63-65.

18 Ibid.

19 Rahul Jacob, "The Big Rise: Middle Classes Explode Around the Globe, Bringing New Markets and Prosperity," *Fortune*, May 30, 1994, p. 78.

20 Gene Bylinsky, "The Digital Factory," *Fortune*, November 14, 1994, pp. 92-107.

21 Kelly Holland, Paula Dwyer, and Gail Edmondson, "Technobanking Takes Off," *Business Week*, 21st Century Capitalism, Special 1994 Bonus Issue, November 18, 1994, pp. 52-53.

22 Paula Dwyer, Pete Engardio, Zachary Schiller, and Stanley Reed, "Tearing Up Today's Organization Chart," *Business Week*, 21st Century Capitalism, Special 1994 Bonus Issue, November 18, 1994, p. 83.

23 Catherine Arnst, "The Networked Corporation," *Business Week*, June 26, 1995, pp. 86-89.

24 "The Global Economy," *The Economist*, October 1, 1994, p. 3.

25 Ibid.

26 Laurence Zuckerman, "Defying Gravity: Trade will make most Asian nations soar in 1994," *The Wall Street Journal Classroom Edition*, February 1994, pp. 12-13.

27 Kathleen Madigan, "In Fast-Growing Asia, Japan is Leaving the U.S. in the Dust," *Business Week*, September 12, 1994, p. 26.

28 David E. Sanger, "More Growth Predicted for New Markets," *The New York Times*, November 4, 1994, p. D1.

Movement Toward Free Trade and Trade Blocs

LEARNING OBJECTIVES

After completing this chapter, you will be able to:

- Discuss potential effects of the growth of regional trade blocs on global free trade.
- Describe the key features of the Uruguay Round of the General Agreement on Tariffs and Trade (GATT) and the World Trade Organization (WTO) and their implications for the conduct of business between member countries.
- Discuss the significance of the World Trade Organization (WTO) to international trade.
- Explain the differences and similarities between a free trade area, a customs union, a common market, and an economic union.
- Describe the important characteristics of the NAFTA and the European Union, ways in which they can be expected to improve business opportunities, and problems associated with their implementation.

The decade of the 1980s saw the beginning of serious efforts by the nations of the world to erase barriers to free trade among themselves. Although efforts to bring about freer trade among nations were begun with the General Agreement on Tariffs and Trade (GATT) negotiations as early as 1948, and with the Treaty of Rome in 1957, which created the European Economic Community, the real impetus to freer trade was given by the recognition by nation-states that, in the long run, the economic benefits of free trade would spread to the peoples of all countries. The success of the European Economic Community, which promoted freer trade among its member countries and raised the living standards of people in the Community, as well as the fall of Communism in the Soviet Union and other eastern European countries, demonstrated the power of the free market and free flow of resources over state regulation of economic activity. These developments played a major role in the global push favoring freer world trade.

There have been major developments favoring free trade which we can place in two categories: (1) the conclusion of the Uruguay Round negotiations of the General Agreement on Tariffs and Trade (GATT) and (2) the emergence of regional trade blocs, such as the North American Free Trade Agreement (NAFTA), the expanded European Union (formerly known as the European Economic Community) and other regional trade arrangements such as MERCUSOR, the Andean Pact, and the Association of South East Asian Nations (ASEAN).

We shall examine these developments in free trade later in this chapter. But first we shall discuss the static and dynamic effects of economic integration, which should put into a proper perspective the ensuing examination of the movement towards free trade among nations and of the various regional free trade agreements.

ECONOMIC EFFECTS OF ECONOMIC INTEGRATION

Economic integration of countries within a region alters tariffs and trade preferences, and thereby changes relative prices and patterns of consumption and production. There are two main categories of effects resulting from economic integration: *static* and *dynamic*.[1] We shall explain how these effects emerge in a **common market** that provides common external tariffs and quotas against third countries, and free movement of people, capital, and goods and services among member countries. Except for an economic union, a common market is the most advanced form of economic integration among countries

Static Effects of Economic Integration

Common external trade barriers and free trade among member countries have both positive and negative effects on trade patterns. The positive trade effect occurs when free trade among member countries leads to the substitution of inefficient domestic production in a common market country for efficient production in another country also in the common market. As an example, in the European Union, German consumers would be better off, after the lowering of tariffs, by importing products produced by a low-cost producer in Spain rather than a high-cost producer inside Germany. Trade is created between Germany and Spain that did not exist before because tariffs on imports made the Spanish products noncompetitive against the German-made products. This is good, as it manifests comparative advantage at work. When such new trade is created among member countries that does not displace third-country imports, it is called *trade creation*. Trade creation is a positive effect of free trade. However, lowering intraregional barriers leaves relatively high barriers on nonmembers. If this leads to a substitution of efficient third-country production by inefficient production in a common market country, it may result in *trade diversion*. Trade diversion would occur when consumers within a common market find that goods produced inefficiently in a member country are cheaper than efficiently produced goods in a country outside of the common market, primarily because of the high tariffs imposed on imports from non-common market countries. As an example, suppose that the unit production cost of a car is $5000 in Germany and $4000 in Japan. If the European Union imposes a 50 percent import tariff on imports of Japanese automobiles, the cost of Japanese cars in Germany and in other European countries would increase to $6000. Consumers in the European Union would therefore be more inclined to buy German cars as opposed to Japanese cars, resulting in a diversion of trade. This is bad: comparative advantage is denied. Why? Because before the free trade was established, exporters of German and Japanese cars faced the same tariff, so the importing country chose its suppliers on price and quality alone. With free trade within the common market, the importer switched to the less efficient supplier in Germany.

Under what circumstances would a common market lead to trade creation as opposed to trade diversion? Trade creation can generally be high when the economies of the member countries are very competitive and not specialized in the production of certain industries or products, i.e., production is overlapping and diffused among member countries. Such conditions provide opportunities for specialization and intra-common market trade. On the other hand, if the economies of the countries prior to the formation of the common market were complementary, then opportunities for *new* trade are limited, because the economies are already specialized with respect to each other. Trade creation is expected to be high also when (1) the member countries in the common market are at similar levels of economic development; (2) the pre-union tariffs of member countries were high, inducing trade creation in products that were once protected from imports; (3) transport costs are low; (4) and the size of the common market is large, because the larger the size, the greater the probability that producers will be able to obtain low cost derived from the scale effect. Trade diversion is more likely to occur in a common market of small economic size, because member countries will be inclined to protect their own relatively less efficient companies (due to higher unit costs because of the absence of the scale effect) against more efficient outsiders by raising the tariff barriers against imports.

The net effect of a common market depends on the size of trade creation relative to trade diversion. Trade creation improves the world's economic efficiency, and thus its potential welfare, by substituting low-cost production for high-cost production. Potential world welfare is lowered when trade diversion causes the substitution of high-cost production within the common market for low-cost production outside the union.

The best solution to ensure trade creation in a free trade area is to insist that "(a) members of a free trade area set a common external tariff (and thus form a customs union) and (b) that the common tariff for any item should be set equal to the lowest tariff applied to that good by any member of the free trade area before the union was formed."[2]

Dynamic Effects of Economic Integration

In addition to the static effects, free trade arrangements can have significant dynamic effects on economic growth. *Market extension* is one benefit of a common market. Producers have free access to the national markets of all member countries, unhindered by import restrictions. Similarly, consumers have access to products produced in all countries of the union. The enlarged market serves as a catalyst for many forces. It promotes *economies of scale,* not only in production, but also in marketing, research and development, and purchasing, as the large market size is able to support larger scale in these functions. Higher capital investment also boosts the returns to skilled labor by improving *productivity,* which in turn increases the accumulation of human capital, thus raising growth further. In common markets, labor mobility also increases productivity and growth as firms are able to hire skilled workers and professionals who are able to move freely in search of jobs where their abilities are most in demand. A larger market size also promotes entry of new competitors and intensifies *competition,* forcing producers to improve product and service quality, and to search for ways to lower costs by improving efficiency in all business functions. Intensified competition fosters the growth of efficient firms and the demise of inefficient ones. Growth of firms, either by internal growth, acquisition of smaller firms, or merger, results in increases in *firm size.* And generally, larger firms have much greater capacity to fund research and development and to compete by marketing innovative products.

WILL REGIONAL TRADE BLOCS PROMOTE GLOBAL FREE TRADE?

Will the already existing trade blocs—such as NAFTA, the EU, and others such as the Andean Pact and MERCUSOR—serve as catalysts for worldwide free trade? Will the trade blocs be able to achieve the vision of global free trade enshrined in the GATT agreement (discussed earlier in this chapter)? Opinion of experts is divided on this issue.

On one side, those who do not believe that trade blocs will lead to global free trade base their opinion on events both in the EU and NAFTA. In the EU, quotas were imposed on imports of Japanese automobiles to protect the European automakers. In NAFTA, quotas restrict imports of some types of steel and textile products. The fear is that companies protected by common external tariff walls against competing imports will become complacent and inefficient, and ultimately demand ever-increasing protectionist measures for their own survival against foreign competition. Professor Jagdish Bhagwati, one of the world's top trade theorists and advisor to the Director General of GATT, believes that "it is all too likely that regional trade blocs will advance the frontiers of liberal trade more slowly than the GATT, because governments will find it harder to resist the argument, put by protectionist lobbies, that 'our market is already large enough.'"[3]

On the other side are those who believe that trade blocs will expand their membership and add countries that do not yet belong. For instance, NAFTA has already made overtures to Chile, and there is speculation that NAFTA may eventually be enlarged to include not only Chile, but Argentina and Brazil as well. By the year 2000 or soon after, NAFTA is expected to add countries from Central and South America to form one huge free trade area to encompass all of North and South America, stretching from Alaska to Argentina. Similarly, the European Union is expected to include all countries of western and eastern Europe during the first decade of the next century.

Finding that they are being discriminated against by the trade bloc countries, those countries that are left out of the trade blocs may seek to form their own trade blocs, or alternatively seek special free trade agreements with existing trade blocs. Such advice is offered to countries like India by Professor Jagdish Bhagwati. Professor Bhagwati believes that, in response to NAFTA and the EU, an Asian bloc may be formed, possibly centered on Japan, and countries such as India that are marginalized on the outside should seek special free trade agreements with it. He believes that the Asian bloc, if it does materialize, would be inclined to seriously consider India's request because of its huge internal market and its potential as a sourcing country for foreign firms.[4] Thus, it is hypothesized that the number of trade blocs will multiply because each new trade bloc will serve as a stimulant for countries left on the periphery to form their own trade blocs.

Proponents of the theory that trade blocs will eventually lead to global free trade also suggest that free trade negotiations between and among trade blocs may lead to their becoming merged with one another. For instance, NAFTA and the EU may initially negotiate free trade in automobiles, which may be extended to other industries, and which in turn may eventually lead to a merger of the two blocs to form one mega-trade bloc that comprises all of the Americas and Europe. However distant this scenario may be to becoming a reality, it is argued that the thrust of the argument, that free trade blocs will lead to global free trade, is no less valid.

Having discussed the benefits and drawbacks of free trade, we shall now review the movement toward global free trade, starting with the General Agreement on Tariffs and Trade (commonly known as GATT) and its successor, the World Trade Organization (WTO).

THE GENERAL AGREEMENT ON TARIFFS AND TRADE (GATT) AND THE WORLD TRADE ORGANIZATION (WTO)

GATT is an organization created in 1947, with twenty-three industrialized countries as the founding members, to set fair and common rules for the way each country must conduct its trade with others. GATT was created after World War II for the principal purpose of reducing tariffs[a] and removing nontariff barriers[b] to international trade.

---

a A tariff (or customs duty) is a tax imposed by a government on physical goods as they move in and out of a country.
b Examples of nontariff barriers are import and export quotas, subsidies to domestic producers or exporters, dumping of products (selling a product in one national market at a cheaper price than in another market), and regulations to imports with respect to safety, health, marketing, labeling, packaging, and technical standards, and local content requirements.

The single most important principle at the heart of GATT is that discrimination poisons trade. In keeping with this principle, GATT strives to ensure that every country in GATT opens its markets equally to every other. GATT upholds the principle of "national treatment," which requires countries to treat foreign businesspeople and foreign companies as they do locals.

To date there have been eight rounds of GATT-sponsored multilateral trade negotiations. From the twenty-three countries that took part in the first round in Geneva in 1947, the number of member countries in the eighth Uruguay round had grown to 117 (each round is identified by the name of the place where it took place).

The Uruguay Round was concluded in Geneva on December 15, 1993, after seven years of strenuous negotiations, and the biggest-ever world trade treaty was signed in Marrakesh, Morocco, on April 15, 1994, amidst hopes of a more equitable and cooperative world economic order. See Box 3-1 for a summary of the agreement's highlights.

Estimated Gains from GATT

The gains to the world's economy from the GATT Agreement by the year 2002, as estimated by the World Bank and the Organization for Economic Cooperation and Development (OECD), range from $213 billion to $274 billion each year—a boost of 6 to 8 percent to the global gross domestic product (see Exhibit 3-1). These numbers are conservative forecasts because they do not take into account gains from liberalizing investment and trade in services.[5]

Estimated gains for the U.S. economy range from a minimum of $100 billion to as much as $200 billion by the year 2005.[6]

EXHIBIT 3-1
The GATT Payoff

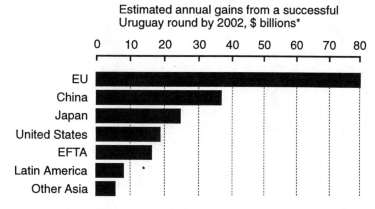

Estimated annual gains from a successful Uruguay round by 2002, $ billions*

Source: "Trade liberalization: Global Economic Implications" by Ian Goldin.
*1992 dollars

BOX 3-1
Highlights of the GATT Accord

Tariffs Tariffs imposed by major industrial countries are to be eliminated, and those of many developing countries either eliminated or sharply reduced. Tariffs would be cut on approximately 85 percent of world trade and eliminated or significantly reduced on a broad range of products, including construction and agricultural equipment, medical equipment, steel, beer, liquor, paper, toys, and furniture. Tariffs on manufactured goods would be slashed by an average of 37 percent, and on industrial goods would drop from an average of about 5 percent to an average of 3 percent. Tariff reductions would be implemented in equal annual increments over five years, although the phase-out period is extended to ten years for textiles.

Agriculture Agricultural export subsidies and trade-distorting domestic farm subsidies are to be reduced by an average of 36 percent. There would be a reduction of 21 percent in the total volume of agricultural products exported with the help of subsidies. Government-paid income support payments for farmers are to be cut by 20 percent. Nontariff barriers, including quotas, are to be phased out. Nontariff barriers will first be replaced by tariffs, then these tariffs will be gradually reduced. Countries with closed markets will have to import at least 3 percent of domestic requirements, rising to 5 percent over six years. Japan, which has maintained a virtual ban on rice imports, must open its market to rice imports equal to 4 percent of domestic consumption, and raise this amount to 8 percent over the next six to ten years. South Korea must import 1 percent of its rice consumption at once, and 2 percent by 1999.

Intellectual Property GATT rules will be extended to intellectual property such as patents, trademarks, and copyrights, which will receive greater protection. Computer programs, semiconductor chip designs, films, music, and books would be protected from piracy. Developing countries would have a ten-year phase-in period to honor patents on drugs. Countries would be obligated to enact laws to enforce this requirement.

Textiles For thirty years, industrial nations have imposed quotas on imports of textiles and clothing from the developing countries under the Multi-Fiber Arrangement. These quotas will be phased out over ten years. The U.S. textile industry will be protected through significantly smaller tariff reductions on textile and apparel imports of just 12 percent, as opposed to the 34 percent U.S tariff reductions on all industrial goods.

Dumping The term "dumping" generally refers to the practice of selling goods in a foreign country below the price charged in the home market, selling at a price that is lower than that offered in other foreign markets, or selling below cost of production. Under GATT regulations, the United States and Europe would be permitted to use existing anti-dumping laws to impose fines or countervailing* duties against countries that are involved in

---

* Countervailing duties are punitive tariffs that are imposed upon products dumped by a company in a foreign country. Aides to Representative Norman Mineta of California were quoted in *The Wall Street Journal* (June 27, 1994, page A14) as saying that, in the United States, the countervailing duties could amount to between $150 and $200 million a year. The steel and semiconductor industries are prominent in anti-dumping suits brought against foreign producers.

BOX 3-1 *(continued)*

dumping. Disputes arising from dumping matters are to be settled under a new, binding, multilateral dispute-settlement mechanism.

Trade-Related Investment Measures (TRIMs)   The Uruguay Round negotiations also yielded trade-related investment measures. For example, the agreements prohibit so-called local content requirements, which force foreign firms to use a set amount of locally produced inputs in production as a condition for granting them the permission to invest in a production facility in the country. It also prohibits "trade balancing" requirements under which a foreign affiliate must export as much of its production as it imports for use as inputs. These requirements have been most troublesome for U.S. firms operating abroad in the past.

Voluntary Export Restraints   Many countries, including the United States, have used the so-called "voluntary export restraints" under which a foreign country is "requested" to hold its exports to a previously agreed-upon fixed quota. For instance, in the mid- to late 1980s, the United States asked, and the Japanese agreed, to establish quantitative limits on the exports of Japanese automobiles to the United States. Similar quantitative restrictions were placed by the European countries on Japanese automobile exports to Europe. The purpose of such export restraints is to protect domestic industry against foreign competitors.

   The GATT agreement prohibits such "voluntary" export restraints and other, similar measures that are often used as safeguards outside GATT rules (GATT sees tariffs as a lesser evil than quotas, although it would prefer to see no tariffs at all).

Services   For the first time, GATT would apply to trade and investment in services, including banking, insurance, accounting, shipping, and telecommunications. The United States was especially interested in applying GATT rules to the $900 billion-worth of services that cross borders and to the $3 trillion-worth of services that are provided domestically in such industries as insurance.[7]

   Negotiators were able to extend, in large part, GATT rules to services under the General Agreement on Trade in Services (GATS). But the agreement on services is much less sweeping than U.S. negotiators had hoped. To realize additional progress, GATS establishes a procedural framework for further negotiations.

Who Wins and Who Loses Under GATT?

The Winners   The obvious winners are countries that are the biggest exporters of merchandise, such as the United States, Germany, and Japan. Exhibits 3-2 and 3-3 show the ten countries that are the leading exporters of goods and services, respectively.

   Europe stands to gain the most. Its exports of everything from wine and cheese to high-tech gadgetry could be most beneficial to the European economies,[8] particularly those that are relatively less affluent.

   The United States also stands to gain as a result of the Uruguay Round. As the biggest exporter in the world and also the most open market to imports, any measures that provide easier and better access to foreign markets should serve as a boost to its economy. The complete

EXHIBIT 3-2
Leading Exporters of Goods

Leading exporters of merchandise

1992	$bn
United States	447
Germany	428
Japan	340
France	236
Britain	191
Italy	175
Holland	140
Canada	135
Belgium/Luxembourg	120
Hong Kong*	118

*Includes re-exports and imports for re-export
Source: GATT

Source: *The Economist*, December 4, 1993, p. 25. © 1993 The Economist Newspaper, Ltd. Reprinted by permission. All rights reserved.

EXHIBIT 3-3
Leading Exporters of Services

Leading exporters of commercial services

1991	$bn
United States	148
France	84
Germany	60
Italy	56
Britain	53
Japan	46
Holland	32
Belgium/Luxembourg	32
Spain	31
Austria	25

Source: GATT

Source: *The Economist*, December 4, 1993, p. 25. © 1993 The Economist Newspaper, Ltd. Reprinted by permission. All rights reserved.

elimination of tariffs in industries in which the United States is a leader, including drugs and medical and construction equipment, should be most beneficial for U.S. economic growth.

The United States is also very strong in most of the service industries that GATT will cover, and which the General Agreement on Trade and Services (GATS) will pursue to liberalize in the future.

American rice, wheat, corn, and other grain growers are by far some of the most efficient in the world, and as such they stand to benefit immensely from GATT, which cracks open previously closed markets, even the rice markets of Japan and Korea.

The Losers   As for the losers from GATT, countries that had kept their markets closed to foreign competitors must open them to foreign companies. Countries such as India, Spain, and Taiwan, which have weak laws for the protection of patents, trademarks, and copyrights, now will have to formulate new laws to protect intellectual property to conform with GATT rules. It will become increasingly difficult for firms in these, and other countries with weak intellectual property protection laws, to produce pirated goods and steal patents, trademarks, and copyrighted materials belonging to foreign companies.

Countries that have very few exports of goods will not gain much from GATT immediately, although they stand to gain from overall global trade liberalization in the long run. For instance, a country like India whose share of world trade is a meager 0.5 percent may see its exports increased by only $1.5 to $2 billion. However, it will be obliged to open its markets to global exporters from the United States and other major exporting countries.

The biggest U.S. loser would appear to be the textile industry, which currently benefits from quotas imposed through bilateral agreements (agreements between two countries) negotiated under the Multi-Fiber Arrangement. GATT requires that these quotas be phased out over ten years. The U.S. textile industry had fought for a fifteen-year phase-out period of these protective measures. However, American consumers should benefit from cheaper textile products.

Paradoxically, for the United States, the GATT accord appears to set governmental policies in opposite directions. For instance, the Clinton administration wants to subsidize the development of a domestic flat-panel display industry. The flat-panel display portends to have numerous applications in medical technology and television sets, in addition to civilian and military aircraft control panels. But ironically, under the GATT accord, sponsored by the same administration, such technology subsidies are permissible only for national security.

The automobile, steel, semiconductor, machine tool, and textile industries all used temporary protection in the 1980s to invest and restructure to become more efficient and competitive in the 1990s. These are tools of national economic development that the United States and other countries are giving up in the new GATT-sponsored global trading order.

What GATT Has Left Undone

The intent of GATT is to remove nontariff barriers altogether, and its new rules are designed to discourage their proliferation. However, it is inevitable that countries will continue to impose nontariff barriers against foreign competitors such as government procurement procedures that favor domestic suppliers, weak enforcement of antitrust laws designed to foster competition, restrictions on inward direct foreign investment, arbitrary application of food safety regulations to block imports, and so on.

The issue of a uniform code for cross-border investments was not addressed by the Uruguay Round. Thus, countries are left with no restrictions on under-the-table subsidies to attract foreign investments. Although the U.S. movie industry won eventual copyright protection worldwide for its movies, U.S. negotiators failed to break a European quota system that limits foreign programming and other domestic film subsidies. Also, much more needs to be done in the area of free trade and investment in services. U.S. negotiators were unable to secure agreement from Asian and developing countries to permit broader entry of U.S. financial services firms into their markets. GATT has contributed significantly to a more harmonious world trade regime. However, new issues such as trade and the environment, competition and anti-trust policies, and regionalism in trade (e.g., NAFTA, which will be discussed later in this chapter) are coming to the fore as the world economy evolves.

The World Trade Organization

The Uruguay Round of GATT created the *World Trade Organization* (WTO) to enforce the GATT agreement. In fact, in 1995 the WTO replaced GATT. GATT was always considered as a halfway agreement among member nations that allowed them to effectively ignore any GATT rulings they did not like. The WTO, by contrast, is an institution, not an agreement, which has the authority to set and enforce rules governing trade between 117 members. Thus GATT, which was set up in 1947 as a temporary entity, was transformed into a permanent trade body.

The WTO, with an elaborate institutional mechanism of councils and committees, oversees the implementation of the GATT agreement by member countries. All members of the WTO, large and small alike, have equal representation in the WTO's Ministerial Conference. The conference meets at least once every two years to vote for a Director General, who appoints other officials.

Settlement of Disputes By the WTO   The disputes settlement procedures call for the establishment of a panel of trade experts who are called upon to resolve disputes. The member countries provide WTO with a list of trade experts. The WTO selects a panel from this list. In case the two countries involved in the dispute are unable to agree on the members of the panel, then the WTO Director General decides who will be on the panel. The WTO must rule on member complaints within one year, which is quite an improvement over the five or more years it took under the old GATT procedures. The panel hears both sides and makes its decision in secret.

Decisions by the trade panels are binding unless overturned by consensus of the WTO membership. As was mentioned earlier, this is quite a departure from the "old" GATT procedures that, absurdly, allowed countries found in violation of fair trade rules to unilaterally block unfavorable panel decisions by merely ignoring them. Under the WTO process, countries that win a case they filed before the WTO receive an automatic green light to undertake retaliatory measures against the offending country if that country does not change its practices. The country that is found guilty of violating fair-trade rules has two choices: It can change its law or face sanctions, most likely in the form of tariffs slapped on its exports by the complaining country.

Fears have been expressed that the WTO will become a foreign-dominated Supreme Court that will result in a loss of national sovereignty of member countries. This charge has been leveled against the WTO especially by its critics in the United States. These critics are afraid that the WTO will make rulings that will put the U.S. environmental, health, and safety laws at risk by labeling them as nontariff barriers, thus requiring the United States to repeal them. In reality, the WTO does not have the legal power to change U.S. laws—only the U.S. Congress can do that. This is equally true for every country in the WTO. No outside body can force a country to do anything it does not want to. However, the fears of the critics are valid to the extent that in choosing not to abide by the WTO rulings, the United States, or any other country, is subjecting itself to sanctions imposed by the complaining country or countries.

However, international business experts believe that because of its economic strength and market size, the United States has little to fear from retaliation. It is reasoned that even countries that win cases before the WTO would hesitate before retaliating, and are more likely to negotiate with each other to arrive at a reasonable compromise.

REGIONAL TRADE BLOCS

There are some who argue that trade liberalization would be much faster under the umbrella of smaller and primarily regional trade blocs, rather than with mammoth and unwieldy global negotiations under GATT and the WTO.

The experience to date is that regional trade blocs, such as the North American Free Trade Agreement (NAFTA), which includes Canada, the United States, and Mexico, have in fact been faster than GATT in promoting the elimination of trade barriers and trade liberalization amongst bloc members.

One or more of the following reasons may explain why regional groupings of countries in trade blocs get formed:

- Geographical proximity and often the sharing of common borders.
- Common economic and political interests.
- Similar ethnic and cultural backgrounds.
- Similar levels of economic development.
- Similar views on the mutual benefits of free trade.

There are four major types of trade blocs:

1. *Free Trade Area (FTA):* In a free trade area, bloc member countries eliminate trade barriers on trade among member countries, but retain the right to impose their own separate trade barriers on trade with countries outside of the trade bloc. According to this definition, NAFTA is a free trade area.

2. *Customs Union:* In a customs union, member countries remove trade barriers on all intra-bloc trade and also have in place common trade barriers on trade with non-bloc countries. The Andean Pact, including Bolivia, Columbia, Venezuela, Ecuador, and Peru, is an example of a customs union.

3. *Common Market:* A common market is a customs union that also allows the free movement of factors such as labor and capital. The European Union is an example of a common market.

4. *Economic Union:* An economic union is a common market wherein the national economic policies of member countries are also harmonized, e.g., harmonization of monetary and fiscal policies, environmental regulations, health and safety measures, a common agricultural policy, technical standards, etc. As opposed to a free trade area, a customs union, and a common market, which are created mainly by the removal of trade restrictions, an economic union demands the transfer of economic sovereignty to supranational institutions. Of all the trade blocs in the world, the European Union appears to be moving the fastest towards an economic union.

The North American Free Trade Agreement

The North American Free Trade Agreement (NAFTA) is a *free trade agreement.* It was ratified by the Congress of the United States in November 1993, and the agreement went into effect on January 1, 1994. NAFTA links the United States, Canada, and Mexico in a free trade area of 350 million consumers and over $6.5 trillion of annual output. NAFTA unites the United States with its largest (Canada) and third-largest (Mexico) trading partners.

Building on the earlier United States-Canada Free Trade Agreement, NAFTA is expected to contribute to productive efficiency, enhance the ability of North American producers to compete globally, and raise the standard of living of all three countries. By improving the investment climate in North America, and by providing innovative companies with a larger market, NAFTA is also expected to increase economic growth. Mexico should benefit from more open and secure access to its largest market, the U.S.; increased confidence on the part of foreign firms to invest in Mexico; a more stable economic environment; and the return from abroad of Mexican-owned capital into the Mexican economy. Canada's benefits are mostly in the form of safeguards: maintaining its status in international trade, no loss of its current trade preferences in the U.S. market, and equal access to Mexico's market.

In addition to dismantling trade barriers in industrial goods, NAFTA includes agreements on services, investment, intellectual property rights, agriculture, and strengthening of trade rules.

There are also side agreements on labor adjustment provisions, protection of the environment, and import surges. The side agreement on labor adjustment was in response to American workers' concerns that jobs in the United States would be exported to Mexico because of the latter's lower labor wages and weak child labor laws and other conditions that afford Mexican labor an economic advantage over its American counterpart. The side agreement is an attempt to manage the terms of the potential change in labor markets brought about by the NAFTA accord. The agreement involves such issues as restrictions on child labor, health and safety standards, and minimum wages. In addition to signing the labor side agreement, the Mexican government has pledged to link increases in the Mexican minimum wage to productivity increases.

The side agreement on environmental cooperation explicitly ensures the rights of the United States to safeguard the environment. NAFTA maintains all existing U.S. health, safety, and environmental standards. It allows states and cities to enact even tougher standards, while providing mechanisms to encourage all parties to harmonize their standards upwards.

The side agreement on import surges creates an early warning mechanism to identify those sectors where explosive trade growth may do significant harm to domestic industry. It also establishes that, in the future, a working group can provide for revisions in the treaty text based on the experience with the existing safeguard mechanisms. During the transition period, safeguard relief is available in the form of a temporary snapback to pre-NAFTA duties if an import surge threatens serious injury to a domestic industry. It is obvious that these three side agreements were negotiated to alleviate the fears of U.S. labor and industry groups that felt threatened by the immediate adverse impact on their members.

The Impact of NAFTA on Firm Operations With the integration of the Canadian, U.S., and Mexican markets into one giant market, companies would re-write their business plans in order to serve the integrated North American market most efficiently. Companies in Mexico, the U.S., and Canada would move quickly to close inefficient plants and concentrate production where it makes the most sense. Whether it is the Mexican company Cemex, the Canadian company Alcan Aluminium, or the American company Ford, each would be able to tap cheap labor for some components and products, and at the same time take advantage of more skilled labor for other components and products. In the foreseeable future, assuming that Mexican worker productivity is equal or close to that of the U.S. or Canadian worker, one would expect that labor-intensive production would be performed in Mexico where workers' wages per hour are less than 50 percent of those in the United States. *Practical Insight 3-1* illustrates the impact of NAFTA on the strategies of Canadian, U.S., Mexican, and European companies.

PRACTICAL INSIGHT 3-1

NAFTA and Cross-Border Integration of Operations

The process of integrating the economies of Canada and the United States did not have to wait for the passage of NAFTA. It began some 30 years ago when free movement of cars and parts began following the signing of the Auto Pact by the two countries. The economies of the two countries were further integrated with the passage of the United States-Canada Free Trade Agreement in 1989, which allowed the free movement of all goods and services between the two countries. Integration of operations across the U.S.-Canadian border gained impetus as companies closed inefficient plants on the Canadian side that once served the small Canadian market. Many Canadian companies moved their operations across the border into the U.S. or closed small but inefficient plants and built larger more efficient plants in their place to serve the enlarged combined market of the U.S. and Canada.

Something similar is happening with Mexico. American companies had already started integrating their production operations with Mexico-based operations in maquiladora plants. Under the maquiladora program, Mexico allowed U.S.-sourced components or raw materials into Mexico duty free, to be used in production or assembly in Mexico, provided that the finished products were shipped back to the United States or third-country markets. The duties imposed upon the imported products were based upon the value added in Mexico. Since labor was so cheap in Mexico the value added was little, and therefore the duties levied were also negligible. It is estimated that there are more than 1500 maquiladoras, most of them U.S.-owned (and several Japanese-owned maquiladoras for assembly and export to the United States) that employ more than 500,000 workers.*

Mexican tariffs fell after Mexico joined the General Agreement on Tariffs and Trade in 1986. And with the passage of NAFTA, the movement towards free trade has reached the apex. Now Mexico could be a gold mine for U.S. and Canadian companies. To satisfy the demand in Mexico for their products American and Canadian companies are boosting exports and, in the process, adding capacity at home. Big multinationals in the automobile and appliance industries are reorganizing their operations to place themselves in a globally superior competitive position by sending some jobs to Mexico while consolidating the rest at home.

Numerous U.S. and Canadian banks are opening subsidiaries in Mexico to capture a market that is expected to grow at a 10 to 15 percent clip over the next several years. Opportunities for insurance companies in Mexico are there to exploit a market that is expected to climb to $50 billion in 15 years from just $5 billion today.

Benefits of deeper levels of economic integration among the three countries is not limited to Canadian and U.S. companies alone. Investment from Mexican companies will also flow northwards. In 1992, Del Monte Fresh Produce was bought by a group of Mexican investors with the objective of adding high-value products to Mexico's mix of agricultural exports. Vitro and Cemex have acquired U.S. companies to take advantage of integrating the North American market.

European companies have also been quick to see the potential benefits from NAFTA. Companies such as ABB, the big Swiss-Swedish electrical engineering and power-generation group, as well as the German industrial group Siemens, have reorganized their production in North

---

* Stephen Baker, "Mexico: A New Economic Era," *Business Week*, November 12, 1990, p. 105.

America on a regional basis to lessen the duplication of their production processes in Mexico, the U.S., and Canada. Nestle, the Swiss food processing giant, runs its U.S., Canadian, and Mexican food operations jointly.

Matsushita, the Japanese conglomerate, says that it hopes to work through Mexico to get better access to the protected markets of South America.

Source: Adapted from E.S. Browning, "NAFTA or Not, Many Foreign Companies View North America as One Market," *The Wall Street Journal*, November 15, 1993, p. A 8; William C. Symonds, Geri Smith, and Stephen Baker, "Border Crossings: NAFTA Would Fulfill the Promise of a Continental Market," *Business Week*, November 22, 1993, pp. 40-42.

In the years ahead, NAFTA will have a significant impact on industries in all three countries. Inefficient industries will fail to survive, as the once-protected industries and markets in a country are exposed to foreign competitors from NAFTA member countries. Following the U.S.-Canada Free Trade Agreement in 1989, the Canadian textile industry suffered from the relatively more efficient factories located in the southern regions of the United States, and in response moved a significant proportion of its production to the United States. Now with the inclusion of Mexico under NAFTA, U.S. factories in textile and other industries will have to break up the value chain in their production processes and distribute the subprocesses among the three NAFTA countries on the basis of the comparative locational advantage of each country. For instance, energy-intensive production processes may be performed in Canada because energy sources like electricity are relatively less expensive in Canada than in the United States or Mexico, high-technology, knowledge-intensive, high-value-added production processes may be located in the United States, and labor-intensive processes may be farmed out to Mexico.

It may appear as though Mexico has a lot to gain from factories and plants moving into that country to exploit cheap labor. Some of this will indeed occur. The phaseout of North American tariffs will draw in billions in investment, which will be good for jobs and economic growth in Mexico. As an example, just on the anticipation of the passage of NAFTA, U.S. direct investment—investment in plants and factories—went up from $13.7 billion in 1992 to $15.4 billion in 1993.[9] However, there is also a downside for Mexico from NAFTA. As the economies of the three countries adjust to the realities of integration, and expose Mexico's most inefficient manufacturing industries to world-class Canadian and U.S. competition, some Mexican companies are sure to lose out to the new competition.

Mexican banks will also be forced to improve their operations in the face of competition from U.S. and Canadian banks. Mexican banks are technologically backward and known for poor service. In order to compete effectively with the technologically superior and customer-oriented banks from its neighbors from the North, Mexico's banks will be compelled to open up their cozy club of bankers, reduce loan rates, and offer better service to corporate clients.[10]

On the retail front, things will not be much different either. Wal-Mart, Kmart, J.C. Penney, and Radio Shack are just a few of the many retail chains that have entered Mexico. Big Mexican chains such as Cifra and El Puerto de Liverpool have formed joint ventures with Wal-Mart and Kmart. J.C. Penney plans to open 17 stores before the year 2000. Fast-food chains from Arby's to Domino's Pizza are adding stores in major cities in anticipation of a growing and bigger middle-consumer class. Large chains such as these will benefit from the growing buying power of the Mexican middle class. However, smaller, mom-and-pop stores may not be able to compete with the attractively priced imports the big chains are featuring.[11] This is a phenomenon that has already occurred in the United States, wherein smaller stores have been unable to compete against large mega-stores such as Wal-Mart. Almost certainly, this U.S. experience will be repeated in Mexico.

Who will benefit from the changes brought about by NAFTA? The consumers in all NAFTA countries stand to gain from the availability of goods and services that are both cheaper and of better quality than pre-NAFTA days. NAFTA should contribute to productive efficiency, enhance the ability of North American producers to compete globally, and raise the standard of living of all three countries. By improving the investment climate in North America, and by providing innovative companies with a larger market, NAFTA is expected to also increase economic growth.

What's Next In the Cards for NAFTA? Both U.S. Presidents Bush and Clinton firmly believe in the benefits of free trade for all countries, and particularly in the potential of NAFTA to serve as the economic generator that would propel North American companies into becoming strong competitors against their counterparts from the European Community and the Pacific Rim countries.

Forecasts by McGraw-Hill and *Business Week* suggest that NAFTA will continue to be the biggest market, as opposed to the European Community and the Pacific Basin countries in Asia.[12] However, direct investments are expected to be the largest in the Pacific Basin, with the European Community coming second and North America falling last.

NAFTA is supposed to be the first step in what is expected to be the creation of a mega-unified market stretching from Alaska to Argentina. This concept is supported by all Latin American countries which are moving away from their protectionist economic policies and toward privatization of state-owned enterprises and free enterprise. Chile, Brazil, and Argentina are considered next in line to join NAFTA.

A study by economists Gary C. Hafbauer and Jeffrey J. Schott of the Institute for International Economics finds that Chile, Venezuela, Barbados, and Trinidad and Tobago rank high as candidates to join NAFTA; followed by Paraguay, Uruguay, Bolivia, and Jamaica. A surprise is Brazil, which ranks all but last because of its high inflation rates and national debt.

Next we shall look into the oldest and probably the most advanced trade bloc, the European Union (EU).

The European Union

The European Union (EU)—most commonly known as the Common Market—is an institutional framework for the construction of a unified Europe. It was created after World War II to unite the nations of Europe through peaceful means and to create conditions for the economic recovery and growth of Europe after the devastation caused by the war. Fifteen countries are now members of the EU, and more than 320 million people share the common institutions and policies that have brought an unprecedented era of peace and prosperity to western Europe.

Take a look at the map of Europe in Exhibit 3-4.

There are many similarities between the European Union and the United States. EU member countries have agreed to pool some of their sovereign powers for the sake of unity, just as the American states did to create a federal republic. In fields where such delegation of national sovereignty has occurred—for example, in trade and agriculture—the EU acts as a full-fledged country, and negotiates directly with the United States and other countries. EU member states retain their full sovereign powers in such fields as security and defense matters. The search for political unity is inspired by the U.S. federative model; however, Europeans realize that Europe will have to construct its own model for unification, one that takes full account of the rich historical, cultural, and linguistic diversity of the European nations.

EXHIBIT 3-4
The European Union

The European Community Origins On May 9, 1950, Robert Schuman, the French Foreign Minister, presented the Schuman Declaration—a bold plan for lifting Europe out of the rubble of World War II. He proposed the pooling of European coal and steel industries as a first step towards a united Europe. Schuman's proposal called for the placement of coal and steel production of France and Germany under a common authority within an organization open to other European countries. The long-term objective of the Schuman Declaration was to lay the foundation for the economic integration of Europe—starting with coal and steel. Belgium, the Federal Republic of Germany, Italy, Luxembourg, and the Netherlands (Holland) accepted the French proposal. The six countries signed the European Coal and Steel Community (ECSC) Treaty in

Paris on April 18, 1951. The ECSC High Authority was created by the six countries, to which each country transferred some of its sovereign power.

The Treaty of Rome   On March 25, 1957, in Rome, the six countries signed two treaties creating the European Economic Community (EEC) and the European Atomic Energy Community (EAEC). Both treaties were ratified by the parliaments of the six member countries before the end of the year.

The EEC was created to merge the separate national markets of the six countries into a large single market within which there would be free movement of goods, people, capital, and services. Common economic policies were also a goal of the EEC.

The EAEC or Euratom was created to promote the use of nuclear energy for peaceful purposes.

The European Community (EC) is in fact three separate entities governed by separate treaties: the European Coal and Steel Community (ECSC), the European Atomic Energy Community (EAEC) or Euratom, and the European Economic Community (EEC). However, the name "European Community" has been in common usage to refer to the three Communities, since together they form a single political whole.

EEC Enlargement   The Community has enlarged its membership from six to fifteen countries. Denmark, Ireland, and the United Kingdom joined in 1973. Greece joined in 1981, and Spain and Portugal became the 11th and 12th member states in 1986. In 1990, the former German Democratic Republic (East Germany) entered the Community as part of a united Germany. Turkey, Austria, Malta, Cyprus, Sweden, Finland, and the new democracies of Eastern Europe have also expressed a keen interest in eventual EC membership. On May 4, 1994, the EEC members voted in favor of admitting Norway, Finland, Sweden, and Austria into the Community. Finland, Sweden, and Austria joined in 1994, however Norway, after a public referendum, refused the EC's invitation.

EC—1992   The first step taken by the European Community toward the creation of a common market was to establish a customs union. This required the removal of tariffs on trade between EC member states and fixing a common external tariff. This process was completed by July 1968. The benefits of the customs union among the six member countries was evident from the massive increase in trade among the six—from $6.8 billion in 1958, when the EEC was established, to $60 billion in 1972, just before the enlargement of the Community to include Denmark, Ireland, and the United Kingdom.

Squabbles over the Common Agricultural Policy coupled with the persistence of some old barriers and the creation of new ones during the 1970s—a period of "stagflation" (high inflation together with low economic growth) for most developed countries—compelled the Community to admit in the mid-1980s that its goal of a real common market was still far from reach. The main source of the Community's poor performance was attributed to the absence of an integrated European-wide market, which prevented European businesses to launch and implement strategies for an integrated European market. The answer was the 1985 White Paper by the EC Commission, which put forth a road map for the completion of an integrated internal market by the end of 1992.

The 1985 White Paper listed almost 300 legislative measures needed to eliminate all physical, technical, and financial barriers to trade and commerce among the member countries. Specifically, it called for:

- An end to intra-EC customs checks and border controls.

- An EC-wide market for services, such as banking, insurance, securities, and other financial transactions.

- The mutual recognition of professional diplomas.

- The harmonization or mutual recognition of technical standards.

- The approximation of national rates and assessment criteria for EC's indirect taxes.

The EC member states signed the Single European Act (SEA) in February 1986. It became effective on July 1, 1987, after ratification by the twelve national parliaments. The SEA contains amendments to the EC treaties necessary to ensure the timely achievement of the 1992 program. The SEA not only aims at the completion of the integrated internal Community market, it also calls for significant developments in economic and monetary policy, social policy and industrial relations, research and technology, and the environment. It also formalized procedures for cooperation in the sphere of foreign policy. Finally, the SEA renewed the commitment to transform relations among the member states into a *European Union*.

At the end of 1992, the internal market became a reality. All frontiers between member countries were removed, as far as goods, services, and capital were concerned. There are no longer any customs controls on the Community's internal borders (between member states). Citizens of non-EC countries have to show their passport and entry visas only at the first point of entry into any EC country, after which they can freely move anywhere within the EC member countries. Travellers may buy as many goods as they wish in any Community country for their own or their family's use, provided that they pay the appropriate tax on the goods in the country of purchase. Community citizens may take up residence in a member state other than their own as long as they wish. Professional qualifications are mutually recognized in all member states.

The Treaty on European Union The success of the Europe 1992 program and the changed political framework prompted the EC members to take a new step along the path of integration, namely the *European Union*.

In Maastricht, the Netherlands, in December 1991, the heads of states of the EC member countries agreed on a Treaty on European Union. It was signed in February 1992, and after ratification by the parliaments of the EC member countries it came into force in November 1993. The Maastricht Treaty on European Union is just one more step on the road to a European Constitution, and is built on the structures that have been handed down. It forms an overall framework for various stages of integration.

What Is New in the Maastricht Treaty The Maastricht Treaty on European Union has several new provisions, principally the following:

- A common European currency by 1999 at the latest.

- Every European in the European Community is eligible to obtain a European passport, which gives the person the right to move freely from one Community country to another.

- Provisions on cooperation in the fields of justice and home affairs, particularly in reference to police and judicial authorities.

- New powers for the European Community to play a more active role in areas such as visa policy, trans-European transport, environmental protection, and consumer protection.

- Special rules on social policy/industrial relations. These are necessary because one member state—the United Kingdom—is against either giving the Community additional responsibilities in this field or even stepping up cooperation.
- Increased enabling powers to the European Parliament to enact legislation.

Of the provisions, the first provision—a common currency by 1999—is worth further examination. In the Maastricht Treaty, the members of the European Community agreed to replace the European Monetary System (EMS) with an **Economic and Monetary Union (EMU)**, a common currency, and a European Central Bank overseeing a single monetary policy.

Let us take a quick look at the EMS, which will serve as the foundation for the building of the common currency. The EMS was created in March 1979 to limit exchange-rate variability among the European currencies. A majority of countries in the EMS agreed to participate in the system's **Exchange Rate Mechanism (ERM)**, under which most member countries were required to maintain their exchange rates within 2.25 percent of "central rates" between their currency and each of the other members' currencies. Under this arrangement, when an exchange rate between two members' currencies moves to the limits of the band, the central banks of both countries are required to intervene to prevent the exchange rate from moving outside the band. Realignments of the country's central rate were permitted only in the event of irresistible pressure on a member country's exchange rate. The EMS has been credited for minimizing currency fluctuations that hampered intra-EC trade and discouraged European firms from undertaking projects across national borders. Because of Germany's unwavering commitment to price stability, the German deutsche mark became the monetary anchor for the EMS. By linking their monetary policies to German policy, other ERM members brought their inflation rates down. French inflation, for example, declined from 10 percent at the start of the 1980s to under 3 percent in 1992.

Under the Maastricht Treaty, progress toward the European Economic and Monetary Union (EMU) would take place in stages, with the final stage—the establishment of a European Central Bank responsible for monetary policy, the creation of an economic and monetary union under which the currencies of the member states are fixed irrevocably to one another at the same exchange rate, and the introduction of a single European currency, the *ECU* (see Box 3-2)—coming no later than January 1, 1999.

The target of the first stage on the road to an eventual economic and monetary union and a common currency has become a reality with the removal of all restrictions on capital movements between member states. Coordination between the central banks of member countries has been intensified in order to monitor the economic policies of member countries.

The second stage began in early 1994 with the establishment in Frankfurt, Germany, of a European Monetary Institute, the forerunner of the European Central Bank. Its main purpose is to pave the way for transition to the final stage through even more intensified efforts to induce countries whose inflation rates and government debt are too high to take steps to remove their "weaknesses" and thereby move closer to those of more stable countries.

Whether or not the goal of the third stage—an economic and monetary union in which the exchange rates of the various currencies of member countries will be irrevocably linked with each other—will be realized before the target date of January 1, 1999, will depend upon the ability of a *majority* of member states to meet the criteria established by the Maastricht Treaty for implementing a common currency and monetary policy before the end of 1996. If a majority of countries meet these common currency criteria the EU can move to a common currency; if not, then at the start of 1999, those that do meet them must begin the final stage of EMU, complete

BOX 3-2
What Is an ECU?

The **ECU (European Currency Unit)** is a "basket" of specified amounts of each EC currency. Amounts are determined in accordance with the economic size of the member countries, and are revised every five years. The value of the ECU is determined by using the current market rate of each member currency. (The exchange rate as of January 1996 was 1 ECU = US$1.24).

In addition to its functions within the EMS, the ECU is also the Community's accounting unit. It has also become popular as a private financial instrument. There are ECU-denominated traveller's checks, bank deposits, and loans, and the ECU is used by some businesses as a currency for invoicing and payment. Significant amounts of ECU-denominated bonds have been placed on international markets. The Community launched the first public offering of these bonds in the United States in 1984. Currently, the ECU ranks among the top ten currencies in international bond issues.

The ECU will probably become the new single European currency within the EMU.

with its single currency. Criteria relating to inflation rates, national debt, exchange rates, and interest rates are stipulated in the Treaty. (Refer to Box 3-3 for the EMU membership criteria.) Price stability is a prerequisite for the stability of the future European currency. Therefore the primary responsibility for maintaining price stability in member countries will lie with the European Central Bank (ECB), which under monetary union will form, in conjunction with the central banks of the member states, the European System of Central Banks (ECSB) that will be responsible for a single monetary policy. The ECB and the central banks will be forbidden to take instructions from politicians and from providing credit facilities to governmental budget deficits. The economic policies of member states will be required to contribute to the stability of the European currency. Countries will be required to avoid excessive budget deficits because

BOX 3-3
Criteria for Membership in the Economic and Monetary Union

Countries acceding to the EMU must meet several strict criteria:

1. The inflation rate must not exceed the average of the lowest three members' rates by more than 1.5 percentage points.

2. The interest rate on long-term bonds cannot exceed those of the three lowest-inflation members by more than 2 percentage points.

3. The country's general government budget deficit must not exceed 3 percent of GDP, and outstanding government debt must not exceed 60 percent of GDP.

4. For at least two years, the country's currency must have remained within its narrow ERM band without realignment.

of their inflationary impact, and if a member country does not control its budget deficits, the Community may impose fines or other sanctions. Sound economic policies, strict price stability, and sound fiscal policies are the conditions for moving a country into the EMU club.

The United Kingdom and Denmark have declared that they are unable at this time to commit themselves to moving to the final stage of EMU. The United Kingdom has agreed to make its position known to member countries in 1996.

What Has Been Achieved to Date Driving along the highways of Europe makes one aware of the reality of a borderless Europe. One can go from Brussels to Amsterdam, a journey of a little over 200 miles, without stopping anywhere for passport checks or customs clearances. The concrete-and-glass immigration and customs booths that marked the frontier between Belgium and the Netherlands are now up for sale. In the old days, travellers had to stop to show their passports and entry visas, and declare imported goods in order to pay the customs duties levied by the customs officials. Nowadays, tourists drive by these relics of the past without having to slow down from the 130 kilometers-per-hour speed that most travel on European highways. Were it not for a road sign that signals that one is leaving one country and entering another, and the necessity of converting the currency, one would not be aware of having entered another country. In fact, this is the reality of the new Europe that one experiences throughout the member countries of the European Union.

Economic integration is progressing rapidly, a fact that is reflected in the trade statistics which show that most of the trade of the European Union countries is with each other. The jury is still out on the question of whether the European Union of fifteen member countries has truly matured into a single unified market like the unified market of the United States. To date, 95 percent of the legislative measures established in the Europe 1992 program have been adopted, and agreement is yet to be obtained on only 17, most importantly on laws relating to intellectual property and corporate law. More remains to be done on deregulating or simplifying regulations that companies have to abide by. Although EU nations have been quite willing to approve pan-European laws regarding the single market, some have been slow to incorporate those measures into their national laws. Paradoxically, Britain and Denmark, the two nations most skeptical of a united Europe, have the best record at enacting national legislation corresponding to EU laws. Greece, Spain, and France have the worst records, and even Germany, who, along with France, is the strongest proponent of a unified Europe, is a laggard.

A survey of 270 companies by the Confederation of British Industries found that 75 percent had made the deliberate strategic decision to focus their trading efforts toward the EU, while 68 percent were successful in boosting their trade with the EU countries. However, of the 270 companies in the survey, only 17 percent said that they had experienced significant cost reductions through the single market, partly because of new costs triggered by the voluminous paperwork associated with the new EU rules on tax declarations. British companies also complained that they were at a disadvantage because of the failure of other EU member states to effectively enforce EU legislation.[13]

The goal of harmonization, or mutual recognition of technical standards, is yet to be achieved. Many companies say that the greatest trade barriers arise when member states refuse to accept technical standards adopted in another EU nation. Exporters still face barriers, particularly in France and Germany, which have both used technical standards to block some imports.

Only 20 to 30 percent of intra-EU goods trade is governed by specific legislation on harmonized standards, while the rest is covered by the concept of "mutual recognition." Under this principle, a product legally produced and marketed in one member country cannot be blocked from free circulation in another member country by requiring it to undergo further testing or modification. But EU legislation permits a member country to do just that, and thereby deny mutual recognition, in the interest of "protecting public health, safety, or morality." Companies complain that member states abuse this exception to the rule, and use "health and safety" as a pretext for protectionism.[14] The industries most affected are food and pharmaceuticals, where national standards still prevail over EU-wide standards.

By contrast, many companies throughout Europe are enjoying significant savings in time, red tape, and transport cost as a result of the removal of formalities in border controls. For instance, Pronuovo SA, a maker of antivibration and noise-control systems located in Belgium, toasts the EU's single market for slashing total trucking costs per truckload from Portugal to Belgium from nearly 100,000 Belgian francs to 50,000 francs. The cost reductions were made possible because "the truckers don't have to stop at all the borders and do all the paperwork, and there's now much more competition among trucking companies because of the greater ease of doing business."[15]

The single EU-wide market has undoubtedly changed the old protectionist business culture in Europe to one that is much more accepting of free trade among nations, unhampered by protectionist laws and practices. Cross-border mergers and acquisitions among EU countries are in vogue. Even the traditionally closed German financial services market has opened up to non-German companies, allowing Crédit Lyonnais SA, a French bank, to tap the lucrative German market by acquiring Bank fuer Gemeinwirtschaft.

Significant differences still remain between the nations. The costs of doing business vary considerably from country to country as wage rates, fringe benefits, and social security systems differ from country to country. For example, firing a worker in Spain can cost twice as much in severance pay and other benefits as in Germany. And the level playing field that was supposed to come with a unified market has not materialized as some governments still continue to give generous subsidies to sick companies. For example, now that the EU governments have agreed to deregulate the airline industry and have liberalized the rules regarding routes and destinations, competition in the airline industry is heating up. But countries such as France, Greece, and the Netherlands still continue to give huge subsidies to their national airlines.

What Are the Prospects for a Single European Currency? As of September 1994, only Luxembourg and Ireland have met the conditions outlined in Box 3-2 for implementing a common currency and monetary policy. Indeed, a strict adherence to the EMU criteria would have disqualified heavily indebted Ireland, except that the treaty has a soft-hearted exemption for countries where public debt is "sufficiently diminishing" at a "satisfactory pace."[16] Even Germany failed to meet the criteria because of its swelling national debt caused by the reunification of East and West Germany. The prospects for a single European currency for all fifteen EU member countries are dimmed because of problems emanating from the two following sources.

National pride is the first source. Countries such as the United Kingdom would find it extremely difficult to abandon the revered British pound, a symbol to the British people of the country's glorious history. Adopting a single currency would also mean abandoning national sovereignty over monetary policy. Because of such nationalistic feelings, it is highly unlikely that the United Kingdom would ever agree to join the EU's economic and monetary union. Similar sentiments are also extant in Denmark, which too may decide to opt out of participation in the EMU and hence the European currency.

Global financial markets are the second source of problems facing the creation of the single currency. High unemployment and a steep drop in economic growth rate in September 1992 led to speculative selling of the British pound. The sell-off of the British pound was caused by the perception of the foreign exchange traders that the British government would be forced to realign or to drop out of the ERM in order to lower interest rates. Finland and Sweden, although not formal participants in the ERM, had been unilaterally maintaining pegged exchange rates, and so faced similar dilemmas as their economies went through deep and prolonged recessions. In September 1992, Finland, the United Kingdom, and Italy decided to allow their currencies to float, which meant that the United Kingdom and Italy, both officially members of the ERM, effectively had dropped out of it. Sweden followed in November. Spain, Portugal, and Ireland all devalued within the ERM between September 1992 and January 1993.

A second crisis occurred in mid-July 1993. A heavy sell-off of their respective currencies forced Belgium, Denmark, France, and Portugal to raise interest rates and intervene heavily in the currency markets to prevent a free-fall of their currencies. Still, the Belgian franc, the French franc, and the Danish krone dropped through the ERM floors. This led to a forced change of the ERM mechanism itself. On August 2, 1993, the bands within which the currencies were allowed to float against each other were widened from +/–2.25 percent to a whopping +/–15 percent. A separate agreement maintains bands of +/–2.25 percent for the German deutsche mark and the Dutch guilder. The wider band brought all currencies well within the new ERM limits, which meant that central banks did not have to intervene and the speculative crisis ended. By the end of 1993, the Belgian, French, Portuguese, and Spanish currencies were within or close to the old ERM limits of +/–2.25 percent relative to the deutsche mark. The United Kingdom aggressively cut interest rates after leaving the ERM in September 1992. Nevertheless, doubts remain about the viability of the ERM system, and of the feasibility of a creating a single currency encompassing all fifteen countries in the EU.

However, optimists had hoped that a majority of the EU members would have met the Maastricht Treaty criteria for the formation of the EMU and a single currency by the end of 1996—hopes bolstered by Finland, Norway, Sweden, and Austria becoming full members of the EU in 1995. At the very least, the European Union hopes that there will be a monetary merger during 1999. Skeptics, however, believe that there could be a single "hard core" currency comprising Germany, France, Belgium, Luxembourg, and Holland.[17] However, as this book goes to print in late 1996, the single European currency—now planned to be called the *Euro*—still appears to be some years off, with a complete changeover to the new currency occurring not earlier than 2002.

What Lies in the Future?[18] Observers of the European Union are speculating that there is a three-tiered Europe in the future—an idea floated by Edouard Balladur, the French Prime Minister, in late August 1994, and reiterated by the parliamentary group of Germany's ruling Christian Democrats 48 hours later. The three-tiered approach calls for the formation of countries arranged in three concentric circles. The inner circle would consist of core countries that would pool their sovereignty and push toward a single currency, common laws, and common defence and foreign policies. The inner core would be led by Germany and France, and would include Holland, Belgium, and Luxembourg. The core group members are expected to meet the conditions for membership into the economic and monetary union, and the common currency before the year 2000. These criteria (See Box 3-2) include the target of public debt of not more than 60 percent of gross domestic product and inflation rates within 1.5 percent of the average for the three EU members with the most stable prices.

The second circle, outside the five-nation inner core, would presumably include the United Kingdom, Denmark, Italy, Greece, Spain, Ireland, and Portugal. It is envisioned that each country in the second circle could join the inner circle when it is ready to apply.

The final and outermost circle would include countries such as Austria, Finland, and Sweden. Each of these countries is small, rich, and already highly integrated with the EU. Of this group, Austria, which has long tied its monetary policy to that of Germany, may wish to jump straight into the inner circle, whereas the others may want to pause outside the core group and join it later.

In the distant future are countries waiting to join the EU. They are the former Soviet-bloc countries of eastern Europe. The EU has made a commitment in principle to allow the eastern European countries to join the club. These countries are many years away from full integration with the innermost circle. The best that the EU would offer them is no more than a free trade zone status.

Other Major Regional Trade Arrangements

LAFTA and CACM   The success of NAFTA and the EU has demonstrated the benefits of regional free trade agreements to the economic well-being of member states. Intra-NAFTA and intra-EU trade has mushroomed and countries in Central and South America and Asia are making rapid moves in the direction of forming their own regional trade blocs. Attempts to form free trade blocs in Latin America were made as early as 1960 when the Latin American Free Trade Association (LAFTA) (consisting of Argentina, Bolivia, Brazil, Chile, Colombia, Ecuador, Mexico, Paraguay, Peru, Uruguay, and Venezuela) and the Central American Common Market (CACM) (which included Costa Rica, El Salvador, Guatemala, Honduras, and Nicaragua) were initiated. Both failed to achieve their objectives because of differing economic conditions and economic policies among member countries that worked against regional economic trade and integration.

In 1980, LAFTA was superceded by the Latin American Integration Association (LAIA) with the same member countries (except Guyana, French Guiana, and Surinam) and Mexico (which is geographically in North America). The LAIA has a modest goal of promoting trade among its members by providing tariff-reduction guidelines to member countries. LAIA also aspires to promote the formation of free trade blocs among some of the members.

When it was formed in 1960, the CACM had among its objectives the establishment of an external common tariff, i.e., a customs union, within five years, followed by convergence to a common market and, eventually, cooperation in monetary and fiscal policies. The CACM failed in achieving its objectives, and it became a political organization in 1980. The original five members of the CACM—Costa Rica, El Salvador, Guatemala, Honduras, and Nicaragua—want to revive it again, this time including Panama.

The Andean Pact   The Andean Pact was signed by six nations—Bolivia, Chile, Colombia, Ecuador, Peru, and Venezuela—in 1969 to create a common market with a common external tariff and the harmonization of economic policies. Chile withdrew from the pact in 1976. The Andean Pact failed to achieve its objectives, but now the five countries still in the pact have relaunched their stalled plans for economic integration. The revival got started with a free trade area among Bolivia, Colombia, and Venezuela, and was later expanded to include Ecuador and Peru. It has since been extended to a customs union. After many years of delay, members of the pact implemented common external tariffs in 1995. In actuality, the maximum tariff will range from 20 percent in Colombia, Venezuela, and Ecuador to 10 percent in Peru and Bolivia.[19] The new tariff policy is one of several efforts aimed at liberalizing and integrating the economies of the five member countries.

The G-3 Pact   Mexico, Colombia, and Venezuela implemented the G-3 trade pact in 1995. The G-3 pact, which includes rules on patent rights and government procurement, will promote free trade of most goods among the member countries after a ten-year period. The three countries were unable to reach agreement on trade in textiles and polyester, but hope to do so within the next two years.[20] The G-3 creates a market of 147 million people with a combined GDP of $432.1 billion.

MERCUSOR   By far the most promising free trade agreement is MERCUSOR, which is composed of Argentina, Brazil, Paraguay, and Uruguay. The MERCUSOR treaty was signed in March 1991. It committed the member nations to cut tariffs every six months, aiming to eliminate tariff barriers altogether by December 31, 1994, and to create a full customs union behind a common external tariff by the end of 1994. To meet the demands of the treaty, governments must continue to deregulate their economies. The aim is to link the four member countries in a market of nearly 200 million people, with a combined gross regional product in excess of $600 billion, and Latin America's largest industrial base.

On August 5, 1994, the presidents of the four countries formally agreed to form a customs union on January 1, 1995. The August 5th agreement fleshed out the details of the previous agreement to form a customs union. Thanks to the massive tariff cuts, intra-MERCUSORial trade jumped from $4.1 billion in 1990 to $9.5 billion in 1993, and this trend should continue with further intra-regional tariff cuts. The common external tariffs which came into force on January 1, 1995, are in the modest range of zero to 20 percent. The MERCUSOR nations have reached their agreement only after agreeing to disagree on areas where much trade takes place. Capital goods, advanced electronics, and petrochemicals, which together comprise 15 percent of the trade, will be treated differently from the rest. For instance, MERCUSOR will have till the year 2001 to implement a common external tariff on capital goods; even then Paraguay and Uruguay will have the grace period of another five years to fall in line. A common external tariff on high-tech goods will not be implemented till the year 2006.

MERCUSOR's founders envisioned free trade not only in goods, but also free movement of capital, labor, and services. Thus far, free trade in goods is almost in place, and steps have been taken to promote free movement of capital. However, there does not appear to be an agreement in sight in the near future for free trade in services or free mobility of labor. Nevertheless, experts in the area suggest that MERCUSOR is on the right track. The reason for such optimism is that technocrats in charge of all four countries are committed to free trade. And there is already talk of inviting Chile, the continent's most liberal economy, to join MERCUSOR.[21]

Association of South East Asian Nations   One major trade bloc in Asia is the Association of South East Asian Nations, commonly known as ASEAN. ASEAN was established in 1967, and is composed of Indonesia, Malaysia, the Philippines, Singapore, and Thailand. Brunei joined the group in 1988. Although some preferential tariffs were implemented, not much progress was made in achieving a free trade zone until September 1994, when economic ministers from the ASEAN countries increased the number of goods targeted for tariff reductions starting January 1, 1995, and agreed that ASEAN would become a free trade zone by the year 2003, five years ahead of schedule. Included also are highly protected agricultural products, which are to be identified later. Significant tariff cuts will reduce the average tariffs from the current 13.4 to 2.6 percent—a reduction of 80.6 percent—by the year 2003. Starting January 1995 member countries began earmarking items for low-duty status from a list of 3141 items. The ministers also agreed to cut in five years, rather than ten, the tariffs on cement, ceramics, chemicals, plastic and leather products, pharmaceuticals, pulp, jewelry, vegetable oils, furniture, electronics, and rubber and textile products.[22]

Will ASEAN evolve from a free trade zone into a customs union with little or no barriers to intra-ASEAN trade and common barriers on trade with non-ASEAN countries? And will it eventually evolve into an ASEAN common market (free movement of people and capital in addition to goods and services) like the European Union?

Presently, ASEAN is aiming to be a free trade zone like NAFTA by 2003. The prospects of ASEAN becoming a common market like the European Union are rather bleak because of a combination of economic, political, and geographical factors. There is little parity among ASEAN countries in economic development. Singapore, with a per capita GNP in 1992 of US$15,750, is much richer than Malaysia (2790), Thailand (1840), the Philippines (770), and Indonesia (670). There are also vast differences in income distribution both within and among ASEAN countries. Socio-economic tensions within countries and within the region could grow in the future, placing a strain on regional cooperation.[23]

Politically, ASEAN countries represent a range of political regimes and philosophies— military-dominated government in Indonesia, personalized leadership in Singapore, Islamic democracy in Malaysia, democratic government in the Philippines, monarchy in Brunei, and constitutional monarchy/democracy in Thailand.

Geographically, the countries are hundreds and, in some cases, up to a thousand miles apart. One strong force contributing to the economic integration among the European Union countries is the geographical proximity and common political borders of most member states, which permits transport of goods and services over land. Such is not the case among ASEAN countries, some of which are separated from each other by the Pacific Ocean. (See Exhibit 3-5.)

Cultural diversity among ASEAN countries is reflected in the variety of religions practiced in the region: Buddhism in Singapore and Thailand; Islam in Brunei, Malaysia, and Indonesia; and Christianity in the Philippines.

The free trade zone, if successfully completed by 2003, may lead to the inclusion in ASEAN of other Asian nations such as Vietnam, Taiwan, and South Korea. Japanese companies have targeted Asia for massive direct investments. From 1987 to 1992, Japanese companies have invested $38 billion worth of manufacturing plants in East Asia, $6.6 billion in 1993 alone. Most importantly, intra-affiliate trade conducted by affiliates of Japanese companies located in ASEAN and other Asian countries play a major role in the integration of the countries in the region.[24] Nevertheless, it is unlikely that Japan will serve as the "hub" to integrate the East Asian, including ASEAN, countries into a more fully integrated market. Japan's historical past in East Asia, involving its brutal attempts to colonize Asia as part of its "Co-Prosperity Sphere," still lingers from northern China to Australia. Korea was brutally colonized by Japan for more than 150 years. However, if NAFTA and the European Union become trade bloc fortresses that block imports produced by Asian countries, ASEAN and other Asian countries may be forced to form an enlarged free trade bloc of their own, as a countervailing force against NAFTA and the European Union.

One last economic organization that warrants mention is APEC, or Asia-Pacific Economic Cooperation. Comprising nearly twenty countries from Asia, North and South America, and the Pacific, APEC is dedicated to speeding up economic liberalization (free trade) in the Pacific area. Current targets of the organization call for the scrapping of all barriers to free trade by all member countries by the year 2020. What will make the progress of APEC interesting to watch is the mix of countries involved—large and small, rich and poor, and politically divergent. As of November 1994, membership included the following countries:

EXHIBIT 3-5
The ASEAN

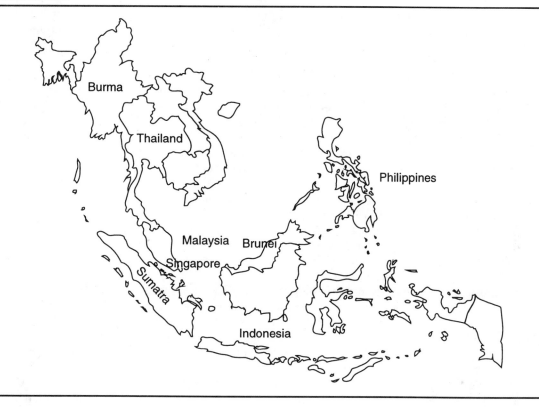

Australia	Hong Kong	New Zealand	Taiwan
Brunei	Indonesia	Papua New Guinea	Thailand
Canada	Japan	Philippines	United States
Chile	Malaysia	Singapore	
China	Mexico	South Korea	

Regardless of their ultimate effect on global free trade, the increasing importance of regional trade blocs will be a major consideration for international managers in the years to come, shaping the environment in which the international company does business. In the next few chapters, we turn to an examination of the three additional dimensions of that environment that we showed in Figure 1-1—the legal, political, and cultural dimensions of international business. While our discussion will generally be from the standpoint of individual country differences, it is important to note that, to the extent countries are united into trade blocs, the blocs themselves may also be a useful focus for addressing these three environmental dimensions.

CHAPTER THREE

SUMMARY

The recent conclusion of the Uruguay Round of the GATT talks is a major development favoring the growth of free international trade. GATT unites more than 100 nations in a system of trade regulations that promotes equal trading opportunities among all members and discourages discriminatory treatment. Safeguards for intellectual property, investments, and other specific assets or transactions among members are also addressed.

The Uruguay Round also created the World Trade Organization (WTO) to resolve trade disputes regarding alleged unfair or discriminatory practices between two or more members. The binding nature of WTO decisions, agreed to by the signatory countries, affords GATT regulations a degree of enforceability that, at least in theory, is a significant step forward for international trade. However, the actual extent of compliance by member countries has yet to be tested.

While GATT has pursued trade liberalization on a global basis, the emergence of regional trade blocs in recent years has proven successful in reducing trade barriers and promoting free trade among bloc member countries. Four types of trade blocs, from lowest to highest degree of integration, are free trade areas, customs unions, common markets, and economic unions.

The recently negotiated NAFTA between Canada, the United States, and Mexico is an example of a free trade agreement. NAFTA liberalizes rules for the transfer of investment capital, jobs, and finished goods and services among the three countries, standardizes regulations for production and marketing, calls for the elimination of many tariffs, and attempts to create a single, unified North American marketplace.

The European Union goes farther than NAFTA, seeking also to create a single European currency, the ECU, for all of Europe, as well as an overarching legal body with the power to make and enforce decisions regarding disputes between member countries. Many of the difficulties in "harmonizing" the many cultural, linguistic, and legal differences among the European nations have been overcome, but significant problems still remain, many exacerbated by strong nationalistic feelings on the part of some member nations.

Other regional trade blocs have been established throughout the world, with ASEAN in Southeast Asia and MERCUSOR in South America two of the more promising. That regional blocs tend to facilitate trade among the member countries seems clear. However, their long-term impact on trade between countries in different blocs is not yet known. As a result, it remains to be seen whether their overall effect on international trade will prove to be beneficial or detrimental.

QUESTIONS FOR THOUGHT AND DISCUSSION

1. What, in your opinion, are the most important features of the Uruguay Round for an international manager? Why do you think so?

2. One key objective of GATT negotiations has been to replace nontariff barriers with tariffs, and then to phase out tariffs. Why do you think tariffs are considered preferable to nontariff barriers? (Hint: what is at the crux, to the U.S., of the ongoing U.S. trade dispute with Japan?)

3. Discuss the differences and similarities between a free trade area, a customs union, a common market, and an economic union. Is it always advantageous to move to a more integrated form of bloc? What factors are necessary to achieve a successful economic union?

4. Explain the concept of harmonization with respect to the European Union and with respect to NAFTA. Is harmonization the same as "becoming identical"? Discuss.

5. You are a manager in a large manufacturing company based in the United States, and have been following the NAFTA debate with great interest. Now that the agreement has been signed, what can your company do to take advantage of NAFTA?

MINI-CASE
A Global European Consumer?

In 1983 Leif Johansson was a manager at Electrolux, a Swedish appliance maker of refrigerators, ovens, and dishwashers. Electrolux was ready for expansion as the Swedish market was just too small. Johansson was swayed by studies that showed Europe was becoming more homogenous. In particular the study showed that unexpected parts of Europe had increased pasta consumption. It was assumed that all types of European markets would begin to show the same type of homogeneity. Johansson envisioned being able to sell the same appliance models across all of Europe as is done in America. He persuaded his superiors to purchase Zanussi, an Italian appliance manufacturer, to increase Electrolux's European market share.

A decade later, Johansson, now Electrolux's president, has found that lifestyles in Europe are not quite as homogenous in the appliance market as they are in the pasta market. The different parts of Europe show drastic differences in preferences when it comes to refrigerators. These preferences are mostly derived from cultural differences. In northern Europe, customers prefer larger refrigerators because they shop weekly in supermarkets. They also prefer to have the freezer on the bottom. In southern Europe, customers prefer smaller refrigerators because they shop almost daily at outdoor markets. They prefer the freezer on top. In Britain, customers prefer mostly freezer, about 60 percent, as they eat lots of frozen foods. Because of such strong preferences, Johansson found that he was unable to pursue his corporate vision of selling the same models of appliances to all of Europe.

In order to compete in Europe, Electrolux has found that it must have 120 basic designs with 1500 variants. The company has come to realize that its strategic vision for Electrolux in Europe was wrong. The idea of only a few brands did not work due to the cultural differences. Johansson had to review his strategic vision and alter it to fit the European market. He found he had to alter his products for each country. His new goal is "... to be a good Frenchman in France and a good Italian in Italy. My strategy is to go global only when I can and stay local when I must." Johansson is still trying to expand the market of Electrolux. He still feels a global strategy is important for Electrolux, only he has learned that culture must be taken into account in each new market. Electrolux is growing. The company has entered the American market and is looking to enter the former Soviet Union and Asia.

Source: Adapted from William Echikson, "Electrolux: the Trick to Selling in Europe," *Fortune*, September 20, 1993, p. 82.

Discussion Questions for Mini-Case

1. How is the European environment different than that in the United States? What factors are responsible for the fragmentation of the European home appliance market?

2. Are there any circumstances under which there will be single homogeneous market for home appliances in Europe?

3. Can you identify products for which there is, or could be, a homogenous market in all of Europe?

4. Identify and explain the functional strategies (e.g., distribution channels, advertising, purchasing, etc.) that a company like Electrolux could use to take advantage of the European Union's common market.

Notes

1 See the classic study by Jacob Viner, *The Customs Union Issue*, Carnegie Endowment for International Peace, New York, 1950.

2 "The Trouble with Regionalism", *The Economist*, June 27, 1992, p. 79.

3 Ibid.

4 Jagdish Bhagwati, "Negotiating Trade Blocs," *India Today*, July 15, 1993, p. 65.

5 "GATT: The Eleventh Hour," *The Economist*, December 4, 1993, pp. 23-24.

6 *Economic Report of the President, February 1994*, United States Government Printing Office, Washington, D.C., 1994, p. 233.

7 "A Guide to GATT," *The Economist*, December 4, 1993, p. 25.

8 "Finally GATT May Fly," *Business Week*, December 20, 1993, p. 36.

9 *Survey of Current Business*, U.S. Department of Commerce, June 1994, p. 74.

10 Geri Smith, "Free Trade Isn't Coming Cheap," *Business Week*, December 6, 1993, pp. 58-59.

11 Ibid.

12 *Business Week*, November 22, 1993, p. 42.

13 Charles Goldsmith and James Pressley, "European Unity Boosts Export Prospects," *The Wall Street Journal*, July 25, 1994, p. B5A.

14 Ibid.

15 Ibid.

16 "European Union: Wishful Thinking," *The Economist*, September 24, 1994, pp. 84-85.

17 Ibid, p. 84.

18 "European Union: Back to the Drawing Board," *The Economist*, September 10, 1994, pp. 21-23; also Bill Javetski and Patrick Oster, "Europe: Unification for the Favored Few," *Business Week*, September 19, 1994, p. 54.

19 "Trade Roundup: A Roundup of Important Trade News in the Americas," *U.S./Latin Trade*, July 1994, p. 12.

20 Ibid.

21 Chile and Bolivia announced on June 25, 1996 their decision to join MERCUSOR making it a free-trade bloc encompassing nearly 210 million people and a combined gross national product of $907 billion.

22 *The Wall Street Journal*, September 22, 1994, p. A4.

23 *Defining a Pacific Community: A Report of the Carnegie Endowment Study Group*, Carnegie Endowment for International Peace, Washington, D.C., 1994, p. 15.

24 Bernard Wysocki, Jr., "In Asia, the Japanese Hope to 'Coordinate' what Nations Produce," *The Wall Street Journal*, August 20, 1990, pp. A1-A2.

The International Legal Environment of Business

LEARNING OBJECTIVES

After completing this chapter, you will be able to:

- Identify the three levels of law that comprise the international legal system for business.
- Discuss the sources and characteristics of international, regional, and national law, and the implications of each for the multinational firm.
- Discuss alternative methods to resolving international disputes through legal channels.

A manager in an international company must have a thorough understanding of the complexity of the international legal environment. The legal requirements for engaging in business activities in foreign countries are determined by the laws of not only the host country but of the home country as well. For example, the United States government has imposed an economic blockade against Cuba that makes it illegal for American companies, and American subsidiaries of foreign companies, to conduct any business transactions with the government or businesses of Cuba. Subsidiaries of American companies in foreign countries may face similar restraints imposed by host country governments on trade with certain countries. For example, for many years in the past China prohibited all business transactions with Taiwan, although such restrictions are gradually being removed as part of the economic liberalization movement in China.

Home and host country legislation is often the outcome of international law, which incorporates the provisions of treaties signed by many countries. For example, member countries of a treaty for the protection of patents are required to mutually provide national treatment to foreign companies—if a country's patent laws give patent protection to domestic patents, then it is obligated to provide the same protection to a foreign company that has applied for a patent in the country and not treat it any differently than it would a domestic company.

The laws of both the host and home countries are quite often the product of legislation drawn up by regional blocs such as the North American Free Trade Agreement (NAFTA) and the European Union (EU). (Trade blocs were covered in depth in Chapter 3.) For example, all members of the European Union have common external tariffs against nonmember countries while allowing free movement of people, goods, and capital within the common market boundaries. Consequently, the EU member countries have been forced to modify country legislation to conform with the EU's rules. International managers who are aware of such legal parameters can take simultaneous advantage of both the EU's common external tariff and the open internal EU market by establishing a production plant in an EU country that provides the most advantages.

There are also significant differences among the laws of countries. Differences exist in laws pertaining to worker rights; protection of patent, trademark, and trade secrets; minimum wage; environmental protection; employee health and safety; product liability; social security and pensions; and so on.

There is no one uniform set of laws governing the business operations and transactions of companies in all foreign countries. Therefore, international managers must be knowledgeable of the laws of each and every country in which they conduct business or are contemplating doing business in the future. Ignorance of laws is not a valid excuse in any country, and breaking a law of a country can prove to be very costly not only in the time and money expended in defending oneself in a foreign court, but also in terms of the damage done to one's reputation by highly publicized court proceedings if the matter cannot be settled out of court.

THE NATURE OF THE INTERNATIONAL LEGAL ENVIRONMENT OF BUSINESS

An international company is obligated to operate within the boundaries of the international legal environment, and specifically within those legal precepts that pertain to international business activities. One could conceptualize the legal environment of international business as consisting of three concentric circles, as shown in Figure 4-1.

In the outermost circle are international *treaties* and *conventions* and international *custom*, which have been and continue to be the most important sources of international legal rules.[1]

In the middle circle are the legal constraints and requirements imposed and incorporated in the laws of nation-states by the over-arching *laws of the regional trade blocs* such as the European Union, North American Free Trade Agreement, Mercusor, etc.

In the innermost circle are the *laws of nation-states* designed to govern the behavior of the nations' citizens and business firms.

FIGURE 4-1
The Legal Environment of International Business

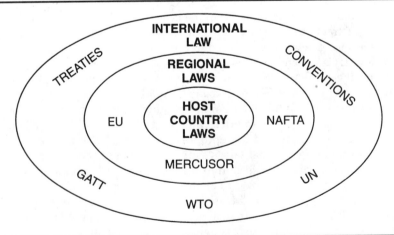

THE CONCEPT OF LAW AND THE
REQUIREMENTS OF AN EFFECTIVE LEGAL SYSTEM

As we shall see later in this chapter, treaties and conventions and customs continue to be the principal sources of international law because the nature of international law fails to meet all of the criteria considered to be prerequisites of an effective legal system. In order to understand the degree to which international law meets the requirements of an effective legal system we shall examine first, the concept of law; second, the requirements of an effective legal system; third, the functions of law; and finally, the degree to which international law meets the requirements of an effective legal system.

The Concept of Law

Law has three basic characteristics in a civilized society. First, law is a norm that prescribes what is assumed to be a proper mode of behavior. It attempts to regulate the behavior of the subjects according to certain standards set by the society or by those who control the society. Second, law not only prescribes a certain pattern of behavior but also requires that the prescribed mode be followed. We are bound to obey the law because it is the official desire of the society in which we live. Third, law includes a process approved by society for applying coercive sanctions against those who do not obey and therefore perform illegal acts. Law is a coercive order. It provides socially organized sanctions and thus can be clearly distinguished from religious and moral orders which are by nature non-coercive.

The Requirements of an Effective Legal System

Several factors determine the effectiveness of a legal system. First, the people in the society must clearly understand and have knowledge of what the society prescribes as legal behavior. Without this knowledge one could not expect the law to be obeyed. Second, the members of society, the subjects of the legal system, must have agreed that the laws deserve to be obeyed; that is, they must regard the laws as being fair and just. And last, an effective system for punishing illegal behavior must be in place. A number of writers have taken the position that an effective system of sanctions is all that is needed to make a legal system effective, and whether the members of society believe that the law is worthy of obedience is immaterial. The position taken in this book is that both prerequisites must be met before a legal system is deemed effective: the belief and sentiment that the law ought to be obeyed as well as a system for sanctioning illegal behavior.

In a democratic society, the government which is duly elected by the people provides the machinery for an effective legal system. The legislative branch of the government makes the laws, and the judicial and executive branches together perform the task of identifying illegal behavior and of applying sanctions on the lawbreaker. A legal system functions effectively when there is a centralized process, like the government, to make and enforce the laws. The more effective that law enforcement is through the government, the lesser the danger that an individual or group might gain enough strength to disturb the stability of a society. At the same time the chances of a government remaining popular and in power are slim if an effective legal system does not exist.[2]

Functions of Law

The principal function of law in a democratic society is to promote law and order with justice. There are four functions of law that promote this principal function.

First, law communicates to individuals in a society their rights and duties in their daily interactions with other people in the society. The definitions of rights and duties of individuals help prevent frequent conflicts among members of the society and also provide a basis for the settlement of disputes among them as they occur.

Second, law helps in controlling and preventing behavior which the society considers undesirable.

Third, governments use law to promote the social and economic welfare of society. Examples of such laws are those concerned with child labor, social security, workmen's compensation, minimum wage, health care, food and drugs, and so on. Such laws promote law and order indirectly and in the long run, in so far as they help lay a solid foundation for an orderly society in the future.

Fourth, laws of a society reflect the norms, values, aims, and general beliefs of a society. To the extent that laws serve this function, they enhance the motivation of the members of a society to obey its laws.

INTERNATIONAL LAW AS LAW

Since the seventeenth century observers of international relations have been plagued with this question: Is international law really law? If international law does exist, does it meet the requirements of an effective legal system? This question has persisted because international law, if it exists, exists in a social system that has no government. International law is true law if (1) there is a general agreement among the nations of the world (and by implications among the people in the world) regarding the nature and types of behaviors by nations and their citizens that are acceptable and those that are not, (2) nations feel obliged to obey the laws, and (3) there is a mechanism for applying sanctions against nations and their citizens if they behave in a manner deemed to be unacceptable according to generally recognized international standards.

The real underlying issue is whether an effective legal system—national or international—can exist without a centralized system—such as a government—that has the legitimacy and power conferred upon it by the subjects to enact and enforce laws that conform with the values and beliefs of the members of the society who are the subjects of the law.

The Nature of International Law

It is generally accepted that there exists in international law what is known as a delict or illegal conduct. One is able to establish that illegal conduct has occurred because international law consists of a set of norms prescribing patterns of behavior, although those patterns are often vaguely defined. For example, expropriating the property of a foreign company without just and fair compensation for the property seized is generally considered to be unacceptable by the world community. Similarly, invasion by one country of another country merely to expand its national boundaries is viewed as illegal aggression under international law.

Secondly, there have been in the past, and continue today, certain norms and reasons obliging states to obey the law. The reasons are usually generated internally rather than from a central source, but they nonetheless exist in a subtle and often unarticulated form.

Finally, there is a system of sanctions in international law that contributes to the coercive enforcement of the law. For instance, the invasion by Iraq of Kuwait led to the Gulf War, in which a United Nations multinational force was involved in ousting the Iraqis from Kuwaiti soil. The United Nations enforced the international law enshrined in the principle that it is illegal for a nation to invade and seize the land and property of another sovereign nation. However, the

United Nations is far from being a world government. The United Nations is in a position to take positive actions against "lawbreaker" states only if all countries that are the permanent members of the Security Council (U.S.A., U.K., France, Russia, and China) agree to not cast a veto against it. Since there is no world government in the true sense of the term, the system of sanctions in international law is not controlled by a centralized force, but is primarily administered according to the principle of self-help.

Therefore, at least in terms of the criteria employed in discussing law in democratic societies, international law can be defined as law. However due to the absence of a single formal supranational institution with the authority delegated to it by the various countries to enact laws, and to force compliance by the countries and their citizens to the laws via enforceable sanctions, international law remains a decentralized or unsophisticated system of law.

The Role of the World Court

The International Court of Justice (The World Court) in The Hague, Holland, the principal judicial organ of the United Nations, is often mistakenly presumed to have the authority to adjudicate commercial disputes between companies and citizens of different countries, and the power to enforce their decrees. There are three scenarios under which disputes could arise: (1) between two countries, (2) between a country and a company, and (3) between two companies. Disputes between two countries can be adjudicated by the International Court of Justice only when *both* governments involved agree to submit to the authority of the International Court of Justice. This limits the scope of this world judicial body. Disputes between a country and a company, or between two companies, can be settled in the courts of one of the parties to the dispute or through arbitration.

Thus, international managers must realize that no centralized judicial body exists to resolve commercial disputes between citizens and companies of different countries. So what mechanisms or provisions are there to resolve international commercial disputes? We shall discuss this topic later in this chapter.

We shall next examine how international law is created and the role that custom and treaties play in this process (the outermost circle in Figure 4-2).

HOW INTERNATIONAL LAW IS CREATED

The two principal sources of national (domestic) law in a country are custom and legislation, whereas the two principal sources of international law are *custom* and *treaties*.

Custom as a Source of International Law

Custom is the oldest method of creating international law, one that was predominant when interactions among states were sporadic and less complex because the rapid modes of communications and transportation characteristic of the twentieth century were nonexistent. Under such conditions habitual patterns of behavior that had evolved over a number of years often reached the level of obligatory rules, i.e., international law, which governed how nations and their subjects interacted with one another. For instance, many of the regulations pertaining to the law of the sea evolved from customary practice. Custom creates law just as legislation does. There are two differences between custom and legislation: (1) Custom is unconscious and unintentional lawmaking. In establishing a custom, men do not necessarily know that they are creating a rule of law by their own conduct, nor do they necessarily intend to create the law. The rule of law is the effect and not the purpose of the activity. Legislation is conscious and deliberate lawmaking—

FIGURE 4-2
The Legal Environment of International Business—First Level: International Law

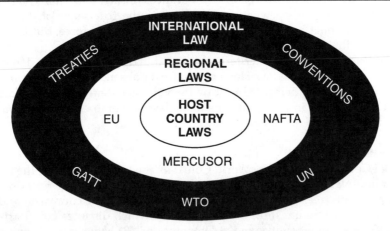

men who legislate know that they are making law and intend by their activity to make law. (2) Customary law is created by individuals themselves who are subject to the law created by their conduct. The individuals creating the law and the individuals subject to the law are at least partly identical. Legislation is lawmaking by a special body of people whose purpose is to make laws, and which is different from, and more or less independent of, the individuals subject to the law created by the body. For instance, in the United States, elected officials in the legislative branch of government have the responsibility to enact legislation. Custom is decentralized creation of law, whereas legislation is centralized creation of law. The law created through legislation is usually called statutory law.

Custom in the form of unwritten but clearly understood norms is a diminishing source of international law because of the increasing interdependence and complexity of the modern world and the expansion of the international legal system beyond the confines of the "Western World." As opposed to bygone days when whatever trade and commerce and political activity that did transpire was predominantly between countries that enjoyed mostly homogeneous cultural values, in today's world such transactions are often between countries in different hemispheres and whose cultural values are anything but homogeneous. Hence efforts are underway through international agencies and bilateral and multilateral agreements among nations to codify traditional customary laws.

Treaties as Sources of International Law

Treaties are the second source of international law. A treaty is an agreement entered into by two or more states under general international law. If the contracting parties consist of only two states, it is called a *bilateral* treaty. A *multilateral* treaty is one in which the contracting parties consist of more than two states. Sometimes a treaty is called an international *convention*, an *agreement*, a *protocol*, or a *declaration*. In most cases the title is not important. However, in the United States a distinction is made between a "treaty" and an "agreement." The U.S. Constitution stipulates that "treaties" are international agreements made by the president of the United States "by and with the advice of the Senate." The Executive Agreements are treaties entered into by the President, or with his authorization by someone else, without consultation with the Senate.

A treaty, like a contract, is a legal transaction by which the contracting parties intend to establish mutual obligations and rights. Countries that have signed the treaty are legally obliged and correspondingly entitled to behave as they have declared that they will behave. Therefore, if they do not behave in conformity with the contract or treaty they are exposed to sanctions and punishment.

A treaty becomes incorporated into the laws of a nation when it is ratified by the nation's legislative body. In the United States, a treaty must be ratified by a two-thirds majority in the Senate.

Treaties are now considered as a major (and by some as *the* major) source of international law. However, one must be careful in taking such a statement too literally. Even taken together, the thousands of treaties made among nations do not create one single general rule of international law. For instance, a commercial treaty between the United States and China, or a treaty to prevent double taxation between France and Morocco, cannot create any rule of conduct for the family of nations. However, there are *law-making treaties*, which are treaties that are made among a number of countries in their joint interest, and which are intended to create a new rule. When a treaty is ratified by many nations, it creates general norms that regulate the mutual conduct among the signatory countries. A law-making treaty, then, is a means by which a substantial number of countries reach an agreement about a particular rule of law. It may promote new general rules for the future conduct of the member countries. A law-making treaty may also cause an existing customary or conventional rule of law to be modified, abolished, or codified. It may lead to the creation of a new international agency. The International Labor Organization is an example of an international agency that was created by a multilateral treaty signed by almost all nations to protect the health, safety, and working hours of workers and to prevent the abuse of child labor. It is this kind of treaty through which conventional international law is created.

Because we live in a world composed of many sovereign states, only member states are obliged to abide by its provisions. If only a few members have joined by signing and ratifying a treaty, the treaty does not create a new rule of general international law but, at best, only a rule of particular or regional application. As more and more states join the treaty, and as a majority of states eventually accept to abide by the treaty provisions, a network of countries is created—a network that binds the network members with each other in a "cobweb" of mutual obligations and rights in accordance with the provisions of the treaty.

COMMERCIAL TREATIES OF SIGNIFICANCE TO COMMERCIAL COMPANIES

There are many different types of treaties in force that govern the behavior of nations and, in turn, their citizens, such as the Law of the Sea, military alliances such as NATO, and treaties that govern global aviation and navigation. However, certain treaties are of particular significance to business enterprises. We shall present an overview of two types of treaties that managers of multinational companies should be acquainted with:

1. Treaties of friendship, commerce, and navigation.
2. Treaties for the protection of intellectual property rights.

Treaties of Friendship, Commerce, and Navigation

When an international company does business in another country, it does so not as a right, but as a privilege. Usually, this privilege and its conditions are negotiated between the host country government and the home country government. The United States has treaties with several dozen nations that formulate the conditions of the privilege under which American firms may do business in these nations, and vice versa. These treaties are generally known as the treaties of friendship, commerce, and navigation (FCN), but are sometimes known as treaties of establishment, or conventions to regulate commerce or navigation. They usually include, among other things, reciprocal pledges by each of the signatory countries to honor the property of the other country's companies located within their respective national borders, and to give the other country's companies *national treatment*, meaning treatment that is no less favorable than that which is given to business firms that are its own citizens. Also included are guarantees that property will not be seized illegally and without proper compensation. Most treaties include in them the *most favored nation* (MFN) treatment clause. The MFN clause obligates the country to give to the imports of goods from the other country with which it has signed a treaty, treatment in terms of tariffs that is no less favorable than that given to imports from third countries. A number of commercial treaties include in them MFN treatment beyond simple tariffs.

A multinational company does not necessarily require a treaty of this kind before it can do business in a foreign country. However, a treaty of friendship, commerce, and navigation, or one like it, affords a degree of legal protection that a multinational firm needs to guard its interests in a foreign country.

Treaties for the Protection of Intellectual Property Rights: An Overview

It is increasingly important for international companies with new technologies to develop patent programs that will protect their inventions throughout the international market. In fact, companies that remain ignorant of foreign patent procedures and apply for patents in the traditional manner—i.e., from a one-nation perspective—can inadvertently destroy their opportunities to obtain foreign patents.

U.S. patents give rights only within the United States. The same rule applies to patents granted in foreign countries. In order to protect its foreign patent rights, a company's patent strategy and business practices must accommodate foreign rules and deadlines, making sophisticated use of complex national, regional, and global patent application strategies. To obtain patent protection in a foreign country or region, companies must ultimately obtain a patent from the appropriate foreign patent office, and the patent must be enforced in that country's or region's courts. By following proper procedures, international companies can achieve these goals. In the following sections we shall review some of the major international treaties for the protection of patents, trademarks, and copyrights.

Patents In the United States, utility patents (patents for "any new and useful process, machine, manufacture, or composition of matter") have a term of 17 years from the date of grant, while design patents have a term of 14 years from the date of grant. However, the life of a patent in other countries varies anywhere from 15 to 20 years. Only the United States, the Philippines, and Jordan have patent systems based on a *"first to invent"* standard; all other national patent systems employ a *"first to file"* standard. When two or more independent inventors file overlapping patent applications, a rule must be applied to determine who will be granted the patent. Under the "first to invent" rule, an inventor who can prove that she was the first to invent a device and diligently pursue its development will obtain the patent rights. In the rest of the world, which uses the "first to file" rule, the first party to file a patent application in a given jurisdiction is awarded the patent.

International companies must be familiar with international treaties for the protection of patents. There are two primary international conventions for patent protection: (1) the Paris Convention for the Protection of Industrial Property and (2) the Patent Cooperation Treaty.

The Paris Convention provides *national treatment* and a twelve-month *priority period* for the filing of patent applications in other Paris Convention member states. This means that from the date a businesswoman files the first application for a patent in a country that is a member of the Paris Convention, she has a twelve-month priority over any other person for filing an application for the same invention in all other Paris Convention member countries. Thus the priority principle gives the businesswoman enough time to apply for patent protection in other countries, and is especially useful in countries whose patent laws stipulate that previous publication of an invention in any country is a bar to patentability. It is important to remember that the twelve-month priority period for patents (and six-month priority period for trademarks) under the Paris Convention runs from the date of application at the U.S. Patent and Trademark Office—not from the actual date that the patent is granted or the trademark is registered. This is a serious error often made by inexperienced U.S. companies, resulting in the loss of potential foreign patent and trademark protection.

Yet another provision of this Convention, which is of significance, is the *independence of patents*. According to this provision, if a company's patent expires in one member country, this does not automatically lead to its cancellation or expiration in other member countries of the Paris Convention.

A majority of the nations of the world are members of the Paris Convention. However, a significant number of countries are not members, notably some of the most rapidly developing countries such as Chile, Hong Kong, India, Pakistan, Singapore, Thailand, and Taiwan.

The Patent Cooperation Treaty permits the filing of a single international patent application which is then reviewed by the patent offices of individual countries. Applicants wishing to obtain foreign patents simply file a single form, checking off the countries from which they wish to obtain patents. Approximately 50 countries are members of this treaty, including all members of the European Union, the United States, Japan, Canada, and China.

Trademarks As a result of the Trademark Law Revision Act of 1988, federal registrations of trademarks and service marks in the United States have a renewable term of ten years (formerly twenty years), provided that the mark is in use in interstate commerce and a specimen proving use is provided to the Patent and Trademark Office. The Paris Convention for the Protection of Industrial Property is the primary international convention protecting trademarks.

As of November 16, 1989, U.S. citizens and firms have been able to file, on the basis of bona fide intended use, a trademark or service mark application, although use must occur prior to registration. Even prior to the 1988 legislation, foreign nationals of countries that were parties to the Paris Convention had the ability to secure federal trademark registrations without prior use in the United States.

Copyrights Copyrights in the United States have a term, in the case of works created on or after January 1, 1987, consisting of the life of the author plus a period of fifty years after the author's death. Unlike patents and trademarks, which require filings in other countries in order to obtain protection in those countries, U.S. copyrighted works are automatically protected in all signatory countries to the Berne Convention for the Protection of Literary and Artistic Works. Berne Convention works that have a country of origin other than the United States are exempted from the requirement that copyrights be registered at the U.S. Copyright Office before an infringement suit can be brought. U.S. origin works continue to be subject to this requirement.

Two global treaties of importance to international companies are the GATT TRIPS Agreement and the U.N. Convention on the International Sale of Goods. Students interested in reading more about these two may refer to the appendix at the end of this chapter.

Problems with Enforcing Treaty Provisions for the Protection of Intellectual Property   While many countries have officially signed the various treaties governing the protection of intellectual property, there is still the serious problem of enforcing the treaty provisions.

A very serious problem facing American industry, and therefore America itself, is the theft of intellectual property—ideas, innovations protected by copyright, patents, and trademarks—due to the absence of effective domestic legislation in other countries for the protection of intellectual property.

The U.S. International Trade Commission estimated in 1986 that American companies lose approximately $60 billion to intellectual property piracy abroad each year. Companies that are hit the hardest are America's most innovative, fastest-growing companies in the computer software, pharmaceutical, and entertainment industries. One can find pirated copies of the latest American movies and audiocassettes and compact discs of the newest American vocalist on the streets of any Asian or Latin American city. In 1985, fully 80 percent of the Japanese market of American films and videos seen there were pirated—usually by entrepreneurs associated with organized crime. Illegal copies of films are available in countries such as Thailand less than two weeks after the official versions are released in the United States. Film companies estimate their annual sales losses in Thailand at $20 million, while album distributors put theirs at $50 million.

The pirating of patented drugs is costing pharmaceutical companies billions of dollars. It takes about twelve years and $299 million to introduce a new medicine in the United States, according to the American Pharmaceutical Manufacturers Association. The introduction of new and more effective drugs is the basis for a competitive edge in the pharmaceutical industry, and pharmaceutical firms must market their products globally in order to obtain enough revenue to finance and support their innovative research. However, these efforts are drastically eroded through drug piracy by foreign companies in countries where no patent protection is available. Such piracy abroad is facilitated by U.S. regulations requiring that domestic companies applying for U.S. patents disclose their formulas in the process. This public disclosure makes copying the drugs and selling them abroad very easy and inexpensive. In many developing countries, where patent laws for drugs do not exist, imitations of patented drugs often beat the domestic company to the market in those countries. For example, Pfizer saw its products Unasyn, an antibiotic, and Diflucan, an antifungal medicine, marketed in Brazil and Argentina before it could get there. Spain is one of the worst offenders in this regard. Unlike most third-world countries, Spain has the technology to copy drugs developed abroad. Moreover, Spanish counterfeiters are "protected" by the Spanish legal system, which takes up to ten years to settle a court case. The pirates are willing to risk paying a fine of a few million U.S. dollars because, while the case against them is in court, they stand to make many millions more than the anticipated fine, which may in fact never be imposed at all.

Companies such as Pfizer spend millions of dollars yearly in battles to defend their patents abroad. Piracy of intellectual property severely hurts global companies not only from lost sales in the country making the pirated goods, but also in lost revenues and market share positions in many other countries having no patent protection. This situation is especially prevalent in Africa and the Middle East, countries to which the pirates export their goods at substantially discounted prices. Exports of faked audiocassettes from Indonesia alone have been estimated at $13 million.[3]

The People's Republic of China is reported to be one of the most risky countries in the world with respect to the safety of computer software, films, and books. U.S. publishers charge that the Chinese government itself is one of the biggest software thieves in China. The International Intellectual Property Alliance, a group of U.S. industry associations, estimates that the illegal copying of software in China cost American companies $400 million in 1990, a figure the U.S. Trade Representative's office says is fairly accurate.[4] The U.S. government has charged that factories in China each year produce $1 billion worth of compact discs, videotapes, and computer programs pirated from the United States without the payment of any royalties or acknowledgement of copyrights to the U.S. owners of patents, copyrights, and trademarks.[5] The U.S. alleges that China does not effectively enforce its intellectual property laws. The USTR had this to say about the Chinese piracy problem:

> "While in general, China has improved intellectual property rights laws and regulations in accord with the 1992 memorandum of understanding, China's enforcement of its laws and regulations is sporadic at best and virtually nonexistent for copyrighted works. Piracy is rampant in the audio-visual, computer software, and publishing sectors, as well as in trademarks. Among the most egregious cases is the establishment of 26 CD and laser disc factories in central and southern China. These factories producing pirated CDs had the capacity to manufacture up to 75 million CDs for export to markets in Hong Kong and Southeast Asia and, recently, Canada."[6]

The Chinese have been insisting that they have taken effective steps to stop copyright infringements, citing as evidence that the authorities in Guangdong Province stopped a truck en route to Hong Kong and confiscated 3,250 pirated compact discs. "A Western diplomat emphasized that Chinese efforts still need to focus on the factories, not on small trucks crossing the frontier to Hong Kong."[7] Mickey Kantor, the U.S. trade representative, observed that during the U.S.-China trade negotiations, pirated American goods were proliferating in shops right outside the meeting room door. Said Mr. Kantor:

> "While our negotiators were just in China last week, during a break in the negotiations, they went down to a particularly notorious street to see if they could buy any pirated U.S. software, computer software, products. They were able to buy a WordPerfect 6.0 and a so-called DOS, MS-DOS product—took it back to the negotiations, and they presented them at the negotiating table, complete with Government-stamped receipts for these products. No action has been taken against these stores to date."[8]

International companies stand to lose from piracy of intellectual property in a number of ways: (1) The international company loses sales in the copycat country itself as it is forced to compete against pirated products. (2) It loses sales in third countries where it has to compete against exported pirated products. (3) Its reputation as a producer of quality products and service suffers because pirated products of inferior quality are quite often sold under the company's brand name (e.g., Polo, Ralph Lauren, Rolex, Gucci, T.G.I. Friday's, Microsoft, Zantac). (4) It may be prevented entry in a foreign market because a company in the foreign market may have established a dominant market share using the international company's pirated technology or trademark.

The problems that companies have to deal with because of pirated trademarks in foreign companies are illustrated in *Practical Insight 4-1*, which portrays problems in Mexico for companies whose logos have already been hijacked.

PRACTICAL INSIGHT 4-1

Is That Our Trademark?

The Sign of "Gucci"

The sign says Gucci. The shop looks like Gucci. It is elegantly situated in the swanky Maria Isabel Sheraton Hotel in the fashionable district of Mexico City. The shop radiates class and good taste and offers customers elegantly arranged displays of leather goods bearing the Gucci logo. The goods are priced upscale but certainly lower than in the U.S. and Europe. The customers can see bargains all over the place. They are told by the sales personnel that the shoes, wallets, and handbags are made in Mexico from "special designs." But is this the real thing? Are those Gucci shoes? No, they aren't! They are fakes counterfeited by Mexican entrepreneurs who have unceremoniously hijacked the Milan-based company's brand.

The Trouble at T.G.I. Friday's

T.G.I. Friday's registered its trademark in Mexico in the early 1980s, intending to open a chain of restaurants south of the border. To their great dismay company executives discovered that there were two T.G.I. Friday's already doing a booming business in prime dining area locations in Mexico City.

The Mexico City T.G.I. Friday's were exact replicas of the 'real thing' in the U.S. The dark wood, the memorabilia, the central bar, the red-and-white striped awnings—it was all there—just like in Los Angeles or Philadelphia, or in Detroit where the popular chain started. After becoming completely enamored with the Friday's concept, the Mexican owners cloned the Detroit Friday's in Mexico City. And it worked. Business boomed within a matter of months.

The T.G.I. Friday's home office in Dallas reached a compromise with the Mexican owners. Rather than pursue the case in the Mexican courts—which would have been a mistake in light of the huge litigation costs and uncertainty of a favorable outcome—they offered the Mexican owners a compromise: "We won't sue, but you must become our franchisee." The Mexicans thought that it was a good idea and agreed to use the T.G.I. Friday's name only if they complied with the franchise agreement. With the franchise agreement came franchise support. The American parent gave the Mexican franchisees trade secrets to make them improve and to become even more like the real T.G.I. Friday's in the U.S.

Soon trouble showed its ugly face. The Mexican franchisees complained that it was too difficult to keep up with the requirements of the franchise agreement. They said that they wanted to get out of the agreement. They agreed to deidentify, removing anything that would identify the restaurant as a T.G.I. Friday's. Actually, they didn't do it. They just changed the name to Freeday. From the American parent's viewpoint, this did not solve anything. In Spanish, there is only a slight phonetic difference between Friday's and Freeday so T.G.I. Friday's is still in the Mexican customers' thinking as they dine at Freeday. The downside of this situation is that the American parent in Dallas often gets complaints about the food and service in "their" Mexican restaurant, which of course isn't their restaurant at all!

Source: Adapted from Candace Siegle, "Toro, Toro, Toro?: A new Mexican law protecting trademarks may not offer much hope for foreign companies whose logos have already been hijacked," *World Trade*, April 1992, pp. 38 and 40.

REGIONAL TRADE LAWS

Up to this point we have studied how international law is created, and the role played by treaties in creating the legal framework under which international companies are obligated to operate. However, international companies must not only live by "treaty law" but also by regional laws that apply to groups of countries, usually trade blocs, such as the European Union and NAFTA (this is the middle concentric circle in Figure 4-3).

Many aspects of the operations of international firms may be constrained by legislation specifically enacted by regional trade blocs. One must understand that such constraints are far too numerous to be covered in this chapter. The purpose here is to point out that regional trade bloc legislation also affects the functioning of international companies and that it is an important ingredient in the international legal environment of business. Box 4-1 on pages 95 and 96, illustrates some of the legislation enacted by the oldest and the most advanced of all trade blocs, namely the European Union, in four areas: (1) duties and taxes, (2) antitrust policy, (3) product liability, and (4) rules of origin.

LAWS OF NATION STATES

Now we move to the innermost concentric circle in Figure 4-4—the laws of nation-states or country laws which, in conjunction with international law (created through treaties and conventions) and regional trade bloc laws, shape the legal environment of international business with which international firms must comply.

We live in a world of sovereign states. Sovereignty grants each independent nation the supreme authority to legislate laws meant to govern those within its jurisdiction. Although a country is obligated to obey the provisions and code of conduct of any international treaty or agreement to which it is party, it still retains the right to make its own laws. The international legal framework as it exists today consists of an umbrella of international law embracing various

FIGURE 4-3

The Legal Environment of International Business—Second Level: Regional Laws

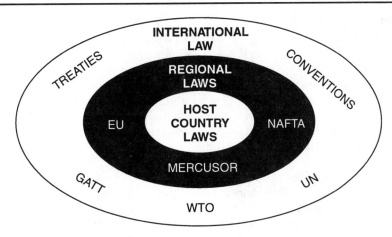

FIGURE 4-4

The Legal Environment of International Business—Laws of Nation-States

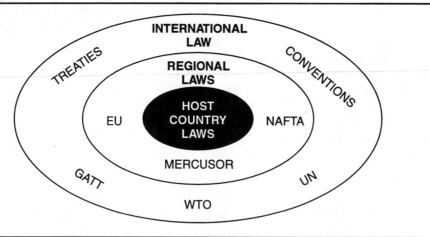

treaties and regional trade bloc law under which are the separate national laws of independent nations.

An international company has to live within this global legal framework. It must comprehend international law, as well as national laws of countries in which it has subsidiaries, and how international and national laws affect the different subsidiaries individually as well as collectively. This can be quite a problem because not only are the legal systems of countries continuously evolving and changing, but quite often the laws of two or more countries might be in conflict. Additionally, international companies must be knowledgeable of not only the treaties that the home country has with other countries, but also of treaties that the host country has with third countries. This is because the foreign subsidiaries must obey the national laws and treaty obligations of both the home and host countries.

The Nature of Common Law, Civil Law, and Islamic Law

Common Law and Civil Law The legal systems of different countries can be grouped into two main categories—common law and civil law. Common law is a set of legal principles that has emerged from the feudal law of medieval England. Civil law, often referred to as "code law" or "Roman law," has its roots in the legal system of the Roman Empire. Civil law was compiled initially by Napoleon Bonaparte. The legal systems of English-speaking countries, such as England, Canada, the United States, and Australia, and of the former British colonies, such as India, Pakistan, Nigeria, Kenya, and Jamaica, are based upon common law. Nations of continental Europe, such as France, Spain, and Italy, and their former colonies base their legal systems upon civil law.

What are the major differences between common law and civil law? Common law is based upon tradition and legal precedents formulated by past court rulings, statutes, and government decrees. Included in common law, therefore, are a set of legal precepts that have gradually evolved over a number of years. Thus the bases for common law are past practices and precedents.

BOX 4-1

Examples of European Union Legislation

Duties and Taxes

As a fully operable customs union, the European Union has a common external tariff structure, while member countries trade duty free among each other.

EU duty rates are applied uniformly by the fifteen member states on products imported from the United States and other industrialized countries. Duties on most products imported from the United States range from 5 to 20 percent. Once duties and taxes are paid, goods are in "free circulation" and can move across borders to other destinations within the Community.

At present, each of the EU member states has a standard value added tax (VAT) that is assessed on the sale of both domestic and imported products. The VAT is a sales or consumption tax imposed on buyers of goods, from the beginning of the production and distribution cycle to the final sale to the consumer. On imported products, the VAT is imposed by EC customs officers on the c.i.f. (cost, insurance, and freight) value of the shipment plus the duty charged on the product.

Antitrust Policy

The primary aim of European competition policy is to ensure that the newly unified single market is not threatened by unfair trade practices. The EU has well-established antitrust regulations which prohibit agreements that distort trade or restrict competition among the member states. Community antitrust laws roughly parallel those in the United States.

Distribution agreements that contain restrictions on territory, non-competition clauses, and grants of exclusivity are banned under EU law. Arrangements between companies that would fix prices, share markets, and limit product or technical development are also in violation of EU antitrust policy. Further, a corporation holding a dominant position within the Community cannot abuse its power.

The elimination of EU national barriers, the expansion of cross-border agreements, and the free movement of goods could contribute to a potential increase in antitrust violations. It is important that U.S. exporters and investors, particularly those that plan cross-border operations in Europe, understand and comply with Community antitrust regulations.

Article 85 (1) of the Treaty of Rome prohibits agreements or practices between two or more companies that restrict competition within the EU. Article 85 (3) of the Treaty, however, permits exemptions from the application of Article 85 (1) for agreements or practices which contribute to the production or distribution of goods or to the promotion of technical progress.

Product Liability

The key provisions of the EU product liability law, adopted in 1985, are similar to U.S. law and include holding the manufacturer of a product liable for damage, loss, or injury caused by a defect in the product. The manufacturer is liable for injuries caused by products, irrespective of fault or other concepts of negligence. The consumer must prove that the defect existed and that it caused damage, loss, or injury. Under the provisions of the law, importers, suppliers, and distributors can be held liable for defective products.

BOX 4-1 *(continued)*

With the free movement of goods across national borders, consumers must have assurances of product safety. The adoption of the product liability directive, along with the harmonization of product standards, provides evidence of the European Union's commitment to consumer protection. As consumer awareness throughout the Community increases, more firms may find themselves involved in product liability litigation.

For U.S. firms exporting to Europe, this means that greater awareness must be exercised to ensure that all products contain adequate warnings, and instructions and products are designed free from potential liability.

American exporters should also be aware that rapid integration of EU product standards plays a key role in product design and product liability. In order to minimize potential product liability problems, U.S. companies should design and manufacture their products to conform to product safety standards.

Rules of Origin

The EU legislation contains preferential rules of origin that are used to determine whether products are eligible for duty-free treatment within the Community. U.S. origin products may be eligible for duty-free treatment within the Community if they have been "sufficiently worked or processed" within an EU country. Depending upon the product in question, "sufficiently worked" can mean that at least 60 percent of the value of the product must originate from an EU country for it to earn a duty-free status.

The above are merely a handful of examples of the numerous regional trade laws enacted by the European Union. Because the member countries of the EU have treaty obligations to abide by EU-wide legislation, EU laws become laws of member countries as well. Similar regional laws have been passed by trade blocs such as NAFTA, MERCUSOR, and others.

Under civil law one finds a comprehensive set of written codes or rules of law, which have been stated in general terms. These codes are then applied to specific cases as they arise. Under civil law the legal system is divided into three codes: commercial, civil, and criminal. Civil law is considered to be far more inclusive than common law. Whereas common law is basically nonlegislative, civil law is legislative in nature.

Civil law recognizes that business problems are often unique and consequently need special status under the law. Therefore, civil law provides a separate code to handle commercial problems. There is no such commercial code specially designed for business under common law, although there is one set of codes that is applied to either civil or commercial disputes. Countries whose laws are based upon common-law principles are making attempts to codify commercial law. However, the bases of commercial law in such cases are still past precedents established by court rulings.

International companies should understand the differences in the natures of these two systems because the due process of law may differ considerably between civil-law and common-law countries.

Islamic Law The *Koran*, the holiest of all holy books in Islam—akin to the Bible for Christians—is the basis for the legal system and the nature of laws in most countries that have a majority of the population belonging to the Islamic faith. Islamic Law (Shari'ah) is the interpretation of the Koran. The word "Islam" means submission (i.e., to the will of God), and the word "Muslim" means one who submits.[9] There are differences in the extent to which Islamic precepts govern the laws of the various predominantly Muslim countries in the world. For example, by far the strictest Islamic country in the world is Saudi Arabia, which has the holy Koran as its constitution. This means that all laws in Saudi Arabia, whether civil or criminal, must reflect the principles enunciated in the Koran. Pakistan is another country that has declared itself an Islamic Republic and which therefore professes to legislate according to Islamic precepts. Countries such as Turkey, Jordan, and Egypt are not as strict as Saudi Arabia in incorporating Islamic precepts in their legislative endeavors.

At the core of Islamic thinking is the right of every man or woman, Muslim or non-Muslim, to own property. Similarly, the importance of business and trade is recognized. The prophet Mohammed was himself a businessman.[10] Islam forbids "excessive" profit, which is considered to be a form of exploitation. Islam preaches moderation and a sharing of wealth with others less fortunate, so individuals are held accountable for the well-being of the community. The concept of sharing of wealth is manifested in the *zakat*, which is the annual tax of 2.5 percent collected annually from individuals and used for the benefit of the community.

Islam also forbids usury or interest. The Islamic law of contracts requires that any transaction must be free of *riba*. Riba is defined as the unlawful advantage by way of excess of deferment, i.e., usury or interest. To Western economists an interest rate should reflect, among other things, "pure time-preference"—i.e., the notion that consumption today is worth more than consumption tomorrow. The interest that is charged by the lender is meant to be a reward for foregone consumption. However, Islamic scholars argue that this justification for charging interest implies that mere hoarding of cash in a safe deposit box at home also deserves an economic reward because it too reflects foregone consumption. Moreover, an economic reward becomes available for distribution only if consumption foregone is translated into investment that yields a real economic return, i.e., the investment creates wealth. They would agree with Western economists that lenders are entitled to have their fair share (in the form of interest) of any such return, but only to the extent that the lenders help to create wealth. This means that lenders must accept a share of the risk. Islamic contract law is very strict in its application of the concept that risks should be shared. It insists that wherever there is uncertainty, contracts that assure one party of a fixed return (interest), even though no wealth was created, are not permitted.[11]

Banks in fundamentalist Islamic nations have banking systems that follow, at least in part, Islamic principles. Some circumvent the prohibition against making interest-bearing loans by buying some of the borrower's stock and selling it back to the company at a higher price. The size of the markup is determined by the riskiness of the venture and the amount and maturity period of the loan. This loan-granting tactic is no different than the traditional criteria used in determining interest rates.[12] This practice is not approved of by strict fundamentalists. Alternatively, banks may buy equity in the venture being financed and share profits as well as losses in the joint ventures.

A variety of partnership agreements allow lending without interest. Schemes such as *mudarabha* and *musharaka* have been designed to allow banks to receive a contractual share of the profits generated by the borrowing firms. Under the mudarabha arrangement the bank supplies capital to a client and in return the bank gets a percentage of the client's net profits every year until the loan is repaid. The bank's share of the profits serves to repay the principal and a profit for the bank which is passed on to its depositors. If the client does not make a profit, the bank, its depositors, and the borrower jointly absorb the loss, thereby putting into practice the Islamic principle that both lenders and borrowers should share in the risks and rewards of an investment.

A musharaka contract is similar to the Western concept of a limited partnership. The bank and the client both share the equity capital, and sometimes even the managerial and technical expertise, of the investment project. Both the bank and the client share the profits or losses of the project according to a previously negotiated ratio.

Such practices for making loans in the face of the Islamic prohibition of interest-bearing loans are examples of how the strict principles of Islamic law can be harmonized with the laws of non-Islamic legal systems.[13]

The practice of Islamic banking in Bank Muamalat Indonesia (BMI) is illustrated in *Practical Insight 4-2*.

Impact of Common Law and Civil Law on National Legal Systems

There are significant differences in the laws of nations, depending upon whether they are common-law or civil-law oriented. For example, a general power of attorney—often used to authorize one person to represent another person—is not accepted in a civil-law country unless it is specifically drawn and notarized. The notary is an important functionary in civil-law countries because almost everything appears to be formalized. A notary certifies all types of documents including marriage agreements. In common-law countries, a notary is, of course, also required, but only for formal documents such as a will or deeds to property.

There is also a significant difference between civil-law and common-law countries in the manner in which they approach the subject of industrial property rights. Under common law, ownership rights to industrial property such as patents, trademarks, processes, and copyrights can be established by prior use. Such is not the case in civil-law countries, because under civil law, ownership of industrial property is established by registration rather than by prior use.

There are also differences between the two legal systems in the field of contracts and sales agreements. Under common law, when two or more parties sign a contract, they must comply with its provisions. Noncompliance with the provisions is inexcusable under any circumstances unless the reason for noncompliance is due to an "act of God," that is, an act of nature such as an earthquake, flood, lightning, drought, and the like, which could not ordinarily be foreseen by either party of a contract. Under civil law acts of God include not only acts of nature but also unforeseeable human acts such as a strike or a riot.

In common-law countries, persons involved in a partnership are individuals before the law. This implies that each person can sue another or be sued as an individual. Consequently, each person's private property is not considered as being legally separate and distinct from the property of the business partnership. Such is not the case in civil law under which the ordinary partnership is regarded as a single legal entity.

Corporations and limited liability companies formed in civil-law countries such as France, Belgium, and Italy differ in many ways from those formed in common-law countries. Under common law, a corporation is considered to be a juridical person. Under civil law, a corporation is considered to have been formed by contract. And so, in many civil-law countries, a certain number of persons are required in order to form a contractual relationship. In France, for example, a société anonyme (S.A.) or public corporation cannot be formed unless there are seven incorporators. If the number falls below seven at any time, the corporation ceases to exist and the stockholders become individually liable for corporate debts.

PRACTICAL INSIGHT 4-2
PROFIT and the PROPHET

Indonesian Bank Offers No-interest Services

Bank Muamalat Indonesia (BMI), Indonesia's first Islamic bank, met with a mixed reaction when it opened its doors for business on 1 May. While many Islamic groups welcomed the new institution, saying it would draw new funds into the banking system, bankers criticized it as being too risky, and political analysts labeled it a thinly veiled attempt by the government to woo Muslim support.

The financial sector in Indonesia, home to the world's largest Muslim community, has risen sharply in the past five years, with funds in the system increasing by more than 200% in 1987-91. Supporters believe BMI will attract business from those Muslims who object to placing their money in banks that violate the Islamic proscription on charging interest on loans.

The principle of Islamic banking is founded on a verse in the Koran in which the Prophet Mohammed forbids the practice of usury. "Usury and interest are synonymous in Islamic terminology," Seyed Ali Asghar Hedayati, a faculty member at the Iran Institute of Banking, said at a Jakarta symposium in October. While a more moderate interpretation defines usury as excessively high rates of interest, BMI subscribes to the stricter view.

The issue is sensitive in Indonesia because the existence of one Islamic bank suggests that conventional banks are violating Muslim teachings. "BMI is an alternative for Muslims," says the bank's managing director, Maman Natapermadi. "If they switch to us, then Allah will forgive them (for banking at conventional banks). If they don't switch, they run the risk of (Allah's) punishment."

An Islamic bank works on a profit-sharing principle. Depositors, treated as investors, are allocated a return based on how profitably the bank invests their money. On the asset side, an Islamic bank acts like a venture-capital investor, injecting funds into companies instead of loans. Islamic banks also participate in a kind of trade financing in which they buy goods and sell them, at a markup, to customers.

BMI divides its assets into three kinds: trade finance, venture capital-type investments and "benevolent lending," in which the bank lends to customers who must repay the principal, but with no interest or additional charges.

Trade finance is the simplest to compute. Instead of lending money to customers for purchases of raw materials or capital goods, BMI acquires the items on its own behalf and re-sells to the customer at a higher price. The markup usually will be equivalent to the rate customers would pay elsewhere for conventional financing.

For its venture-capital investments, BMI will provide start-up capital, and the client will manage the business. "Together, we share the risks and rewards," says Natapermadi.

To depositors, BMI offers products that are similar to demand and savings deposits. In an Islamic bank, the latter are called profit-sharing deposits and are distinguished by the absence of a pre-determined reward.

Theoretically, the return that depositors receive depends on how well the bank "invests" its available funds. The bank and the depositor agree to a "revenue-sharing ratio" which stipulates how much of the bank's profits are kept and how much are to be paid out to the depositor.

In practice, BMI's depositors will receive a return close to that offered by conventional banks. "We don't want our depositors to make less than they would make elsewhere," says Natapermadi.

PRACTICAL INSIGHT 4-2 *(continued)*

Periodically, BMI will adjust the revenue-sharing ratio so that the portion of profits allocated to depositors will be close to the rate of interest offered by other banks.

Source: Adam Schwarz, "Profit and the Prophet: Indonesian Bank Offers No-interest Services," *Far Eastern Economic Review,* May 21, 1992, pp. 44-46.

A major difference also exists between civil law and common law in the way in which each perceives the role of a board of directors of a corporation vis-à-vis the stockholders. In common-law countries, the board of directors is responsible to the stockholders and acts as trustees on their behalf. In civil-law countries, the board of directors does not have a fiduciary responsibility to the stockholders. Rather, its responsibility is to the corporation, although it is subject to general control similar to the auditing controls found in American companies.

Peculiarities of Country Laws

Different nations have their own peculiar laws, which in one way or another affect the international operations of multinational companies. In the following paragraphs we shall take a brief look at a few such laws. The examples given in this section are by no means all-inclusive. There are certainly many more interesting differences in the legal requirements of various countries, all of which cannot be presented here not only because of time and space limitations, but also because the purpose of this exposé is merely to acquaint the reader with situations that may be legal in one country but not be in another. Multinational companies need to give particular attention to the impact of national laws on such crucial areas as advertising, patent protection, ownership of subsidiaries, finance, and personnel.

Differences in the ways in which various countries treat patents and trademarks were emphasized earlier in this chapter and therefore need no reiteration.

Many countries place various restrictions on the use of premiums in the promotional efforts of companies. Premium offers are normally not allowed in Austria because any cash reductions that cause discriminatory treatment of buyers are considered illegal. In France it is illegal to offer a product for sale at a cost less than its cost price, or to offer a buyer an inducement such as a gift or a premium conditional upon the purchase of another product. It is also illegal in France for a company to offer products that are different from the kind ordinarily handled by the firm. For example, a soap manufacturer cannot legally offer glassware or cups as inducements to the buyer. Thus premiums are practically illegal in France.

Foreigners are not allowed to operate radio and television stations in many countries. The United States does not issue radio or television broadcasting licenses to noncitizens. Magazine publishing firms in Brazil have to be wholly owned by nationals alone; in Mexico they must be more than 50 percent owned by Mexican nationals. The radio and television industry is nationalized in several countries. Commercial radio and television is not available in countries such as Belgium, Denmark, Norway, and Sweden. In Germany, advertisers are permitted to sponsor programs on television but are allowed spot announcements only between certain hours in the evening.

Many countries place severe restrictions on the employment of foreigners. For example, the Swiss and Japanese governments place strict restrictions on the employment of foreign labor.

The problem of environmental pollution is worldwide. Subsidiaries operating in industrialized countries wherein air pollution has become a major problem must comply with the local air pollution standards or face stiff penalties. It is debatable whether air pollution curbs in the United States are any stricter than in many European countries. The Dutch and Swedish pollution laws are said to be stricter than the American laws, and those in Germany may be just as strict or even stricter.

Restrictions are placed on what can be advertised on television in some countries. Cigarettes cannot be advertised in the United States, England, or Italy. Italy forbids the advertising of cigarettes in any medium, whether it be the newspapers, radio, or television.

In Germany, a company cannot compare its product in its advertisements with that of a competitor, or claim that its product is the best unless it can prove it conclusively. Thus, a company selling gasoline or beer cannot advertise that its brand is just as good or better than that offered by another company, or that it is the best on the market. However, such claims can be made in the United States without any penalties.

There are restrictions placed by some countries on the purchase of land by foreigners. Swedish law does not permit any company that is more than 20 percent owned by foreigners to own land or do business in Sweden without special permission from the government.

Some countries do not allow private ownership of certain industries. For example, oil wells cannot be privately owned in Argentina, Brazil, Mexico, or India. It is said that the purpose of this law is to prevent this vital industry from falling into foreign hands. Private exploration is now allowed in Argentina, but not ownership of oil wells.

A company could have serious problems with a subsidiary located in a country that requires that a certain percentage of the components and subassemblies used in the production of a product must be sourced from local suppliers. Such laws are in effect in India, the United States, Chile, Spain, and in several other countries. Problems arise when local suppliers are not in a position to meet the quality standards of the subsidiary and/or supply the inputs at competitive world prices.

It should be obvious from the preceding discussion that the legal climate for multinational operations varies widely from country to country. Even for a given country, laws affecting investment policies and operating decisions can change markedly and quickly as different political regimes and changing economic circumstances alter a nation's goals and priorities. Supranational influences (such as GATT worldwide, NAFTA for Mexico, Canada, and the United States, or the EU in Europe) also may result in significant changes in trade-related laws. Failure to keep abreast of changes in the various legal environments in which the multinational firm operates can subject the firm and its assets—financial, plant, and intellectual property—to unnecessary risk, or even to loss. Equally unacceptable is a failure to take full advantage of the often substantial investment incentives offered by many developing countries, when the investment being encouraged is in line with the firm's strategic objectives. Table 4-1 illustrates some of the differences commonly found among national legal environments that may impact a firm's ability to be competitive in those markets. Space limitations preclude more than just a smattering of examples, but the table should make clear the importance of a thorough investigation prior to any significant investment decision.

RESOLVING INTERNATIONAL DISPUTES THROUGH LEGAL CHANNELS

Lawyers experienced in resolving international commercial disputes recommend that if a dispute cannot be resolved privately between the parties concerned through direct negotiations, then the

TABLE 4-1

Examples of Host Country Laws

Country	Patent Protection*	Foreign Investment
Brazil	Inventions—15 years Industrial designs—10 years Pharmaceuticals cannot be patented	Discouraged or prohibited in such sectors as mining, basic telecommunications, and petroleum production and refining Incentives for import substitution
China	Product and process inventions (including pharmaceuticals)—20 years	Multi-tiered screening process Encouragement for advanced technology and export-generating ventures
Germany	All inventions—20 years	Foreign firms receive national treatment No limit on percentage of equity foreigners may own, or on size of foreign investment
India	Inventions—14 years Patents prohibited for foods and drugs, although production processes may be patented	For 34 "high priority" industries, up to 51% foreign equity is automatically approved All other foreign investments require approval of Foreign Investment Promotion Board
Japan	Awarded on 'first to file' basis Paris Convention rights protected only when patent filed in Japan	No requirements or limitations regarding local equity, export performance, or local content
Mexico	All inventions—20 years	Foreigners may not own land, water, or mineral rights in Mexico Certain sectors unavailable to foreign investors, e.g. electricity, oil, railroads, communications satellites
Saudi Arabia	Applications may be submitted only by Saudi nationals. Government may declare specific areas of technology unpatentable, effectively removing protection for inventions in those areas	Saudi partners are necessary for venture to qualify for investment incentives Saudi law requires projects involving capital to result in economic development and transfer needed technology

* Information in the first four columns is extracted from *International Business Practices*, U.S. Department of Commerce, International Trade Administration, August, 1994.

Table 4-1 *(continued)*

Taxation	Repatriation of Capital	Marketing issues**	Work week
Corporate tax rate—30%	Capital may be repatriated without tax up to the amount brought into Brazil, with a 25% tax on any additional amount. Repatriation subject to Central Bank approval No guarantee against currency inconvertibility	Maximum allowable footage of foreign content in TV commercials is 30% Foreign payments prohibited for advertising films	Monday-Friday
33% of pre-tax income	Regulated by Bank of China and the government Generally must balance foreign exchange receipts and expenditures	Advertising cannot belittle other products of the same kind Cigarette advertisements forbidden on radio and TV	Monday-Friday
Branches of foreign corporations—46%	No restrictions	Time restrictions placed on radio and TV advertising	Monday-Friday
Public companies—45% Branches of foreign companies—65% All others—50%	Stringent controls due to India's foreign exchange shortage No guarantee against currency inconvertibility	Commercial breaks on radio and TV must not occur during program time Use of promotional contests, lotteries, and games of chance and skill is proscribed	Monday-Friday
Corporate tax rate—37.5%	No restrictions	Tobacco and cigarette advertising OK if it does not suggest that smoking is harmless Overall, not severely regulated	Monday-Friday
Official corporate tax rate—35%	No restrictions	Advertising that causes corruption of the Spanish language and is contrary to good morals is prohibited No comparative advertising allowed in any media	Monday-Friday
Sliding scale based on annual taxable income—25% to 45%	No controls	Alcohol and pork products cannot be advertised Careful attention must be paid to advertisements featuring women—if such advertising is permitted	Saturday-Wednesday

** *Source:* Barbara Sundberg Baunot, *International Advertising Handbook: A User's Guide to Rules and Regulations.* Lexington, MA: Lexington Books, 1989.

next best alternative is to submit it to voluntary arbitration. Taking a case to a foreign court is not recommended except as a last resort, because winning in a foreign court is seldom worth all the tangible and intangible costs incurred in litigation, such as court costs and lawyer's fees, delays in getting a court hearing date (up to ten years or longer is not uncommon in countries like India), difficulty in collecting a judgment, danger of creating a poor image in the host country, and the possibility of not getting a fair hearing in a foreign court. Other factors that contribute to the delay, expense, and uncertainty may include language barriers, distance between the litigants, the necessity to hire and depend upon foreign lawyers, and the overall unfamiliarity with foreign laws.

To avoid such inconveniences, businesses the world over turn to voluntary arbitration for the settlement of disputes. Not only is it less expensive but it is also private and faster, and it assures the parties of a hearing and judgment by persons (arbitrators) who are competent to judge the issues in the business involved.

Voluntary Arbitration

Under voluntary arbitration, the parties to the dispute select one or more impartial experts to judge the merits of the arguments presented by each of them. These experts hear and examine the case and weigh and appraise the evidence. The inquiry is limited to the issues agreed to in the arbitration agreement between the disputants. The experts then resolve the dispute according to universal mercantile standards and established business practices. This method of informally resolving disputes has been generally quite effective. However, in most cases the parties take their disputes to arbitration before one of the following formal domestic and international arbitration groups:

- The American Arbitration Association.
- The International Chamber of Commerce Court of Arbitration.
- The Inter-American Commercial Arbitration Commission, which arbitrates disputes among firms located in Latin America and the United States.
- The Canadian-American Commercial Arbitration Commission.
- The Arbitration Institute of the Stockholm Chamber of Commerce, which has functioned as an international arbitration institution since 1976, particularly in contracts dealing with East-West trade.
- The London Court of International Arbitration, which is jointly controlled by the City of London, the London Chamber of Commerce and Industry, and the Chartered Institute of Arbitrators. This is the oldest and fastest-growing center for international arbitration, and its fees are modest.
- The International Center for Settlement of Investment Disputes (ICSID), created in 1966 by the World Bank.

Arbitration Clauses

Companies that deal with foreign businesses should include in any legal contract a clause that calls for arbitration to settle disputes. Unless a provision for arbitration of any dispute is included in the contract, the likelihood that one or both parties to the dispute will agree to take the issue to arbitration is greatly diminished.

The American Arbitration Association suggests that the following standard clause be included in contracts:

> Any controversy or claim arising of or relating to this contract, or the breach thereof, shall be settled by arbitration in accordance with the rules of the American Arbitration Association, and judgment upon the award rendered by the Arbitrator(s) may be entered in any Court having jurisdiction thereof.

The model clause recommended by the International Chamber of Commerce is as follows:

> All disputes arising in connection with the present contract shall be finally settled under the rules of conciliation and arbitration at the International Chamber of Commerce by one or more arbitrators appointed in accordance with the said rules.

Enforcement of Arbitral Awards

An arbitration clause can help to avert problems; however, in many circumstances enforcing arbitration agreements and arbitration awards can be a significant problem in its own right. Companies may refuse to take a dispute to arbitration, or even refuse to honor the arbitrator's award after first agreeing to arbitrate the dispute according to the arbitration clause in the contract. What can a company that has won in the dispute do in such circumstances?

In most countries, courts will recognize arbitration clauses and are willing to enforce them. This process is facilitated by several treaties and conventions for enforcing foreign arbitral awards, of which the most important are the following:

- The United Nations Convention on the Recognition and Enforcement of Foreign Arbitral Awards, also known as the New York Convention, has been signed by 89 countries including the United States. The Convention obligates member countries to recognize and enforce, under their respective laws and jurisdiction, arbitration awards made in other member countries, and it prevents courts from adjudicating disputes that the parties have agreed to arbitrate. The Convention permits member countries to limit application to certain types of disputes. Some countries, including the United States, limit application of the Convention to commercial transactions only.

- The Inter-American Arbitration Convention, of which the United States and many Latin American countries are members.

- There are numerous bilateral treaties of friendship, commerce, and navigation (FCN Treaties) between the United States and foreign countries that contain clauses permitting enforcement of arbitrations conducted abroad (which may be used if a country is not a party to either the New York Convention, the Inter-American Arbitration Convention, or any other convention that provides for the enforcement of foreign arbitral awards).

Enforcement of Foreign Court Judgments

Managers in international companies must know that not every country in the world is a member of a convention or treaty for the enforcement of foreign arbitral awards, in which case the inclusion in the contract of a clause calling for arbitration to resolve disputes becomes irrelevant. What can an international company do when faced with a dispute with a company based in such a country? There are several alternatives that the company can pursue:

1. It must try to resolve the dispute out of court through conciliation or mediation, if at all possible. For reasons discussed earlier, taking a dispute to court is not advisable in many countries because of the lack of fair play involved in the local court system.

2. As a plaintiff it can sue in the foreign court. If it wins the case then it may be able to collect the damages from the defendant company.

3. There are instances in which the defendant may not have sufficient assets to satisfy the judgment. If the defendant has assets in other countries, it becomes important to determine whether those countries will recognize and enforce a foreign judgment. In fact, courts have long recognized and enforced foreign judgments in certain circumstances.[14]

4. A company that has obtained a foreign judgment could sue again for the same grievance in its home (domestic) court. The domestic court would then examine the case on its merits and make its own judgment which could be different than that of the foreign court.

5. The company could bring suit in the domestic court on the basis of the foreign judgment. The domestic court would then make its own judgment on whether the foreign judgment should be enforced.

Managers in American international companies must be aware of the fact that the United States is not a party to any international convention governing the recognition and enforcement of foreign judgments. However, U.S. courts have traditionally been quite liberal in recognizing and enforcing foreign judgments (i.e., so long as there are no serious due-process violations). But U.S. judgments have not received similar treatment in foreign jurisdictions. This is a major problem facing international companies, and its magnitude is likely to grow with the expansion of international business and increasing frequency of transnational litigation.

There are three multilateral money judgments conventions, however, currently in force:

• Brussels Convention on Jurisdiction and the Enforcement of Judgments in Civil and Commercial Matters adopted in 1990 by the European Union countries.

• Lugano Convention on Jurisdiction and the Enforcement of Judgments in Civil and Commercial Matters adopted in 1989 by the European Union countries and former European Free Trade Association (EFTA) members (Austria, Finland, Iceland, Liechtenstein, Norway, Sweden, and Switzerland).

• Inter-American Convention on the Extraterritorial Validity of Foreign Judgments and Arbitral Awards adopted in 1979 by the members of the Organization of American States (OAS), namely Argentina, Colombia, Ecuador, Mexico, Paraguay, Peru, Uruguay, and Venezuela.

Although the United States is not a member of any of the above conventions, international managers must be aware of their existence because the foreign subsidiaries of international companies might be located in countries that are members of these conventions and therefore subject to their provisions.

However, as we have shown throughout this chapter, there is not yet a comprehensive, enforceable international legal system to which to resort. The international legal environment for business is a dynamic one, continuously evolving into a more coherent, effective system through such developments as the GATT TRIPS Agreement (Appendix 1). But the fact remains that the current international legal system is a complex composite of national and regional laws and international conventions, held together by the mutual consent of sovereign states, not by an overarching supranational body with effective enforcement power. So long as this central authority is lacking, the often fundamental differences among national and regional legal systems will place special demands and challenges on the managers in international companies charged with decision making in a multinational context.

From our look at the international legal system and its implications for the international manager, we now turn, in Chapter 5, to the international political system and its importance as part of the environment within which the international firm operates.

SUMMARY

The international legal environment can be viewed as comprising three concentric levels around the company: the laws of the nation-states within which the firm operates, laws of the regional trade blocs to which those nation-states belong, and international law.

To be effective, a legal system must (a) be understood by the people subject to it, (b) be accepted as fair and just by those same people, and (c) have an enforceable system for punishing illegal behavior. The lack of the third element sets international law apart from national legal systems—international law is implemented by the mutual agreement of nation-states, not through the power of a central enforcement authority.

International law, the outermost level of the legal environment, may be based on custom—the historical practice of generally accepted patterns of behavior—or on treaties and conventions—signed agreements governing activity between sovereign states. Treaties may be bilateral or multilateral, depending on the number of signator countries. We discussed two types of treaties of particular importance to international companies: treaties of friendship, commerce, and navigation (FCN) and treaties for the protection of intellectual property rights.

Protection of intellectual property—patents, trademarks, and copyrights—is a primary concern of international companies. Laws governing what can and cannot be protected and for how long vary widely among nations. While many countries are party to the Paris Convention, which standardizes and simplifies intellectual property protection, practical problems of enforcement are still widespread. The recently completed Uruguay Round of GATT also attempts to improve intellectual property protection.

Ineffective enforcement of provisions for intellectual property protection opens the door to piracy—the unauthorized and illegal use of the intellectual property of another company. Piracy is a serious problem, particularly in many developing countries. Companies may also be damaged by copying activities which have the same effect as piracy, but that are technically not illegal due to differences among the protection laws of different nations.

The second level of the international legal environment of business is the regional laws that have developed along with the various regional trade blocs in recent years. These laws, particularly well-developed in the European Union, standardize activity and requirements among the member nations, and are designed to facilitate intraregional trade.

The third level of the international legal environment is the laws of nation-states. National legal systems are generally based on either common law, civil law, or Islamic law, and reflect the social, cultural, and religious norms of the people. Accordingly, there are many significant differences and peculiarities among the laws of different nations. Activity or behavior that is perfectly acceptable in one country may be illegal in others. Managers in international companies must research and be aware of these differences as they affect foreign investment and operations.

The resolution of business disputes in the international context is generally better handled informally between the parties or through voluntary arbitration than through the courts. Legal proceedings can be expensive, often damaging to a firm's reputation, and legal judgments may be difficult or impossible to enforce. Several nonpartisan international bodies are available to arbitrate disputes.

QUESTIONS FOR THOUGHT AND DISCUSSION

1. We mention in the chapter that a number of writers believe that an effective system of sanctions is all that is needed to make a legal system effective, and that whether the members of society believe that the law is worthy of obedience is immaterial. What do you think? Why?

2. Can you suggest a system for effectively establishing and enforcing international laws? What would be the key features? How would you "sell" your plan to a group of national leaders from both developed and developing countries? What objections might they raise to your proposal?

3. Discuss the difference between actual piracy, or illegal counterfeiting, of intellectual property, and legal copying, such as occurs in the pharmaceutical industry due to the nonpatentability of drugs in certain countries. Which is more damaging to the company being victimized, and why? What strategy or strategies would most effectively combat the "copycat" activity in the two cases?

4. Is the regional law being developed by trade blocs more closely analogous to international law or to the laws of nation-states? What characteristics of each does it share?

5. Can you think of examples (other than those given in the text) of activity or behavior that is legal in one country but illegal in others? What specific reasons can you suggest for the difference in legal treatment by the two countries?

MINI-CASE
See You in Court: Lehman Brothers Sues Chinese Giants

Early in 1993, two giant state-owned Chinese firms, Sinochem (China National Chemicals Import and Export Corporation) and Sinopec (China National Petroleum and Chemicals Corporation), launched a joint venture baptized Unipec. The event was celebrated in grand style at a reception held in Beijing's huge "Great Hall of the People." Senior representatives of every major American investment bank attended the ceremonies. Indeed, in the words of one guest, a Hong Kong-based staffer at a major United States investment bank, the newly born Unipec was to be the engine of "China's integration with world oil markets." Thus, according to the same source, "it was natural that everyone would run after them to do business."

Eighteen months later, Unipec is no longer courted but still sought out: this time as a defendant in a breach-of-contract suit filed by a major subsidiary of the U.S. investment bank, Lehman Brothers. The suit, one of two filed by Lehman Brothers in New York on November 15, 1994, charges Unipec with failing to honor obligations stemming from foreign exchange and swap transactions. The second suit is against Minmetals International Non-Ferrous Metals Trading and its parent, China National Metals & Minerals Import & Export Corporation.

The action in court is an attempt to recover some US$100 million Lehman claims the two Chinese companies—Unipec and Minmetals—owe on swaps and currency trades that went bad starting in May 1994, after foreign exchange markets were roiled by a sudden weakening in the U.S. dollar. The two Chinese firms agreed to accept U.S. jurisdiction in their dispute with Lehman, and each has 30 days to answer the charges. Neither has made a formal response, although Unipec has issued a statement rejecting all accusations of wrongdoing.

Lehman's lawsuits offer a striking and dramatic example of what foreign businesses have known for years: the Chinese do not always pay their bills and China can quickly become a financial quagmire for those investors who do not take the necessary precautions.

For the Chinese, however, the lawsuits represent a rather novel experience. Indeed, eager as they are to keep a foot in the China market, few aggrieved foreign firms have dared go public with default problems, let alone play hardball to recover damages.

In its daring confrontation with China's often lax attitude toward settling debts, Lehman has many silent supporters. Says the executive director at a competing firm: "If they lose on this in New York, we'll see a tidal wave of Chinese walking away from obligations."

The suits haven't prompted a major reassessment of China's sovereign risk. "Why should this change people's perceptions?" asks the head of financing at a Lehman competitor in Hong Kong. "Didn't we all know China was like this?"

The concern over credit risk in China is pervasive. Most Western financial houses require extensive approvals, authorizations, and guarantees, especially when hard currency is involved. "China is one big black box," says the New York-based head of commodities dealing for a major U.S. investment bank, "Who has the authority? Who can you rely on for guarantees? What do you ever really know?"

Today, more than ever, business dealings with China are full of perils; indeed, a 15-month austerity program has left many Chinese companies strapped for cash. "Everyone must be looking at their China portfolios," said the head of financing at a Lehman competitor, "especially to determine whether their exposure is to branches or subsidiaries or the head office. And where a letter of comfort would do in the past, now people will seek guarantees instead."

The suits Lehman is bringing in New York are more serious because they involve the head offices of the Chinese companies rather than subsidiaries, and because Lehman has marshalled considerable documentation to buttress its claims. That evidence suggests it'll be much harder for Unipec and Minmetals to sustain their cases.

According to Lehman's New York lawsuit, the bank began trading with Sinochem in June 1992, and with Unipec the following April. By June 1994, Lehman says, it had executed more than 100 transactions with Unipec. The suit alleges that Unipec President Jiang Yunlong provided written authorization for Deputy Manager Yin Jian to enter into swaps with Lehman, and frequently met with Lehman officials to discuss foreign exchange dealings.

The market, however, turned against Unipec, and Lehman began to make margin calls, or demands for cash, which Lehman says the Chinese company failed to pay in full. Shortly thereafter, in May 1994, Unipec stopped meeting margin calls altogether, and refused to post letters of credit to cover them. In July, Lehman placed stop-loss orders on all foreign exchange dealings with Unipec. By the time the suit was filed in New York, Lehman claims the Chinese company owed it about US$44 million.

Lehman's relationship with Minmetals developed in a similar fashion. It had written authorization from Minmetals President Cao Yongfeng allowing a vice president to deal with Lehman. It also had a written guarantee from Minmetals' parent, China National Metals, as further assurance for its trades with Minmetals.

Unipec and Minmetals now claim the trades were not legal. Their major argument is that the actual losses occurred in the subsequent transactions Lehman made with other American financial institutions after swapping with Unipec or Minmetals. Unipec has decided to counter-sue Lehman for the losses that it has already suffered as a result of Lehman's "mishandling of transactions." According to Lehman, however, the Chinese never complained as long as they were making money: Minmetals made US$28.7 million in its 1993 foreign exchange dealings with Lehman, which claims Minmetals owes it US$52 million.

Some competitors suggest Lehman should have known what it was getting into. Neither Unipec nor Minmetals were regarded as China's official foreign exchange windows—entities whose debt is considered sovereign because it is explicitly guaranteed by the State Administration of Exchange Control (SAEC). "Had these two been covered by the SAEC and then walked away—that would have been scary," says the managing director of a U.S. investment bank.

Moreover, both Unipec and Minmetals are known as aggressive traders; for instance, there is often no ceiling for the amount of swap transactions. As clients, that makes them both desirable and dangerous for commission-hungry salespeople.

Other foreign firms had carefully appraised the two Chinese companies and found them far too risky. One New York investment bank, trying to establish whether Unipec's foreign exchange trading was a matter of legitimate hedging or simply speculation, flew the head of its finance department from New York to Beijing. The senior officer learned that Sinochem had little need for hedging because it sells oil in China for hard currency. The U.S. firm decided that Unipec's bets on the dollar versus such illiquid, volatile currencies as the Swedish krona and the Spanish peseta, were too far removed from its main business and declined to set up currency-trading lines with Unipec.

A second U.S. firm refused to deal in currencies with Minmetals when it couldn't gather enough information about the company to make a credit decision. Other investment banks declined foreign exchange dealings with the Chinese companies after learning that neither would have SAEC guarantees.

"We always believe in staying in the line of business these companies have a charter to do," said the New York-based head of oil trading for a New York investment bank a week before Lehman filed suit. "If the Chinese side stays in the original area, they can hide their losses in the system. But they can't hide foreign exchange losses. The people who get hurt in China are the people who have strayed from that principle."

Many competitors wonder why Lehman waited so long to act. Morgan Stanley says it sends up warning flags as soon as a business partner's debt reaches US$1 million. Smith Barney Shearson says it automatically clears outstanding positions after 30 days. Moreover, it isn't clear whether contracts governing these trades offered Lehman as much protection as many of its counterparts would have demanded in terms of standby letters of credit and penalty interest rates on deficits. Lehman declines to comment.

Lehman can ill afford to get hurt in China, or anywhere else at present. Like other investment banks, it faces lean times as a result of adverse moves in the world financial markets. The filing of the lawsuit, according to Lehman's auditors, will allow the firm to avoid having to take an immediate loss for the money it is owed. Also, Lehman could have faced lawsuits in the U.S. by its own shareholders had it failed to sue over the China losses.

This is the second time in recent months that Lehman has run into problems with a Chinese business partner. Along with about a dozen other firms, it is also trying to settle outstanding positions with the Shanghai subsidiary of China International Trust & Investment Co. (Citic) for contracts on the London Metals Exchange. The amount is undisclosed, but insiders claim it is under US$10 million. The case has not gone to court.

Source: Written by Dr. Yadong Luo, Assistant Professor of International Management, University of Hawaii at Manoa. Copyright © 1997 by Arvind V. Phatak.

Discussion Questions for Mini-Case

1. Domestic business disputes are settled in U.S. courts according to U.S. law. International business disputes involving firms from different countries present a major dilemma: whose law is applicable? Should there be a set of international laws governing financial transactions?

2. Why does Lehman have "silent supporters" and why have these supporters remained "silent"?

3. Consider the case of Lehman winning its lawsuits. What are the benefits derived? Are there any disadvantages? Why or why not?

4. The U.S. is a legalistic society where individuals and firms rely heavily on the legal code to protect and promote their interests. Other societies, for historical or cultural reasons, may shy away from open confrontation in general, and court arbitration of dispute in particular. When U.S. firms are dealing internationally, should they seek to solve disputes through channels other than the U.S. courts? Why or why not? Suggest some alternatives if your answer is affirmative.

APPENDICES

1. The GATT Uruguay Round TRIPS Agreement

The GATT Uruguay Round on Trade Related Aspects of Intellectual Property Rights (TRIPS) establishes substantially higher standards for protection for a wide range of intellectual property rights than are embodied in current multilateral agreements and provides for the effective enforcement of such standards both internally and at the border. The TRIPS Agreement requires all GATT members to provide at least a baseline level of protection and enforcement for patents, trademarks, copyrights, trade secrets, semiconductor chip layout designs (mask works), and industrial designs. Members are free to provide a higher level of protection than that required in the TRIPS Agreement as long as the provisions of the TRIPS Agreement are not violated.

The TRIPS Agreement resolves many long-standing trade irritants for U.S. patent interests, especially pharmaceutical and agricultural chemical companies. Some of these benefits include: (1) product and process patents must be available for virtually all types of inventions, including product patent protection for pharmaceuticals and agricultural chemicals; (2) meaningful limitations are imposed on compulsory patent licensing (a practice that is common in most developing countries which prohibits the grant of exclusive patent rights to only one company, and thereby requiring that it be shared with others who may wish to use it); and (3) patents must have a term of 20 years from the date of filing.

The TRIPS Agreement addresses a number of international trademark problems experienced by U.S. industry. Some of the prominent provisions of the Agreements are: (1) it requires member countries to register service marks as well as trademarks; (2) enhances protection for internationally well-known marks; and (3) forbids the compulsory licensing of trademarks.

The TRIPS Agreement resolves some key trade problems for U.S. copyright-based industries by: (1) protecting computer programs, requiring member countries to grant owners of computer programs and sound recordings the right to authorize or prohibit the rental of their products; (2) establishing a 50-year term for the protection of sound recordings; and (3) setting a minimum term of 50 years for the protection of motion pictures and other works where companies may be the author. The TRIPS Agreement also obligates member countries to comply with the substantive provisions of the 1971 Paris text of the Berne Convention for the Protection of Literary and Artistic Works, other than the Berne Convention's requirements on moral rights of authors.

2.   The U.N. Convention on the International Sale of Goods

The U.N. Convention on the International Sale of Goods (CISG) entered into force in the United States on January 1, 1988. If applicable to a given transaction, the CISG supplies "gap filling" rules that govern contract formation and set forth the rights and obligations of the buyer and seller. The CISG provides, however, that express contractual provisions take precedence over the default provisions of the CISG. Thus, contracting parties remain free to specify whatever law or terms they wish to apply to their transaction, and may exclude altogether the application of the CISG to their contractual relationship.

As of December 1993, the CISG had entered into force in the following 35 countries:

Argentina	Lesotho
Australia	Mexico
Austria	Netherlands
Belarus	Norway
Bulgaria	People's Republic of China
Canada	Romania
Chile	Russian Federation
Czech Republic	Slovakia
Denmark	Spain
Ecuador	Sweden
Egypt	Switzerland
Finland	Syria
France	Uganda
Germany	Ukraine
Guinea	United States of America
Hungary	Yugoslavia
Iraq	Zambia
Italy	

The Treaty Section of the United Nations' Office of Legal Affairs maintains the most up-to-date listing of countries that have ratified, acceded to, or otherwise adopted the CISG.

The CISG applies only to the international commercial sales of goods. Each of these elements constitutes an important limitation on the scope of CISG's applicability. First, the sale must be international in character. A sale is considered "international" if it involves "parties whose places of business are in different States." In ratifying CISG the United States stipulated that, absent express agreement to the contrary, CISG would not apply to contracts between a U.S. party and a party whose place of business is in a country that has yet to adopt CISG.

Second, CISG covers the sale of goods, and does not automatically apply to services contracts. Where a contract includes both goods and services elements, CISG will apply when the sale of goods constitutes the "preponderant part of the (seller's) obligations. . ." Contracting parties are free to apply CISG to services (or predominantly services) contracts, so long as this choice of law is made explicit in the contract itself.

Finally, CISG only applies to commercial transactions, i.e., sales between merchants of goods. Among other limitations, it does not cover consumer sales, auction sales, sales of negotiable instruments or securities, or sales of ships, vessels, or aircraft.

Adoption of CISG by the United States provides important benefits to U.S. exporters. Parties negotiating international sales contracts often find the "choice of law" issue to be among the most contentious. Each party is familiar with its own domestic sales law, and prefers that its local rules apply to the transaction. CISG enables the parties to avoid difficulties in negotiating "whose law will govern" by putting into place internationally accepted substantive rules on which contracting parties, courts, and arbitrators may rely.

Notes

1   William D. Coplin, *The Functions of International Law,* Rand McNally Company, Chicago, 1966, pp. 8-9.

2   Ibid., pp. 3-4.

3   Faye Rice, "How Copycats Steal Billions," *Fortune,* April 22, 1991, pp. 157-164.

4   "Beijings Blatant Piracy Could Slash Its U.S. Trade," *Business Week,* April 22, 1991, p. 46.

5   Edward A. Gargan, "U.S. May Thwart China's Trade Goal," *The New York Times,* July 24, 1994, p. 14; Patrick E. Tyler, "China Pressing to Join Trade Club," *The New York Times,* November 14, 1994, p. D1.

6   Thomas L. Friedman, "China Faces U.S. Sanctions in Electronic Copyright Piracy," *The New York Times,* July 1, 1994, p. D2.

7   Patrick E. Tyler, "China Pressing to Join Trade Club," *The New York Times,* November 14, 1994, p. D2.

8   Thomas L. Friedman, "China Faces U.S. Sanctions in Electronic Copyright Piracy," *The New York Times,* July 1, 1994, p. D2.

9   Jessica M. Bailey and James Sood, "The Effect of Religious Affiliation on Consumer Behavior: A Preliminary Investigation," *Journal of Managerial Issues,* Vol. 5, No. 3, Fall 1993, p. 333.

10 Mushtaq Luqmani, Zahir A. Quaraeshi, and Linda Delene, "Marketing in Islamic Countries: A Viewpoint," *MSU Business Topics,* Summer 1980,

11 "Banking Behind the Veil," *The Economist,* April 4, 1992, p. 76.

12 Luiz Moutinho and M. Hisham Jabr, "Perspective on the Role of Marketing in Islamic Banking," *Journal of International Consumer Marketing,* Vol. 2, No. 3, 1990, pp. 29-47; Geraldine Brooks, "'Riddle of Riyadj' Islamic Law Thrives Amid Modernity," *The Wall Street Journal,* November 9, 1989, p. A1.

13 "Islamic Banking Rules Spell More Paperwork but the Same Result," *Business Asia,* March 11, 1991, p. 81.

14 Michael Litka, *International Dimensions of the Legal Environment of Business,* Second Edition, PWS-KENT Publishing Company, Boston, 1991, p. 214.

The Political Environment of International Business

LEARNING OBJECTIVES

After completing this chapter, you will be able to:

- Describe the components, relationships, and interactions involved in the political systems model, and explain how the one-nation model can be extended into a global business context.

- Explain the reciprocal nature of the dynamics between political and economic systems, policies, and relations.

- Define and differentiate among the various types of political risk, and discuss their implications for the multinational firm.

- Discuss a comprehensive framework for assessing political risk, from a global as well as a single-country perspective.

- Describe Gurr's model of civil strife, how it relates to the assessment of political risk, and how it can be used to estimate the probability or intensity of civil strife.

In the previous chapters, we have discussed in detail several important dimensions of the global business environment—elements that shape the context within which international business must be conducted. We continue that discussion in the present chapter by considering the political environment facing the international business manager and the problems it can pose for international operations in the form of political risk.

Politics and political interests are powerful forces in every country throughout the world, and their ability to support or disrupt business operations is of major interest to the global manager. Only through an understanding of the fundamental elements and dynamics of political systems can a manager adequately appreciate their effect on the multiple operating environments facing the global firm, and properly assess the degree of political risk involved in commencing or continuing operations in each. To this end, we begin the chapter with a discussion of a generic political system and its properties before proceeding to a more specific treatment of the dynamics of the interface between political and economic environments, especially as it involves the nature and type of political risk facing the firm.

THE POLITICAL SYSTEM

In order to understand the nature of the international political system and how it works, we should understand just what a political system is and what its characteristics are. In the following section we shall examine a generic model of a political system and after that we shall assess to what extent this generic political system model is replicated in the international political arena.

The generic model of a political system is presented in Figure 5-1. Please refer to this exhibit in the following explanation of the nature of the political system.

The "Players" in the Political System

The political system consists of a set of "players," each with their own unique set of aspirations and goals which are often in conflict with those of the other "players" in the system. The *government* is only one of many players in this system, although a key one, as it alone has the legitimacy to make authoritative decisions and to enforce those decisions by force. The other key players in the system are the various significant *groups* that exist in a society. Examples of societal groups are labor unions, environmental activists, the National Rifle Association, Mothers

FIGURE 5-1
The Political System

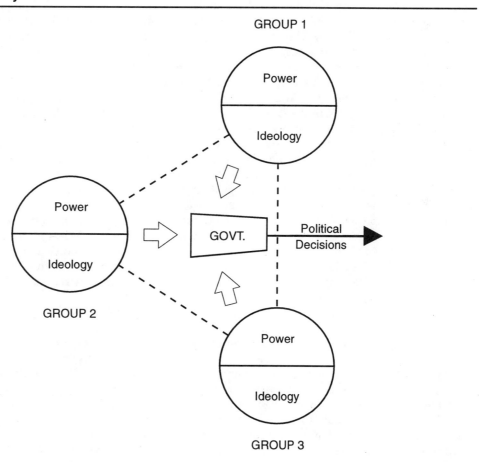

Against Drunk Driving, the Christian Coalition, the Irish Republican Army (in the United Kingdom), the Mafia, political parties, the church, the armed forces, and so on. Some of these groups, such as the political parties, the armed forces, labor unions, and the church are significant institutions of society; other groups such as the National Rifle Association and Mothers Against Drunk Driving are primarily lobby groups; and the Mafia and the Irish Republican Army are illegal groups in that they exist without the approval of the government.

Each of these groups has a certain amount of **power** it can exert to control and influence the behavior of other groups and of the government. The amount of power in the hands of each group is not equally distributed—some groups may be more powerful than others. The power of each group is derived from the total number of people who are firmly committed to the group's ideals and goals, and from the group's stockpile of key financial, technical, and human resources.

Each societal group also has its unique **political ideology**. Ideology has been defined as "a set of closely related beliefs, or ideas, or even attitudes, characteristic of a group or community."[1] Similarly, a "political ideology is a set of ideas or beliefs that people hold about their political regime and its institutions and about their position and role in it."[2] The ideology of a group is the set of values and beliefs pertaining to the way in which society should be organized—politically, economically, morally—that are shared by its members. For example, in the United States the ideology of the National Rifle Association is grounded in the belief that every person has the right to bear arms, whereas on the opposite side is Hand Gun Control, Inc., which is committed to restricting the possession of handguns by lay members of the society. The labor unions have as their primary objective the protection of workers from unfair treatment by the employer. The Democratic Party in the United States and the Labor Party in the United Kingdom are committed to worker welfare, whereas the Republican Party in the United States and the Conservative (Tory) party in the United Kingdom are committed to the development and growth of business firms with little or no interference by the government.

Various groups within a society "at given times and under given conditions, challenge the prevailing ideology. Interests, classes, and various political and religious associations may develop a "counter ideology" that questions the status quo and attempts to modify it. They advocate change rather than order; they criticize or reject the political regime and the existing social and economic arrangements; they advance schemes for the restructuring and reordering of the society; and they spawn political movements in order to gain enough power to bring about the changes they advocate. In this sense, a political ideology moves people into action. It motivates them to demand changes in their way of life and to modify the existing political, economic, and social relations, or it mobilizes them on how to preserve what they value.[3] Thus two all-important features characterize all ideologies: a given ideology rationalizes the status quo, whereas competing ideologies and movements challenge it.

One must make note of the fact that institutions and groups that appear to be alike may perform different functions in different countries. For example, in the United Kingdom labor unions have a leftist ideology and are politically affiliated with the Labor Party, whereas in the United States the labor unions are basically "business unions" with an ideological bias in favor of private enterprise and a capitalist society. In the United States, the Republican party members believe that the Democratic Party is politically left of center, whereas outside the United States the Democratic Party is seen as a right of center party. It should be noted that the United States never had politically viable socialist or communist parties. Such is not the case in many countries such as Italy, India, Sweden, and Greece. The role played by the church also varies from country to country. For instance, the Catholic Church played a crucial role in the "liberation" of Poland from Soviet domination and in the overthrow of the Marcos dictatorship in the Philippines, as opposed to the Catholic Church in India which is politically totally neutral.

The Concepts of Legitimacy and Consensus[4]

Every group in the political system has its own objectives and aspirations, and they all attempt to influence the government and thereby translate their particular interests into authoritative political decisions. A key prerequisite for the efficient functioning of any political system is the presence of a high level of "consensus." *Consensus* is the widespread acceptance of the decision-making process in the political system by the individuals and groups in the system. Consensus is the instrument by which a government itself becomes legitimized. *Legitimacy* is the use of the power of the state by officials in accordance with prearranged and agreed-upon rules. A legitimate act is also legal, but a lawful command is not always legitimate. For example, the commands issued by the Nazi government in Germany were legal; however, they were not legitimate because they violated a code of civilized behavior and morality that brought into question their legitimacy. Legitimacy and consensus are key indicators of the effectiveness and performance of the political system. Conversely, the absence of legitimacy and consensus can cause an undermining instability of the system. A government that has no legitimacy does not have the right to issue authoritative directives, and as such is likely to lead to political instability unless it is backed up by massive coercive force to keep it in power, e.g., the dictatorships in Cuba, China, and North Korea.

The Political Process

The political process constitutes a political bargaining process in which different groups representing different interests conflict over different preferred outcomes. The outcomes of the political process are the myriad political decisions made by the government in response to the pressures applied by the different interest groups. Group conflict is common in an effective political system, and the strength of the political system is its ability, through the agency of the government, to resolve the intergroup conflicts peacefully. Group conflict occurs, for example, between groups that favor free trade and lower tariff barriers and those that advocate protectionism. The role of the government is to engage in the constructive management of conflict among the various interest groups.

THE GLOBAL POLITICAL SYSTEM

Now let us apply this generic framework of a political system to the international political system. The international political system, like the political system of a nation, also consists of numerous players, each of whom have their own particular interests, goals, and aspirations. The various countries of the world, the various regional trade blocs (e.g., NAFTA, the European Union, MERCUSOR) and the different international organizations (e.g., the United Nations, The World Bank, the International Monetary Fund) are the major participants in the international political system. "In domestic politics, goal-seeking behavior is regulated by government which has the authority to make decisions for a society and the power to enforce those decisions. The characteristic that distinguishes international politics from internal politics is the absence of government. In the international system, no legitimate body has the authority to manage conflict or achieve common goals by making and enforcing decisions for the system; instead, decision-making authority is dispersed among many governmental, intergovernmental, and non-governmental groups."[5]

Over the centuries, nations have deliberately, or as a result of custom or tradition, devised rules, institutions, and procedures to manage international conflict and cooperation. For example, the nineteenth century imperial European powers, after experiencing much conflict and warfare over who could control the trade routes and resources of the world, agreed to carve the world into their respective spheres of influence. Consequently, England colonized India and parts of Africa and West Asia, while France controlled their colonies in North Africa and Southeast Asia. Holland and Germany too had their colonies around the globe. Consequently, each colonial power had well-established markets in their colonies for products produced at home. In 1994 we witnessed the birth of the World Trade Organization (the successor to GATT), which is empowered by an international treaty signed by over one hundred countries to regulate world trade and investments in accordance with the rules of the treaty provisions. The World Trade Organization has the power to adjudicate in trade disputes between countries and to impose punitive measures against those that are found to be guilty of violating the treaty provisions. Similarly, international law, characterized by treaties such as the treaty for the protection of intellectual property (as we discussed in the previous chapter), is designed to manage conflict and cooperation in the area of intellectual property rights.

Because of the absence of a legitimate "world government" with the capability for making and enforcing authoritative decisions, it has been up to the various nations and international groups to create the appropriate rules, institutions, and procedures that manage international conflict and cooperation. Within this framework, conflict occurs within agreed-upon limits, and cooperation among nations is enhanced. However, when there are no effective rules, procedures, and institutions to manage conflict and cooperation, international conflict may rise to undesirable levels, and may even escalate into war.

THE INTERACTION BETWEEN INTERNATIONAL POLITICS AND INTERNATIONAL ECONOMICS

In today's world the international economic system and the international political system do not function independently of each other. The international economic relations between nation-states are determined to a large extent by their political and diplomatic relations, while the reverse holds true as well. The interdependence between international economics and international politics is illustrated in *Practical Insight 5-1*, which exemplifies the duality of (1) maintaining a fruitful dialogue with the Chinese government on political issues while (2) simultaneously imposing trade sanctions against Chinese exports to the United States because of the Chinese piracy of American products, trademarks, patents, and other intellectual property.

PRACTICAL INSIGHT 5-1
Chinese Invite U.S. to Resume Talks on Trade
By David E. Sanger

WASHINGTON, Feb. 6 — On Saturday, the Clinton administration announced the imposition of 100 percent tariffs on a range of Chinese goods as punishment for China's failure to crack down on piracy. The administration did not say whether, to meet American demands, China would have to close the 29 plants that are producing 70 million compact discs and video-discs annually.

Presumably the United States would be satisfied if the factories licensed production of the movies and music, paying royalties. But that would so increase the cost that the business might no longer be viable for the Chinese manufacturers.

Today's announcement of China's willingness to act came as the White House held a meeting over how to handle the increasingly complex web of issues surrounding the American relationship with China on trade; on the transition of power as the country's paramount leader, Deng Xiaoping, lies gravely ill; on human rights; and on China's shipment of missile technology abroad.

"There is a sense that there is not a lot of order to all of this, and we have to get it together," one participant in the meeting said today.

The confusion of priorities will be particularly evident later this month, when Energy Secretary Hazel R. O'Leary arrives in Beijing on a mission to get the Chinese to spend billions of dollars on American-made electric-power systems.

But Ms. O'Leary will also be carrying another message, State Department officials say. She will be urging China to accept Secretary of State Warren Christopher's offer to begin regular discussions on Chinese missile exports, including an offer to forgive past violations in return for a full accounting of past sales.

At roughly the same time, Mr. (Mickey) Kantor's (the United States trade representative) deputies will be reopening the trade talks and telling the Chinese that commercial relations between the world's largest and third-largest economies will be gravely threatened if Beijing does not meet American demands to stop copying music and software.

Mr. Kantor and his aides said last week that they believed the announcement of sanctions would bring the Chinese back to the negotiating table, much as a similar action did last year in a lower-profile dispute over textiles.

But with the Chinese leadership in considerable disarray, some American diplomats expressed concern today that there were still powerful interests in Beijing arguing against an accommodation with the United States, in part because an agreement to crack down on the disc makers would interfere with one of the most profitable businesses in which China's military has a stake. That comes just as the Pentagon is trying to deepen its relations with China's military leaders, setting up regular consultations and even discussing the possibility of allowing port calls by each nation's naval vessels and other such arrangements.

"We've got the Pentagon trying to build a better relationship with these guys, and Mickey Kantor cutting off their revenue," an administration official involved in the issue said.

Much of that revenue comes from the 29 plants that produce compact discs and video-discs sometimes bringing out hit movies before they are sold or rented in the United States ("Jurassic Park" being a recent example of that). Almost all of the products are then exported to South Korea, Taiwan, Singapore, Malaysia and other markets where American movies are popular.

Within hours of Mr. Kantor's announcement of trade sanctions on Saturday, China angrily responded that it would place 100 percent tariffs on American-made goods, ranging from video games to cigarettes and alcohol. Still, both country's lists were notable for what they excluded.

The American list, for example, has no toys and few electronics, China's No. 1 and 2 exports to the United States. American officials decided that a doubling of the wholesale price of Chinese-made toys would hurt large and small American retailers—to say nothing of making the White House akin to the Grinch—and that placing tariffs on electronics parts would hurt American computer makers.

The main beneficiary of such a move on electronic components would probably be Japan, where producers would not be paying a tariff on their purchase of components.

Some shoes and winter apparel are included on the American list, but these items represent only a fraction of such products that are shipped to the United States by China. Other items that Washington picked for tariffs include fishing rods, surfboards, and bicycles, all of which are available from American producers or are imported to the United States by manufacturers in other nations.

China excluded from its list aircraft and aircraft components, which are among its biggest imports from the United States.

Up until recently, students of international politics who analyzed the interaction between international economic and political events almost always focused on how economic reality had an impact on politics. There is a school of thought that maintains that a nation's economic resources determine its strategic and diplomatic power. Most of us tend to view a country's gross national product, the resources that it possesses—such as petroleum reserves and precious metals—and its international trade and financial strength to be the essential ingredients that determine its political and military power. And there is considerable historical evidence that supports this point of view. The early industrialization of Great Britain in the nineteenth century, for instance, served as a significant resource base for British political power and an important factor in Great Britain's domination of that century's global economic and political structure. Similarly, in the twentieth century, the United States' economic power was instrumental in promoting its military and political dominance on the world arena.

The idea that the international economic system influences the international political system has received universal acceptance. An excellent example of this relationship is the European Union, which was the outcome of an economic reality that was shared by the European nations that the division of their economies along the political boundaries of nation-states was untenable in the long run in the face of the growing clout of the economic might of the United States and multinational corporations (of primarily American origins). The so-called invasion of American multinational corporations brought to the attention of European countries the benefits resulting from the removal of economic barriers separating their economies and the formation of a single unified European common market that would allow European companies the market size necessary to take advantage of scale economies primarily in production and distribution of goods and services. Now the fifteen-member European Union has a political body called the European Parliament that enacts laws in a variety of areas ranging from labor laws to environmental regulations that are applied throughout the Community. This is a classic example of how the international economic system impacts upon the international political system. The political landscape in Europe has changed dramatically, and the impetus for this change was provided by the economic reality of ensuring the survival of European industry and European companies in face of global economic competition mainly from the United States and U.S.-based multinational corporations.

On February 4, 1995, the Clinton administration imposed severe trade sanctions on exports of Chinese goods to the United States. The trade sanctions imposed 100 percent punitive tariffs on more than $1 billion of Chinese exports to the United States. The sanctions were meant to send a message to the Chinese government that, because of piracy by Chinese entrepreneurs of

American software, movies, music, brand names, and trademarks, American companies were incurring losses in revenue amounting to billions of dollars, and that the refusal by the Chinese government to move against the Chinese pirates was unacceptable to the U.S. government. The Clinton administration had ignored China's alleged human rights violations and extended favorable trade conditions to the Chinese in 1994. Finding that the Chinese government was not inclined to rectify its stance on piracy by Chinese entrepreneurs, the Clinton administration slapped the punitive tariffs on Chinese exports to the United States. This decision was made after the complete recognition and acceptance of the fact that this action by the U.S. government was certain to cause a serious rift in the political and diplomatic relations between the United States and China. However, it was taken in response to the intense pressure from the American business community whose economic interests were at stake. The diplomatic relations between the United States and China deteriorated as a result of the sanctions. This is yet another example of how economic concerns shape the foreign (political) policy of nations. This phenomenon is embodied in *Practical Insight 5-2*.

PRACTICAL INSIGHT 5-2

A Trade Tie That Binds: China Effort Survives, U.S. Officials Stress

WASHINGTON, Feb. 4—Nearly a year and a half ago, the United States decided that it had to end the deterioration in relations with China by embracing rather than isolating the government in Beijing.

Since then, there has been a steady stream of high-level diplomatic, economic, and military contacts. There have been setbacks on American initiatives concerning human rights, weapons proliferation, Taiwan, trade, culminating in today's decision to impose the toughest trade sanctions in American history. . . .

China is still a one-party Communist state, but it is the third-largest economy in the world, and economic concerns have taken center stage in the administration's foreign policy. The administration's decision to renew China's trade benefits despite its poor human rights record was a decision to help American business; so was today's decision to punish China for its rampant pirating of American goods and services.

In imposing the sanctions, the United States trade representative, Mickey Kantor, made clear that business had won out over diplomacy, that he had paid no attention to China's internal decision-making process or the declining health of China's leader, Deng Xiaoping.

"I have one job: to protect American workers and create markets for U.S. products and exports," he said in an interview on Friday. "I cannot control what China's leadership does. That is none of my business."

Source: Elaine Sciolino, "A Trade Tie That Binds: China Effort Survives, U.S. Officials Stress," *The New York Times*, February 5, 1995, p. 1. Copyright © 1995 The New York Times Company. Reprinted by permission.

So far we have focused on the influence of economic factors and concerns on political outcomes. Students of international politics, however, have often overlooked the "flip side" of this coin: the political dynamics of international economics.

Joan Edelman Spero has identified three ways in which political factors affect economic outcomes: "*First, the political system shapes the economic system,* because the structure and operation of the economic system is, to a great extent, determined by the structure and operation of the international political system. *Second, political concerns often shape economic policy,* because economic policies are frequently dictated by overriding political interests. *Third, international economic relations themselves are political relations,* because international economic interaction, like international political interaction, is a process by which state and nonstate actors manage, or fail to manage, their conflicts and by which they cooperate, or fail to cooperate, to achieve common goals."[6] What follows is a look in some detail of these three political dimensions of international economics.

The Influence of the International Political System on the International Economic System

The influence of the international political system on the international economic system is apparent when we review the political developments during three distinct periods in history. The first is the period of nineteenth century imperialism, the second is the post-World War II era of cold war between the Soviet Union and the Western free world led by the United States, and the third is the post-Berlin wall demolition and the demise of the Soviet Empire era.

Nineteenth Century Imperialism and the International Economic System The nineteenth century imperialism and mercantilism was driven by two major political factors: (1) powerful nation-states in Europe—the United Kingdom, France, Germany, and Holland—of nearly equal military power and (2) rampant nationalism practiced by these powerful nation-states which drove each nation to engage in practices designed to enhance national pride, national identity, self-sufficiency, wealth, and economic power. National independence, rather than collective or cooperative relations among nation-states, was in vogue. These two conditions led to the pursuit of "empire building" characterized by the policy of colonialism under which each European power engaged in colonizing countries in Asia, Africa, and Latin America. The objective of the colonial powers was to obtain the raw materials and minerals from the colonies, to process them into finished products at home, and to market the products in the captive markets of the colonies. The overriding objective of the colonial powers was to accumulate wealth and power and to provide full employment to their citizens, at the expense of the colonized countries whose markets and production capabilities were totally controlled by the imperial powers. The European colonial powers divided the world into parts that each controlled. Thus Britain controlled most of West and South Asia and parts of Africa. The French controlled Southeast Asia and Northwest Africa. The Dutch controlled Indonesia and parts of Central and South America, and the Germans took control of parts of West Africa. Wars erupted between the colonial powers as each attempted to increase their respective power by colonizing more countries. Thus the British and the French fought for the control of India, and the British and the Dutch fought for parts of Africa. European imperialism determined the patterns of trade and investments—each colonial power concentrated on trade and investments within its colonial empire. Thus the international economic system of the colonial era was determined by a political system characterized by colonialism and empire.

The Cold War Era and the International Economic System The imperialist system and the residual domination of the United Kingdom in the West ended following the end of World War II. Two major superpowers emerged in the post-World War II period, namely the United States and the Soviet Union. A new political and economic system emerged based upon the rivalry between these two superpowers for world political and economic domination. Politically, the new system was bipolar and hierarchical. The United States was the leader of the West and a weakened Japan, as well as the dominant military power; the Soviet Union was the dominant military power and leader of the so-called Soviet bloc in the East, which was composed of countries behind the "iron curtain." The developing countries of the third world, most of which had gained their freedom from the old imperial powers, remained politically subordinate to their once colonial "mother" countries. On the global arena, the United States and its allies confronted the Soviet Union and its allies in the Cold War. Such was the political system that determined the post-World War II international economic system.

For political reasons, the West and East were isolated in two disparate economic systems. The United States and its allies in the West adhered to the capitalist system which championed the free enterprise and free market economic system. In the East, the Soviet Union and its allies in the Communist bloc adhered to the Socialist/Marxist economic model that called for centralized control of the economy by the government and the absence of private property. In the West, the United States was the dominant economic power, and its free market vision shaped the economic order in the West; trade and commerce and capital flows occurred predominantly amongst the free market economies. In the East, the Soviet Union forced the Eastern bloc countries to adhere to the socialist model for their economies, and for political reasons made them economically dependent on the Soviet Union and economically isolated from the West. Thus politics shaped economics in the post-World War II period.

The Demise of the Soviet Union and Its Impact on the International Economic System As before, the changing political scene in the late 1980s and the 1990s caused the breakdown of the post-World War II international economic system. The birth of democracy in Poland and Hungary, the demolition of the Berlin Wall that resulted in the union of East and West Germany into one nation, and the subsequent breakup of the Soviet Union caused a sea change in the international economic system. Countries that once loathed capitalism and a free enterprise economy acknowledged its superiority over the socialist model, and gradually adopted its salient features. Russia became a democracy, and China, Vietnam, and India opened up their respective markets to foreign investments and trade.

Political Concerns and Economic Policy

In addition to influencing the international economic system, political concerns influence a nation's economic policies as well. Internal political processes play a role in determining a national economic policy. Economic policy is the outcome of the political bargaining process, which is responsible for resolving the conflict over the outcomes preferred by different groups, each representing distinct and often conflicting interests. The outcome of the political conflict is determined by the relative power of each group vis-à-vis other groups. For instance, conflict occurs between labor unions that want to protect domestic employment and are therefore opposed to free trade and business organizations that favor free trade, with the group that has more power exerting stronger influence on determining the international economic policy.

The overriding political and strategic interests of a nation very often determine its international economic policy. In effect, international economic policy becomes a tool to fulfill a nation's strategic and foreign policy objectives. For example, *embargo* has been used as a tool of political warfare throughout history, as when the United States placed an embargo on trade with Cuba after Fidel Castro came to power in that country. Similarly, the United Nations placed an embargo on all trade and investments in South Africa in the 1980s as a means of dismantling the apartheid system in that country.

International economic policy, driven by political considerations, can sometimes be beneficial to international companies. For example, because of larger political and strategic interests such as maintaining a correct political balance of power among countries, nations have often overlooked the human rights violations committed by repressive governments or the rape of democratic freedoms by military coups, and continued to promote trade, commerce, and investments with such nations. An example of this strategy is the huge investments by Western nations and Japan in communist China, which by all accounts has an overtly repressive regime.

At times, political considerations cause a nation to take actions in the economic sphere that prove to be detrimental to the interests of private enterprise. For example, *Practical Insight 5-3* illustrates how GM Hughes Electronics lost out on significant sales of satellites to the Chinese government because of the politically motivated decision by the U.S. government to ban the exports of satellites to China.

PRACTICAL INSIGHT 5-3
The Long March Back to China

Earthbound businesspeople often moan about the meddling of politicians, but the space industry has a particularly tough time of it. Consider the world's largest market for communications satellites: China. Last year the American government banned satellite exports to Beijing after it caught the Chinese discussing missile sales to the Middle East. In October China signed a binding agreement not to sell its M-9 and M-11 missiles to Arab countries—and the administration let American aerospace firms off the leash. The result? Up to $2 billion worth of satellite orders that the Chinese were on the brink of handing to Germany may now go to California.

The Chinese market (including Hong Kong) could easily require 20-30 new telecommunications satellites over the coming decade to cope with the mushrooming amount of data traffic, telephone calls, and television broadcasts. Before the trade sanctions went into effect a year ago, the world's largest satellite manufacturer, GM Hughes Electronics, a Los Angeles-based subsidiary of General Motors, was close to signing a deal for supplying at least ten of the satellites. The embargo is believed to have cost Hughes and other American satellite builders $400 million a year in lost business.

Partly to punish the Americans, but also to broaden their own access to foreign technology, the Chinese government gave the go-ahead a year ago for China Aero-Space Corporation (CASC) to form a 50-50 partnership with Deutsche Aerospace (DASA), which is part of Germany's giant Daimler-Benz conglomerate. The joint venture, EurasSpace of Munich, plans to develop a series of telecom and earth-observation satellites in much the same class as Hughes's big HS 601 spacecraft. When launched in 1996, the partnership's first satellite, called Sinosat-1, will carry data traffic for the People's Bank of China.

With some justification, Hughes feels that it was knocked out of the running for the Sinosat series of spacecraft for political reasons—and the DASA won the contract for the first three satellites by default.

Source: The Economist, November 5, 1994, p. 67. © 1994 The Economist Newspaper, Ltd. Reprinted by permission. All rights reserved.

International Economic Relations and International Political Relations

Earlier in this chapter, we discussed the nature of the international political system as being characterized by the absence of a legitimate body like a "world government" to manage conflict or achieve cooperation among and between the various members in the system (such as the nation-states, global companies, and various financial and nonfinancial institutions such as The World Bank, the OPEC oil cartel, and Amnesty International). In the absence of a "world government" with the requisite authority and legitimacy to make and enforce decisions for the political system, decision-making authority to manage conflict and cooperation among the various members of the political system is dispersed among the members of the system.

International economic relations may be viewed as the outcome of the political process involving the management of conflict and cooperation over the acquisition of scarce resources among the various members of the political system in the absence of a centralized "world government." As with all international political interaction, economic interaction ranges from pure conflict to pure cooperation. The conflict among the members of the political system is often rooted in a struggle for greater power and national sovereignty. National sovereignty is associated with national wealth. A country that is not independently wealthy becomes dependent on others and hence loses some of its national sovereignty. Therefore, the pursuit of wealth is the goal of most members in the political system, and the pursuit of this goal in the presence of scarce resources frequently leads to conflict among the system members. The conflict between producer countries and consumer countries over the price of oil is an example of economic warfare among members of the political system over which group or country will get a bigger share of a scarce resource, namely oil. It also displays a direct challenge by the oil producers, and especially by the OPEC countries, to the power of both the developed countries and the oil companies.

There is a high level of cooperation in the international economic system. For instance, most states are interested in free trade, and this has been manifested in the emergence of the World Trade Organization (the successor to GATT) to promote expanded free trade in the world. And the International Monetary Fund plays a critical role in promoting stability in the international currency markets as well as in maintaining the stability of currency exchange rates.

Like the debate over which came first, the chicken or the egg, the debate over whether the international political system influences the international economic system or whether the international economic system influences the international political system will continue unabated. However, when one accepts the fact that nations interacting with each other are the dominant players in both economic and political systems, then unquestionably the political interests embodied in national power and national sovereignty will be the primary determinants of their political as well as economic relations with other nations in the world community of nations.

Now that we have discussed, from a somewhat theoretical perspective, the general nature of the international political process and ways in which it may interact with economic processes, we will turn to the more specific issue of the interface between the international firm and its political environment. We can now begin to apply what we have learned about political dynamics to the operating and strategic challenges facing the firm. We have seen through Practical Insights and from historical examples the magnitude of the impact that political policies and relations can have on trade. From the firm's standpoint, the question facing the international manager is: "What is the likelihood that political forces may affect my operations in country X, how much of what sort of an impact might there be, and how should I plan to best deal with this potential impact while maintaining the highest practical profit?" The answer to this question lies in identifying and assessing the nature and extent of the *political risk* facing the firm, the subject of the remainder of this chapter.

POLITICAL RISK AND THE INTERNATIONAL FIRM

Political Risk Defined

Political risk is the likelihood that political forces will cause unexpected and drastic changes in a country's environment that significantly affect the opportunities and operations of a business enterprise.

This definition of political risk puts emphasis on political forces as being the primary determinants of political risk in a country's environment. Political forces are the different participant groups in the political system. Earlier in this chapter we examined the characteristics of a political system, and the role played by the major political groups in a society in influencing the authoritative decisions of the government in power. Political risk is the degree of uncertainty associated with the pattern of decisions made by the government. There is no political risk when there is certainty about the future decisions made by the government. The higher the degree of uncertainty regarding the policy decisions made by the government, the higher is the political risk perceived by those most affected by governmental decisions.

Countries in which the government does not show consistency in the pattern of decision making are more likely to be perceived as risky than those in which the decisions show a pattern of consistency. Two major emerging economies—India and China—are cases in point. Since 1990 the Indian government has embarked on a slow but steady program of opening the huge Indian market to foreign competition and investments. Billions of dollars of foreign investments, mostly from the United States, have entered the Indian market. Although, in the opinion of many observers, the rate at which the Indian government is opening up the market is rather slow, the (adverse) political risk that is perceived by firms doing business in India is moderate to low. In contrast, China, which also has a huge market potential for many business firms, has made much bigger strides in opening the market to foreign firms. However, the perception of the degree of political risk is much higher in China than is the case with India. This is because China as yet does not have an effective legal system, a reliable commercial code that establishes the rules of commercial interactions and obligations does not exist, and decisions made by one agency of the government are often negated by decisions of some other agency. The following story from *The Philadelphia Inquirer* illustrates the nature of political risk faced by McDonald's in China:

> In a move that may chill the confidence of foreign investors, Beijing said last week that McDonald's must pull down the golden arches on the city's choicest corner.
>
> The city reneged on its promise to give McDonald's 20 years at the site after giving a Hong Kong developer the same prime location—the busy corner of Wangfujing street and the Avenue of Eternal Peace.
>
> The Wangfujing outlet, just two blocks from Tiananmen Square, has become one of the most lucrative of the 22 McDonald's in China in the two years since it opened.
>
> Now the 1.2 million square-foot site surrounding the restaurant is destined to become the Oriental Plaza, a commercial, office, and residential complex planned by developer Li Ka-shing, the richest man in Hong Kong.
>
> An official in Beijing's Foreign Liaison office who requested anonymity said McDonald's would have a site within the new complex once it is completed in about three years. Details of its location and of the compensation to be paid are to be negotiated between the land developer and McDonald's, he said.

McDonald's representatives in Beijing and Hong Kong said they had not been officially notified of the city's decision. McDonald's officials had said earlier that they had no intention of vacating the site, and that they believed they had a legal right to stay in the building they had built.

The city's decision to break the land-use agreement raises doubts about other such contracts.

To encourage investment while retaining public ownership of land, Communist China usually grants investors the right to use land and build on it for several decades, sometimes longer.

But a construction boom has made prime property of all central Beijing as well as other cities, tempting governments to break those pledges for the sake of higher profits.

Beijing officials granted McDonald's the right to use the Wangfujing site after the army crackdown on pro-democracy protests on Tienanmen Square in 1989.

Then, most foreigners were suspending or backing away from their Beijing investments. When McDonald's said it wanted that corner, the city was glad to oblige.[7]

The experience of McDonald's in China exemplifies the devastating impact that an unanticipated decision by government officials can have on the operations of an enterprise. This potential for government officials to unexpectedly change their economic and legal policies and procedures is the very essence of political risk.

The Nature of Political Risk

Political risk need not necessarily be unfavorable in its impact on businesses—favorable consequences may accrue as well. For example, despite the presence of political risk in China, the Chinese government has made a mammoth policy change that now allows foreign investments in China. Not many years ago, few observers would have predicted such an opening of the Chinese economy to foreign trade and investments. This newly open Chinese market has provided companies worldwide with new business opportunities, and illustrates the potentially favorable impact of political risk. The same can be said about the changes that have occurred in Russia, which has embraced capitalism and the free enterprise system following the demise of what once was the Soviet Union. Hence political risk can be positive as well as negative depending upon how it affects company operations.

There is no established relationship between the political ideology of the government and the nature of risk incurred. Regardless of the government's ideology, it is the behavior of the government that determines the degree of risk prevalent in a country. A government with a capitalist ideology may pose more risk to businesses if it abruptly changes its policies than a socialist government which has a record of maintaining consistent policies over extended periods of time.

The form of government is also not necessarily associated with the amount of risk generated in a country. Dictatorships may pose the same amount of risk as democracies. Once again it is the behavior of the government that determines the amount of risk present in a particular country.

One would normally conclude that a stable government presents less political risk than one that is unstable, and in most instances this is true—but not always! For example, both France in the 1950s and Italy in the 1980s and early 1990s experienced considerable instability in their respective governments. Both countries experienced frequent changes in government, however, the economic policies of the government showed only insignificant changes. Political risk therefore was quite low in France and Italy, notwithstanding the frequent changes in the government in both countries. On the other hand, India has had considerable political stability with the Congress party in power since 1947, except for a brief period of two years or so in the mid-1980s. Still, the economic policies of the government have varied widely and frequently, creating considerable political risk for businesses until the more consistent P.V. Narasimah Rao government assumed power in the late 1980s.

Political risk can be country, company, or project specific. *Country-specific* political risk is manifested in the mutual hostility between Israel and Syria. One would expect that Israeli companies would find little support in Syria, and the same would apply for Syrian companies in Israel. *Company-specific* risk invokes either a favorable or unfavorable response aimed at a particular company. For example, companies known for their technological superiority, such as Motorola and Hewlett-Packard, may receive favorable treatment in some countries in the form of special incentives as inducements to form joint ventures or to establish wholly owned subsidiaries. On the other hand, large companies may not be welcomed in a country that is afraid that they may destroy local firms. *Project-specific* risk involves special treatment bestowed on a certain type of project. For example, countries such as Libya and Iran that are very unfriendly to foreign investments from the United States are nonetheless eager to collaborate with American oil companies in oil exploration and drilling.

Types of Political Risk

The impact of political decisions can be felt in three different ways: (1) transfer risk, (2) operational risk, and (3) ownership risk.

Transfer risk is the change in the degree of ease or difficulty experienced in making transfers of capital, goods, technology, and people in and out of a country. Capital controls include restrictions placed on the remittance of money to or from a country through foreign exchange controls. Similarly, governments may impose controls over the flow of goods into a country through quotas and high tariffs. Technology transfer may be constrained by government policy. For instance, the United States government has forbidden the export of technology that could be used to develop products with military applications, such as missiles and nuclear weapons. Similarly, most countries require work visas for foreigners, while some place limits on the number of foreign nationals who can be employed in a company, thereby limiting the flow of human resources among the subsidiaries of international companies.

Operational risk is the impact on the operations of a firm caused by changes in the government's policies. For example, the enforcement of strict new environmental protection legislation may cause a firm to shift its production site from one location to another within a country, or to another country altogether. Similarly, a change in minimum wage laws may induce a company to farm out some production work to contractors in countries with more competitive wage rates.

Ownership risk involves a change in the proportion of equity owned by a company in a foreign subsidiary. Until the late 1960s and early 1970s, the nature of the ownership risk experienced by international companies was predominantly negative. The nationalistic ideology of most developing countries—countries which had become independent from the bondage of colonialism—called for economic independence and self-sufficiency. This ideology fomented a wave of nationalization, expropriation, or forced divestment of equity of foreign companies in such countries as India, Egypt, Zimbabwe, Zambia, and Indonesia. Since the 1980s and 1990s, however, there has been a rise in the wave of sentiment in favor of foreign enterprise. The thirst for foreign technology and access to foreign markets, both of which international companies are in a good position to provide, has motivated governments in countries that once abhorred foreign companies to now throw them a welcome mat. Foreign companies that were once asked to divest their share of equity in foreign subsidiaries are now being asked to increase their share to a majority or wholly owned status. In these cases, ownership risk has now shifted from negative to positive.

The Scope of Political Risk

The scope of transfer, operational, and ownership risk may range from **macro** to **micro**. Macro and micro risk can be looked at as two ends of a continuum. Like heat and cold, there are degrees of macro and micro risk. One can conceive of macro risk as one in which all private enterprise is confiscated or nationalized, as was the case when Cuba became a Communist country. A macro risk of lesser scope could be when only foreign companies or only certain industries are nationalized. At the other extreme is micro risk, which may entail a specific action against a specific company by a group or government. The bombing of the offices of the El Al Airlines by the PLO, or the pressure put on Coca-Cola by the Indian government in 1977 to reveal its secret syrup formula (which forced Coke to abandon the Indian market) are examples of micro risk.

The table in Exhibit 5-1 shows the relationships among the three types of risk—transfer, operational, ownership—and the scope of such risks—micro and macro. The table shows that for country XYZ, there are six different categories of political risk: transfer, operational, and ownership, with each of these types of risk falling anywhere along the macro–micro risk continuum.

For instance, in the table in Exhibit 5-1, company A in country XYZ is experiencing a medium level of micro/transfer risk, a low level of micro/operational risk, and a high level of macro/ownership risk.

EXHIBIT 5-1
Classification of Types of Risk for Company A in Country XYZ

	RISK	SCOPE
RISK TYPE	Macro Risk	Micro Risk
Transfer Risk		**
Operational Risk		*
Ownership Risk	****	

Legend: ***** = High   * = Low

Assessing Host Country Political Risk

Doing business internationally requires that the business risks caused by the political climate be assessed in every host country in which the international firm conducts business. A valid and reliable evaluation of the host country political risk provides managers with a realistic view of the probability of being able to achieve the proposed venture's objectives. Armed with this information, managers are in a position to determine the minimum levels of expectations from the venture in areas such as the rate of return (discounted for the level of risk), market share, and profits, and to employ this knowledge in the ensuing negotiations with either the foreign government officials or potential business associates.

Assessing the political risk in a host country should begin with an exhaustive study of the political system and the corresponding political process in the country. (Review Figure 5-1.) As stated earlier in this chapter, the political process constitutes a political bargaining process in which different groups in the political system, representing different interests, conflict over different preferred outcomes. Assuming that the government in power has the legitimacy to govern, the outcomes of the political process are the various political decisions made by the government. The government's decisions are in response to the lobbying efforts by the various interest groups in favor of their respective viewpoints.

An exhaustive study of the political process involves the following:

1. Study the relative power of the dominant groups in the society and become familiar with their ideologies. Groups that are more powerful are more likely to have their way with the politicians in the government than those with less power. Look for any dominant coalitions among one or more groups whose political aspirations may be overlapping. Coalitions among groups may help less powerful groups gain more influence in the political process than would be possible if each of the relatively less powerful groups were to operate on its own.

2. Study the decision-making process in the government. Which political parties are represented in the legislative branch of the government? For example, the British Parliament includes members whose party affiliations include Tory, Labor, Liberal, and Communist. The United States Senate and House of Representatives include members who are either Democrat or Republican. Understand the ideologies of the political parties in the legislative branch and the dominant groups in society whom they represent. For instance, the British Tory party and the Republican party in the United States both represent the interests of the various business associations within their respective business communities.

2a. Evaluate the relative strength and bargaining power of the political parties in the legislative branch. Assess the relative bargaining power of the various dominant coalitions in the legislative branch. The political party(s) and dominant coalitions that have greater bargaining power are more likely to have their ideologies implemented through legislation that is enacted by the legislative body.

    In a parliamentary democracy there is no separation between the legislative branch and the executive branch of government as the Prime Minister (the Chief Executive) is chosen by the majority party in the parliament. However, in the presidential system the legislative branch is separate from the executive, and therefore, as has often been the case in the United States, the party in power in the legislature may not be the same as the party to which the President belongs. Therefore, in a presidential system one must evaluate the relative power between the President, who represents the executive branch of government, and the dominant political party in the legislative branch, because in this form of government the political decisions made by the government are outcomes of the bargaining and negotiations between the legislative and the executive branches of government.

3. Study who the key decision makers are in both the legislative and executive branches of government. The key decision makers are those who have the most influence on the policy choices of the government. The key person may be the chairperson of a sub-committee of the parliament or congress, or a senior civil servant in a governmental agency. Occasionally the most influential person may not be in the government at all. For example, Senior Minister Lee (the former Prime Minister) is supposedly the person who is most influential in developing the policies of the Singapore government, although he is not officially part of the government itself. Identifying the key decision makers may provide valuable clues on the future policy initiatives of the government.

4. Study the path traveled by the government in power over the past several years in terms of its economic, social, and foreign policies. This information in conjunction with the information accumulated in the aforementioned three steps may be used to make informed judgments as to the future policy initiatives of the government.

5. Evaluate the impacts on the industry and your company of the anticipated political decisions of the government, i.e., the political risk facing the industry and company in the host country. Assess the nature of the political risk—transfer, operational, or ownership? Will the risk be macro or micro? What is the probability of the political risk and what is the timeframe within which it is likely to materialize?

Diligently following the five steps outlined should provide international managers with a fairly good picture of the probability, intensity, and nature of the political risk that their companies are likely to face in the target country.

CIVIL STRIFE AND POLITICAL RISK

Civil strife in a country can cause a government to change its policies or alternatively may cause a government to fall and be replaced by another with a different political ideology. In any such event, there is the likelihood that a new set of political decisions will be made by the government in power which may sow the seeds of political risk for businesses in the country.

Recent examples of countries in which civil strife has either brought about a change in government or a change in government policies are the former Soviet Union, Poland, Hungary, Iran, and South Africa. Political scientists have made some progress in identifying the causal factors of civil strife. Ted Gurr offers an approach to evaluate the probability and degree of civil strife in a country. His framework is shown in Figure 5-2.

Gurr postulates that civil strife of any kind must have as a precondition "relative deprivation," which he defines as the citizens' "perceptions of discrepancy between their value expectations (the goods and conditions of the life to which they believe they are justifiably entitled) and their value capabilities (the amounts of those goods and conditions that they think they are able to get and keep)."[8] The citizens' response to perceived deprivation is discontent and anger, which may ultimately find an outlet through aggressive acts. The more intense and widespread deprivation is among the people of a country, the greater is the potential for civil strife.

131

FIGURE 5-2
A Framework for Assessing Country Civil Strife

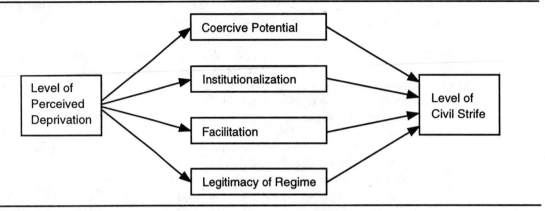

Source: Ted Gurr, "A Causal Model of Civil Strife: A Comparative Model Using New Analysis," *The American Political Science Review,* Vol. 62, No. 4, December 1968, pp. 1104-1124.

Gurr further postulates that discontent and anger do not necessarily result in civil strife because of the mediating effects of four variables.[9] They are as follows:

1. Coercive potential: The government could apply high levels of coercion, which could limit the extent of strife. Also, the more loyal the coercive forces are to the government, the more effective they are in deterring strife.

2. Institutionalization: "The extent to which societal structures beyond the primary level are broad in scope, command substantial resources and/or personnel, and are stable and persisting."[10] Societal structures such as labor unions and political parties serve two purposes. First, they provide alternative means by which the citizens can attain their value satisfactions. Second, they provide citizens with outlets to channel their dissatisfactions and anger in a nonviolent manner. Therefore, the greater the institutionalization, the lower the magnitude of strife is likely to be.

3. Facilitation: Social and structural conditions in a country might promote the outbreak and persistence of strife. Examples of such conditions are (a) the belief held by the population, partly based upon the historical experience of chronic civil strife, that violence is justified as a means of overcoming deprivation; (b) the transportation network and terrain of a country; (c) the presence of organized groups that facilitate social strife; and (d) the extent of foreign assistance to the initiators of strife. "The greater the levels of past strife, and of social and structural facilitation, the greater is the magnitude of strife."[11]

4. Legitimacy of the regime: This variable refers to the popularity of the regime. "The greater is regime legitimacy at a given level of deprivation, the less the magnitude of consequent strife."[12]

Thus, in assessing the magnitude of civil strife, not only is it necessary to establish the level of perceived deprivation but also an evaluation of the *cumulative* impact of the aforementioned four mediating variables. Staff groups in multinational companies specializing in political risk forecasting could devise ways of composing indices to measure the level of deprivation, coercive potential, institutionalization, facilitation, and legitimacy of the regime in a country. These indices could then be used conjuctionally to obtain the magnitude of civil strife in the country. Indices based upon uniform parameters could be constructed for various countries, which would in turn facilitate the comparison of potential political risk in two or more countries.

To sum up, the magnitude of civil strife in a country would depend upon the level of perceived deprivation among the people, the relative strength of the mediating variables, that is, coercive potential, institutionalization, facilitation, and legitimacy of the regime. Civil strife is likely to occur if the mediating variables cannot neutralize the discontent, anger, and the resultant aggressive and violent behavior emanating from the peoples' perceived deprivation.

Civil strife, as was pointed out earlier, either forces the government of a country to be changed or causes the existing government to change its policies and practices. In either case there is the likelihood of a change in the government's policies towards foreign-owned firms. Executives in a company, who are responsible for making foreign investment decisions, should ask these questions:

1. To what extent would the new political group in power and/or the government's revised policies be favorably inclined towards (a) foreign firms operating in the country and (b) new foreign investments in the country?

2. How would the new government policies affect the various business sectors in the economy? Would there be greater or lesser control of the economy by the government?

3. Are any particular industries likely to be affected more than others? Is our company in such an industry?

4. Are selected foreign firms—not the entire industry—likely to be expropriated?

The answers to these questions can help executives decide the mode of entry that would best exploit the opportunities in the target market. For example, licensing would be preferred in a high-risk political environment as opposed to a foreign direct investment which needs a political environment that is relatively more stable and risk-free. However, if the company already has direct investments in a country in the form of a manufacturing plant or assembly operation, then executives would be in a better position to decide—again on the basis of the answers to the above questions—whether to (a) make more direct investments in the country, (b) withdraw its investments from the country, (c) form a joint venture with local partners, or (d) use financial techniques to minimize company losses.

The country of Iran is a good example of how civil strife led to a change of the regime in power—the Shah of Iran was replaced by the Ayatollah Khomeini—which eventually resulted in unacceptable risks and the withdrawal of American firms from that country. Other countries in which civil strife has resulted in a change of governments include the Philippines, Poland, South Africa, Hungary, Romania, and the former East Germany. Civil strife also led to the break-up of Yugoslavia into several smaller countries.

The Global Framework for Assessing Political Risk

Up to this point we have focused upon the process for evaluating political risk in a particular country. The proposed frameworks for making such an evaluation have assumed that the host country was insulated from forces and events outside of the country's political boundaries.

However, in the real world of interdependent nation-states such is really not the case, since the political risk faced by a company is caused not only by the events and environmental changes occurring in the host country, but also by those occurring in the home country and in the international political system.

Figure 5-3 depicts a framework with four basic environments: host country, home country, international environment, and international events. The framework can help the international manager identify the key factors and developments affecting an analysis of political risk.

One always first considers the host country. Analysis of political risk in the host country may follow the frameworks offered earlier in this chapter, and forecasts of the anticipated probability, degree, and nature of risk faced by the enterprise in the target country can be made by international managers.

However, there are many ways in which the home country can also be the source of political risk to a company's operations in the host country. Policy decisions by the home country government directed at a particular foreign country can have a serious impact upon the operations of companies that have business dealings and operations in that country. For instance, the home country government can place restrictions on technology transfers to the target country, or it may impose economic sanctions on goods exported to, and imported from, the target country. Companies that do business in the targeted country would be affected by such home country actions. Thus, the political risk can be sourced not just in the host country, but in certain cases the home country can also become a major source of political risk for an international company.

The international environment is also a source of political risk for an international company. The international environment consists of the various groups that transcend the political boundaries of any one country. Those groups that are localized within the political borders of one country fall under the category of "country environment." Examples of international groups include Amnesty International, the various Islamic fundamentalist groups that have branches in numerous countries, the Irish Republican Army and its branches worldwide, the World Trade Organization, the International Monetary Fund, the United Nations and its various agencies, etc. International groups can create political risk for an international company through the influence that they can exert on the political decisions of nation-states. For instance, the United Nations sanctions on trade and investments in South Africa, aimed at bringing down the minority white government in that country, forced countries to pass laws that prohibited trade and investments in that country. Companies such as Polaroid, IBM, and many other large and small companies worldwide were affected by the U.N. sanctions.

FIGURE 5-3
Global Risk Assessment Framework

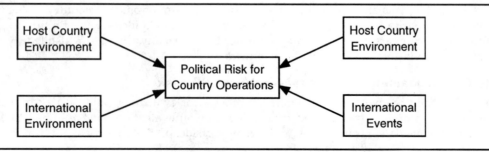

International events are also the cause of political risks faced by international companies. For example, the oil crisis of 1974 affected countries and companies worldwide. An economic recession is no longer confined to one country alone, rather it spreads rapidly throughout the world. A financial crisis such as the external debt crisis that hit Mexico in 1995 had its repercussions felt not only in the United States but throughout the world. The actions taken by the United States and the International Monetary Fund involving a loan guarantee of up to $40 billion to the Mexican government was an effort to curtail the global impact of Mexico's financial crisis. Events such as the global oil crisis and the Mexican debt crisis can have significant impact on transfer risk and operational risks experienced by international companies.

From the above discussion, the need for conducting a realistic and thorough assessment of the political risk facing a firm should be obvious. The potential loss to a company from unanticipated political forces or actions can be substantial, even to the point of expropriation of its capital assets. We have explored two frameworks that can be of value in risk assessment. Their use, along with a proper categorization or classification of the specific type(s) of anticipated risks, can provide international managers with the information they need to make smart decisions that best manage the political risk inherent in a given scenario. These "tools" will be most effective for the manager who has a solid understanding of the fundamental elements and dynamics of political systems, and the ways in which they interact with economic systems and policies in forming the political environment of the international firm. As with the other environmental dimensions that we discuss in this text, the presence and potentially aversive nature of the political environment of the international business presents a distinctive challenge for the global manager.

The economic, legal, and political dimensions of the international business environment that we have discussed in the past three chapters are similar to each other in that the specific nature of each facing an international firm can generally be ascertained rather directly by researching a nation's economic statistics, legal code, and any of various sources regarding the nature of the political system. The cultural dimension, which we address in the next chapter, is somewhat different, in that many of the key variables—such as attitudes and values—are invisible. The problem facing the manager is one of recognizing these underlying cultural factors, not concerning himself solely with the more obvious behavioral traits they cause. Thus, this last aspect of the international environment that we discuss in this book in some ways poses the greatest managerial challenge.

SUMMARY

A political system is composed of a set of players, each of which has a unique ideology and some degree of power which it uses to control and influence the behavior of other groups. One group, government, has an additional attribute—legitimacy—which it uses along with its generally greater influence to make and enforce authoritarian decisions. It does so by means of the political process, the bargaining process by which the conflicting interests and relative power of different groups are constructively managed in attaining political decisions.

This simple political model can be applied in a global context as well, with the competing groups including international organizations such as the United Nations and The World Bank, regional trade blocs such as NAFTA, the EU, and MERCUSOR, and individual nation-states. The lack of an overarching, legitimate "world government" to manage conflict among these groups results in a less stable network of relationships that are dependent upon voluntary cooperative agreements in the form of treaties or conventions to establish and enforce acceptable behavior.

Today's international economic and political systems and processes are highly interdependent. Economic relations between countries are shaped to a large extent by their political relations, and vice versa. As a result of this complex interaction, political considerations can generate actions by nation-states in the economic sphere that may be detrimental to the interests of private enterprise.

The likelihood that such political forces will unexpectedly and drastically affect a firm's operations is embodied in the concept of political risk. High levels of political risk are generally associated with low levels of stability and consistency in the political system of a nation-state. Political risk may be felt in three ways: transfer risk, operational risk, and ownership risk. Each of these three types of risk can be further classified as macro or micro in nature, depending on the particular circumstances.

Valid and reliable assessment of a host country's political risk is an essential element of doing business internationally. A structured analytical framework involving thorough evaluation of the individual groups, ideologies, relative power relationships, and decision-making processes of the host country's political system can facilitate such an assessment.

A key determinant of political risk in many countries is the likelihood of civil strife, a mass uprising that would result in destabilizing the incumbent political system. Ted Gurr has proposed a useful framework for assessing the likelihood of civil strife based on the level of perceived relative deprivation of the population as mediated by the coercive potential and legitimacy of the government, the degree of institutionalization in the society, and the extent to which factors that facilitate civil strife are present.

Although political risk is generally discussed in the context of one particular country at a time, today's global firms are exposed to such risk on a much broader front. The complex nature of the dynamics between political and economic relations requires that the modern firm extend its risk assessment framework to include not only the host country environment, but the home and international environments as well, and the role of current international events in shaping those environments.

QUESTIONS FOR THOUGHT AND DISCUSSION

1. Using the political system model from the chapter, outline at least five different types of groups that can influence the government's decision-making process. As best you can, identify the ideologies involved, the relative power relationships, and the decision-making process. If your class has students from another country, repeat the exercise using their home country as a model. How are the two political systems similar? How are they different?

2. Newspapers are full of examples of the dynamic interdependency between political and economic concerns in today's international arena. Find an article that deals with the micro (on one firm) effects of macro (between two nation-states) political considerations. Was the effect an intended one? Explain the cause-effect relationship involved.

3. What effect has the demise of the Soviet Union had on the level of political risk for multinational firms in the NIS (Newly Independent States)? Should this be considered a short-term or a long-term effect? Why?

4. Apply the political risk assessment framework presented in the chapter to your own country. What areas of concern (if any) would you convey to a foreign multinational considering doing business there? Compare your assessment with one prepared on the same country by a foreign student in the class. How do the two assessments differ? If your company was considering

investment in another country, would you prefer an assessment from a native of that country or from someone else? Discuss.

5. Assess the probability of civil strife in a country of your choice, using Gurr's framework as presented in the chapter. Support your position with specific examples for the required precondition and each of the mediating variables. How likely is the probability to stay the same? If the situation indicates a high likelihood of strife, what, if any, action could or should be taken to reduce that likelihood? If strife erupts, would the impact on foreign multinationals be positive or negative? Explain.

MINI-CASE
Business as Usual After Tiananmen Square?

Bing Wang* was a student leader at Beijing University in the heady days of May 1989. It was during Gorbachev's official visit to China that Chinese students, emboldened by the presence of the champion of glasnost (political openness) and the foreign news media, publicly voiced their opposition to the power of the Communist Party and pressed for democratic reform. The movement grew stronger every day, as massive demonstrations converging on Tiananmen Square became a daily event in Beijing, well after the departure of the Soviet leader.

Bing Wang was a major organizer of the student protest movement. He was active in all aspects of the groundswell that had began to attract many ordinary citizens: rural migrants, factory workers, and housewives, young and old alike. As the editor of the student union paper, Bing Wang spent many sleepless nights preparing articles that for the first time in decades were free of censorship. As an organizer, he decided, along with others, on the slogans to be carried or leaflets to be distributed. Indeed, caught in the excitement of the new era that seemed to dawn in China, Bing Wang worked tirelessly and with unbounded enthusiasm.

All this came to an abrupt end on the night of June 4, 1989. The army had encircled the city for several days, but no one really believed that it would move against the demonstrations. On that fateful night, it did. Those who attempted to oppose the tanks that were rolling toward the city center were killed or wounded. Bing Wang narrowly escaped arrest. He spent many days and nights in the houses of trusted friends, always managing to stay one step ahead of the police. After several months in hiding, he left Beijing for Shenzheng, where a high-placed government official, secretly a pro-democracy sympathizer, helped him cross into Hong Kong. Soon afterwards, Bing Wang resurfaced in New York, where he settled and became a prominent voice and leader of an association of exiled Chinese intellectuals. He organized letter-writing campaigns, addressed members of the United States Congress, and in denouncing the human rights abuses of the Chinese government urged U.S. trade sanctions against China, in particular the withdrawal of the Most Favored Nation (MFN) status that had been granted by the U.S. government.

Bing Wang and his American and Chinese friends were not entirely unsuccessful. Indeed, President Clinton had decided in 1993 to make the renewal of the MFN status for China contingent on an improvement of the human rights situation in Bing Wang's homeland.

Bill Turner* has never met Bing Wang. Indeed, up to two years ago he knew little about China beyond a general appreciation for its growing role in Asia. It was only recently that, as one of the star executives in the Chrysler Corporation, he was given the challenging and difficult mission

---

*This is a fictitious name.

of winning a fiercely competitive battle against formidable European and American competitors for building a $1.2 billion minivan plant in Guangdong province. The contract could represent a major boost for the fortunes of the Detroit auto company, which faces a mature and increasingly competitive domestic market. Bill Turner knew, however, that Europeans, in particular Germany's Daimler-Benz corporation, were also bidding for the contract. The Chinese buyers, masters in the art of negotiations and boosted by the importance of their rapidly growing economy, were determined to drive a hard bargain. Bill Turner knew that, but he was also confident that Chrysler could win the bid, thus providing him with his most important professional achievement: ensuring employment for thousands of Americans and securing a crucial foothold for the Detroit auto maker in a country poised to become a major global economic power.

The news reports from Washington were disturbing. President Clinton had threatened to withdraw China's MFN status, in spite of the risk that such an action could pose for American business interests. To his chagrin, the Chinese delegation that was scheduled to visit Chrysler's Detroit facilities had postponed its visit, awaiting the announcement from the White House.

The Chinese authorities had made clear that they would not tolerate any meddling by outsiders in what they considered an internal matter—the human rights situation in China. They had warned that a suspension of China's MFN status would have a negative impact for U.S.-Chinese relations, and by extension for American business interests as well. Bill Turner, along with many other American businesspeople, was concerned about the American government policy. Large companies such as Boeing and Chrysler, as well as a myriad of smaller companies, stood to lose lucrative markets to their Japanese and European competitors. When Secretary of State Christopher visited Beijing before the official U.S. announcement on the MFN status, his mission was to obtain a concession or at least a symbolic gesture from the Chinese on human rights, thus paving the way for a favorable decision in Washington. During private talks, however, the Chinese were unbending. Asked by reporters to comment on the negotiations, the Secretary of State reportedly replied laconically: "I wish it were as good as the lunch was."

Not only did Christopher not gain any concessions from the Chinese, he also had to contend with the frustration of the American business community in Beijing. In meeting with the Secretary of State, the expatriates made clear to him that their position converged with that of the host government: they wanted the renewal of the MFN status and the disassociation of politics from trade and business issues.

It is not that Bill Turner or other American executives did not feel sympathy or compassion for the victims of repression in China, such as Bing Wang; indeed, practically all were deeply hostile to the Communist ideology which had nurtured and guided the Chinese leadership over the years. However, many felt that openly punishing the independent-minded Chinese over the issue of human rights would be counterproductive. The development of China's foreign trade and the prosperity that had followed economic reforms could conceivably lead to a more relaxed political atmosphere in the future. At a more fundamental level, Bill Turner and his peers argued that slapping sanctions on China would harm American companies and simply benefit their rival European and Japanese companies who did not have to contend with such politically motivated constraints. Moreover, many business executives as well as legislators and government officials in the United States felt that the interests of the American workers, consumers, and shareholders should be placed above the plight of foreign nationals.

In May 1994, the Chrysler executive, along with many other opponents of sanctions, anxiously awaited the presidential decision.

As for Bing Wang, on the day before the fateful announcement, he looked from the window of his office toward the Statue of Liberty, visible in the distance. He remembered the replica that student demonstrators had dubbed "the Goddess of Democracy" and carried boldly through the streets of Beijing, five years earlier, almost to the day. He felt confident about the upcoming presidential announcement.

While deploring the continued human right abuses in China, President Clinton declared on May 26, 1994, that the United States would renew China's MFN status, and would not, in the future, link trade decisions to the domestic Chinese political situation.

Source: Written by Dr. Yadong Luo, Assistant Professor of International Management, University of Hawaii at Manoa. Copyright © 1997 by Arvind V. Phatak.

Discussion Questions for Mini-Case

1. What effects will the Clinton administration decision have on the bilateral relations between China and the U.S.A.? What reaction do you expect from the Chinese?

2. What are the benefits from the renewal of the MFN status for China? for U.S. exporters? for American consumers?

3. Political risk can originate from a number of sources. Identify the sources of political risk for subsidiaries of U.S. companies in China.

4. If you were a U.S. exporter of products, what possible measures could you adopt to minimize the political risk arising from governmental policies of either the home or host country that might hurt your exports to China?

Notes

1 John Plamenatz, *Ideology*, Praeger Publishers, New York, 1970, p. 15.

2 Roy C. Macridis, *Contemporary Political Ideologies*, 5th ed., Harper-Collins Publishers, Inc., New York, 1992, p. 2.

3 Plamenatz, p. 2.

4 For more on the concepts of consensus and legitimacy please read Roy C. Macridis and Bernard E. Brown, (Eds.), *Comparative Politics: Notes and Readings*, 3rd. ed., The Dorsey Press, Homewood, Ill., 1968, pp. 107-114.

5 Joan Edelman Spero, *The Politics of International Economic Relations*, 4th ed., St. Martin's Press, New York, 1990, p. 9.

6 Ibid., p. 4.

7 Elaine Kurtenbach, "Beijing cuts McDonald's deal short," *The Philadelphia Inquirer*, November 27, 1994, p. A1.

8 Ted Gurr, "A Causal Model of Civil Strife: A Comparative Model Using New Analysis," *The American Political Science Review*, Vol. 62, No. 4, December 1968, p. 1104.

9 Ibid., pp. 1105-1106.

10 Ibid., p. 1105.

11 Ibid., p. 1106.

12 Ibid.

The International Cultural Environment

LEARNING OBJECTIVES

After completing this chapter, you will be able to:

- Define culture and discuss four critical value differences between Western and non-Western cultures.
- Discuss some examples of problems that may arise from an international manager's insensitivity to cultural differences.
- Describe two frameworks for analyzing cultural differences, and some managerial implications of an analysis conducted with them.

The multinational operations of companies have brought executives into face-to-face contact with the cultures of different nations and regions, many of which seem very strange. The importance of understanding the cultures of countries in which a company operates—as well as the similarities and differences between those cultures—becomes clear when one looks at the multitude of blunders international executives have made because of insensitivity to cultural differences.[1] Investigators who have studied the performance and problems of corporations and individuals abroad have concluded that it is usually the human problems associated with working in a different culture that are likely to be critical to the success or failure of their endeavors.[2] Analyses of problems and failures abroad have shown that the techniques, practices, and methods that have proved effective in one country may not work as well in other countries. One dominant, interfering factor is culture.

The following old oriental story vividly dramatizes the consequences of ignorance, and it is an appropriate metaphor for the kinds of problems that can arise when people of diverse cultures come into contact without preparation.

> Once upon a time, there was a great flood; and involved in this flood were two creatures, a monkey and a fish. The monkey, being agile and experienced, was lucky enough to scramble up a tree and escape the raging waters. As he looked down from his safe perch, he saw the poor fish struggling against the swift current. With the very best of intentions, he reached down and lifted the fish from the water. The result was inevitable.[3]

Just as the monkey in the story assumed that the fish's environment was similar to his and behaved accordingly, so do many international executives unconsciously assume that all people think and feel the way they do. Management practices that are suited to their own cultural environment may bring about undesirable, perhaps terrible, consequences in another culture. In international business dealings, then, ignorance of cultural differences is not just unfortunate; it is bad business.

To avoid such problems, the international manager must understand his or her own culture first. A person's behavior is based on a commonly shared cultural system of values, beliefs, and attitudes of the society. When the international manager fully comprehends his or her own culture, as well as that of the country into which the business plans to expand, the manager can be certain of not unconsciously expecting the foreign nationals to behave like the "normal" people of his or her own culture. The manager must recognize the cultural imperatives abroad, making appropriate changes in his or her own interpersonal behavior and managerial practices.

In this chapter, we shall examine the concept of culture and the value orientations that are typical of American and most Western societies. We shall study how these value orientations differ from those of non-Western societies and how problems occur when the diverse Western and non-Western value orientations interact with each other as people from these cultures come face to face.

A manager living abroad needs a framework in which to analyze and understand the differences between his or her own culture and that of the host society. We shall examine two frameworks for evaluating cultural differences. Before we go on with our study of culture in international management, let us first take a test. Look at *Practical Insight 6-1* and answer the questions that test your understanding of cultural differences.

PRACTICAL INSIGHT 6-1
Are You World Wise?

Going Global? Before you buy your plane tickets, test your business etiquette knowledge (some questions have more than one answer):

1. During business meetings, use first names in:
   a) Great Britain, because everyone is oh, so chummy.
   b) Australia, because informality is the rule.
   c) China, because the first name is the surname.
   d) Japan, because the last names are easy to mispronounce.

2. In China, offer expensive gifts to your hosts:
   a) Every time they ask for one.
   b) When you need help getting out of the country.
   c) Never—if they can't reciprocate, they'll lose face.

3. In which country is a business card an object of respect?
   a) Japan: An executive's identity depends on his employer.
   b) Taiwan: It explains a person's rank and status.
   c) France: Especially cards describing a man's mistress.

4. When doing business in Japan, never:
   a) Touch someone.
   b) Leave your chopsticks in the rice.
   c) Take people to pricier restaurants than they took you.
   d) All of the above.

PRACTICAL INSIGHT 6-1 *(continued)*

5. Power breakfasts are inappropriate in all but:

   a) Italy: They like to bring the family along.
   b) Mexico: They don't bother to get to work till 10 a.m. anyway.
   c) United States: We invented them.
   d) France: They're at their most argumentative in the morning.

6. In some countries, colors are key. Which is true?

   a) For Koreans, writing a person's name in red signifies death.
   b) In China and Japan, gifts wrapped in white or black should only be presented at funerals.
   c) Purple suits in Great Britain represent lack of taste.

7. Which of these choices are obscene gestures?

   a) The okay sign in Brazil.
   b) A hearty slap on the back in Switzerland.
   c) Doing anything with the left hand in Saudi Arabia.
   d) Thumb between second and third finger in Japan.

Answers: 1-b, c; 2-c; 3-a, b; 4-d; 5-c; 6-a, b; 7-a, c, d

Source: Business World, May 1990, p. 27.

THE MEANING OF CULTURE

There are as many definitions of culture as there are books in anthropology. Culture is the way of life of a group of people. It is "that complex whole which includes knowledge, belief, art, morals, customs, and any other capabilities and habits acquired by man as a member of society."[4] In other words, it is the distinctive way of life of a group of people; their complete design for living.[5] A person is not born with a given culture; rather, he or she acquires it through the socialization process that begins at birth. An American is not born with a liking for hot dogs, or a German with a natural preference for beer; these behavioral attributes are culturally transmitted.

Dressler and Carns list the following characteristics of culture:

1. Culture exists in the minds of individual human beings who have learned it in their past associations with other human beings, and who use it to guide their own continuing interaction with others.

2. Human cultures vary considerably, one from another.

3. Although different in some respects, cultures resemble one another to a considerable extent.

4. Once a culture has been learned and accepted, it tends to persist.

5. All cultures are gradually and continuously being changed, even though human beings tend to resist these changes.

6. Different individuals of the same society may behave differently in response to a given situation, even though all have internalized certain elements of the same culture.

7. No person can escape entirely from his culture.[6]

Dressler and Carns also offer the following as functions of culture:

1. Culture enables us to communicate with others through a language that we have learned and that we share in common.

2. Culture makes it possible to anticipate how others in our society are likely to respond to our actions.

3. Culture gives standards for distinguishing between what is considered right and wrong, beautiful and ugly, reasonable and unreasonable, tragic and humorous, safe and dangerous.

4. Culture provides the knowledge and skill necessary for meeting sustenance needs.

5. Culture enables us to identify with others; that is, include ourselves in the same category with other people of similar background.[7]

CRITICAL CULTURAL VALUE DIFFERENCES

The nature of most of the problems encountered by international managers abroad may be perceived as this: a conflict exists between the basic values held by two or more groups of people. The problems and misunderstandings occur because of the ethnocentric attitudes of members of each group, who take for granted that their values, especially those that tend to be acted on unconsciously, are correct and indeed best. In the following section, we shall identify and discuss some specific values held by Americans which frequently are at odds with those of people of other cultures. These values may not be characteristic of all Americans—after all, America is considered the melting pot of many different cultures and nationalities—but they do represent values common to many Americans and tend to distinguish the United States culture from other contemporary cultures.

Individualism

Individualism describes the attitude of independence of a person who feels a large degree of freedom in the conduct of his or her personal life. In American culture, this individualism may motivate personal accomplishment, and self-expression is considered to be of the greatest worth. By contrast, individualism is not considered important in other cultures. In the Chinese and Japanese cultures, the group is preeminent in social life; so conformity and cooperation are values that rank higher than individualism. Individual successes or failures are shared by the family, clan, or community.

No country in the world exemplifies the characteristics of "groupism" better than Japan. We can speak of Japan as a country whose society could be organized into several concentric circles. The outer circle consists of Japanese society at large with its long history and the feudal traditions of the Shogun Dynasties. Historically, Japan has been an isolated country. Until the fifteenth century, Japan was insulated from foreign influence by the natural barrier of its surrounding seas. In spite of the dramatic changes in the rest of the world brought about by the maritime power of Western countries, the political policies of the Tokugawa Shogunate kept foreigners out of the country. Until the mid-nineteenth century, Japan was the country least influenced by western

CHAPTER SIX

European culture. Its maritime barriers not only kept foreigners out, they also prevented people from leaving the country. The mountains in Japan made travel difficult within the country, which in turn led to the further isolation of social groups.

Because of the mountains, only 10 percent of the land can be cultivated. So, if one uses people per square mile of arable land as a measure, Japan is the most densely populated country in the world. Thus, isolation from the outside world and crowding inside the country have contributed to making the Japanese into a tightly knit, organized society that places a high value on obedience, cooperation, and interpersonal and group harmony, and which abhors the independence, equality, and individuality that are so characteristic of American society.[8]

Within the outer circle—consisting of the Japanese social structure—lies an inner concentric circle consisting of the various social groups and institutions in Japanese society. These groups include the family and other organized groups such as business groups, labor unions, governmental agencies, political parties, consumer groups, and so on. The societal values that put a high premium on cooperation and collaboration encourage the social groups in the inner circle to work together in a collaborative mode for the good of Japanese society at large. It is precisely because of the high premium placed on collective behavior that one sees such a high degree of collaboration between the government, business firms, labor unions, and financial institutions in Japan. The objective of this collaboration is to fight against a common "enemy" of Japan, which in contemporary terms means the other nations of the world with whom Japan competes for world dominance.

One also sees this collaboration principle in almost all companies and in all industries in Japan. For example, the labor unions in Japan are not adversarial in nature as they are in the United States. Trade unions in the United States cut across company boundaries, while in Japan labor unions are predominantly company unions, with each company having its own separate labor union. In such a labor union, the loyalty of the members is to the company to which they belong and not to a union that transcends company boundaries. The objective of union leadership in Japan is to promote harmony in labor-management relations and to work things out amicably. Consequently, the number of man-days lost to strikes or labor unrest in Japan are minuscule compared to the number lost in the United States, which amount to thousands of man-days per year. The loyalty of the Japanese worker is to her or his group, and it also extends to the company, which is the larger group to which she or he belongs. In return, the company shows loyalty to its employees by treating them as members of a family, providing them with long-term and often life-long employment.

An enlightening example of the groupism concept is presented in *Practical Insight 6-2*. It refers to the tradition of enshrining deceased employees in a company memorial, a practice that is unheard of in the United States.

PRACTICAL INSIGHT 6-2
Japanese Companies Keep Employees Together—Even the Dearly Departed

OSAKA, Japan—One gray December day, the president of Asahi Breweries Co. secretly gave hundreds of employees the low-down on the firm's results. But none of them rushed to call their brokers. Where they are, they don't need brokers. Like tens of thousands of other loyal—and deceased—workers in Japan, the names of 673 Asahi employees have been enshrined at a company memorial after their deaths. On the rice-paper pages of a barley-color book, their names, job titles, tenures, and dates of death are meticulously kept by the company. Twice a year or so, Asahi's top executives show up at the two-year-old, 500 million yen ($3.6 million), winged black-marble shrine to install new names and appease their late colleagues' souls with detailed reports on the company's progress.

Common Consciousness

"Workers spend more than half their lives at the company, and we should return their commitment," says Asahi spokesman Noki Izumiya. "One of the unique Japanese characteristics is a common consciousness. We want to preserve it."

And so, as if the exercising together each morning, laboring and drinking together into the night, and playing golf together on weekends weren't enough, more and more Japanese companies now offer their employees eternal corporate togetherness. In most cases, that means having your name included on a permanent record attached to a stone monument.

"It may look unusual to Americans that people belonging to different religions and backgrounds are enshrined in the same monument," says a spokesman for candy company Ezaki Glico Co., which has memorialized 88 employees. "But to be enshrined gives a feeling of relief to Japanese workers. Their spirits can be together always." Employees seem to like the idea. A survey of a few dozen workers at Asahi's main brewery found that five out of six want to spend forever with their coworkers. "I want to leave a footnote showing that I existed in this company," says 28-year-old Kimito Kawamura.

Management experts say shrines foster loyalty. Malcolm Salter, a professor at Harvard University's graduate business school, visited Asahi's shrine and declares the sentiments it fosters "not phony at all." The practice of "honoring and remembering employees is part of the ongoing renewal of the company."

Companies don't expect employees' attitudes to change just because of a shrine. "We aren't expecting employees to appreciate the company for this," says Eiro Hamada, a personnel manager at Kubota Corp., an industrial group that has kept a shrine since 1952. "Our way of thinking is simply to tie what employees of the past have done to what employees today are doing. It is very Japanese."

Actually, it is very Kansai, the region around Osaka. Companies in Tokyo and elsewhere in Japan sometimes help employees' families arrange burial plots. But few have company shrines. The Kansai companies that do pay up to $5 million for them, and memorial services cost as much as $100,000 each year. That may be one reason it's mainly companies with strong earnings, such as Asahi, who keep the shrines. Unlike Asahi, most Japanese companies in this area keep their memorials in Koyasan, a 1,000-year-old Buddhist mission in the lush, steep mountains outside Osaka.

A stroll among the graceful stone memorials is like a walk through an industrial park. There, under the towering Japanese cedars, Matsushita Electric Industrial Co. remembers thousands of its late employees in a rough-hewn granite temple. Embossed on a polished, black-marble slab is a testament to hundreds of Sharp Corp.'s workers. A bronze statue of two uniformed workers marks Nissan Motor Co.'s memorial. Komatsu Ltd., the heavy-equipment maker, is just up the path from a temple to the World War II infantrymen who died in Japan's North Borneo campaign.

PRACTICAL INSIGHT 6-2 *(continued)*

Lavish Designs

What sets the corporate memorials apart from the more traditional temples are their expansive, sometimes lavish, designs. Kirin Brewery Co. boldly displays its trademark mascot, a stylized, mythical animal. And one small technology company's shrine boasts a space rocket. Most peculiarly Japanese of all are the squat stone or wood boxes at the shrine entrances. They are for depositing business cards, meishi in Japanese. "Companies with business relationships will put their meishi in to show that they are thinking of their old business connections," says Taiei Gotoh, a dark-robed, 31-year-old Buddhist priest.

As the local authority on company shrines, Mr. Gotoh also is knowledgeable on recent Japanese corporate history. He remembers, for example, that Matsushita bought a rival refrigerator maker in 1973, because that's when Matsushita took over the smaller company's shrine. He knows how companies are doing because he sits in on the sort of corporate updates that Asahi's president delivers.

Source: Marcus W. Brauchli, *The Wall Street Journal*, July 10, 1989, p. A6. Reprinted by permission of *The Wall Street Journal*, © 1989, Dow Jones & Company, Inc. All Rights Reserved Worldwide.

Informality

The American culture is not one that attaches a great deal of importance to tradition, ceremony, and social rules. This informality has caused serious problems for businesses operating in other cultures. Latin American countries, for example, are extreme cases of a formal society. The Latin American likes pomp and circumstance and is quite at ease with it. He or she likes lavish public receptions and processions and would expect that an outsider would carefully observe all the amenities of personal etiquette and hospitality. An American, when immersed in a culture like this, is likely to feel ill at ease; he or she must take special precautions to avoid appearing blatantly casual and informal in words and deeds in order not to offend the Latin hosts.

Another value related to informality is the American inclination not to "beat around the bush"; to get to the point of the matter in business meetings and conversations. In Saudi Arabia or Latin American countries, however, it is customary to converse first about unrelated matters before embarking on the business discussions for which the meeting was arranged. An American should realize that people of other cultures often feel it is important to get to know one another and develop mutual trust before getting down to business negotiations or problems. Barging straight into the business issue, without the informal small talk at the beginning, may make a Saudi Arabian or Latin American so uncomfortable that the American who insists on such an approach may well not get what he or she came for.

Materialism

The United States has been blessed with abundant natural resources, a fact which seems to have made Americans, in the eyes of foreigners, wasteful in their consumption of both resources and material goods. Visiting foreigners are often astonished to see cars less than ten years old heaped in junkyards. These cars would probably still be on the road in most countries, because other cultures seem more inclined to foster an awareness of the need for conserving resources and preserving material goods. The more wasteful American attitude has been said to arise from the American Frontier philosophy that humans are the masters of nature and should therefore conquer, change, and control nature for the benefit of humankind. This philosophy is at total variance with the philosophies of the people of India, Korea, and Egypt. In India and Korea, worship of nature is part of the religious dogma.

Even for persons for whom religion is not the significant determinant of behavior, the river Ganges in India and the Nile in Egypt are revered for their power over the economic and physical well-being of the people. An American must strive to be aware of the differences between his or her own attitude toward nature and those of other cultures. All of us should be careful not to judge other cultures on the basis of the quality or quantity of physical goods present in daily life.

There is also a tendency in Western cultures to attach status to certain physical objects, such as a suit made by a famous clothing manufacturer or a recent-model car. Many non-Western cultures foster no interest in acquiring such symbols; rather, the emphasis is on finding and enjoying aesthetic and spiritual values. An understanding of these differences in values is important for the international manager, because behavior that may seem strange to an American may be the necessary expression of fundamental values held by a person from a different culture.

Change

Societies differ in their attitudes toward change and progress. Although change is inevitable, non-Western people look upon change as a phenomenon that occurs naturally, and as part of the overall evolution of humans and their universe. Change in such societies is accepted, but passively, without any deliberate effort to bring it about. The people in Western societies, however, feel that the future is not predestined and that humans, by actions and deeds, are capable of manipulating the environment in which they shall live in the future, and of changing it to their liking.

These differences in attitudes toward change may account for the often fatalistic attitude of non-Western people, and their passivity may be partially responsible for the difficulties encountered by Western managers and technicians when introducing innovations into non-Western societies.

Time Orientation

Time can be considered a communication system, as are words or languages. Like different spoken languages, the languages of time are also different. These so-called unspoken languages "are informal, yet the rules governing their interpretation are surprisingly ironbound."[9] Western cultures, and particularly Americans, perceive time as a resource—and an extremely scarce one that is continuously depleting. Americans, therefore, emphasize the efficient use of time. Phrases such as *time is money, time never comes back,* and *time is the enemy* are often used to promote the effective use of time. This orientation is due to the Western belief that there is a limited amount of total time available to a person—that which he or she has from birth to death—and, therefore, one should make the most of it. This perception of time has made Americans conscious of the need for establishing deadlines for work to be done and to stick to them. It also accounts for Americans being very fastidious about making and keeping appointments.

In contrast, Eastern cultures view time as an unlimited and unending resource. For a Hindu, time does not begin at birth nor end at death. Scholars in Hinduism postulate that belief in reincarnation gives life a nontemporal dimension. Time is perceived to be an inexhaustible resource. This attitude towards time makes people in Eastern cultures quite casual about keeping appointments and deadlines, an indifference which makes Americans dealing with them very anxious and frustrated.

In the United States, the time spent waiting outside a person's office beyond the appointed time is seen as a measure of the importance of the person kept waiting. Americans therefore get very upset if they are kept waiting for thirty minutes or more and consider this to be a personal affront. In the Middle East there is no such interpretation; a businessperson may keep a visitor waiting for a long time, but once the businessperson does see the visitor, the interview will last as long as may be necessary to complete the business at hand. But this approach means that the businessperson is likely to keep the next visitor waiting for hours, too.

An excellent and contemporary example of the differences in time orientation is given in the following incident during Secretary of State Warren Christopher's visit to Saudi Arabia.

> Secretary Christopher was on a visit to Saudi Arabia to discuss critical Middle East issues with King Fahd. The King kept his guest waiting more than six hours beyond the expected meeting hour, before meeting him shortly before 10 P.M. Mr. Christopher used the free time to tour the old section of Jedda, rest, and have dinner. The King did apologize for the delay but offered no explanation. The whole incident was written off by the U.S. State Department saying that it was nothing personal and that such things happen all the time in that part of the world.[10]

The above incident would have created a diplomatic furor had it occurred in the United States, England, or probably in any European country.

There are many other value orientations in which Western cultures differ from non-Western cultures. The scope of this chapter does not permit the discussion of every one of them. However, the purpose of the preceding discussion of value orientations was to point out that differences in behavior are due to differences in the value orientations of societies.

PROBLEMS CAUSED BY CULTURAL DIFFERENCES

We have seen that the international manager can face, or cause, many problems in a foreign host country because of cultural differences. This section gives a few examples of problems created by cultural insensitivity. One such example follows: Some years ago, in 1946, an agricultural extension worker introduced a new type of hybrid maize into a community of Spanish American farmers in New Mexico. He was already well known and liked. He was able to demonstrate that the new seed yielded three times as much as the seed the farmers normally planted, and he was certain that he was doing right in persuading them to grow it. They followed his advice, but within three years they had nearly all gone back to growing their old low-yielding variety.

This sounds almost incredible, but it can be explained quite simply. The farmers ate the maize they grew. They ground it into flour, and with the flour, their wives made tortillas, the flat round cakes that formed the staple of their diet. But the new type of maize gave a flavor to the cakes the people did not like. The people valued the high yield but did not like the price they had to pay in taste, and the innovation failed because the agency had overlooked the need to test for taste as well as yield before the seed was given to the farmers.[11]

The preceding example shows the influence of cultural preferences and the difficulties we can encounter if we assume that others have the same tastes as we do, or the same priorities.

The following incident shows the impact of the differences in time orientation. In Western societies, one can suffer severe penalties for not completing work on time, and enjoy significant rewards for meeting work schedules and deadlines. The Western worker feels that he or she is duty bound to keep promises, and believes that his or her reputation will be tarnished for failure to deliver on time. When two persons involved in a business transaction have two totally opposite orientations toward time schedules, a lot of difficulty will result. The following is an example.

> The Middle Eastern peoples are a case in point. Not only is our idea of time schedules not part of Arab life, but the mere mention of a deadline to an Arab is like waving a red flag in front of a bull. In his culture, your emphasis on a deadline has the emotional effect on him that his backing you into a corner and threatening you with a club would have on you.

One effect of this conflict of unconscious habit patterns is that hundreds of American-owned radio sets are lying on the shelves of Arab radio repair shops, untouched. The Americans made the serious cross-cultural error of asking to have the repair completed by a certain time.

How do you cope with this? How does the Arab get another Arab to do anything? Every culture has its own ways of bringing pressure to get results. The usual Arab way is one which Americans avoid as "bad manners." It is needling.

An Arab businessman whose car broke down explained it this way:

> First, I go to the garage and tell the mechanic what is wrong with my car. I wouldn't want to give him the idea that I didn't know. After that, I leave the car and walk around the block. When I come back to the garage, I ask him if he has started to work yet. On my way home for lunch I stop in and ask him how things are going. When I go back to the office I stop by again. In the evening, I return and peer over his shoulder for awhile. If I didn't keep this up, he'd be off working on someone else's car.[12]

Language can also pose a problem for international managers. The problem with language is not just with having to learn a new vocabulary. Many international managers have learned from experience that one word or idiom may have a different meaning and implication in another culture that uses the same language. For example, in the United States, the word "homely" means not attractive, plain, not good-looking or handsome, not elegant or polished. However, in England and India it has a totally different meaning. "Homely" in those countries means a home that is friendly, warm, and hospitable. Students from India and England are therefore advised never to say to their American family hosts: "You have a homely family."

World travellers generally see signs written in languages that are foreign to the host country. One sees signs at airports welcoming tourists that are written in Japanese, Spanish, French, or English. International companies have to translate documents and directions for using various products and operating instructions for machines in a variety of languages. One has only to look at the instructions manuals for electric razors, camcorders, and CD players to see the number of languages that the instructions are written in. And it is sometimes quite amusing to see the choice of words used to communicate in the English language, especially when the product is made by a Chinese or Japanese company. *Practical Insight 6-3* includes several humorous examples of innocent mistakes made by non-English speaking business enterprises in different countries.

PRACTICAL INSIGHT 6-3
Signs in English All Over the World

Here are some signs and notices written in English that were discovered throughout the world.

In a Tokyo hotel:
Is forbidden to steal hotel towels please. If you are not a person to do such a thing is please not to read notis.

In a Bucharest hotel lobby:
The lift is being fixed for the next day. During that time we regret that you will be unbearable.

In a Leipzig elevator:
Do not enter lift backwards, and only when lit up.

In a Belgrade hotel elevator:
To move the cabin, push button wishing floor. If the cabin should enter more persons, each one should press a number of wishing floor. Driving is then going alphabetically by national order.

In a Paris hotel elevator:
Please leave your values at the front desk.

In a hotel in Athens:
Visitors are expected to complain at the office between the hours of 9 and 11 A.M. daily.

In a Yugoslavian hotel:
The flattening of underwear with pleasure is the job of the chambermaid.

In a Japanese hotel:
You are invited to take advantage of the chambermaid.

In the lobby of a Moscow hotel across from Russian Orthodox monastery:
You are welcome to visit the cemetery where famous Russian and Soviet composers, artists and writers are buried daily except Thursday.

In an Austrian hotel catering to skiers:
Not to perambulate the corridors during the hours of repose in the boots of ascension.

On the menu of a Swiss restaurant:
Our wines leave you nothing to hope for.

On the menu of a Polish hotel:
Salad a firms' own make; limpid red beet soup with cheesy dumplings in the form of a finger; roasted duck let loose; beef rashers beaten up in the country people's fashion.

Outside a Hong Kong tailor shop:
Ladies may have a fit upstairs.

In a Bangkok dry cleaners:
Drop your trousers here for best results.

Outside a Paris dress shop:
Dresses for street walking.

In a Rhodes tailor shop:
Order your summer suit. Because is big rush we will execute customers in strict rotation.

PRACTICAL INSIGHT 6-3 *(continued)*

From the **Soviet Weekly:**
There will be a Moscow Exhibition of Arts by 150,000 Soviet Republic painters and sculptors. These were executed over the past two years.

A sign posted in Germany's Black Forest:
It is strictly forbidden on our black forest camping site that people of different sex, for instance, men and women, live together in one tent unless they are married with each other for that purpose.

In a Zurich hotel:
Because of the impropriety of entertaining guests of the opposite sex in the bedroom, it is suggested that the lobby be used for this purpose.

In an advertisement by a Hong Kong dentist:
Teeth extracted by the latest Methodists.

In a Rome laundry:
Ladies, leave your clothes here and spend the afternoon having a good time.

In a Czechoslovakian tourist agency:
Take one of our horse-driven city tours—we guarantee no miscarriages.

Advertisement for donkey rides in Thailand:
Would you like to ride on your own ass?

In a Swiss mountain inn:
Special today—no ice cream.

In a Copenhagen airline ticket office:
We take your bags and send them in all directions.

On the door of a Moscow hotel room:
If this is your first visit to the USSR, you are welcome to it.

In a Norwegian cocktail lounge:
Ladies are requested not have children in the bar.

In a Budapest zoo:
Please do not feed the animals. If you have any suitable food, give it to the guard on duty.

In the office of a Roman doctor:
Specialist in women and other diseases.

In an Acapulco hotel:
The manager has personally passed away all the water served here.

In a Tokyo shop:
Our nylons cost more than common, but you'll find they are best in the long run.

From a Japanese information booklet about using a hotel air conditioner:
Cooles and Heates: If you want just condition of warm in your room, please control yourself.

PRACTICAL INSIGHT 6-3 *(continued)*

===

From a brochure of a car rental firm in Tokyo:
When passenger of foot heave in sight, tootle the horn. Trumpet him melodiously at first, but if he still obstacles your passage then tootle him with vigor.
Two signs from a Majorcan shop entrance:
English well speaking
Here speeching American.

Source: From an AIR FRANCE BULLETIN, December 1, 1989.

The phrase *come any time* can have different interpretations: Visiting time involves the question of who sets the time for a visit. George Coelho, a social psychologist from India, gives an illustrative case. A U.S. businessman received this invitation from an Indian businessman: "Won't you and your family come and see us? Come any time." Several weeks later, the Indian repeated the invitation in the same words. Each time the American replied that he would certainly like to drop in, but he never did. The reason is obvious in terms of our culture. In America, *come any time* is just an expression of friendliness. You are not really expected to show up unless your host proposes a specific time. In India, on the contrary, the words are meant literally that the host is putting himself at the disposal of his guest and really expects him to come. It is the essence of politeness to leave it to the guest to set a time at his convenience. If the guest never comes, the Indian naturally assumes that he does not want to come. Such a misunderstanding can lead to a serious rift between people who are trying to do business with each other.[13]

American brand names can also take on strange meanings when translated into a foreign language. American Motors' Matador became *killer* in Spanish. Ford's problems with the Spanish language are also well known. Its low-cost truck Fiera, when translated into the Spanish language, meant *ugly old woman*. Similarly, Fresca soft drinks in Mexico did not do too well; there the word is slang for *lesbian*. And the famous Pepsi-Cola slogan *Come alive with Pepsi* was translated in Germany as *Come out of the grave* and in Taiwan as *Bring your ancestors back from the dead*. More recently, Goodyear expanded its Servitekar tire specialty stores from Indonesia and Malaysia into Japan, and found customers snickering. It seems that the word means *rusty car* when pronounced in Japanese.[14]

The experience of Federal Express when it first entered the European market illustrates the problems that ethnocentric attitudes can create for global companies. Federal encountered serious problems breaking into the European market, partly because it had not done its homework regarding how people there live and work. For instance, all company brochures, promotional material, and shipping bills were in English. And to keep arrival times constant, package pickup deadlines were set for 5:00 p.m. even though the Spanish, for example, work as late as 8:00 p.m. Federal had assumed that lifestyles and work schedules were the same in Europe as in the United States, and that was a big mistake.[15]

Cross-national joint ventures, mergers, and acquisitions are being forged with increasing frequency in today's global economy. One sees such "marriages" between companies from diverse cultures when, for example, a Japanese company forms an alliance with an American company. Sometimes such alliances between companies having quite different cultures can cause problems when executives from the companies involved begin to work in teams. A good illustration of this point is the acquisition of the American company, Firestone Tire & Rubber Company, by the Japanese tire giant, Bridgestone Corporation. Cultural differences between the Japanese and American managers, especially regarding language and the difficulties in adjusting to two different styles of work, caused major problems. The Japanese, who are used to working until 9:00 p.m., could not understand why the Americans would not stay that late, and the Americans could not get used to Japanese arrangements, such as open offices and desks facing each other.[16]

In the American culture, it is generally expected that when a manager asks her or his subordinate if a task could be completed by a certain date, the latter will say yes or no and give the reasons why if the answer is no. But once the subordinate has agreed to complete the task on time, she or he is expected to abide by the promise. Western society emphasizes the value of truthfulness in interpersonal behavior. However, in Egypt, Pakistan, or India a person is likely to make a promise to do something while knowing quite well that it cannot be kept. The reluctance to say no to a request is due to the person's reluctance to displease someone with a negative answer, and also to save the embarrassment of having to admit that one is incapable of doing what she or he has been asked to do.

The war against Iraq in 1991 involved many American soldiers in the Allied effort to drive Saddam Hussein out of Kuwait. Most foreign troops in the Allied effort were stationed in Saudi Arabia. Saudi Arabia is a very conservative Islamic country, home to some of the holiest places of Islam. In fact, the Koran is the constitution of Saudi Arabia. It is as if the Bible were the Constitution of the United States. Many forms of behavior which would be considered quite normal in Western cultures are totally unacceptable in Saudi Arabia, such as the displaying of affection between the sexes in public, displaying the sole of one's shoe while crossing one's legs, dancing in public, driving by women in public, and the exposing by women of their legs, neck, and arms. Consequently, American soldiers in Saudi Arabia were given a crash course in the etiquette and social customs of that country. An illustration of the cultural background training which was given to American soldiers is illustrated in *Practical Insight 6-4.*

PRACTICAL INSIGHT 6-4
In Preparation for Joint Saudi-U.S. Exercises, Marines Get the Word on Kisses and Crucifixes

NORTHERN SAUDI ARABIA—Silver crucifixes gleaming on the collar of his camouflage fatigues, Chaplain Stan Scott paces the sand before a group of U.S. Marines. The men, squatting in the sun with their M-16s beside them, listen raptly as the chaplain gives what he calls "a down and dirty on 2,000 years of history." In just over an hour, his talk sweeps from the caravans of ancient Arabia to the contemporary mores of Saudi society. Topics include table manners ("If you've had enough coffee, wiggle your cup. Don't put your hand over it or he'll just keep pouring and you'll end up with a burned hand"), women's veils ("You may see it as a bummer but for them there's prestige that goes with it"), and dissatisfaction with colonially drawn borders ("The Arabs do have some gripes out here").

Too Close for Comfort

To show how Arab men traditionally greet their friends, he hauls a burly Marine out of the front row, kisses him three times on the cheek and locks him in a tight embrace. "You feeling comfortable now?" he asks. The Marine's eyes roll in embarrassment. "We have a bubble of

PRACTICAL INSIGHT 6-4 *(continued)*

privacy," he says. "The Saudis don't have that. Male embracing and hand-holding don't have sexual overtones. Don't impose on this culture your indicators of homosexuality."

Chaplain Scott is giving this talk because these troops, the weapons company of the First Battalion, Third Marine Regiment, are about to move north for five days of combined training with Saudi forces. Three months into the Gulf crisis, such exercises are still extremely rare among ground forces. Most U.S. troops have yet to meet a Saudi. With Arab forces—mostly Saudis, with some Egyptians, Kuwaitis, Moroccans, and Syrians—stationed close to the northern border, chances are that in an initial battle some would have to pass through U.S. lines. Confusion, as U.S. troops tried to tell Arab allies from enemies, could cost lives. "So far, U.S. Marines have had some limited training with Saudi marines and national guardsmen," says Brig. Gen. Thomas Draude, assistant division commander. "But combined training has taken a back seat so far in the rush to get U.S. troops deployed."

"The Saudis are very patient about organizing combined exercises," says Capt. Michael Callaghan, whose troops are taking part in this week's training. "We don't want to rush into anything overambitious and offend their sensibilities."

Mistaken Intentions

The few U.S. troops who have so far met Saudis have found that that's quite easy to do. One Marine private recently shared guard duty with a Saudi soldier. Touched by the Saudi's generosity in sharing his food and water, the Marine tried to reciprocate by showing him a magazine with a picture of a woman in a bathing suit. "He said 'no, no' and looked real embarrassed," the Marine recalls.

The chaplain's briefing is meant to head off such misunderstandings. To explain the Saudis' approach to women, the chaplain tells an anecdote from his earlier tour of duty in the country between 1979 and 1982. His wife, he said, would get offended when the landlord would come with workmen to fix something in the apartment and pass by her at the door without speaking. "She'd tell me when I got home, 'That son of a gun can't even be polite enough to say good morning.'" In fact, Chaplain Scott explains to the troops, the landlord was being very polite by not presuming to invade her privacy by speaking to her without her husband present. "He was honoring her the best way he knew how."

As a further gesture to Saudi sensitivities, the company has checked its prepacked meal rations to be sure that no pork or ham entrees are included in supplies being taken north.

But a few Marines think all this sensitivity is too much. Michael Austin, a 25-year-old corporal from Elgin, Ill., asks why Marines were told not to wear crucifixes. "I don't see how any man should be asked to hide his faith," he says.

Chaplain Scott explains that Marines can wear their crosses so long as they wear them under their T-shirts. He adds that Saudis adhere to an especially strict branch of Islam and feel special responsibilities as custodians of Islam's two holiest mosques in Mecca and Medina.

"The concessions that this country has made to allow me to be here are phenomenal," says the chaplain, who wasn't permitted to wear his crosses on his uniform nor to openly identify himself as a clergyman on previous visits to Saudi Arabia. "You might not see it," he tells the troops, "but I see it as a tremendous step forward in religious dialogue."

Source: Geraldine Brooks, *The Wall Street Journal*, October 10, 1990, p. A16. Reprinted by permission of *The Wall Street Journal*, © 1990, Dow Jones & Company, Inc. All Rights Reserved Worldwide.

ANALYZING CULTURAL DIFFERENCES

An international manager needs a conceptual scheme to analyze cultural differences between his native culture and the foreign culture. One approach that may be useful in identifying the various dimensions along which cultural differences can be measured was developed by Geert Hofstede,[17] who undertook an enormous questionnaire survey of 117,000 IBM employees in 88 countries. His study found that national cultures can be differentiated along four major dimensions:

1. Individualism/Collectivism

2. Masculinity/Femininity

3. Power Distance

4. Uncertainty Avoidance

A fifth dimension, called "Confucian Dynamism," was identified by Michael H. Bond.

Individualism/Collectivism

Individualism exists when people look at themselves primarily as individuals and secondarily as members of groups. Self-interest motivates behavior, and everyone is expected to look after themselves and their immediate families. *Collectivism* is the opposite of individualism. In collectivist societies, people see themselves primarily as members of groups and secondarily as individuals. The group (family, clan, tribe, organization, social club) is the main determinant of individual beliefs and values. The United States is supposed to have an individualistic culture, whereas Japan is said to have a collectivist culture.

Masculinity/Femininity

Masculine cultures emphasize assertiveness and the acquisition of money and things as opposed to a concern for people. *Feminine* cultures have dominant values that emphasize concern for others and relationships with people. Masculine cultures, like macho men, are supposed to be tough and assertive. Feminine cultures, like tender females, are supposed to be gentle and caring of the feelings of others and with the quality of life. Masculine societies define gender roles more rigidly than do feminine societies; e.g., feminine societies would be far more accepting than masculine societies of women driving trucks and of men as nurses or ballet dancers. Japan, Mexico, and Italy scored high on the masculinity scale in Hofstede's study, with Japan scoring the highest points. Norway, Finland, Sweden, and Denmark scored high on the femininity scale.

Power Distance

Power distance is a measure of the extent to which those who have less power in society accept that power is distributed unequally among members of the society, and therefore some members of the society have the "right" to have more power than others. For example, in high power distance countries such as India, Mexico, and Brazil, employees accept the concept that the boss must be obeyed because he/she is the boss with the right to issue orders. In contrast, in low power distance countries such as the United States, Australia, and Denmark, employees would tend to obey the boss only if they believe that he/she has the competence to make the right decisions, or that the boss' way is the right way to get things done.

Uncertainty Avoidance

Uncertainty avoidance measures the extent to which a culture programs its members to feel either uncomfortable or comfortable in unstructured situations. People in high uncertainty avoidance cultures feel threatened by risky, uncertain, or unknown situations. Uncertainty avoidance cultures try to minimize the possibility of such situations by establishing strict laws and rules, high degrees of formalization, and intolerance of behaviors and opinions that differ from their own. Countries such as Japan, Argentina, Italy, and Israel scored high on the uncertainty avoidance scale in Hofstede's study. Countries scoring low on this dimension included the United States, Great Britain, Sweden, and Denmark.

Confucian Dynamism

Michael Bond, of the Chinese University of Hong Kong, has identified a new, fifth cultural dimension that he calls Confucian dynamism, which was not identified by Hofstede in his IBM study. Bond identified this cultural dimension in his Chinese Value Survey that was administered to 50 male and 50 female students in a variety of disciplines in each of 22 countries selected from all five continents.[18]

"Confucian dynamism is an acceptance of the legitimacy of hierarchy and the valuing of perseverance and thrift, all without undue emphasis on tradition and social obligations which could impede business initiative."[19] The study showed that four of the Five Dragons—Hong Kong, Taiwan, Japan, and South Korea—scored the top positions on the Confucian dynamism scale. Brazil, India, Thailand, and Singapore got the next highest scores. The Netherlands, Sweden, and West Germany took the middle positions. The English-speaking countries of Australia, New Zealand, the United States, Britain, and Canada scored on the lower end, as did Zimbabwe, Nigeria, the Philippines, and Pakistan.[20]

A very intriguing finding of the study was the relationship between the prevalence of Confucian dynamism in the culture of a country and its economic growth. Employing two samples of 18 and 20 countries and economic growth data for the periods 1965-80 and 1980-87, the results of the study showed that Confucian dynamism had the most consistent explanatory power for most of the differences in national economic growth rates. Confucian dynamism appears to explain the relative success of the East Asian economies of Hong Kong, Taiwan, Japan, and South Korea.[21]

Managerial Implications of Cultural Dimensions

One would expect many consequences for management practices resulting from cultural differences along Hofstede's four dimensions discussed previously. For instance, in high power distance countries a leader characterized as a benevolent autocrat would be most effective, whereas in low power distance countries a leader who is people-oriented and participative in his leadership style would be most effective.

In countries that are high on individualism, the most appropriate reward system would reward individuals for their own performance (as opposed to group performance). Competition between individuals for monetary and nonmonetary rewards, such as status and promotions, would be encouraged. In collectivist societies, rewards to individuals based upon the performance of their group would be most appropriate. Yearly bonuses based upon the profitability of the whole company, or divisional profits, are illustrative of group performance-based rewards.

Countries characterized by masculine cultures expect women to play certain roles, such as staying home and taking care of the children, or working as nurses or secretaries. Japan, which has a masculine culture, has the reputation for a very low "glass ceiling" for women. It is not uncommon in Japan to see women get fired because of marriage. And women in Japan are not expected to assume responsible managerial positions at any time. Similar conditions exist in Italy and Mexico, both of which are known for their "macho" men. In feminine cultures like Sweden, Finland, Norway, and Denmark, women have equal status with men. This is reflected in the societal expectation that women should work, and businesses are required to make this easier for women by providing both men and women with paid paternity or maternity leave to take care of newborn children.

In high uncertainty avoidance cultures, one finds organizations that have clearly formulated rules and procedures which reduce uncertainty about what should be done in certain circumstances, what is acceptable or unacceptable behavior, and so on. People in such cultures appreciate stability and the certainty that accompanies it. Hence, one finds that in such cultures people do not change jobs readily, but prefer to stay with a company for their entire career. This is typical of Japan and Italy, which are high uncertainty avoidance countries. Low uncertainty avoidance countries, such as the United States and Great Britain, favor organizations that provide managers with freedom to take prudent risks. These countries are also known for very high rates of job mobility.

Another approach to understanding cultural differences is that which has been developed by Herskovits.[22] He lists five dimensions of culture:

1. Material Culture
2. Social Institutions
3. Man and the Universe
4. Aesthetics
5. Language

Material Culture

Material culture affects the level of demand for goods and the quality and types of products demanded. It is composed of two aspects: technology and economics. Technology refers to the techniques used to produce material goods, as well as the technical know-how of a country. Economics can be described as the manner in which a culture makes use of its capabilities, and the resulting benefits. A multinational company involved in selling electrical appliances, for example, should analyze the material culture of the proposed foreign market. For instance, a firm may be able to sell microwave ovens in England and France, but will find few buyers in New Guinea. It would be good to be able to anticipate that outcome by understanding the material cultures of the three nations.

Social Institutions

Social institutions—whether they be of a business, political, family, or social-class nature—influence the behavior of individuals. An American in Japan, for example, must recognize that in Japan, social institutions favor a paternalistic leadership style and decision making that is by nature participative and consensus-oriented. In India, a fair amount of nepotism is a feature of the joint-family system.

Man and the Universe

This dimension is composed of the elements of religion and superstitions, both of which have a profound impact on the value and belief systems of individuals. Making light of superstitions when doing business with other cultures may prove to be an expensive mistake. In parts of Asia, for example, ghosts, fortune telling, palmistry, and soothsayers are all integral parts of the culture and must be understood as being influential in people's lives and in business dealings as well.

In the United States and many Western countries, the owl is a symbol of wisdom. Temple University in Philadelphia has an owl as its mascot. Temple University has several campuses abroad in places such as Tokyo, London, and Rome. Should Temple decide to open yet another campus in Bombay, India, it may well have to change its mascot, at least for its India campus, and in all of its advertisements and publications sent to India. In many parts of India the owl is looked upon as a symbol of death. Superstitions are quite pervasive in the Chinese culture as well. As you will see in *Practical Insight 6-5*, numbers have a very special meaning—good or bad—depending upon the particular number or combination of numbers being considered.

PRACTICAL INSIGHT 6-5
By the Numbers Superstition Is Bottom Line for Some Chinese

Emblazoned in three-foot-high characters on the side of a medical office building in Monterey Park are the numbers 941-943. The numbers are merely the building's address, but when the numerals 9, 4, 1, 3 are pronounced in Mandarin or Cantonese dialects, they sound like a common Chinese saying: "Nine die; one lives." "It means the possibility of surviving is almost zero," said one real estate agent, shaking his head in disbelief. "Imagine a medical building with that number? I won't even mention the property to a client."

Now consider the BMW 528e, that trendy symbol of the American yuppie. In Cantonese, the model number is easily recognizable as the phrase: "Not easy to prosper." The first two digits of the Volvo 240 have the even more horrifying pronunciation: "Easy to die." "They're not popular cars" among Chinese, said Gregory Tse, owner of Wing On Realty in Monterey Park, the only city in the nation with a majority Asian population.

Such is the world of Chinese numerology, an amalgam of linguistic coincidences and age-old superstitions from the Far East that is exerting a quirky effect on American life in places where Asians have settled. The superstition has influenced choices on buying cars, selecting telephone numbers, picking lucky Lotto combinations, and even determining wedding dates.

But nowhere has it had a more far-reaching effect than in the world of commercial and residential real estate, especially in the San Gabriel Valley with its burgeoning Chinese population. Real estate agents say fear of the number four, which, when translated, sounds like the word "death," and the popularity of the number eight, which sounds like "prosperity," have become factors in the marketplace. Some deals have dangled in escrow waiting for a lucky date to close, prices have been determined by the number of eights in the final figure, and even hardened investors have become squeamish when a property has the number four in its address.

While many Chinese speakers are aware of the superstition, only some actually believe it.

Double Meaning Recognized

For example, in the Monterey Park building on 941-943 South Atlantic Boulevard, two of the eight offices are rented to Chinese. Yu Dafang, an acupuncturist who has an office in the building, said he recognized the double meaning of the address the minute he saw it, but decided it was unimportant. "At first, people said things, but not anymore," he said. "It's not polite."

Nonetheless, awareness about the effect of the superstition has spread to the point where even non-Chinese are now watching their numbers.

Last year, Toni Foster-Quiroz, president of Cosmic Escrow Corp. in Monterey Park, opened a new office on Garvey Avenue. One of the first things she did was pay the city $500 to change the building's address from 114 to 116 to remove the number four. "I don't believe it, but if it makes my clients feel better about coming here, it's OK with me," she said: "It gives us a little edge."

The key to the superstition lies in the tonal nature of Chinese in which one pronunciation can have many meanings depending on which tone is used. Mandarin, the dialect spoken by those from Taiwan and parts of mainland China, has four tones. Cantonese, the dialect of Hong Kong and Guangdong province, has nine.

The Cantonese, by most accounts, are the main followers of the superstitions. In that dialect, every digit except seven and zero has a clear dual meaning. The number one is the same as "certainly," two is "easy," three is "life, birth, or to do business," four is "death," five is "no or not," six is "happiness, wealth, or continuous," eight is "prosperity," and nine is "long lasting."

The fascination with numbers is more extensive in Hong Kong, Taiwan, Singapore, and other parts of Asia. In Singapore properties are sometimes offered at a discount because of unlucky addresses, and in Hong Kong vehicle license plates with lucky numbers, which are competitively bid, can cost thousands of dollars to obtain.

The most notorious of the numbers is four, and some buildings such as the Bank of Trade building in Chinatown have no fourth floor just because of the connotation of death. Woe be to the person with the address of 14, which sounds like the phrase: "certain death." The number 24 is a slight improvement, "easy to die." Watch out for 424, which in Mandarin is pronounced in the same way as "die and die again."

Just having four anywhere in an address can be unsettling. Three years ago, architect C. K. Moh bought a rental house in Monterey Park with the address 434. Moh said he was not worried about the address when he bought the property but later paid the city $500 to have it changed to 438 after he became involved in a lawsuit related to the property. "I don't really believe in it, but, well, I'm trying to avoid bad luck," he said. "I'm playing it safe."

City officials in Monterey Park report they receive two or three requests a month for address changes. The vast majority of applicants, who pay $500 for the service, are Chinese. Arcadia gets about 40 requests a month, all of which are futile because the City Council about two years ago banned address changes, said Joseph Lopez, director of public works. "There was such a large volume of requests," Lopez said. "If we made a change for every request, it would really create an intolerable work load."

Four can be lucky in certain combinations, such as the number 154, which sounds like the phrase: "No way to die." Likewise, the pronunciation of the number 148 closely resembles: "A lifetime of prosperity."

Eight is by far the most sought-after number, and the arrival of Aug. 8 last year—8/8/88—sparked a flurry of weddings, banquets, and Lotto purchases in areas with large Chinese populations, such as San Francisco and Los Angeles.

The reputation of the number is such that some sales people have latched onto it as a gimmick to attract Chinese buyers. Georgene Neely, a San Marino real estate agent, said she has noticed in recent years that more home sellers are using the number in asking prices, such as a house that was recently on the market for $988,000. "It's an obvious ploy to appeal to the foreign buyer,"

PRACTICAL INSIGHT 6-5 *(continued)*

she said, adding that she views the practice as unprofessional. Neely said buyers also have asked to add the number eight to real estate prices for good luck, such as a recent lease agreement involving several thousand dollars in which the tenant added $1.88 to the final figure.

But these digits are the easy cases. The meanings of other combinations can be open to a wide range of interpretation. Numbers that sound one way in one dialect can sound entirely different in another.

Take the number 169. Mandarin speakers would shrug their shoulders, but to a Cantonese, "It's one of the worst numbers you can have," said Valiant Chiu, the head of Garfield Realty in Monterey Park. The number is pronounced like an obscene slang term.

How much effect all this really has on business is uncertain. Richard Brooks, spokesman for BMW of North America Inc., said he was unaware of the meaning of the BMW 528e, which coincidentally was discontinued last year. But George Sarrade, sales manager of Century Motor Sales, a major BMW dealership in Alhambra, said he has noticed that the dealership has sold few 528e models to Chinese. "Son of a gun," he said. "It might have something to do with that."

Most real estate agents say superstition's power to affect the market has been blown way out of proportion. Jimmy Shen, manager of Huntington Realty in San Marino, said a good house at a good price will always sell no matter how bad the number. Shen, for example, lives in a house with the street number 404. "It's been a lucky number for me," he said. "I don't even care. This is America."

Tse of Wing On Realty agreed that the superstition plays only a small role in business. "It's minor," he said. To prove his point, Tse mentions the recent sale of a house with the street number 664—a terribly inauspicious number that sounds like the phrase: "continuous death." "We just cleared escrow on the house," he said. Only later does he explain that the sale to a Chinese family was contingent on changing the address from 664 to 662, which means "always easy."

Number Superstitions

In various Chinese dialects, some numbers sound like threatening phrases. Houses with such numbers may be considered unlucky; cars with such numbers may be shunned. On the other hand, the number 8 sounds lucky. Here are a few numbers and their "translations" in Chinese:

In English	In a Chinese Dialect
9,4,1,3	"nine die; one lives"
(BMW)528	"not easy to prosper"
4	"death"
8	"prosperity"
14	"certain death"
424	"die and die again"
154	"no way to die"
148	"a lifetime of prosperity"
664	"continuous death"

Source: Ashley Dunn, *Los Angeles Times*, May 28, 1989, pp. 12, 19. © 1989, The Los Angeles Times. Reprinted by permission.

Aesthetics

This category includes the art, folklore, music, and drama of a culture. The aesthetics of a particular culture can be important in the interpretation of symbolic meanings of various artistic expressions. Failure to correctly interpret symbolic values can be problematic for multinational companies. For instance, folklore has established the owl as a symbol of bad luck in India, so clearly the owl should not be used in advertising.

Language

Of all the cultural elements that an international manager must study, language is probably the most difficult. One needs more than the ability to speak a language; one also needs the competency to recognize idiomatic interpretations that are quite different from those found in the dictionary. Thus, the international manager cannot take for granted that he or she is always communicating effectively in another language. Small nuances of the local tongue may elude a foreigner who has not been immersed in the foreign culture for a long time.

Religion

To the list compiled by Herskovits we could add one more category—religion. We saw that religion can reasonably be considered a part of the man-and-the-universe dimension, but it could well be a dimension by itself, especially in cultures in which religion is a central, organizational feature. Religion in such societies has a profound effect on how business is conducted.

For example, international hotel chains in Israel must make sure their business practices conform with the Jewish religious beliefs. Not doing so means risking the loss of rabbinical sanction and, eventually, customers. Hence, on the Jewish Sabbath they program elevators to stop automatically at designated floors so that guests do not have to violate religious proscriptions against pressing the buttons themselves. Rabbinical supervisors inspect their kitchens. And their room service staff will refuse to deliver milk and meat on the same plate or on the same order, even if they are for different guests, because Jewish religious laws prohibit the mixing of dairy products and meat.[23]

Consumption of pork is forbidden by law in Islam and Judaism. Therefore, companies are not able to market hot dogs and sausages containing pork as one of the ingredients in countries where those religions are practiced. Instead, all-beef hot dogs and sausages and beef bacon, already marketed in the United States and Europe to serve the needs of Jewish customers, would have to be introduced in Islamic countries of the Middle East, such as Saudi Arabia, Iraq, and Iran, and in the Southeast Asian countries of Indonesia and Malaysia. *Practical Insight 6-6* discusses problems that fast-food chains like McDonald's have encountered in Israel and India due to religion-based dietary restrictions.

PRACTICAL INSIGHT 6-6
Are You Ready for Kosher Hamburgers, or Burgers Without Beef?

Omri Padan owned a successful chain of clothing stores. But he has given that up just so that he could start a chain of McDonald's hamburger restaurants in his native land. After all, who does not like McDonald's hamburgers? Mr. Padan owns the McDonald's franchise in Israel and he wants to make the "golden arches" a mammoth success in the holy land.

PRACTICAL INSIGHT 6-6 *(continued)*

But there looms on the horizon what could be a potentially big problem—should McDonald's sell kosher or non-kosher hamburgers in the Jewish State? "And what exactly does kosher mean?" is a quandary for Mr. Padan. Because of the sensitivity of the issue, McDonald's executives in Oak Park, Illinois, would rather not talk about it, which will not help Mr. Padan. Mr. Padan is aware that even large segments of the Israeli population who are not Orthodox believers prefer that their food be prepared according to Jewish dietary laws. Of course he knows that Jewish dietary laws do not allow mixing meat and dairy products like milk and cheese, but the term "kosher" has many different interpretations amongst the Israelis. He will therefore conduct surveys to learn how, exactly, Israel's 4.1 million Jews define "kosher."

Mr. Padan knows that his McDonald's restaurants are not obligated to serve kosher fare. There are many non-kosher restaurants across Israel. He has watched Wendy's and Wimpy's chains enter Israel and serve kosher food, and neither has proven to be a huge success. But Mr. Padan is a pragmatic businessman who wants to succeed. He wants his cheeseburgers and milk shakes to be the fast-food of choice of all Israelis.

Mr. Padan appears to have made a pragmatic business decision. The first McDonald's restaurant opened its doors in Israel on October 13, 1993. It serves its traditional and non-kosher menu: hamburgers, cheeseburgers, french fries, and shakes. "Our figure is that 20 percent of Israelis will not enter a non-kosher restaurant, but on the other hand 80 percent will enter this restaurant although it is not kosher," said Jim Skinner, senior vice president of McDonald's International.

However, the situation in India is quite different.

McDonald's In India

The problem for McDonald's in India, as in Israel, is the dietary imperatives imposed by religious beliefs. The Indian government has given McDonald's permission to open 20 restaurants throughout the country. McDonald's is eager to do well in a country of 850 million people with a middle-class population that is larger than that of the United States. However, there is a problem that McDonald's must face head-on. Four out of five Indians are Hindu and eat no beef. Can McDonald's make a beefless hamburger and still call it a Big Mac? It could look at the success of local competitors such as Nirula's, which has 18 restaurants in New Delhi and three in Nepal. Nirula's is "India's McDonald's" says one customer who frequently patronizes the restaurant in busy Connaught Circus in the heart of New Delhi. "Look at their menu," he says. "They serve hamburgers, milk shakes, and cola, just like McDonald's in America." However, the hamburgers at Nirula's are made from ground mutton, not beef. And they are a lot more spicy than the bland version handed out in the typical McDonald's. "Indians like their food a bit more spicy than most Westerners," he says. And they like their hamburgers made of mutton, not beef, thank you!!!

So for the first time ever, McDonald's will exclude beef from its menu. In its Indian franchises, McDonald's instead will serve chicken and fish, as well as vegetable burgers.

Source: Adapted from Clyde Haberman, "Jerusalem Journal: Dishing Up Lunch for a Land That Isn't All Kosher," *The New York Times*, April 16, 1993, p. A4; "A McDonald's Opens in Israel," *The New York Times*, October 14, 1993, p. D15; "In India, Beef-Free Mickey D," *Business Week*, April 17, 1995; and personal observations and experiences of the author in India.

In Christian societies, Sunday is the day of rest, whereas in Islamic countries it is Friday, and in Israel it is Saturday. American executives working in Islamic countries experience a mild culture shock when they are forced to get dressed and go to work on Sunday. This was reported to have happened to many American expatriates who, while working on construction projects in Saudi Arabia, had to get used to violating their own religious precepts of not working on Sundays in order to abide by the religious norms of the host nation.

Islam forbids "excessive" profit, which is considered to be a form of exploitation. Islam preaches moderation and the sharing of wealth with others less fortunate, so individuals are held accountable for the well-being of the community. The concept of sharing wealth is manifested in one form called *zakat*, which is an annual tax of 2.5 percent collected from individuals and used for the benefit of the community. Islam also forbids usury; hence, banks in fundamentalist Islamic nations take equity in financing ventures, sharing profits as well as losses in the joint ventures. The prohibition of usury means that using credit as a marketing tool is not acceptable if the interest charged is deemed to be "excessive" by local standards. Companies operating in such cultures would have to create other forms of selling inducements for the customer, such as discounts for cash transactions and raising prices on products purchased on an installment basis. One would therefore suspect that credit card companies such as MasterCard and VISA, which charge high interest on unpaid balances, would have a difficult time in very orthodox Islamic countries.

Muslims are expected to pray facing the holy city of Mecca five times every day. Western companies in Islamic countries must be aware of this religious ritual and make the necessary adjustments that would allow employees to stop working during prayer time. It is not considered unusual in Saudi Arabia and in contemporary Iran for managers and workers to put a carpet on the floor and kneel to pray several times during a typical work day. Therefore work schedules, meeting times, and sales calls must be planned accordingly.

Our discussion in this chapter concludes this section of the text on the dimensions of the international business environment. Now that we have gained an appreciation for the complexity of the economic, legal, political, and cultural environments facing the international manager, we turn in the next section to the topic of managing effectively in the international context. The first of the seven topics we will cover in this area is that of international business negotiations, an important element of many of the business operations of the international firm.

SUMMARY

In this chapter we focused on the cultural environment of international management. Culture was defined as "that complex whole which includes knowledge, belief, art, morals, customs, and any other capabilities and habits acquired by man as a member of society." It has been emphasized throughout the chapter that most problems facing managers who live abroad are those arising from conflicts between the value orientations of different cultures.

Some specific values held by Americans that frequently conflict with those of peoples of other cultures were discussed: individualism, informality, materialism, attitude toward change, and orientation toward the concept of time. Next, we looked at several illustrations of problems caused by cultural differences. Finally, we considered Hofstede's and Herskovits' frameworks for analyzing cultural differences.

QUESTIONS FOR THOUGHT AND DISCUSSION

1. Why should an international executive understand cultural differences?

2. Even though the United States has been described as a "melting pot," are there any significant differences in the observed behavior of ethnic groups (Italian, Irish, Asian, Polish, German) that can be attributed to cultural differences?

3. Discuss the differences between the following cultural dimensions identified by Hofstede: (a) Individualism/Collectivism, and (b) Masculinity/Femininity.

4. Discuss the following concepts: (a) Power Distance, (b) Uncertainty Avoidance, (c) Confucian Dynamism.

5. Where does the United States rank in comparison with some other countries on each of Hofstede's cultural dimensions?

6. Explain the role of religion in international management.

MINI-CASE

Any Talk of a Baseball Strike Is Foreign to the Japanese

Tokyo—Nobuhisa Ito clutched a little blue book in each hand.

"This one," said Ito, a Japan pro baseball official, raising his left hand, "is the basic agreement that governs baseball in your country. It is a contract between players and owners, yes?"

He lowered that book and lifted the other.

"This one," he said, "governs Japanese baseball. It is a contract, too. But it is a contract between owners of the Central League and owners of the Pacific League. Owners and owners. Not owners and players."

In other words, Marvin Miller (the former director of the American Major League Baseball Players Association) couldn't get to first base here.

"The idea of a players' strike here is inconceivable," said Peter Miller, Marvin's son and the Japanese representative of the Major League Baseball Players Association. "Absolutely inconceivable."

So don't lose any sleep worrying that a strike might someday cancel the Japan Series—this country's version of the World Series, a best-of-seven championship that began yesterday at the Tokyo Dome, pitting the Yomiuri Giants against the Seibu Lions.

To powerless players in Japan, where employers are viewed as benevolent father figures, that notion is as incomprehensible as drive-by shootings. Players here don't demand more money, because to do so, they believe, would be placing their own wishes above the interests of the team.

On the surface, perhaps, player-management relations don't appear much different than they do in America. But scratch a little and you'll discover it's all illusions.

While there is a Japanese players association, it has no authority. "They offer suggestions to the owners," explained Ito. While there is arbitration, it has no teeth. "The impartial arbitrator," said Miller, "is the commissioner." While there is free agency, it's so incredibly restrictive that in 1993, its first year, just four players switched teams. While the average salary is about $420,000, team payrolls are kept secret so negotiating players can't use them for comparison.

"They have no idea about unions, no idea what other shortstops or other center fielders are paid," said Dan Gladden, the ex-big-league outfielder who now plays for the Giants. "They don't have any grasp of how much revenue they might be generating for the team. They're kept in the dark about stuff like that, even their salaries, and they like it that way. They don't want to cause any trouble."

So the Japanese player happily lives in a dormitory, gets one month off a year—plus an extra week, if his team wins a championship—practices for hours each day, must attend daily meetings and film studies, possesses little bargaining leverage, and, on a few teams, can't smoke, drink, or grow a mustache.

"It's different, that's for sure," said Gladden. "In their defense, though, these guys can have a job with the organization for life, if they want it."

There are functioning unions in Japan, and occasionally the rail workers or coal miners will walk out for 12 hours. But they don't carry the weight of their American labor counterparts.

"Labor law in the United States is what made the Players Association there so successful," said Miller. "The whole idea of a baseball union was objectionable to many people at first, but they eventually learned that a whole body of labor law, in effect, offered them protection. That body of law doesn't exist here."

But it's not simply legal differences that make the Japanese player appear so powerless. This is a culture that shuns confrontation, and players here, as naive as it sounds, see themselves as merely servants to the greater needs of owners and fans.

"I know it might sound strange," said Miller, "but even if these players here got a union and an issue arose that looked like it might lead to a strike, they still wouldn't do it, unless they had the approval of the fans.

"I don't mean that they would take a referendum or anything like that, but they would have to be convinced that the whole idea was acceptable to their fans. That's why, after a loss here, it's not unusual to see whole teams bowing in apology to their fans."

Ito, the assistant director of baseball operations for the 60-year-old, 12-team league, said despite its American roots, baseball has been customized to mesh with the Japanese philosophy.

"Things are very different in this nation," said Ito. "In our society, things work through consensus and compromise, not through confrontation. The players meet with the owners, occasionally, and make their suggestions. The Players Association is very comfortable with that."

To Miller, though, that spirit of compromise was born of frustration. The average Japanese, he said, had no recourse but to yield to power.

"They're always telling you how they get things done through compromise," he said. "Well, that's because the social order doesn't allow litigation to succeed. It takes at least 30 years to get anything accomplished in the courts here. There's no opportunity for confrontation.

"These people are just so docile," Miller said. "They accept anything. The consumers are gouged by ridiculous prices, but they don't fight back. The notion that it's them against the world is so deeply ingrained in them that that's how they view everything. And that thinking carries over into baseball."

Within the last few years, the owners, most of them large corporations, instituted systems of arbitration and free agency. Let's just say they will never be mistaken for the American versions.

In what few arbitration cases there are, the commissioner decides. A Japanese free agent must have ten years' experience. He can't sign for more than 150 percent of his old salary. And if he switches teams, his new club must award both the player's previous salary and a player.

"In Japan, we do not change jobs like you do in the U.S. We stay with a company for life," said Ito. "Someone who changed jobs here would be viewed as discontented."

As a result, out of sixty players eligible for free agency in 1993, only five filed, four of them signing with new teams.

Gladden learned just how taboo the subject of a baseball strike was shortly after big-league players walked out in August.

"When some of the Japanese guys on our team first heard about the strike (in the U.S.A.), they began to ask me what it was all about," the Giants outfielder said Friday, after his club's final practice session in preparation for yesterday's series opener. "Some people on the club heard about that, and they told me not to make any more comments about the strike. They didn't want me to educate the players about a union."

Even answering a question on the subject spooked Gladden, a 37-year-old in his first Japanese season.

Asked if a strike were possible, he clutched a reporter's arm and marched him to a safe spot on the otherwise crowded Tokyo Dome field. He glanced around suspiciously. Finally, seeing that the interpreter for the Yomiuri Giants was nowhere close, he began to speak quietly. "I can get in trouble for talking about this," he said.

A short while later, surrounded by reporters, a few of them American, Giants outfielder Hideki Matsui was asked his thoughts on the baseball strike.

"I really don't know anything about it," he said through an interpreter.

Could it happen here?

"I have no comment," he said.

Source: Frank Fitzpatrick, "Any Talk of a Baseball Strike is Foreign to the Japanese," *The Philadelphia Inquirer*, October 23, 1994, p. C1.

Discussion Questions for Mini-Case

1. "The idea of a players strike here (in Japan) is inconceivable," says Peter Miller, son of Marvin Miller (president of the American Baseball Players Association). Do you agree with Peter Miller that one of the reasons for no strikes in Japanese baseball is that the players are powerless to strike? Do you agree with him that the spirit of compromise was born of frustration and that the average Japanese has no recourse but to yield to power?

2. Is there an underlying system of values in Japanese society that is reflected in the Japanese labor law which discourages strikes by employees?

3. Nobuhisa Ito, Assistant Director of the 12-team baseball league says: "Despite its American roots, baseball has been customized to mesh with the Japanese philosophy." Discuss the so-called Japanese philosophy that Ito is referring to.

4. Evaluate the opinion of Miller that the Japanese are a very docile people, will accept anything, and will not fight back. Is this what you have seen of Japanese behavior historically in the political and economic arena?

5. How much does Miller understand Japanese society and culture?

MINI-CASE
The Controversy Over the Islamic Head Scarf: Women's Rights and Cultural Sensibilities

Taraneh Assadipour walked briskly through the international arrival terminal of the Orly airport in Paris. Her flight from Tehran had landed a few minutes earlier and Taraneh, accompanied by her thirteen-year-old daughter Shireen, was back in the city she had known as an undergraduate student, more than twenty years ago. She felt exhausted: it had been only a six-hour flight from Tehran, but a long and arduous journey for the forty-four-year-old woman. Taraneh was leaving behind the constraints and rigors of life under the strict Islamic code enforced in her homeland to start a new life abroad.

She had not left Iran for fifteen years, and the sight of bareheaded, smartly dressed Parisian women was startling. Taraneh loosened her scarf and let her neatly combed black hair free. Her daughter looked on disapprovingly; the slightly built teenager, her round face enveloped by a tightly knotted white scarf, had been reluctant to leave the only country that she had ever known. In contrast to her mother, she wholeheartedly embraced the Islamic code of behavior and vehemently rejected any suggestion that they restricted women's basic rights.

Shireen had been raised in an environment where gender segregation was the norm. Women were separated from men in all public places, in schools as well as on city buses, at cultural and sporting events, even on the beaches . . . Shireen maintained, with all the conviction of her thirteen years, that the constraints imposed on women, such as the mandatory use of head scarves and loose-fitting garments in public, actually enhanced the status of women. Toeing the arguments put forth by the fundamentalists rulers of Iran, the young girl denounced western attire as demeaning to women: fashionable clothing made them physically attractive to men, she said, thus reducing them to mere objects of desire. Modesty, on the other hand, underscored the Moslem woman's dignity.

Taraneh, a professional woman who had fought to preserve women's rights in her country, and had suffered subsequently the consequences of their loss, had resigned herself to her daughter's intransigence. She felt confident that once Shireen was exposed to a different environment, her views would moderate. One day, maybe, they could understand each other better. For now, however, mother and daughter were walking silently side by side.

A sensation of freedom seized Taraneh: she felt eager to rush forward and embrace a new life full of promise as well as uncertainties. Memories, however, kept racing through her mind . . .

She remembered the heady days of 1979, when like so many other young Iranians, she had left a lucrative job abroad to come home and help build the new post-revolutionary Iran.

"How enthusiastic and naive we were!" she thought to herself. Like many other members of the secular middle class, she had been slow to acknowledge the ominous signs of a new dictatorship taking shape: anti-clerical publications were shut down, peaceful demonstrations were repeatedly and violently disrupted by young toughs—the self-described members of a shadowy and nebulous "Party of God," and increasingly stringent demands were raised for the so-called Islamization of public life.

As the noose of the newly established theocracy tightened, fear fast replaced the enthusiasm of yore.

Taraneh vividly recalled how the newly consolidated regime required all women to wear the "hijab," either a full-length cloth covering from head to toe; or, at the very minimum, a head scarf concealing the hair.

To protest these new restrictions on clothing, a group of educated urban women, braving the rising tide of intimidation, had called for a demonstration on the International Woman's Day, March 8, 1980.

Taraneh could never forget that day: as demonstrators gathered to march, they were quickly surrounded by young toughs, some carrying clubs or chains, who mercilessly threatened and taunted them, before actually assaulting many. Taraneh remembered the fear that gripped her as the bearded young men lunged at her, chanting "Yah roossaree, yah toossaree!" ("either scarf on the head or blows to the head!") and the stream of insults, especially the cries of "Prostitute! Prostitute!" leveled at female demonstrators.

Soon, panic set in, and the demonstrators, some wounded or badly beaten, dispersed.

That night, Taraneh watched in dismay as the state television news broadcast reported that "the outraged citizens of our Islamic country spontaneously stopped a group of provocateurs, remnants of the ousted imperial regime and other counterrevolutionaries, from defiling the dignity of the Moslem woman."

The short-lived transition period between the fall of the imperial tyranny and the consolidation of the new dictatorship, which had witnessed the blossoming of freedoms and the rise of great expectations, had drawn to an end.

Most people withdrew from the public sphere and took refuge in their private lives. Many women were forced to resign from their jobs in public and private institutions as the expropriations and policy uncertainties contributed to deepen an economic downturn. Then came the Iraqi attack and a protracted and bloody war that was to last eight years. It was a time of extreme hardship with scant hope for better days. It was also then that Taraneh met Behrooz.

Like Taraneh, Behrooz had pursued graduate studies in the United States. It was difficult and risky to meet and virtually impossible to go out together, given the extraordinary circumstances of war and the newly enacted rules banning intermingling and socialization between the sexes as being tantamount to debauchery and perversity. As a result, the two married before they could get to know each other well. It was an unhappy marriage. The only fleeting moment of joy came when Shireen was born. After several years of strained relations, Taraneh sought a divorce. She then discovered, much to her dismay, that profound changes had taken place in the country's judicial system: the civil laws had been replaced by an Islamic code in various legal areas, from business practices to laws governing family matters. The rights of women, in particular, had been severely curtailed. Taraneh could not get a divorce unless her estranged husband consented to it. Further, the courts gave custody of children to fathers, in most cases.

For four long years, Taraneh tried to obtain a divorce and leave the country to join her brother Khosrow in France or her sister Afsaneh, a resident of the United States.

Finally, shortly after Behrooz met and married another woman, he consented to the divorce and gave his first wife the custody of their daughter.

It took Taraneh another year to sell off her belongings and secure the necessary documents to travel. She had eagerly awaited the day when she could start a new life abroad and that day had finally arrived.

Taraneh quickened her pace, tugging Shireen along. After undergoing extensive questioning by stern and suspicious immigration officials, the mother and daughter emerged into the crowded arrival hall. Khosrow was waiting there, beaming. The brother and sister embraced. Khosrow then turned to the niece he had never met. Shireen gingerly stepped back and extended her arm. They shook hands.

It took several months for Taraneh to adjust to the new environment. France had much changed from the days when Taraneh haunted the hallways of its venerable universities. The number of immigrants from third-world countries had risen and so had resentment against them. This hostility extended to the French-born children of immigrants, especially those of North African origin. Known as "Beurs," these young French citizens of Arab origin were mostly the offspring of unskilled workers who had settled in France during the 1960s and 1970s to work in the factories or to take menial jobs that the French-born increasingly shunned. They grew in the sprawling housing developments that ringed the major cities. As economic conditions deteriorated in the 1980s and 1990s, unskilled immigrants were the first to lose their jobs and many became dependent on public assistance. The younger generation of people of North African ancestry was also besieged by a high incidence of unemployment. Some of its members had turned to petty larceny or other illegal activities. Most felt alienated from their parents' culture, and at the same time rejected by French society.

Indeed, populist and outright xenophobic political parties were successfully exploiting the resentment and fears of the populace. The National Front, in particular, had grown from a marginal and insignificant organization of the extreme right in the 1970s into a major political party of the 1990s, capturing 15 percent of the popular vote in the 1995 presidential elections. Its leader, the charismatic Jean-Marie Le Pen, repeatedly demanded that France be for the French, denouncing the loss of national character, rising crime rates, unemployment, and empty public coffers, all allegedly resulting from the presence of immigrants and their offspring.

A National Front mayoral candidate darkly warned of a future where a mayor could be named Mohammed, while others raised questions about the influence of Islamic fundamentalists among the several million Moslems living in France. The specter of a rising Islamic tide lapping at the borders of the secular French republic and threatening its very foundations had become a popular and entrenched image. Moslem residents, especially observant or pious individuals, were facing deep suspicion. Although many among them rejected religious intolerance they were widely viewed as the Trojan horses of fundamentalism.

Taraneh was anxious. She was especially concerned about her daughter Shireen, who steadfastly refused to take off her head scarf in public. Shireen had made great strides in learning French and had started to attend the local public school. Her attire, however, had given rise to strong objections from the school administrators.

The principal and her associates were well-prepared to manage the situation. As early as 1989, indeed, in the Paris suburb of Creil, a schoolgirl's insistence on covering her hair with a scarf had caused a nationally publicized confrontation. School authorities considered that wearing the scarf was tantamount to religious proselytism, and thus incompatible with the secular nature of the French republic and its institutions. The public school system was always considered a pillar of secularism and a conduit through which children of immigrants could be inculcated with ideas and beliefs that would facilitate their insertion in the French society. Thus the defiance of Moslem schoolgirls, first in Creil and later in a number of other localities, was considered a serious threat that had to be thwarted. The tug-of-war between school administrators and a majority of instructors on the one hand, and devout Moslem girls and their parents on the other, resulted in several expulsions of students and a call for national guidelines. In the fall of 1994, Francois Bayrou, then minister of education, issued a decree, formally prohibiting the use of any "ostentatious religious signs" in public schools and mandating punishments, starting from initial warnings to eventual expulsions, for those who did not obey the new regulations. As a result, scores of Moslem high school students were forced to stop attending the public school system.

Taraneh had tried to coax her daughter into removing her scarf during school hours, but to no avail. The school had already issued several warnings to Shireen, and Taraneh knew that, ultimately, she may have to leave for a country where her daughter's beliefs, as well as her own, could be accommodated. In fact, Taraneh had decided to move to the United States, should the pressure on her daughter become unbearable. She had already contacted the Houston, Texas, company where she had worked in the late 1970s, and knew that she could be rehired.

One day Shireen came home in tears. "I am not allowed to go to school anymore," she announced. Taraneh took her daughter into her arms, and while consoling her tried one last time to persuade her to submit to the school regulations. "Never!" cried out the adolescent girl "it is not my head scarf that they hate, it is me!"

Three months later, Taraneh was sitting in the personnel manager's office of the Houston company, listening intently.

"Things have changed a lot since you were last here, Terry—I can call you Terry, right?" The lanky Texan continued without waiting for an answer: "Our company has grown tremendously, but we have maintained our employee-friendly orientation: indeed, we are very much aware of the diverse backgrounds of our staff and try to be very responsive to their special needs. In particular, we are committed to creating an environment where cultural diversity can thrive. As you have noticed, you will be working with people of many different ethnic backgrounds. Our company has been a leader in promoting multiculturalism in the workplace."

Source: Written by Farid Sadriech, Ph.D. student in International Business, Temple University. Copyright © 1997 by Arvind V. Phatak.

Discussion Questions for Mini-Case

1. It is said that a person's freedom ends where it encroaches on another person's rights. Give your interpretation of this idea using examples. Do freedom and individual rights have a universal meaning or should they be defined differently in different countries?

2. Consider the head scarf controversy as a symbol of the broader debate on the status of women. Develop a cultural relativist approach and take sides in the events depicted in the case accordingly. What can you say about the mandatory use of head scarves in Iran? About their mandatory removal in French public schools?

3. In the controversy over head scarves in French schools, many liberals and intellectuals have found themselves siding with extreme rightists and nationalist groups denouncing the use of head scarves. What are the likely motivations of the first group and what probably incites the nationalist groups to oppose head scarves?

4. What may explain American society's greater tolerance for publicly expressed differences in religious or cultural behavior? Does the emphasis on multiculturalism reduce the possibility for minority groups to fully participate in mainstream society? How could it strengthen or weaken the national unity and sense of purpose of a country?

5. What factors affect the status of women in a society beside the cultural tradition? In what way are the attitudes toward women in conservative Moslem countries reminiscent of those prevailing in America, at an earlier time?

6. Imagine that you are the manager of a French subsidiary of an American multinational company. How would you handle the problem of several of your French managers objecting to the Islamic dress code observed by immigrant women secretaries?

Notes

1 For an excellent documentation of incidents illustrating such blunders, see David Ricks, Marilyn C. Fu, and Jeffrey S. Arpan, *International Business Blunders*, Grid, Inc., Columbus, Ohio, 1974.

2 See, for example, Harlan Cleveland, Gerard J. Mangone, and John Clarke Adams, *The Overseas Americans*, McGraw-Hill Book Co., New York, 1960; John D. Montgomery, "Crossing the Culture Bars: An Approach

to the Training of American Technicians for Overseas Assignments," World Politics, Vol. 13, No. 4, July 1961, 544-560; George M. Foster, *Traditional Cultures, and the impact of technological change,* Harper and Brothers, New York, 1962; John Fayerweather, *The Executive Overseas,* Syracuse University Press, Syracuse, 1959; and Conrad M. Arensberg and Anther H. Niehoff, *Introducing Social Change: A Manual for Americans Overseas,* Aldine Publishing Co., Chicago, 1964.

3 Don Adams, "The Monkey and the Fish: Cultural Pitfalls of an Educational Advisor," *International Development Review,* Vol. 2, No. 2, 1969, p. 22.

4 Melville J. Herskovits, *Man and His Works,* Alfred A. Knopf, New York, 1952, p. 17.

5 Clyde Kluckhohn, "The Study of Culture," in Daniel Lerner and Harold Laswell (eds.) *The Policy Sciences,* Stanford University Press, Stanford, 1951, p. 86.

6 David Dressler and Donald Carns, *Sociology, The Study of Human Interaction,* Alfred A. Knopf, New York, 1969, pp. 56-59.

7 Ibid., p. 60.

8 John L. Graham and Yoshihiro Sano, *Smart Bargaining: Doing Business with the Japanese,* Ballinger Publishing Co., Cambridge, Mass., 1989, p. 18.

9 Edward T. Hall, "The Silent Language in Overseas Business," *Harvard Business Review,* May-June 1960, p. 138.

10 Adapted from Elaine Sciolino, "Christopher Confers with Saudi King on Aid and Arms," *The New York Times,* March 13, 1995, p. A7.

11 Thomas R. Batten, *Communities and Their Development,* Oxford University Press, New York, 1957, pp. 10-11. Reprinted by permission.

12 Edward T. Hall and William Foote Whyte, "Intercultural Communication: A Guide to Men of Action," *Human Organization,* Vol. 19, No. 1, Spring 1960, p. 9. Reproduced from *Human Organization* by permission of the Society for Applied Anthropology.

13 Ibid., pp. 8-9.

14 *Business Week,* March 7, 1988, p. 28.

15 Daniel Pearl, "Federal Express Finds Its Pioneering Formula Falls Flat Overseas," *The Wall Street Journal,* April 15, 1991, p. A8.

16 Thomas F. O'Boyle, "Bridgestone Discovers Purchase of U.S. Firms Creates Big Problems," *The Wall Street Journal,* April 1, 1991, p. A1.

17 Geert Hofstede, *Culture's Consequences: International Differences in Work-Related Values,* Sage Publications, Beverly Hills, 1980; Geert Hofstede, "Motivation, Leadership, and Organizations: Do American Theories Apply Abroad?" *Organizational Dynamics,* Summer 1980, pp. 42-63.

18 Geert Hofstede and Michael Harris Bond, "The Confucius Connection: From Cultural Roots to Economic Growth," *Organizational Dynamics,* Vol. 16, No. 4, Spring 1988, pp. 4-21.

19 Richard H. Franke, Geert Hofstede, and Michael H. Bond, "Cultural Roots of Economic Performance," *Strategic Management Journal,* Vol. 12, 1991, p. 167.

20 Hofstede and Bond, pp. 16-17.

21 Franke, Hofstede, and Bond, pp. 165-173.

22 Herskovits, p. 17.

23 Clyde Haberman, "Jerusalem Journal, Dishing Up Lunch for A Land That Isn't All Kosher," *The New York Times,* April 16, 1992, p. A4.

Further Reading

Adams, Dan, "The Monkey and the Fish: Cultural Pitfalls of an Educational Advisor," *International Development Review,* No. 2, 1969.

Arensberg, Conrad M., and Arthur H. Neihoff, *Introducing Social Change: A Manual for Americans Overseas*, Aldine Publishing Co., Chicago, 1964.

Batten, Thomas R., *Communities and Their Development*, Oxford University Press, New York, 1957.

Cleveland, Harlan, Gerard J. Mangone, and John C. Adams, *The Overseas Americans*, McGraw-Hill, New York, 1960.

Dressler, David, and Donald Carns, *Sociology, The Study of Human Interactions*, Alfred A. Knopf, New York, 1969.

Fayerweather, John, *The Executive Overseas*, Syracuse University Press, Syracuse, 1959.

Foster, George M., *Traditional Cultures, and the impact of technological change*, Harper & Brothers, New York, 1962.

Francis, June N.P., "When in Rome? The Effects of Cultural Adaptation on Intercultural Business Negotiations," *Journal of International Business Studies*, Vol. 22, No. 3, Third Quarter 1991, pp. 403-428.

Glover, M. Katherine, "Do's & Taboos: Cultural Aspects of International Business," *Business America*, Vol. 111, No. 15, Aug. 13, 1990, pp. 2-6.

Hall, Edward T., "The Silent Language in Overseas Business," *Harvard Business Review*, May-June 1960.

——*The Silent Language*, Anchor Press Doubleday, Anchor Books Edition, Garden City, N.Y., 1973.

Hall, Edward T., and William F. Whyte, "Intercultural Communication: A Guide to Men of Action," *Human Organization*, Vol. 19, No. I, Spring 1960.

Harris, Philip R., and Robert T. Moran, *Managing Cultural Differences*, 2nd ed., Gulf Publishing Company, Houston, Texas, 1987.

Herskovits, Melville J., *Man and His Works*, Alfred A. Knopf, New York, 1954.

Lerner, Daniel, and Harold D. Lasswell, eds., *The Policy Sciences*, Stanford University Press, Stanford, 1951.

Luqmani, Mushtaq, Zahir A. Quraeshi, and Linda Delene, "Marketing in Islamic Countries: A Viewpoint," *MSU Business Topics*, Summer 1980.

Montgomery, John D., "Crossing the Culture Bars: An Approach to the Training of American Technicians for Overseas Assignments," *World Politics*, Vol. 13, No. 4, July 1961.

Ricks, David, Marilyn Y. C. Fu, and Jeffrey S. Arpan, *International Business Blunders*, Grid, Inc., Columbus, Ohio, 1974.

Terpstra, Vern, *The Cultural Environment of International Business*, South-Western Publishing Company, Cincinnati, Ohio, 1978.

Townsend, Anthony N., Scott K. Dow, and Steven E. Markham, "An Examination of Country and Culture-Based Differences in Compensation Practice," *Journal of International Business Studies*, Vol. 21, No. 4, Fourth Quarter 1990, pp. 667-678.

Ueno, Susumu, and Sekaran Uma, "The Influence of Culture on Budget Control Practices in the U.S.A. and Japan: An Empirical Study," *Journal of International Business Studies*, Vol. 23, No. 4, Fourth Quarter 1992, pp. 659-674.

International Business Negotiations

LEARNING OBJECTIVES

After completing this chapter, you will be able to:

- Identify key elements of both the environmental and immediate contexts within which international business negotiations take place and how they can affect the conduct and outcome of negotiations.
- Outline the preparations necessary to a successful negotiation.
- Discuss ways in which cultural differences can impact international business negotiations and ways to minimize the adverse effects of these differences.

We see negotiations occurring all around us. Children negotiate curfew times with their parents, employees negotiate for wages and benefits with their employers, and companies negotiate with each other for the sale or purchase of a good, service, or technology.

There can be no international business without the presence of at least two parties, each coming from different countries, sitting face-to-face and negotiating a business deal. International business negotiations precede all international business transactions, whether it is the sale of a product to a foreign buyer, the formation of a joint venture between two companies of different nationalities to develop a new technology or to share distribution channels in a third country, an acquisition of a company by a foreign company, or the licensing of a technology by a company to a foreign producer. It is inevitable that negotiations between two or more sides will take place whenever a certain outcome is impossible to obtain unilaterally without incurring unacceptable political, legal, or economic consequences.

Negotiations take place because the parties involved have to or want to. If a company does not have the power to get what it wants from another company—e.g., a patent for a process technology—it will use negotiations to get what it wants, at a negotiated price, from the company that holds the patent. Even in circumstances when a company has the power to impose its will on another company, it may choose not to do so and may find itself negotiating with the weaker side. For example, a large company like the Ford Motor Company may have the power to impose its will in terms of the price that it is willing to pay to a supplier for a component such as a crankshaft or an engine. However, knowing that the relationship with the supplier would suffer irreparable damage if it were forced to accept Ford's take-it-or-leave-it offer, Ford may instead choose to negotiate with the supplier a price for the component that the supplier could live with.

Negotiations Defined

Negotiation is a process through which two or more parties—be they individuals, groups, or larger social units—interact in developing potential agreements to provide guidance and regulation of their future behavior.[1] Simply put, negotiation is a process in which one person or party tries to change the attitude, beliefs, or behavior of another person or party. Such negotiation is conducted between nations—as in the tri-partite negotiations between the United States, Canada, and Mexico to forge the North American Free Trade Agreement (NAFTA), or in the ongoing negotiations between the United States and Japan aimed at opening up Japanese markets to American goods and service; between companies—as in the alliance between British Air and U.S. Air to share routes, airport gates, and reservations systems; and between any two or more parties that need to cooperate or bargain to attain certain common or conflicting ends.

THE NEGOTIATIONS CONTEXT

Whenever two parties negotiate, the entire negotiations process occurs under two umbrella contexts: (1) the environmental context and (2) the immediate context.

The *environmental context* refers to the forces in the environment that are beyond the control of either party involved in the negotiations, such as cultural differences between negotiators, legal requirements that constrain the scope and outcome of negotiations, and external stakeholders who have a keen interest in the negotiations outcomes such as labor unions, government agencies, competitors, and so on. International business negotiations are conducted under the contextual umbrella of the environmental factors. The immediate context—which will be discussed next— is impacted by the environmental context.

The *immediate context* includes aspects like the relative power of the negotiators and the nature of their interdependence, and the level of conflict between the negotiators at the start of the negotiations. Figure 7-1 shows the conceptual framework for international business negotiations and the various dimensions of the environmental and immediate contexts of international business negotiations. It shows the environmental context, in the outer circle, consisting of eight dimensions, and the immediate context, in the middle circle, composed of five dimensions. Furthermore, Figure 7-1 conveys that the environmental context has an impact upon the immediate context, which in turn impacts upon the process and outcome of the negotiations process.

Both the environmental context dimensions and the immediate context dimensions will be discussed in the context of international business negotiations. Although there are many features that are common in both purely domestic business negotiations and international business negotiations, international business transactions, as a group, are influenced and molded by certain basic common factors that are not to be found in purely domestic business transactions. These international business factors give international business negotiations, of whatever type, a conceptual unity, while at the same time differentiating them sharply from purely domestic business negotiations. Furthermore, these factors basically mold the process of international business negotiations of all sorts, and therefore they must be thoroughly examined.[2]

THE ENVIRONMENTAL CONTEXT OF INTERNATIONAL BUSINESS NEGOTIATIONS

We shall first explore the nature of the environmental context—the outermost circle in Figure 7-1—starting with the dimension called *legal pluralism*.[3] (Please refer to Figure 7-1 throughout the coverage of the environmental context.)

FIGURE 7-1

Framework for International Business Negotiations

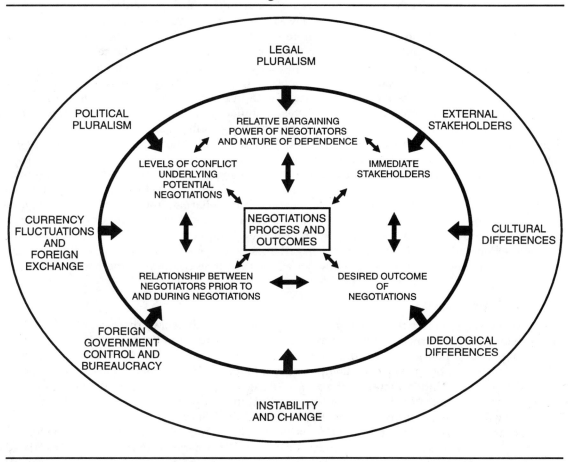

Legal Pluralism

The principle of national sovereignty gives every nation-state the right to make laws which are supposedly in its national interests. Therefore, every country in the world has its own legislation in areas such as exports, anti-trust, labor, environmental protection, patent and trade-mark protection, product liability and marketing, minimum wage, taxation, and so on.

An international business transaction must comply with the laws of countries involved in the transaction. Certain laws prohibit certain types of transactions. For example, an American company that is negotiating to transfer technology or sell a product to an Indian company must ensure that the transaction is legal both in the United States and in India, i.e., the transfer of the technology or product is allowed under both U.S. laws as well as Indian laws. A case in point is the proposed sale by Cray Computer Company of a supercomputer to the Indian government. The U.S. government disallowed the sale on grounds that the sale was illegal as it hurt the national

175

security interests of the United States. The United States has legislation that lists the various types of technologies—especially those with potential military applications—whose exports are prohibited. Negotiators must therefore ensure that the outcome of the negotiations does not violate the laws of the countries involved. Thus, the laws of nation-states put limits on matters that could be negotiated among nationals of two or more countries.

There are laws that put limits on some types of transactions. For instance, certain sectors of the economy such as telecommunications and automobile industries are often kept off-limits to wholly owned foreign investments. For instance, a foreign company can enter the Indian and Chinese markets only by forming joint ventures with indigenous companies. General Motors, Ford, Volkswagen, and Mercedes have established manufacturing plants in India in joint ventures with Indian companies; and Volkswagen, Citroen, and Peugeot have joint ventures in China. The negotiations between these car companies and the local companies in India and China were conducted under the constraint that only a joint venture agreement could be signed. The joint venture requirement undoubtedly had an impact on the negotiations between the two sides over other important aspects such as managerial and quality control, global marketing rights, valuation of technology transferred to the joint venture, profit-sharing, and royalty payments.

Negotiators would be wise to be forewarned about the legal traps that could transform a supposedly good agreement into a nightmare if the legal implications of the transaction are not carefully examined. It is imperative that negotiators be extremely careful in avoiding the risk of doing something illegal under the laws of either the home country or the host country.

Political Pluralism

The world consists of more than one hundred countries, each with its own distinct political system and foreign policy. International businesspersons often get caught in the cross-fire of sometimes conflicting foreign policies of two or more countries. For example, an American executive in a French subsidiary of an American company must be aware of the foreign policy of France as well as that of the United States as it applies to engaging in a business relationship with an organization in Cuba or North Korea. A business deal that may be in the political and economic interests of France may run counter to those of the United States.

An example of such a situation is the construction of the Trans-Siberian pipeline in the former Soviet Union in the 1980s. Several European subsidiaries of American companies had negotiated contracts to supply equipment such as transformers, generators, and construction services for the pipeline. With the Soviet invasion of Afghanistan, American foreign policy turned quite hostile towards the Soviet Union, and the U.S. government demanded that the American companies (and their subsidiaries) not supply the equipment and services. The European governments demanded that the subsidiaries of American companies based in European countries be permitted to fill their contracts with the Soviets, claiming that the pipeline supply contracts were in the national interest of the host European countries. Only diplomacy at the highest level finally resolved the problem.

Presently the policy of the United States is to forbid the sale of any products, technology, or services that may be used by a foreign government or company to make nuclear weapons or equipment (e.g., aircraft or missiles) that could deliver nuclear warheads. To further its foreign policy objectives, the U.S. government forbids the export or licensing of dual-purpose products and technology which can be used in military as well as non-military applications. Such dual-purpose items include sophisticated computers, certain types of aircraft engines, and nuclear power plants.

This discussion of the impact of the foreign policies of countries on international business transactions highlights the importance of studying thoroughly the potential political fallout of an international business deal before it is negotiated and the agreement is signed.

The foreign policy of the host country also impacts upon the conduct of international business negotiations. For example, the Datuk Seri Mahathir Mohamad, the Prime Minister of Malaysia, is known for his anti-European, and in particular his anti-England, political stance. In a circumstance like this, English companies engaged in negotiating a business deal with Malaysian companies would have to try extra hard to get the deal, especially if there are non-European and especially non-English companies from countries that are friendly with the Malaysian government that are also in the fray to obtain the deal.

The above discussion on political pluralism highlights the importance of understanding the constraints imposed on the process of international business negotiations by the foreign policies of countries that are directly or indirectly impacted by the outcome of such negotiations.

Currency Fluctuations and Foreign Exchange

The Wall Street Journal reported on December 28, 1994, that "the Mexican currency lost almost 36 percent of its value against the dollar since the currency crisis began a week ago, and 43 percent since the beginning of the year."[4] This event highlights the significance of the impact of currency value fluctuations on international business negotiations. International firms that have negotiated business deals or operations in Mexico hopefully had taken the risk of the peso devaluation into account during their negotiations with Mexican firms. A devalued peso will make Mexican products cheaper in foreign currency and therefore more competitive in foreign markets. Consequently, exports from Mexico would get a boost. Foreign-made products would be more expensive for Mexican consumers and therefore imports would suffer. American firms that have established manufacturing plants in Mexico for making components for export to the United States stand to gain from the devaluation of the peso. On the other hand, American firms that are exporting components made in the U.S. for assembly and distribution in Mexico stand to lose from the peso devaluation.

Unlike purely domestic business transactions, international business transactions take place in a world of multiple currencies, the values (foreign exchange rates) of which fluctuate on a daily basis. Most major currencies in the world are allowed by their respective governments to let the world currency markets determine their exchange rates. However, there are many countries in which the governments fix the currency exchange rates. In either case, there is always the risk that the value of a currency may either appreciate or depreciate in response to macroeconomic conditions. The change in the currency value may be brought about either by market forces (currency supply and demand conditions in the market) in the global currency markets, or by a unilateral decision by the government.

A business deal that is not effectively structured to compensate and protect against foreign exchange fluctuations is bound to be a prelude to a disaster or a windfall if the underlying currencies in which payments are to be received have a precipitous decline or appreciation in value against the recipient company's home currency or against other stable currencies. The following example illustrates this concept.

Let us suppose than an agreement has been made between an American and a Mexican company that requires the Mexican company to pay the American company in Mexican pesos for goods received by the Mexican company in an export deal, or for licensing fees in a technology transfer agreement. The following scenarios would unfold depending upon whether the peso depreciates or appreciates against the U.S. dollar:

(1) If the peso depreciates against the U.S. dollar, the U.S. company will lose revenues in U.S. dollars equal to the percentage of the peso devaluation against the U.S. dollar.

(2) If the peso appreciates against the U.S. dollar, the U.S. company will stand to gain in revenues received; the gain will equal the percentage of the peso appreciation against the U.S. dollar.

In the situation described above, it would be prudent if negotiators for both the American and Mexican companies were to obtain realistic "most likely" forecasts of the exchange rates for the Mexican peso and the U.S. dollar from reliable sources such as international banks and currency futures markets, and to build into the agreement contingency clauses that would protect either side from wild swings in the exchange rates of their respective currencies, or engage in currency hedging contracts. International business negotiations are always conducted under the cloud of the possibility of currency value fluctuations. Negotiators have to take into consideration the likelihood of currency devaluation or appreciation as they haggle over the financial aspects of a business deal.

Foreign exchange controls by many governments also influence international business negotiations. Foreign exchange controls are the restrictions placed by the government on the inflow or outflow of both foreign and local currencies. Foreign exchange permits are required in order to exchange local currency for foreign currency and vice versa. The ability of a company to pay for imported raw materials, or to repatriate profits or dividends to a foreign parent, is dependent upon the willingness of the host government to make the necessary foreign exchange available for such transactions. Negotiators for a foreign company must ensure that in whatever agreement is negotiated—whether for a foreign direct investment, a joint venture, or a simple licensing agreement—there are provisions that would avoid or blunt the effect of these controls. For instance, in the face of foreign exchange restrictions, an international company could negotiate a "countertrade" deal by which payment is made in goods, rather than cash.

Foreign Government Controls and Bureaucracy

Americans are constantly complaining about the bureaucratic hassles and government intrusion and control of business in the United States. However, the extent of governmental interference in business in many nations is far more intrusive and extensive than is ever experienced in the United States. For instance, government agencies have the authority to control the total output of an industry, and the absolute control over the granting of permits to expand production capacity. A company that feels that it has the potential to increase market share is obligated to obtain the necessary license to expand capacity, which is often denied by government bureaucrats. A company may also need a license to implement a strategy designed to expand its product line. As a case in point, in the mid-1980s, the Indian subsidiary of Procter & Gamble had to plead with the Indian government to grant it the permission to market Proctor & Gamble's consumer products in the Indian market. Such intrusion into the "private" affairs of companies is unheard of in the United States and in most developed countries, however, it is quite routine in most developing countries such as China, Indonesia, Egypt, and India. Efforts at liberalization and privatization in these countries has reduced the pervasive interference by government bureaucrats into the affairs of private enterprise; however, the level of such interference is still far more than one normally encounters in the more economically advanced countries such as Germany, France, or the United States.

Government agencies control entire industries in many countries. For instance, until recently the entire telecommunications field was in the sole domain of government-owned enterprises in

Brazil, Argentina, Chile, and India. Now, private enterprise is allowed in these sectors in joint ventures with government enterprises. In many countries private enterprise is forbidden in sectors such as oil and gas, shipping, and airlines, and in some industries the government firms compete with private enterprise as is the case in India.

Governmental agencies in such countries have control over almost every major decision made in a business enterprise, such as plant expansion, product and business diversification, and the financial structure of a firm. Bureaucrats in government agencies exercise considerable power and influence over the private sector. It is not unusual for a government agency to take years to grant a license to a company to do something that would be considered quite mundane in the United States.

> While India last year approved $1.1 billion of U.S. investments, up from $80 million two years earlier, it still takes three or four years for companies to get through the red tape before they can operate. India's bureaucracy isn't the straitjacket it used to be, but its capacity to meddle and postpone remain daunting.[5]

Negotiations in the sort of business environment described above almost always include the government as one of the parties that a foreign firm is negotiating with, directly or indirectly. For example, a foreign firm that is negotiating a joint venture with a domestic firm to manufacture a product is simultaneously negotiating with the domestic firm in the host country and with the host government agency as well. The government agency may not be physically present at the negotiating table, but its silent presence is felt throughout the negotiations process because every issue that is negotiated has to be considered in light of the pertinent relevant governmental regulations.

Instability and Change

Heraclitus is quoted to have said that "there is nothing permanent except change." Change is omnipresent. It engulfs us with new challenges every day. Domestic as well as international firms must cope with risks emanating from unanticipated changes in the political, economic, legal, technological, and cultural segments of the external environment. However, the scope and magnitude of risks that the international business environment imposes on international firms is far greater than for firms that operate only in single-country environments. International transactions are frequently afflicted by such traumas as war and revolution, currency devaluations, unexpected political changes, sudden changes in government policies, and coups d'etat. The following quote illustrates the nature of the political uncertainty that international companies have to live with.

> . . . Americans need to accept that economic adjustments forged by democracies sometimes are perceived as halting and half-hearted. For democracies, bolder reforms can bring political backlash if they don't produce quick gains.
>
> In Poland and Hungary, for instance, voters jarred by the difficult transition to capitalism have brought droves of former Communists back into office. No one expects these new officials to reinstate discredited command economies, but they are likely to slow reforms.[6]

During the 1980s and the early 1990s we witnessed such unexpected events as the fall of the Soviet Union, the Gulf War, significant peace prospects in the Middle East between the PLO/Arab States and Israel, and the economic liberalization and opening of markets to trade and foreign investments in China, India, and Russia. Each of these events brought forth threats or opportunities for international firms. The opening of the Chinese, Indian, and Russian markets have created tremendous business opportunities for foreign companies in such fields as infrastructure projects, energy development, and marketing of consumer products, just to name a few. However, such opportunities also are associated with risks in other areas:

> A more immediate worry for investors is that if inflation is not checked, China's currency, the yuan, could be devalued. Investors only have to think back a few years to a period when China's government was devaluing the currency every few months. Growth is nice, but so is capital preservation.
>
> Political risks seem to be rising, too. Can the market keep liberalizing without creating a strong desire among citizens for more freedom in other areas of life leading to another bloody confrontation with the old-line Communist leaders? And what happens to China's power structure after Deng Xiaoping dies? Such concerns do not negate the long-term case for China, but they do make it less of a sure bet. Investors need patience, smarts, and a strong stomach for volatility.[7]

To cope with volatility and risks, negotiators should be prepared with advice from experts on the probability of economic and political risks in the target country. Armed with valid and reliable information on the most likely economic and political scenarios, international managers would be on a firmer footing to negotiate effectively the very best deal possible with their host country company counterparts. Without such data, negotiators stand the chance of signing a bad agreement. The political risk in China is causing companies to put a premium on the expected rates of return on investments in that country:

> With China's risks rising, so must the expected returns. Morgan Stanley, which has been investing there for ten years, calculates the country's risk premium at 19 percent, meaning an investment in China must offer a prospective return that beats U.S. Treasury bills by at least 19 percentage points. That assumes that the Chinese investment is liquid, as a stock is. An illiquid investment has to do even better, by far. Direct investment fund managers say the potential returns they are offering investors today must be 30 percent or more.[8]

International negotiators must have the expertise and the knowledge of not only the global business environment but also of the target country. Knowledge of global opportunities and risks for the international company's product, service, or technology is most useful for the negotiator because it serves as a benchmark against which he or she can evaluate the costs and benefits of doing business in a particular country. For example, a British company that is negotiating the setup of a joint venture with a Chinese enterprise to produce cars for the Chinese market would be in a much better bargaining position knowing that an equally good opportunity exists in India. It could then bargain with the Chinese enterprise from a position of strength knowing it could possibly go for a joint venture in India in the event that it is unable to negotiate an acceptable business arrangement in China. Knowing that such an option exists would be most valuable to the British company in negotiating the best deal that is beneficial to both sides. This outcome would be even more likely if the Chinese enterprise is also made aware of the opportunity in India for the British company.

Ideological Differences

Ideology may be defined as the body of ideas on which a particular political, economic, or social system is based. The political ideology of the United States stresses freedom, which may be defined as (1) the right to participate in determining the form of government, (2) choosing the officials of government, and (3) playing a role in making the laws that govern the various aspects of individual behavior. The economic ideology of the United States can be best described as one that stresses (1) the primacy of private enterprise, (2) the right of a person to own private property, and (3) the right to earn a surplus or profit from putting one's property to proper use. The social system in the United States is based upon egalitarian principles which stress that all men and women in society should have equal political, economic, and social rights, as well as religious freedom.

An international manager will be shocked—unless he or she has been adequately briefed beforehand on what to expect in a foreign country—to find that the very basis of life in the United States that he or she has always taken for granted may not exist in a foreign land. For example, the right to own private property does not exist in Communist countries like Cuba, North Korea, and China. In some segments of the economy in these countries where private enterprise does exist, that right is delegated to the individual by the State. This concept is quite contrary to the ideology of the United States wherein individuals have the birthright to own property. Political freedom is limited in countries like Egypt which allow only one political party to exist. Political freedom is totally absent in China. Equality does not exist among members of society, especially between men and women, in countries like Saudi Arabia. Discrimination based upon religious beliefs is prevalent in fundamentalist Islamic countries.

The profit motive is denounced by society in some countries. In countries like India, Pakistan, and most countries in Africa, public displays of one's wealth are a sign of greed and selfishness, and business and businessmen are viewed with disfavor.

Countries such as India, Nigeria, Malaysia, Egypt, Indonesia, and others which were once the victims of colonization by Western powers like England, France, Belgium, and Holland have had a history of antipathy towards foreign investment. Foreign investment is mistakenly perceived as another form of foreign domination. Although the attitude toward foreign investment in these countries has changed dramatically since the beginning of the decade of the 90s, there is still present a significant political force comprising left-wing political parties and labor unions that continue to blame global companies for the countries' problems.

The conflict in political ideologies makes it necessary for the negotiators to find a "middle ground" that is acceptable to both sides, and to frame the language and content of the negotiated contract in a pattern that is acceptable to both sides.

Cultural Differences

International business negotiations involve interactions between managers from different cultures. We have examined in the chapter on culture (Chapter 6) the variety of ways in which culture affects individual and interpersonal behavior. Cultural differences between the negotiators and the cultural norms of the negotiators have a significant influence on how the negotiators behave both before and during the negotiations, as well as after the negotiations have been completed. For instance, the building of trust and relationships is extremely important for the Japanese, Chinese, Mexicans, and most Latin Americans. Before the start of negotiations in these cultures, it is considered essential to spend some time together in getting acquainted with each other and in building a certain amount of "comfort level" before sitting down at the negotiating table. By contrast, Americans are known for their impatience to "get down to business" after a few pleasantries.

During the negotiations, Americans are inclined to make small concessions early to establish a relationship and to keep the negotiations process moving forward smoothly, whereas the Japanese have the tendency to hold back making major concessions until very late in the negotiations. Differences also exist on how much and what type of information is shared with the other side. American negotiators are inclined to share large amounts of significant information about their company's needs, limitations, urgency to obtain desired negotiated outcomes, and so on, the premise being that the other side will reciprocate upon seeing how open you are. The Japanese see no such need to provide meaningful information to the other side and therefore provide only the smallest crumbs of information in exchange for the information of real value they receive from the Americans.

To Americans the contract signals the conclusion of negotiations—the terms of the contract establish the rights, responsibilities, and obligations of the parties involved. However, to the Japanese, a company is not forever bound to the terms of the contract, and in fact the contract can be renegotiated whenever there is a significant shift in the company's circumstances. For instance, an unexpected change in the government's tax policy, or a change in the competitive environment, are considered legitimate reasons for contract renegotiation. To the Chinese, a signatory to an agreement is a partner with whom they can work, and therefore to them the signing of a contract is just the beginning of negotiations.

Most international business negotiations never fulfill their potential expectations because of cultural "faux pas" on one side or the other during the negotiations. International business negotiators would be better off provided that they are well versed in the cultural nuances and unspoken language of the negotiators at the other end of the table. The greater the understanding of the cultural differences of one's own culture as well as that of the other side, the greater is the likelihood of a mutually satisfactory outcome of the negotiations.

Later in this chapter we shall examine in some detail the subject of cultural differences and their impact on the negotiating styles and behavior of managers from different countries.

External Stakeholders

External stakeholders are the various persons and organizations that have an interest or stake in the outcome of the negotiations. Examples of such stakeholders are competitors, consumers, labor unions, organized business groups such as the chamber of commerce and industry associations, and the company's shareholders.

Competitors are likely to apply pressure by lobbying against a proposed business arrangement, such as a joint venture, if the outcome of the negotiations is the introduction of a formidable new competitor in the market. Lobbying strategies may include the launch of a public relations campaign against the deal—illustrating the real or contrived harmful effects of the joint venture—through newspapers and television or through efforts to deny key permits and approvals by the government to the proposed venture.

Consumers that are affected by the outcome of the negotiations may get involved in ways that may help or hinder the negotiations process. If the outcome is deemed to be favorable, consumer groups may lobby for a speedy conclusion of the negotiations. But if the outcome is perceived to be unfavorable to the consumers, they are likely to do their very best to scuttle the negotiations. For example, the United States has been negotiating for decades with the Japanese government to provide greater access to the Japanese market for American goods and services. The Japanese consumers are in favor of opening the Japanese market to foreign competition because it would result in the Japanese consumer getting cheaper and a wider variety of goods, so they have been lobbying for it. However, the various industry groups in the electronics, automobile, and agricultural sectors have been opposed to any opening of the Japanese market to foreign competitors and to date have been quite successful at blocking any substantial market-opening measures.

Labor unions are generally opposed to any business transaction that is likely to reduce employment opportunities for their members. Caterpillar, the American manufacturer of earth-moving equipment, has had several strikes at its plants in the U.S. organized by labor unions. One of the principal grievances of the union against the company is the loss of manufacturing jobs in the U.S. resulting from the transfer of manufacturing jobs overseas by Caterpillar's management in search of low-cost production sites. Caterpillar has several manufacturing joint ventures abroad, and the reaction of the labor unions in the U.S. must surely be having an impact on the negotiations process for any new production joint ventures abroad that have the potential to result in job losses for workers in the U.S.

The attitude of organized business groups like the country's chamber of commerce can influence the ambiance for international business negotiations. For example, with the opening of markets in China, India, and Russia, the U.S. Chamber of Commerce has organized several groups of top-level executives from major American corporations to visit these countries in search of joint ventures with Chinese, Indian, and Russian enterprises. The positive attitude of a country's chamber of commerce gives the required boost to successful negotiations. The chambers of commerce in each country involved can help clear many hurdles such as unnecessary bureaucratic red tape. The hundreds of joint ventures established in China, India, and Russia for technology transfer and production of consumer and industrial goods could never have materialized had it not been for the proactive stance of the chambers of commerce of the involved countries.

The progress of negotiations can be either stimulated or inhibited by the reaction of the shareholders. Studies have shown that if a company's stock is traded in the country's stock exchange, the appreciation or decline in the price of the stock sends a clear signal regarding the attitude of the shareholders to a proposed merger or strategic alliance. It appears inevitable that the executives involved in the negotiations would be influenced by the attitude of the shareholders. For instance, a company whose shareholders are opposed to a merger will either withdraw from the negotiations or try to change the attitude of the shareholders by making changes in their negotiations stance to include demands from the other side that would appease its shareholders. The shareholders are always the "invisible man" present at the negotiations table, watching over the proceedings, and signalling their approval or disapproval of the content of the negotiations.

This concludes our coverage of the environmental context of international business negotiations. We have examined several dimensions that together constitute the environmental context: legal pluralism, political pluralism, currency fluctuations and foreign exchange, foreign government controls and bureaucracy, instability and change, ideological differences, cultural differences, and external stakeholders. Each of these dimensions—singly and in conjunction with one another—impact upon the immediate context of negotiations.

THE IMMEDIATE CONTEXT OF INTERNATIONAL BUSINESS NEGOTIATIONS

In the middle circle in Figure 7-1 is the immediate context of international business negotiations. The immediate context consists of influences that impact on the negotiations process, including the negotiating strategies and negotiations outcomes. It consists of five dimensions: the relative bargaining power of negotiators and the nature of dependence, the levels of conflict underlying potential negotiations, the relationship between negotiators prior to and during the negotiations, the desired outcome of negotiations, and the immediate stakeholders.

Relative Bargaining Power of Negotiators and Nature of Dependence

Power is the ability to influence the behavior of another person. The greater the ability that one has to induce another to conform to one's wishes, the greater is one's power over that other person. Here we have referred to power as a capability of a person. It is the ability to get things done the way one wants them to be done. However, in a real sense groups and organizations also possess power. An organization has power when it can induce or force another person or organization to obey its dictates. An organization has power when it can bring about a desired outcome independently, without the help of others.

In the context of negotiations, the relative bargaining power of the negotiators is the ability of each side to independently obtain the desired outcomes, i.e., without the cooperation of the other side or with the cooperation of some other parties. The nature of dependence existing between the two sides in the negotiations determines the relative power of one side vis-à-vis the other. The nature of dependence can be classified into three different types: independence, dependence, and interdependence.

If one party is totally independent of the other then there is no need for negotiations because it has the power to achieve its goals without the need to cooperate with anyone else. For example, a company that has the financial resources to enter a foreign market on its own with a wholly owned subsidiary has independent power.

Negotiations will also not occur if one party is totally dependent on another. Total dependency implies that the dependent party has no power and must accept and accommodate the demands of another person or company that is capable of fulfilling its needs. An example of total dependency is that of a supplier of a component whose entire output is purchased by a single buyer, in which case the supplier must either accept the transaction terms dictated by the buyer, or find another buyer if there is one.

There can be no negotiations unless both sides need to cooperate with each other to achieve their respective goals, i.e., there is some measure of interdependence between them. Negotiations involve a give-and-take between two sides. Interdependent relationships are characterized by interlocking goals—both sides need each other to accomplish their goals. For example, many large global pharmaceutical companies have consummated joint ventures with small start-up biotechnology firms to develop breakthrough cures for a variety of diseases. Interdependence is characterized by the small biotechnology firms' need for financial resources which only large companies are in a position to provide, and the craving by large pharmaceutical companies to place their bets on the development of several risky projects by hooking up with as many promising small companies as possible. This interdependence motivates the two sides to negotiate with each other.

The relative bargaining power of each individual or company can be assessed by the simple measure of how much each side needs the cooperation of the other to achieve its goals. The more one side is dependent on the other's help in fulfilling its needs, the less power it has in the negotiations relative to the other side. Similarly, the greater a company's capability to independently achieve its goals, the greater power it has in the negotiations vis-à-vis the other side.

The negotiating strategies adopted by a company thus depend upon that company's relative power in the negotiations. A company with greater power is more likely to adopt an aggressive "take it or leave it" stance, whereas a company that has less power will most likely adopt a far more submissive stance.

Levels of Conflict Underlying Potential Negotiations

Very few negotiations begin with a neutral relationship. The relationship between the negotiators could range from very hostile to very supportive.

The more that two sides agree on key issues, the lower will be the level of conflict between them. In the same vein, an increase in the degree of disagreement between them will raise the level of conflict.

The level of conflict on key issues underlying a potential negotiation establishes whether the relationship will be supportive or hostile. The greater the conflict between negotiators, the greater will be the level of hostility. Similarly, the lower level of conflict, the more supportive the relationship between the negotiators is likely to be.

In summation, the more that the negotiators agree on key issues, i.e., the more "common ground" both sides share, the less conflict there will be between them, and therefore the more supportive of each other their relationship will be. On the other hand, the more that they disagree on the key issues underlying the negotiations, the greater will be the conflict between them, which will result in a more hostile relationship.

The likelihood of a supportive relationship between the negotiators is enhanced in "win-win" situations. In negotiations characterized by a win-win situation—also known as a non-zero sum game or integrative bargaining—the goals of the two sides are linked with each other in such a way that the extent to which one party achieves its goals determines the extent to which the other party achieves its goals as well. In a win-win situation, both sides emerge as the winners, i.e., the more that one party gains from the outcome of the negotiations, the more the other party's gains will be. The basic premise of an integrative, win-win situation is that one party's gain is not at the expense of the other party, and that it is possible for both parties to achieve their respective goals. An example of a win-win situation is an agreement between a multinational company and a host country government which says that the number of items that the multinational company could sell in the country market would be equal to the number of items of the product exported by the multinational company from the host country. In this case, both the multinational company as well as the host government win—exports help the host country to earn foreign exchange, and sales in the host country allow the multinational company to increase its total revenue and market share.

Conflict between the two sides is inevitable in "win-lose" situations. In such a situation—also known as a zero-sum game or distributive bargaining—the gains of one side come at the expense of the other side. In a win-lose situation it is assumed that there is a limited amount of resources available, i.e., there is a "fixed pie," and both sides may want to be the winner, with each wanting more than half of the pie. For example, two companies negotiating the percentage of the total equity of each in a joint venture are involved in win-lose negotiations, because any increase in the equity over 50 percent for either side would result in the other getting less than 50 percent of the equity.

Relationship Between Negotiators Prior to and During Negotiations

The nature of the relationship between the two sides prior to the very first negotiations session would have a significant impact on their relationship during the negotiations. If the two sides have had a harmonious prior relationship—e.g., they might have had a long and positive business relationship, or the two sides may have engaged in mutually beneficial win-win negotiations previously—then the negotiating strategies adopted by each side would tend to be supportive of another win-win outcome.

The entire negotiations process actually consists of a series of negotiations sessions. Therefore the experience—positive or negative—of each prior session serves as a backdrop for the next one, and this process continues to the culmination of the entire negotiations process. Consequently, each "positive" negotiations session serves to facilitate a favorable outcome at the next session, whereas a "negative" session has the potential to do damage to the atmosphere of the next session. Therefore, the relationship of the negotiators prior to and during each negotiations session is instrumental in determining the ultimate success or failure of the negotiations.

Desired Outcome of Negotiations

The outcome of negotiations can be both *tangible* and *intangible*. Tangible outcomes include agreement on matters such as profit sharing, technology transfer, royalty rates, laws for the protection of intellectual property, equity ownership, and other such outcomes that represent assets having real substance and which can be appraised for value. Intangible outcomes include the goodwill generated between the two sides in the negotiations, the desire to make concessions to enlarge the stockpile of goodwill among the parties, and the overall desire to attain win-win outcomes through collaboration and compromise.

The desired outcome of negotiations may be governed by one of the following three antecedent forces impacting on the negotiations: (1) the outcome negotiated is a one-time deal and the two sides will cease to be associated with each other after the negotiations have concluded, (2) the two sides wish the negotiated outcome to be a building block of a long-term relationship with each other, and (3) the relative emphasis placed on tangible vs. intangible outcomes.

The strategies adopted by the negotiators during the negotiations will be conditioned by the short-term vs. long-term relationship desired by the two sides. For instance, it would be reasonable to expect both sides to compromise on the tangible outcomes in favor of intangible outcomes if indeed the long-term relationship is the preeminent objective of both sides. On the other hand, if a short-term relationship is all that is desired, the negotiators are likely to aim for those tangible results that do not require goodwill between the two sides for their fulfillment.

The U.S.-Japan trade negotiations are an example of negotiations in which, while tangible results are crucial, the long-term relationship between the two sides is even more important than the immediate tangible results of opening up the Japanese market to foreign goods and services and reducing the yearly U.S. trade deficit with Japan of approximately $60 billion (of which about $30 billion is in auto parts alone). An indication that the two sides wish the negotiations to be the building blocks of a fruitful long-term relationship is illustrated in the following item in *The Philadelphia Inquirer*:

> President Clinton and Japanese Prime Minister Tomiichi Murayama concluded a low-key summit yesterday highlighting mutual efforts to address the North Korea nuclear problem while playing down the yawning trade imbalance between the two countries. Clinton did note that "further progress must be made to open Japan's markets to U.S. autos and auto parts, which account for nearly 60 percent of America's deficit with Japan. But in contrast to a contentious U.S.-Japan summit a year ago, both sides went out of their way to stress the trade agreements that have been reached rather than the differences that remain . . . . During the joint news conference, Clinton noted that the often-stormy framework negotiations to open Japan's markets had produced several agreements since October

in the areas of government procurement, flat glass, insurance and—just this week—in financial services. "But further progress must be made, especially in the areas of autos and auto parts, which make up the bulk of our trade deficit with Japan," the President said. "We must redouble our efforts to assure further progress."[9]

It must be emphasized that most tangible outcomes in international business negotiations require goodwill and long-term relationships for them to become a reality. For example, the transfer of technology by an international company to a foreign enterprise is a tangible outcome, however, for this transaction to become effective generally takes months, and often years, making goodwill and harmonious relations between the two sides a vital commodity.

Impact of Immediate Stakeholders

The immediate stakeholders comprise (1) the negotiators on each side and their characteristics and (2) the company's negotiators, employees, and the board of directors.

The *characteristics of the negotiators* include aspects such as the cumulative experience of the negotiators in past international business negotiations and their cultural background.

It is generally accepted that the more experience one has in a certain activity, the more proficient one is likely to be in that activity, i.e., efficiency and effectiveness in performing the activity is expected to increase. This is the learning curve or experience effect. This precept applies to international business negotiations as well. A negotiator who has negotiated numerous international business deals in the past will have a body of knowledge in her repertoire which could be quite an asset in impending business negotiations. For instance, a negotiator who has negotiated with the Chinese in the past will be far more adept than someone who is a novice at reading the "unspoken language" during negotiations with other Chinese businesspersons. Choosing which approaches and strategies work and which do not, in the context of a given negotiation, is an art acquired through the practice of negotiations.

The negotiator's cultural background has perhaps the most profound impact upon the negotiations process. After all, there can be no international negotiations without the interaction between at least two persons of different cultural backgrounds. And culture, which is the amalgam of a set of values, beliefs, and norms that have been internalized by people in a society, has a definite role to play in how and why people behave the way they do, including in the context of international business negotiations. For example, the American culture is known for the importance placed on punctuality and the effective use of time. To an American time is a depleting resource. It is an "asset" that is slowly but surely depreciating, i.e., the amount of time at one's disposal now is less than it was a minute ago. The concept of time is quite different in Mexico, India, and in many countries in Asia. To an Indian or an Egyptian, punctuality and meeting one's commitment on time is important but it is not the most important thing in one's life. The general attitude may be summarized in the following comment made by an Indian student of mine: "Americans will get ulcers worrying over time wasted, we Indians have a much more relaxed attitude, we consume our time, we don't allow time to consume us." This cultural difference between Americans and other cultures comes into play in international business negotiations, with Americans sometimes emerging on the losing side because they made unnecessary concessions due to perceived time pressures.*

---

* Culture-based styles of negotiations will be covered later in this chapter.

The personal stakes of the negotiators, employees, and board of directors in the outcome of the negotiations have a bearing upon the strategies chosen, and on any offers and counter-offers made during the negotiations process.

All three groups—managers, employees, and board of directors—may have one or more of the following different types of stakes in the outcomes of the negotiations: financial, career advancement, ego and prestige, personal power, wages and employment, or economic security. Managers are likely to think twice before negotiating an agreement that would erode any of their personal stakes, or those of the employees or the board of directors. For example, as we previously mentioned, Caterpillar, the producer of earth-moving equipment, has suffered numerous breakdowns in labor-management negotiations and several strikes at its Peoria, Illinois, plant because the company has been negotiating with foreign governments and companies the terms for transferring several labor-cost sensitive operations to locations wherein wages are far more competitive than in its U.S. plants. Caterpillar's labor union is unhappy because of potential job losses at the Peoria plant caused by the exports of jobs to cheaper labor wage countries. But Caterpillar was forced to follow this strategy because in a global industry like earth-moving equipment, in which there are strong global competitors such as the Japanese company Komatsu, Caterpillar had to make significant productivity and labor efficiency improvements to remain globally competitive.

Let us refer again to Figure 7-1. By now, we have examined the dimensions of both the external (outer circle) and the immediate (middle circle) context of international business negotiations. Next we shall examine the innermost circle in Figure 7-1, which is the negotiations process that brings the two sides to the negotiating table. Specifically the focus will be on the steps in the negotiations process.

STEPS IN THE NEGOTIATION PROCESS

All negotiations—international or domestic—go through several steps in the negotiation process. These steps are:

- Preparing the background information
- Assessing the needs of both sides
- Understanding who the negotiators are
- Preparing the issues
- Establishing the bargaining positions
- Conflict and cooperation
- Compromise and common ground

Preparing the Background Information

The time invested in collecting and digesting critical information prior to the start of negotiations can pay huge dividends during negotiations and obtain the most favorable outcome for one's side. What sort of information about the other side is critical? At the very least one should try and obtain as much data as possible on the environmental context, illustrated in Exhibit 7-1, under which the negotiations are to occur. Exhibit 7-1 is not comprehensive, nevertheless it is illustrative of the types of information that could be collected on the other company and country.

There are a variety of sources of background information. The company may have negotiated with the company or country in the past and therefore executives who were involved in previous

EXHIBIT 7-1
Useful Background Information

Data You Need on the Company

- Products: characteristics, life cycles, development, differentiation, hierarchy, R&D policy.
- Pricing strategy: objectives, elasticity.
- Profits and profitability.
- Purchasing strategy.
- Markets (local and international). Customers. Sources of materials. Demand. Market share. Competitors. Marketing strategy. Advertising and promotional strategies/agents.
- Channels of distribution and distributors. Transportation.
- Labor relations. Recruitment policies. Training facilities. Salary structures and fringe benefits. Labor relations between local members of your culture.
- Financial data. Financial statements and other reports. Debt ratios.
- Communication facilities.
- Type of company: legal status. Importance of family ties. Patron-client relationships.
- Organizational structure, strategies for change. Structures of control and communication. Structures for planning, motivation, and resolving conflict. How decisions are made, communicated, and implemented. Organizational culture.
- Technology and plant.
- Record in negotiating and in implementing negotiations: delivery and quality performance. Legal history.

Data You Need on the Industry

- National and international competition.
- Market growth. Industry forecasts.
- Market research.
- Upstream and downstream industries, local and/or foreign.
- The categories relating to the company, where they apply to the industry.

Data You Need on the National Environment

- Economic and financial data: currency, exchange rates and requirements, conditions for repatriation of capital, national and company investment policies, subsidies, tax structure, tariffs, customs duties, expected time for customs clearance. Inflation rate. GNP. Average incomes.
- Infrastructure: transportation, communication systems.
- Labor resources: skills demanded and supplied, trained manpower, training facilities, educational structure.
- Laws relating to trade and industry. Plant location, pollution and the environment.
- Laws relating to employment, recruitment, and dismissal procedures, severance payments, salary structures, fringe benefits.
- Laws relating to ethical problems.
- Laws relating to ownership of land, plant, technology, intellectual property.

Exhibit 7-1 *(continued)*

- The political system and structures: opposition groups within and outside of the political structure.
- Country risk.
- Geography and climate. Hot, wet, cold seasons. (When is the best time to negotiate?)
- Public holidays, work hours.
- Names and addresses of contacts.

Data You Need on the Cultural Environment

- Typical cultural attitudes towards time, nature, human relationships, modes of activity. Power distances, needs to avoid uncertainty, degree of individualism versus collectivism, degree of masculinity versus femininity.
- Attitudes towards planning, motivation, conflict, decision making, implementation of decisions.
- Face-to-face relationships in business.
- Evidence of and attitudes toward cultural change.
- Values associated with innovation and technology.
- Attitudes toward non-members and members of your culture.
- Degree of legalism in negotiating and implementing negotiations.
- Social, religious, ethnic, economic, political groups. Inter-group conflicts.
- Languages used and language groups. Correlations between language groups and social, religious (etc.) groups.

Source: Richard Mead, *Cross-Cultural Management Communication*, John Wiley & Sons, New York, 1990, pp. 167-168.

negotiations may be able to provide invaluable insights that may be impossible to get from published sources. Most countries have trade officials in their embassies and consulates who may offer advice. The United States has trade officials based in the Commerce Department who are responsible for keeping tabs on the changing economic and political climate in other countries. International banks and international organizations such as the International Monetary Fund (IMF) and The World Bank publish country reports containing volumes of data that may be relevant to the current negotiations.

Assessing the Needs of Both Sides

Determine the fundamental motivations and driving forces that have brought the other side and your side to the negotiating table. What do you want to get out of the negotiations? What does the other side want to get out of the negotiations? On the surface, is there likely to be a common ground that both could agree on? How convergent or divergent are the basic interests of both sides? Answers to questions such as these should give the negotiators some idea about the climate that is likely to exist during the negotiations.

Understanding Who the Negotiators Are

Understanding and knowing who the persons representing the other side are, how many of them there are, and what their rank and functions are, allows you to choose who and how many from your side should be involved in the negotiations. For instance, cultural factors influence the size and composition of a negotiating team. Consensus is important to the Japanese and so they bring a large negotiating team that includes everyone who would be involved in implementing the outcome of the negotiations. The Chinese also bring large teams, but authority rests with the senior managers in the team.

It is also important to know who in the negotiating team has the most authority, and whether that person has the authority to sign an agreement. It is generally understood that members of an American negotiating team are given the authority to negotiate an agreement, however, the final authority to approve it remains in the hands of a senior executive in the company headquarters.

Preparing the Issues

International business negotiations are seldom restricted to a single issue nor are both sides necessarily negotiating for the same outcomes. For example, Company A may be interested in establishing a joint venture in Japan with Company B because this may be the easiest and fastest avenue for marketing its patented product in the Japanese market. However, Company B may be interested only in a licensing agreement with Company A in order to obtain the manufacturing and marketing rights for Company A's patented product. There may be other issues involved in the negotiations as well, such as the percentage of equity that each side would hold, the royalty rate to be charged for the technology transferred, the buy-back of the finished product by the licensor, and so on.

Establishing the Bargaining Positions

There is a price that the seller wants to get and the buyer wants to pay for each item or issue that is subject to negotiation. For instance, in a licensing agreement there is a price in the form of the royalty rate for a technology that the licensee (buyer) must pay to the licensor (seller). Similarly, there is a price that must be set for technical assistance given by the licensor to the licensee. In an export import transaction, the price paid by the importer will depend upon issues such as the terms of payment, sale of replacement parts, and service after the sale provided by the exporter.

Each side must establish the maximum and minimum that it can *realistically* hope to get from the other side on each item or issue. These are the ceiling and floor prices, respectively. Each issue may not be equally important or critical, and in order to keep focused on those issues that are essential to the success of the venture or project, negotiators would be prudent to prioritize items under such categories as (1) must obtain, (2) like to obtain, and (3) concession bait.

Conflict and Cooperation

The "floor" and "ceiling" positions on key issues taken by each side establish the "bargaining range" in the negotiations. The bargaining range lies in the area between the "ceiling price" of the buyer (bid ceiling price) and the "floor price" of the seller (offer floor price). The give-and-take on each item in the "bargaining package" being negotiated causes the bargaining range to expand or contract. Figure 7-2 illustrates this concept. Adding an item to a "package" will cause the bid ceiling price to rise, while deleting an item from the package will have the opposite effect. This process continues until finally an agreement is reached on all issues being negotiated.

FIGURE 7-2
Bargaining Range

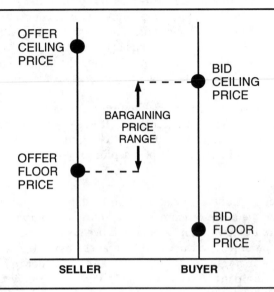

Compromise and Common Ground

Throughout the process, each side should address the following questions: What are the key issues as perceived by each side? Where lies the room for agreement? Disagreement? What are we negotiating for and what can we offer in return to the other party?

The key to effective negotiating is to create new issues and thus increase the alternatives for each party to benefit, i.e., find a win-win alternative by which both sides can benefit. How a win-win solution helps both sides is exemplified in the following.

> There were two sisters arguing over the possession of an orange. One sister wanted to drink the juice, the other to use the peel in baking a cake. They agreed to cut it in half, and thereby overlooked the alternative by which both would double their benefits: one take all the peel and the other take all the juice.[10]

This example is illustrative of numerous conflicts that occur when two parties fight over an issue (who gets the orange) and end up with a win-lose or lose-lose solution, rather than a win-win solution. The key is to find a common ground, a common interest, over which both sides can agree and emerge from the negotiations as winners.

HOW CULTURAL DIFFERENCES AFFECT NEGOTIATIONS

In Chapter 6 we studied the subject of cultural differences in some detail. You may wish to review that chapter once again, because in the following we shall be examining how cultural differences influence international business negotiations. Dean Foster[11] identifies eight different ways in which culture can influence negotiations.

The Definition of Negotiation

The meaning of the term "negotiation" and what it is meant to achieve can vary from one culture to another. Whereas Americans see negotiations as an opportunity to resolve contentious issues, the Japanese, Chinese, and Mexican cultures view negotiations as a vehicle to establish a relationship; resolving problematic issues is never the first goal. "The Japanese view the negotiation as a collaborative process of 'mind-meeting,' which can mandate several meetings before substantive issues are even discussed . . . . Americans tend to view negotiating as a competitive process of offers and counteroffers, while the Japanese tend to view the negotiation as an opportunity for information sharing."[12]

Selection of Negotiators

The criteria used to determine who would be best equipped and qualified to participate in negotiations can vary across cultures. These criteria can include age, sex, family connections, status, competence, and experience. Americans generally choose their negotiators on the basis of expertise of the issues at hand. However, the Japanese choose their negotiators on the basis of seniority and status; it is rare to see a woman as a member of a Japanese negotiating team.

Protocol

Cultures differ in the degree to which protocol or formality in interpersonal interactions is observed. The Americans are supposedly one of the world's most informal cultures. Americans are quite casual in aspects such as calling others by their first names, ignoring titles while addressing others, dressing informally, physical contact, and not giving due "respect" to business cards. The Japanese are very fussy about using business cards. In Japan, a business card not only conveys one's name and company affiliation, but more importantly it establishes one's status in relation to another businessperson. For instance, the bigger the company that one works for, the higher one's status vis-à-vis someone from a smaller company, even though they both may have the same title. Therefore, upon receiving a business card from a Japanese business, one is expected to review it carefully and treat it with respect. Just taking it and dropping it in a coat pocket can be perceived by the Japanese as highly insulting. The Europeans are very fussy about status and titles. Calling a German, Englishman, or a Frenchman by his or her first name is considered very insulting. Employees in French companies address their superiors by last name even after working together for years. In Germany, not addressing a person by his or her proper title (Herr Doktor, Herr Professor) is considered extremely rude.

Communication

Both verbal and nonverbal communication is affected by culture. On a verbal to nonverbal scale, the United States is clearly on the verbal side. Americans believe in the spoken word as the primary means of communication. Other cultures rely on unspoken means of communication such as body language—the use of silence, eye contact, and intonation of speech. A word may have different meanings in different cultures. For example, the word "homely" means friendly or warm in England but ugly in the United States. An international negotiator must be cognizant of not only the meaning of words in different cultures but also of the nonverbal cues that are sent by the other side. *Practical Insight 7-1* offers an interesting current example of the problems inherent in cross-cultural communication.

PRACTICAL INSIGHT 7-1
A Simple 'Hai' Won't Do
By Reiko Hatsumi

TOKYO—When a TV announcer here reported Bill Clinton's comment to Boris Yeltsin that when the Japanese say yes they often mean no, he gave the news with an expression of mild disbelief.

Having spent my life between East and West, I can sympathize with those who find the Japanese yes unfathomable. However, the fact that it sometimes fails to correspond precisely with the Occidental yes does not necessarily signal intended deception. This was probably why the announcer looked bewildered, and it marks a cultural gap that can have serious repercussions.

I once knew an American who worked in Tokyo. He was a very nice man, but he suffered a nervous breakdown and went back to the U.S. tearing his hair and exclaiming, "All Japanese businessmen are liars." I hope this is not true. If it were, all Japanese businessmen would be driving each other mad, which does not seem to be the case. Nevertheless, since tragedies often arise from misunderstandings, an attempt at some explanation might not be amiss.

A Japanese yes in its primary context simply means the other person has heard you and is contemplating a reply. This is because it would be rude to keep someone waiting for an answer without supplying him with an immediate response.

For example: a feudal warlord marries his sister to another warlord. (I am back to TV.) Then he decides to destroy his newly acquired brother-in-law and besieges his castle. Being human, though, the attacking warlord worries about his sister and sends a spy to look around. The spy returns and the lord inquires eagerly, "Well, is she safe?" The spy bows and answers "Hai," which means yes. We sigh with relief thinking, "Ah, the fair lady is still alive!" But then the spy continues, "To my regret she has fallen on her sword together with her husband."

Hai is also an expression of our willingness to comply with your intent even if your request is worded in the negative. This can cause complications. When I was at school, our English teacher, a British nun, would say, "Now children, you won't forget to do your homework, will you?" And we would all dutifully chorus, "Yes, mother," much to her consternation. A variation of hai may mean, "I understand your wish and would like to make you happy but unfortunately . . ." Japanese being a language of implication, the latter part of this estimable thought is often left unsaid.

Is there, then, a Japanese yes that corresponds to the Western one? I think so, particularly when it is accompanied by phrases such as "sodesu" (It is so) and "soshimasu" (I will do so). A word of caution against the statement, "I will think about it." Though in Tokyo this can mean a willingness to give one's proposal serious thought, in Osaka, another business center, it means a definite no. This attitude probably stems from the belief that a straightforward no would sound too brusque.

When talking to a Japanese person it is perhaps best to remember that although he may be speaking English, he is reasoning in Japanese. And if he says "I will think about it," you should inquire as to which district of Japan he hails from before going on with your negotiations.

The Value of Time

In Chapter 6 we discussed the differences in the orientation towards time in different cultures. In the context of international business negotiations, cultural differences in the value placed upon the use of time as a resource can influence whether negotiations succeed or fail. Americans are known to be fastidious about punctuality, getting things done as promised on time, and not wasting time. Americans like to focus upon the issues at hand and resolve them as quickly as possible. However, the Chinese, Japanese, and Mexicans do not mind spending a lot of time on socializing for long periods of time, sometimes even days, before getting down to business. They do not see this activity as a waste of time. On the contrary, they see it as an effective use of time to build proper trust before talking business. As mentioned earlier, Americans perceive time as a depleting resource that must be used efficiently. The Mexicans and Chinese see time as an endless continuum, a context rather than a constraint, in which we live.

Risk Propensity

This dimension is similar to Hofstede's uncertainty avoidance dimension discussed in Chapter 6. Some cultures are risk-takers while others are risk-averse. Risk-taking cultures are likely to produce negotiators who are entrepreneurial and apt to take the risk of making quick decisions in the face of incomplete information. Risk-averse negotiators may tend to be conservative, slow, and deliberative in making decisions. According to Foster, Americans are high-risk takers, the so-called Asian dragons—Taiwan, Singapore, Malaysia, Thailand, and Indonesia—are even more risk oriented, and Japan and Mexico are quite risk-averse.[13]

Individual vs. Group Orientation

This dimension is similar to the individualism/collectivism dimension covered in Chapter 6. Individualistic cultures place a premium on independence, self-interest, assertiveness. In individualistic cultures like the United States one person is likely to have the authority to make decisions. In group-oriented or collectivist cultures the group is preeminent, and one is expected to place group interests above individual interests. In such countries, for example Japan and China, decisions in the negotiating team will be made by group concensus. And decisions probably will not be made at the negotiating table, but rather will be discussed among team members after the meeting is over.[14]

Nature of Agreements

Cultural factors also have an important effect both on the motives for arriving at an agreement and upon the meaning of the term "agreement." In the United States, objective factors such as price and quality are crucial in deciding who gets the business. However, while other cultures such as Japan and Mexico do appreciate objective criteria and rational arguments in negotiating a deal, who eventually gets the deal may depend upon factors such as family or political connections.

In addition, agreements do not mean the same thing in all cultures. Foster notes that the Chinese like to issue "memorandums of understanding" which are supposed to be the "spirit" of the agreement.[15] And the Chinese are notorious for breaking contracts. In such cases the problem lies in the difference in the way in which Americans and the Chinese perceive the purpose of negotiations. Americans view an agreement as the end of negotiations. For the Chinese, an agreement is merely an understanding that they can do business with each other. As such, an agreement is just the beginning of negotiations. To them an agreement is a broad framework to work together and to accommodate each other's needs when and if circumstances require it.

COUNTRY-SPECIFIC NEGOTIATING STYLES*

Countless books have been written on the negotiating styles of various countries. It is beyond the scope of this single chapter to present in detail what these books contain.[16] Our objective here is to give you a sampling of the literature by including brief descriptions of the negotiating styles of three countries in the Pacific Rim that have significant business relationships with the United States—South Korea, Japan, and China. Although all three are geographically in the same region, the similarities and differences in styles among them make for interesting comparisons.

South Korea

As one of the fastest-growing economies in the Pacific Rim, South Korea is gaining increasing importance as a trading partner for western nations. Generally speaking, Korean business negotiators have displayed a much greater familiarity to date with Western negotiating style and practice than Westerners have displayed of the Korean style. Rosalie Tung has sought to remedy this disparity through her study of eighteen cooperative ventures between U.S. and Korean firms, proffering three distinguishing characteristics of the Korean negotiating style along with a list of five "common denominators" to successful negotiations with Korea.[17]

Three features that characterize the Korean negotiating style are the relative speed of decision making (compared to other Asian countries), personal considerations versus Western logic, and the profit motive. The tendency of Koreans to make binding decisions more quickly than negotiators from, for example, Japan or China, Tung attributes to the fact that most Korean businesses are still family owned and controlled. This makes for a shorter "chain of command" than in a firm whose control lies with a relatively distant board of directors or with a state agency, and facilitates a faster response. This is a generalization, and is not to say that talks will not stall, either as a deliberate bargaining tactic or because the Korean negotiators at the table may not, in fact, have the authority to make decisions without further consultation.

A second characteristic of the Koreans is that they may respond more to a sense of personal consideration, or ego fulfillment, than to a purely logical (in the Western sense) argument. This may result in emotional, even abusive, displays during negotiations that would never be exhibited by a Japanese or Chinese team. This same attribute may also cause Korean negotiators to take and maintain what their Western counterparts consider to be an irrational position, exasperatingly defying all attempts at "logical persuasion."

The third aspect of the Korean negotiating style that Tung addresses is the importance, or *un*importance, attached to monetary profit. In this, the Koreans are similar to the Japanese and other Asians in that they may well assign more weight to market share and growth than to short-term profit. As a result, persuasive efforts based on the type of quick return so attractive to Western firms may encounter stiff opposition from across the table.

In addition to the three characteristics of the Korean negotiating style discussed above, Tung's study also found patience, respect for cultural differences, building and nurturing personal relationships, and a long-term commitment to be of great importance in successfully completed

---

* This section is written by John Volkmar, Ph.D., a student in International Business at Temple University.

negotiations. In these areas, Korea is not unlike Japan, China, or other East Asian countries, although it is interesting to note that Koreans stress more than the others the importance of a knowledge of the Korean culture and language. Koreans share the view of the Japanese and Chinese that contracts are only starting points to a business partnership, subject to change in response to changing circumstances. Similarly, the importance of establishing relationships to demonstrate a long-term commitment to the agreement between the parties is very similar to Japan. In both countries, the preferred business relationships are long-term ones, with a great deal of trust and consideration exchanged between the parties.

Japan

Much has been written about the characteristics of the Japanese negotiating style and decision making, but two key elements that are consistently cited are the strivings for harmony and for conflict avoidance. Indeed, many of the more specific attributes of negotiations with the Japanese derive from these two fundamental inclinations. The Japanese are a group-oriented society, and maintaining the harmony of the group is of paramount importance. Accordingly, the exercise of individual authority in decision making is practically unheard of; rather, every effort is made to obtain a consensus. The use of intermediaries in the resolution of disagreements is a device to avoid the loss of face (disharmony) that would accrue to one or both parties to the confrontation. Similarly, the Japanese do not appreciate "surprises" at the bargaining table, as they are disruptive to the carefully planned order of the negotiation process.[18]

This overarching desire for harmony is also one cause of the oft-cited lack of emotion on the part of Japanese negotiators, because of the feeling that open displays of emotion would stand in the way of the proper conduct of the proceedings. However, this inscrutability is also attributable in part to the concept of *tatemae*,* the masking of one's true feelings (*honne*) in order to avoid revealing too much of one's "hand" at the bargaining table.

The use of the spoken language or, sometimes more importantly, the *non*use of it is also a key aspect of negotiations with the Japanese. Unlike Americans and many other Westerners, the Japanese are quite comfortable with what Westerners consider to be oppressively long periods of silence in the course of a business meeting. They also have learned that in many cases they may capitalize on this fact and the impatience such silences may engender in the other negotiating team. In contrast, what is spoken by a Japanese negotiator may not have the same meaning for him as it does for his Western counterpart across the table. Such disparities have resulted in significant misunderstandings in the past (see *Practical Insight 7-1*).

As is the case with other Asian countries, the negotiation of a contract does not signify the end of a process for the Japanese, but rather the beginning of what is hoped to be a long and productive relationship. Because of the importance and permanence of the arrangement, the process of getting to know one another and establishing the requisite degree of trust and confidence is essential to any successful negotiation. Hence the series of social events and gift-exchanges that precede meaty negotiations. Westerners must be patient with this process, even though they may regard it as irrelevant to the matter at hand; to their Japanese counterparts, these preliminaries are as essential, if not more so, to a successful business relationship than the actual negotiations.

---

* "Tatemae" can be translated as the official stance, and "honne" as the "true mind" or the real intentions.

Because the business arrangement being negotiated is viewed by the Japanese as a long-term give-and-take relationship between two interdependent parties rather than merely as a legal contract, the agreement itself is viewed by the Japanese as a dynamic framework, subject to modification with changing circumstances. This is not to say that the basic principles will be abandoned, but that the details may be reinterpreted in terms of the overall objective of the agreement—i.e., a productive, long-term relationship. On this point, Japan, China, and Korea are very similar.

In general, the keys to successful negotiations with the Japanese are supreme patience and a sensitivity and demonstrated respect for the differences between the two cultures represented at the bargaining table. Because of the tremendous differences in culture and language, the use of a knowledgeable native Japanese throughout the negotiations to advise on the more subtle aspects of the spoken and unspoken language and attitudes is highly advisable.

China

Like their counterparts in Japan and Korea, the Chinese are known to be extremely tough negotiators. Likewise, many of the same cultural and attitudinal features that distinguish the negotiating styles of other East Asian countries are equally applicable to China. The single most significant difference in China is the immeasurable importance of politics and the state to any business dealings of consequential size. The overriding concern of a Chinese negotiator that he may make a mistake for which the state may hold him accountable results in a calculated deliberateness in considering proposals and possible responses. Also, seldom do the Chinese negotiators at the bargaining table have the actual power or authority to make binding decisions on the matters at hand; matters must be presented to the proper government officials for resolution. This process takes time, requiring patience on the part of the other negotiating team. The Chinese, like the Japanese, are well aware that Westerners like to "get down to business" and become very uncomfortable and impatient at delay. Like the Japanese, they use this to their advantage whenever possible.

Harmony is an important and desirable goal for the Chinese as it is for the Japanese. There is also a strong attitude favoring ethics and moral principles in business dealings, in contrast to the more legalistic approach espoused by most Western negotiators. Somewhat incongruent with these sentiments is the observed penchant for the Chinese, unlike the Japanese and the Koreans, to employ "hardball," or pressure, tactics during the course of negotiations, such as good guy-bad guy and lowballing. A first-hand account of one company's experience negotiating with the Chinese is offered in *Practical Insight 7-2.*

The view of business partners in terms of a long-term relationship of trust has the same importance in China as in Korea and Japan, and negotiating teams going to China can expect similar preliminaries involving social interaction and gift-giving. The Chinese tend to attach great importance to reaching agreement on the general principles governing the relationship being negotiated—with the feeling that if there is agreement on the higher objectives, the detailed specifics will, in a sense, look to themselves. This is consistent with the view, common to Japan and Korea as well, that the completed contract is a flexible document, subject to change to accommodate changing circumstances.

The requirements for patience and for a respect for the differences in culture that apply to negotiations with the Chinese are the same as we have discussed with respect to Japan and Korea, while recognizing that the omnipotence of the state, and its role in business negotiations, is the essential difference.

PRACTICAL INSIGHT 7-2
Round and Round

(To survive your business negotiations, you'll need patience, skill—and perhaps an extra coat)

Let a hundred renegotiations bloom! For in China, there's no end to the art of the deal. Just when you thought you had pinned down every last detail, your counterpart smiles and starts again—at the top of the list.

Indeed, negotiating in China will test your cunning, your sense of humor—and your digestive tract. You had better learn quickly, because the person across the table has all sorts of strategies to wear you down.

Such as literally giving you the cold shoulder. That's what happened to Clinton Dines, who remembers virtually being held hostage in remote Xiangfan in 1980, when his efforts to buy ball bearings from a Chinese factory hit an impasse. At the time, he was working for Jardine Matheson Holdings Ltd., and he had traveled to Xiangfan in the middle of winter to wrap up contract discussions. Instead, factory officials suddenly jacked up their price.

"It was freezing cold, and the guest house at the factory had no heat," Mr. Dines recalls. "There was no hot water and no shower. I wore gloves in the dining room." After four days of haggling, Mr. Dines decided to leave town.

No way, said the officials. They told Mr. Dines that they couldn't get him a train ticket, and that the shuttle van to the station was busy with other things. It remained busy for two days. Mr. Dines stood his ground, shivering. Finally, embarrassed, the Chinese let him go.

"They figured once they got someone in their clutches, they'd change the price, says Mr. Dines, who advises not giving an inch when bullied.

A lot has changed since then, but renegotiating the deal is still a favorite tactic in China. Here are some others.

MANIPULATING THE DEADLINE: Foreigners, particularly Americans, are impatient. Everyone knows it. And the Chinese are experts at playing it to their advantage, says Richard H. Solomon, former assistant secretary of state. When Henry Kissinger went to Beijing in 1975 to negotiate a communique, Chinese officials kept him on edge until the last moment.

"They invited us out to a picnic in the Western Hills," Mr. Solomon says. "Kissinger was going crazy. Instead of negotiating, the Chinese were dragging things out. Then they gave him an unacceptable document at midnight on the last day of his visit," hoping the Americans would cave in rather than miss their self-imposed deadline.

The lesson: Don't go to China hamstrung by a specific timetable. There's always room for more negotiation, says Mr. Solomon.

SWITCHING NEGOTIATORS: Mr. Dines cites one recent deal in which, after four years of talks, the Chinese side came to the table with a new official—and a new contract. The Australian side revolted and canceled the deal. A week later, their bluff called, the Chinese reinstated the former terms.

If this happens to you, stick to your guns. Keep in mind that China is heavily bureaucratic, and that your counterparts may not want the new official at the table any more than you do.

PSYCHING YOU OUT: During negotiations, every gesture has a deeper meaning—even the "friendly" banquet. Joseph Massey, a U.S. trade negotiator from 1987 to 1992, remembers one fancy dinner that the Chinese threw for their American counterparts. Arrayed over huge mounds of rice, Mr. Massey says, was the specialty of the house: marinated, deep-fried scorpions with their stingers intact.

PRACTICAL INSIGHT 7-2 *(continued)*

"It was both a joke and a test," says Mr. Massey, who downed the delicacy. "You had to laugh and pass the test to maintain the fiction of cordiality." (For the curious, fried scorpion tastes, well, liked fried grasshopper.)

PLAYING THE UNDERDOG: "We're just a poor country, so you should give us special concessions." When you hear that line—and you WILL hear it—buy into it at your own risk. And remember: Japan also used to plead poverty.

OTHER RULES TO KEEP IN MIND:

- The negotiations will always continue even after the deal is done.

- The Chinese believe there is a winner and a loser in every transaction.

- Only senior officials have the authority to spend money, so don't assume your negotiating adversary can make the commitment.

- The Chinese negotiate, not to tie up every loose end, but to develop a relationship and a commitment to work together.

- It's sometimes best to deliver a tough message through a third party.

- Don't let your chief executive officer fly in, get enchanted, and make a promise that will later handcuff your negotiators. The Chinese love it when they know a company's negotiators are under pressure from the boss to close the deal.

Source: Sarah Lubman, *The Wall Street Journal*, Dec. 10, 1993, p. R3. Reprinted by permission of The Wall Street Journal © 1993 Dow Jones & Company, Inc. All Rights Reserved Worldwide.

The three country briefs presented reinforce the basic theme of this chapter that there are a multitude of factors shaping the context within which negotiations take place, and that the ability to identify and to accommodate these often conflicting, cross-cultural forces is essential to negotiating a successful international business deal. Unlike negotiations between parties that share a common culture, and therefore common beliefs and expectations about the negotiations process itself, the international dimension may well require modifying one's fundamental ideas about the purpose and process of negotiations to succeed, or at least recognizing that the other party brings a different set of expectations and priorities to the table.

Now that we have an understanding of the purpose and nature of international business negotiations, and their importance to the international company, we turn in the next chapter to discussion of the planning process itself, its essentiality to the firm, and the types of strategic decisions and problems that confront the international manager.

SUMMARY

Negotiation—a process by which one party tries to change the attitudes, beliefs, or behavior of another party—is essential to the conduct of international business transactions. The negotiations process can be viewed as occurring within two umbrella contexts: an *environmental context* of forces beyond the control of either party to the negotiations, and an *immediate context*, the set of relationships and attributes that characterizes the negotiations process itself.

The environmental context of international business negotiations comprises several unique dimensions beyond those that apply in strictly domestic negotiations. These include legal and political pluralism, the impact of currency fluctuations, foreign government controls and bureaucracy, instability and change, differing ideologies and cultures, and external stakeholders.

The environmental forces also serve to shape the nature of the immediate context of negotiations, which includes the relative bargaining power of negotiators, levels of conflict underlying the negotiations, the relationships between negotiators, the desired outcomes of the negotiations, and the immediate stakeholders.

A successful negotiating strategy entails identifying the nature and strength of the various forces of both the environmental and immediate contexts, and incorporating a consideration of those forces. Careful preparation is also necessary in collecting background information, assessing the needs of all the parties, even in understanding who the negotiators are. The establishment of proper bargaining positions is critical to success, as is a reasoned plan for when and how strongly to maintain those positions.

Cultural differences between the negotiating parties may also have a substantial influence on the negotiations. From differences in the very meaning and objectives of the negotiation process, to misperceptions and miscommunications due to differing attitudes about time, risk, protocol, etc., there are a multitude of threats to a successful negotiation. Doing one's homework on the specifics of the negotiating style of the other party is absolutely essential.

QUESTIONS FOR THOUGHT AND DISCUSSION

1. Which do you feel has a greater impact on the international business negotiation process—the environmental or the immediate context? Support your answer with material from the chapter.

2. In Chapter 4 we discussed the lack of an overarching legal authority as a key aspect of the legal environment for international business. For companies engaged in international business negotiations, what implications does this fact have with respect to the concepts of legal and political pluralism introduced in this chapter?

3. Find an article in the current business press that addresses an international business negotiation. Identify some of the external and immediate stakeholders in this negotiation (they may not all be listed in the article). How might each attempt to influence the negotiation? How would this affect the negotiators on both sides?

4. Using Figure 7-2, show how the bargaining range between a car buyer and a car salesperson is established. What is the significance of the "bid floor" and the "offer ceiling" prices in this case? Does the bargaining range remain fixed throughout the negotiations? Explain.

MINI-CASE
Both Sides Claim Victory in Trade Deal

Brief Background

Consistently huge trade deficits with Japan during the past several years ranging from $50—$65 billion a year led President Bill Clinton of the United States to threaten punitive tariffs in the form of 100 percent import duties on Japanese luxury cars if an agreement were not reached by midnight of June 28. The Japanese government threatened retaliation against U.S. imports to Japan if the punitive tariffs were implemented. The trading partners of both countries firmly believed that the trade dispute should be settled by the newly created World Trade Organization (WTO). The Japanese believed that their side would win their case before the WTO. Japan and the U.S. were friends and allies since World War II, and a trade war between the two largest economies in the world was something that neither side relished.

Geneva—With a possible trade war at stake, Mickey Kantor agonized all night about closing a deal with the Japanese, alternating from confidence to self-doubt to relief when the two sides finally reached an historic agreement.

Kantor, the U.S. trade representative, had flown here Sunday to try to wrap up negotiations on auto trade with the Japanese. At the time, some thought he would merely rubber-stamp a deal his aides had put together in lower-level talks last week. Instead, he spent much of three days in intense, face-to-face talks with Japan's fiesty trade minister, Ryutaro Hashimoto. A lengthy interview with Kantor during his ride to the airport, hours after the United States and Japan announced their trade deal, reveals that the talks nearly collapsed Wednesday in the early morning hours.

Kantor rode out through the gates of the Japanese mission here Wednesday morning at 2 a.m. He had just finished his fourth meeting with Hashimoto. A deal seemed within sight.

Negotiations continued among lower-level officials. But things were going badly. And there wasn't much time to work with: The U.S. and Japan were facing a countdown to a potential trade war, starting at midnight ET Wednesday.

Kantor returned to the Geneva offices of the U.S. trade representative in the U.S. consulate. But aides at the Japanese mission a couple of miles away in a quiet residential neighborhood began calling Kantor with gloomy reports. "The situation was deteriorating," Kantor said. "But that sort of thing often happens in negotiations. What do they say? 'It's always darkest before the dawn.'"

Still, Kantor was worried. He asked himself whether he'd made a mistake by leaving the talks.

At 6 a.m., after staying awake all night, he showered, shaved, changed clothes and waited for Hashimoto to arrive for another round of face-to-face discussions.

U.S. negotiators had prepared two statements: one announcing success—an agreement to begin opening Japan's auto market; the other, to announce failure—and the imposition of 100 percent tariffs at midnight ET Wednesday on thirteen luxury car models sold in the United States.

Hashimoto's Mercedes-Benz arrived at the trade representative's office promptly at 8:45 a.m. "Hashimoto came in, and we had a good productive meeting," Kantor said.

Significantly, Hashimoto had brought with him the voluntary plans from the five major Japanese automakers for increasing purchases of U.S. parts, stepping up auto production in the U.S., and increasing imports of foreign-made auto parts into Japan.

It was the first time Kantor had seen the plans. But U.S. negotiators had long hoped Japanese automakers would step forward with commitments to buy more U.S. parts. The Japanese government had balked at agreeing to numerical targets on behalf of its auto industry.

But these voluntary agreements by Japanese car companies would allow Hashimoto to say that the Japanese government had refused to accept numerical targets.

Kantor asked an aide, David Burns, to go over the numbers. Burns and a Japanese trade official examined the data for several hours.

"Then (Burns) came in and he said, 'This is what we wanted,'" Kantor said. At that moment— around noon Wednesday, Geneva time—he knew there would be a deal.

Not long afterward, Kantor took a call from President Clinton. "Hey, Mick, it sounds like you did great," the President told Kantor.

Kantor said he could not explain why the morning negotiations with Hashimoto went so smoothly after a night that U.S. officials called "a roller coaster." Perhaps, Kantor says, Japan's suddenly hard-line position a few hours earlier was merely "pre-buyer's remorse."

The key may have been that Hashimoto "wanted this to work," Kantor said. After negotiating on a variety of trade issues for more than two years, Kantor and Hashimoto have developed a good working relationship. "I have great respect for him and have become friends with him," Kantor says.

For his part, Hashimoto said at a joint press conference with Kantor, the key to reaching a deal was "Ambassador Kantor's realistic approach and persistent efforts."

The announcement pre-empted the U.S. threat of tariffs on Japanese luxury cars.

Sanctions could have sparked a trade war with Japan and jeopardized the 50-year security relationship between the two nations. Failure also could have meant the end of Japanese luxury cars in the United States, threatening the survival of hundreds of auto dealerships.

Kantor insists the deal was no compromise: The U.S. got most of what it wanted, he says. But the Japanese maintain they didn't give in on what they considered the most important issue: the U.S. demand that they agree to numerical targets designed to measure whether they were opening their markets to U.S. autos and auto parts. Most observers say both sides gave ground, the U.S. more than Japan.

The breakthrough came after three days of nearly around-the-clock negotiations.

The deal done, Kantor and Hashimoto shook hands in a ballroom at the posh Intercontinental Hotel here. Then both left through a hotel kitchen to avoid an army of journalists covering the talks from countries around the globe.

Outside the hotel, Kantor quickly climbed into a dark blue Ford Scorpio for the short drive to the United Nations complex here. Kantor was using the United Nations' television studio for a series of short interviews with U.S. TV networks. While claiming success, Kantor was careful not to say the Japanese had given in. "It was not a matter of who blinked," he said in one TV interview. "We all can win if we have good, strong trade agreements."

Kantor had been awake for 38 hours straight by the time he boarded a U.S. military jet in Geneva Wednesday night for a flight to Denver for a trade conference.

He didn't look like a man who hadn't slept in a day and a half. "The adrenaline keeps you going," he said.

Kantor said the threatened U.S. sanctions played a key part in bringing the Japanese to the table. He said the Japanese were convinced that Clinton would allow the sanctions to take effect.

Kantor said the agreement is "solid, meaningful, and concrete" and "a significant step to fundamental change" in the way Japan does business. But the agreement will not be the final work on opening Japan's market.

"This agreement will not solve every problem. Let's not give hyperbole a bad name," Kantor said.

"All of this is in the best interest of American workers," Kantor said. "This is a very big step in a long road," Kantor said at his joint press conference with Hashimoto. "What it will do is make a significant difference in opening the most important sector in Japan."

Source: Michael Clements, *USA TODAY*, June 29, 1995, pp. 1B & 2B. © 1995, USA Today. Reprinted by permission.

Discussion Questions for Mini-Case

1. Why was Mickey Kantor, the U.S. trade representative and chief U.S. negotiator, careful not to say that the Japanese had given in?

2. Look at Figure 7-1. Identify and discuss the dimensions in the *external context* which might have come into play in the negotiations between the two sides.

3. Identify the most important dimensions in the *immediate context* that could have influenced the outcome of negotiations between Mickey Kantor and Ryutaro Hashimoto.

4. Obtain information from the library or from the Internet on the history of U.S.-Japan trade relations over the past two decades, and identify the problems that led to President Clinton's ultimatum of trade sanctions against the Japanese.

Notes

1. Jack Sawyer and Harold Guetzkow, "Bargaining and Negotiation in International Relations," in Herbert C. Kelman, (ed.), *International Behavior: A Social-Psychological Analysis*, Holt, Rinehart and Winston, New York, 1965, p. 466.

2. Jeswald W. Salacuse, "Making Deals in Strange Places: A Beginner's Guide to International Business Negotiations," *Negotiation Journal*, January 1988, pp. 5-13, reprinted in Roy L. Lewicki, Joseph A. Litterer, David M. Saunders, and John W. Minton, *Negotiation: Readings, Exercises, and Cases*, Richard D. Irwin, Burr Ridge, Illinois, 1995, pp. 521-529.

3. Some concepts for this section have been borrowed from Jeswald W. Salacuse, "Making Deals in Strange Places: A Beginner's Guide to International Business Negotiations," *Negotiation Journal*, January 1988, pp. 5-13.

4. Craig Torres, "Mexico's Woes Accelerate as Peso Falls Further," *The Wall Street Journal*, December 28, 1994, p. A3.

5. Tim Carrington, "U.S. Visit by India's Prime Minister Was Reminder of Hard Balancing Act," *The Wall Street Journal*, May 23, 1994, p. A10.

6. Ibid.

7. John J. Curran, "China's Investment Boom," *Fortune*, March 7, 1994, p. 117.

8. Ibid., p. 118.

9. Martin Crutsinger, "Clinton-Murayama downplay trade gap," *The Philadelphia Inquirer*, January 12, 1995, p. A3.

10. Mary Parker Follet, "Constructive Conflict," in H.C. Metcalf and L. Urwick, (Eds.), *Dynamic Administration: The Collected Papers of Mary Parker Follet*, Harper, New York, 1940.

11. The eight categories are adapted from Dean Allen Foster, *Bargaining Across Borders*, McGraw-Hill, Inc., New York, 1992, pp. 272-293; however, the ideas are derived from this source as well as from the author's own viewpoints.

12. Dean Allen Foster, *Bargaining Across Borders*, McGraw-Hill, Inc., New York, 1992, p. 272.

13. Ibid., pp. 287-288.

14. Ibid., p. 289.

15. Ibid., p. 292.

16. For a comprehensive and detailed treatment of the negotiating characteristics and patterns of different countries, the reader is referred to Frank L. Acuff, *How to Negotiate Anything with Anyone Anywhere Around the World*, AMACOM, New York, 1993; or to Dean Allen Foster, *Bargaining Across Borders: How to Negotiate Business Successfully Anywhere in the World*, McGraw-Hill, New York, 1992.

17   Rosalie L. Tung, "Handshakes Across the Sea: Cross-Cultural Negotiating for Business Success," *Organizational Dynamics*, 19:3, Winter, 1991, pp. 20-30.

18   Frank L. Acuff, *How to Negotiate Anything with Anyone Anywhere Around the World*, AMACOM, New York, 1993.

Strategic Planning in a Global Setting

LEARNING OBJECTIVES

After completing this chapter, you will be able to:

- Explain the importance of strategic planning and its role in the international firm.
- Discuss external and internal issues and problems that may affect the strategic planning process of an international manager.
- Describe some of the consequences of a company's failure to properly plan for entering a new foreign market.
- Identify the steps involved in developing a global corporate strategy.

This chapter is about the strategic planning function in a global setting. The international setting is complex; hence the problems and issues confronting global strategic planning are equally complex. Lack of strategic planning would almost certainly result in the misallocation of resources and a disappointing performance by the company's global operation. A well-designed global corporate strategy allows a company to set realistic objectives and to deploy and use its resources efficiently on a global scale.

The focus of this chapter is on strategic planning at the parent company level of an international company. At the core of this presentation are the issues that top management at headquarters must come to grips with in developing strategies for the company's international involvement.

WHAT IS STRATEGIC PLANNING?

Strategic planning is one of the basic functions in the management process. Every manager must have plans in order to reach maximum organizational effectiveness. Strategic planning involves assessment of the environment for opportunities and threats in the foreseeable future, evaluation of the strengths and weaknesses of the enterprise, and the formulation of objectives and strategies designed to exploit the opportunities and combat the threats.

All planning is concerned with the future; it is concerned with deciding what an enterprise wants to be and wants to achieve, how to attain these aspirations, allocate resources, and implement designs. Russell A. Ackoff says that "planning is the design of a desired future and of effective ways of bringing it about."[1] He goes on to say that "planning is a process that involves making and evaluating each of the set of interrelated decisions before action is required, in a situation in which it is believed that unless action is taken a desired future state is not likely to occur, and that, if appropriate action is taken, the likelihood of a favorable outcome can be increased."[2] To George A. Steiner, "planning deals with the futurity of present decisions."[3] This, he says, can mean one of two things—or both. "Planning examines future alternative courses of action which are open to a company. In choosing from among these courses of action an umbrella, a perspective, a frame of reference is established for current decisions. Also it can mean that planning examines the evolving chains of cause and effect likely to result from current decisions."[4]

WHAT IS GLOBAL STRATEGIC PLANNING?

All the aspects of strategic planning just mentioned are applicable to global strategic planning as well. In addition, global strategic planning is concerned with the assessment of the multinational environment, determining future worldwide opportunities and threats, and formulating the global objectives and strategies of the enterprise in light of this environmental assessment, as well as an internal audit of the enterprise's strengths and weaknesses. Global strategic planning includes the formulation of short and long-term goals and objectives and the allocation of resources, people, capital, technology, and information globally to achieve the enterprise's global aims.

CONSEQUENCES OF A LACK OF PLANNING

An international company should have an overall plan and a well-designed strategy for entry into foreign markets. Too many companies have entered foreign markets via licensing, contract manufacturing, or production facilities without a deliberate plan for foreign market penetration, only to find that the particular strategy chosen was wrong in light of later developments. For example, a company may begin its involvement in a foreign market in the form of export sales in response to inquiries from foreign distributors. As export sales grow, the company may begin to experience problems supplying the foreign market via exports because of a variety of tariff and nontariff barriers and import restrictions imposed by the local government. Believing that the foreign market should be protected, company management may resort to licensing a local company to produce the product. This may turn out to be the wrong strategy if, in fact, the market for the product expands and becomes large enough to support a local production facility. The option of production abroad would be unavailable to the company now because a local company is already producing the product. Had the company looked into the future and made sales forecasts for the product in the foreign market, it might not have given the license to the foreign company to produce the product, and instead could have commenced production itself.

Lack of planning may also "lead to a sub-optimum deployment of corporate resources overseas and a consequent loss of the potential benefits of multinational operations. An important advantage of multinational business as contrasted with purely domestic operations is that it provides management with the broadest possible dimension of enterprise in which to take full advantage of worldwide investment opportunities that offer the highest returns. However, this strength can be realized only when alternatives are systematically examined and compared on a global basis."[5]

Absence of effective planning may result in the company's allocating its resources to ventures that may not represent the best among the available global market opportunities. A company that does not have a formalized program for the evaluation of foreign market opportunities is not likely to discover the best ones among the many available; therefore, it might make an unwise investment abroad merely because the prime opportunities were never identified as such. Proper timing of entry into foreign markets can often make the difference between success or failure of a foreign venture. Establishing a production facility before the market is large enough to support the required volume for optimum plant utilization results in excess plant capacity and higher per-unit production costs. However, waiting too long is always equally undesirable because the first entrant in the market has the distinct advantage of being able to capture a huge share of the total sales volume. The experience of many companies has shown how difficult it is to take sales and market share away from a competitor who already has a large proportion of the total market. Timing of foreign market entry is thus critical, and needs very careful planning.

The availability of adequate resources, both financial and managerial, is often overlooked by firms when they decide to venture abroad. At issue is not the availability of such resources in absolute terms; companies with genuine opportunity can generally manage to find them. What is crucial is that the resources be at hand when they are needed. For instance, a company may be making fine profits, but if its capital is tied up in the development and marketing of many new products that experience a net cash outflow, it may not have the necessary cash to start new ventures abroad—especially if it does not have a portfolio of mature products that can serve as cash cows. Or, a company could establish many foreign affiliates in rapid succession, only to find, to its dismay, that it does not have adequate managerial personnel to send out from the home office, or hire abroad, to manage these operations. Planning of foreign market entry could avoid such problems.

Finally, lack of planning may cause numerous operating problems after the foreign venture gets under way. For example, a company may assume that marketing channels similar to those at home are available in the foreign market, only to find that there are no existing channels that it can use for marketing its products. In the United States and other advanced Western countries, a company has a choice between establishing its own distribution network or using one already there, such as a chain of department stores or retail food outlets. Most developing countries do not have such alternative distribution networks, so companies must set up their own, which can be quite expensive. Furthermore, the company may not have anticipated the need to hold a far greater stockpile of inventory of raw materials and components than the level generally kept in the home country. Such stockpiling could be necessary if the items must be imported due to local nonavailability, and this stockpiling will probably mean higher inventory costs than anticipated.

STEPS IN DEVELOPING A GLOBAL CORPORATE STRATEGY

The aforementioned problems that arise from poor strategic planning point out the acute need for the development of a strategy for international business operations. In the following pages, we shall be concerned with how such a strategy may be developed by a company that is considering entering foreign markets, and we shall also look at some issues involved in the development of the strategy.

A company that is considering foreign market opportunities should begin by asking the following basic question: Should we go international? If the answer to this question is in the affirmative, then the next questions to consider are Where, throughout the world, should we look for opportunities? How soon should we embark on our first venture abroad? What is the best way of exploiting foreign opportunities? Although on the surface it may appear that there are many business opportunities abroad, it is important to recognize that such opportunities vary signifi-cantly among industries and individual firms. Besides, different firms have unequal abilities to exploit foreign markets successfully. Hence, in evaluating the value of entry into foreign markets, management should:

1. Evaluate the opportunities in foreign markets for the firm's products and technology, as well as the potential threats, problems, and risks related to these opportunities.

2. Evaluate the strengths and weaknesses of the firm's managerial, material, technical, and functional (finance, marketing, etc.) competence to determine the degree to which the firm has the resources to successfully exploit potential foreign opportunities.

Step 1 is generally known as *environmental analysis*, and step 2 as the *internal resource audit*.

The assessment of the international opportunities and of the strengths and weaknesses of the resource base should permit the company's management to define the scope of its international business involvement. The next step is to formulate companywide global business objectives; then develop pertinent global corporate strategies aimed at achieving those objectives.

To summarize, the development of a global corporate strategy involves the following steps:

1. Evaluate the opportunities, threats, problems, and risks.

2. Evaluate the strengths and weaknesses of the firm to exploit foreign opportunities.

3. Define the scope of the firm's global business involvement.

4. Formulate the firm's global corporate objectives.

5. Develop specific corporate strategies for the firm as a whole.

It should be noted that although the steps are listed sequentially, in practice the process is iterative, and there is, typically, considerable backtracking as one progresses from one step to the next. For example, if global business objectives are formulated, but then managers cannot develop creditable strategies to achieve them, the objectives must be changed and steps 4 and 5 redone. The process is illustrated in Figure 8-1.

Let us now examine the steps in global corporate strategy formulation.

FIGURE 8-1
Global Corporate Strategy Process

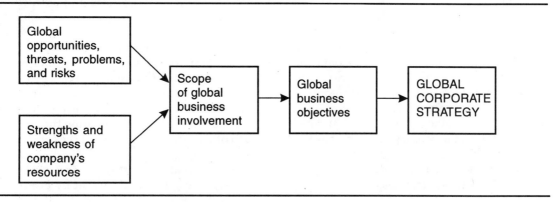

CHAPTER EIGHT

Analyzing the Global Environment

Environmental analysis focuses on the discovery and evaluation of business opportunities, and on the threats, problems, and risks associated with them. It involves the analysis of certain factors in the environment that could have a significant positive or negative impact on the operations of a firm, and over which the firm has little or no control. Environmental factors with a positive impact may create future opportunities, whereas those with a negative impact may represent future threats, risks, and problems for the firm. Such factors—which we shall call *critical environmental factors*—are the focus of an environmental analysis. Hence, when a firm conducts an environmental analysis it should zero in on the critical factors in the economic, political, legal, and cultural segments of the total environment in which the firm operates.

Global environmental analysis is the conduct of this activity on an international scale. However, in an international company, environmental analysis should be conducted on at least three different levels: (1) multinational, (2) regional, and (3) country. At the multinational level, environmental analysts at the company headquarters are concerned with the identification, forecasting, and monitoring of critical environmental factors in the world at large. The analysis is very broad in nature, and devoid of much detail; its focus is on the significant trends and events unfolding over time. For example, corporate environmental analysts may study global technological developments, trends in governmental intervention in the economies of nations, or the overall changes occurring in the values and lifestyles of people in industrialized versus developing countries. Then, the analysts would make judgments about the probable nature of these trends and the degree of impact on the internal operations of the company—now and in the future.

Environmental analysis at the regional level focuses on a more detailed study of the critical environmental factors within a specific geographic area such as western Europe, the Middle East, or Southeast Asia. Here, the intent is to identify opportunities for marketing the company's products, services, or technology in a particular region. Analysts also research the types of problems that may occur and the appropriate strategies to counter them. For example, an automobile company may find that significant growth anticipated in the gross national product and per capita incomes of a population has created a potentially large market for automobiles; however, because of the absence of good roads and skilled auto mechanics, cars sold in the region must be sturdy, with engines of a basic design that do not require complicated repair procedures. Similarly, a company making electronic equipment may find that low wages in the Far East or southern Asia provide an opportunity to significantly lower production costs by transferring labor-intensive operations to those areas. But it may also face problems in dealing with a labor force that has a different cultural background. Regional environmental analysis pinpoints countries in regions that seem to have the most market potential. These become the focus of country environmental analysis—the next level of analysis.

Environmental analysis at the country level is concerned with an in-depth analysis of the critical environmental factors—economic, legal, political, cultural—in a small number of countries. In each country, an evaluation is made of the nature of the opportunities available. The kinds of questions analysts ask include (1) How big is the country market for our products, services, or technology? (2) How can the market be served—by exports, licensing, contract manufacturing, or local production? (3) Which of these is the best strategy for entering the country market? (4) Can the country serve as a base for exports to other countries, including the company's home market?

Country analysis also identifies the nature of the potential threats, risks, and problems associated with each form of market entry. For instance, serving the local market by exporting to it may carry with it the risk of government restraints in the future, such as higher tariffs or import quotas. However, establishing a local production facility may also be risky because the government may, in the future, insist that the equity of the foreign affiliate be shared with the local population. Thus, country environmental analysis must be oriented to each of the market entry strategies for it to be meaningful for planning purposes. A suggested procedure for conducting this analysis is as follows: First, identify the critical external conditions or factors that must exist for the success of a particular market entry strategy. Next, evaluate the critical environmental factors associated with each market entry strategy. A matrix similar to that shown in Exhibit 8-1 may be used for this purpose. Evaluations of the critical environmental factors (economic, legal, political, cultural) that can affect each form of market entry are made and recorded in each cell in the matrix. The individual evaluations in each cell may be "averaged" to arrive at a cumulative index of the quality of the critical environmental factors for each market entry strategy, thus permitting a comparison among them. Similar market entry strategy evaluations may be conducted for each country under consideration. Examples of different types of critical environmental factors for each form of market entry strategy are presented in Exhibit 8-2.

Before closing the subject of global environmental analysis, we must stress that the external environment is always changing—hence the critical environmental factors favorable at one time may become unfavorable later, and vice versa. Therefore, multinational, regional, and country environmental analysis must be done continuously. Moreover, the focus of such analysis must be upon forecasting the future characteristics of critical environmental factors, so that the company may have sufficient lead time to make appropriate modifications in its strategies.

Making an Internal Resource Audit

The focus of an external environmental analysis is on the environmental conditions that must be present for the successful implementation of a market entry strategy. Now our attention is

EXHIBIT 8-1
Market Entry Strategy Evaluation Matrix

Entry Strategy \ Critical Environmental Factors	Economic	Legal	Political	Cultural	Cumulative Strategy Index
Export	A	C	B	B	B
Licensing	B	A	A	E	A-
Contract manufacturing	C	B	A	E	B
Local Production	B	B	C	B	B-

A = Excellent   D = Poor
B = Good   E = Not acceptable
C = Fair

EXHIBIT 8-2
Examples of Critical Environmental Factors for Market Entry Strategies

Export	*Contract Manufacturing*
Import tariffs	Quality of local contractor
Import quotas	Capital repatriation
Distance from nearest supplier country	
Freight costs	*Local Production*
	Political stability
	Size of market
Licensing	Market structure
Patent and trademark protection	Currency stability
Quality of license	Capital repatriation
Legal limit on royalty rate structure	Local attitude toward foreign ownership

turned to the internal resource audit, which is concerned with an evaluation of the conditions internal to the company that must exist if the company is to succeed in a specific business in a particular country. The aim of an internal resource audit is to match the company's managerial, technical, material, and financial resources with those required for success in a business.

The internal resource audit is business-related rather than environment-related. The *key business success factors* (KBSF) may be different from those needed in another business. For example, the factors needed to succeed in the baby food business are different from those required for success in the fast-food industry. The internal resource audit is also country-related; for example, the total amount of resources that a firm must be able to generate internally to succeed in a country such as Mali may not be the same as the amount required to succeed in Japan. A well-developed capital market and banking industry in Japan, for instance, allows a firm to borrow locally for working capital or plant expansion purposes. It does not have to have this money internally. But the absence of such facilities in Mali would force the firm to finance the foreign affiliate's capital requirements from its internal sources, such as retained earnings. Thus, in order to succeed in a business in Mali, a firm must have the capacity to generate the required funds from internal sources.

Along the same lines, a firm in a business that requires effective channels of distribution—businesses such as vending machines or food markets (such as "Seven-Eleven")—for marketing its products must have the resources to develop its own distribution system. In a country that does not have well-developed channels of distribution, it will have to induce independent retail shop owners to carry and promote its products. Such a problem would not occur in an advanced country like Germany, but would in a developing nation such as Sudan.

The preceding examples show that there is a close link between the strengths and weaknesses of a firm and the environment in which it does business; a firm may have ample resources to do business in one country, but may match up very unsatisfactorily with the setting another country provides. Each environment places constraints on the availability of resources required to succeed in the business in that country's market. These constraints determine the amount of resources that the firm must be able to generate on its own in order to succeed. The ability to generate resources determines the firm's strengths and weaknesses. This relationship between the environmental constraints and the firm's strengths and weaknesses is shown in Figure 8-2.

FIGURE 8-2

**Relationship Between External Environmental
Constraints and the Strengths and Weaknesses of a Firm**

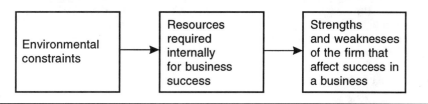

The conceptual process needed to evaluate the strengths and weaknesses of a company is as follows: (1) Determine the key business success factors, that is, those in which the firm must excel in order to succeed in the business. (2) Match the firm's available resources against those required to score high and do better than competitors in each of the areas identified by the key business success factors. (3) Assess the strengths and weaknesses of the firm. This process is illustrated in Figure 8-3. Examples of key business success factors are presented in Exhibit 8-3. The key business success factors can and do change from one period to another. For example, fuel efficiency was not a critical factor for success in the automobile industry prior to the oil crisis and its resultant increases in the price of gasoline (since 1974), but now it is. Therefore, a company must maintain an effective program for continuously monitoring and forecasting the key factors for success in each of the businesses in which it is involved. And an international company must conduct an evaluation of its strengths and weaknesses to succeed in every country in which it already has business operations or is planning to start them in the near future.

Defining the Scope of Global Business Involvement

The next step in international corporate strategy formulation is the definition of the scope or basic perimeter of the firm's global business activities. Knowing the scope helps company management identify those foreign market opportunities that may be considered for an in-depth study before

FIGURE 8-3

Conceptual Process to Evaluate the Strengths and Weaknesses of a Firm

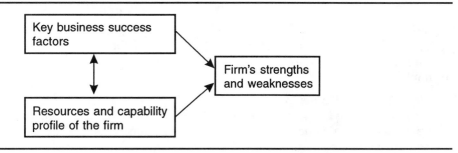

EXHIBIT 8-3
Examples of Key Business Success Factors

Automobile Manufacturer	*Pharmaceutical Company*
Styling	Efficacy of products
Fuel efficiency	Product innovation
Quality	Patents
Price	Company image
Service	
Distribution system	

Soft Drinks Producer
Channels of distribution
Taste
Sales promotion
Brand identification
Price

resources are committed for their exploitation. Those that clearly fall outside the scope can be ignored. A thorough investigation of a foreign market can be costly and time-consuming; however, defining the company's scope of global business involvement helps the company weed out market opportunities that, given the company's strengths and weaknesses, it cannot exploit.

The scope of the company's global business may be defined in terms of the following dimensions: *geography, product, technology, ownership, size of commitment, risk, time span, form of market entry,* and *level of economic development.* The following questions must be answered for each dimension.

Geography Should the company limit its international business involvement to certain geographic regions of the world, or should it become truly global by going after opportunities that are attractive irrespective of their geographic location?

Product Should the company's global business involvement be limited to only some of its products? Should the stage in the product life cycle determine a product's global involvement—that is, should only mature products be involved in international business, leaving those that are at the development or growth stage for the home market first?

Technology Shall the company limit its global activities to those opportunities that involve the use of older or nonproprietary technology? Or should the global thrust be founded on the best and most advanced technology available? How important is patent protection in the transfer of technology abroad?

Ownership Should foreign ventures be one hundred percent owned by the company, or can ownership be shared with local partners abroad? Is majority ownership acceptable in areas where complete ownership is not allowed by local legislation? Under what conditions will a minority ownership be acceptable?

Size of Commitment   Should there be limits placed on the magnitude of commitments the company is willing to consider in a given market? Should maximum and minimum limits be placed on the size of commitments that can be made in one country?

Risk   How much risk is the company willing to assume in a venture, given the size of the commitment involved and the benefits expected? What is the balance among risk, commitment, and benefits that is acceptable in each venture? Should risks be diversified by products and regions?

Time Span   What proportion of the company's total resources should be committed to foreign opportunities in any given year? Should the company enter by phases into foreign markets?

Form of Market Entry   Will the company consider only opportunities that are exploitable by local production, or will it consider those that lend themselves to exporting, licensing, or other market entry strategies?

Level of Economic Development   Should the company limit its global involvement to developed countries only, or will it consider opportunities in both developed and developing countries?

A deliberate and careful study of these issues will serve to define and limit the scope of the company's global business involvement. For example, one firm may conclude that, given its strengths and weaknesses, it should limit its initial foreign involvement to establishing a firm foothold via licensing in the European Common Market, and it might limit such involvement in the early stages to only one of its major product lines. Another firm may decide to look worldwide for market opportunities, and to exploit them only by establishing wholly owned manufacturing facilities. Thus, defining the scope of global business involvement specifies the types of foreign business opportunities the firm is interested in, and allows it to ignore those that do not meet the chosen criteria.

Formulating Global Corporate Objectives

The next step in international corporate strategy formulation is the determination of what the company hopes to achieve from its international operations. Global corporate objectives are the objectives of the company as a whole. They serve as the umbrella under which the objectives of each of its corporate divisions and foreign affiliates are formulated. Divisional and affiliate objectives are expected to be consistent with, and contributory to, global corporate objectives. This relationship between global corporate, divisional, and affiliate objectives is presented in Figure 8-4.

Global corporate objectives are formulated in areas such as profitability, marketing, production, finance, technology, host government relations, personnel, research and development, and the environment. There may be other areas in which global corporate objectives can be formulated. The general guideline is to formulate objectives in areas that directly and vitally affect the survival and prosperity of the company. While developing corporate objectives, top management must recognize the objectives of the claimants on the corporation—the stockholders, customers, employees, suppliers, and the public located in geographically dispersed regions. But most importantly, top management must make every effort to ensure that the company's foreign operations make positive contributions toward meeting the goals of each host country.

Often the objectives of these various groups conflict with each other, in which case top management must establish their relative importance to the long-run survival and growth of the company. Management must also assess the comparative political influence of each claimant, then

FIGURE 8-4
The Hierarchy of Objectives

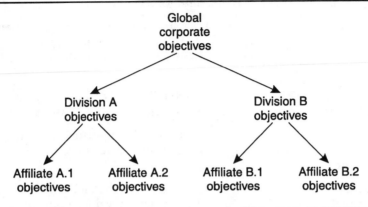

reformulate the international corporate objectives in the company's long-range interests. "The importance of recognizing the objectives of the various claimants is brought into sharp focus when we realize that several American multinational companies could have avoided expropriation of their properties in Latin America had they recognized the values and expectations of the host countries and incorporated them in their overall company objectives and plans.[6] The different areas in which a company may formulate (and revise) its global corporate objectives are presented in Exhibit 8-4.

The next critical task for top management is deciding how the objectives are to be achieved. This decision involves the formulation of the company's corporate strategies.

Developing Specific Corporate Strategies

A strategy may be defined as a course of action designed to achieve a desired end result. *Corporate strategy development* is concerned with the deployment of the company's resources in order to achieve its global corporate objectives. Corporate strategies, therefore, should be developed in each area in which corporate objectives have been developed.

A corporate strategy establishes the framework for the formulation of strategies at the divisional and foreign affiliate level. For example, a corporate financial strategy that states that all company growth objectives will be financed only by retained earnings implies a very conservative way of financing growth. In this case, all foreign affiliates must abide by this company-wide strategy and finance their own growth plans only by retained earnings. Similarly, a corporate marketing strategy calling for the adaptation of products to suit local tastes and conditions allows foreign affiliates to make appropriate changes in the basic product, but it forbids the introduction of new products. For example, a company involved in the marketing of coffee worldwide may allow the local affiliates to modify its taste to suit local preferences, but it will not allow an affiliate to sell a product such as cocoa, which may be new to the company.

Corporate strategies affect the fundamental design of a company's overall operations. An analogy with the design of an aircraft may help to explain this concept. An aerospace engineer who changes the design of an airplane to achieve its performance objectives is involved in

EXHIBIT 8-4
Areas for Formulation of Global Corporate Objectives

Profitability
Level of profits
Return on assets, investment equity, sales
Yearly profit growth
Yearly earnings per share growth

Marketing
Total sales volume
Market share—worldwide, region, country
Growth in sales volume
Growth in market share
Integration of country markets for marketing efficiency and effectiveness

Production
Ratio of foreign to domestic production volume
Economics of scale via international production integration
Quality and cost control
Introduction of cost-efficient production methods

Finance
Financing of foreign affiliates—retained earnings or local borrowing
Taxation—minimizing tax burden globally
Optimum capital structure
Foreign exchange management—minimizing losses from foreign fluctuations

Technology
Type of technology to be transferred abroad—new or old generation
Adaptation of technology to local needs and circumstances

Host Government Relations
Adapting affiliate plans to host government developmental plans
Adherence to local laws, customs, and ethical standards

Personnel
Development of managers with global orientation
Management development of host country nationals

Research and Development
Innovation of patentable products
Innovation of patentable production technology
Geographical dispersion of research and development laboratories

Environment
Harmony with the physical and biological environment
Adherence to local environmental legislation

"corporate strategy" formulation, and the design of all components of the airplane must conform with the overall airplane design. Similarly, the design of the company's overall operations constrains and influences the design of the divisional and affiliate operations.

Although corporate strategies are formulated in areas that are of major concern to a company, and will therefore vary from one company to another, international companies do develop strategies in some areas in common. Consider the following:

- Methods of entering foreign markets
- Growth—internal development versus acquisitions
- Geographical diversification
- Product diversification
- Product portfolio optimization
- Foreign exchange risk management
- Human resources development
- Organization structure

The construction of corporate strategy is a difficult process. It requires an objective assessment of the strengths and weaknesses of the company's resources and of its managerial practices. Adoption of new strategies may mean the abandoning of old and familiar ways of running a business and therefore may, as a prerequisite, involve a change in the fundamental attitudes of top management. However difficult the process may be, top management must evaluate corporate strategies periodically and keep them in tune with the dynamic environment.

To repeat a point that was made earlier in this chapter, the entire corporate strategy formulation process is by nature iterative. The essence of the entire process is to keep the organization adaptable and responsive to changes. Hence, every step in the corporate strategy formulation process that we have discussed must be performed in view of both the present and forecasted characteristics of the firm's environment.

SUMMARY

This chapter was about the process of strategic planning in an international company from the point of view of the top management personnel at the headquarters of an international company.

Planning is one of the basic functions of management. It is a process that involves the assessment of the environment for opportunities and threats, the evaluation of the strengths and weaknesses of the enterprise, and the formulation of objectives and strategies designed to exploit future opportunities and combat threats.

International strategic planning is planning in an international context. Strategic planning in an international company is far more complicated than in a domestic company because the multinational environment in which an international company's operations and activities occur is far more complex than that of its purely domestic counterpart.

After discussing briefly the nature of the problems created when a firm enters foreign markets without proper strategic planning, the chapter concluded with a coverage of the steps involved in the development of an international corporate strategy.

QUESTIONS FOR THOUGHT AND DISCUSSION

1. Discuss some of the issues and problems that international companies must confront in planning their global operations. Are any of these faced by companies that do not operate internationally?

2. Why is the formulation of an overall plan and a well-designed strategy for entry into foreign markets so critical for an international company?

3. Discuss the three levels at which environmental analysis must take place in an international company. Why should country environmental analysis be oriented to each market entry strategy?

4. The internal resource audit is both business- and country-related. Discuss this statement, giving examples.

MINI-CASE
Tapping India's Potential

India has been identified by investors worldwide as one of the ten big emerging markets. After decades of standing stubbornly in the way of foreign investors, the Indian government is now rolling out its best Kashmiri carpets. The country is irreversibly on the path of economic reforms aimed at more market-oriented capitalism, economic liberalization, and deregulation of the economy. Unlike China, "India is a society in which private property and profit have existed uninterrupted for centuries, thus imbuing the long-established business community with a genuine understanding and respect for both. China's 20th century history wiped out those traditions, and today's China has little understanding of the basic capitalist concept that business can be a win-win game to enlarge an economic pie . . . . India offers what in a competitive world may be the most valuable software of all—minds that have been permitted to be open, inquisitive and creative and men and women who are fluent in the global language of business, English."[a]

About two-thirds of India's population lives in villages, far removed from the metro and urban centers. The road system connecting the villages and cities is weak and undeveloped, however, India boasts of a large network of railroads connecting major cities and towns throughout the country. Journey to a village often requires travel by bus or bullock cart.

India's per capita soft drink consumption is a paltry 0.7 liters per year, much lower than that of neighboring Pakistan (3 liters) or Sri Lanka (5.7 liters). The size of India's population is nearing 900 million.[b] About 40 million Indians live in households with annual incomes of over Rs.900,000, or $30,000; in purchasing power terms that approximates an income of $600,000 in the U.S. Down the ladder is India's middle class: the 150 million people who live in households with incomes of Rs.30,000 ($1,000) and up. In local purchasing power, $1,000 is the equivalent of around $20,000 in the U.S. Most of the middle-class population can afford 20-inch color televisions, washing machines, motorcycles, and mopeds. This group is growing at the rate of 5 to 10 percent a year, and therefore should account for 400 million people within a decade.[c]

a Karen Elliott House, "Two Asian Giants, Growing Apart," *The Wall Street Journal*, February 24, 1995, p. A10.
b Sugeeswara Senadhira and Havis Dawson, "Raising India," *Beverage World*, February 1994, pp. 46-48.
c Peter Fuhrman and Michael Schuman, "Now we are our own masters," *Forbes*, May 23, 1994, pp. 128-138.

The annual soft drink growth rate is about 1 percent per year; experts believe that heightened marketing could speed up this growth to between 5 and 10 percent per year. It is estimated that India's market for all soft drinks amounts to $353.3 million.

One key to greater volume is increased rural sales. Urban centers account for about 80 percent of soft drink sales. Per-person soft drink consumption in New Delhi—the nation's largest market—is about 45 servings of 8-ounce bottles, and in Bombay it is about 26 servings, as opposed to about 3 such servings across India as a whole.

There is a distinct pattern of seasonality to soft drink consumption in the country. The peak season falls during April, May, and June. May alone accounts for 16 percent of the year's business.

The road system outside the major highways does not make for decent returnable glass business. Nevertheless, India will remain a returnable-glass market for a long time. Cans will come, too, but at today's prices aluminum is very expensive, making a regular-size soft drink can almost twice as expensive as a regular-size soft drink bottle. Consumers have experienced cans bursting in the sweltering summer heat that sends temperatures soaring as high as 116 degrees.

Most consumer products such as soap, toothpaste, breakfast cereals, candy, and soft drinks are sold through millions of kiosks and small mom-and-pop stores sprinkled in cities, towns, and villages throughout the country. Supermarkets and convenience stores similar to those in developed countries are nonexistent.

Blue Bell Beverages

Blue Bell Beverages is in the soft drink business. The company produces and markets soft drinks primarily in the United States and western Europe. The company's product portfolio consists of carbonated and non-carbonated fruit drinks, mineral water, and carbonated cola and non-cola soft drinks. Company-owned bottling plants, as well as franchised bottlers in the U.S. and Europe, produce, bottle, and distribute the soft drinks in assigned markets.

Blue Bell is the tenth-largest soft drink company in the global soft drink industry. Market share battles in the industry are heavily dependent on creating brand image and brand recognition through expensive marketing, promotion, and advertising campaigns using newspapers, billboards, and television advertising. Two giants, Coca-Cola and PepsiCo, have dominant market shares globally in the industry.

Bill Christine, Vice-President of Strategic Planning, Blue Bell Beverages Inc., is presiding over a meeting of the strategic planning committee that reports to the board of directors:

> Bill Christine: "We ought to take a good hard look at the Indian market. I have read in *The Wall Street Journal*, *Business Week*, *Fortune*, and *The New York Times* that the Indian market is likely to be one of the biggest within the next fifteen years or so. Yes, we must seriously consider an entry into the Indian market."
>
> Raj Phatak (V.P. International): "Penetrating the Indian market is not going to be an easy task. We ought to investigate what it will take to succeed in that market. I suspect that we will need a different set of capabilities and skills to succeed in that market—capabilities and skills not necessarily the same as those needed in the American and European markets."
>
> Rhoda Harris (V.P. Marketing): "Do the Indians like cola drinks or do they prefer non-cola drinks instead? I am told that one of the most popular is a mango-flavored drink called 'Mangola.' Which of our soft drinks should we go with first? We must also think about how we will distribute our products."

Tim Brooks (V.P. Finance): "How much is this going to cost? Can we take our profits out of India? How stable is the Indian rupee?"

Bill Christine: "We should ask the president to authorize a market survey of the Indian soft drink market and then we will be in a position to decide whether we should make plans to enter it."

All members of the strategic planning committee agreed to ask President Randy Gaboriault for a budget to conduct a survey of the Indian market.

Source: Arvind V. Phatak, Copyright © 1997

Discussion Questions for Mini-Case

1. Discuss the variety of data about the Indian market that Blue Bell Beverages ought to collect in order to determine the attractiveness of the Indian soft drink market.

2. What information must the strategic planning committee have at its command in order to evaluate the capabilities of Blue Bell Beverages to succeed in the Indian market?

3. Depending upon your knowledge of India, in what ways do you expect the Indian soft drink market to be different than markets in Europe or in the United States?

4. Obtain information from the library of the entry strategies used by PepsiCo and Coca-Cola to tap into the Indian market. What advice can you give to Blue Bell Beverages based upon your library research?

Notes

1. Russell A. Ackoff, *A Concept of Corporate Planning*, Wiley Interscience, New York, 1970, p. 1.
2. Ibid., p. 4.
3. George Steiner, *Top Management Planning*, Macmillan, New York, 1969, p. 6.
4. Ibid.
5. M. Y. Yoshino, "International Business: What Is the Best Strategy?" *Business Quarterly*, Fall 1966, p. 47.
6. Arvind V. Phatak, *Managing Multinational Corporations*, Praeger Publishers, New York, 1974, p. 162.

Further Reading

Ackoff, Russell A., *A Concept of Corporate Planning*, Wiley & Sons, New York, 1970.

Davidson, William H., *Global Strategic Management*, John Wiley & Sons, New York, 1982.

Hamel, Gary, and C. K. Prahalad, "Do You Really Have a Global Strategy?" *Harvard Business Review*, July-August 1985, pp. 139-148.

Harrell, Gilbert D., and Richard O. Kiefer, "Multinational Strategic Market Portfolios," *MSU Business Topics*, Winter 1981, pp. 5-15.

LaPalombara, Joseph, and Stephen Blank, *Multinational Corporations in Comparative Perspective*, The Conference Board, New York, 1977.

Phatak, Arvind V., *Managing Multinational Corporations*, Praeger Publishers, New York, 1974.

Schwendiman, John S., *Strategic and Long-Range Planning for the Multinational Corporation*, Praeger Publishers, New York, 1973.

Shanks, David C., "Strategic Planning for Global Competition," *Journal of Business Strategy*, Winter 1985, pp. 80-89.

Simon, Jeffrey D., "A Theoretical Perspective on Political Risk," *Journal of International Business Studies*, Winter 1984, pp. 123-143.

Steiner, George A., *Top Management Planning*, Macmillan, New York, 1969.

Walters, Kenneth D., and R. Jose Monsen, "State-Owned Business Abroad; New Competitive Threat," *Harvard Business Review*, March-April 1979, pp. 160-170.

Yoshino, M. Y., "International Business: What Is the Best Strategy?" *Business Quarterly*, Fall 1966.

The Nature and Scope of International Integration Strategies

LEARNING OBJECTIVES

After completing this chapter, you will be able to:

- Discuss the functional and geographic structure of the international company in terms of dispersal and reintegration of the firm's value chain.
- Explain the ethnocentric, polycentric, and geocentric attitudinal orientations as they apply to international firms.
- Describe a three-dimensional framework for classifying international firms.

WORLDWIDE DISPERSAL AND REINTEGRATION OF THE VALUE CHAIN, FUNCTIONAL AND GEOGRAPHIC

International companies are rapidly moving to put in place integrated systems of international production and distribution capable of most effectively achieving the three categories of objectives examined in Chapter 1: efficiency in current operations, managing risks, and global learning and innovation. Such a system incorporates (1) the dispersal of the company's various activities and functions in the value chain and their location in different parts of the world to take advantage of national differences, and (2) a reintegration of the dispersed activities and functions to benefit from scale and scope economies. We shall examine the characteristics of this system. First we shall study the functional scope of the value chain dispersal and reintegration strategies, to be followed by a description of the geographic scope of such strategies.

The Functional Scope of Value Chain Dispersal and Integration Strategies

In the initial stages of internationalization, products are exported by the company to foreign markets from the home country. As the company expands its markets abroad to include several countries, it may choose to perform one or more activities in the value chain in foreign locations with the principal purpose of taking advantage of national differences, scale economies, and scope economies.

The foreign location where a particular activity is performed may, or may not, be in a country where its products or services are currently marketed. Factors such as the following induce companies to disperse the different activities in the value chain to various locations throughout the world:

- comparative advantage of the country (competitive input costs, low levels of political risk, market size, proximity to major markets or supply sources, availability of knowledge and skills in the population, etc.);
- efficiency gains from economies of scale and scope derived from an increased internal functional specialization and international division of labor;
- competitive pressures from domestic and foreign-based companies and the necessity to compete in the competitors' home and third-country markets;
- the benefits of flexibility and risk reduction derived from multiple sourcing points and destination points for components, products, and capital;
- global and country-based political, legal, and economic risk; and risk from exchange rate fluctuations;
- the opportunities to innovate and learn from diverse cultures and economic systems;
- the fact that human, capital, material, and knowledge-based resources are dispersed throughout the world and not concentrated in any one country or region; and
- tariff and nontariff barriers that prevent market penetration via exports.

Having dispersed the value chain activities in different parts of the world, international companies implement plans to reintegrate those activities in response to a global strategy designed to enable the company to achieve its objectives most efficiently and effectively, under an umbrella of an acceptable level of risk.

The level of integration varies from company to company. We shall categorize the level of integration into three categories: (1) stand-alone, (2) simple integration, and (3) complex integration.

A value chain of a firm describes how it organizes and performs the many discrete activities that add value to the goods and services produced and marketed by it. Some of these activities are vertically and sequentially linked, and others are linked horizontally and cut across the various vertical links in the value chain.

Figure 9-1 is an example of a value chain. The vertically linked activities are inbound logistics, components manufacture, assembly, distribution, marketing, and after-sales service. The horizontally linked activities include research and development, human resource management, procurement, finance, accounting, and other management functions such as planning, organizing, and controlling. The horizontally linked activities are performed in all links of the value chain, e.g., human resource management—which includes salary administration and staffing—is carried out in each and every operation in the vertically linked value chain. The same can be said of the other horizontally linked activities.

How effective and efficient a firm is in managing the most critical links in the value chain is what ultimately determines how competitive it will be in the industry.

Stand-Alone Strategies Figure 9-2 on page 226 is an illustration of a stand-alone strategy. Under such a strategy, each foreign affiliate is responsible for the performance of almost all of the required activities in the value chain in the host country. The output produced by an affiliate is marketed primarily in the host country, although some of the output may be "exported" to other affiliates and to the parent company. The foreign affiliate may also "import" the output produced by other affiliates for sale in the host country market. For instance, an affiliate in France may produce camcorders, another in Germany may produce VCRs, and the parent company may produce television sets. Each unit may export their respective outputs to the other two (as shown in Figure 9-2), and each would then have three products to sell in each country market.

FIGURE 9-1
A Value Chain

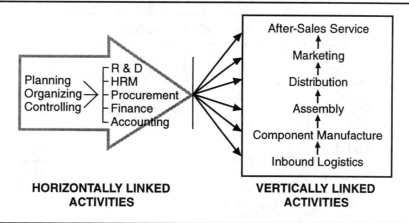

Except possibly for the export and import of outputs, there is no integration of value chain activities among the affiliates themselves or between the parent and affiliates. The principal linkage between the parent and an affiliate is through ownership, supply of long-term capital, and transfer of technology. The parent does not interfere in the activities of an affiliate as long as the affiliate is profitable and does not deviate from the company's mission and business portfolio.

Factors such as trade barriers (tariffs and quotas), high transportation costs, and communications barriers may cause a company to establish a stand-alone affiliate abroad. Stand-alone strategies are particularly prevalent in service industries. Services such as fast-food restaurants, advertising agencies, computer services, management consulting, banking, insurance, and engineering and construction services are not tradeable, and hence affiliates in these industries are established as self-contained units, mirroring the "production" organization of their parents.

Simple Integration Figure 9-3 on page 227 illustrates a simple integration strategy. A simple integration strategy calls for the integration of a few activities in the value chain among some or all affiliates of an international company. In the figure, only assembly and component manufacture in the affiliates are integrated.

The integration might be unidirectional or multidirectional. In unidirectional or one-way integration, one affiliate might be responsible for producing components for use in another affiliate. Or an affiliate in a country like Switzerland or Singapore might be responsible for raising funds for use in other affiliates, or to serve as a cash cow for investments in other functions such as research and development or advertising expenditures to gain a bigger market share in a key country market.

In multidirectional integration, there is interdependence among the affiliates and between the affiliates and the parent. For example, an English affiliate might manufacture and export an engine to an Italian affiliate and in return it may import a transmission manufactured by the Italian affiliate. Or the parent might import and assemble different components produced in

FIGURE 9-2
Stand-Alone Strategy

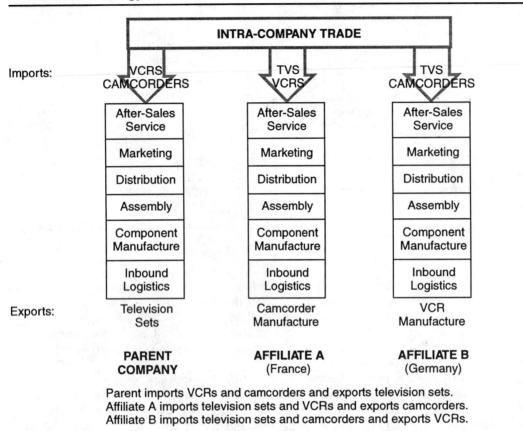

Parent imports VCRs and camcorders and exports television sets.
Affiliate A imports television sets and VCRs and exports camcorders.
Affiliate B imports television sets and camcorders and exports VCRs.

different affiliates, and subsequently export the assembled products to the affiliates for marketing through their respective distribution channels.

The practice of outsourcing by some international companies represents simple integration in its most popular form. Outsourcing is performing some activities in the value chain in foreign countries and linking them to work done elsewhere, mainly in the home country. International outsourcing is the farming out of some value chain activities to countries other than the home country and the major market countries of the product or service. The unit producing the outsourced product may be controlled by the international parent either through equity control or through non-equity contractual arrangements with non-affiliated foreign contractors. Outsourcing enables an international company to focus on certain activities in the value chain and to delegate other activities in the chain to subcontractors who can specialize in those activities. Contractors who have associated with an international company for many years in effect become part of the value chain of the international company. In such cases, contractors not only produce a component but also design it for the international company. Levi Strauss & Company (jeans),

FIGURE 9-3
Simple Integration Strategy

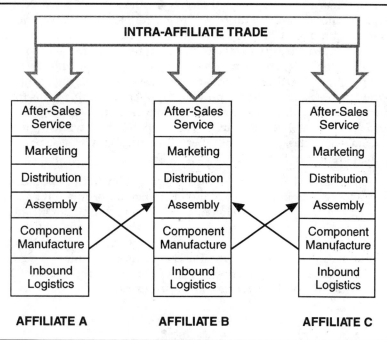

Reebok (athletic shoes), Wal-Mart (clothing), and Marks and Spencer (clothing) have significant outsourcing operations in countries like Bangladesh, Turkey, and China. Many software developers use foreign affiliates or subcontractors to process data or write software. Advances in telecommunications have made possible the transfer of computer programs by communications satellites. India, for example, has the second largest information technology base in Asia after Japan,[1] and it has emerged as the primary development center for sophisticated software and hardware for international companies such as IBM, Motorola, and Hewlett-Packard.

To a large extent, outsourcing is cost-driven as companies search for locales that offer cheap production inputs such as labor, raw materials, and energy. However, companies also source abroad in more than one locale, through affiliates or subcontractors, as a hedge against economic, political, and currency risks. Having more than one source country allows an international company to reduce the risk of overdependence on only one source of supply. Thus, all other things being equal, a company that has operations in Japan as well as in Italy could easily shift its supply source from Japan to Italy in response to an exorbitant rise in the value of the Japanese yen or in the Japanese wage rates that make imports from Japan expensive and economically unviable.

Firms that play the role of subcontractors need to be functionally integrated into the parent company's value chain through the establishment of functional linkages. Thus, integration of some functions of the parent company with those of the subcontractor is necessary. For example, in the $300 million retooled Chrysler plant in Sterling Heights, Michigan, which produces the

227

Chrysler Cirrus and Dodge Stratus compact cars, suppliers were hired earlier in the design process than ever before and had more time to improve quality and iron out problems. In the past, suppliers bid for contracts and were selected largely on the basis of price. Now Chrysler gives the business to a "supplier-partner" who helps create the part. The way prices are set for the purchased parts is also unique. Chrysler establishes the price that customers will pay for a car or truck and then works backwards to determine a target price for each part. Suppliers are expected to meet or beat that price. More parts are being assembled outside the plant into modular systems and are brought to Sterling Heights for final assembly. Toyota, which makes only 25 percent of its own parts, does not bother to provide suppliers with blueprints for a part. Instead, suppliers are given the exterior dimensions and performance characteristics, and are then expected to design the part.[2] In a similar vein, affiliates in various parts of the world who serve as suppliers of parts or subassembly modules, or for some other value chain activities, also must be functionally integrated with the parent (see Box 9-1).

Complex Integration   Major changes in the world economy including diminishing market barriers in developed and developing countries; the liberalization of international trade; the emergence of trade blocs like the European Union, NAFTA, and MERCUSOR; advances in global telecommunications and computer networks; and the spread of information technology have made it easier for international companies to transfer goods, services, components, capital, technology, and information among the parent and affiliate companies. This business-friendly environment has precipitated the entry of new firms from developed and developing countries, which has led to *intensified global competition* in most industries.

BOX 9-1
Integrated Outsourcing in the Auto Industry

Beginning in October, all auto manufacturers will be required to label their cars so that customers know the country of origin. Perhaps the manufacturers should declare the company of origin too. Like blending Scotch and vintage wine, today's cars are made from a combination of ingredients, only a fraction of which come from the company whose name goes on the trunk lid.

More and more, automakers are turning to independent suppliers to provide such critical components as instrument panels, seats, and electronics. By assembling these parts off site, then bolting them into the car on the assembly line, the auto companies are behaving more like computer makers than traditional, vertically integrated manufacturers. . . . Now the auto industry is disintegrating. In a world where organizations are networked together by information technology, auto parts can often be made more cheaply by someone else. . . . Don't confuse this fragmentation with the industry's infatuation with outsourcing. That meant sending detailed specifications for a particular part around the world in search of the low-cost producer. Today's automakers are seeking suppliers capable of not just making the part but also designing it, engineering it, integrating it with surrounding parts, and delivering it globally.

Source: Alex Taylor III, "The Auto Industry Meets The New Economy," *Fortune*, September 5, 1994, pp. 52-60. © 1994, Times Inc. All rights reserved.

Convergence of consumer tastes for some products (refrigerators, automobiles, television sets, personal computers, VCRs, camcorders, etc.) have reinforced the *standardization of products* across national boundaries. Standardization of products provides companies with the opportunity to reduce unit production costs through *economies of scale*. There is still the simultaneous need to engage in *product adaptation* to make some products suitable to local and regional tastes. For example, refrigerators are half the size in Europe as in the United States; and washing machines in Europe are side-loaded with a horizontal rotating drum, whereas those in the United States are top-loaded with an agitator action. *Shortened product lifecycles* and the corresponding imperative to develop *new and innovative products* have propelled companies to search for new ideas and human capital throughout the world.

In response to these conditions, international companies are beginning to redesign the pattern by which they manage and organize their physical, financial, technological, and human assets worldwide. Through *complex integration strategies*, international companies are transforming their geographically dispersed affiliates and fragmented production, financial, and marketing systems into functionally integrated regional or global networks of affiliates.

Complex integration strategies are characterized by a dispersal of the value chain into discrete functions—component production, assembly, finance, research and development, distribution, etc.—and their location in whichever place in the world they can be best carried out in response to the overall goals and strategy of the firm as a whole. Any affiliate may be selected by the parent to perform functions for the international company as a whole (either by itself or in close interaction with other affiliates or the parent company) on the basis of a sophisticated intra-firm division of labor. For example, an affiliate in England may be responsible for research and development for the whole company, an affiliate in Switzerland for finance, and those in the United States and Belgium for marketing of products in North America and Europe, respectively. Similarly the production chain for the manufacture of an electric fan might be dispersed as follows: purchasing done by a central purchasing office in France; components manufactured in Mexico (frame), Germany (motor), and India (blades) for final assembly in Singapore (electric fan); and marketed in North America and Europe by affiliates in the United States and Belgium, respectively. An illustration of a complex integration strategy is displayed in Figure 9-4.

Complex integration strategies create a network of linkages among the various affiliates including the parent. The linkages among the various units represent substantial unidirectional and multidirectional flows of technology, people, products, services, components, capital, and information. The distinction between the parent and affiliates becomes blurred in the corporate network as an increasing number of affiliates assume primary responsibilities for functions that are supposed to serve as inputs to other functions performed elsewhere in the network.

Complex integration represents the most advanced level of globalization of a company. Firms that have a complex integration strategy in place are not just a collection of discrete affiliates at home and abroad, but rather a system of interdependent affiliates in which each affiliate's functions are designed and carried out in response to a unified strategy for the company as a whole. The design of a complex integration strategy is formulated in response to questions such as the following:

1. Where in the world should we manufacture components A, B, C, etc.?
2. Where in the world should we assemble products A, B, C, etc.?
3. Where in the world should we source products A, B, C, etc. for country X, country Y, country Z, etc.?
4. Where in the world should we raise capital for investment in our global operations?

FIGURE 9-4
Complex Integration Strategy

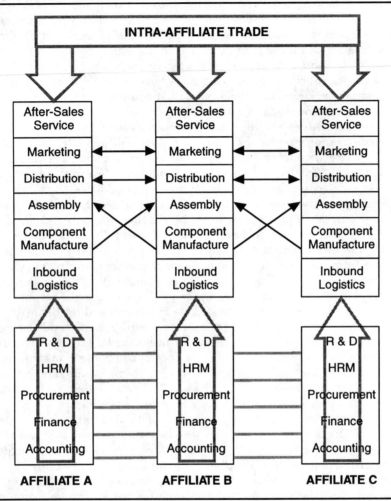

5. In which currency should the company's funds be denominated?
6. Where in the world should we conduct research and development?
7. Where in the world are the potential markets for the company's products and services, now and in the future?
8. Where in the world should we recruit personnel for our management team?

The Geographical Scope of Value Chain Dispersal and Integration Strategies

The coverage of the integration strategies focused upon the degree of integration—ranging from stand-alone strategies to simple integration strategies to complex integration strategies. The strategies can also be arranged along a geographical continuum with multidomestic strategies at one end of the continuum and global strategies at the other, with multifocal and regionocentric strategies somewhere between these two extremes:

Multidomestic_____Multifocal_____Regionocentric_____Global

The organization of value chain activities in the company is largely affected by which of these strategies is adopted by the company.

Multidomestic Strategies   A multidomestic strategy requires that each foreign affiliate primarily serves the host country market. Products and services are customized to the needs of each country market. Marketing strategies are fully tailored for each country. All or most of the value chain is reproduced in every country. Few efforts are made by the parent company to integrate the operations in host countries with parent company operations or with operations in other host countries, although some functions in the value chain may be integrated across countries. Competitive moves are made without consideration of their impact on other countries. Multidomestic strategies allow for differentiated strategic approaches across country locations.[3] The strategy of each affiliate is driven by local conditions. Affiliates have considerable autonomy to respond effectively to local conditions. Stand-alone and simple integration strategies (discussed earlier) would be most commonly found in multidomestic strategies.

Highly differentiated national tastes and habits, or trade barriers such as high tariffs, import quotas, and local content requirements are some factors that have motivated companies to establish stand-alone affiliates in some countries.

Multifocal Strategies   In multifocal strategies, a company develops some strategies driven by local market conditions in each country while simultaneously integrating other activities worldwide.[4] Thus a company in the food business might formulate product strategies that are suited to the climatic conditions and taste preferences of a country, while at the same time implementing complex integration strategies in most other value chain activities. Nestle, the Swiss global company, has adopted a global strategy for marketing its popular brands, however, it manufactures chocolate in almost two dozen countries for local distribution. Nestle's chocolates are suited to the local conditions, for instance, those manufactured in warm countries like India are much harder in order to prevent meltdowns due to the hot climatic temperatures, whereas those manufactured in Europe and the United States are soft and easy on the teeth. Apart from its global brand management strategies, the company's financial and raw materials strategies are integrated across country markets.

Regionocentric Strategies   In regionocentric strategies, a company develops strategies driven by regional market conditions. Integrated networks of distributed value chain activities primarily along regional lines are established in support of the regionocentric strategies. The creation of economic unions—like the European Union and free trade areas such as the North American Free Trade Agreement, which promote free trade and foreign direct investment and economic integration among member countries—have increased the desire of companies to develop regionocentric strategies. Several examples of regionocentric strategies are offered in *Practical Insight 9-1.*

Global Strategies   Looking at the whole world as the marketplace and selecting key country and regional markets as target markets for building significant share are the underpinnings of a global strategy. The key markets may not necessarily be the most profitable in their own right, the

PRACTICAL INSIGHT 9-1
Regionocentric Strategies of Companies

The formation of the European Union, which has created a unified market in almost all of Europe, has served as a catalyst for companies to reorganize their operations on a Europe-wide basis. The following are a few examples of this phenomenon.

Thompson (France) has specialized plants that manufacture television sets on a regional basis. The German plant concentrates on high-feature, large-screen sets, the French plant focuses on high-volume products, and plants in Spain and the United Kingdom assemble low-cost, smaller sets. Marketing of the products is handled by a separate regional marketing and distribution organization.

From 1973 to 1989, Unilever has cut the number of factories in Europe from thirteen to four. Each of the four factories, located in Austria, France, Italy, and the United Kingdom, produces a separate line of products which are marketed throughout Europe. Unilever has also combined its sixteen separate affiliates into a single cleaning and hygiene business called Lever Europe. Lever Europe manages product development, sales, and distribution in Europe. This new structure allows the simultaneous introduction of products in all European countries. Plants specialized in food production produce products for all of Europe. The Italian plant for frozen meals manufactures products that are distributed throughout the region.

Sourcing of raw materials and components is also organized on a regional basis in some companies. Hoechst, the German company, has set up a central European purchasing unit that purchases materials and components on behalf of its European subsidiaries.

Procter & Gamble (USA) has set up Eurobrand teams to coordinate its European affiliates. Each key brand team is headed by a general manager from a "lead country." Included in the Eurobrand team are the advertising and brand managers of all countries in which the product is sold and the appropriate functional managers from the European headquarters. Typically, the country subsidiary with the most resources, the leading market positions, or the most commitment to the product is given the lead role so that it can spread its knowledge, expertise, and commitment throughout Europe. The lead country's responsibility is to coordinate the introduction, standardization of the product formula, promotion, and packaging for all of Europe. The team concept is also aimed at avoiding unnecessary duplication of the brand's management and coordination of activities across all European subsidiaries.

Quaker Oats (USA) has established a separate European headquarters to integrate all activities in Europe under a single umbrella. The European headquarters sets the overall strategy for Europe, although marketing is done by local affiliates and adapted to local conditions.

Regional manufacturing networks have been set up by automobile manufacturers. For example, in the Pacific Basin countries Japanese companies have established manufacturing systems in which separate components are manufactured in specialized plants in different countries, with the final assembly done in each country. Thus each country gets all components needed to assemble a product, but none manufactures all of them. Mitsubishi, Toyota, and Nissan have manufacturing systems based upon this model in the Pacific Basin.

Sources: J. Howelles and M. Wood, *The Globalization of Production of Technology,* Commission of European Communities, Commission Dossier 2, October 1991, pp. 77-78; Peter J. Williamson, "European Single Market: the toughest test yet for sales and distribution," *Multinational Business,* No. 3, Summer 1992, pp. 57-76; Bernard Wysocki, Jr., "In Asia, the Japanese Hope to 'Coordinate' What Nations Produce," *The Wall Street Journal,* August 20, 1990, pp. A1 and A2.

implication being that a company may establish an operation in a country that may be unattractive in most respects, such as profitability and growth prospects. A company might make inroads in such a market if it holds strategic global significance for the company's global operations, e.g., the market may be the home market of a major competitor. Presence in a competitor's home market provides the company with the opportunity to attack it with resources generated in other units of the company's integrated network of affiliates.

Companies with global strategies aim to have standardized products with strong brand names that have global recognition. Adaptations to local or regional conditions and tastes are kept to a minimum. Marketing strategies are designed to be implemented uniformly worldwide, except for minor modifications to suit local and regional differences in cultural attributes and legal requirements. Competitive moves in any particular country market are undertaken only after forethought of their impacts on other country markets.

Not all products or services lend themselves to the development of a global strategy. Products like soft drinks (Coca-Cola), alcoholic beverages (Miller, Heineken, Budweiser), aircraft (Boeing, Lockheed, Airbus), various entertainment electronic products (Sony, Panasonic), and computers (IBM, Apple, Toshiba, Compaq) offer the most opportunities for developing global strategies. Others, like food products, insurance, and legal services, need either a multidomestic, multifocal, or regionocentric strategy.

An integrated network of interdependent value chain activities supports the global strategy. The value chain is broken up and activities are strategically placed in different parts of the world to take advantage simultaneously of locational advantages, risk reduction, and counterattack capability against a competitor.

The relationship between the functional integration strategies (stand-alone, simple integration, complex integration) and their geographical scope is portrayed in Exhibit 9-1.

EXHIBIT 9-1

**Relationship Between Functional Integration
and Geographical Integration in a Company**

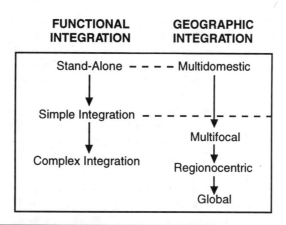

Adapted from: World Investment Report 1993, United Nations, New York, 1993, p. 154.

233

Complex/Global Integration at the Ford Motor Company

The reorganization of the Ford Motor Company to develop a "world car" envisions projected savings of billions of dollars through eliminating duplication of efforts worldwide. The company has combined its North American and European operations into a single group that will consolidate the North American and European vehicle operations. Additionally, it will reduce purchasing costs of almost $37 billion a year through a worldwide production purchasing operation which will replace regional purchasing operations that handled parts procurement. To cut vehicle development costs the company has reorganized product development of "world cars" into five teams called vehicle platform centers (VPCs)—four in Dearborn, Michigan, responsible for large front- and rear-drive cars, light trucks, and commercial lorries; and one in Europe split between Germany and Britain, responsible for small, front-wheel drive models. *Practical Insight 9-2* describes Ford's complex/global integration strategy.

PRACTICAL INSIGHT 9-2
Ford 2000

It's early 1995, you are scanning the headlines, and you can't believe your eyes. The No. 2 automaker in the world has a New Year's resolution. What can it be? The company seems to be driving on cruise control. It has just reported earnings of $5.3 billion and record revenues of $128 billion for 1994. Everything seems to be fine, right? Not according to Ford Motor Company's Chairman, Alex Trotman. He's gearing up to get his company ready for the next century. His philosophy is to be global and local. Ford will look for global products and economies of scale, but not overcentralize. Ford has restructured its organization, with the hope of achieving efficiency and economies of scale.

In April 1994, Alex Trotman announced his plan to integrate Ford Motor's worldwide operations and "get more firepower from Ford's resources." In the new year the plan became reality. Ford's North American and European engine and transmission units were combined to form one organization. Chairman Alex Trotman said that the trick would be to get "these two big elephants to dance."

The restructuring won't end with North America and Europe. Next year, South American and Asian operations will integrate with the new company. Also, the company doesn't want to stop with just engines and transmissions. Its ultimate goal is to tear apart Ford's current structure and combine auto operations into one single global company. Trotman feels that it is important to correct any problems before the next downturn. Also, due to the restructuring, he hopes to make a push into emerging markets.

Ford may be coming off a record year, but Alex Trotman believes there is room for improvement. In the past, Ford has spent too much money and time designing new cars. Competitors of Ford are more efficient at getting new models to the market faster. For example, the Ford Taurus took five years to redesign, whereas Chrysler was able to design its Neon in approximately half the time.

In the past, Ford has wasted time and money duplicating design efforts between the North American and European companies. The new restructuring is designed to reduce these problems. Currently, Ford uses six different four-cylinder engines in Europe and North America. Not for long, because Trotman believes that six different engines aren't necessary. Now the company will only use two different four-cylinder engines. By eliminating four of the six engines, Ford should be able to save millions of dollars.

The restructuring has begun with the merger of the U.S. and European product development operations. Product development has been organized into five teams, called vehicle platform centers. Four of the centers will be located in Dearborn, Michigan, and one in Europe, split between Germany and Britain. The company is globalizing product development in its quest to create a world car that should hit the market in 1997.

Creating a world car means efficiently developing vehicles which, with minor modifications, can sell in several parts of the world. Ford has such a car, known as the Mondeo in Europe and the Ford Contour/Mercury Mystique in the U.S. However, it cost $6 billion to develop, and Ford executives have learned from this program. The company will spend far less on future world cars.

The company hopes to achieve economies of scale by using common parts and global suppliers. Currently, European and American parts have no parts in common. The goal is to cut costs by negotiating better deals. Ford will buy a larger number of parts from fewer global suppliers. Also, the company will cut the number of suppliers for goods other than auto parts. The savings are estimated to be $1 billion. Mr. Trotman said, "We are using resources around the world more than we have in the past."

Each vehicle platform center is devoted to a segment of the market. Trotman hopes to improve productivity by utilizing product-oriented teams. For example, engineers are permanently assigned to work on the Ford Taurus and they will work closely in teams with designers and marketers to build products for individual countries.

To ease the transition, managers from both sides of the Atlantic also engaged in a massive reengineering program. The goal of this reengineering program was to cut costs and minimize any cultural disputes that may occur due to the merger. Last year, approximately 500 Ford employees from different countries spent nine months in Dearborn, Michigan.

One objective of the program was to search for the most efficient practices used in designing a car. The employees accomplished this by comparing how jobs were done in North America and Europe against benchmarks from outside Ford. Previously, Ford was not very efficient in machining new engine prototypes. However, due to the program, the employees found that many tasks could be done simultaneously. The employees determined that by breaking down the task of machining a new engine prototype into several stages that can be done simultaneously, Ford could cut the time to get an engine from design to testing from two years to a little over three months. The company is so zealous about improving efficiency that it devotes three-fourths of its research in hopes of achieving it.

New technology has played an integral part in this restructuring. Ford is utilizing video conferencing and linked computer networks. Designers around the world can work together without being at the same site. Also, engineers can run a "crash test" without making costly prototypes, and manufacturing experts can see how to build a new design cheaply.

In the past, Ford has had too much bureaucracy. It used to take twenty-two meetings over two months to get approval for a project. Now, it takes less than a month. To lessen bureaucracy, Trotman convinced 400 out of 2,000 managers to take early retirement.

Allan R. Kammerer is the head of Ford's Escort vehicle line. He's working on designing a car for efficient production in many markets. He has found savings by using the best method employed by each organization. For example, the U.S. system for coordinating the redesign of

PRACTICAL INSIGHT 9-2 *(continued)*

prototype parts is the most efficient, whereas Europe's practice of monitoring the engineering work that arises from warranty claims at the factory is better. Now he is pondering which practices to use in the Escort redesign.

Ford Motor is restructuring with the goals of achieving efficiency and economies of scale. There are many risks involved in designing a world car, but Alex Trotman remains confident that he will succeed. He states, "Ford 2000 ain't gonna fail."

Source: Written by Joe Casey, MBA student at Temple University, from the following sources: James Braham, "Ford shifts R&D into overdrive," *Machine Design,* December 12, 1994, pp. 18-20; Paul Ingrassia and Jaqueline Mitchell, "Ford to realign with a system of global chiefs," *The Wall Street Journal,* March 31, 1994, p. A3; Neal Templin, "Ford's Trotman gambles on global restructuring plan," *The Wall Street Journal,* April 22, 1994, p. B4; Oscar Suris, "Retooling itself, Ford stresses speed, candor," *The Wall Street Journal,* October 27, 1994, p. B1; Robert Keatley, "Ford reorganizes to stay competitive and reach new markets in the world," *The Wall Street Journal,* July 22, 1994, p. 4A; Kathleen Kerwin, "Alexander J. Trotman/Ford: Getting two big elephants to dance," *Business Week,* Bonus Issue 1994, p. 83; James B. Teese, Kathleen Kerwin, and Heidi Dawley, "Ford: Alex Trotman's daring strategy," *Business Week,* April 3, 1995, pp. 94-104; "Ford's Reorganization: Another new model . . .," *The Economist,* January 7, 1995, pp. 52-53.

To conclude our brief look at the different types of global strategies that a firm may employ in its international activities, we have summarized the three integration strategies in Exhibit 9-2. The exhibit illustrates the intra-firm linkages, degree of integration, and environmental characteristics most associated with each functional integration strategy.

THE ATTITUDINAL ORIENTATIONS OF COMPANIES

Howard V. Perlmutter[5] has identified three states of mind or attitudes that can be inferred from examining the managerial practices of international firms. He calls them *"ethnocentric," "polycentric,"* and *"geocentric."*

An ethnocentric attitude is one that looks upon everything that is domestic as the best in the world. This includes managerial personnel, management techniques and practices, products, marketing techniques, and so on. The approach of ethnocentric companies is to extend to foreign subsidiaries that which has proved to be effective at home.

A polycentric attitude is one that assumes that there are vast differences among the various countries because of differences in culture, language, race, and in their economic, political, and legal systems. Because of the great differences in these aspects, it would be impossible for the home country nationals to really understand the foreign environments. Hence, management in the parent company should give foreign subsidiaries as much freedom as is possible to manage their own affairs.

A geocentric attitude is one that is world-oriented. Managers at the parent company and in the foreign subsidiaries are in close communication with one another and are aware of the objectives of the entire enterprise. Decisions are made at the parent company level as well as in subsidiaries only after a thorough analysis of worldwide opportunities and threats. The geocentric attitude is characterized by an absence of parochial thinking within the parent and subsidiaries. This does not mean that the host countries' needs are ignored. On the contrary,

EXHIBIT 9-2
Integration Strategies and Antecedent Factors

Integration Strategy	Type of Intra-Firm Linkage	Degree of Integration	Environment
Stand-alone, e.g., multi-domestic	Ownership, technology, intracompany trade in goods and services	Weak, self-contained affiliates	Host country barriers; market entry allowed via direct investment
Simple integration	Financial, technology, components, uni- or multidirectional	Strong at some links in the value chain, frequent outsourcing to independent contractors	Moderate financial, political, currency risks; significant differences in comparative advantages of countries; free trade
Complex integration, multifocal, regionocentric, global	All functions, multi-directional network	Strong linkages throughout value chain	Free trade, trade blocs, convergence of consumer tastes, intense competition from global competitor

a geocentric firm wants to be a good citizen of the host country and makes its global plans after taking into account the aspirations of host countries. The incentive system is designed to motivate each subsidiary manager to attain not only the objectives of the subsidiary but also those of the entire international company. Unlike a polycentric firm, managers of foreign subsidiaries in a geocentric firm have the opportunity to move into parent company management. This is in response to the philosophy of a geocentric firm to place in each job the person who can do it best, regardless of nationality or other considerations like race or religion—provided that mobility across national borders is permitted by immigration laws of sovereign states. Exhibit 9-3 illustrates how ethnocentric, polycentric, and geocentric attitudes are expressed in determining the managerial process at home and abroad.

THE MULTIDIMENSIONAL INTERNATIONAL COMPANY

Many scholars and observers have chosen to classify companies with international operations into four categories: international, multinational, global, and transnational. In the following we shall explain these four categories. (As noted earlier, we use these terms interchangeably in this book.)

An international company is defined by some as one in which the focus of the top management is upon domestic operations, and the international operations are treated as accessories whose main purpose is to support the domestic operations by providing critical raw materials or components or incremental sales of the domestic product lines.

EXHIBIT 9-3
Three Types of Headquarters Orientations
Towards Subsidiaries in an International Enterprise

Organization Design	Ethnocentric	Polycentric	Geocentric
Complexity of organization	Complex in home country, simple in subsidiaries	Varied and independent	Increasingly complex and interdependent
Authority; decision making	High in headquarters	Relatively low in headquarters	Aim for a collaborative approach between headquarters and subsidiaries
Evaluation and control	Home standards applied for persons and performance	Determined locally	Find standards which are universal and local
Rewards and punishments; incentives	High in headquarters low in subsidiaries	Wide variation; can be high or low rewards for subsidiary performance	International and local executives rewarded for reaching local and worldwide objectives
Communication; information flow	High volume to subsidiaries orders, commands, advice	Little to and from headquarters; little between subsidiaries	Both ways and between subsidiaries; heads of subsidiaries part of management team
Identification	Nationality of owner	Nationality of host country	Truly international company but identifying with national interests
Perpetuation (recruiting, staffing, development)	Recruit and develop people of home country for key positions everywhere in the world	Develop people of local nationality for key positions in their own country	Develop best men everywhere in the world for key positions everywhere in the world

Source: Howard V. Perlmutter, "The Tortuous Evolution of the Multinational Corporation," *Columbia Journal of World Business*, January-February 1969, p. 12.

A multinational company is defined as a company whose top management appreciates the importance of foreign operations to its overall profitability and competitive strength. Companies in this category adopt products, strategies, and management practices country by country. Their worldwide strategy is an amalgam of the multiple, country-based approaches of its foreign subsidiaries. Multinational companies have a multidomestic strategy. This approach is analogous to the stand-alone strategy described earlier in this chapter.

A global company is described as one that searches for commonality among countries in aspects such as consumer tastes and preferences, market segments, and lifestyles. As such, global companies attempt to standardize products and marketing approaches that are sold globally, and they also find ways to squeeze efficiency from the production function by manufacturing the products on a global scale in a few very efficient plants strategically located in different parts of the world. Such companies require a considerable degree of coordination among the various worldwide operations, and generally it is provided by various product or business managers with worldwide responsibility. Strategic decisions are made at the parent company level and foreign subsidiary managers are expected to play the role mainly of implementers of centrally designed strategies. Some aspects of the simple and complex integration strategies discussed earlier are present in the functioning of a global company.

Transnational companies are described as those that attempt to balance the need to be responsive to host country markets through adaptation of the product, marketing strategies, and management practices to suit local conditions, and at the same time try to obtain global efficiencies by linking and coordinating the dispersed operations. The resources and activities are distributed to specialized foreign operations, and they are integrated into an interdependent network of worldwide operations. The complex integration strategies described earlier are representative of the functioning of a transnational company.

Reality Check

In reality, of the hundreds of companies that have international operations, very few fall in the purely international, multinational, global, or transnational category. This is because the attributes of a typical international company are far too diverse and complex to be placed in one particular category. All companies exhibit some attributes of each of these categories. For instance, in some aspects, like marketing, a company might have a global strategy, but its production strategy might be multidomestic.

Earlier in the chapter we examined the **functional** (stand-alone/simple/complex) and **geographic** (multidomestic/multifocal/regionocentric/global) scope of value chain dispersal and integration strategies. We also studied the **attitudinal** orientations of international companies. In Figure 9-5 we have pulled together the three dimensions—functional, geographic, and attitudinal—and the subdimensions that one would find in a company with international operations. For instance, as illustrated in Figure 9-6, Company A's international strategy is functionally complex and geographically global, coupled with a geocentric managerial attitude. This strategy and attitudinal configuration is different than that of Company B, which has a stand-alone, multidomestic strategy and a polycentric attitude. One could envision any number of different combinations of the ten subdimensions, each resulting in a unique specimen of a company with international operations.

We do acknowledge that companies may be classified into distinct categories such as international, multinational, global, and transnational. However, the contents of this book address issues that are equally applicable to any company that has international operations and is not limited to any particular archetype. *This is the reason that we use terms such as international, multinational, global, and transnational interchangeably to mean **all** companies that have international operations.*

SUMMARY

In this chapter, we used the concept of the value chain to illustrate the functional and geographic scope of integration strategies available to the international firm in responding to different environmental contexts. Stand-alone strategies are based upon a high degree of autonomy for

FIGURE 9-5
The Three Dimensions of International Strategy

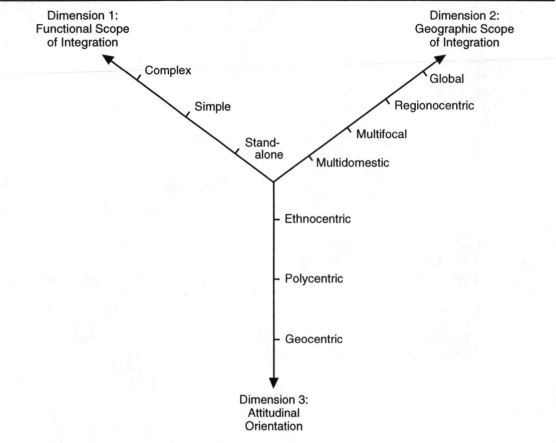

operating units and require the least amount of centralized coordination. Simple and complex integration strategies offer more opportunity to capitalize on global economies of scale and scope, but also require greater degrees of coordination and control among the different subunits.

We concluded the chapter by presenting the ethnocentric, polycentric, and geocentric attitudes that the international firm may exhibit, and offered a three-dimensional framework for classifying international firms on the basis of those three attitudinal orientations and the functionally and geographically orientations to integration strategies described earlier.

QUESTIONS FOR THOUGHT AND DISCUSSION

1. Decisions that change a company's international value chain integration strategy are documented every day in the business press. Find a current article that talks about such a decision

FIGURE 9-6

The Three Dimensions of International Strategy—Two Configurations

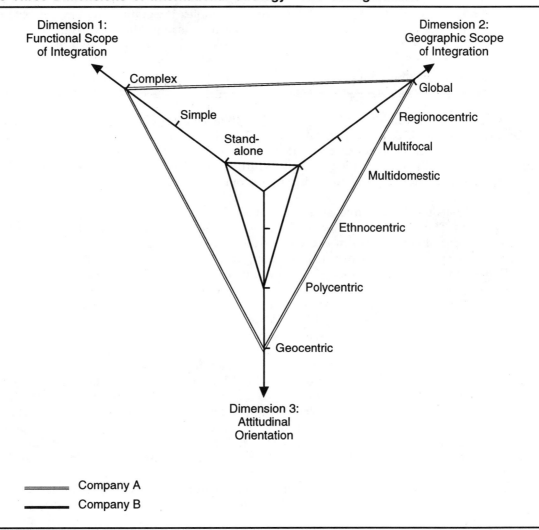

and describe how the article illustrates the basic points addressed in the text about the choice of strategy.

2. Can you think of a well-known international company that could be characterized as having an ethnocentric attitude? Why do you think so? How about companies with a polycentric or a geocentric attitude? Do you feel that one attitude may be more characteristic of successful companies than the others? Why or why not?

3. Choose several companies that you know something about, and plot how you think they would appear on the three-dimensional framework (Exhibit 9-4) shown in the chapter.

4. How would you explain the difference between a complex integration strategy, a global orientation, and a geocentric attitude? Or do they mean the same thing? Explain.

MINI-CASE
The Globalization of Whirlpool

When Whirlpool, the well-known U.S. household appliance manufacturer, decided to transform its largely domestic (U.S.) operation into a global leader in the industry, its first step was to acquire the appliance business of the Dutch consumer-goods giant Philips Electronics. After purchasing a minority stake in Philips in 1989, Whirlpool acquired 100 percent ownership in 1991, changing the name from Philips to Whirlpool Europe. The total price was approximately one billion dollars.

The newly-acquired company needed prompt attention, as it had been steadily losing market share for years. The subsidiaries established in the different European countries operated virtually independent of one another in everything from product design and advertising to supply sourcing and warehousing. There was little, if any, attempt to integrate these functions across subsidiaries. Each national company was concerned only with its own market. Philips was considered even by its industry peers to be "a company that had lost its way."[6]

Whirlpool immediately took steps to rationalize and coordinate both production and distribution across its entire appliance business. At the heart of this strategy was the decision to develop common 'platforms' for each major product line that would allow different models to be built around the same core components—power supply, chassis, etc. In this way, technology and suppliers could be shared and redundant costs significantly reduced.

One example of this 'platform' approach is with Whirlpool Europe's line of household ovens. Before the acquisition, Philips had manufactured a line of mid-range ovens and marketed them under the Philips' name. It also had marketed a high-end line of ovens under the Bauknecht brand, but had subcontracted manufacture of this line to its archrival Electrolux. Philips did not offer a low-end line. As part of the rationalization strategy, Whirlpool established a no-frills line called Ignis, and now manufactures all three lines itself on the same assembly line in Italy, all built around a common interior.

Marketing received similar attention. Philips had maintained eleven separate national advertising agencies that touted their own product lines to their own national market. Coordination among them was rare, with the result that dissimilarities and even conflicts regarding the information they produced about Philips' products was common; that is, there was no Europe-wide consistent image associated with Philips' products. At the same time, the Whirlpool name was virtually unknown in Europe. Whirlpool tackled this problem by launching a dual-branding campaign all across Europe that coupled the known but inconsistently perceived Philips' name with that of Whirlpool. In just a few years, the Philips' name was dropped from most products, completing a smooth transition to the Whirlpool brand.

Whirlpool's efforts appear to have paid off: excess plant capacity has been closed, the number of warehouses has been reduced by a factor of four, the number of suppliers has been halved, and inventories have been reduced by one-third. After the first three years of Whirlpool Europe, operating profits are up over 80 percent, and market share has increased over 13 percent against its well-established European competitors.

The benefits of coordination have not been restricted to Whirlpool's European operations. Newly-established pan-European research and design teams are encouraged to collaborate with their U.S. counterparts. This has enabled the exchange of product and process innovations between the two continents, contributing to further cost-saving commonalities in production.

Some analysts feel that Whirlpool's efforts to integrate and rationalize its manufacturing and marketing in Europe and the United States have put the company in a powerful position to assert global leadership in the appliance industry. The key to Whirlpool's success is considered to lie in its efforts to standardize design, production, and marketing across the different markets in which the company operates. In the words of CEO David R. Whitwam, "This business is the same all over the world. There is great opportunity to leverage that sameness."[7] However, not everyone has the same opinion. Bosch-Siemens, one of Whirlpool Europe's toughest competitors, offers that "Whirlpool sees Europe as a uniform market, but we also see the differences in customer demands and needs from country to country."[8]

Even while the debate between proponents of standardization and differentiation strategies continues in Europe, the playing field is being extended to other regions of the world. Whirlpool, in an attempt to repeat its success with Europe's Philips, has agreed to acquire majority ownership in India's largest refrigerator manufacturer, Kelvinator of India, Ltd. Whirlpool's rivals are also planning moves into the fast-growing Asian markets. With the high stakes involved, the competition in these new Asian markets is sure to be keen.

Source: Adapted from Patrick Oster and John Rossant, "Call It Worldpool," *Business Week*, November 28, 1994, pp. 98-99.

Discussion Questions for Mini-Case

1. What was the overarching driving force that led to Whirlpool's acquisition of the appliance business of Philips in Europe and of Kelvinator in India?

2. Identify the changes implemented by Whirlpool in Philips' production system. How did the changes support Whirlpool's global strategy?

3. What did Whirlpool do to create a uniform brand image in Europe?

4. Can you identify the steps taken by Whirlpool to (a) achieve efficiency and (b) transfer knowledge and learning from one region of the world to another?

5. How did Whirlpool take advantage of (a) scale economies and (b) scope economies?

MINI-CASE
Endaka and Transnationality of Japanese Firms*

There seems to be no end to sight in the continuing saga of the ever rising yen. The all-powerful currency climbs against all other currencies to unprecedented levels, leaving in its wake distraught Japanese business executives wary of the loss of competitiveness of their products in markets overseas. Their fears are confirmed by tumbling stock market share prices in Tokyo.

---

* Written by Dr. Yadong Luo, Assistant Professor of International Management, University of Hawaii at Manoa. Copyright © 1997 by Arvind V. Phatak.

Indeed, many Japanese company fortunes are closely tied with success abroad and a strong yen spells disaster for them and leads to a vote of no confidence from the financial market.

Meanwhile in Washington, some Commerce Department officials can barely hide their satisfaction: they smugly predict that Japan's colossal trade surplus will finally be cut to size.

The developments described above seem all too familiar. They may remind many of the latest tussles in the trade wars across the Pacific. However, they depict events taking place almost a decade ago, in late 1985, just weeks after the finance ministers of the G7 countries, meeting at New York's Plaza Hotel, agreed to devalue the dollar against major world currencies. This marked the beginning of the *endaka*, or strong yen, era.

Today (1995), a new bout of yen appreciation has driven the yen to a postwar high of around ¥88 to one U.S. dollar. Once again the familiar ritual is being played out. "We are not ready for 90 yen to the dollar," laments Yoshikazu Hanawa, Nissan Motor Co.'s executive vice-president for product planning and development. And "the yen is killing us," says Richard B. Thomas, who heads the Acura division of Honda Motor Co. in the U.S.

The complaints mask the extraordinary resilience of Japanese exporters. Indeed, Japanese manufacturers have grown adept at surviving yen shock and even benefiting from it. They are using the yen's strength to quickly and cheaply set up integrated manufacturing bases in Asian countries with currencies pegged to the dollar. In addition, earlier investments in the U.S., Mexico, and Europe have led to the emergence of many Japanese companies as true multinationals, which allows them to play both sides of the yen-dollar swings, using cheaper dollar-denominated parts and materials to offset higher yen-related costs.

Indeed, the era in which Japan simply made finished products at home and shipped them out to the world is over. The most dynamic companies are parting with stay-at-home Japanese suppliers and ceding more decision-making authority to overseas subsidiaries, particularly in the U.S. Their geographic diversification is such that "the losses and dislocations from the most recent yen revaluations won't be as high as they might have been," says Mark Mason, a Japan watcher and associate professor at Yale University School of Management. "To a very great extent, they've been cushioned."

The multinationality of Japanese manufacturers and the flexibility they have acquired in shifting production to offset currency swings may explain why the neoclassical economic theory seems increasingly unable to explain trade flows. Most economists had expected that currency movements would eventually offset trade imbalances. However, *endaka*—which should theoretically make Japanese products less price-competitive abroad—hasn't reduced Japan's record $121 billion global trade surplus, at least not yet. Export volume, up 9.6 percent in 1994, has increased steadily during the 1990s. Although a flood of cheap imports should lower the Japanese trade surplus by about 5 percent in 1995, Japanese bureaucrats' half-hearted efforts to remove import barriers will keep the surplus, and consequently the yen's value, high.

There is no denying that the soaring yen has meant plenty of pain for Japan. The 18 percent decline in 1995 in the Nikkei 225 average owes much to worries that the high yen will clobber corporate earnings. Salomon Brothers Inc. says *endaka* will keep economic growth below 1 percent in 1995. Worse, an exodus of manufacturing jobs overseas threatens Japan's lifetime job-security compact. "The best manufacturers, like automakers, will leave, while we keep the less efficient ones," frets Nomura Research Institute analyst Richard Koo, author of *Good Endaka, Bad Endaka*. Undoubtedly, the value of the yen vs. the dollar is important to Japanese manufacturers because of what it can mean to their revenue: at 115 yen to the dollar, the sale of a $20,000 car in the U.S. brings Toyota 2.3 million yen; at 88 yen to the dollar the sale is worth 1.76 million yen—a 23.48 percent drop.

Lower costs lure Japanese companies abroad and some choice jobs will be lost at home. The fact remains, however, that many manufacturing companies would probably have gone under in high-cost Japan had they not moved operations to other countries. Take the electronics powerhouse Hitachi Ltd., which has set up eight manufacturing operations in the U.S. since 1985. Its line of projection televisions, assembled in Mexico, is very much the result of a global effort. The small picture tubes come from a Hitachi subsidiary in Greenville, S.C., while its chassis and circuitry are made by its affiliate in Malaysia.

Can the projection televisions still be considered Japanese? Well, some parts are still produced in Japan, namely computer chips and lenses, which represent only about 30 percent of the value of the parts being used. Hitachi executives are quietly pleased that their decade-long efforts to ride out trade friction with the U.S. have given them such flexibility. They've been able to avoid any price increases for the projection TVs, which retail between $2,800 to $4,400, according to the model.

The most recent yen appreciation is forcing the Japanese manufacturers in the U.S. to take further measures to cope. Mitsubishi Electric Corp. is attempting to "Americanize" its production of big-screen televisions in Cypress, Calif. The chairman of the American subsidiary, Tachi Kiuchi, is turning his company into a much more self-managing entity. Mitsubishi Electric America Inc. has indeed taken control of Mexican assembly plants away from headquarters in Japan. Purchasing, now done out of Kyoto and Singapore, has been moved to the U.S.

As a result of these steps, the yen-based content in Mitsubishi's TVs is shrinking dramatically. "A year ago, all of our 35-inch picture tubes were coming from Kyoto," says Jack L. Osborn, president of Mitsubishi Consumer Electronics in Norcross, Ga. "By next year, they'll all be coming from North American manufacturers." Overall, Mitsubishi Electric estimates that Japanese content is only 20 to 25 percent of the value of the goods it sells.

The results of *endaka* are also perceptible in other industries. For example, Japanese cars built in the U.S. have tended to become even more American. Initially, when Japanese automakers began building U.S. cars in the 1980s, they relied heavily on parts imported from Japan. However, as the yen continued to climb against the dollar—making shipments from Japan even more expensive in terms of the U.S. currency—the car makers have steadily increased the local content in their cars. For instance, 75 percent of the parts in the Toyota Camry built in Georgetown, Ky., are from the U.S., up from 60 percent when Toyota started building the car there in 1988. The Honda Accord built in Marysville, Ohio, has domestic content rising from 75 percent before 1993 to above 80 percent in 1994.

An increase of local content can be realized by using more locally made parts or through expanding local investment. Toyota Motor Corp. has sought to protect itself from the strong yen by investing £200 million to more than double the annual production at its car plant in Derbyshire, England. The expansion, to be completed by 1998, will increase Toyota's production to an annual level of 200,000 cars from the current 90,000. The new facility will produce the Corolla model and use 80 percent European-made parts in the cars. At a news conference, Yukihisa Hirano, managing director of Toyota U.K., said the production increase was mainly influenced by the yen's strength. Similarly, Honda Motor Co. is planning to build minivans with the capacity of 90,000 a year in one of its Ohio assembly plants as soon as 1998 to replace the Odyssey minivan currently built in Japan.

These measures have consequences that go beyond simply protecting the U.S. market share of Japanese companies. Japanese companies are also using the strong yen to buy cheaper components from around the world and ship them home for assembly. This pattern of sourcing provides a competitive edge in Japan itself. Sanyo recently signed a deal with the Mexican appliance maker Mabe to produce compressors to be used in refrigerators assembled in Japan. Similar strategies in China and Vietnam have contributed to an earnings turnaround at Sanyo. This "reverse export" trend has been developing even within Japan's flagship auto industry. Toyota Motor Corp. in 1995 will make 348,000 engines in the U.S., up from 233,000 in 1994. The increased output is expected to reduce the number of costly Japanese-made engines in U.S.-assembled cars. Japanese auto parts makers are beginning to ship components produced in their U.S. plants back home. About 26,000 engines will be exported back to Toyota plants in Japan.

While holding the line on the price of consumer durables such as automobiles, some Japanese producers are able to pass along currency-related cost increases whenever they don't face real competition. Theoretically, if they want to maintain profit margins as the yen strengthens, Japanese exporters have four options: raise prices, cut costs, invest overseas, or source components offshore. In a few cases, some companies have been able to opt for the first choice. With about 45 percent of the world's liquid crystal display market, Sharp is considering export price hikes that analysts say will be about 5 percent. Assemblers of computers in the U.S. may have little choice but to accept such increases. Similarly, NEC has raised prices on its high-end video cassette recorders. It has been able to do that because there are few non-Japanese competitors producing high-end VCRs. Most competitors, many from South Korea, make only low-cost VCRs. But the overwhelming majority of firms, Tadahiro Sekimoto, CEO of NEC says, have to either locate the production site or source parts in low-cost countries.

Financial hedging strategies have also been exploited by Japanese firms to minimize the negative effect of *endaka*. For example, Sony Corp. sold forward 70 percent of the dollars it expects to earn at a favorable rate, and Toshiba has hedged its currency exposure sufficiently to ensure that the yen's strength won't have a major impact on earnings.

There is a big difference between the current Japanese foreign investment wave and the first outpouring of Japanese money a decade ago. Back then, the Japanese were seeking a new export platform, and the target markets were still Europe and North America. This time around, emerging economies closer to home are also considered as havens offering a reprieve from *endaka* and promising markets for new investments. In locating large amounts of industrial assets in the Asian dollar zone, Japanese manufacturers hope to dominate local sales and fend off U.S. competition while furthering their own exports to the rest of the world. Minebea Co., for example, announced recently that it will spend $22 million on a new bearing plant in Shanghai. Fuji-Xerox is moving more production of its copier machines and other office equipment from Japan to Malaysia and India. Audio gear maker Aiwa Co. will lay out $43 million to double its output in Malaysia. Suntory Ltd. is expanding its brewery in China's Jiangsu province. And Osaka-based fiber maker Kanebo Ltd. is putting $18 million into an Indonesian subsidiary.

What impact will such a world-girding system have on Japan's trade surpluses? The betting is that Japan's global surplus will fall by about 5 percent in dollar terms this year. But the Japanese trade surpluses will still be painfully large, especially as sales to the rest of Asia continue to soar. And a high yen won't do much to shrink those surpluses since most large Japanese companies have become truly global multinationals.

Source: Neal Templin, "Japan Car Firms Unveil Cheaper Luxury Models," *The Wall Street Journal*, February 9, 1995, p. A4; Neal Templin, "Japan Auto Makers Buy More U.S. Parts," *The Wall Street Journal*, August 24, 1993, p. A2; Brian Bremner, Edith Updike, Larry Armstrong, and James B. Treece, "What the Strong Yen Is Breeding: Japanese Multinationals," *Business Week*, April 10, 1995, pp. 118-119; Mark Memmott, "Japanese Firms Adapt to Strong Yen," *USA Today*, November 10, 1994, p. 2B; Larry Holyoke and Dave Lindorff, "The Cheap Buck Gives Japan a Yen for Asia," *Business Week*, May 23, 1994, p. 52.

Discussion Questions for Mini-Case

1. Mr. Smith is the president of a U.S. firm that uses local suppliers to sell on the domestic market. At a recent meeting at his headquarters, one of his managers pointed out the turbulence in the currency markets and the rising value of the yen against the dollar, and wondered what effect this might have for the American company. Mr. Smith's reaction was dismissive, stressing that his company was small, centered to a local market, and was far removed from global trade movements. Do you agree with Mr. Smith's assessment? Why or why not?

2. Mr. Yakomoto is the owner of a small Japanese company producing highly specialized machine tools. Most of his production is exported to North America and Europe. The market for these machine tools is very restricted and their production requires highly skilled labor. What strategies do you suggest for Mr. Yakomoto's company, in order to cope with *endaka*?

3. What factors other than *endaka* should Japanese firms consider in formulating geographical strategies of offshore sourcing and overseas investment? Explain.

Notes

1 K.S. Nayar, "A Showcase for Information Technology," *India Abroad*, May 5, 1995, p. 30.

2 Doron P. Levin, "'Flexible' Plant for Fast-Changing Chrysler," *The New York Times*, September 9, 1994, p. 37; Alex Taylor III, "The Auto Industry Meets The New Economy," *Fortune*, September 5, 1994, pp. 56 and 58.

3 Kendall Roth and David Ricks, "Goal Configuration in a Global Industry Context," *Strategic Management Journal*, Vol. 15, 1994, pp. 103-120; George S. Yip, "Global Strategy in a World of Nations?" *Sloan Management Review*, Fall 1989, pp. 29-40.

4 Roth and Ricks, pp. 103-120.

5 Howard V. Perlmutter, "The Tortuous Evolution of the Multinational Corporation," *Columbia Journal of World Business*, Vol. 3, No. 1, January-February 1969, pp. 9-18.

6 Patrick Oster and John Rossant, "Call It Worldpool," *Business Week*, November 28, 1994, p. 98.

7 Ibid., p. 99.

8 Op. cit.

Further Reading

Kobrin, Stephen, "An Empirical Analysis of the Determinants of Global Integration," *Strategic Management Journal*, 1991, pp. 12, 17-31.

Kogut, Bruce, "Designing Global Strategies: Comparative and Competitive Value-Added Chains," *Sloan Management Review*, Summer 1985, pp. 15-28.

——"Designing Global Strategies: Profiting from Operational Flexibility," *Sloan Management Review*, Fall 1985, pp. 27-38.

Kogut, Bruce, and Nalin Kulatilaka, "Operating Flexibility, Global Manufacturing, and the Option Value of a Multinational Network," *Management Science*, 40(1), 1994, pp. 123-139.

UNCTAD, *World Investment Report, 1993, Transnational Corporations and Integrated International Production,* United Nations, New York, 1993.

Modes of Entry into Foreign Markets

LEARNING OBJECTIVES

After completing this chapter, you will be able to:

- Identify the alternative modes of entry into a foreign market that are available to the international company.

- Describe different forms of countertrade and their importance to the international firm.

- Discuss the advantages and disadvantages of licensing agreements as a mode of entry into foreign markets.

- Explain the types of equity-based ventures available to the firm, the conditions influencing the selection, and the pros and cons of international joint ventures.

- Discuss the factors influencing an international company's choice of entry mode, and describe a comprehensive framework for determining the appropriate mode to employ.

An international company can avail itself of several different modes of entry into foreign markets such as:

- Exporting
- Countertrade
- Contract manufacturing
- Licensing
- Franchising
- Turnkey projects
- Equity-based ventures—wholly owned/joint ventures

Typically, an international company engages in all of the above foreign market entry modes in different world markets. And in any one country market, a subsidiary may be engaged in one or more of the above entry modes. The parent company of the international enterprise decides which foreign affiliate will be responsible for which of the above international business activities.

In this chapter, we shall first examine each entry mode. Some—e.g., exporting, countertrade, licensing, and equity-based joint ventures—will be reviewed in greater detail than others because of their relatively greater importance in international business. Later in the chapter we shall review the significant factors that research has shown to have an impact on the choice of a particular entry mode for a particular foreign market. Now let us begin our discussion with a look at the most basic of the market entry strategies, exporting.

EXPORTING

A U.S. company has many methods to choose from for exporting its products. In some instances the company itself does nothing more than supplying the products for export. For example, the company may deal with a U.S.-based export merchant who buys on his own account, sells abroad through his own affiliates or branches, and often maintains his own warehouses, shipping docks, and transportation facilities. A company could also sell through an export commission house or through an export buyer, who acts as a purchasing agent for various foreign buyers. For the company these processes are exporting in name only, since the sales transactions take place in the home country itself; the actual export activity is accomplished by the buyer of the company's products.

There are two basic methods of export management—the indirect approach and the direct approach. It is not uncommon for a company to use both approaches simultaneously.

The Indirect Approach

A global company would not generally resort to this method of exporting. However, small- and medium-sized companies, particularly those just getting started in export, may prefer to begin with the indirect approach by entering into a contract with a combination export manager or with a manufacturer's export agent, both of which would be based in the company's home market.

A **combination export manager (CEM)** acts as the export department of the company. The CEM sells the company's products together with allied, but noncompetitive, lines of other companies through its own network of foreign distributors, who conduct business in the name of the company they represent. To potential buyers abroad, the CEM is the export department of the product manufacturing firm. Contracts with buyers are negotiated in the manufacturer's name. Correspondence may be on the manufacturer's letterhead, thus affording it an opportunity to establish its brand name abroad. All quotations and orders are also subject to approval by the manufacturer. Most CEMs operate mainly on a commission basis. A CEM often takes over all risks and problems of export. The manufacturer on his part has to see that the orders placed by the CEM get filled.

The CEM provides a manufacturer with one of the fastest routes of entering foreign markets, as well as the CEM's ready-made experience—a very important factor in international marketing because of the differences between the markets in various countries in areas such as culture, channels of distribution, product liability laws, and so on. The CEM is actually a ready-made export department for the manufacturer, considering that the CEM not only researches foreign markets but also chooses the type of distribution channel to be used and does his own advertising and sales promotion. He also gives credit assistance to the manufacturer where buy-and-sell arrangements are involved. It is essential, therefore, for the manufacturer to maintain a close liaison with the CEM on policies concerning advertising, sales promotion, pricing, financing, and credit extension.

If for some reason exporting the manufacturer's product appears to be no longer profitable or feasible, the CEM can also act as a middleman in helping the manufacturer to identify manufacturing or licensing opportunities abroad.

The contract with the CEM may be on a global or regional basis. The CEM is far more attractive to the company when he has branch offices in several key markets abroad. The manufacturer has a great deal of control over the marketing of his product, although not to the same degree that he would normally have over his own sales organization. Nevertheless, the CEM can be very useful to a company that is just getting involved with exporting and which does not have the capability or the funds to set up its own elaborate export sales organization.

An alternative to hiring a CEM is engaging a **manufacturer's export agent**. A manufacturer's export agent, unlike the CEM, does not make sales in the name of each manufacturer she represents, but retains her own identity by operating in her own name. She works on a straight commission basis. Unlike a CEM, a manufacturer's agent does not assume responsibility for advertising and financing.

Some of the advantages and disadvantages of indirect exporting follow:

Advantages of Indirect Exporting

1. A full-scale export program can be easily and quickly established.
2. A minimum financial commitment is required of the manufacturer.
3. Experts in international marketing are entrusted with the task of exporting and developing markets abroad.
4. The volume of exports can be built up relatively quickly by experts who know where the markets for the manufacturer's products are.
5. A minimal risk is involved on the part of the manufacturer.

Disadvantages of Indirect Exporting

1. The manufacturer does not have direct control over the export of his products and their marketing.
2. Middlemen have to split their attention over products of different companies, and therefore may not promote those products that are less profitable.
3. The company's own personnel may not get an export orientation because of their non-involvement with export activities.
4. Middlemen may abruptly decide to drop a company's product.

The Direct Approach

Direct exporting happens when a company sells its products *directly*, without an intermediary, to an importer or buyer located in a market abroad. The direct approach involves more expense and detail than the indirect approach. However, over the long haul, the results can be far superior in comparison with the indirect approach.

A company may at first conduct its direct exports through a "built-in" operation, in which a sales executive responsible for exports uses the services of the existing departments and personnel. The traffic department, for instance, routes and arranges the export shipment, perhaps in conjunction with a foreign freight forwarder.

A *foreign freight forwarder* advises and assists the export sales executive on invoicing, placing, and labeling shipments, picking them up at the factory, seeing them through with proper documentation to the foreign port, and so on. He may also assist the export sales executive in obtaining shipping space, transferring shipments to dockside or airport, arranging for marine insurance, procuring consular invoices or consular certified bills of lading, and clearing through customs. In exchange for his services and expenses, the foreign freight forwarder charges a fee to the company.

A separate *export department* may be created by the company to enable its own staff to concentrate on developing new markets abroad. An export department is a distinct, self-contained department that handles most of the export activities. The export department may be organized by territory, product, customer, or any combination of these. A separate export department enables exporting to be handled by specialists in the area who are committed to its success.

Some companies, that want to separate international marketing from its domestic counterpart have formed a separate *export sales subsidiary*. An export sales subsidiary is a semi-independent corporation, that is, a separate corporation wholly owned by the parent company. Very often the export sales subsidiary is made a profit center to enable the parent company to better monitor how successful its foreign marketing efforts have been. A major advantage of an export sales subsidiary is that it can be organized as a domestic international sales corporation (DISC), a western hemisphere trade corporation (WHTC), or an export trade corporation—any of which, if properly utilized, could accrue substantial tax benefits to the parent company.

A *manufacturer's representative* may be used by a company to directly export to foreign markets. A manufacturer's representative handles the noncompetitive products of a number of firms in the foreign market. He covers his selling expenses with commissions on sales within a specified territory of which he is a national. He usually does not assume any credit risk, nor does he maintain an inventory of products. Many companies often choose to tap a foreign market through a foreign distributor. A *foreign distributor* buys on his own account, maintains his stock, and generally sells at prices which he decides. A foreign distributor assumes all promotional costs and servicing responsibilities for a company's products if he is given an exclusive territory by the company.

Companies that feel the need for closer supervision over the sales of their products in a certain market may choose to establish their own selling offices abroad functioning as *foreign sales branches* of the U.S.-based company. Foreign sales branches are usually located only in large markets because the sales volume must justify the cost involved in establishing and operating a branch office. The sales branch handles all sales and promotional activities in a specified market and generally sells to wholesalers, dealers, and at times to industrial users. Usually, a foreign sales branch is established only after representatives and distributors have developed a market for the company's products.

In time, the foreign sales branch may be incorporated by the company as a *foreign sales subsidiary*, the foreign counterpart of the home-based export sales subsidiary. A foreign sales subsidiary is far more independent than a foreign sales branch because of its foreign incorporation and domicile. The staff of the subsidiary can evaluate the market, suggest product changes, and judge the effectiveness of advertising, public relations, and promotional efforts from the foreign consumer's point of view.

It is beyond the scope of this chapter to cover the various export procedures. The U.S. Department of Commerce and the international divisions of commercial banks are excellent sources of information and assistance to companies in this respect.

COUNTERTRADE

It is estimated that between 25 and 40 percent of the world's total exports are generated via countertrade, which clearly sets such transactions in the realm of big business. In "normal" business transactions, goods or services flow in one direction while the money being paid for them flows back in the other. The term countertrade is used to refer to arrangements whereby the flow of goods or services in both directions (and possibly even more!) is an integral element of the specific terms of the business transaction. Of the many varieties of countertrade, we will discuss the five principal ones: pure barter, clearing arrangement, switch trading, counterpurchase, and buy-back.

Pure Barter

In *pure barter*, both sides in the business arrangement agree to accept each other's goods as payment for the transaction. For example, in an agreement with Russia, PepsiCo trades its syrup for cases of Stolichnaya vodka. Russia markets Pepsi domestically under a franchising arrangement with PepsiCo, which receives an equivalent value of Stolichnaya vodka in return for the franchise rights and syrup that it sells to the Russians. PepsiCo in turn markets the Russian vodka in the United States.

In Mexico, PepsiCo adopted a creative barter arrangement that helped the company to grow in a country where price controls and a big drop in the local currency against the U.S. dollar would have resulted in lower U.S. dollar profits.

During Mexico's economic collapse in 1982, the Mexican government imposed price controls and devaluated the peso several times. Seeing their profits in U.S. dollars dropping precipitously, many U.S.-based companies such as Anderson Clayton and Nabisco sharply cut back their Mexican operations. Not so for PepsiCo, which elected to build instead. It is now cashing in on one of the world's most promising economies. How did PepsiCo do it? PepsiCo's ingenious strategy was to use the Mexican pesos earned from local sales to buy from local producers wheat, frozen juices, and pineapples—hardly considered PepsiCo's core businesses—for export to the United States, where they were sold to third parties. In 1991, this business was worth $30 million.

Rather than run away from a problem currency and difficult economic conditions, PepsiCo chose to stick around and, by using a creative barter arrangement, was able to convert the profits generated in Mexico into U.S. dollars without suffering the losses incurred in currency conversions from pesos to dollars. In 1991, PepsiCo was Mexico's largest consumer products company, with an estimated $1.2 billion in sales—larger than Procter & Gamble or Colgate-Palmolive.

It is alleged that American companies have a much shorter perspective than Japanese companies. The former are supposedly much more concerned about quarterly profits, whereas the latter are known to stress long-term growth and market share, hoping that profits will eventually come to those who wait patiently. But perseverance and creative strategies are what it takes to penetrate foreign markets. Fortunately, PepsiCo had both in its approach to Mexico, as this example illustrates.[1]

In another interesting deal in Ukraine, PepsiCo has agreed to sell Ukrainian-built commercial ships in the world market in exchange for the opportunity to market Pepsi and open several Pizza Hut restaurants (which PepsiCo owns) in Ukraine. This arrangement between PepsiCo and the Ukrainian government, and another between McDonnell Douglas and the Ugandan government in which McDonnell Douglas and the Ugandan government will exchange helicopters and fruit concentrate, is presented in *Practical Insight 10-1*.

Clearing Arrangements

Under a *clearing arrangement* two countries agree to exchange products by signing a "purchase and payment agreement." This agreement specifies the goods to be traded, their monetary value, and the settlement date. Any deficit on either side at the end of the contract is "cleared" either by accepting unwanted goods or by paying the balance in a specified currency such as U.S. dollars or West German marks.

PRACTICAL INSIGHT 10-1

Pepsi and McDonnell Douglas Sell Ships and Passion Fruit;
Countertrade Deals Make Life Interesting for Global Firms

Pepsi for Commercial Ships

For more than 20 years, PepsiCo Inc. has been engaged in countertrade with the former Soviet Union. Under the agreement with PepsiCo, the Soviet Union obtained the right to market Pepsi in the Soviet Union and PepsiCo, in exchange, received Stolichnaya vodka, which it marketed in the U.S.A. A much more unique version of countertrade was a deal signed by PepsiCo with the Soviet Union in the early 1990s. Under this agreement, PepsiCo agreed to accept not only Russian vodka but also ships built in Ukraine as a way to conduct commerce in Russia, which lacked convertible currency. PepsiCo sells the vodka and the commercial ships in the world market. Now, in an effort to further boost its sales in the former Soviet Union, PepsiCo has entered a joint venture with Ukraine worth $1 billion to market in the world market commercial ships built in Ukraine. Under the agreement, Pepsi will cooperate with three Ukrainian companies to market the ships. Some of the proceeds from the ship sales will be reinvested in the ship-building venture, and some will be used to build five Pepsi bottling plants and to buy soft drink equipment. The balance will be used to finance the opening of 100 Pizza Hut restaurants in Ukraine. Pepsi also owns the Pizza Hut chain. Since Ukraine does not have the hard currency, this type of arrangement will be very beneficial to both PepsiCo and Ukraine.

Helicopters for Passion Fruit

Uganda wanted to buy 18 helicopters to help eradicate elephant and rhino poaching but didn't have the $25 million to pay for them. Enter McDonnell Douglas Helicopter. McDonnell Douglas set up several projects in Uganda to generate the hard currency required. It set up a plant to catch and process Nile perch and a factory which produced pineapple and passion fruit concentrate, for which McDonnell Douglas found buyers in Europe. Uganda received the badly needed 18 helicopters and McDonnell Douglas got paid in the convertible currency.

Sources: Adapted from "Why Countertrade Is Getting Hot," *Fortune*, June 29, 1992, p. 25; and Michael J. McCarthy, "Pepsi Seeking To Boost Sales To Ukrainians," *The Wall Street Journal*, October 23, 1992, p. A9.

Switch Trading

Switch trading is trade involving three or more countries. For instance, England agrees to trade computers worth $500,000 to Brazil in exchange for coffee that has an equivalent market value of $500,000. The English may not want the coffee and so, with the help of a switch specialist, they sell the coffee to an Italian company for $450,000. England gets the cash for the sale minus the 5 to 10 percent that may be paid to the switch trader. Because the English side knows in advance that the coffee will be sold elsewhere at a discount, it will have hiked the price of the computers upward to compensate for the discount and the commission paid to the switch trader.

Counterpurchase

In a *counterpurchase* deal, Country A exports to Country B, and in return promises to spend some or all of the receipts on imports from B. The details of those imports need not be specified, but they must be bought within a particular period—usually three years.

Buy-Back

Buy-back involves licensing of patents or trademarks, selling production know-how, lending capital, or building a plant in another country and agreeing to buy part or all of its output as payment. In one case of buy-back, General Electric provided Poland with the technology and equipment to manufacture electrocardiogram meters, which, in turn, Poland shipped back to General Electric. In another famous deal, Fiat built an automobile factory in Russia, and the Russians paid Fiat for the factory partly in Russian-made Fiats.

CONTRACT MANUFACTURING

A contractual agreement between a company and a foreign producer under which the foreign producer manufactures the company's product is called *contract manufacturing*. Under this agreement the company retains responsibility for the promotion and distribution of its product. For example, an American pharmaceutical company may contract a company in India to manufacture its cough syrup. The Indian company manufactures it and does all the packaging of the product as per the requirements of the American company. Then the American company takes the packaged product and markets it in India or even globally.

LICENSING

An alternative route to markets abroad, one which falls somewhere between exporting and manufacturing abroad, is licensing. In a foreign *licensing* agreement the international company, or licensor, agrees to make available to another company abroad, the licensee, use of its patents and trademarks, its manufacturing processes and know-how, its trade secrets, and its managerial and technical services. In exchange, the foreign company agrees to pay the licensor a royalty or other form of payment according to a schedule agreed upon by the two parties. The licensing agreement could be between the parent company of the international enterprise and one or more of its foreign affiliates, or it could be between the international enterprise and an independent foreign, private, or government enterprise. For example, Firestone has given a license to the Mody Group in India to manufacture and market tires in the Indian domestic market. Similarly, General Foods has licensed the Kothari Group in India to market Tang, the soft drink mix.

Foreign licensing involves more risk than straight exporting from the home country, but it does not have in it the risks that go with the start-up of foreign manufacturing facilities abroad. The licensor is in fact exporting his know-how instead of products.

Reasons for Licensing

There are many reasons why a company might decide to use licensing as a means of tapping foreign markets. The following are some such reasons.

- To obtain extra income from technical know-how and services.
- To spread the costs of company research and development programs.
- To maximize returns from research findings and accumulated know-how.

- To retain established markets that have been closed or threatened by trade restrictions.
- To reach new markets not accessible by export from existing facilities.
- To enter or expand foreign markets quickly with minimum effort or risk.
- To gain cost or other advantages of local manufacture without committing capital abroad.
- To augment limited domestic capacity and management resources for serving foreign markets.
- To provide overseas sources of supply and services for important domestic customers.
- To accommodate military needs of home or foreign governments.
- To develop market outlets for raw materials or components made by the domestic company.
- To build goodwill and acceptance for other company products or services.
- To develop sources of raw materials or components for other company operations.
- To discourage possible infringement, impairment, or loss of company patents or trademarks.
- To bolster a minority ownership role.
- To diversify sources and types of company income.
- To pave the way for future investment.
- To acquire reciprocal benefits from foreign know-how, research, and technical services.

This list is not homogeneous and all-inclusive, nor does it distinguish between long-run and short-run objectives of the licensors. Also, it includes reasons that may be unacceptable to some companies. At the very least, however, most companies have the following objectives when they negotiate a license agreement.

1. To obtain a foothold in a foreign market which is inaccessible via exporting, or too risky through direct foreign investment.
2. To obtain know-how developed by foreign companies through reciprocal licensing arrangements.
3. To earn extra revenue to support company research and development.
4. To develop markets for components or other products made by the company.

Types of License Agreements

License agreements are defined by the nature and content of the rights granted by the licensor to the licensee. A simple licensing agreement is limited to a patent or trademark. But more complex licensing agreements include the delivery by the licensor to the licensee of one or more of the following.

- A patented product or process.
- A trademark or trade name.
- Manufacturing techniques and other proprietary rights generally referred to as company or industry know-how.
- Supply by the licensor to the licensee of components, materials, or equipment essential to a manufacturing process.

- Technical advice and services of various sorts.
- Marketing advice and assistance of various sorts.
- Capital and/or managerial personnel.

No two licensing agreements are alike. Licensing is a flexible and variable working arrangement, which can be tailor-made to the needs of both the licensor and the licensee.

Generally, a foreign licensing agreement is between two independent companies. However, it is not unusual in contemporary agreements for either the licensor or the licensee to be a government-owned enterprise. Several American pharmaceutical companies have licensed their patents, manufacturing process, and technical know-how to government-owned firms, mostly in developing countries. It is also commonplace for licensing agreements to be negotiated between the parent company and its wholly owned subsidiaries or branches. A company may also have a licensing agreement with its foreign joint venture partners in which it has either a minority or a controlling equity interest.

These are just a few examples of the variety of licensing agreements that exist in international business today.

Advantages of Licensing

Licensing has several advantages. It opens the way to getting a foothold in a foreign market without a large capital investment. Thus it can be less risky than starting a manufacturing operation. Equipment and know-how can be transported quickly to a foreign enterprise and operations set into motion. It eliminates the work of procuring personnel, buying land, constructing a building, and doing many of the other things ordinarily required in establishing a manufacturing subsidiary.

Licensing is most attractive to firms that are new to the international business arena. Most countries require that patents and trademarks be used within a certain number of years of their grant and registration, respectively, or get cancelled, which makes licensing a viable option for protecting the company's patents and trademarks.

Import restrictions and tariffs that are suddenly imposed after a company has established a market for its products in the country through exports pose a difficult problem for the company: Should it abandon the proven market for its products? Should it establish a manufacturing facility in the country? Is licensing the best alternative, given the global strategic interests of the company? It may resort to licensing if it decides not to jump over the trade barriers by establishing its own manufacturing plant in the country. Licensing of the products to a local company enables the firm to retain a foothold in such markets, which would otherwise be completely lost.

There are fewer currency exchange problems involved in licensing arrangements. Moreover, the licensor may find it to be the best way of tapping a foreign market if the market potential in the country is too small to optimally support a manufacturing plant. Licensing is a good method of securing business in foreign countries that have nationalized industries such as radio, television, telephone, transportation, oil, steel, and public utilities.

Some licensors consider the acquisition of patents from foreign patent holders to be one of the major benefits of foreign licensing operations. Reciprocal license grants are frequently made by the licensee as partial compensation for the rights and know-how made available by the licensor.

Disadvantages of Licensing

The disadvantages of licensing as a technique for penetrating foreign markets should be recognized and clearly understood by multinational companies. Let us examine some of the more important disadvantages.

Every licensee is a potential competitor of the licensor. If the original licensing agreement does not stipulate the region within which the licensee may market the licensed product, then there could be problems for the licensor if the licensee insists on marketing the product in third-country markets in competition with products already served in the market by the licensor.

The licensee may develop a formidable market with the use of licensed patents, trademarks, technology, or process, and reap huge profits, much to the chagrin of the licensor who did not foresee the huge markets developing, and therefore is receiving a comparatively negligible royalty under the license agreement in effect at the time.

The experience of many firms indicates that it is very difficult for the licensor to have complete satisfactory control over the licensee's manufacturing and marketing operations. This could result in damage to the licensor's trademark and reputation.

Several companies have had difficulties with licensees who refuse to pay royalties, claiming that the original product or process was altered and no longer in use. Moreover, if the licensing agreement calls for a payment of royalties in local currency, devaluation of the local currency would result in a decline of the value of royalty payments in the home country currency.

Key Factors to Be Considered Prior to Foreign Licensing

It is extremely important for a company to consider how its licensing program fits into its overall long-range strategic objectives and policies. If a company can establish its own manufacturing and sales facilities, it should do so, because it is to its advantage to develop and run its own business abroad and reap maximum benefits from the global markets for its products. Possible repercussions on domestic, export, and other foreign operations as well as prospective return in terms of resources and risks involved must be carefully determined prior to signing any license agreement with a foreign firm. If a company does decide to enter into a licensing agreement then it should consider the following steps. Before entering into a licensing agreement, the licensor must know the market's potential and the cost of developing it. The company must do its own research and gather its own information and not rely solely upon data provided by the licensee. It is important that the company does not underestimate or overestimate the market potential. If it does the former it might sell itself short, whereas if it does the latter it may make unrealistic demands of the licensee in terms of royalties and market development expectations. One company made just such arrangements in a foreign country. It oversold its franchise, demanded unrealistic results, and then expected the licensee to expend unreasonable sums of money to develop the market without hope of commensurately adequate compensation. The result was disastrous. Legal proceedings ensued with the licensor demanding compensation for loss of profits, and the licensee counterclaiming on the grounds that he had been deliberately misled on the value of the franchise.

The company must clearly state in the licensing agreement what it expects in terms of income from royalties and the effort to be expended in terms of financial and managerial resources by the licensee to develop the market. Unrealistic demands should not be made of the licensee, who should be fairly compensated for the time, effort, and money spent by him or her on the task. A successful licensing arrangement should result if both parties to the agreement feel that they are getting a fair bargain for their efforts.

The quality of the partner must be thoroughly investigated by the licensor company. The licensee need not be a big firm; however, it must have the managerial and financial strength to carry out its side of the agreement. It is also important that the licensee have a good image in the host country.

Serious problems could occur if a multinational company does not retain control over the production and marketing of its products by the licensee. A company can retain control over production by providing for quality control in the agreement. Agreement could be reached with the licensee that provides for the permanent stationing of a technical representative in the licensee's plant to check on the quality of the products produced or the process being used. Or, the licensee could be required to submit samples of production runs to the multinational company for approval. Periodic visits by the multinational company's production and quality control personnel to the production site could also help prevent the marketing of inferior quality products.

A special marketing company can be created through a contractual agreement between the licensor and the licensee with the stipulation that the marketing company would have the exclusive right to market the licensed products. Ownership of the marketing company could be shared by the licensor and the licensee, with controlling interest preferably in the hands of the licensor. If the licensee insists on owning a controlling equity in the company, all is not lost if the multinational company has a big enough minority interest to ensure a voice in the management of the marketing company. However, in this case, it is advisable to make a prior agreement with the licensee that would allow the licensor to buy a majority stock interest in the marketing company as its sales and profits increase over the years.

Several studies and company experiences reported in the popular business press have reported the following success factors for company licensing programs.

- Choice of a reliable, competent, and compatible licensee.
- Inherent value of the patents, trademark, or know-how licensed.
- Thorough advance research and understanding of the market.
- Mutual confidence and respect for each other's interests and objectives.
- Some participation in ownership and/or management.
- Close personal contact and public relations efforts with licensees.
- Prestige and favorable reputation of the licensor and the licensed product.
- Margin of technical and research lead maintained by the licensor.
- Provision of merchandising and sales assistance to licensees.
- Organized supervision and servicing of licensees by a special licensing staff.
- Scale of activity and amount of effort and attention devoted to it.
- Active support of top management.
- Flexibility of approach and administration.
- Correct timing and pacing of licensing activity.
- Anticipation and detailed listing of contract obligations and relationships.
- Effective coordination with other parts of the foreign trade program.

As for the failure of licensing, the following reasons appear to be the most important.

- Inadequate market analysis by licensor.

- Product defects not known or understood by licensing executives.
- Higher start-up costs than licensee anticipated.
- Insufficient attention, interest, and support from licensee's top management, marketing, engineering, and production executives.
- Poor timing.
- Competition (not just local, but from competitors from home and third countries).
- Insufficient marketing effort on the local scene by licensor and/or licensee.
- Inadequate licensee "after-sales" effort.
- Weakness in licensee market research and competitive intelligence.

Among the most troublesome factors to determine are accurately gauging the size of the market; obtaining meaningful clues as to the nature of the market—e.g., customer (industry, government, or individual) buying habits; the nature of the expected competition; and the verification of such information through effective test marketing or market research. Some companies reported their failure to realize that their "new" products would not be sufficiently "new" or different to capture the overseas public's fancy. One food company executive said he discontinued one of his products because consumers would not use it properly. Housewives insisted on adding milk rather than water, making it uneconomical to use! Most troublesome of all: accurately gauging the size of the market; obtaining meaningful clues as to the nature of the market—customer (industry, government, or individual) buying habits: probable competition and verifying such information by effective test marketing or market research.

The License Contract

The license contract contains specifics pertaining to the use of the rights conferred on the licensee and the limitations of those rights. The owner of the patent must decide whether he should license his property rights exclusively to one company in a country or nonexclusively to several. He may grant the licensee exclusive manufacturing rights in the country but deny her the exclusive rights to distribute the product in the world markets. Or the licensor may grant the licensee the exclusive rights to distribute the product in specified neighboring countries only. Some American companies have such an arrangement with Japanese companies by which the Japanese licensee is given an exclusive right to manufacture the products in Japan and exclusive rights to market them in Japan as well as in the countries of the Pacific Basin. The denial of exclusive rights to the licensee to market the products worldwide is meant to provide a healthy inducement for the licensee to develop the full potential of the markets allocated to her.

At times the licensor may grant the licensee exclusive manufacturing rights in a country but deny the licensee the right to use the licensor's trademark.

The specific rights and privileges included in a contract are governed by factors such as the bargaining positions of the two parties and their respective long-range regional or global production and marketing plans. Patent, trademark, and antitrust regulations of both home and host countries, as well as the current and anticipated political, economic, and financial risk in the host country, also have a major influence on the provisions of a licensing agreement.

The following specific questions should be considered by a company before drafting a license contract.

- How may patents, processes, or trademarks be used?
- How will technical assistance be rendered?

- Which products are included in the agreement, and to what extent?
- What territory is to be covered by the license?
- How should the licensee be compensated?
- What happens if compensation cannot be paid by the licensee?
- If sublicensing is permitted, how should it be carried out?
- What are the provisions as to duration and cancellation?
- What rights does the licensor have in developments by the licensee?
- What visitation and inspection privileges are held by the licensor, and on what terms and conditions are they to be exercised?
- Can the parent company inspect accounts?
- What provisions are there for satisfactory promotional and sales performance and for adequate quality control?
- What government approvals are required?
- What tax factors are involved?

This concludes our overview of the licensing mode of entering foreign markets, which is frequently used by international companies.

FRANCHISING

Another form of licensing is *franchising*—a transfer of technology, business system, brand name, trademark, and other property rights by a franchisor to an independent company or person who is the franchisee. There has been an explosion of franchising throughout the world in recent years. Usually a company initially establishes a brand name for its products, service, quality, and so on in the home market, and a standardized business system to operate the business. It then franchises the entire business system, including the trademark and brand name, to the franchisee in a foreign country. The franchisee operates the business under the franchisor's trademark or brand name and is contractually obligated to adhere to the procedures and methods of operation prescribed in the business system. The franchisor generally maintains the right to control the quality of the franchisee through quality control of products and service so that the franchisee cannot harm the company's image. In exchange the franchisor receives a fee based on the volume of sales. Sometimes the franchisor mandates that the franchisee must buy from it the equipment and some key ingredients used in the products. For example, Burger King and McDonald's require the franchisee to buy from the company cooking equipment, patties for the burgers, and other products that bear the company name. Coca-Cola and Pepsi send the syrup which is the key ingredient in the soda to its franchisees who bottle and market the drink. Marriott, Holiday Inn, Hilton, McDonald's, Burger King, Avis, Hertz, Coca-Cola, and Pepsi are examples that have become household names throughout the world using the franchising entry mode.

The advantages and disadvantages of franchising are similar to those of licensing. The main advantages are franchising is an inexpensive way of exploiting a foreign market, there is little or no political risk involved, and it is a fast and relatively easy avenue for leveraging globally a company's assets such as a brand name and standardized business system.

Franchising has disadvantages as well, however. The franchisee may spoil the franchisor's image by not upholding the standards for quality established by the franchisor. Even if the franchisor is able to terminate the agreement, the franchisee may still stay in business by slightly altering the company's brand name or trademark. For example, the former franchisee of TGI Friday's in Mexico City merely changed its name to TGI Freeday and continued to do business. Thus a franchisee may actually help to establish a competitor.

TURNKEY PROJECTS

When an international company engages in setting up a *turnkey* operation abroad, it assumes responsibility for the design and construction of the entire operation, and, upon completion of the project, it hands over the total management to local personnel whom it has trained. In return for the completion of the project, the international company receives a fee, which can be quite substantial. Turnkey operations generally involve projects such as the construction of airports, dams, electric power stations, roads, and factory complexes such as steel mills, refineries, chemical plants, and automobile plants.

Examples of American companies that have completed turnkey projects abroad include Bechtel and Fluor, who have constructed many foreign plants and projects. Cogentrix, the American power company, is building a $1.4 billion electric power generation plant in India. An entire automobile plant was constructed in Russia by Fiat, the famous Italian company. Foreign companies have built hospitals in Saudi Arabia, and South Korean, Chinese, and Indian companies have built highways in Africa and the Middle East under turnkey contracts.

EQUITY-BASED VENTURES

As opposed to the modes of entry discussed above, equity-based foreign market entry involves the equity ownership and control by an international company of a foreign venture. The foreign venture may serve several purposes. It may be established to obtain raw materials for use by the company in production in other countries, or for sale on world markets. Companies in the petroleum, aluminum, steel, and copper industries have established numerous foreign ventures for these purposes.

An *equity-based venture* may also be established to produce components or products that are mainly exported to the home country or to third countries. A company may establish such an enterprise in a foreign country to take advantage of the availability of labor, energy, or other inputs at competitive prices. International companies, especially in the electronics industry, have established sourcing subsidiaries in Mexico, China, and many countries in the Pacific Basin for this purpose.

An equity-based foreign venture need not necessarily involve production. A company may establish one that is involved in the distribution of the company's products, or in the marketing of a service such as advertising, accounting, engineering, legal, or management consulting.

An international company may decide to establish an equity-based venture in a foreign country to produce and/or market a product or service mainly to serve the foreign market itself. It may export some of the production to the home market or to third-country markets, however, the host country market is the principal target market for the products produced by the venture. For example, several Japanese multinational automobile companies such as Nissan, Honda, Toyota, Subaru, and Mazda have set up manufacturing plants in the United States that have the latest manufacturing technology and management techniques. Their purpose is to give the Japanese companies the greatest competitive edge in serving the domestic U.S. market as well as a base for sales to Europe, which tightly limits imports from Japan but not from the United States.[2]

An equity-based venture abroad could be a greenfield investment, which involves setting up the venture from the ground up, or it may involve the acquisition of an existing firm. It may finance the new venture abroad from its own funds, or it may borrow the necessary funds from financial institutions and equity markets in the home, host, or third-country markets.

An equity-based venture could be wholly owned by the parent international company or it could be a joint venture in which the international company shares its ownership with another company. Managing a wholly owned foreign subsidiary is a relatively less complex endeavor than managing a joint venture. The complexity of managing a joint venture is caused by the sharing of the management of the enterprise with a foreign partner. The joint venture route is a popular mode for foreign market entry among international companies.

Although many companies shun joint ventures, insisting upon wholly owned subsidiaries as a mode of foreign market entry, an increasing number of companies often conclude that under certain circumstances a joint venture mode of market entry can be mutually beneficial to all parties involved in its formation.

In the following sections, we shall examine the nature of joint ventures, their advantages and disadvantages, and how they can best be utilized by international companies.

What Is an International Joint Venture?

An international joint venture is a business collaboration between companies based in two or more countries who share ownership in an enterprise established jointly for the production and/ or distribution of goods or services. Pure trade agreements are excluded from our concept of a joint venture.

Of particular interest to us in this chapter are joint ventures in which one of the partners is an international company and the other is a national of the host country.

Conditions that Influence the Choice of the Joint Venture Mode

The affinity of companies for joint ventures abroad is influenced by several factors. The following are some of the most influential.

Legislation The laws in some countries mandate that foreign firms must form joint ventures with local partners (as opposed to wholly foreign-owned subsidiaries) in order to conduct business within their borders. Often this rule is applied for certain industries only. At times no such legal requirement may exist, but nevertheless the attitude of the host government may be so heavily biased in favor of joint ventures that it becomes the only practical entry mode available to a foreign company.

Protecting a Profitable Market Tariffs or import barriers imposed by a local government may threaten a profitable export market developed in a country by an international company. If the local government has policies that discourage or disallow wholly owned subsidiaries, then the multinational company can choose to effect a licensing agreement with a local company. However, if the international company decides that neither licensing nor contract manufacturing are attractive alternatives to pursue, then it is left with two alternatives: (1) form a joint venture with a local partner or (2) abandon the market altogether. Only if an international company has a firm policy of its own of not forming joint ventures under any circumstances will it decide to abandon the market despite its already established position.

Technological Characteristics Companies that have products whose value is based upon a unique production process, trademark, brand name, or trade secret are quite hesitant to form joint ventures because of the danger that the production process and trade secret may be leaked to third parties. Such companies hesitate to form joint ventures also because of the risk of eroding the value and prestige associated with the quality of their product, brand name, or trademark, which could happen if the joint venture is unable to maintain the original quality standards.

Integrated Network of Subsidiaries Companies that have several subsidiaries abroad that are integrated globally or regionally in a network of production-assembly-distribution systems are likely to oppose joint ventures because joint ventures with local partners decrease their flexibility as well as increase the control required to optimally integrate the different subsidiaries involved in this network. For example, local partners are more likely to be interested in the profitability of the joint venture and would therefore be inclined to oppose any plans to curtail production in the joint venture and shift it to another subsidiary, or to supply third markets from another subsidiary, even though the multinational company considered such plans to be in the interests of its global operations. Therefore, a joint venture that has been established primarily to produce products for the national market only may be more suitable for an international company than one that may have to be integrated in a global or regional network of subsidiaries, unless the international company has an overwhelming majority equity interest in the joint venture which gives the international company a veto power over the decisions made by the joint venture management.

Acquisition of Expertise Companies seek joint ventures when they need expertise that can best be provided by a local, such as a well-developed marketing and service organization, well-established and proven contacts with important officials in the host government, an established name and place in the host country's industrial sector, a competent management team and labor force, and so on.

Types of International Joint Ventures

International joint ventures can take many forms depending upon the needs and circumstances of the partners and the conditions under which the collaboration agreement is consummated. International joint ventures can vary depending on such factors as the percentage of the total equity in the joint venture held by each partner, the number of partners involved in the joint venture, and the characteristics of the partners.

An international company's ownership of a joint venture may vary from a majority to an equal to minority participation in the total equity capital of the joint venture.

The number of partners involved in a joint venture may also vary. There might be only two or three partners involved when firms or small groups of interests from two or more countries form a joint venture. For example, companies from England, France, and Holland are partners in the development and production of the Airbus that is so popular in the airline industry. However, numerous partners are involved when the equity of the joint venture is dispersed in the hands of the general public through the sale of stock. Several American companies have formed such joint ventures in India. Such an arrangement allows the international company to maintain effective managerial control over the joint venture and at the same time satisfies the requirement of the government that a majority of the equity be in the hands of its citizens.

An international company could have a variety of partners in a foreign joint venture. The partner could be a local company, another international company, the host country government, or the general public in the host country.

Advantages of a Joint Venture

A joint venture may be the only possible way to set up a business in a country. This may be particularly true in the case of certain industries that are regarded as politically sensitive, such as the petroleum industry, aircraft manufacture, or transportation or utility companies.

A firm with limited resources is able to enter a greater number of markets through the joint venture route than would be possible with a policy of establishing only wholly owned subsidiaries abroad. In some developing countries in particular, where large local firms do have capital but are short of technical and managerial know-how, a multinational company can form a joint venture with a local firm, without making any capital outlays, by receiving equity in the joint venture in exchange for its patents and know-how.

In countries where the fervor of nationalism is high, a joint venture with a local firm or government agency could help in substantially lowering the governmental and societal hostility against a foreign firm.

In many instances, the local partner is able to circumvent red tape and bureaucratic harassment which afflict multinational companies in many countries. Through well-established contacts with the right people, the local partner is often able to obtain important permits and licenses for imports, foreign exchange, plant expansion, water and electricity supply, and so on.

First-class managerial talent is difficult to find everywhere, but this is particularly evident in developing countries. The best way of obtaining high-quality managerial talent that is knowledgeable about local conditions is often through a joint venture with a successful local firm.

Another advantage of an intangible nature is the effect on the local employees of a joint venture. It was reported that in India the sale of 10 percent of the stock of a once wholly owned subsidiary to the Indian public had a significantly positive impact on the morale of the Indian staff.

Government contracts are sometimes given only to domestic firms. International firms in certain industries are therefore obliged to form joint ventures with local companies in order to qualify for government contracts.

Developing countries have been insisting on joint ventures with the government because of an historical distrust of foreign countries arising from their experience with colonialism. This distrust is transferred to foreign companies who, it is feared, might exert undue political and social influence. A minority participation of the government in a joint venture would allow its representatives to sit on the board of directors, thus permitting direct scrutiny of the workings of the joint venture. The allaying of such anxiety, however ill-founded it may be, may be a valid motive for a multinational company to form a joint venture with the government. Civil servants on the board of directors can also be helpful in obtaining favorable rulings from the government on vital matters such as price increases and import permits. As a partner in the joint venture, the host government is in a position to examine the problems and needs of the joint venture, as well as its contributions to the country's economy, from the inside.

International companies are often confronted with a peculiar problem that forces them to form joint ventures. For example, foreign companies planning to establish manufacturing facilities in a country may find that certain prominent local business firms have managed to corner permits that are no longer granted by the government, but are required to produce products that the international company wants to produce. Hence they are compelled to form joint ventures with local firms that own the required permits to produce the products.

Many companies form joint ventures with local firms that have the ability to provide the foreign partner with a steady stream of quality raw materials and/or components. A joint venture with a local firm is especially useful when imports of the required materials have been cut off by the government and when a license for their production has been given to the local firm.

Disadvantages of a Joint Venture

Joint ventures can have several disadvantages as well, and therefore international companies should carefully weigh the advantages against the disadvantages of joint ventures before deciding for or against them. We shall examine some of the most prominent disadvantages of an international joint venture.

A company with a planning system attempts to mobilize and deploy its worldwide resources with the aim of achieving its global objectives effectively and efficiently. This requires that actions be taken based upon decisions that are in the interests of the company as a whole, even though the interests of one or more of its subsidiaries may have to be suboptimized in the process. A multinational company can take such actions only if the subobjectives of each of its subsidiaries are derived from, and dovetail with, the global company objectives. Problems with achieving global objectives could arise if a foreign joint venture partner refuses to go along with decisions of the international company that may be in the best interests of its global objectives but which may not be in the best interests of the joint venture partner. For example, the local partner may resist efforts by the international company to have one of its wholly owned subsidiaries, rather than the joint venture, serve third-country markets. A multinational company may like to make such a shift if it is feasible, especially because, in the case of a wholly owned subsidiary, the increased profits emanating from higher sales do not have to be shared with anybody, which is not true in the case of a joint venture. The local partner is likely to resist the shift even more, particularly when exports are essential to keep the joint venture operating at full capacity.

Sourcing of components and raw materials could also cause problems in a joint venture. For example, it might be cheaper to manufacture certain components in a third country and have them imported (if the import legislation permits it) for final assembly in the joint venture. The local partner is not likely to look favorably upon this idea, especially if, as is very often the case, the local joint venture partner is capable of making the components, and importing them would mean an increase in costs and a decrease in the joint venture's profits.

Problems could arise if the local partner—in the absence of any prior agreement precluding any such action—insists on exporting the products of the joint venture into world markets. A multinational company may find itself in a very grave predicament if the products of the joint venture begin to compete in third-country markets with similar products produced by its subsidiaries. Worse still would be for the joint venture products to find their way into the home market of the multinational company itself.

Conflicts between the partners could also occur if the local partner owns rival distribution channels for the products produced by the joint venture. Such conflicts forced Grace Company to sell out its share to Pinturas Colombianas, its Columbian partners.

The above are examples of how a joint venture could disrupt a multinational company's plans for a regional or worldwide integration of its production-assembly-marketing operations in view of its total company objectives.

There are also other areas in which problems could arise. The long-term success of a joint venture depends not only on how and to what extent the capabilities and contributions of each of the partners reinforce each other, but also on the combination of their respective risk/gain and time/return attitudes. Let us see how the risk/gain and time/return attitudes of the partners could affect a joint venture's prospects.

The desire for growth and the propensity to assume corresponding risks to achieve it may differ between partners. For example, a multinational company, because of its bigger size and stronger financial position, might be willing to assume financial risks on projects that have prospects of high returns. Such high risk-high return projects might appear as reckless behavior to the local partner, who might be relatively more conservative because of her smaller size and weaker financial position. Because of the differences in the willingness to assume risks, friction could arise between the joint venture partners on issues such as the extent to which the joint venture company is an aggressive price leader, the debt/equity ratio assumed, whether some budget items are capitalized or expensed, the handling of employee pension funds, the amount of resources committed to marketing capabilities to exploit new markets, and the aggressiveness of marketing policies.

The time/return attitudes of the two partners might also vary and cause problems. This is not to be confused with the conservative/liberal attitude towards risks, which has to do with a company's propensity to take risks. The time/return attitude of a company is concerned with its tendency to wait in anticipation of a future return. For example, the local partner might be unwilling to commit the company's resources to research and marketing programs that may promise high long-term returns but which sacrifice the joint venture's short-term competitive edge and immediate profits.

Conflicts could also occur due to the different tax laws and foreign exchange considerations affecting the two partners. A U.S. international company, for example, may wish to forgo dividends in order to defer U.S. taxes on dividends repatriated to the United States. But this may conflict with the desire of the local partner for dividends and immediate cash.

An international company that has a joint venture in a country with a history of currency devaluations would prefer to keep the joint venture's current assets to a minimum to limit its losses from local currency depreciation. It would also prefer to borrow from the local capital markets to meet the joint venture's working capital needs. This again may not be acceptable to the local partner, who has no such losses to worry about, and who may therefore object to the idea of incurring heavy interest payments by borrowing for working capital requirements. Joint ventures could, in this way, reduce the flexibility of an international company to respond strategically to exploit profit opportunities arising from differences in tax laws and currency fluctuations.

Disagreements also could arise over staffing practices in the joint venture. In some countries it is a common practice for top management personnel to be recruited from a certain social class. It is also common in some countries, like India, for owners of firms to give good jobs to family members or members of the same community. An international company, which desires to employ competent managerial personnel in the joint venture, might have a conflict with the local partners who might want to hire their own relatives or members of the same class or community for important managerial posts.

Maintaining Control Over a Joint Venture

Maintaining control over a joint venture is crucial for an international company with a plan to integrate it into its global production-assembly-marketing plan. However, it is also necessary to maintain control of some sort over the joint venture even if the international company has no such plans.

There is no control problem if the joint venture is wholly owned by a multinational company or when it owns a majority of its equity. However, how can a company minimize problems in a joint venture in which it has minority or 50-50 ownership of the equity? Following are some techniques that have been used by international companies.

An international company can negotiate a management contract with the local partner giving it the authority to manage the joint venture. This method has been frequently used by international companies in developing countries. The developing countries are often willing to give up managerial control of joint ventures if they do not have the trained personnel necessary to manage them. Managerial control can be obtained in various ways. One method is to give an international company a majority representation on the board of directors. This method was used by the English firm Metal Box in its joint venture in Tanzania with the Tanzanian government as partner. If a majority cannot be obtained, then the next alternative is to have equal representation by the two sides on the board of the joint venture but to provide in the joint venture contract that the views of the international company would be upheld in the event of a deadlock. If the local partner does not agree with this alternative, then the international company may be able to negotiate an agreement that gives it the right to veto any unacceptable policy decision.

Another method of obtaining managerial control is to negotiate the authority to appoint members to the executive committee of the joint venture. The executive committee is concerned with the day-to-day management of the enterprise, whereas the board of directors is concerned with the formulation of the major policies and plans of the enterprise. The board of directors also has the responsibility of overseeing the total management of the enterprise and appointing the key management personnel. Technically, the board of directors can overrule the decisions of the executive committee. But in the event that an international company cannot obtain control over the joint venture's board then it may have to settle on the right to name the executive committee members. A company can also negotiate the right to select the managing director and/or the technical director of the subsidiary, which in essence gives it the authority to make strategic decisions for the joint venture.

Some joint ventures provide for the voting control, and hence the control of the enterprise, to remain in the hands of the multinational company. This is not legally possible in some countries. If it is allowed by local laws then the means of achieving voting control without a majority ownership of the equity is to issue two types of shares with one class of shares having no votes or multiple votes.

Taking local financial institutions such as banks and/or insurance companies as majority partners in a joint venture is a device often used by multinational companies. Financial institutions quite often take little or no interest in the actual day-to-day management of the enterprise, thus enabling the multinational company to retain control over its management.

A multinational company could obtain a controlling interest in a joint venture, although it may not hold a majority interest, by taking two or more local firms as partners. For example, an international company could own 40 percent of a joint venture with the balance owned by two or more other partners. Although it is theoretically possible for the other partners to collude and form a voting bloc against the international company, in reality the odds are against this outcome.

Selling sufficient stock on the local stock market is one variation of the above method that can be used to prevent bloc voting by local partners. The public issue of shares represents an ingenious technique of local public participation because the public is generally not interested in taking an active role in the day-to-day management of the joint venture. So, even if a multinational company holds a minority of the voting shares, it can still exercise effective control.

267

Actual control over a joint venture can be exercised by an international company through a license agreement. When the joint venture cannot operate effectively without the license, and the license is terminable by the international company, the significance of the license to the control of the joint venture is obvious. Similar results can be obtained through the lease of equipment and various types of technical and financial assistance agreements.

A multinational company could also negotiate a contract which gives the local partner a controlling equity interest in the joint venture with the stipulation that all output of the enterprise, or at least that which is exported, be marketed by a separate marketing company that is wholly owned by the international company. It is not uncommon, however, for the local partner to own up to 49 percent of the voting shares of the marketing company. The key is for the multinational company to control its management. This device is used to prevent the local partner from disrupting the global marketing plans of the international company. In the absence of this type of control by the international company over the marketing of products, the local partner could start to export the products produced by the joint venture to third-country markets already served by the international company's subsidiaries in other countries.

The Joint Venture Agreement

The joint venture agreement should be a carefully pre-planned document that specifies in clear language the rights and obligations of the partners in the joint venture. It is suggested that any joint venture agreement should cover the following points.

- The legal nature of the joint venture, its name, and the parties to it.
- The purpose of the joint venture and the terms under which it can be dissolved.
- The constitution of the board of directors and voting power of the partners.
- The managerial rights and responsibilities of the parties.
- Constitution of the management and appointment of the managerial staff.
- The conditions under which equity capital could be increased.
- Constraints on the transfer of shares or subscription rights to nonpartners.
- The responsibilities of each of the partners in respect to assets, finance, personnel, R&D, and so on.
- The financial rights of the partners with respect to dividends and royalties.
- The rights of the partners with respect to the use of licenses, know-how, and trademarks in third-market countries.
- Limitations, if any, on sales of the joint venture products to certain countries or regions.
- An arbitration clause indicating how disputes between partners are to be resolved.
- Conditions under which the articles of the joint venture agreement may be changed.

Before concluding any joint venture agreement, care should be taken to ensure that the joint venture does not violate any antitrust laws of the home and/or host countries involved.

Now that we have examined the seven modes of entry, we shall review what we know of the factors that have a significant bearing upon which mode of entry is chosen by a company to enter a foreign market. Our review will include findings of previous research on the subject of entry mode choice.

FACTORS INFLUENCING THE ENTRY MODE
CHOICE BY INTERNATIONAL COMPANIES*

The choice of the mode of entry in a foreign country by a firm is perhaps one of the most widely researched areas in the international business arena. It ranks with the most significant decisions that a firm will make as it embarks upon a global strategy to penetrate foreign markets.[3] The choice of an entry mode is critical in a firm's globalization strategy because, as shown in Table 10-1, each entry mode discussed earlier in this chapter differs in the degree of control, the degree of systemic risk experienced, the degree of dissemination risk experienced, and the amount of the firm's resources committed. *Degree of control* is the authority over operational and strategic decision making that a company has over its foreign operations.[4] *Systemic risk* is the level of political, economic, and financial risks faced by the particular entry mode. *Dissemination risk* is the risk that firm-specific advantages in know-how will be expropriated by a partner in a foreign venture.[5] *Resource commitment* refers to the amount of resources invested in revenue-generating assets in a foreign venture such as plant and equipment, training imparted to personnel, or the costs of penetrating a foreign market, all of which cannot be redeployed to alternative uses without incurring substantial sunk costs.[6]

As shown in Table 10-1, the degree of control of a foreign operation ranges from low for exporting, countertrade, and licensing to high for wholly owned subsidiaries. Systemic risk

TABLE 10-1
Characteristics of Entry Modes

Type of Entry Mode	Degree of Control	Systemic Risk	Dissemination Risk	Resource Commitment
Exporting	Low	Low	Low	Low
Countertrade	Low	Low	Low	Low
Contract Manufacturing	Medium	Medium	Low to medium	Low
Licensing	Low	Low	High	Low
Franchising	Low to medium	Low	Medium	Low
Turnkey	Low	Low	Low	Low
Equity-based entry: Joint venture	Medium	Medium	Medium to high	Medium to high
Equity-based entry: Wholly owned subsidiary	High	High	Low	High

* The following material was written by Raman Muralidharan, lecturer in Management, Indiana University at South Bend.

269

varies from low for exporting, countertrade, licensing, franchising, and turnkey projects to high for the wholly owned entry mode. Dissemination risk is highest for licensing, and resource commitments are highest for wholly owned ventures.

Several theoretical perspectives, such as transaction cost economics, industrial organization, and strategic behavior, have been advanced to explain the choice of entry mode by global companies. Over the past two decades, researchers have empirically tested several existing explanations for this phenomenon, and new explanations have been offered.

More than twenty-five different variables have been empirically tested for their influence on the entry mode decision. We will synthesize and categorize the previous research findings into five dimensions. Research findings on the significance of variables in terms of their impact on choice of entry mode have been conflicting. We shall therefore focus on only those variables from various research findings which have consistently shown to be significant in terms of their impact on the entry mode decision.

Findings of Previous Research

Research on entry mode strategies has yielded twenty-five different factors as determinants in the entry mode choice. However, there has not been an agreement among the research findings on the significance of some of these factors. Some studies identify certain factors as being significant in their impact on the entry mode decision, and others negate such conclusions. We have therefore selected seventeen variables that were tested and found to be statistically significant in eight empirical studies conducted between 1987 and 1992. The eight studies were built upon the accumulated knowledge and findings of previous research, and therefore reflect the key findings of earlier studies as well as new developments in the area. In the following we present a brief review of each of these seventeen variables.

1. **Firm Size.** Firm size is one of the measures of managerial capabilities and resources of a firm, and as such could influence the choice of entry mode. Empirical evidence shows that there is a positive impact of firm size on foreign direct investment, i.e., generally one would expect firm size to have a positive correlation with foreign market entry, and in particular with entry through wholly owned or joint venture modes.[7]

2. **Multinational Experience.** Multinational experience reduces the uncertainty associated with assessing the true economic worth of entry into a foreign market. It follows, therefore, that firms with little or no experience with international business or multinational operations would seek to limit their risk exposure. Such firms would prefer low control/low resource, non-investment-type entry modes such as exporting or licensing.[8] In contrast, firms with significant multinational experience would prefer high control/high resource, investment-type modes such as joint ventures or wholly owned affiliates.

3. **Industry Growth.** Industry growth in the target country is an indicator of the degree of competition and profitability that a firm would experience in that country. Industry growth is therefore expected to influence the entry mode choice. Kogut and Singh found that the entry mode preference of a firm is dependent upon competitive assumptions.[9] They also found evidence (albeit weak) for the proposition that the joint venture entry mode is encouraged when the industry is growing.

4. **Global Industry Concentration.** Hamel and Prahalad have argued that in a global industry characterized by global competition, firms that function under a global strategy umbrella respond to their competitor's competitive moves not only in their home market but also

in the competitor's home market, or in third-country markets.[10] For such firms it is imperative that they have control of their foreign affiliates, without which it would be impossible to implement a global response to a competitor's onslaught.[11] Assuming that high global industry concentration would be associated with a high degree of global competition, firms operating in such industry conditions would prefer high control entry modes such as wholly owned subsidiaries.

5. **Technical Intensity.** Failure of markets[12] to mediate the exchange of technology and tacit knowledge is given as the reason by most studies that firms in technically intense industries prefer the wholly owned affiliate entry mode. However, an entering firm that is seeking technology and tacit knowledge is more likely to enter the foreign market through a joint venture with a firm that has the needed technology.

6. **Advertising Intensity.** When a firm's involvement is in an industry that is characterized by high advertising intensity, it is inclined to shy away from joint ventures and be favorably inclined to seek entry modes which provide full control over the foreign venture.[13]

7. **Country Risk.** Firms prefer to avoid countries with high political risk like expropriation or nationalization, or economic risk like restrictions on remittances of assets and limitations on operational and managerial choice. But if they do choose to make an entry into such countries, they would do so utilizing non-investment (low control) entry modes.[14]

8. **Cultural Distance.** Firms entering culturally distant countries will prefer licensing agreements or joint ventures over wholly owned affiliates.[15]

9. **Market Potential.** In high market potential countries, firms are inclined to pursue joint ventures or wholly owned entry modes since such modes provide higher profitability and market presence.[16]

10. **Market Knowledge.** Firms can be expected to pursue the wholly owned entry mode relative to a joint venture as firms gain experience and learn more about the local environment.[17] Firms are likely to use high control entry modes when following a client into a country market.[18] Therefore, prior experience with a country market and/or client following is expected to be associated positively with high control entry modes.

11. **Value of Firm-Specific Assets.** If the value of the firm-specific assets involved in the venture is high, then firms are likely to prefer entry modes that allow full control, and avoid joint ventures with local partners due to the fear of opportunism by the latter. Researchers have used different variables to capture the value of firm-specific assets. Agarwal and Ramaswami used the firm's "ability to develop differentiated products."[19] Gatignon and Anderson used the "value of firm specific know-how" to represent the value of firm specific assets involved in a venture.[20]

12. **Contractual Risk.** If the cost of making and enforcing contracts to prevent opportunism by local partners is high, then the firm will prefer entry modes that offer high control over their assets and skills.[21] Therefore, when the contractual risk is high, firms are likely to pursue high control entry modes.

13. **Tacit Nature of Know-How.** If the nature of the firm-specific know-how is tacit, then wholly owned operations increases the firm's ability to utilize the accumulated tacit knowledge.[22] Therefore, tacit know-how is expected to be positively associated with degree of control.

14. **Venture Size.** Gatignon and Anderson (1988) have argued that the size of the operation will have an impact on the extent of control sought by the entrant.[23] Empirical evidence[24] supports the proposition that firms shy away from wholly owned entry modes in favor of joint ventures when the size of the venture is big.

15. **Intent to Conduct Joint Research and Development.** Market-determined governance structures may not provide the requisite control to manage the complex judgmental tasks involved in conducting research and development.[25] Therefore if the intent of a firm entering a foreign market is to conduct research and development work in conjunction with a partner, it will be inclined to favor a joint venture as opposed to other low control governance structures.

16. **Global Strategic Motivation.** It has been argued by researchers[26] that foreign market entries are motivated by strategic factors that go beyond immediate efficiency considerations. Strategic goals, such as establishing a strategic outpost and developing a global sourcing site, or moving into a market to deny a profit sanctuary for competitors, motivate firms to prefer wholly owned or joint venture entry modes as opposed to low control licensing agreements.[27]

17. **Global Synergies.** Firms seek hierarchical control over affiliates when there is a high degree of interaction between and among the foreign affiliates and the parent company in pursuit of an integrated global strategy.[28] Therefore, when the potential synergies from global integration of companywide strategies are high, firms are likely to pursue high control entry modes like wholly or majority owned affiliates.

A COMPREHENSIVE FRAMEWORK FOR ENTRY MODE CHOICE

The roots of entry mode choice lie in the early stages of the theory of the multinational enterprise. The earliest non-neo-classical trade and finance-type explanations for FDI or no foreign involvement came from the industrial organization perspective.[29] The Industrial Organization school focused on the structural imperfections in the market to explain FDI.[30] Notable work in this perspective includes the classic dissertation of Stephen Hymer.[31]

The transaction cost paradigm stresses the transactional imperfections in the market.[32] The transaction cost school predicts that firms will choose the mode of entry that minimizes the production and transaction costs.[33] Transaction costs are costs incurred to ensure the proper performance of fiduciary promises of business partners.[34] Work in this paradigm includes Dunning,[35] Beamish and Banks,[36] Hennart,[37] and Anderson and Gatignon.[38]

The evolutionary view of a multinational enterprise emphasizes multinational experience as a factor affecting the entry mode choice. Numerous studies such as Erramilli,[39] Gatignon and Anderson,[40] Agarwal & Ramaswami,[41] and Kogut and Singh[42] have used multinational experience explicitly in their explanations of choice of entry mode.

Researchers in strategic management have claimed that a firm's entry decisions are not based upon immediate efficiency considerations alone.[43] Hill, Hwang, and Kim incorporated strategic variables in their entry mode choice model.[44] Kim and Hwang found empirical support for the inclusion of strategic factors in the entry mode choice model.[45]

In summary, the industrial organization paradigm explains entry mode choice on the basis of variations in industry structure. The transactions cost paradigm uses minimization of production and transaction costs as the basis for the choice of entry mode. The evolutionists believe that as firms acquire more multinational experience, they pursue higher control entry modes, i.e., the higher the multinational experience of a firm, the higher the control over its foreign operations sought by it, and vice versa. The strategic management theorists argue that the entry decisions go beyond the narrow scope of immediate efficiencies, or transactions costs, and that a firm's strategic needs determine the choice of entry mode.

The rationale for choice of entry mode offered by the aforementioned four schools of thought apply simultaneously in explaining the entry mode choice. Drawing upon these four paradigms, we have developed a comprehensive framework for an entry mode choice decision. This framework is five-dimensional and incorporates the seventeen variables reviewed earlier (see Figure 10-1). A brief description of the five dimensions follows.

FIGURE 10-1

A Comprehensive Framework for Entry Mode Choice

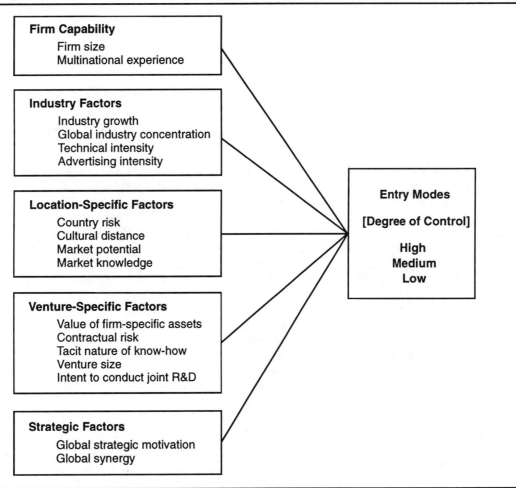

1. **Firm Capability.** Firm capability refers to the capabilities and competencies of the firm as a whole. The variables included in this dimension are firm size and multinational experience. This dimension represents the evolutionist view of the determinants of entry mode.

2. **Industry-Specific Factors.** Industry factors are characteristics of the industry, and include industry concentration, technical intensity, advertising intensity, and industry growth. This dimension represents the industrial organization school's view of entry mode choice determinants.

3. **Location-Specific Factors.** The four variables—country risk, cultural distance, market potential, and market knowledge—represent the location-specific factors. This dimension draws on the transaction costs paradigm.

4. **Venture-Specific Factors.** These are firm-specific factors that are relevant to the specific entry as opposed to the firm as such. The variables that form this dimension are value of firm-specific assets, tacit knowledge, contractual risk, size of the venture, and intent to conduct joint research and development. This dimension also draws on the transaction costs paradigm.

5. **Strategic Factors.** Strategic factors are the two strategy variables global strategic motivation and global synergy. This dimension represents the strategic management perspective on the determinants of entry modes.

Table 10-2 summarizes the impact of the five dimensions on the degree of control associated with each entry mode.

The five-dimensional framework presented here can serve as a useful tool for evaluating the potential merits of any particular market entry mode decision with respect to the internal and external factors specific to the situation.

As we have seen in this chapter, there is a wide selection of different entry modes available to the firm, from the relatively low-risk and low-investment requirements of simple exporting and licensing to the more risky but substantially more profitable equity-based ventures. It is up to the management of each firm, facing each new entry decision, to select the particular mode most appropriate to the firm's capabilities, risk propensity, and objectives in each case. It is important that each entry mode decision be considered in light of its own specific context—the various environmental factors that we addressed in the earlier chapters of this text. This allows the international firm to effect a strategy that derives the maximum possible benefit from the different markets in which it does business, a key source of the strong competitive position of the global firm.

We looked in this chapter at the factors affecting an international company's choice of mode for entering a foreign market. Generally, markets are entered to improve a company's competitive position, as an outgrowth of the corporate strategic process that we discussed in Chapter 8. In the next chapter we will focus on four types of strategies embraced by international companies in their search for a global competitive advantage.

SUMMARY

A company desiring to enter foreign markets can choose from among several different modes of entry: exporting, countertrade, contract manufacturing, licensing, franchising, turnkey projects, and equity-based ventures. Each mode involves differing levels of capital investment, risk, and potential returns.

TABLE 10-2

**The Five Dimensions and Their Effect on the
Degree of Control in the Mode of Entry: A Summary**

DIMENSION & VARIABLES	EFFECT ON DEGREE OF CONTROL
FIRM CAPABILITY	
Firm size	+
Multinational experience	+
INDUSTRY FACTORS	
Industry growth	−
Global industry concentration	+
Technical intensity	+ / − @
Advertising intensity	+
LOCATION-SPECIFIC FACTORS	
Country risk	−
Cultural distance	−
Market potential	+
Market knowledge	+
VENTURE-SPECIFIC FACTORS	
Value of firm-specific assets	+
Contractual risk	+
Tacit nature of know-how	+
Venture size	−
Intent to conduct joint R&D	+
STRATEGIC FACTORS	
Global strategic motivation	+
Global synergy	+

"+" indicates a positive association with degree of control.

"−" indicates a negative association with degree of control.

@ This prediction depends on whether the entrant is seeking or is in possession of the technology. If the entrant is seeking technology, the prediction is "−"; if the firm is in possession of technology, then the prediction is "+".

Exporting, the selling of one's goods or services in another country, is the simplest means of entering foreign markets, and usually the first step for a company going international. Exporting can be accomplished either indirectly, via an agent or forwarder, or directly by an organizational subunit or subsidiary of the exporting company.

Countertrade refers to transactions involving a two- or more-way flow of goods or services, and is an important aspect of world trade, especially with developing and controlled economies. Countertrade can ease problems with inconvertible and fluctuating currencies, but also requires the ability to profitably dispose of the goods acquired through the countertrade agreement.

Licensing agreements allow a foreign company to use, in exchange for fees or royalties, another's patents and trademarks, manufacturing processes and know-how, trade secrets, or managerial and technical services. Foreign licensing involves more risk than straight exporting or countertrade, but is less risky than direct investment in foreign production. Essentially, the firm is exporting its know-how instead of its products. Franchising is a special type of licensing agreement.

Equity-based ventures involve some degree of ownership and control of a foreign venture by the international company, and includes both wholly owned and joint ventures. The choice of joint venture will be influenced by company, industry, market, and country conditions. Maintaining the necessary control over a joint venture is crucial for the international company.

The choice of entry mode by an international firm is among the most significant decisions that a firm will make, and is influenced by firm capability, industry factors, location-specific factors, venture-specific factors, and strategic factors. Risk and resource requirements must be balanced in a manner appropriate to each entry mode decision.

QUESTIONS FOR THOUGHT AND DISCUSSION

1. In the chapter we indicate that countertrade is most commonly a part of trade arrangements involving developing or controlled economies. What specific reasons can you suggest why this might be so? Similarly, discuss some reasons why countertrade is less frequently found in transactions between developed countries.

2. Some writers attribute much of the global success of Japanese companies over the past half century to the fact that the Japanese developed technology and know-how that they acquired legally through licensing agreements and other strategic alliances with American and European firms into a competitive advantage over their former partners. If this is so, what, in your opinion, are the implications of this idea for the desirability of licensing as a mode of entry? How could a licensing agreement be made "safer"? Discuss.

3. We mentioned in the chapter that restrictions placed by some countries on foreign ownership preclude wholly owned, and in some cases even majority owned, ventures as a mode of entry. Even in a country where no such legal restrictions exist, can you think of reasons why a minority ownership venture might be more attractive than a majority position? Give specific examples to illustrate your answer.

4. You work for a global pharmaceutical company that desires to expand into new markets. Select three countries—one each from Africa, from the Newly Independent States (NIS) in Central Europe, and from Asia. Using whatever knowledge you have about these countries, apply the entry mode selection framework (Figure 10-1) and recommend an entry mode for each country. Address the advantages and risks involved in the choices you recommend, and support your opinion with concrete factors.

MINI-CASE
The Health of Nations
By Richard B. Egen*

Since 1985, notes a recent McKinsey & Co. study, the formation of international joint ventures involving American corporations has increased by 27 percent a year. However, the study adds, at least a third of those fail to meet the expectations of the companies involved.

---

* Richard B. Egen is president and CEO of Clintec International Inc., Deerfield IL.

Among those who have successfully entered the global joint venture arena is Clintec International Inc., which got underway in 1989 after nearly a decade of planning. Nearly four years later, this joint venture between Baxter International Inc., the Illinois-based, international health care giant, and Nestle S.A., the Swiss-based world leader in food and nutrition products, has sales of almost $400 million annually, operations in North America and Europe, and clinical nutrition products on the market in Latin America, Africa, and Asia.

What has allowed Clintec to succeed where so many other joint ventures have not? Clintec's experience suggests that several key factors affect the likelihood of success.

To start with the potential must be large enough to command the attention—and the commitment—of the companies. For Clintec, the opportunities are significant. Clinical nutrition, which involves products used for patients who cannot be fed by normal means or who require a nutritional supplement, is one of the most promising areas in medicine and one of the fastest-growing markets in the health care industry.

The opportunities in clinical nutrition are directly related to an expanding knowledge base. In recent years, studies have demonstrated that nutritional intervention can help shorten hospital stays and improve clinical outcomes for patients. Enteral nutrition in particular, which runs the gamut from naso-gastro tube feeding to special supplementary oral diets, fits well with long-term trends toward less invasive, more cost-effective therapies. At the same time, medical educators and researchers are showing greater interest in the field, which increases the possibility of new and more effective products in the future.

The growth potential is important not only for attracting the attention of the parent companies in the first place, but also for sustaining interest and investment levels later on.

In Clintec's case, one example is that the cost of developing new products, which often require well-documented clinical studies, runs into millions of dollars. Without opportunities proportionate to the effort and expense, Clintec's parents might be less inclined to support such expenditures, which as a percentage of sales far exceeds the amount they spend on their own less R&D-intensive businesses.

The Strategic Complement

Size and growth potential are only part of a successful partnership. It is equally important that the partners bring different or complementary strengths to the table.

Baxter is historically strong in the parenterals business—which includes products that deliver nutrition intravenously or through a catheter—and also has extensive experience with medical markets, both with hospitals and home-care or "alternate-site" patients. But the company had virtually no experience with enteral products, which represent the fastest-growing segment of the clinical nutrition market. Moreover, its manufacturing, marketing, and distribution capabilities in parenteral nutrition are mainly focused on North America.

On the other hand, in addition to being the leading food company worldwide, Nestle has a strong background in basic nutrition. As a major firm in the infant formula business, it had a growing interest in adult nutrition products, world-class research and development capabilities, and a strong presence in all major worldwide markets. What it lacked was experience with medical markets.

By combining the strengths and skills of both, Clintec has grown rapidly, particularly in enteral products and markets outside of North America, to become the second largest clinical nutrition company in the world. There is no other single competitor that combines both parenteral and enteral products with the company's geographic reach.

Although complementary and different strengths are critically important for joint ventures, such differences must be reconciled through an underlying level of compatibility and trust. Joint ventures are often compared to marriages, and there are some similarities. For example, it helps if the partners share basic attributes and attitudes. Although Nestle is a Swiss company and Baxter is American, both are large multinational corporations that promote an open management style.

Easy Does It

Yet, even when the partners have so much in common, the courtship can't be rushed—especially when it represents a first major joint venture, as it did for both Baxter and Nestle. Informal talks between the companies began in the early 1980s. These discussions eventually produced an agreement in 1986 that created a Clintec division within Baxter to distribute Nestle enteral products in the U.S. This working arrangement, in turn, enhanced the comfort level of the partners over several years and led to the establishment of a formal joint venture in 1989.

This step-by-step process undoubtedly increased the trust and understanding between the partners, and it helped them to anticipate problems. For example, as part of the initial arrangement in 1986, the partners agreed (after a year of discussions) on a price Nestle would pay for a half interest in Baxter's U.S.-based parenterals business. With the creation of the worldwide joint venture in 1989, it became necessary to value other Baxter businesses in Canada and the United Kingdom. Rather than spending years determining a value for each, Nestle simply agreed to apply a formula based on the earlier arrangement. Without the high level of trust developed during the intervening years of successful cooperation, such a solution probably would not have been proposed, much less adopted.

Just as in a marriage, partners in a joint venture must build on their compatibility and put their trust to the test every day. Decisions must be made and agreement reached. So consensus is a fourth critical component. Prior agreement on key goals and strategies is essential.

For example, in addition to the technical aspects of the joint venture plan worked out in 1989, the partners also agreed on Clintec's basic mission. It committed the company to seeking a significant position in both the parenteral and enteral sides of the market and to doing business in all major geographic areas. It was an ambitious agenda, with major implications for the future. To make sure that the mission was accomplished, the partners set aggressive top-line sales growth as the company's primary strategic objective.

From this goal, in turn, came specific strategies. In North America, Clintec invested heavily in sales and marketing to develop an enterals business from the ground up. In Europe, it made several strategic acquisitions—some designed to expand the geographic base in parenterals, another to strengthen its enteral capabilities. Such actions required considerable investment spending, but because everyone had previously agreed on Clintec's mission and goals, the "strategic" investment decisions were much easier.

The Cultural Evolution

The importance of consensus also extends to values and matters of corporate culture. Clintec, for example, is managed by people drawn largely from Baxter, Nestle, and the companies Clintec has acquired, all of whom have come together in a relatively short period of time. So considerable effort was spent developing a set of values and operating principles that managers could use in their new roles to guide decision making.

The values highlight such issues as identifying and meeting customer requirements better than the competition, employing the best people, acting with honesty and integrity, collaborating effectively with other management team members, fostering open and honest communication, making informed decisions, promoting transnational ability, and being held accountable for results. These ideas were developed and discussed at the senior management level. We then convened the top twenty-five executives to plan for communicating the values throughout the company.

Some would suggest that such effort is superfluous, that you can't legislate culture. Although that's probably true, culture will evolve whether or not we plan for it. Well-understood values can help guide that evolution, especially when starting from scratch, as one does with a joint venture. At Clintec, these values and operating principles help mediate disputes and define a "Clintec way of doing business" that is legitimately different from that of either parent company.

For example, at the time the joint venture was created, Nestle had few management bonus plans and long-term incentive programs in Europe, except for its most senior executives. But, because the partners had articulated the values of employing the best people and holding them accountable for results, Nestle readily agreed to support performance-driven compensation plans within Clintec.

Formal written values, however, can only go so far. Consensus is also a day-to-day affair, so flexibility and common-sense compromise are equally important. In international ventures, this is especially true on a strategic level.

Habit Forming

American managers, for example, are generally more short-term oriented than their counterparts overseas. Therefore, a venture involving an American and a European firm has to deal with this difference. At Clintec, for example, research and studies on new products in clinical nutrition take time—typically five years or more. Although Nestle was comfortable with that kind of time frame in terms of investment, Baxter had to become more flexible.

Similarly, Baxter has traditionally been oriented toward growth from within. Nestle has been more acquisition-minded. Clintec's strategy in Europe, driven by the needs of the business and the opportunities available, has focused thus far on acquisitions. Again, Baxter supported that strategy because it was right for the venture as a whole.

Flexibility and compromise are essential in small as well as large ways. With board members in both Europe and North America, the question of where meetings are held becomes significant. At Clintec, we've simply compromised and said two out of the four meetings will be held on each continent each year.

Other examples are more subtle. European managers typically want to plan meetings well in advance. Americans are much more inclined to compress the scheduling timeframe and get to a meeting by plane. Similarly, many European managers like to communicate by memorandums and fax. Americans often want to pick up the phone and talk to a person.

As a result, everyone learns to adjust. One of my top European executives rarely telephones me when I'm in my U.S. office, preferring to send faxes instead. I try to respond in kind during the week but usually by Friday I pick up the phone and we talk.

The Value of Continuity

A sense of continuity is very important in an international joint venture. Combining different companies and cultures and creating strategy from the ground up is difficult enough without having to deal with major or frequent changes in personnel and policies. In fact, continuity is so important that it is often worth bending the rules in other areas.

Clintec, for example, is organized as a 50/50 joint venture and is governed by an advisory board of directors originally composed of five people—myself, two Baxter executives, and two from Nestle, one of whom was named chairman of Clintec.

When this individual subsequently retired from Nestle, he was asked to remain as board chairman because of the need for continuity. However, in order to maintain an appropriate representation of active Nestle management, a sixth board member was added; this created a technical imbalance in Nestle's favor. Meanwhile, one of the Baxter executives on the board now works with an independent company spun off from Baxter. Again, because continuity is important, we asked that member to remain on Clintec's board even though he technically is no longer a "Baxter" appointee.

This kind of continuity has allowed Clintec to maintain a consistent focus and strategy. The working relationships built up over time also help in the decision making and implementation process. In a company and an industry where growth and change are so important, stability in key areas and among key people helps keep the long-term picture in focus.

Source: Richard B. Egen, "The Health of Nations," *Journal of Business Strategy*, Vol. 14, March-April 1992, pp. 33-37. Reprinted with permission of Faulkner & Gray, Inc.

Discussion Questions for Mini-Case

1. For a successful joint venture, the partners must bring different or complementary strengths to the table. What strengths did Baxter International bring to the joint venture? What did Nestle S.A. contribute?

2. Although complementary and different strengths of the partners are important to the success of an alliance, they do not guarantee that the joint venture will succeed. List the factors identified by Mr. Egen that laid the foundation for a successful alliance between Baxter International and Nestle S.A.

3. What steps were taken by both partners to create compatibility and trust between them?

4. Why was it so important to reach a consensus on the mission, key goals, and strategies of Clintec? How did it promote the success of Clintec?

5. Describe the steps taken to develop the corporate culture of Clintec. Why was it critical to ensure that Clintec had its own unique culture?

6. Describe the values and operating principles that govern the decision making of managers in Clintec.

7. Explain the differences between Baxter International and Nestle S.A. on matters such as (1) time horizons (short term versus long term) of managers, (2) growth strategy (internal growth versus acquisitions), and (3) meetings and methods of communicating with each other.

8. How did managers of Clintec demonstrate flexibility and compromise in handling the differences cited in question 7?

MINI-CASE
Mercedes to Build in Alabama*

On Saturday, July 31, 1993, Governor Jim Folsom, Jr. of Alabama was relaxing at home when the telephone rang. It was Billing Joe Camp, the state's development director. The governor immediately decided to take the call. There must be new developments in the Mercedes-Benz deal, he thought as he picked up the phone.

The governor was right: Camp told him that the German automaker was about to make the final selection in the multi-state scramble for a $300 million U.S. assembly plant for its sport-utility vehicles. The plant was expected to provide 1,500 jobs directly and create another 10,000 new jobs through the ripple effects of the investment in just five years. Alabama's Troy State University's economists had predicted that the Mercedes project would attract autoparts and service companies, help beef up local salaries, build up the local tax base, and promote local retail sales in an area that was badly in need of new investment. Many other states, however, were also courting the German auto manufacturer for a project that Governor Folsom called "an industrial crown jewel." On that hot summer day in Montgomery, Camp strongly urged the Governor to immediately plan a trip—it would be his second to the German headquarters of the automaker— to lobby for the Alabama site. The site was at a former railcar-repair depot near Vance, a small town between Tuscaloosa and Birmingham, covering 1,000 acres of land. State officials had led Mercedes-Benz executives in several inspection tours of the site, including one by helicopter, and had pitched tirelessly the many benefits the state offered. To sweeten further the deal, they promised more than $200 million in job training and tax breaks, and even offered to rename a section of Interstate 20/59 the "Mercedes-Benz Autobahn."

In early August 1993, Governor Folsom, accompanied by Camp and two state legislators, left Montgomery for Stuttgart in an all-out effort to win the Mercedes-Benz project. The German automaker finally narrowed its choice of the potential factory site to three locations. Alabama remained in the race, but so did its two competitors, South Carolina and North Carolina. However, unlike the latter states who had failed to meet all of Mercedes's demands for job training or tax breaks, Alabama was ready to offer preferential tax breaks, training support, subsidies, and other benefits likely to reduce production costs. For instance, Alabama promised to pay the salaries of trainees and this amount was about double that offered by other states. "The Mercedes project simply was worth more to us than it was to any other state, and we knew the primary reason that Mercedes decided to move its manufacturing base from Germany to U.S. was to reduce its high production costs and enhance its productivity," says Camp.

In addition, a group of Alabama businesses, led by the politically active utility concern Alabama Power Co., agreed to provide their own $11 million subsidy to the Germans, and many large companies promised to buy Mercedes vehicles. Local hotels, clubs and businesses offered their services for free; local government agencies offered low-interest loans.

In mid-August, Alabama passed its tailor-made tax law, helping to finance Mercedes's $300 million plant construction. Mercedes says it agreed to limit itself to using just $42.6 million in income and payroll tax credits; Alabama officials say that was all Mercedes expected to be able to use, based on profit projections. It also allowed Mercedes to escape more than $9 million a year in property taxes and other fees, as permitted under existing law.

---

* Written by Dr. Yadong Luo, Assistant Professor of International Management, University of Hawaii at Manoa. Copyright © 1997 by Arvind V. Phatak.

CHAPTER TEN

When Mercedes needed more land than Alabama had anticipated, officials in Tuscaloosa County, home of Alabama's site, went door to door for three weeks, negotiating to buy people's homes so the land could be given to Mercedes for $100. A detailed topographical map, which normally takes four months to prepare, was finished in four weeks and sent to Mercedes's consultants in South Carolina by chartered jet to avoid missing a deadline even by a few hours.

The all-out effort paid off: Alabama was declared the winner in the race, beating 34 other states. This victory would enable Alabama to get a big economic boost from the planned factory. But the German automaker had even more riding on the choice. The new plant and Jeeplike sports-utility vehicle scheduled for production there in 1997 are key elements of Mercedes's desperate bid to reinvent itself. The company has a 30 percent cost disadvantage against Japanese and U.S. competitors, and has seen its share of the luxury market slip in the past four years. Mercedes's "costs are too high," says Andreas Renschler, the 35-year-old president of Mercedes-Benz Project Inc., the subsidiary that will run the U.S. venture. For decades, Mercedes officials concede, the company's engineers have pursued automotive excellence with little regard to costs.

Labor costs in Germany are the world's highest (the average hourly wage was $25.56 in 1993, including benefits). The cost of providing universal medical care, generous pensions, and long vacations has become prohibitive. Energy, raw materials, even a phone call—all are more expensive in Germany than in the United States or Japan. "Production costs were so high that our trademark quality risked becoming unaffordable," said Helmut Werner, Mercedes-Benz Chairman. "It seemed provincial at a time when rivals were expanding around the globe," he supplemented.

Strong unions limit the kind of slash-and-burn cost-cutting that is common in the United States—especially with unemployment already near or above 10 percent in most European countries. The high cost of hiring and firing workers discourages companies from doing either. "The cost crisis has in no way been overcome," Klaus Murmann, the president of the German employers federation, said at a news conference in June 1994.

The ongoing transformation of Europe into a single market, which offered the promise of economies of scale, has not lived up to the expectations of most companies, which complain that trade remains inhibited by continuing legal, regulatory, taxation, and cultural differences among nations. In addition, labor costs in other European countries are also high.

A study by Massachusetts Institute of Technology in the late 1980s found German factories among the least efficient in the world. In some, the space for repairing finished autos equaled the entire square footage of Japanese plants. The resulting productivity gap is what explains Mercedes-Benz Chairman Helmut Werner's recent vow to cut 27,000 jobs by 1995 and the pressure from parent Daimler Benz to slash $2.3 billion from Mercedes's car and truck operations.

In 1992, McKinsey & Co. surveyed nine industries in the major industrialized countries, the United States, Germany, and Japan. The Germans lagged behind their rivals in productivity in all nine industries (Japan led in five, including auto parts and steel, and the United States in four, including computer and beer).

Along with BMW and Volkswagen, Mercedes-Benz has slipped in the United States in recent years. This decline can be attributed to the high value of the German mark—which continued to climb against the dollar, making German products more expensive—and Japanese competition, which has introduced high-quality imports such as the Acura, Infiniti, and Lexus to the American market. Mercedes-Benz is expecting to have much lower labor costs in Alabama than in Germany because of the weak dollar.

Not only labor but also capital is likely to be of foreign origin in the future: indeed the capital needs of Daimler, the parent of Mercedes, are now filled abroad; in October 1993, it became the first German company to be listed on the New York Stock Exchange. "We definitely want to become less German and need to set a global strategy to offset the weakness seen in Germany," explained a senior executive involved in strategic planning.

The U.S. sports-utility assembly plant project is indicative of this new global orientation of the German automaker. In accord with its efforts at regeneration, Mercedes did not select the management of the new venture from among its established executive ranks. Instead, Renschler, a deputy to Werner, who had joined the company only four years earlier, was named to head the project. He assembled a team of about 25 youthful product planners, engineers, and marketers. They set up shop in a temporary office in Stuttgart's industrial Unterturkheim district, where they routinely worked 16-hour days, subsisting on delivered pizzas.

Renschler's mission was ambitious: find a site outside Germany and produce at least 10 percent of Mercedes's total output by the end of the decade abroad. All Mercedes autos had always been built in Germany, except for a few thousand assembled from imported kits in "screwdriver" plants in such places as South Africa. The team narrowed the search to North America, figuring the combined costs there of labor, shipping, and components, as well as exposures to currency fluctuations, would be lowest. Since the Multiple Purpose Vehicle (MPV) will be built only in the United States and Mercedes expects to export at least half the production, transportation costs and currency fluctuation impacts on investment and operations are as important as labor costs. As a result, the team zeroed in on areas near the Atlantic or Gulf seaports, major highways, and rail lines.

Keeping a lid on costs remains crucial. Mercedes plans to price the MPV under $30,000— about the same as a fully loaded Jeep Grand Cherokee. However, the plant's small scale (65,000 vehicles per year production) places it at a disadvantage relative to volume producers such as Chrysler Corp., which builds twice as many Grand Cherokees. Mercedes hopes to match the Grand Cherokee's labor productivity rate (10 hours per vehicle) while maintaining the high quality standards that are the hallmark of Mercedes. Werner says that the plant should break even at production levels as low as 40,000 vehicles per year.

On April 5, 1993, Werner and other Mercedes officials had outlined their plans and promised to break ground in 1997. They began to look at more than 100 sites in 35 states from California to the East Coast. By the mid-summer, when Governor Folsom of Alabama received the urgent call of the state's development director, Mercedes had narrowed its list of contenders to a few states. On September 13, 1993, the 12-member site-selection team assembled in the small, second-floor meeting room in the Unterturkheim headquarters. From 8 a.m. until 2 p.m. the group discussed the merits of the three finalists—North Carolina, South Carolina, and Alabama. From the outset, everyone seemed to agree on Alabama as the best choice except for two construction consultants who argued for North Carolina. Eventually they, too, were won over.

On October 1, the state of Alabama shook off its decades-long image as a redneck, racist backwater to officially become the location for the leading German company's first U.S. car plant.

Source: Adapted from E.S. Browning and Helene Cooper, "States' Bidding War Over Mercedes Plant Made for Costly Chase," *The Wall Street Journal*, November 24, 1993, p. A6; Audrey Choi, "Deutsche Babcosk Sets Global Strategy To Offset Weakness Seen in Germany," *The Wall Street Journal*, January 1, 1994, p. B5; James Bennet, "Mercedes Selects Alabama Site," *The New York Times*, September 30, 1993, pp. D1 and D6; Richard W. Stevenson, "Europe Inc. Has a Novel Idea: Cut Costs," *The New York Times*, July 17, 1994, p. 6F; David Woodruff and John Templeman, *Business Week*, October 11, 1993, pp. 138-139.

Discussion Questions for Mini-Case

1. What were the major reasons explaining Mercedes's decision to assemble its vehicles in Alabama? Why did Mercedes-Benz not choose countries with cheaper labor costs such as China or India as a production site?

2. What are some of the financial, economic, and political risks that Mercedes faces as a result of locating a production plant in Alabama?

3. Was the Alabama government justified in making tax and other concessions and offering subsidies? What are the potential costs and the expected benefits of the project for Alabama?

4. How does the decision affect German workers and German consumers?

Notes

1   Claire Poole, "Pepsico's Newest Generation," *Forbes*, February 18, 1991, p. 88.

2   *Business Week*, March 7, 1988, p. 55.

3   Sanjeev Agarwal and Sridhar Ramaswami, "Choice of Foreign Market Entry Mode: Impact of Ownership, Location, and Internalization Factors," *Journal of International Business Studies*, Vol. 23, No. 1, 1992, pp. 1-27.

4   Charles W. Hill, Peter Hwang, and Chan W. Kim, "An Eclectic Theory of the Choice of International Entry Mode," *Strategic Management Journal*, Vol. 11, 1990, pp. 117-128.

5   Ibid.

6   Ibid.

7   Agarwal and Ramaswami, pp. 1-27.

8   Krishna M. Erramilli, "The Experience Factor in Foreign Market Entry Behavior of Service Firms," *Journal of International Business Studies*, Vol. 22, No. 3, 1991, pp. 479-501.

9   Bruce Kogut and Harbir Singh, "Entering United States by Joint Venture: Competitive Rivalry and Industry Structure," in Farok Contractor and Peter Lorange, (Eds.), *Cooperative Strategies in International Business*, Lexington Books, Lexington, MA, 1988, pp. 241-251.

10 Gary Hamel and C. K. Prahalad, "Do You Really Have a Global Strategy," *Harvard Business Review*, July-August, 1985, pp. 139-148.

11 Hill, Hwang, and Kim, pp. 117-128.

12 Oliver E. Williamson, *Markets and Hierarchies: An Analysis of Antitrust Implications*, Free Press, New York, 1975; David J. Teece, "The Multinational Enterprise: Market Failure and Market Power Considerations," *Sloan Management Review*, September 1981, pp. 3-17.

13 Kogut and Singh, pp. 241-251.

14 Agarwal and Ramaswami, pp. 1-27.

15 Chan W. Kim and Peter Hwang, "Global Strategy and Multinationals' Entry Mode Choice," *Journal of International Business Studies*, Vol. 23, No. 1, 1992, pp. 29-53.

16 Agarwal and Ramaswami, pp. 1-27.

17 Bruce Kogut and Harbir Singh, "The Effect of National Culture on the Choice of Entry Mode," *Journal of International Business Studies*, Fall, 1988a, Vol. 19, No. 3, pp. 411-432.

18 Krishna M. Erramilli and C.P. Rao, "Choice of Market Entry Modes by Service Firms: Role of Market Knowledge," *Management International Review*, Vol. 30, 1990, p. i2.

19 Agarwal and Ramaswami, pp. 1-27.

20 Hubert Gatignon and Erin Anderson, "The Multinational Corporation's Degree of Control Over Foreign Subsidiaries: An Empirical Test of a Transaction Cost Explanation," *Journal of Law Economics and Organization*, Vol. iv, No. 2, 1988, pp. 305-336.

21 Agarwal and Ramaswami, pp. 1-27.

22 Kim and Hwang, pp. 29-53.

23 Gatignon and Anderson, pp. 305-336.

24 Gatignon and Anderson, pp. 305-336, and Kogut and Singh, *Effect of National Culture*, pp. 411-432.

25 Richard N. Osborn and Christopher C. Baughn, "Forms of Inter-Organizational Governance for Multinational Alliances," *Academy of Management Journal*, Vol. 33, No. 3, 1990, pp. 503-519.

26 Hamel and Prahalad, pp. 139-148.

27 Kim and Hwang, pp. 29-53.

28 Ibid., pp. 29-53.

29 John H. Dunning and Alan M. Rugman, "The Influence of Hymer's Dissertation on the Theory of Foreign Direct Investment," *AEA Papers and Proceedings,* May 1985.

30 Ibid.

31 Stephen H. Hymer, *The International Operations of National Firms: A Study of Direct Foreign Investment,* MIT Press, Cambridge, 1976 [1960].

32 Williamson.

33 Kogut and Singh, *The Effect of National Culture*, pp. 411-432.

34 Williamson.

35 John H. Dunning, "The Eclectic Paradigm of International Production: A Restatement and Some Possible Extensions," *Journal of International Business Studies*, Spring 1988, pp. 1-31.

36 Paul W. Beamish and John C. Banks, "Equity Joint Ventures and the Theory of the Multinational Enterprise," *Journal of International Business Studies*, Summer 1987, pp. 1-16.

37 Jean-Francois Hennart, "A Transaction Costs Theory of Equity Joint Ventures," *Strategic Management Journal*, Vol. 9, 1988, pp. 361-374.

38 Erin Anderson and Hubert Gatignon, "Modes of Foreign Entry: A Transaction Cost Analysis and Propositions," *Journal of International Business Studies*, Fall 1986, pp. 1-26.

39 Erramilli, pp. 479-501.

40 Gatignon and Anderson, pp. 411-432.

41 Agarwal and Ramaswami, pp. 1-27.

42 Kogut and Singh, "The Effect of National Culture on the Choice of Entry Mode," *Journal of International Business Studies,* Vol. 19, No. 3, pp. 411-432.

43 Hamel and Prahalad, pp. 139-148.

44 Hill, Hwang, and Kim, pp. 117-128.

45 Kim and Hwang, pp. 29-53.

Strategies for International Competitiveness

LEARNING OBJECTIVES

After completing this chapter, you will be able to:

- Describe the four common forms that a strategic alliance may take and the key features of each.
- Discuss the reasons that an international company may participate in a strategic alliance.
- Identify the risks and problems associated with strategic alliances, and describe actions the international company can take to make an alliance work.
- Explain core competencies, and how the international firm can leverage its core competencies into competitive advantage.
- Discuss the concept of a counterattack strategy, and its implications for the international firm.
- Define "glocalization" and explain its role in the strategy of an international company.

In the last chapter, we examined the process of determining the best mode of entering a new foreign market. Now we will focus on the content of strategies that global companies have embraced and implemented in search of a global competitive advantage in a variety of industries. We shall look at the following four types of strategies adopted by global companies:

- Strategic alliances
- Core competency leveraging
- Counterattack
- Glocalization

STRATEGIC ALLIANCES

Not a week goes by without an announcement in the business press of a strategic alliance between two or more companies. Almost every internationally minded company trying to become global will consider forging a strategic alliance with another company as a fast track to that goal. A strategic alliance is a collaborative arrangement that a company makes with competitors, suppliers, customers, distributors, or firms in the same or different industries in order to develop, produce, distribute, or market a product or service. A strategic alliance can take a variety of forms. Among the most common are the following:

- Collaboration without equity
- Joint venture
- Equity ownership
- Cash-neutral exchange of assets

Collaboration Without Equity

In collaboration without equity there is a loose association between companies. An example is the alliance between the Japanese company Mitsubishi and the German company Daimler Benz. The two companies are working on eleven joint projects involving cars, aerospace, and integrated circuits. Sony, the dominant Japanese firm in the electronics and entertainment industries, has forged such alliances with several small, high-technology companies in the United States. The company is sharing its research staff, production facilities, and even business plans for specific products with small companies. Sony is working with Panavision Inc. to develop a lens for high-definition television cameras, with Compression Labs Inc. on a video-conferencing machine, and with Alphatronix Inc. to develop rewritable, optical-disk storage systems for computers.[1]

Joint Venture

The joint venture form of strategic alliance was covered in considerable detail in Chapter 10.

In this collaborative arrangement, a new venture firm is created, with its own identity and management structure in which each of the partners owns equity. For example, Texas Instruments (TI) and Acer Inc., the personal computer company in Taiwan, have formed a jointly owned company in Taiwan called Acer-TI to make 1 Mb and 4 Mb DRAMs. The plant will cost at least $250 million. The benefits of this alliance to TI are evident in their getting a new memory chip factory at little cost, as Acer is financing most of that cost. The benefits for Acer include getting an assured supply of parts to its core operations.[2]

In another joint venture, Japan's Mitsubishi Motors Corporation, AB Volvo, and the Dutch government each own 33 percent of a car production facility in the Netherlands. The trio jointly produce a new generation of midsize cars, replacing Volvo's 300 and 400 series currently produced at the Netherlands plant. The partners will invest a total of $3.7 billion to develop the cars. Mitsubishi will contribute its production and design expertise, a key weakness of Volvo. For Mitsubishi, buying into an existing factory in a joint venture arrangement was an attractive option, given the risk implied by the European Community's having imposed quotas on Japanese car imports into Europe, and the strong likelihood that such quotas will also include cars manufactured by Japanese transplant factories in Europe.[3]

In an unusual alliance, two of the world's largest global corporations, Coca-Cola Company and Nestle S.A., plan to form a joint venture to cash in on a potentially rich market in ready-to-drink coffees and teas. The venture, in which each company will invest $50 million, is designed to exploit the combined strengths of Nestle brand dry foods, like instant coffee and tea, with the massive, global distribution system of Coca-Cola. This venture will make possible the delivery of coffee and tea products to worldwide markets much faster than either company could alone.[4] Both companies stand to save considerable sums of money—Coca-Cola by not having to develop its own products and Nestle by not having to develop the massive distribution channels required to compete effectively in the beverage industry.

Equity Ownership

Equity ownership involves either a one-way or a mutual purchase of equity. Examples of the former are the 24 percent equity that Ford holds in Mazda, and Hong Kong's Semi-Tech (Global)

Ltd., which owns 20 percent of Emerson Radio. Ford nameplates are on 12 percent of the cars Mazda makes and sells in Japan. The Semi-Tech and Emerson alliance gives Emerson a much needed cash infusion, and Semi-Tech, which owns Singer sewing machine operations as well as its consumer electronic and durable outlets, gains access to Emerson's contract production facilities in the Far East. An example of mutual purchase of equity is the alliance involving alcoholic beverages between Japan's Suntory and Great Britain's Allied-Lyons. Suntory holds 2.5 percent in Allied-Lyons, while Allied-Lyons has a 1 percent stake in Suntory.

Cash-Neutral Exchange of Assets

In a cash-neutral exchange of assets, the partnership does not involve any cash. Rather, each company has a stake in the other and they trade assets. It is believed that such cash-neutral transactions may become a trend in a credit-sensitive, post-junk-bond era. An example of such an alliance is the unusual marketing alliance between U.S.-based Delta Airlines and U.K.-based Virgin Atlantic Airways, which will allow Delta to offer its U.S. passengers access to London's Heathrow Airport for the first time—on Virgin Aircraft. Under this agreement, Delta purchases a designated number of seats on Virgin flights between London Heathrow and Boston, Los Angeles, Miami, Newark, New York, Orlando, and San Francisco. Delta will buy space in each class—upper, mid-class, and economy—and then independently price, market, and sell the seats. The deal is estimated to be worth up to $150 million in increased revenues to Virgin. Delta stands to benefit even more because the higher-yield travelers prefer Heathrow over Gatwick airport in London.

This alliance should strengthen the position of both airlines in the important transatlantic market. This alliance is not like the British Airways' code-sharing and equity agreement with USAir. (Code-sharing is explained later in this chapter. With code sharing, airlines advertise and sell a flight as if they were single continuous flights on just one airline.) The Delta-Virgin code-sharing is strictly eastbound, and Virgin has no seat allocation on Delta flights. Nevertheless, it provides Virgin a strong U.S. partner, with better connecting schedules and pricing from the U.S. gateways to the 165 cities Delta serves in the U.S., Puerto Rico, and Virgin Islands, in addition to the points served by the Delta Connection commuter carrier; an expanded frequent flyer program that permits Delta passengers to earn miles on Virgin flights to London and Virgin frequent-fliers to redeem their miles to any Delta destinations worldwide; as well as space in Delta's terminal at JFK airport in New York. According to Virgin's chairman Richard Branson, this agreement will allow Virgin to remain independent and competitive in the face of an increasing number of global alliances in the airline industry. Delta, on the other hand, gains access to Heathrow airport, something restricted to them due to the current U.S.-U.K. bilateral agreement, which allows only American Airlines and United Airlines to land there. This pact is expected to enhance competition on routes dominated by British Airways, American, and United.[5]

Reasons for Creating Strategic Alliances

In the previous discussion regarding the variety of forms that strategic alliances could take, we have seen some of the reasons for the creation of strategic alliances. There are, of course, other reasons for strategic alliances, some of which are as follows.

- Penetrate new foreign markets
- Share the risk of giant investment
- Share research and development costs and risks

- Launch a counterattack against competitors
- Pool global resources
- Learn from partners

Penetrate New Foreign Markets Companies form strategic alliances as a cheap and more efficient way of entering either a partner's home market or a third-country market in which a partner is especially strong. For example, General Mills and Switzerland's Nestle S.A. have created a partnership in a newly formed company called Cereal Partners Worldwide in order to launch General Mills' cereal business in Europe. Nestle has strong distribution channels in Europe, and its first assault will be on France, Spain, and Portugal with General Mills' Golden Grahams and Honey Nut Cheerios. The joint venture has also acquired the British breakfast cereal operations of Ranks Hovis McDougall PLC, giving it a foothold in one of the world's biggest cereal-eating countries. The average English person eats thirteen pounds of cereal a year, the average French person one pound a year, and in Japan people eat less than one quarter of a pound. An average American eats ten pounds of cereal a year. Therefore, the global cereal market is seen as fertile ground by the cereal industry and the Nestle-General Mills venture expects sales of $31 billion in Europe by the year 2000. This partnership represents General Mills' first venture outside North America.[6]

AT&T and British Telecom (BT), the American and British telecommunications giants, have as their vision to become the first truly global phone companies serving households and businesses on every continent. To reach this lofty vision, both companies have been forging strategic alliances with phone companies around the world to get a foothold in as many world markets as possible. To start with, BT has formed a major strategic alliance with MCI, the second largest U.S. long-distance company, by acquiring a 20 percent stake in the company. *Concert*, the BT-MCI team, has signed up Norwegian Telecom, Tele Denmark, and Telecom Finland as partners and allies. AT&T owns a stake in phone companies in the Ukraine and Venezuela. AT&T's *WorldPartners* alliance includes Kokusai Denshin Denwa (KDD)—Japan's largest international carrier—and Singapore Telecom. AT&T, KDD, and Singapore Telecom own 50 percent, 30 percent, and 20 percent respectively of *WorldPartners*, which also includes several other Asian carriers as nonequity partners. *WorldPartners* has announced a plan to form a joint venture with Unisource, a consortium owned by Dutch KPN, Spanish Telefonica, Swedish Telia, and Swiss PTT. "Stringing networks to all those distant places would be impossibly expensive. Therefore, AT&T and BT are squaring off against each other in what looks like a variation of the popular global board game, Risk. Through various alliances, partnerships, and consortiums, each company is trying to get a presence in as many countries as possible."[7] "The game is how you develop your pieces around the world, for once the squares are taken by rivals, your options are constrained,"[8] says Sir Ian Vallance, chairman of BT.

And now, in response to the forays in the global telecommunications market by competitors, Deutsche Telekom AG of Germany, France Telecom, and the U.S. company Sprint are moving toward the formation of a global telecommunications venture to compete with AT&T and BT/MCI. The three companies hope that their joint venture, called Phoenix, will offer an array of global telephone services to multinational corporations and smaller phone companies.[9]

The aim of the global linkups is to provide so-called virtual private networks for international business customers, and ultimately ordinary consumers, that could vastly simplify international communications. For instance, a person using a virtual private network at a company's headquarters could dial any of the firm's international subsidiaries using only four- or five-digit extensions, avoiding the need for 14-digit international codes.[10]

Share the Risk of Giant Investment   Nowhere do we see the risk of giant investment as strong a motive for forming alliances as in the aircraft industry. The costs of creating jets are so enormous that aerospace companies are forced to join hands in coproduction agreements with actual or potential rivals, even when they would prefer to invest alone for fear of losing vital technological and other company secrets to their partners. Boeing has formed an alliance with Fuji, Mitsubishi, and Kawasaki—all Japanese companies—to help defray the estimated $4 billion cost of building the new 777 jetliner. The Japanese will build 20 percent of the airframe. By contracting out a large portion of the design and manufacture, Boeing hopes to speed up market introduction of the aircraft and beat the competition from Airbus A330 and A340 aircraft. Boeing has a contract with United Airlines to deliver thirty-four planes worth $323 million each.

Larry Clarkson, the senior vice-president of Boeing's commercial group, explains why such a dominant company needs partners. "The day of an airplane being a sole Boeing product has passed," he says. "What's unique about the big-jet business is that it takes a lot of dollars and involves high risk, a long-term investment, and a limited customer base. If we make another large airplane, we would have to have international involvement."[11]

Share Research and Development Costs and Risks   This reason for a strategic alliance has been the principal motive for linkups in the high technology and biotechnology sectors. In 1988, Texas Instruments and Japan's Hitachi Ltd. entered into a technology agreement to develop 16-megabyte (Mb) dynamic random access memories (DRAMs). Texas Instruments has several cross-licensing agreements with Fujitsu, Sharp, Toshiba, NEC, and Mitsubishi Electric. "No memory chip company can compete globally unless it has $1 billion of manufacturing plant,"[12] says Stan Shih, president and CEO of Acer, Taiwan's leading computer firm.

To underscore the importance of strategic alliances, consider that before such alliances became popular, companies were often forced to spend huge sums of money to acquire required technologies. For instance, in 1985 General Motors spent $5 billion to acquire Hughes Aircraft in order to obtain Hughes' advanced aerospace technologies. GM could have fulfilled the same goal through a strategic alliance and with no investment.[13]

America's Big Three automakers—General Motors, Ford Motor, and Chrysler—have undertaken joint projects to develop basic technologies which, upon development, each will share. The three companies have agreed to join hands because none has the resources to undertake alone the several expensive and risky basic research projects that must be financed in order to gain an edge over their Japanese rivals in state-of-the-art technologies. *Practical Insight 11-1* explains how the three auto giants are sharing the costs of developing new technologies under the auspices of the United States Council for Automotive Research (USCAR).

PRACTICAL INSIGHT 11-1
The Big Three Collaborate to Win Joint Patent

In what may be the first of many such future joint endeavors, the big three automakers in America—General Motors, Ford Motor, and Chrysler—have achieved something that would have been unthinkable ten years ago. The trio, better known for fierce competition with each other, have collaborated and successfully produced their first joint patent. The patent, a manufacturing process for a lightweight material that could replace steel in car bodies, is a milestone for the Big Three's accelerated efforts to pool basic research under the umbrella of the United States Council for Automotive Research (USCAR).

PRACTICAL INSIGHT 11-1 *(continued)*

Why would the once cut-throat competitors agree to make peace with each other? There are several reasons. First, the U.S. automakers must find a way to cut costs and improve global competitiveness. Second, no one company, including General Motors, has the financial clout to support the broad array of research projects that must be funded to develop the state-of-the-art technologies to get an edge on the Japanese. This was evident when General Motors scaled back its efforts to single-handedly build an electric car, and instead started sharing its concepts with Ford and Chrysler. Third, there is a clear incentive to share costs for basic research whose payoff may be uncertain and far into the future. This is true of the process patent granted jointly to the Big Three automakers that took five years of collaborative research, and which may not deliver a payoff in production for several more years.

The existence of USCAR has been made possible as a result of the relaxation of prohibitions against joint research under U.S. antitrust laws. There are now ten consortia operating under the USCAR umbrella, and more are expected. One of the biggest is the U.S. Advanced Battery Consortium (USABC), a $225 million four-year project partly funded by the U.S. Government's Department of Energy, to research new technology to improve lead-acid battery technology. The goal of this project: to be the first in the race with Japan in developing a practical electric vehicle power supply. USCAR's existence is a clear signal that American automakers cannot go it alone when it comes to funding expensive basic research projects whose prospects for success are uncertain and whose payoffs are unknown and in the long term.

Source: Adapted from Oscar Suris, "Big Three Win Joint Patent, Marking a First," *The Wall Street Journal*, April 13, 1993, pp. B1 and B13.

Launch a Counterattack Against Competitors IBM, the powerful computer giant, found itself losing market share in the personal computer business in Europe to companies like Toshiba, Compaq, Hewlett-Packard, Olivetti, and Mitsubishi Electric. Simultaneously, it saw European rivals such as the Netherlands' Philips getting weaker, and in that situation there was a danger that IBM's rivals would fill the vacuum. In 1990, Fujitsu had acquired International Computers Ltd., Britain's flagship company, and Mitsubishi Electric had bought Apricot, the personal computer manufacturer. In the mainframe market, Hitachi was growing faster than IBM; and in April 1991, NEC Corporation was negotiating to buy a stake in France's troubled computer maker, Groupe Bull.

IBM perceived the battle for the European computer market as a winner-take-all contest against the Japanese. IBM's response has been to launch an all-out attack to hold its ground in Europe by forming several alliances with its European rivals. It has teamed up with Germany's Siemens to develop high-capacity 64-megabyte chips. IBM will forge a critical research and development link between the United States and Europe as a new member of a European project called JESSI. The project is designed to conduct advanced chip research, an area in which the Japanese have a dominant position worldwide. As rivals like Toshiba, Compaq, and Olivetti have lured IBM's prized dealers away, IBM has sought to regain their loyalty by pumping equity capital into the dealerships. The company has invested $100 million in two years into nearly two hundred joint ventures and partnerships, including European software suppliers, a Danish supplier of network services, and a German software maker. Says Fausto Talenti, IBM Europe's

291

director of strategy and business development, "We're trying to put agreements in place with all the Europeans and challenge Japanese dominance with all our means."[14]

IBM's strategy of forming partnerships with rival European computer makers such as Siemens, and with software and service suppliers, is a classic example of a company launching a counterattack against aggressive, newer entrants into a market that it considers of vital importance to its global strategy.

Pool Global Resources Companies in the same industry or line of business sometimes join together to eliminate unnecessary duplication or to share resources and facilities. This strategy is proving to be very popular in the airline industry. For example, United Airlines and British Airways have a strong alliance, especially on key flights through Chicago to London. In the airline industry, a formidable barrier to entry into the industry is the availability of gates at key airports in major world cities. No airline can land at an airport without a gate. Therefore, airlines of different countries are forging alliances in order to share gates. Also, access to foreign markets is often limited by restrictive air treaties and by the huge costs of mounting their own flights; therefore many U.S. carriers have teamed up with European and Asian airlines, and many non-U.S. airlines have teamed up with U.S. airlines to obtain increased access to the big U.S. air market.[15] USAir and British Airways have a "code-sharing" arrangement. With code sharing, airlines advertise and sell a flight as if they were single continuous flights on just one airline. Such code-sharing agreements make it easier for travel agents to sell international airline tickets and, airlines say, provide passengers with a more hassle-free trip. For example, code-sharing connects passengers on USAir flights from Syracuse, Rochester, and Cleveland with British Airways flights between Philadelphia and London. The same arrangement is extended to passengers transferring from USAir to British Airways flights between London and Pittsburg and Baltimore, two other USAir hubs. Exhibit 11-1 illustrates the code-sharing partnership between British Airways and USAir.

In a similar code-sharing arrangement, Northwest Airlines advertises and sells flights between Amsterdam and 30 cities in Europe and the Middle East as Northwest flights that actually are flown by Northwest's partner, KLM Royal Dutch Airlines. Conversely, KLM can sell, as its own, Northwest flights to 88 U.S. cities from Northwest gateways in Minneapolis, Boston, and Detroit.[16]

When passengers take a USAir flight from Syracuse to Philadelphia with a linkup to a London-bound British Airways plane from Philadelphia, their tickets are listed in the reservation system as British Airways flights with one connection in Philadelphia. This practice extends British Airways' reach, through USAir flights, deep into the heartland of the United States. Similarly, passengers from Seattle, Washington, can take a Northwest flight deep into a European or Middle Eastern destination city on a KLM ticket.

As is true for many global industries, brand loyalty is most important as a competitive weapon for the airlines industry. Ideally, the airlines would prefer to acquire carriers around the world and merge them under one name. However, governments would block such mergers; so, in order to provide the necessary bonding, airlines have resorted to buying equity stakes in each other. For example, British Airways has invested in excess of $300 million in USAir, KLM Royal Dutch Airlines has a 20 percent equity stake in Northwest Airlines, and Delta and Singapore airlines have a 5 percent stake in each other.

Learn from Partners The desire to learn critical aspects of a business from an alliance partner is a legitimate reason for consummating an alliance. An alliance that is famous as an example

EXHIBIT 11-1

Code-Sharing Between British Airways and USAir

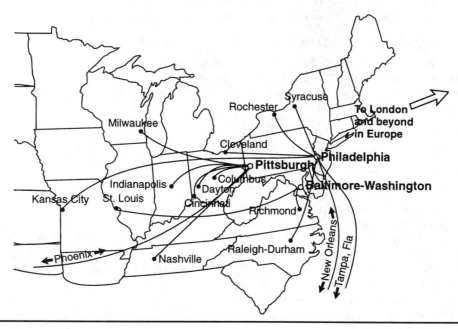

Source: Tom Belden, "British Airways Is Happy with its USAir Alliance," *The Philadelphia Inquirer*, October 21, 1993, pp. D1 and D8.

of this motive is the one between General Motors and Toyota who, in 1984, formed New United Motor Manufacturing Inc. (NUMMI). The alliance, which is managed by Toyota, took over an old General Motors plant in Fremont, California. Toyota's objective in the partnership was to learn from General Motors how to deal with plants, suppliers, and labor in the United States, while General Motor's goal was to learn the Toyota method of managing and manufacturing. Toyota has surely achieved its objective, considering that it has opened two more plants on its own in the United States since NUMMI was formed. How much did General Motors learn? It certainly learned a great deal from Toyota, but academics and consultants criticize General Motors for spreading NUMMI graduates too thinly throughout its huge bureaucracy. Rather than concentrating them in one place, GM has diluted their beneficial impact on the company as a whole.[17]

Some academics claim that, in the numerous alliances forged between American and Asian companies, it is the Asian companies that benefit the most because Asian companies enter into partnerships to learn from the other side. Such is not the case with most American companies, which often enter into alliances to avoid investments. They are more interested in reducing the risks and costs of entering new businesses or markets, and not as much in acquiring new skills from their partners. The Japanese company NEC has been able to gain a leading position in telecommunications, computers, and semiconductors through a series of collaborative ventures. It has enhanced its technology and product competencies in spite of having invested less in research and development than competitors like Sweden's L.M. Ericsson, Texas Instruments, and Canada's Northern Telecom. NEC astutely leveraged its in-house research and development over two decades via its string of alliances, especially with Honeywell.[18]

Risks and Problems in Managing Strategic Alliances

We have covered some of the most commonly observed reasons for forming strategic alliances. It is assumed, incorrectly of course, that all strategic alliances are successful. In fact, many alliances are terminated due to a variety of reasons. Among the most common reasons for the failure of alliances are the following.

- Clash of cultures
- Unrealized partner expectations
- Surrender of sovereignty
- Risk of losing core competence to a partner

Clash of Cultures When two companies from different countries with very different cultures come together in an alliance, problems can arise due to a misunderstanding of the different ways of thinking, behaving, and communicating of each culture. For instance, in a Japanese-U.S. company alliance, the long-term orientation that is so typical of Japanese management could conflict with the relatively short-term orientation of American managers in decisions related to issues such as reinvesting profits in the business for long-term benefits, versus declaring dividends in order to keep shareholders happy.

For the most part, Japanese companies are primarily interested in the welfare of their employees and not that of the shareholders; the opposite is the case with most American companies. Therefore, this fundamental difference in attitude toward employees versus shareholders impacts upon decisions that are made in almost all functional areas, from employee layoffs in production to financial decisions such as the expected payback period on a new investment in the plant and equipment that could have implications for employment.

Unrealized Partner Expectations Difficulties in partner relationships are often caused by one of the partners in the alliance thinking that the other partner is not doing its share, or is not making the expected contributions to make the joint venture succeed. Sometimes such problems occur because it is difficult for the partners to accurately assess each other's capabilities during the negotiation stage of the alliance. Consequently, unrealistic expectations are created that lead to disillusionment later on.

Surrender of Sovereignty Big companies are increasingly turning to close alliances with small companies (see Exhibit 11-2). Through joint ventures, equity investments, and other deals, big companies get quick access to new technology and entrepreneurship. The small companies get the much-needed cash and credibility that a big corporate partner can provide. For example, Glaxo, the giant British pharmaceutical company, has formed an R&D deal with Gilead Sciences Inc., a biotechnology concern. Under this deal, Glaxo will fund Gilead's development of a new anti-cancer drug. In return, Glaxo obtains rights to market the drug internationally.[19]

However, there is always the danger of the larger partner buying out the smaller partner in the alliance when the smaller partner cannot keep up with an increasing demand for equity, needed to maintain its share in the alliance as the venture grows. The larger partner's share in

EXHIBIT 11-2

Some Strategic Alliances

Large Company	Small Company	Date	Type of Alliance
IBM	Geographic Systems	1989	Marketing and development
Motorola	Applied Intelligent Systems	1990	Product development
Sony	Panavision	1988	System development
Glaxo	Gilead Sciences	1990	Sales and marketing
Upjohn	Biopure	1990	Sales and marketing
Chesapeake	Stake Technology	1990	System development
Kodak	Immunex	1988	Technology development

Source: Udayan Gupta, "How Big Companies Are Joining Forces with Small Ones for Mutual Advantage," *The Wall Street Journal*, February 25, 1991, p. B1. Reprinted by permission of *The Wall Street Journal*, © 1991 Dow Jones & Company, Inc. All Rights Reserved Worldwide.

the venture grows as its contribution increases, and eventually the smaller partner is bought by the bigger company in the alliance.

The danger of a takeover is not limited just to small companies, as was the case when, in 1990, Fujitsu bought 80 percent of the British computer company ICL. Furthermore, a survey by McKinsey and Company, a management consulting firm, showed that of 150 companies involved in alliances, 75 percent had been taken over by the Japanese.

Risk of Losing Core Competence to a Partner Earlier we discussed the desire to learn from a partner as being one of the reasons for forging strategic alliances. However, unless there is mutual and equal learning by all parties involved in an alliance, the partner who learns the most from the partnership stands to emerge as the strongest among the alliance partners. The greatest danger is one partner learning the most critical or core skills from the other partner, and later using the knowledge gained from the partnership to compete in the industry against its former allies. This turn of events is precisely what happened in the case of Borden Inc. and Japan's Meiji Milk Products.

Borden and Meiji Milk had an enviable partnership. Under a licensing agreement with Meiji Milk, Borden marketed its premium ice cream throughout Japan through Meiji's vast distribution network. Meiji Milk, in the meantime, learned the technique of processing cheese, margarine, and ice cream, which were still unfamiliar to Japanese producers. In time, Borden had over 50 percent of the Japanese market. But competition from Pillsbury Company's Haagen-Dazs and a string of domestic brands began to eat into Borden's market share.

Unhappy with Meiji Milk's efforts in fighting the competition to maintain market share, Borden decided to dissolve the partnership. However, much to Borden's dismay, Meiji Milk then introduced two competing brands of premium ice cream, one of which was named Breuges, a brand that even Meiji Milk marketers concede is similar in price and content to Borden's "Lady Borden." Here is an example of a partner, in this case Meiji Milk, learning a core technology from its partner and then competing against it when the partnership sours.[20]

Making Strategic Alliances Work

Although there are no magical prescriptions to ensure the success of strategic alliances, there are some guidelines that could enhance the chances of their survival.

Trust Is Built in Small Steps   Trust among partners is critical to the success of any alliance. But trust cannot be written into a legal document in the form of a contract. It is each other's observed behavior that builds trust in any relationship, and this fact is true in a strategic alliance as well. Alliance partners must keep trust in mind and behave in an open manner that enhances the bonds of that trust between them. Each of the partners must attempt to find ways of working together without either one feeling that the other is trying to steal technology or take advantage in any way. Such trust takes time to develop, and relationships based upon trust need to be developed in a deliberate fashion.

Select a Compatible Partner   To begin with, the alliance must be important enough to make a strategic impact on the future well-being of both partners. If one of the partners considers the alliance of merely peripheral importance, the seeds of dissolution are sown. Cultural compatibility is an absolute prerequisite for the success of any partnership. Therefore, if the partners in an alliance have greatly divergent cultures, it would be advisable to have one of the partners play a dominant role in the day-to-day management of the venture once the strategic intent of the alliance has been mutually agreed upon. This arrangement is the one under which the NUMMI partnership between General Motors and Toyota is being administered, with Toyota managing the venture on a daily basis.

Create and Maintain an Alliance with Equal Power   An alliance in which one of the partners is more powerful than the other is in danger of collapsing, unless the more powerful partner treats the weaker partner as an equal. Power derives from one's ability to deliver something—technology, capital, information, or resources—to another, something that the other party cannot obtain in the marketplace or develop by itself at an acceptable cost. The power that a company can muster in an alliance is not necessarily associated with its relative size vis-à-vis its partner. For example, a company that has the proprietary knowledge and expertise to develop a breakthrough drug for the treatment of a fatal disease, or that can develop a better and faster computer chip, will have the power to deal on equal terms with a much larger company. The power balance in an alliance is what matters. A small company may have the technology, but a large firm can provide the required capital to develop and commercialize it. As long as the relationship maintains a power balance, the partnership should not expect trouble. However, when a power imbalance develops in an alliance, the company emerging as the more powerful should be careful not to act as such in order for the alliance to survive.

Be Patient   An infinite amount of patience is needed on both sides during the various stages of an alliance. During the initial negotiation phase, patience is necessary to ensure that the alliance is properly structured in terms of who is responsible for what types of decisions, and so forth. Spending extra time and effort on ironing out such issues early in the alliance helps prevent future problems. Patience is also needed when the alliance begins to function. Expecting immediate results can prove fatal. Managers on both sides must recognize that delays and unexpected technical- and people-related problems will emerge in any organization, and that the chances of such problems arising when two companies are engaged in a collaborative effort are that much greater.

CORE COMPETENCY LEVERAGING

Building strategic alliances is one of the principal strategies that astute multinational companies have successfully adopted in order to attain global competitive advantage and superiority. Another strategy is being used by companies that are gaining prominence in a variety of businesses, a strategy that is not readily apparent to their less perceptive competitors. This strategy is to gain superiority by building on one or more core competencies. Fundamental to the concept of core competence is the recognition of the distinction among core competence, core product, and end products.[21]

Core competence may be defined as the distinctive ability to excel in a key area, upon which a company can build a variety of businesses and develop new generations of products, some of which customers may need but have not yet imagined. Core products are the intermediate linkages between core competencies and end products. They are the subassemblies or components that actually make significant additions to the value of the end products. To be in a position of world leadership, a company must be in a position of strength at all three levels—core competencies, core products, and end products. For example, Honda developed core competence in engines and power-train technology that was physically embodied in its core product—the engine—which it skillfully incorporated in a variety of end products such as lawn mowers, generators, marine engines, motorcycles, and cars. At the core competence level, the goal is to attain state-of-the-art, world-class leadership in a key field. For example, Sony developed the capacity to miniaturize, and Canon's competencies are in optics, imaging, and microprocessor controls.

At the core products level, the goal is to maximize world manufacturing share. This goal is achieved by manufacturing a core product for sale to both internal and external customers. For instance, in the 1970s the Japanese company JVC established several VCR supply relationships with American and European consumer electronics companies. Such arrangements enabled JVC to garner the cash and market feedback on its products, and to surpass Sony and the Dutch company Philips. A similar strategy is being used by Korean companies such as Goldstar, Samsung, and Daewoo. They have set up supply relationships with Western companies, their objectives being to build core product leadership in such diverse areas as displays, semiconductors, and automotive engines. Another strategic objective of the Korean companies is to prevent their potential American and European customer competitors from making manufacturing investments in the Korean companies' core products, and thus displacing them from value-creating activities.

Serving as a manufacturing base for Western companies gives core product manufacturers such as Goldstar and Samsung an opportunity to build manufacturing share without the risk and expense of building downstream brand share. Product feedback received from buyer companies provides free and invaluable market research data on customer preferences and market needs. Such information is used by a core product manufacturer to improve the core product. Furthermore, this kind of information serves as a lever to develop the end product by itself and to enter the end product market independently. This strategy was used quite effectively by Japanese television makers like Sony and Hitachi in their quest to enter the U.S. market. They first served as original equipment manufacturers (OEMs) of private-label, black and white television sets for American department stores. Then they used the experience and knowledge gained in the process to upgrade their presence in the United States from OEMs to independent marketers of color TV sets under their own brand names. More importantly, in doing so the Japanese companies managed to destroy American TV manufacturers like RCA, GE, and Sylvania.

A dominant world manufacturing share in a core product may not necessarily mean an equally strong position in the market for end products. For example, Canon supposedly has a dominating world manufacturing share in desktop laser printer engines; however, its brand share in the laser printer business is actually quite small. Similarly, Matsushita has a huge market share worldwide in compressors, its core product. Its brand share in the air conditioner and refrigerator businesses, however, is negligible. Clearly, the strategic objective for obtaining the maximum possible manufacturing market share for core products is to generate revenue and customer feedback, which in turn can be used to improve and extend core competencies. The focus should be fixed on enhancing and replenishing a company's core competencies and leveraging them to develop and market a variety of end products, with core products serving as their backbone. Examples of companies that have effectively leveraged their core competencies are Casio, 3M, and Canon. Casio drew on its expertise in semiconductors and digital displays by producing calculators, small-screen television sets, musical instruments, and watches. The 3M Company combined competencies in substrates, coatings, and adhesives to produce Post-it pads, magnetic tape, photographic film, pressure-sensitive tapes, and coated abrasives—quite a diversified product portfolio driven by only a few shared core competencies. Canon has leveraged its competencies in optics, imaging, and microprocessor controls to produce copiers, laser printers, cameras, and image scanners. Core competence is important because, in the short run, the quality of a company's product and its performance determine its competitiveness. In the long run, however, the global competitiveness of a company depends more upon its ability to grow through internal development, licensing deals, or strategic alliances. Its core competencies, however, are what give birth to new generations of products, and at a rate faster than the competition.

In the above discussion we focused on technological core competence. However, companies can develop core competencies in a variety of functional areas. For example, the Maine-based catalogue sales retailer L. L. Bean's core competence is in logistics and distribution, and Philip Morris is unbeatable in its ability to identify emerging market segments for consumer products, which it has leveraged in businesses other than cigarettes, like soft drinks and fast foods. Core competence may also be developed in other functions such as purchasing, service after sales, product design, and advertising. For instance, the Italian company Benetton, retailer of sportswear and casual clothing, has a celebrated expertise in developing extremely successful and relatively inexpensive, albeit often controversial, advertising campaigns.

COUNTERATTACK

With the increasing globalization of industries, U.S. companies in such industries have come to realize that a competitive attack against their home market can be launched by foreign companies who, at the time of the attack, may have a relatively small presence in the U.S. market. In the past, the typical response of U.S. companies was to assume that foreign companies, especially those from Japan and the Pacific Basin countries, were able to effectively compete in the U.S. market because of lower costs derived from cheap labor rates in their own countries.

In response, U.S. companies established offshore assembly and manufacturing sites in Asia to lower their own production costs. American companies also observed that the Japanese were taking advantage of lower costs from scale economies derived from production in large world-scale plants. In response, American companies followed suit and also established world-scale plants. However, such strategies did not prevent a market share decline in the U.S. market of American companies as Japanese companies continued to take over the market share. What American companies did not recognize, and what Japanese companies apparently did, was that a strategy based on low labor costs was vulnerable to fluctuating exchange rates and rising labor costs. This phenomenon is exactly what has taken place in Japan. Wage rates there have risen significantly in the last three decades, high enough to make them noncompetitive in comparison to wage rates in other Asian countries such as Malaysia, Thailand, and Sri Lanka. Moreover, the strategy of lowering production costs through scale advantages derived from large-scale plants also proved to be vulnerable to technological improvements in the production process brought about by such factors as robotics and computer-aided, flexible manufacturing. Today, global competition is characterized by a series of competitive attacks and counterattacks by global companies in each other's home and third-country markets. Companies that cannot engage in such battles are doomed to lose market share, both at home and abroad.[22] For example, an American company that is attacked by a Japanese company cannot spend its resources only on defending its home market, while the Japanese company faces no such threat in its own home market. The American company must be capable of attacking the Japanese company in the Japanese market or in a third-country market where the Japanese company is vulnerable. The Japanese aggressor, when attacked by the American defender on his (Japanese) home ground, is forced to divert his resources towards defending his home market and away from attacking the foreign American market. In actual military combat, a defender must be able to attack the enemy in the enemy's home territory in order to repel the enemy's attack. The same holds true in business warfare. In order to launch a counterattack, however, one must have the required "firepower" which, in business terms, is the cash flow to launch an attack.

Cash flows are needed to develop the various capabilities required to make an effective attack or counterattack. The types of capabilities needed are (1) channels of distribution through which to direct an attack, (2) investment in key core competencies, and (3) a wide range of products that can benefit from the same distribution channels. With these capabilities in place in major world markets, companies can engage in cross-subsidizing across countries and markets.[23]

Cross-subsidization involves the deployment of resources generated in one area or country for use in another location. For instance, using cash flows generated in Japan or elsewhere, a Japanese company can launch an attack on an American company in the U.S. market, or in a third-country market in which the American company is weak. Such an attack might involve lowering the Japanese company's prices in the U.S. market just enough to squeeze the profit margins of the U.S. company. The objective here is to reduce the cash flows of the American company, and drain them away from activities such as marketing and research and development. Without channels of distribution in the foreign company's home market, the American company is in no position to cross-subsidize and counterattack. The American company is thus weakened, and unable to make necessary improvements in its products or to launch expensive advertising and marketing campaigns. Consequently, the American company loses market share and the Japanese company then proceeds to raise its prices and increase its margins, which are, in turn, used to continue such attacks in other countries and markets.

Cash flows are also required to develop effective channels of distribution in major markets of the world. It is generally accepted that, to be a global player in a global industry, a company must have an effective presence in three areas of the world; namely, the United States, Europe, and Asia. Developing channels of distribution is an expensive endeavor for which enormous amounts of cash are needed.

Cash flows are also vitally needed to develop core technologies and core competencies, which, as just discussed, are key requisites of a global company's competitive advantage. Companies that can generate such competencies can leverage them in the ways that were discussed earlier.

Cash flows are also needed to develop a large enough portfolio of contiguous products that can be funneled through the existing distribution channels to utilize the channels to their maximum capacity.

Each of these activities, carried out on a global scale, requires cash flows. These activities, in turn, generate necessary cash flows, and the cycle of cross-subsidization, attack, and counterattack continues on a global scale. Companies that do not perceive the strategic intent of global companies playing the game of cross-subsidization—weakening the competition in one market after another in order to capture market share and accompanying cash flows—are paving the path to their own extinction. The strategic intent of global competitors is to wage battles worldwide. They want not only to capture world volume but to generate the cash flow necessary to support the creation of new core technologies; enhance core competencies; establish strong distribution channels; acquire or build world-class, efficient plants; and achieve global brand recognition through massive advertising and marketing campaigns. An excellent example of an effective counterattack strategy is the invasion by Eastman Kodak of the home market of Japan's Fuji Photo Film.[24] Kodak launched the attack against Fuji in response to Fuji's attack on Kodak's lucrative markets in America and Europe, where for decades Kodak had maintained a dominant market share in the color film business. Fuji's attack shrank Kodak's margins and forced it to cut prices. Realizing that it faced a global challenge from Fuji that would only grow stronger, Kodak struck back and invaded its rival's home market. The results have been dramatically favorable for Kodak. Kodak's sales have jumped sixfold to an estimated $1.3 billion in 1990. It has put Fuji on the defensive; Fuji's domestic margins have been squeezed, and some of Fuji's best executives have been recalled to Tokyo. In Kodak's estimation, its invasion of the Japanese market forced Fuji to divert its resources from overseas in order to defend its home market, where it had enjoyed a commanding 70 percent share of the market in color film. *Practical Insight 11-2* presents a complete picture of Kodak's counterattack strategy.

PRACTICAL INSIGHT 11-2

The Revenge of Big Yellow Eastman Kodak Has Struck Back at Fuji Photo Film Where It Hurts Most—at Home in Japan. Yes, It Can Be Done.

Throughout the 1980's, Eastman Kodak looked like just one more fat-and-unhappy American company incapable of defending itself against a Japanese onslaught. Fuji Photo Film attacked the American and European markets, where for decades Kodak had enjoyed a lucrative dominance in color film. It squeezed Kodak's margins and forced it into a divisive and not always successful panic to slash costs. "Big Yellow," as Kodak is known on Wall Street because of its bright yellow boxes of film, received the thumbs down from investors. Its share price underperformed the market for years, prompting rumors of eventual breakup.

Then Kodak struck back. Its executives in Rochester, New York, admitted to themselves that their company faced a global challenge from Fuji that would only grow. They decided to invade their rival's home market. Since reentering the Japanese market in 1984, Kodak's local operation has grown from a pokey office housing 15 people to a business with 4,500 employees, a fancy headquarters in Tokyo, a corporate laboratory in nearby Yokohama, manufacturing plants, and dozens of affiliated companies. Meanwhile, Kodak's sales in Japan have soared sixfold, to an estimated $1.3 billion this year. All this has been achieved against fierce resistance from Fuji and Konica, the entrenched Japanese film suppliers.

PRACTICAL INSIGHT 11-2 *(continued)*

Kodak's push into the Japanese market has not been cheap. Its Japanese operations are now making an operating profit, but it may be years before they pay back the $500 million spent to build them up. But Kodak spotted that the Japanese market is the world's second largest. It judged that its invasion would put Fuji on the defensive, forcing it to divert resources from overseas in order to defend itself at home, where it had enjoyed a 70 percent share of the market in color film. Some of Fuji's best executives have now been pulled back to Tokyo. Fuji's domestic margins have been squeezed. Fuji has proved as vulnerable to attack in Japan as Kodak was in America. Kodak has been selling photographic materials in Japan since 1889. But after World War II, the American occupation forces persuaded most American firms, including Kodak, to leave Japan to give war-torn local industry a chance to recover. Kodak handed over the marketing of its products to Japanese distributors. Over the next four decades, Fuji gained its 70 percent share of the Japanese market and then launched its export drive. Konica, a latecomer, grabbed 20 percent of domestic sales, leaving Kodak and a handful of European firms to share a miserable 10 percent. By 1984, repeated rounds of trade negotiations had dismantled most of the postwar barriers protecting the Japanese film market. Kodak set out to make its yellow-packaged boxes as familiar and friendly to Japanese customers as any local product. Its strategy was to boost:

Distribution. Kodak realized that it had to get control of its own distribution and marketing channels. "Using a trading company helps at the start," says Mr. Albert Seig, the president of Kodak's Japanese subsidiary, "but few trading companies take a strategic view." Rather than go it alone, Kodak established a joint venture with its distributor, Nagase Sangyo, an Osaka-based trading company specializing in chemicals. Kodak won the support of Nagase's 1,500 employees with two years of patient wooing.

Local investment. To nurture relations with its suppliers, Kodak also took equity stakes in them. It now has 20 percent of Chinon Industries, a supplier of 35mm cameras, videocamera lenses, printers, and other computer accessories which Kodak sells under its own label. Kodak has acquired a good deal of manufacturing know-how from Chinon and is expected to increase its holding in it still further. When Kodak needed to hire 100 systems engineers quickly, it invested in Nippon Systems House. Likewise, Kodak Imagica, a photo-finisher that provides developing facilities around Japan, is 51 percent owned by Kodak. Kodak Information Systems, formerly part of a microfilm and electronic-imaging equipment supplier called Kusuda, is now a wholly owned subsidiary.

Promotion. At a time when Fuji and Konica were committed to heavy spending on promotion abroad, Kodak spent three times more than both of them combined on advertising in Japan. It erected mammoth Sim neon signs as landmarks in many of Japan's big cities. Its sign in Sapporo, Hokkaido, is the highest in the country. It sponsored sumo wrestling, judo, tennis tournaments, and even the Japanese team at the 1988 Seoul Olympics, a neat reversal of Fuji's 1984 coup when it won the race to become the official supplier to the Los Angeles Olympics.

Kodak's cheekiest ploy was to spend $1 million on an airship emblazoned with its logo. It cruised over Japanese cities for three years, mischievously circling over Fuji's Tokyo headquarters from time to time. To Fuji's chagrin, Japanese newspapers gleefully picked up the story. The Japanese firm was forced to spend twice as much bringing its own airship back from Europe for just two months of face-saving promotion in Tokyo.

Half of all Japanese consumers can now recognize Kodak's goods instantly. This brand awareness has helped Kodak grow in Japan at about twice the pace of Fuji or Konica. Kodak's share of sales to amateur photographers has grown by a steady 1 percent each year for the past six years. Kodak now has a 15 percent slice of that market and is expected to overtake second-place Konica within the next few years. Kodak's success in Tokyo has been even more impressive. It now has 35 percent of the amateur market there, even though amateur photography is not Kodak's biggest business in Japan. Medical x-ray film and photographic supplies to the graphic arts and publishing industries are bigger. In these markets Kodak's share reaches 85 percent.

Kodak's counterattack has been possible only because of an abrupt change in attitude back in Rochester. Kodak has shed the worst of its fabled parochialism, even though the parent company still has no foreigners on its main board. Technically brilliant, the company had become complacent and slipshod in marketing. It was not until 1984 that Kodak started printing in Japanese on its packaging in Japan—and not until 1988 that it launched a film (Kodacolor Gold) that offered the more garish colors which Japanese consumers prefer.

Today, Kodak thinks just like a Japanese company—at least in Japan. Apart from a small unit headed by Mr. Seig which liaises with Kodak's headquarters, the rest of the local subsidiary is entirely Japanese, complete with a Japanese boss and Japanese management. There are only 30 foreigners among Kodak's 4,500 people in Japan. So thoroughly Japanese has Kodak become that it even has its own keiretsu—a family of firms with cross holdings in one another. And so thoroughly has it been accepted that some of Kodak's largest business customers are asking that Kodak take a small equity stake in them too. That is a significant gesture of both market anticipation and goodwill. The global battle with Fuji will continue, but it is now being waged on both sides of the world.

Source: *The Economist,* November 10, 1990, pp. 77-78. © 1990 The Economist Newspaper, Ltd. Reprinted with permission. All rights reserved.

Implications of Counterattack Strategy

The implementation of a counterattack strategy has several critical implications for the management of a global company. This section examines some of the most important ones.

In order to assist a parent company in a global counterattack, the foreign affiliates in the company have to relinquish much of their autonomy to the parent company or to divisional management. The relationship between and among the affiliates and the parent company has to be one of resource interdependence rather than independence. The strategies and implementation plans of each affiliate have to be coordinated with those of the parent company and the other affiliates. This coordination is necessary so that resources required for launching offensive or preemptive cross-subsidization strikes against competitors can be marshalled from the most appropriate sources within the global network of the company. The managerial philosophy underlying a counterattack strategy is that in a global industry, competition in an affiliate country does not always emanate from other local companies; rather, it can come from affiliates of foreign companies that are members of powerful networks of global companies having worldwide access to resources. Therefore, a foreign affiliate left to fend for itself with only its own country-based resources would be no match for an aggressive global company's attack without help from sister affiliates or the parent company. Collaboration among the affiliates and the parent company in the sharing of resources through cross-subsidization is the only way to deflect an attack by a global company against a weak sister affiliate.

At the parent company level, divisional management and strategic business units (SBUs) have to abandon a "my division" or "my business unit" attitude and think more in terms of inter-divisional and cross-SBU relationships. Like foreign affiliates, they too have to collaborate and share resources among themselves, and seek to agree on, and implement, strategies that add value and strength to the company as a global whole.

Investments abroad in manufacturing, research and development, marketing, and other functional areas have to be made for strategic reasons, such as establishing a beachhead in major markets of the world or in the home market of a foreign competitor. Such investments are based primarily on their strategic importance to any future offensive or defensive counterattack strategies, and not necessarily on financial considerations, such as return on investment or profitability.

GLOCALIZATION

In discussing the three strategies—strategic alliances, core competency leveraging, and counter-attack—it is quite clear that the parent company plays a central role in coordinating its network of globally dispersed affiliates. The parent company makes the network operate as one inte-grated, collective global unit. Global companies, however, must be careful that, in their zealous pursuit of an effective global strategy, they do not neglect managerial initiative at lower levels in the organizational hierarchy, especially at the regional and subsidiary levels. *Glocalization*, which means thinking globally but acting locally, includes an optimal mix of parental control where it counts, and local initiative at regional and subsidiary levels. This structural balance has proved to be most fruitful for well-managed, global companies.

A successful strategy incorporates the glocalization of the following interrelated elements:

- Management
- Foreign affiliates
- Exports
- Products
- Production

Glocalization of Management

Adopting a global strategy that does not stifle local initiative involves a delicate balancing act. It often means giving regional and subsidiary managers the freedom to develop their own implementation plans for products, marketing, financing, and production that are consistent with local political, economic, legal, and cultural demands. For example, Levi Strauss & Company, the jeans maker, maintains tight headquarters control where it matters most. As a company that cherishes brand identity and quality, Levi's has organized several foreign manufacturing subsid-iaries rather than rely on a patchwork of licensees that are hard to control. It has also exported its pioneering use of computers to track sales and manufacturing, and in so doing, keep a step ahead of fashion trends. Levi's also allows local managers to make decisions about adapting products to suit local tastes. In Brazil, Levi's local managers make decisions regarding distri-bution. For example, local initiative and knowledge of the market enabled Levi's to establish a chain of 400 Levi's Only stores, some of them in tiny, rural towns in Brazil's fragmented market.

In 1990, the stores accounted for 65 percent of Levi's Brazilian sales. Levi's approach represents a slogan that is symbolic of what glocalization stands for: "Be global, act local."[25]

In the Sony Corporation, apart from the long-term strategy handed down from Tokyo, regional managers make all their own investment and product decisions on the spot. Top managers from Sony's subsidiaries around the world meet twice a year to hammer out the basic details of the company's operations.[26] Insiders say that this international top meeting arrangement is the main reason for Sony's ability to respond to market changes and launch new products so swiftly.

A glocalization of management philosophy is also evident in Toshiba and Matsushita Electric Industrial, which have delegated decision-making authority to regional headquarters. Toshiba has a tri-polar regional management structure for Asia, Europe, and the United States. Each area manager has decision-making authority for manufacturing, sales, and some research and development. At Matsushita Electric, which has regional headquarters for Asia, Europe, and the United States based in Singapore, London, and New Jersey, respectively, most local decisions are now made locally, and the three top regional heads are all members of Matsushita Electric's board of directors. Again, each region has manufacturing, marketing, and product-related research and development capability, and Matsushita plans to develop some regional, basic research facilities as well.[27]

Glocalization of Foreign Affiliates

Strong presence in a foreign market requires the physical presence of manufacturing facilities in the market itself. Governments are making it easier for companies to enter markets, provided there is a commitment on the part of company management to base production of the product in the foreign country as soon as possible. Companies are also realizing that, as good corporate citizens, they ought to make a significant contribution to the economic development and social welfare of their host countries. Transferring production technology to the host country and increasing the ratio of locally produced items in the production process or the final product are ways to contribute to a host country's economic well-being. Training and developing local suppliers of components and subassemblies enhances the technological base of a nation. Such a transfer of technology could be brought about by entering into technical collaboration agreements with local partners, forming joint ventures with local capital, or establishing a wholly owned subsidiary—that is, owned by the parent company. The economic and political conditions in a country or region, as well as market size and the capabilities of the local partner, often dictate the mode of collaboration. For example, Japanese manufacturers have chosen to enter European markets mainly through joint ventures because of a preference, in Europe, for such collaborations and the hostility toward wholly owned Japanese plants exhibited by European governments. In the United States, Japanese companies have shown a preference for wholly owned plants, although they have also established several joint ventures with American companies. For example, Honda has wholly owned manufacturing subsidiaries in the United States, is collaborating with the Rover Group in Britain, and has a joint venture to produce motorcycles in Thailand.

Glocalization of Exports

Using foreign production plants as export bases to third-country markets is yet another way to become a "local" company in a foreign country. The Japanese have been exporting U.S.-made Japanese automobiles back to Japan and to European markets. Similar strategies have been adopted by global companies, which export from developing countries in Asia and other parts of the world. Following a glocalization of production strategy, Sony now has its own network of factories in each of the company's main markets—America, Europe, and Asia. Levi Strauss has a global manufacturing network with a mix of eleven sewing plants and contract manufacturers that enables it to supply customers from nearby factories.

Glocalization of Products

Should a company standardize its product or service throughout the world—sell the same product without making variations to suit differences in local taste and use—or should the product or service be tailored and customized to comply with local taste and use? This issue has been debated ad infinitum, and the answer to the question is that, to the extent that standardization is possible, a company should attempt it. There are some products and services that can be standardized globally, such as fax machines and telephones. On the other side of the scale, however, are products, such as coffee and soups, that must be modified to make them more palatable to the tastes of people in various countries and cultures.

Companies are resolving this dilemma by realizing that some products have certain core technologies, subassemblies, or components that can be standardized on a worldwide basis, while other parts or configurations of the same product require adaptation to local conditions. For example, Whirlpool Corporation saw a growing market in India for washing machine sales to the growing number of middle-class, two-income families in that country. The washing machines sold in Europe and America, however, were not suited to wash the traditional, five-yard-long saris worn by Indian women. Whirlpool formed a joint venture with an Indian partner to produce and market a Western-style automatic washing machine that is compact enough to fit into Indian homes and incorporates specially designed agitators that will not tangle saris. Variations of the same machine, internally dubbed the "World Washer," are also built and sold in Brazil and Mexico. In the aftermath of the glocalization of exports strategy discussed previously, Whirlpool is considering the export of these machines from factories in those countries to other Asian and Latin American markets. Except for minor variations in controls, the three bare-bones washers are nearly identical; they all handle only eleven pounds of wash, which is about one half the capacity of the typical U.S. model.[28] Whirlpool illustrates the slogan of product glocalization, which is: Standardize worldwide what you can, and adapt what you cannot.

Glocalization of Production

Companies are splitting up the production process and farming out parts of it to different countries. They are doing so in order to exploit the advantages of lower costs derived from scale economies, of international specialization—some countries are better at doing certain things than others—and of locational advantages such as proximity to markets, cheap labor, freedom from significant political risk, and local incentives such as tax holidays and government subsidies. Japanese automobile companies have targeted Asian countries for the expansion of their production activities because of the long-term growth potential of markets there. For example, one result of the Japanese expansion is the beginning of a parts-supply network that spans Southeast Asia. To achieve economies of scale, Japan's car makers produce different parts in different countries. Nissan, for example, wants to concentrate on production of diesel engines in Thailand, mechanical parts in Indonesia, wire harnesses in the Philippines, and clutches and electrical parts in Malaysia. Toyota has earmarked $215 million for investment in facilities to support a similar parts-production program.[29]

The farming out of production to different countries also extends to finished products. For instance, a company that produces a variety of models of the same product might assign a subsidiary in one country to specialize in the production of one model and a subsidiary in yet another country to specialize in a second model. The two subsidiaries then export to each other the models they produce. In this way, both subsidiaries have two models to market in their respective regions, but each is responsible for the production of only one of them. This strategy is quite common in the global automobile industry, and General Motors and Ford already practice it in Europe.

In this chapter, we discussed the strategies that a company can employ in its quest for a sustainable global competitive advantage. To be effective, these strategies should be part of a comprehensive planning process, as discussed in Chapter 8, and should be consistent with other strategic decisions made by the firm, such as choice of entry mode. Additionally, the successful implementation of a sound plan requires other elements as well—for example, without an organizational structure that can support the company's objectives, the international firm is unlikely to see its strategic objectives realized. In the next chapter, we look at the issue of the international firm's organization, and discuss the relationship between that structure and corporate strategy.

SUMMARY

This chapter was about the principal strategies that global companies have adopted to gain worldwide competitive superiority in global industries. Four such strategies were discussed: (1) strategic alliances, (2) core competency leveraging, (3) counterattack, and (4) glocalization.

Strategic alliances are collaborative agreements among firms in the same or different industries that may be forged for a variety of reasons: the necessity to penetrate foreign markets, to share the risk of huge investments needed for various projects, to share research and development costs and risks, to launch an attack against a competitor by teaming up with a competitor's common enemy, or to learn critical skills from the alliance partner. There are a variety of strategic alliances. Some involve collaboration without an investment in equity capital, while others are in the form of a joint venture between the partners in which a daughter company is formed, and in which both partners have an equity interest. Yet another type of strategic alliance is one in which there is either a one-way or mutual purchase of equity among the partners. A strategic alliance can also be cash-neutral, meaning that each company trades assets with the others and no cash changes hands.

There are risks and problems with strategic alliances about which one should be cautious. Problems can and do arise, due to a clash of the divergent cultures of the partners, or because of unrealized expectations from the alliance, the surrender of sovereignty by one of the partners to the other, or the danger of losing core competence to a partner who later uses it to compete with its former alliance company. The strategy of leveraging core competencies is based on the premise that a company must have a core competence—some strength that it excels in vis-à-vis its competitors—in one or more areas, and that it can build a variety of businesses and new generations of products on that competence. A core product is the link between a core competence and the final product, and for a company to achieve a position of world leadership in a business, it must excel in all three aspects of leveraging—core competence, a core product, and end products.

Counterattack strategy is based on the premise that global competition is characterized by a series of competitive attacks and counterattacks by global companies in each other's home and third-country markets. Companies that cannot fight such battles risk losing market share superiority both at home and abroad. In order to wage a counterattack strategy, companies must generate enough cash to cross-subsidize businesses and regions and to support and develop counterattack weapons that include the following: (1) strong distribution channels in major current and potential markets, (2) core technologies and core competencies, and (3) a portfolio of contiguous products that can also be funneled through the company's distribution channels in order to make maximum use of them.

The final global strategy discussed was glocalization, the essence of which is, "think globally, but act locally." To implement this strategy, companies must glocalize their managerial practices, foreign affiliates, exports, products, and production.

QUESTIONS FOR THOUGHT AND DISCUSSION

1. What is a strategic alliance? Discuss reasons for the formation of strategic alliances.

2. Identify and explain the different types of strategic alliances that are possible in a global business.

3. Scan some recent issues of *Business Week* and *The Wall Street Journal* and bring to class items that report on a recently created strategic alliance. Identify and describe the type of alliance it is.

4. Discuss reasons that could cause an alliance to fail.

5. Explain the concept of core competence. What is the difference between a core competence and a core product?

6. Discuss the relationship among a core competence, core product, and end product.

7. Explain the meaning of cross-subsidization. How is cross-subsidization utilized globally in a firm's competitive battles?

8. What is the strategic intent of companies that engage in the practice of cross-subsidization?

9. Explain the relationship between cross-subsidization and global cash flows. Why is it important for companies to understand this relationship?

10. What is the meaning of the term glocalization? Can a company that is implementing a global strategy simultaneously implement a glocalization strategy?

11. Explain glocalization of each of the following aspects of a multinational company's business: management, foreign affiliates, exports, products, and production.

MINI-CASE
Bury Thy Teacher

In October [1992] Chicago's 97-year-old Schwinn Bicycle Co., the grand name in American bicycles, filed for bankruptcy. On the other side of the world, Antony Lo took a breather from promoting his high-priced mountain bikes at the Tokyo International Cycle Show to deliver an eloquent eulogy for Schwinn, the company that Lo helped bury.

"Without Schwinn, we never would have grown to where we are today," said Lo, the polished president of Taiwan's Giant Manufacturing Co., now the world's largest bike exporter. "We learned many basic things from them: quality, value, service."

Down in Hong Kong, in his office in a converted factory near the colony's mammoth container port, Jerome Sze, the managing director and a large shareholder of Shenzhen, China's publicly traded China Bicycles Co., also pays his respects to the American company that helped him grow. "Schwinn," says Sze, "helped to promote our products in the U.S."

This is a story about how a great American company lost its way and, through management blunders, created powerful competitors that ultimately did it in. Says Scott Montgomery, president of Cannondale Japan, a wholly owned unit of the successful Georgetown, Conn., high-end bike company: "After Schwinn built them up [Giant and China Bicycles], they ate Schwinn." But this isn't just about Schwinn. In an intensely competitive global economy in which joint ventures with foreign partners are becoming the norm, what befell Schwinn can befall any company.

By the time Edward Schwinn, Jr., the great-grandson of founder Ignaz Schwinn, took over the company in 1979, the managerial blood had begun to run a bit thin. Schwinn's share (by units) of the U.S. bicycle market has eroded from over 25 percent in the 1960s to 7 percent in recent years and maybe only 5 percent in 1992. Analysts put Schwinn's output at 500,000 to 600,000 units and revenues at under $200 million a year—and falling—the past couple of years.

By contrast, Giant is growing rapidly; measured by value, it is now the world's largest bicycle exporter. It began selling under its own brand name outside Taiwan only in 1986, but it is already the top branded import to the U.S., Europe, and Japan. This year 70 percent of Giant's worldwide sales of 1.35 million units will be under its own brand name. Revenues: about $230 million in 1992.

Measured by volume rather than value, CBC is the world's largest bike exporter. Though it began making bikes only in 1985, total output is already 1.8 million units and is projected to rise to close to 2.3 million bicycles next year. CBC now sells nearly 30 percent of its bikes under the Diamond Back brand name, a U.S. label it acquired in 1990 for $17 million.

Schwinn's fortunes began to unravel in the 1980s. In the 1970s Schwinn still had a strong ten-speed business; this was based on its powerful retail distribution network and brand name. But in the 1980s the market shifted to mountain bikes, now 60 percent of the entire market, and to exotic bikes for adult enthusiasts, built of lightweight materials such as aluminum and carbon fiber. Once the innovator, Schwinn became the market follower. It never led the innovation in mountain bikes. Says J.C. McCullagh, editor and publisher of *Bicycling*, the industry's leading trade publication: "Schwinn had the best bike engineers in the country but it lost its edge because its management didn't respond quickly enough."

Schwinn had grown flabby in other areas. Until fairly recently, for example, it hadn't bothered to develop much of a presence in overseas markets, a deficiency because specialty bikes—not unlike cars—are global, fast-changing products. Explains Paul Brodek, director of Trek Japan, a wholly owned subsidiary of Trek USA: "We've learned things in Germany and Japan, the most demanding markets, that have improved the quality of our bikes in the U.S." From nothing in the early 1980s, Waterloo, Wisconsin-based Trek (revenues, $175 million) has become one of the world's most powerful specialty bikemakers.

Going overseas in the 1970s, Schwinn was more concerned with moving production out of the U.S. than with selling abroad. "Schwinn was obsessed with cutting costs," says Cannondale Japan's Montgomery, "instead of innovation."

Schwinn began its foreign campaign by sourcing many of its bicycles from Japan. By 1978 the expanding Taiwanese bike industry was already beating Japanese producers on price.

Again Schwinn was forced to react. This time it did so by importing a small quantity of Taiwanese-made Giant bikes, on which Schwinn slapped its nameplate.

Then, in 1981, another nail in the coffin: The workers went on strike at Schwinn's main factory in Chicago. Management panicked. Instead of negotiating a settlement, Schwinn closed the plant and sent its engineers and equipment to Giant's factory in Taichung, a port city in western Taiwan.

Recalls Giant's Antony Lo: "Schwinn thought that if the strike went on a long time, it would kill Schwinn dealers. They asked for our help in increasing capacity quickly."

As part of its new partnership with Giant, Schwinn handed over everything—technology, engineering, volume—that Giant needed to become a dominant bikemaker. In return, Schwinn imported the bikes and marketed them in the U.S. under the Schwinn name. Says an executive of a U.S. competitor: "Schwinn gave the franchise to Giant on a silver platter." (Schwinn declined to be interviewed for this story.)

By 1984 the Taiwanese tail was wagging the American dog. Giant was shipping 700,000 bicycles a year to Schwinn under the Schwinn nameplate, fully 70 percent of Schwinn's and Giant's sales.

According to the U.S. competitor, Schwinn could have driven a much harder bargain in Taiwan. "If Schwinn had gone to any bicycle maker in Taiwan and told them they would give them 700,000 units, they could easily have gotten a 50 percent share of the company," he says. But privately owned Giant refused to sell any equity to Schwinn, and Schwinn declined to press the point.

As a result, the Americans had no control over Giant's strategy. They could not, for instance, later prevent Giant from using the knowledge gained about specialty bike dealers to launch its own brand name in the U.S. ·

Which is what the Taiwanese did. Armed with Schwinn's technical specifications but able to produce at lower prices, Giant introduced its own brand-name bikes in Europe in 1986 and in the U.S. in 1987. No copycat, Giant later improved upon Schwinn's technology. By 1990, for example, it had become the world's largest manufacturer of carbon fiber frame bikes. Its best-selling bikes retail for $400 to $600, more than Schwinn's popular models.

The clever student quickly stole business from its old American teacher. "Giant bought market share in the U.S. by telling dealers its bikes were the same as Schwinn's, but 10 percent to 15 percent cheaper," says Ash Jaising, president of the independent Boston-based Bicycle Market Research Institute. To build its U.S. distribution, Giant hired several former Schwinn executives. Among them was William Austin, a former Schwinn vice president and now president of the Taiwanese company's U.S. subsidiary, Giant Bicycle Inc.

Dazed by Giant's aggressive brand-name push, Schwinn tried to protect itself by forging a new alliance, this time with Jerome Sze's China Bicycles Co. It began buying CBC's bikes and selling them under the Schwinn name. This time Schwinn demanded and got some equity in the venture with CBC, buying a 33 percent stake in 1987 (since diluted to 18 percent after CBC went public on the fledgling Shenzhen stock exchange early this year).

Until Schwinn went into business with China Bicycles, CBC's main business in the U.S. was supplying commodity house-brand bikes to Sears and other mass merchandisers from its low-cost factory in Shenzhen, in the heart of southern China's capitalist revolution (*Forbes*, Aug. 5, 1991). But Schwinn taught CBC about the U.S. specialty dealer market, raised the Chinese factory's quality standards, and lent it credibility.

"CBC came light-years in a short period of time because of a lot of technology transfer from Schwinn," says *Bicycling*'s McCullagh. Sze subsequently used all the knowledge he gleaned from Schwinn to help bolster his business supplying bicycles to the European operations of bike companies such as Scott and France's MBK (owned by Japan's Yamaha).

Burned once by Giant, Schwinn tried to dissuade China Bicycles from developing its own brand-name business in the U.S. But that didn't stop Sze. In 1990, despite Schwinn's opposition, Sze and his Shenzhen partner together acquired a medium-size U.S. bicycle importer and distributor, which owned the Diamond Back name. That gave CBC its own U.S. brand name and distribution channels. Diamond Back competes directly with Schwinn and is particularly strong on the West Coast.

With Giant, China Bicycles, and other competitors taking big bites out of its market share, Schwinn was finally forced to file for bankruptcy in October [of 1992]. It still imports bikes from its two former students and sells them under the Schwinn name. But production of its own bikes in the U.S. is down to under 10,000 units a year, sold under the Paramount name of high-priced racing bikes.

Interestingly, Giant's Lo and China Bicycles' Sze believe China, not the West, will be their best growth market. Sze says American-image mountain bikes are all the rage in China. He expects to sell over 30 percent of China Bicycles' output in 1993 on the domestic Chinese market, up from 15 percent this year and under 10 percent last year.

China Bicycles opened its second factory—the world's largest bike plant—this summer. Situated just north of Shenzhen, it will eventually produce 2.5 million units a year. Giant's Antony Lo says that in 1994 Giant will open a 1.5-million-unit plant in Shanghai. At least half of its production will be earmarked for the Chinese market.

What will happen to Schwinn? It still has a strong brand name and established distribution, plus a successful line of fitness products. China Bicycles' Sze says he's interested in acquiring Schwinn. Doing so would make sense for CBC, which hasn't progressed as far as Giant in establishing its brand name. Schwinn's shareholding in CBC was recently worth $45 million at Shenzhen stock exchange prices, enough to clear over half of Schwinn's estimated debt of $80 million. But Schwinn can't recapitalize itself by selling off its stake in China Bicycles: A joint venture agreement controlling CBC says none of the three major shareholders (Schwinn, Sze and the Shenzhen government) can sell without approval of the other two. In this matter, too, Schwinn's destiny is controlled by others.

On the other hand, if Sze were to buy Schwinn, he would be repurchasing a big piece of China Bicycles' equity as well as getting the rights to one of the world's best-known bicycle brand names and an excellent distribution system.

When Ignaz Schwinn founded his company nearly a century ago, Chicago was the world's bike capital, with about 90 manufacturers. Schwinn is the last major one. Who could have thought that its fate would lie in the hands of a publicly traded company in a communist country—a company Schwinn itself helped nurture into a formidable competitor?

Source: Andrew Tanzer, "Bury Thy Teacher," *Forbes*, December 21, 1992, pp. 90-95. Copyright © 1992 Forbes Inc. All rights reserved.

Discussion Questions for Mini-Case

1. What were the strategic blunders committed by Schwinn Bicycle Company that led to its downfall in the global bicycle market?

2. What strategic measures should Schwinn have taken to prevent the growth of Giant Bicycle Company and China Bicycles Company?

3. What lessons can we learn from the mistakes of Schwinn regarding the risks and dangers in forming international strategic alliances?

Notes

1 Udayan Gupta, "Sony Adopts Strategy to Broaden Ties with Small Firms," *The Wall Street Journal*, February 28, 1991, p. B2.

2 Stuart M. Dambrot, "Foreign Alliances that Make Sense," *Electronic Business*, September 3, 1990, p. 68.

3 Stephen D. Moore, "Volvo Contract on Joint Facility Appears Near," *The Wall Street Journal*, April 26, 1991, p. A12.

4 Michael J. McCarthy, "Coke, Nestle Get Together Over Coffee," *The Wall Street Journal*, November 30, 1990, p. B1.

5 Carole A. Shifrin, "Delta Travelers To Reach Heathrow On Virgin," *Aviation Week and Space Technology*, May 23, 1994, p. 28.

6 Richard Gibson, "Cereal Venture Is Planning Honey of a Battle in Europe," *The Wall Street Journal*, November 14, 1990, pp. B1 and B8.

7 Julia Flynn, Catherine Arnst, and Gail Edmondson, "Who'll be the First Global Company," *Business Week*, March 27, 1995, p. 117.

8 Ibid.

9 Douglas Lavin, "Sprint's Venture With Germany, France, Takes Step Forward Amid Many Delays," *The Wall Street Journal*, May 31, 1995, p. A12.

10 David P. Hamilton, "Nippon Telegraph & Telephone to Align With AT&T for Long-Distance Service," *The Wall Street Journal*, March 1, 1995, p. B2.

11 Jeremy Main, "Making Global Alliance Work," *Fortune*, December 17, 1990, p. 124.

12 Michael Selwyn, "Making Marriages of Convenience," *Asian Business*, January 1991, p. 26.

13 Jordan D. Lewis, "Competitive Alliances Redefine Companies," *Management Review*, April 1991, p. 14.

14 Jonathan B. Levine and Gail E. Schares, "IBM Europe Starts Swinging Back," *Business Week*, May 6, 1991, pp. 52-53.

15 Susan Carey, "Airline Ties Boost Revenue, GAO Says, But Transportation Agency Is Criticized," *The Wall Street Journal*, May 5, 1995, p. B4B.

16 Ibid.

17 Main, p. 124.

18 Gary Hamel, Yves L. Doz, and C. K. Prahalad, "Collaborate with Your Competitors and Win," *Harvard Business Review*, January-February 1989, p. 134.

19 Main, pp. 121-122.

20 Yumiko Ono, "Borden's Breakup with Meiji Milk Shows How a Japanese Partnership Can Curdle," *The Wall Street Journal*, February 2, 1991, p. B7.

21 For an excellent expose of the concept of core competence, see C. K. Prahalad and Gary Hamel, "The Core Competence of the Corporation," *Harvard Business Review*, May-June 1990, pp. 79-91.

22 Craig M. Watson, "Counter-Competition Abroad to Protect Home Markets," *Harvard Business Review*, January-February 1992, pp. 40-42.

23 Gary Hamel and C. K. Prahalad, "Do You Really Have a Global Strategy," *Harvard Business Review*, July-August 1985, pp. 139-148.

24 "The Revenge of Big Yellow," *The Economist*, November 10, 1990, pp. 77-78.

25 Maria Shao, Robert Neff, and Jeffrey Ryser, "For Levi's, A Flattering Fit Overseas," *Business Week*, November 5, 1990, pp. 76-77.

26 Nicholas Valery, "Consumer Electronics Survey," *The Economist*, April 13, 1991, p. 17.

27 "The Goal Is Genuine Internationalism," *Business Week*, July 16, 1990, p. 80.

28 David Woodruff, "A Little Machine that Won't Shred a Sari," *Business Week*, June 3, 1991, p. 100.

29 Amy Borrus, "Japan Streaks Ahead in East Asia," *Business Week*, May 7, 1990, p. 55.

Further Reading

Babbar, Sunil, and Arun Rai., "Competitive Intelligence for International Business," *Long Range Planning*, Vol. 26, No. 3, June 1993, pp. 103-113.

Erdmann, Peter B., "When Businesses Cross International Borders: Strategic Alliances and Their Alternatives," *Columbia Journal of World Business*, Vol. 28, No. 2, Summer 1993, pp. 107-108.

Hamel, Gary, and C. K. Prahalad, "Do You Really Have a Global Strategy?" *Harvard Business Review*, July-August 1985, pp. 139-148.

——"Strategic Intent," *Harvard Business Review*, May-June 1989, pp. 63-76.

Hamel, Gary, Yves L. Doz, and C. K. Prahalad, "Collaborate with Your Competitors and Win," *Harvard Business Review*, January-February 1989, pp. 133-139.

Maruyama, Magoroh, "Lessons from Japanese Management Failures in Foreign Countries," *Human Systems Management*, Vol. 11, No. 1, 1992, pp. 41-48.

Ohmae, Kenichi, "The Global Logic of Strategic Alliances," *Harvard Business Review,* March-April 1989, pp. 143-154.

Sugiura, Hideo, "How Honda Localizes Its Global Strategy," *Sloan Management Review*, Fall 1990, pp. 77-82.

Turpin, Dominique, "Strategic Alliances with Japanese Firms: Myths and Realities," *Long Range Planning*, Vol. 26, No. 4, August 1993, pp. 11-15.

CHAPTER TWELVE

Organizing for International Operations

LEARNING OBJECTIVES

After completing this chapter, you will be able to:

- Describe the stages of the product life cycle and how they parallel the early patterns of development in the international company.
- Explain the differences between the international division and global structures for organizing international companies.
- Discuss the relative advantages and disadvantages of global product, global area, and global functional organizational structures.
- Describe the matrix structure as it pertains to the international company.
- Explain the relationship between strategy and the organizational structure in the international company.

Organizations are created to link the behavior of individuals; to collect and pool information, skills, or capital; to engage in related actions toward the achievement of a set of goals; to monitor performance, initiate corrections, and to define new goals.[1] In a strictly domestic enterprise, these aims can be achieved with a two-dimensional organization—an organization that concerns itself with resolving the potentially conflicting demands of functional (production, finance, marketing, etc.) and product line requirements.

A two-dimensional organization is, however, not the appropriate structure for a multinational enterprise because it must not only be able to resolve functional and product line demands, but also be able to deal effectively with geographic area concerns. Thus, a more appropriate organizational form for a multinational enterprise should combine three dimensions: (1) functional expertise, (2) product and technical know-how, and (3) knowledge of the area and country. The manner in which these three dimensions are combined should and does differ from one international company to another. There is no one best way for organizing an international company, and each company will combine these three dimensions in an organizational structure that it tries to make consistent with its own particular strategy.

Michael Duerr and John Roach point out that a firm's international organization is generally determined as a response to three major strategic concerns:

- How to encourage a predominantly domestic organization to take full advantage of growth opportunities abroad.

313

- How to blend product knowledge and geographic area knowledge most efficiently in coordinating worldwide business.
- How to coordinate the activities of foreign units in many countries while permitting each to retain its own identity.[2]

Responses to each of these concerns will differ, depending on the firm's situation and the overall philosophy of top management. In this chapter we focus on the organizational design of international enterprises; that is, on the formal arrangement of relationships between the various domestic and foreign organizational units in the multinational network and the mechanisms provided for their coordination into a unified whole. Our treatment will be limited to the level of the senior managers who report directly to the president's office. We shall not be concerned with the organizational structure of foreign affiliates; rather, the emphasis will be on the structure inside the parent company, whose purpose is to plan and control the multinational network, and on the structure of the network itself. Our treatment of the organizational structure excludes recognition of the legal or statutory features of an enterprise. The legal structure is classified in accordance with government regulations for tax and cash flow purposes, and seldom reflects the actual manner in which an enterprise is managed. Because this chapter is concerned with managerial aspects of an international company, the legal structure has been ignored.

Six basic organizational structures of multinational companies will be covered: the pre-international division phase, the structures of the international division, the global product division, the global area division, the global functional division, and the multidimensional global form.

BASIC ORGANIZATIONAL DESIGN OF INTERNATIONAL ENTERPRISES

In most cases, a multinational firm's organizational structure is neither predetermined nor permanently fixed, but rather evolves continuously to correspond with changes in the firm's strategy. As a firm's operations grow and spread to new foreign markets, its organizational structure typically becomes overburdened. As the strain intensifies and threatens organizational structure, the firm normally is compelled to experiment with alternate organizational forms.

Eventually it chooses an organizational form consistent with its new international expansionist strategy and capable of handling its expanding operations. The replacement structure chosen is typically influenced by the structure that preceded it because the experience of the company with one structure provides a building block for future structures.

Although there is no one best organizational structure for multinational enterprises, it does not follow that every firm's organizational structure is completely unique or that there is no rationale for a firm's structural development. On the contrary, there are certain regular organizational patterns that firms of like strategy develop, and through which multinational firms with changing strategies evolve.

PRE-INTERNATIONAL DIVISION PHASE

A firm with a technologically advanced product in the new product stage is well positioned to exploit foreign markets. Generally, initial exploitation occurs through exports—the first stage in the evolution of a multinational company. At this stage, the firm is relatively small by multinational enterprise standards, and its activities are generally confined to a few products and markets. (Different stages in the evolution of a multinational enterprise were covered in Chapter 1.) The firm has to deal with a comparatively limited number of strategic dimensions, most of which are related to the domestic market, and which can be addressed directly by the president with input from managers who report directly to him. Since the firm's technologically advanced product stands on its own, there is little need to develop expertise in the foreign markets in which the firm sells. Assistance in exporting is usually provided initially by an independent export management company and later by an in-house export manager. In most cases, an in-house export manager is thought of as an adjunct to marketing, whose principal communication needs are with the marketing vice president and others in the marketing group. The organizational arrangements for a firm in this stage of multinational development are rather simple, with an export manager reporting to the chief marketing officer in an organization with a narrow product line; or directly to the chief executive officer in an organization with a broad product line (see Figure 12-1).

As the firm's exports increase and its product matures, certain pressures develop that tend to threaten the firm's foreign market share. Such threats can originate from one of two sources: (1) others at home and abroad begin to share the firm's special knowledge and special skills, thus the threat of competition becomes more tangible; (2) as local demand and sales volume increase in a country, an importing country begins to encourage local production by imposing "buy local" policies on its government agencies and other public buyers, and by enacting import restrictions such as tariffs and quotas.

FIGURE 12-1
Typical Organization of International Company
Primarily Engaged in Exporting to Foreign Markets

A. Company with narrow product line

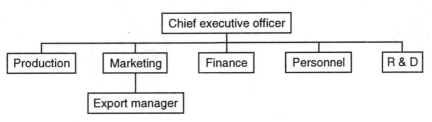

B. Company with broad product line

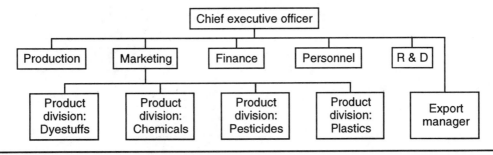

Source: Arvind V. Phatak, *International Dimensions of Management, Fourth Edition*, Cincinnati: South-Western Publishing Co., 1995, p. 153.

Faced with increased competition from other producers and higher comparative costs resulting from freight and tariff costs, the exporting firm feels pressed to defend its foreign market position by establishing a production facility inside the foreign market. Once established, the foreign production unit supplies the foreign market as the former technologically advanced product matures, or makes its way through the maturity stage and into the standardized product stage of the product cycle. The same cycle may be repeated by the firm in the markets of other nations as the firm tries to protect its market share by establishing local production units to supply local markets. At first the management of the newly formed foreign subsidiaries remains quite decentralized. A typical organizational arrangement for a firm at this early stage of foreign production is shown in Figure 12-2. Here, the foreign subsidiaries report directly to the company president or other designated company officer, who carries out his responsibilities without assistance from a headquarters staff group. As the firm increases its investment in foreign operating units, however, and as these become more important to the firm's overall performance, greater emphasis is placed on international product coordination and operations control.

Thus, there is pressure to assemble a headquarters staff group to assist the officer in charge and to develop a specialized international expertise. While originally responsible for the firm's foreign operating units, the group essentially takes control of all international activities of the firm and evolves into a separate international division in a new and comparatively more complex organizational structure.

INTERNATIONAL DIVISION STRUCTURE

In the international division form of organization, all international activities are grouped into one separate division and assigned to a senior executive at corporate headquarters. The senior executive is often given the title of vice president of the international division or director of international operations, and is at the same level as the other divisional and functional heads of the company in the organizational hierarchy (see Figure 12-3).

The head of the international division is generally given line authority over the subsidiaries abroad, and the international division is made into a profit center. The formation of the inter-

FIGURE 12-2

Typical Organization of Company at Early Foreign Production Stage

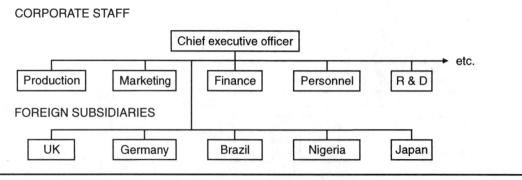

Source: Arvind V. Phatak, *International Dimensions of Management, Fourth Edition,* Cincinnati: South-Western Publishing Co., 1995, p. 154.

FIGURE 12-3
International Division Structure

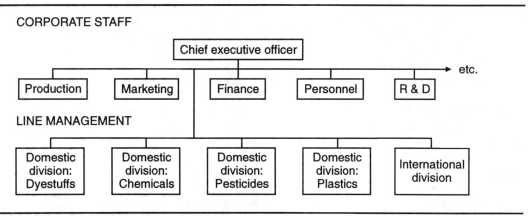

CORPORATE STAFF

Chief executive officer

Production   Marketing   Finance   Personnel   R & D   → etc.

LINE MANAGEMENT

| Domestic division: Dyestuffs | Domestic division: Chemicals | Domestic division: Pesticides | Domestic division: Plastics | International division |

Source: Arvind V. Phatak, *International Dimensions of Management, Fourth Edition*, Cincinnati: South-Western Publishing Co., 1995, p. 155.

national division in effect segregates the company's overall operations into two differentiated parts—domestic and international. As far as the top management at headquarters is concerned, the international division is expected to manage the nondomestic operations, and therefore to be the locus of whatever international expertise there is or should be in the company. There is not much contact or interaction between the domestic and international sides, and whatever coordination there is between the two segments of the company occurs at the company's top management level.

Organizationally, the formation of an international division lessens the autonomy of the foreign subsidiaries, because authority to make strategic decisions is pulled up into the hands of the head of the international division. However, this change is also accompanied by a far greater measure of guidance and support from the top to the foreign subsidiaries.

Who Adopts the International Division Structure?

In general, companies that are still at the developmental stages of international business involvement are likely to adopt the international division structure. Other factors favoring the adoption of this structure are limited product diversity, comparatively small sales (compared to domestic and export sales) generated by foreign subsidiaries, limited geographic diversity, and few executives with international expertise.

In the international division, executives are able to supervise the establishment and growth of one or more product lines in several foreign markets and, at the same time, develop new opportunities for expansion in others. In this structure, executives are providing the concentration of managerial expertise necessary for the effective promotion of the company's international efforts. During the period in which the company is establishing itself in international markets, international operations tend to remain, in the minds of the corporate executives of domestic operations, a sideline of minor importance. There are several advantages to the use of an international division structure. The concentration of international executives within the division

317

ensures that the special needs of emerging foreign operations are met. The presence of the head of international operations as a member of the top management planning team serves as a constant reminder to top management of the global implications of all decisions. The international group provides a unified position regarding the company's activities in different countries and regions as it makes an effort to coordinate the operations of foreign subsidiaries with respect to the various functional areas—finance, marketing, purchasing, and production. For example, central coordination of international activities enables the company to make more secure and more economic decisions about where to purchase raw materials, where to locate new manufacture, and from where to supply world customers with products. Also, when the financial function of the international division is coordinated, investment decisions can be made on a global basis and overseas development can turn to international capital markets, instead of just local ones, for funds.[3] The international division also will not strain the capabilities of product or functional managers within the domestic divisions because these persons are not required to work with unfamiliar environments.

There are several drawbacks to the international division structure; hence a company will use this structure only if the benefits from its adoption as a coordination mechanism clearly outweigh the costs. One principal disadvantage of the international division structure is the separation and isolation of domestic managers from their international counterparts, which may prove to be a severe handicap as the company continues to expand abroad. If foreign operations should approach a level of equality with domestic ones in terms of size, sales, and profits, the ability of domestic managers to think and act strategically on a global scale could be critical to the success of the company. Also, an independent international division may also put constraints on top management's effort to mobilize and allocate the resources of the company globally to achieve overall corporate objectives. Even with superb coordination at the corporate level, global planning for individual products or product lines is carried out awkwardly at best by two "semiautonomous" organizations—the domestic company and the international division.[4]

Conflicts occasionally occur between the domestic product divisions and the international division, particularly when the international division asks for help from the domestic divisions and gets what it considers to be inadequate technical support and second-rate staff members for special assignments abroad. Still another problem with the international division is that the firm's research and development remains domestically oriented. Consequently, new ideas originating abroad for new products or processes are not easily transmitted to and enthusiastically tackled by the research and development personnel who remain, after all, in the domestic setting of the organization.

When Is an International Division No Longer Appropriate?

As international sales and production capacity grow, and as more markets are entered, product lines begin to diversify to serve a variety of end users. Considerations such as transfer pricing (charging a higher or lower price between divisions than is charged to an outside buyer) then come into play; the international division structure gets a strained to its limits and is unable to fulfill its former role. Faced with this situation, the company may continue to use the international division structure by subdividing further as a response to diversification either by product line, if product diversification is causing the problem, or by area, if regional diversification is straining the organization (see Figure 12-4). Product or area managers, reporting to the international division head, are then established within the division to coordinate the expansion of the firm into new markets.

FIGURE 12-4
Divisions Within the International Division

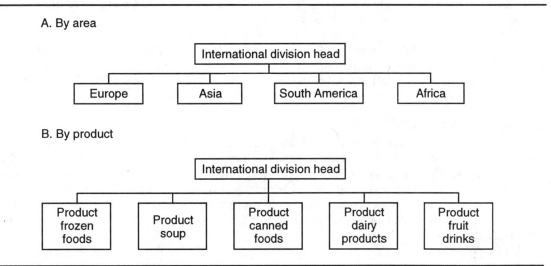

A. By area

B. By product

Source: Arvind V. Phatak, *International Dimensions of Management, Fourth Edition*, Cincinnati: South-Western Publishing Co., 1995, p. 158.

Another alternative is to take the profit responsibility from the international division and reorganize the entire company on either a product or area division basis, keeping the international division in an advisory capacity. (Product and area-based structures will be discussed later in the chapter.) If given an advisory role, executives in the division can function as generalists, monitoring environmental trends and conditions, and advising their functional, product, or geographical counterparts in the company. If the firm chooses to reorganize on a product basis, the international staff might be assigned to monitor the legal, political, cultural, and economic environments of major country and regional markets. If a geographically based structure is chosen, the international staff may serve as global coordinators, spotting trends and continuing to investigate the potential for new markets.

A Business International research report identifies the following factors as indicators that the international division is no longer an appropriate structure for an international company.

- The international market is as important as the domestic market.
- Senior officials of the corporation have both foreign and domestic experience.
- International sales represent 25 to 35 percent of total sales.
- The technology used in domestic divisions has far outstripped that of the international division.[5]

Other studies have shown that the pressures to reorganize on an integrated, worldwide basis by dismantling the international division mount when the division has grown large enough to be equal in size to the largest product division.[6] This is to a large extent due to the struggles that take place between the international and domestic divisions over capital budgeting and transfer pricing issues.[7] But most importantly, it is the structural conflict between the geographic orientation of the international division and the product orientation of the domestic divisions that motivates top management to reorganize the company in a fashion that merges the domestic and international sides of the business into one integrated global structure.

Dowling and others have noted that European companies have tended to take a different structural path than U.S. companies. Research studies have revealed that European companies often moved directly from a functional "mother-daughter" structure to a divisionalized global structure (worldwide product or area division) or matrix structure without the transitional stage of an international division.[8]

GLOBAL STRUCTURES

Up to this point we have been concentrating on the typical stages in the evolution of the organizational structure of a company as it becomes increasingly involved in international business activities. As the firm gains experience in operating internationally, the initially limited involvement in foreign direct investment gradually turns into a full-fledged commitment. Top management begins to perceive the company as a truly multinational enterprise, the company enters a new phase in its evolution, and the domestic/foreign bifurcation is abandoned in favor of an integrated, worldwide orientation.

Strategic decisions that previously were made separately for the domestic and international parts of the company are henceforth made at the corporate headquarters for the total enterprise, without any distinctions of domestic versus foreign. Top management considers the home market to be only one of many, and operational and staff groups are given global responsibility. Under such an attitudinal setup at corporate headquarters, corporate decisions are made with a total company perspective, and for the purpose of achieving the company's overall mission and objectives. These decisions include where to establish a new production facility, where to raise capital, what businesses and products to be in, where to obtain resources, what methods to use for tapping foreign markets, what subsidiary ownership policies to adopt, and so on.

The shift to a global orientation in company management must be accompanied by the acquisition and allocation of company resources on the basis of global opportunities and threats. These changes require an organizational structure that is consistent with, and supportive of, this new managerial posture. The new organizational structure includes, as all structures do to varying degrees, three types of informational inputs: product, geography, and function. Although the structures adopted by various companies differ, the structure an international company adopts is certain to be based on one of these basic orientations: a worldwide area or a worldwide product (or occasionally, a worldwide function). Depending on which is chosen, delineation of the other dimension[s] . . . are accounted for, in sequence. For these secondary and tertiary forces, they are subdivided (and hence duplicated) with each primary grouping, and/or they are centrally positioned in the form of corporate staff.[9]

We shall begin our look at global structures by first examining the product structure.

The Global Product Division

When the international division is discarded in favor of a global product division, the domestic divisions are given worldwide responsibility for product groups. The manager in charge of a product division is given line authority and responsibility for the worldwide management of all functional activities such as finance, marketing, production, and so on related to a product or product group. Within each product division, there may exist an international unit or even a more refined subdivisionalization on an area basis (see Figure 12-5).

FIGURE 12-5
Global Product Division Structure

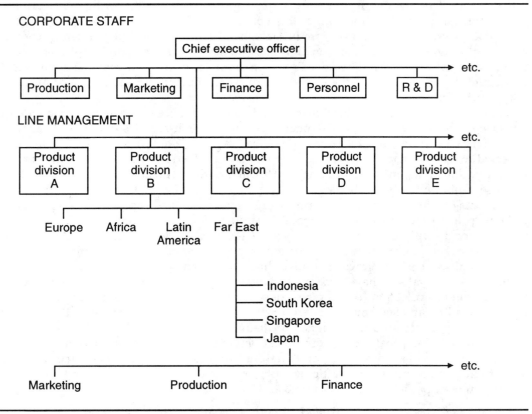

Source: Arvind V. Phatak, *International Dimensions of Management, Fourth Edition*, Cincinnati: South-Western Publishing Co., 1995, p. 161.

Each product division functions as a semiautonomous profit center. Divisional management has considerable decentralized authority to run the division because of the unique multinational environmental pressures under which it must operate. However, corporate headquarters provides an umbrella of companywide plans and corporate strategy. This umbrella provides both the protection and the constraints under which product divisions are expected to formulate divisional plans and strategy. A product division receives general functional support from staff groups at the corporate level, but at the divisional level it may also have its own functional staff, specialized to provide services tailored to the division's unique market situation. The product division head is given worldwide responsibility to develop and promote his or her product line.

When Is a Global Product Division the Best Choice? Conditions favoring this structure are as follows: the firm manufactures products that require different technologies and that have dissimilar end users; there is little use of common marketing tools and channels of distribution among the firm's products; there is a significant need to integrate production, marketing, and research related to the product; abroad, there is little need for local product knowledge and product adaptation; or the products involved need continuous technical service and inputs and a high level of technological capability, requiring, therefore, close coordination between divisional staff groups and production centers abroad.

Some products require close, product-oriented technological and marketing coordination between the home market affiliates and foreign affiliates. This interdependence between the home and foreign affiliates—the latter needing help from the former in matters pertaining to the production and promotion of the growth product in a foreign market—calls for products, and not markets, as the primary organizing dimension.[10]

In order to maximize the benefits of divisionalization based on a global product structure, a firm must be able to produce a standardized product that requires only minor modifications for individual markets, and for which world markets can be developed. Division managers are expected to take advantage of the structure to generate global economies of scale in production, resource acquisition, and market supply. This makes the structure particularly suited to firms that use capital-intensive technology.

The major advantages of this form of organization are the ease and directness of flow of technology and product knowledge from the divisional level to the foreign subsidiaries and back, which tends to put all facilities, regardless of location, on a comparable technological level. Additionally, the global product form preserves product emphasis and promotes product planning on a global basis, it provides a direct line of communications from the customer to those in the organization who have product knowledge and expertise, thus enabling research and development to work on the development of products that serve the needs of the world customer, and permits line and staff managers within the division to gain expertise in the technical and marketing aspects of products assigned to them.[11]

In addition, the global product division structure facilitates the coordination of domestic and foreign production facilities according to natural resource availability, local labor cost and skill level, tariff and tax regulations, shipping costs, and even climate, in order to produce the highest quality product possible at the lowest cost.

What Are the Drawbacks of a Global Product Division? There are several critical problems associated with a global product structure. One is the duplication of facilities and staff groups that takes place as each division develops its own infrastructure to support its operations in various regions and countries of the world. Another is that division managers may pursue geographic areas that offer immediate growth prospects for their products, and neglect other areas where the current prospects may not be as bright but may have a greater long-run potential. A far more serious problem is that of "motivating product division managers to pursue the international market when the preponderance of their current profits comes from domestic business and most of their experience has been domestic."[12]

International companies have tried to alleviate these difficulties by adopting a multidimensional structure, which we will discuss later in this chapter.

The Global Area Division

Firms abandoning the international division as a structure may also choose to coordinate their global operations by using area (or geography) as the dominant organizational dimension.

In the international division structure, the company's worldwide operations are grouped into two regions—domestic and international. Thus, in a way, the international division structure is also an area-based structure. But in a truly area-based global structure, the company's worldwide operations are grouped into several co-equal geographical areas, and the head of an area division is given line authority and responsibility over all affiliates in the area. There is no one fixed pattern for carving up the geographical areas. Obviously, each enterprise has its own circumstances and needs that determine how countries get grouped into regions. Factors such as locations of affiliates, customers, and sources of raw materials influence the grouping of countries into manageable geographic units.

The Domestic Market as One of Many   An area structure reflects a very significant change in the attitudes of top management towards international operations and the allocation of the company's resources. In the international division structure, the domestic/nondomestic bifurcation of the company's global operations reflects the point of view of top management that the domestic side of the business is as important as all the international operations together. The area structure embodies the attitude that the domestic market is just one of many markets in the world (see Figure 12-6).

The manager in charge of an area is responsible for the development of business in his or her region. However, his or her area plans and strategies have to be consistent with those of the company as a whole. Area managers and their counterparts participate in the formulation of companywide plans and strategies. Such participation in total company planning gives each area manager an appreciation of how his or her area operations and results fit with total company plans and performance.

When Is Global Area Division the Best Choice?   A global area structure is most suited to companies having the following characteristics: they are businesses with narrow product lines;

FIGURE 12-6
Global Area Division Structure

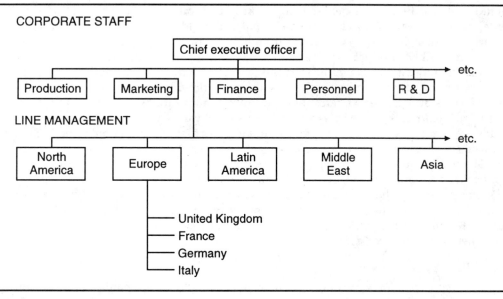

Source: Arvind V. Phatak, *International Dimensions of Management, Fourth Edition*, Cincinnati: South-Western Publishing Co., 1995, p. 164.

they have high levels of regional product differentiation; and they have the opportunity to attain high levels of economies of scale in production, marketing, and integrated resource procurement on a regional basis. Industries with these characteristics that favor a global area structure include pharmaceuticals, cosmetics, food, beverage, automotive, and container companies.

The principal advantage of an area structure is that the authority to make decisions is pushed down to the regional headquarters. This means that decisions on matters such as product adaptation, price, channels of distribution, and promotion can be made near the scene of action. For example, a company that makes soups, coffee, and prepared frozen foods must take into account regional and even country differences. The Italians and Turks like dark, bitter coffee, whereas Americans like the lighter and less bitter variety. The English like bland soups, whereas the French prefer those with a blend of mild spices. Different countries have different taste preferences. By and large the peoples of the Middle East and Asia like their foods spiced, whereas those in Europe and America like theirs bland. Information on such differences among regions and country markets can be considered at lower levels in the organizational hierarchy, which helps in the making of plans and strategies consistent with the existing regional and country conditions.

The other advantage of the area structure is that it promotes the finding of regional solutions to problems. Ideas and techniques that have worked in one country are easier to transfer to other countries in the region. And the area manager can resolve conflicts between subsidiaries by finding solutions that optimize the operations in the region as a whole. For example, when a new country market opens up, which subsidiary in the region is in the best position to serve it through exports? Conflicts could occur if more than one subsidiary attempts to export to the new market, but with the area structure, the area manager is in a position to resolve such problems.

What Are the Drawbacks of a Global Area Division? The main disadvantage of the area structure is the difficulty encountered in reconciling product emphasis with a geographically oriented management approach. This can be particularly difficult if the company's product line is diverse and if it has to be marketed through different types of distribution channels. Since a certain amount of product expertise has to be developed by the area unit, a duplication of product development and technical knowledge is often required. At the same time, there is an overlap of functional staff responsibilities with the worldwide headquarters. All of this adds to overhead costs and creates an additional tier of communications.

Other difficulties reported by executives in a study by the Conference Board are that "research and development programs are hard to coordinate, that global product planning is difficult, that there is no consistent effort to apply newly developed domestic products to international markets, and that introduction to the domestic market of products developed overseas is too slow, or simply that 'product knowledge is weak.'"[13]

In many respects, the advantages of a global area structure are the disadvantages of a global product division structure, and vice versa. The answer to the product/area dilemma may be in an organizational structure that incorporates in its authority, responsibility, and communications lines a blend of these two dimensions.

Global Functional Division

The functional division is not commonly used by international companies; however, one important exception is the extractive industry companies that extract oil or metals. In this form of organization, global operations are organized primarily on a functional basis and secondarily on an area or product basis, with marketing and production being the dominant functions. This structure is most appropriate for firms with narrow, standardized product lines for which product knowledge is the significant factor (see Figure 12-7).

The main advantages of this form of organization are these: there is an emphasis on functional acumen; it provides tight, centralized controls, requiring a relatively lean managerial staff, and it ensures that the power and prestige of the basic activities of the enterprise will be defended by the top managers. The disadvantages of the structure are the following: coordination of manufacturing and marketing in an area (for example, Europe) is problematic; multiple product lines can become difficult to manage because of the separation of production and marketing into departments with parallel lines of authority to the top of the hierarchy; and only the chief executive officer can be held accountable for the profits.

A variant of the global functional structure is the functional process structure used by the petroleum industry. Here, specialized functions such as exploration, crude production, tanker and pipeline transportation, refining (manufacturing), and marketing are organized and managed on a global basis through centralized functional departments. These global functional departments may, in turn, be divisionalized on a geographic area basis (see Figure 12-8). In the functional process structure, all oil exploration in the different regions is centralized under the control and direction of the specialized exploration department. Similarly, production of crude oil is managed by the production department. The transportation of crude oil to the refineries located in different countries, and the shipping of gasoline and other petroleum distillates such as kerosene, diesel oil, and lubricating oil to various world markets by railroads, ships, pipelines, and trucks, is coordinated by the transportation department. The marketing of petroleum products in world markets is the responsibility of the marketing department.

Companies that favor the global functional process structure are those that (1) need tight, centralized coordination and control of an integrated production process consisting of stages that

FIGURE 12-7
Global Functional Structure

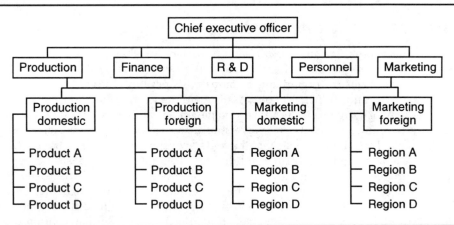

Source: Arvind V. Phatak, *International Dimensions of Management, Fourth Edition,* Cincinnati: South-Western Publishing Co., 1995, p. 166.

FIGURE 12-8
Global Functional Process Structure

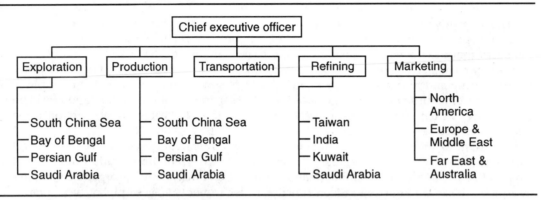

Source: Arvind V. Phatak, *International Dimensions of Management, Fourth Edition,* Cincinnati: South-Western Publishing Co., 1995, p. 167.

are carried out on a global basis and (2) are involved in a major way in transporting products and raw materials across national boundaries, and from one geographic area of the world to another.

A global functional structure has proved to be quite unstable; most companies that adopt it eventually have to abandon it, owing to the problems of integration of supply and distribution caused by a global dichotomy between production and sales. Commenting on the instability of this form of organizational structure, Stanley M. Davis says, "The lesson is, don't organize global structures around functions unless you are in extractive raw materials industries, and even then you will find that they are unstable and will have to share primacy with geographic factors and, in some instances, with product differences."[14]

MULTIDIMENSIONAL GLOBAL STRUCTURE

In deciding whether to organize on a functional, product, or area basis, managers of international companies must weigh the benefits of each against the costs. The particular dimension that is chosen as the primary basis for organizing a company's operations should be that which offers the best benefits/costs ratio. When one of these three dimensions—function, product, or area— is chosen as the primary organizational form, management still tries to utilize the advantages of the remaining two dimensions at lower levels in the structure. For example, a company that is organized on a product division basis may have its own functional staff at the divisional level, and each of the divisions may be further subdivided on a geographic basis. However, many international companies have found that none of the global structures discussed is a totally satisfactory means of organizing because some problems remain untouchable, and therefore unsolved. For instance, the problem of coordinating subsidiaries in different divisions on a regional basis in a global product division structure still remains. Similarly, in an organization based on global area, problems still occur in coordinating products on a global basis and across area division lines.

Some companies have attempted to cope with these problems by establishing product committees in area-based structures and area committees in product-based structures. Membership of such committees is comprised of divisional managers and staff specialists who are assigned the collective responsibility for coordinating transactions that cut across divisional lines.

Another alternative is to create staff positions for advisors and counselors. For instance, a product division structure might have area specialists for each of the major regions served by the company. These persons are given the task of exploring new opportunities and developing new markets for the company's products in their respective regions, thus maintaining the distinct advantages of the product structure without losing sight of the unique characteristics of each regional market. Similarly, in an area-based structure, the position of product manager would have responsibility for the coordination of the production and development of his or her product line across geographic areas.

In each of the preceding structural arrangements, there is an implicit assumption that an organizational structure can have only one dominant dimension. Because the advantages of the other dimensions are lost when only one is chosen, an attempt is sometimes made to correct the situation by overlaying the dominant dimension with some aspects of the others.

Some international companies are rejecting the notion that there must be a clear line of authority flowing from the top to the bottom in an organizational hierarchy—with a manager at a given level reporting to only one superior at the next highest level in hierarchy. This so-called principle of the unity of command has been cast aside by companies that have adopted what is known as the matrix structure. In a matrix, the organization avoids choosing one dimension over another as the basis for grouping its operations; instead it chooses two or more: "The foreign subsidiaries report simultaneously to more than one divisional headquarters; worldwide product divisions share with area divisions responsibility for the profits of the foreign subsidiaries."[15]

For instance, a subsidiary manager may report to an area manager as well as a product manager. In a pure product division or area structure, only the manager in charge of the dominant dimension has line authority over a foreign subsidiary in her or his unit. In a matrix structure, both product and area managers have some measure of line authority over the subsidiary. Thus the unity of command principle is abrogated in favor of a coordinating mechanism that considers differences in products and areas to be of equal importance. Firms using the matrix structure are attempting to integrate their operations across more than one dimension simultaneously (see Figure 12-9).

Firms should consider adopting the matrix structure if conditions such as the following exist.

- Substantial product and area diversification.
- Need to be responsive simultaneously to product and area demands.
- Constraints on resources requiring that they be shared by two or more divisions—product, area, or functional.
- Significant problems created and opportunities lost due to emphasis on just one dimension, product, or area.
- Formulation of corporate strategy requiring the simultaneous consideration of functional, product, and area concerns.

Adoption of a matrix structure requires a commitment on the part of top management, not only to the structure itself, but to the essential preparation required for it to be successful. Executive

FIGURE 12-9
The Matrix Structure

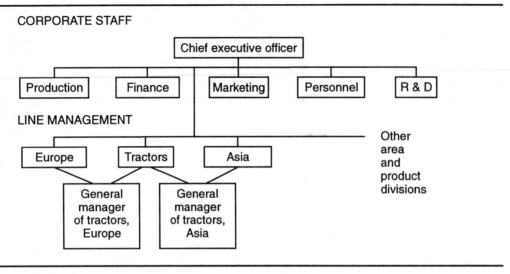

Source: Arvind V. Phatak, *International Dimensions of Management, Fourth Edition,* Cincinnati: South-Western Publishing Co., 1995, p. 169.

ground work must be laid; executives must understand how the system works, and those who report to two or more superior managers, such as the subsidiary managers, must be prepared to work through the initial confusion created by dual reporting relationships. As noted by Davis and Lawrence, a "matrix organization is more than a matrix structure. It must be reinforced by matrix systems such as dual control and evaluation systems, by leaders who operate comfortably with lateral decision making, and by a culture that can negotiate open conflict and a balance of power."[16] Thus, the mere adoption of a matrix structure does not create a matrix organization.

Adoption must be followed by some fundamental changes in technical systems and management behavior. Managers must recognize the need to resolve issues and choices at the lowest possible level, without referring them to a higher authority. A delicate balance of power must be maintained among managers face to face. A tilt in favor of one organizational dimension or another would cause the organization to fall back to the old single-dimensional, vertical hierarchy, with a resulting loss of the benefits of a matrix structure. Absence of cooperation between facing managers, even when a perfect power balance exists, could cause so many unresolved problems and disputes to be referred up the hierarchy that top management would become overloaded with interdivisional matters.

The benefits of a matrix structure flow directly from the conditions that induce enterprises to adopt it. A matrix organization can respond simultaneously to all environmental factors that are critical to its success. Decision-making authority can be decentralized to an appropriate level. Policy decisions are made in concert with people who have relevant information, and the design also facilitates a flow of information that promotes better planning and the implementation of plans.

The matrix structure does take time, effort, and commitment by executives to make it work. Although Peter Drucker says that it "will never be a preferred form of organization; it is fiendishly difficult," he nevertheless concludes that "any manager in a multinational business will have to learn to understand it if he wants to function effectively himself.[17]

An example of effective use of the matrix structure is that of ABB Asea Brown Boveri, the Swedish-Swiss diversified company that was created following the merger of Sweden's Asea and Switzerland's Brown Boveri. How the company has organized its matrix management structure is presented in *Practical Insight 12-1*.

PRACTICAL INSIGHT 12-1
Company Profile: GLOBAL HERO

When the electromechanical activities of Switzerland's BBC Brown Boveri merged with the Swedish engineering company ASEA in 1988, the newly forged giant received a mixed reception: applause for the swiftness and secrecy with which the deal was executed, skepticism over whether the instant conglomerate could work.

Four years later, the doubts have been replaced by almost universal admiration. ABB Asea Brown Boveri has 1,300 companies and 214,000 employees operating in 65 business areas in 140 countries. It is a world leader in the generation, transmission, and distribution of electricity, in industrial process automation, in systems and products for environmental control, and in rail transport systems. It is also a management model of a new type of conglomerate that achieves global reach through a network of deep local roots, a model from which other conglomerates, notably IBM, draw inspiration. "ABB is extremely focused," says research analyst Martin Neusome of Goldman Sachs in London. "It knows what it wants to be and goes about it very quickly."

The helmsman who has steered ABB through its great leap forward is its president and chief executive, Percy Barnevik, a lean and bearded Swede who was formerly managing director of ASEA . . . . .

His strategy for ABB is based on three internal contradictions. "We want to be global and local, big and small, radically decentralized with centralized reporting and control," he says . . . . .

Barnevik manages this many-tentacled operation by way of a matrix system. A 12-member executive committee, which he heads, sets strategy and reviews the performance of the whole. Each committee member manages one of eight business segments—power plants, power transmission, power distribution, transportation, industry, environmental control, financial services, and a miscellaneous segment, called 'various activities,' which embraces robotics and telecommunications—and/or a country or region. Each reports to the group at meetings held every three weeks in a different country. At the same time a centralized reporting system, named Abacus, collects performance data on the company's 5,000 profit centres, compares them with budgets and forecasts, converts them into dollars to enable cross-border analyses, and consolidates or breaks them down by segment, country, and local company.

The group is then divided vertically by business area and horizontally by country. Business area leaders set the rules on a global level, determining strategy, organization, manufacturing and product development. They also allocate export markets to specific factories. Country managers run line operations, establishing balance sheets and income statements and administering their own career ladders, while fulfilling their obligation to respect ABB's worldwide objectives—not always an easy task, Barnevik admits. "Thirty of the companies we have bought had been around for more than 100 years," he says. "We have to convince country managers that they gain more than they lose when they give up some autonomy." Answering to both business area managers and country managers are the bosses of the myriad local companies.

"The only way to structure a complex, global organization is to make it as simple and local as possible," Barnevik says. "ABB is complicated from where I sit, but on the ground, where the real work gets done, all our operations must function as closely as possible to stand-alone operations. I don't expect most of our people to have global mindsets, to do things that hurt their business but are 'good for ABB'." . . . . .

The ambiguity of evolving a multi-cultural environment with a multiple management structure is a further problem, raising the possibility of conflict or confusion. "The matrix management does not dissolve centrifugal forces within a company," says Miles Saltiel, a research analyst at the Nomura Research Institute in London. To avoid such confusion, ABB has set out its values in a 40-page booklet. They include ethics, individual responsibility and initiative and, crucially, openness to foreign cultures. "The goal is to accept them," Gasser says. "The challenge is to live up to them." . . . . . .

Source: Romy Joyce, "Global Hero," *International Management*, September 1992, pp. 82 and 85.

THE IMPACT OF STRATEGY ON ORGANIZATION STRUCTURE

One of the main purposes of an organization structure is to serve as a vehicle for the implementation of the firm's strategy. An organization structure must facilitate information flows vertically, horizontally, and diagonally throughout the length and breadth of an enterprise in support of managerial decision making and implementation of strategic plans. A structure that is not in tune with the strategy that it is supposed to help implement must be replaced by one that does. There are numerous examples of companies that have reorganized in response to a change in company strategies. We shall examine a few of them in the following.

With the objective of bringing costs down and catering more effectively to a global clientele, IBM has reorganized its marketing and sales operations into fourteen worldwide industry groups overseen by an umbrella unit called Industry Solutions. The fourteen groups are communications, utilities, travel, cross-industry, distribution, process, education, finance, government, petroleum, health, insurance, manufacturing, and transportation. The new units are intended to make it easier for customers to deal with IBM on a global basis and to increase "mass customization" of industry-specific computer products and services. In making this change in the structure, IBM is moving away from a structure based on geography to one that is focused on industry and the customer. As an example, under the new industry-based structure, IBM serves the global needs of Chase Manhattan Bank—one of its largest customers—by funneling all of Chase's business through a single, industry-savvy sales representative in the finance and banking group.

The new industry structure has eliminated the once highly decentralized country operations, each complete with a chairman and board, sales force, financial staff, technical experts in various operations, and total control over all aspects of the country operations. The new structure has greatly reduced the clout of country and regional managers. Each region, e.g., IBM Europe, will now have industry sector teams. Each industry sector team will have the responsibility of serving clients within a region most effectively. The new structure transforms IBM from a checkerboard of competing fiefdoms to a more streamlined, global organization. The main goal of the reorganization is to globalize control over product development, sales, and marketing. Before, it was nearly impossible for global companies to do business with IBM as a single entity. Now, a single contract could be drawn up to serve a customer globally. In moving away from a geographic organization structure, IBM hopes to eliminate turf wars and make itself more responsive to customer needs.[18]

It is appropriate to make the connection between the strategy of complex global integration of Ford and the structural changes that were brought about by this strategy. As was explained in Practical Insight 9-2 in Chapter 9, the Ford Motor Company has merged its product development, manufacturing, and sales in North America and Europe into one organization. And in a move towards a more horizontal structure, five vehicle platform centers have been created with worldwide responsibility to develop new cars and trucks. In the very near future Latin America and Asia are expected to merge with the new organization. The goal of Ford is to combine the global auto operations into a single global company. The new organization structure of Ford was created in response to its strategy of integrating its once disparate operations in North America and Europe into a single integrated operation. The goal of this strategy is to achieve efficiency through economies of scale, and through sharing learning and knowledge flows between the two regions.

The growth and development of regional trade blocs have given birth to regional headquarters. The regional headquarters are physically located in one country within a region and are responsible for coordinating the operations of all affiliates within a region, as well as for implementing the parent company's product, manufacturing, marketing, and other functional strategies for each business in its portfolio for the region. Several American and Japanese companies have established regional headquarters in Europe to coordinate the operations of affiliates that were established in anticipation of the single unified European common market. Several others have set up similar regional headquarters in Asia, the Pacific Basin, and North America. For example, Quaker Oats has set up a European headquarters in Brussels, and Hitachi, Nissan, Sony, and Toshiba all have regional headquarters in both North America and Europe.

Many companies move the headquarters of important business units abroad because they want the decision-making authority to be close to key customers and tough competitors in dynamic markets far from home. This is especially true of diversified companies who acknowledge that they cannot effectively manage all of their worldwide businesses, some of which are far away from home, from one single location. For example, American Telephone and Telegraph has located the headquarters for its corded telephone business in France. Examples of other companies that have followed suit are presented in Exhibit 12-1.

Several companies have established functional headquarters outside their home countries that specialize in carrying out a particular function such as marketing, research, manufacturing, or procurement for the entire company or for all affiliates in a certain region. Here the strategy is to gain efficiency and lower costs in performing a particular function through economies of scale, exploiting country-based advantages such as cheap labor or highly skilled workers, and improvements that accrue by way of learning that occurs from performing an activity over a period of time—also known as the learning or experience curve. Swissair has all its revenue accounting done by a Bombay-based affiliate, Airline Financial Services India. ITT, an American firm, has centralized paper buying in Belgium for the yellow-page directories which it produces in eight countries.[19]

EXHIBIT 12-1
Moving the Home Base to Foreign Soil

Some multinational corporations moving global headquarters of major business units overseas:

COMPANY	HOME COUNTRY	NEW LOCATION	OPERATION SHIFTED	YEAR MOVED
AT&T	U.S.	France	Corded telephones	1992
Du Pont	U.S.	Japan	Electronics	1992
Hyundai Electronics Industries	South Korea	U.S.	Personal computers	1992
IBM	U.S.	U.K.	Networking systems	1991
Siemens	Germany	U.K.	Air-traffic management	1991
Siemens	Germany	U.S.	Ultrasound equipment	1991
Du Pont	U.S.	Switzerland	Agricultural products, and parts of fibers and polymers businesses	1991
Hewlett-Packard	U.S.	France	Desktop personal computers	1990
Siemens	Germany	U.S.	Nuclear-medicine products and radiation-therapy equipment	1989
Cadbury Schweppes	U.K.	U.S.	Beverages	1987*
Du Pont	U.S.	Switzerland	Lycra business	1987

Moved back to London in 1991.
Note: Every relocated operation previously had its headquarters in same country as parent company.

Source: Joann S. Lubin, "Firms Ship Unit Headquarters Abroad," *The Wall Street Journal*, December 9, 1992, p. B1. Reprinted by permission of The Wall Street Journal, © 1992 Dow Jones & Company, Inc. All Rights Reserved Worldwide.

The examples of companies such as IBM, Ford, Quaker Oats, Hitachi, Nissan, Sony, Toshiba, American Telephone and Telegraph, Swissair, and ITT illustrate the association between strategy and structure of a company. As a company changes its strategies, its priorities change as well. This in turn requires that the company's organization be changed as well in order to coordinate and bring to the forefront the most important tasks that need to be effectively performed in order to implement the strategy. There has been a debate among scholars in the international business field whether strategy determines organization structure, or whether, in fact, structure determines the strategy of a company. Undoubtedly, the current organization structure distributes authority and power to people within the command structure of the company. To the extent that structure distributes power to people who determine company strategy, structure does influence the strategy of the company. However, once the strategy is set by management, the structure does need to be changed if it does not effectively help in implementing the company's strategy.

In this discussion on the organization of the international firm, we have focused on the way the company configures its internal organizational subunits to best accomplish its strategic objectives. However, no matter how well the organizational structure fits the firm's strategy, a good structure does not, by itself, guarantee success—another essential component is the people who fill out the structure. Personnel and staffing are important concerns of the international manager, and in the next chapter we examine some of the problems associated with international staffing, along with the issue of compensation.

SUMMARY

This chapter was concerned with the typical stages in the evolution of the basic structures of international companies. Six organizational patterns were discussed: the pre-international division phase, international division structure, global product division structure, global area division structure, global functional division structure, and the multidimensional global structure. Reasons for the adoption of each of these organizational types, as well as the advantages and disadvantages of each, were explained.

Finding the organizational structure best suited to a company's global corporate strategy is a challenge that an international company's top management executives must meet effectively and efficiently. The imperative to coordinate the three dimensions—function, product, and area— has created problems and tensions in the internal transactions and management of international companies. Companies usually modify the structures and make tradeoffs among the various approaches while attempting to integrate their geographically far-flung operations.

Another challenge facing international company managers is that, after finding a suitable structure for a particular global corporate strategy at a certain point in time, they must keep modifying the structure to suit evolving company strategy as well. This requirement for change is ever present in international enterprises.

QUESTIONS FOR THOUGHT AND DISCUSSION

1. Discuss the salient features of the international division structure. What factors are responsible for its adoption by an international company?

2. How does a global product division differ from a global area division? What conditions favor the adoption of each of these structures?

3. Why is the matrix structure adopted by international companies? What are the advantages of the matrix structure? What conditions must accompany the adoption of a matrix in order for it to be successful in an organization?

4. What is the relationship between an international company's strategy and its organizational structure? Describe how changes in a company's strategic objectives might change its structure.

MINI-CASE
Digital Shows Doctrine the Door

When Digital Equipment's chief executive announced last week that the company was taking yet another huge charge against earnings in yet another effort to revive the staggering computer giant, he also announced an end to the company's decades-old management system.

"Matrix management at our company is dead," Robert B. Palmer, Digital's president and chief executive, told reporters. "For Digital, that statement is monumental."

Monumental indeed. "Matrix management" may sound like some business school arcana. But many people inside and outside Digital say the system of management by consensus has sapped energy and efficiency from product development efforts. They also see it as a leading factor in Digital's $4 billion of losses over the last four years, a figure that does not include the $200 million fourth-quarter loss Digital is expected to report next week.

The Urge to Streamline

And so, Mr. Palmer is putting in place a system that makes his top executives more clearly accountable for the success or failure of their divisions. No more interminable meetings before making any decisions. No more need to delay a customer's call for help while tracking down someone in marketing, engineering, manufacturing, or sales authorized to supply an answer.

And no more of the other forms of consensus building that may have once helped Digital become the nation's second-largest computer maker but more recently have been seen as reducing the company to a plodding, unfocused giant in an industry where speed and flexibility are now keys to success.

Analysts blame the matrix organization, at least in part, for leaving Digital poorly positioned in several crucial markets. These include personal computers, work stations based on cutting-edge RISC chips, and computers using the industry-standard Unix software operating system.

To be sure, Digital is taking other steps to right itself besides dropping matrix. It plans to cut 20,000 jobs in the next twelve months. And yesterday, as part of its effort to focus on its core computer systems and components business, Digital said it was selling its disk drive operations to the Quantum Corporation for $400 million.

But the move that may fundamentally change Digital more than any step the company has taken since Kenneth H. Olsen founded it in 1957 is the decision to scrap Mr. Olsen's cherished matrix management.

"This is not a shift in boxes on an organizational chart," said Enrico Pesatori, whom Mr. Palmer promoted to vice president of the newly formed computer systems division, which encompasses 90 percent of Digital's business. "This is a total redesign of the core business of Digital."

It was Mr. Pesatori who helped Digital play catch-up in the personal computer business, turning the company into one of the fastest growing suppliers of desktop machines in just two years. And he did that by operating outside the matrix structure, overseeing his own engineering, manufacturing, sales, and marketing.

As practiced at Digital, matrix management was characterized by strong functional groups like engineering, sales, marketing, and manufacturing. Constellations of these groups would form around the business units whose job it was to design and develop products—often in competition with one another.

When Mr. Olsen started the matrix system in 1964, the seven-year-old Digital was an $11 million adolescent. He was looking for a way to keep up with the rapid growth that would turn the company, based in Maynard, Mass., into the international power that had $14 billion in sales and 130,000 employees at its peak in 1989.

For years the pace of change in the industry was slow enough to allow for Mr. Olsen's matrix bureaucracy. Digital was able to turn out innovative products, like the PDP minicomputer in the 1960s, and its successor, the VAX, which reigned throughout the 1980s and still provided the bulk of Digital's declining sales.

But by the time Mr. Palmer arrived in 1985 to head Digital's semiconductor operations, matrix was already a management style out of step with the industry. No wonder Mr. Palmer spent his first several months at the company inadvertently offending other Digital managers.

"It never occurred to me to check with a manufacturing person in the Scotland plant about a decision I was making," he said. "I remember Ken Olsen telling me how few from outside survive. He said to me, 'You probably won't survive either.'"

More Than Survival

Mr. Palmer not only survived his tenuous start, he eventually mastered Digital's disconcerting culture enough to end up as Mr. Olsen's successor as president and chief executive when Mr. Olsen was forced out two years ago by Digital's board.

Now, having labored unsuccessfully since then to return the company to profitability, Mr. Palmer has decided to abandon the system. Some analysts have criticized Mr. Palmer for taking too long to kill matrix. Others wonder whether, with matrix management so deeply ingrained in Digital's culture, the changes can be made quickly enough to revive the $143 billion company.

"I don't know why he didn't do this two years ago," George Colony, president of Forrester Research in Cambridge, Mass., said. "He's making moves that were obvious moves two years ago."

In any case, Mr. Colony and many other analysts agree that Mr. Palmer now sits in a very hot seat, with the Digital board nearing the limit of its patience. It will be crucial, they say, for Mr. Palmer to make good on his stated hope that the company can become profitable by the year's end.

Mr. Palmer, in an interview on Monday, said matrix management was the reason Digital's costs exceeded those of its competitors. "Each engineering group required someone to work with manufacturing, deciding where it will be build, how it will be built, negotiating with the plants," he said. "There's an enormous amount of internal decision making, and at the end of the day, customers won't pay for that."

Terry Shannon, an analyst with Illuminata, a consulting firm in Hollis, N.H., said the matrix legacy had hurt Digital in the technology on which the company intended to build its future: the Alpha AXP chip, based on an approach known as RISC, for reduced instruction set computing.

Mr. Shannon lauded Digital's engineering efforts on Alpha AXP technology, which since late 1992 has made its way into a broad range of high-powered personal computers, work stations, and network "server" computers. But because matrix management has parceled responsibility for Alpha out among various product groups, there has been too much infighting and "they've never really had a clear, coherent Alpha marketing strategy," Mr. Shannon said.

All that is supposed to change, if Mr. Pesatori can carry out Mr. Palmer's no-matrix mandate.

Mr. Pesatori said his division would forgo internal debate to focus on one goal: profitability. He intends to break the division into three units—personal computers, larger computer systems, and a client accounts group handling the 1,000 largest customers.

And as part of the overall job cuts previously announced by Digital, Mr. Pesatori said he planned to cut 14,000 workers from the computer systems division's 35,000 within twelve months.

Source: Glenn Rifkin, "Digital Shows Doctrine the Door," *The New York Times*, July 20, 1994, pp. D1 and D6. Copyright © 1994 by The New York Times Company. Reprinted by permission.

Discussion Questions for Mini-Case

1. What are the principal reasons cited in the case for the scrapping of matrix management at Digital?

2. Is matrix management suited for small and medium-sized companies, but not in large companies?

3. Why did matrix prove to be effective in ABB Asea Brown Boveri (Practical Insight 12-1) but not in Digital?

4. What role does the company president play in making the matrix management work in a company?

Notes

1 Raymond Vernon and Louis T. Wells, Jr., *Manager in the International Economy*, 3rd ed., Prentice-Hall, Englewood Cliffs, N.J., 1976, p. 31.

2 Michael G. Duerr and John M. Roach, *Organization and Control of International Operations*, The Conference Board, New York, 1973, p. 5.

3 Stanley Davis, "Basic Structures of Multinational Corporations," in Stanley Davis, Ed., *Managing and Organizing Multinational Corporations*, Pergamon Press, New York, 1979, p. 202.

4 Gilbert H. Clee and Wilbur M. Sachjan, "Organizing a Worldwide Business," *Harvard Business Review*, Vol. 42, No. 6, November-December 1964, p. 60.

5 Business International, *Organizing the Worldwide Corporation*, Research Report No. 69-4, Business International, New York, 1970, p. 9.

6 John M. Stopford and Louis T. Wells, Jr., *Managing the Multinational Enterprise*, Basic Books, New York, 1972, p. 51.

7 Stanley M. Davis, "Trends in the Organization of Multinational Corporations," *Columbia Journal of World Business*, Summer 1976, p. 60.

8 Peter J. Dowling, Randall S. Schuler, and Denice E. Welch, *International Dimensions of Human Resource Management*, Wadsworth Publishing Company, Belmont, California, 1994, p. 27.

9 Davis, "Basic Structures," p. 203.

10 Ibid., p. 205.

11 Arvind V. Phatak, *Managing Multinational Corporations*, Praeger Publishers, New York, 1974, p. 183.

12 Duerr and Roach, p. 12.

13 Ibid., p. 10.

14 Davis, "Trends in the Organization," p. 66.

15 Stopford and Wells, p. 87.

16 Stanley M. Davis and Paul R. Lawrence, "Problems of Matrix Organizations," *Harvard Business Review*, May-June 1978, p. 4.

17 Peter Drucker, *Management: Tasks, Responsibilities, Practices*, Harper & Row, New York, 1974, p. 598.

18 Bruce Caldwell, "Industrious IBM?" *Informationweek*, May 23, 1994, p. 15; Ira Sager, "Big Blue Wants the World to Know Who's Boss," *Business Week*, September 26, 1994, p. 78.

19 "...and Other Ways to Peel the Onion," *The Economist*, January 7, 1995, p. 52.

Further Reading

Clee, Gilvert H., and Wilbur M. Sachtjan, "Organizing a Worldwide Business," *Harvard Business Review*, Vol. 42, No. 6, November-December 1964.

Davis, Stanley M., "Trends in the Organization of Multinational Corporations," *Columbia Journal of World Business*, Summer 1976.

——*Managing and Organizing Multinational Corporations*, Pergamon Press, New York, 1979.

Davis, Stanley M., and Paul R. Lawrence, "Problems of Matrix Organizations," *Harvard Business Review*, May-June 1978.

Denali, Jacquelyn, "Keeping Growth Under Control," *Nation's Business*, Vol. 81, No. 7, July 1993, pp. 31-32.

Drucker, Peter, *Management: Tasks, Responsibilities, Practices*, Harper & Row, New York, 1974.

Duerr, Michael G., and John M. Roach, *Organization and Control of International Operations*, The Conference Board, New York, 1973.

Goggin, William C., "How the Multidimensional Structure Works at Dow Corning," *Harvard Business Review*, January-February 1974.

Organizing the Worldwide Corporation, Research Report No. 69-4. Business International, New York, 1970.

Phatak, Arvind V., *Managing Multinational Corporations*, Praeger Publishers, New York, 1974.

"Stages of Global Development," *Chief Executive*, Jan/Feb 1993, pp. 6-9.

Stopford, John M., and Louis T. Wells, Jr., *Managing the Multinational Enterprise*, Basic Books, New York, 1972.

Vernon, Raymond, and Louis T. Wells, Jr., *Manager in the International Economy*, 4th ed., Prentice-Hall, Englewood Cliffs, N.J., 1981.

Vincent, Edgar, "Developing Managers for an International Business," *Journal of Management Development*, Vol. 7, No. 6, 1988, pp. 14-20.

International Human Resources Management

LEARNING OBJECTIVES

After completing this chapter, you will be able to:

- Identify the three main sources from which the international company can draw its pool of managers and describe the pros and cons of each source.

- Discuss the important characteristics for success in a foreign assignment and the methods international companies use to select managers for foreign assignment.

- Explain the role of training programs in preparing managers for foreign assignments and describe the subject areas such programs should address.

- Explain why repatriation plans are an important aspect of managing international staff and suggest elements that a repatriation plan should include.

- Define the ethnocentric, polycentric, and geocentric attitudes and the types of staffing decisions that are associated with each.

- Describe the problems associated with international executive compensation and the different forms that salary differential mechanisms may take.

- Discuss the advantages and disadvantages of global stock option plans as a means of compensating international management staff.

In this chapter we shall take an overview of the human resources management process in an international company. This is a very important topic which has been covered in depth in several books on the subject.* Our intent in this chapter is to examine the salient features of topics in this area that an international manager must be familiar with.

As the international business involvement of a company increases, so too does its need for well-qualified executives who are willing and able to manage abroad. Not everyone who has been successful as a manager in one country can be successful in another. It takes a person with a unique set of characteristics to succeed in diverse foreign environments.

---

* For an excellent coverage of the various issues involved in international human resource management, the reader is directed to Peter J. Dowling, Randall S. Schuler, and Denice E. Welch, *International Dimensions of Human Resource Management,* Wadsworth Publishing Company, Belmont, California, 1994.

Many costly managerial failures abroad can be avoided by the use of effective selection methods and predeparture training programs. Frequently, good managers who are good candidates refuse to go abroad on managerial assignments because they fear that a foreign stint might have a negative impact on their career paths. To eliminate this problem, companies need a planned and communicable program for the repatriation of the manager who serves abroad. A sound international executive compensation program is another essential component of an international staffing program. Thus, in this chapter we will also examine the main features of compensation for foreign assignments.

THE EXPANSION OF INTERNATIONAL STAFFING

With the growth of companies' global ambitions, the ranks of "international executives"—i.e., executives who are sent abroad to work in foreign markets—have been increasing. For example, Nynex Corporation has seen the number of U.S. executives overseas increase from zero in 1988 to more than one hundred. General Motors has more than 500 U.S. managers overseas.[1] It is estimated that several thousand U.S. managers are now working abroad. The situation in European and Japanese companies is no different. The number of expatriate managers is bound to increase as more and more companies—not only from the United States, Europe, and Japan, but also from the newly industrializing countries like South Korea, Taiwan, Singapore, Malaysia, Thailand, and India—spread their "business wings" to cover foreign markets. And the demand for international executives should continue to increase as the once-closed markets of China, Russia, India, and the countries that were part of the former Soviet Union continue to open their doors wider to foreign investments and trade.

An assignment abroad is now considered by managers to be the fast track to senior management positions. Companies like Gerber and Gillette emphasize foreign assignments as part of normal career development for executives. The experience of working abroad is seen by managers as an asset that sets them apart and gives them an edge over colleagues who have no such experience. This is a far different attitude to foreign assignments than existed among U.S. executives a decade or so ago. Up until the late 1980s, the focus of American businesses was on the booming domestic markets. International companies routinely sent executives abroad, but they returned home only to find that their foreign experience was not fully appreciated by the home office executive staff, whose attention was mainly devoted to implementing a predominantly domestic strategy. As a result, many managers concluded that a foreign assignment was a career killer.

That attitude has changed with the growing globalization of industries and companies, and the importance attached to success in foreign markets as a prerequisite for success in one's domestic business. As a consequence of this attitudinal change towards foreign markets, companies look to place their very best managers in key foreign markets, and they search for the top talent at home and abroad. As executives at companies like General Motors, Ford, General Electric, and Procter & Gamble, with years of experience abroad, move into top management positions, they are changing the image of a successful executive. Now, the road to the top of the organizational hierarchy zigzags through one or more foreign assignments.

SOURCES OF MANAGERS

There are three main sources from which managers can be recruited to fill international management positions, both in the headquarters and in the foreign subsidiaries. They are home country nationals, host country nationals, and third-country nationals. Home (or parent) country nationals are the citizens of the country in which the headquarters of the multinational company is based. Citizens of the country that is hosting a foreign subsidiary are the host country nationals. Third-country nationals are the citizens of a country other than the parent or the host country—for example, a French executive working in a German subsidiary of an American multinational company. Most multinational corporations use all three sources for staffing their international operations, although some companies exhibit a distinct bias for one of the three types.

Home Country Nationals as Managers

Historically, multinational companies have had the tendency to staff the key positions in their foreign affiliates with home country nationals. Some classic reasons include the unavailability of host country nationals having the required managerial or technical expertise; the desire to provide the company's more promising managers with international experience and thereby equip them for more responsible positions; the need to maintain and facilitate organizational coordination and control; the company's view of the foreign operation as short-lived; the host country's multiracial population, which might mean that selecting a manager of any one race would result in political or social problems; the company's conviction that it must maintain a foreign image in the host country; and the belief of some companies that a home country manager is the best person for the job.[2]

Research has shown that the most important motives for staffing foreign subsidiary management positions with home country nationals are (1) their technical expertise and (2) during the start-up phase it is considered advantageous to have them there.[3] In a newly acquired subsidiary, the desire to ensure that the foreign subsidiary complies with overall company objectives and policies induces headquarters to staff it at the top with a home country national.

Third-Country Nationals as Managers

Although the data on third-country nationals are not as extensive as those on home and host country nationals, the main advantages for using them are their technical expertise and the belief that the third-country national is the best person for the job.[4]

U.S. corporations tend to use third-country nationals only from advanced countries. The selection criteria for third-country nationals are identical to those applied in the selection of home country nationals for foreign assignments. However, the company's final objectives for the two types of international managers are often different. In the case of the home country manager, most often the objective is to train and develop the manager for a top management position in parent company headquarters. But for a third-country national, a top management position at the subsidiary is usually envisioned as the ultimate goal in the manager's career development.

There are advantages and disadvantages in employing third-country nationals. One advantage is that the salary and benefit requirements of a third-country national may be significantly less than those of home country nationals. However, the salary scales for the two groups are approaching parity—reflecting the rapidly evolving management salary structure in many industrialized countries, particularly those of western Europe. This equalizing trend applies particularly to third-country nationals working in regional or international division headquarters.[5]

Another advantage of the third-country national is that he or she may be better informed about the host environment. For example, the candidate may speak the host country's language—such as a Belgian who could work in France easily because French is the language spoken in both countries. Or a candidate's country may have a special relationship with the nation in which the subsidiary is located. Thus a French citizen could adapt fairly readily to working in the Ivory Coast. For these reasons, many American companies have hired English or Scottish executives for top management positions in their subsidiaries in countries that were former British colonies, such as Jamaica, India, and Kenya.

Two distinct drawbacks may arise from the use of third-country nationals. First, in certain parts of the world, animosities of a national character exist between neighboring countries—for example, India and Pakistan, Greece and Turkey. Transfers of third-country nationals must take such factors into account because an oversight in this area could be disastrous. The second disadvantage is associated with the desire of the governments of developing countries to upgrade their own people into responsible managerial positions. It is often more palatable to these governments to accept a home country national than to accept a third-country national, even though the third-country national might be better qualified for the position.

Host Country Nationals as Managers

Most multinational corporations use host country nationals in middle- and lower-level management positions in their foreign subsidiaries located in developing countries. This may be because local law requires that they do so. But perhaps the corporation would fill all managerial positions with host country nationals if there were not a scarcity of managers with the necessary qualifications for top jobs. In any event, it would be very difficult to staff the numerous middle-level positions totally with foreigners, even if local legislation permitted it.

When it comes to top management positions, the picture is not clear. Massey-Ferguson's Thornbrough asserts that "for all the talk, some North American companies still have the specific, rigid policy that key people in units abroad must be American."[6] This charge is refuted by a number of executives in other companies. The assistant general manager of the International Department at DuPont, David Cronklin, states, "Nationals head about half of our wholly owned subsidiaries in Europe, and in only three of our eleven Latin-American subsidiaries are there American top executives on a long-term basis."[7] George Young, who is vice president for international operations at Abbott Laboratories, says, "Abbott starts out by hiring [host country] nationals for foreign operations. Second choice is third-country nationals. Third preference is Americans. Out of 5,000 employees overseas there are maybe three or four Americans at most."[8]

An important factor in determining to what extent host country nationals are selected for management positions is the increasing pressure by some governments for foreign firms to expedite the "nativization" of management. This pressure takes the form of sophisticated government persuasion through administrative or legislative decrees. For example, Brazil requires that two-thirds of the employees in a Brazilian subsidiary be Brazilian nationals, and there are pressures on multinationals to staff upper-management positions in Brazilian subsidiaries with Brazilian nationals. In response to such pressure, many multinational corporations are subscribing to a policy similar to that described by a Standard Oil Company executive:

> While in the past we did employ substantial numbers of people for assignment overseas on a career basis, today, in keeping with our policy of utilizing nationals of the host country to the maximum extent possible, our practice is to assign domestic North American employees on a relatively short-term transfer or loan basis.[9]

Research by Rosalie Tung on U.S. multinational corporations throws more light on the staffing of foreign subsidiaries. She found that U.S. multinational corporations have a tendency to use host country nationals at all levels of management to a much greater extent in the more advanced regions of the world than in the less advanced regions. This may be understandable, considering that the advanced countries are more likely to have a large pool of trained personnel with the necessary qualifications to occupy managerial positions. The executives in the survey said that the most important reasons for hiring host country nationals were (1) their familiarity with the local culture and language, (2) the lower costs incurred in hiring them as compared to home or third-country nationals, and (3) the improved public relations that resulted from such a practice.[10]

There are other reasons as well for the hiring of host country nationals to manage foreign subsidiaries. For instance, host country managers are believed to be more effective in dealing with local employees and clients than their foreign counterparts because they adhere to local patterns of management. There is also greater continuity of management because host country nationals tend to stay longer in their positions than managers from other countries. But more important is the avoidance of low morale that results when host country managers are not given opportunities to move into upper-management positions. The following argument by an Italian manager in a U.S. multinational company's subsidiary in Italy illustrates this point:

> We feel we are the hurt and wounded part of Italian management. In an earlier time having . . . [Americans] here as managers was a good idea. As we have now developed our own management skills, some of those early advantages have disappeared. The right philosophy hasn't taken hold . . . [and] the long hand of the parent is now a bad idea. I insist we who have been in the company ten, fifteen, or more years should have as much of the parent's confidence as do American managers. They sometimes come in here in fact for the . . . reason of stopping in Italy as birds of passage on their way to brilliant careers with the parent.[11]

The Immigrant Expatriate

A variation of the host country national is a group of managers whom we shall label as the *immigrant expatriate*. An immigrant is a person who has legally emigrated from his or her country of birth to another country. An immigrant may or may not have taken the citizenship of the adoptive country in which he or she has assumed a permanent resident status. For example, most immigrants assume the citizenship of the United States; however, there are thousands of immigrants who are permanent residents in the United States, but who are not citizens and therefore are still legally the citizens of other countries.

International companies have discovered that the well-educated professional immigrants from foreign countries can serve as a rich reservoir of managerial talent for foreign assignments, especially those involving a return to the immigrants' motherland. Empirical evidence suggests that with the opening up of markets in China and India, international companies have begun to tap into the huge immigrant pool of U.S.-trained and educated professionals from those countries for managerial and technical assignments "back home." Most Chinese and Indian immigrants are sent to China and India to spearhead the development of a new business venture in those countries. Generally companies prefer to recruit Indians or Chinese professionals initially for entry-level or middle-management jobs in the parent company, with the understanding that they would eventually be sent to work in their respective mother countries. A year or two of work experience in the parent company is designed to give the potential international executive an understanding of the company's culture, policies, business functions, and practices. Yet another incentive—and a very strong one—to hire a professional immigrant is the ease with which he or she can transcend the cultural barriers separating the adoptive and mother countries.

We call this group of immigrant professionals "immigrant expatriates" because most managers in this category have as a goal to return to the adoptive country (e.g., the United States) after an extended stay in the mother country. Some do come back to the adoptive country, and others do not. However, the goal of eventually returning to the adoptive country is an important factor that separates this group of international managers from the host country cadre of managers. *Practical Insight 13-1* illustrates the phenomenon of the Indian immigrant expatriates.

PRACTICAL INSIGHT 13-1
The Indian Immigrant Expatriate

For most American companies with Indian interests, the expatriates are the natural choice for an Indian assignment, combining as they do the American result-oriented approach with Indian savvy—which are equally important for the success of a foreign enterprise in India.

While local managerial talent is available in India, companies prefer non-resident Indian (NRI)* executives who have trained and worked in America to take over key Indian posts because they can communicate with both the head office and the Indian staff.

Prakash Chandra, chairman of the Silicon Valley Indian Professionals Association, whose members are California-based Indian computer professionals, said: "Such a combination is essential for starting a venture in a country where the language, culture, and environment are very different."

It was for this reason that IBM chose its foreign-born executives to pilot its establishments in Latin America, Hong Kong, and Singapore, Chandra said.

Familiar with Local Conditions

P. K. Basu, who monitors South Asian countries for the world economic forecasters, WEFA, agreed. "The reason why multinational companies tend to send NRI executives to India," he said, "is that they feel expatriates understand local conditions, markets, and dynamics better."

"This is natural," Basu said. "In ventures of the U.S. companies in Taiwan, Taiwanese executives have been sent, and in the Chinese ventures Chinese executives have been assigned."

Polly Howes, a Coca-Cola spokeswoman, said: "Within Coca-Cola we move the people in the system as new positions come up. They can be sent anywhere in the world."

Matching People with Tasks

"One of the key considerations," she said, "has always been to match the people with the best possible qualifications wherever a position opens up. Several veteran Coca-Cola employees who are natives of India were chosen to work in Coca-Cola's new offices in India, and that is based on their business background and experience within the system."

Several NRI executives working for the company have gone to India, but Howes declined to say how many. She said their assignments spread across the board, from marketing to administration to other general activities.

She emphasized, however, that Coca-Cola operates in 195 countries and has employees of various nationalities, and that company policy for selecting somebody for a particular position is guided purely by merit, and that nationality is not the most important thing.

---

* A non-resident Indian (NRI) is classified by the Indian government as a person of Indian origin who has established legal residence outside of India.

Local Talent also Suitable

There are also those who find the local talent in India good enough. Kumar Mahadev, corporate vice president of business development (Asian region) of Dun & Bradstreet, the information and database company, said: "We will in all likelihood be recruiting people locally in India for two reasons: First, the quality of Indian talent is good enough and comparable to anybody else in the business; second, the cost of expatriate packages tends to be too high."

Anthony T. Hebron, manager for corporate publicity of Kellogg—which is building a ready-to-eat cereal manufacturing plant and plans to make and market Kellogg's cornflakes in India, said that the company now has only a small staff in India to oversee construction.

Bombay Plant Cited

But "in Kellogg operations around the world, most management and production positions are held by nationals and we expect this to be the case in India when the Bombay plant opens in 1994."

He added: "The Kellogg company is committed to employing and promoting to management positions people of all races, colors, and national origins. We provide them management opportunities within Kellogg operations in their country and our facilities around the world. We anticipate that over time a number of our Indian managers will receive international assignments."

In the case of high-tech companies, where the human element is crucial, the quality and attitudes of personnel are extremely important. To start an Indian venture, a couple of executives are enough to get the ball rolling, before handing over charge to local recruits.

Hewlett-Packard Policy

As for Hewlett-Packard, it was Sanjay Rajpal who went to India five years ago to get the HP-Hindustan Computers Ltd. collaboration off the ground. He was joined by a few more NRI executives. Rajpal is still in India.

Intel set up its Bangalore operation with two NRI executives, Siddharth Aggarwal and Vikram Modak. The Oracle Corporation, a $1 billion software company, opened a Delhi office three months ago with the help of an NRI. McKensie & Co., another U.S. company, sent an NRI executive, Anil Kumar, to start its Indian office.

According to Chandra of the Silicon Valley group, Indian executives working for American computer companies often take the initiative to set up an Indian venture—for instance, in the form of a collaboration—"and they are assigned to start the operation."

When It's the NRI's Idea

Chandra himself has been hired by 3-Com, a $700 million software company for which he plans to set up a local operation and sales outlet in India within six months.

In most Silicon Valley companies the idea of starting Indian operations was conceived and implemented by Indian executives. "The expatriate executive here plays the role of a catalyst for the Indian venture before being assigned to implement it," Chandra said.

The NRI's inducement is usually a longing to return to India, or a desire to start a business venture there on behalf of his company. Such experience also looks good on an executive's resume. The perks are an added advantage, but the Indian government taxes 50 percent of what an NRI executive is paid in dollars, Chandra noted.

Office Culture No Obstacle

As for the work culture, it is hardly an obstacle. Many foreign companies have set up offices in India, which they manage to run quite efficiently. "Once you step into their offices, you cannot tell the difference between India and America," Chandra said.

He explained: "There are about 50,000 NRI executives in the computer industry here in the U.S., and a large number of them are interested in going back to India to start a venture."

But the NRI executive also usually ends up returning to the West because, having achieved what he set out to do in India, he finds himself at a dead end again. As Chandra pointed out: "The NRI has to leave India to move on to something new."

Source: O. P. Malik and Nirmal Mitra, "When the Expatriate Is the Expert," *India Abroad*, November 19, 1993, p. 24.

WHAT ARE THE TRENDS IN INTERNATIONAL STAFFING?

Is there any pattern that can be detected in the international staffing practices of international companies? Research on this subject shows that changes in international staffing policies tend to coincide with predictable stages of internationalization of multinational corporations. For instance, in the first stage of internationalization—exports—most companies prefer to hire host country nationals. The company's greatest need is to adapt to local conditions, so local nationals are the logical choice. However, as the local market becomes large enough to support local manufacture of the product, home country managers are sent abroad, at least during the first few years of the foreign manufacturing operation.

As the process of national market development approaches maturity, host country managers again replace home country managers as the senior staff of local subsidiaries. Some even get promoted to top managerial posts at regional headquarters. Some host country managers are also used to manage subsidiaries in third countries.

As more and more companies become globalized, and their corporate agendas shift from a local focus to one that is regional or global, there is an increasing need for managers who can work effectively in several countries and cultures. This is especially true in Europe, where unification in 1992 is forcing many companies to manage several aspects of their businesses from a pan-European perspective. Because of all the changes that are already occurring in Europe, there is a need for *"Euromanagers."* These are executives who are able to think in terms of a European-wide big picture, and at the same time appreciate and understand local nuances and differences in tastes and preferences. In many respects, they are "glocalized" in their attitudes and behavior. Among their other more important attributes are flexibility in managing people of a different cultural heritage and nationality, skills in bringing a diverse team together, and the willingness to learn at least one foreign language. Firms are facing difficulties finding Euromanagers for their European operations. *Practical Insight 13-2* is about the Euromanager phenomenon and how global companies such as ICI, Colgate-Palmolive, Unilever, 3M, and Honeywell are facing and handling the difficulties of hiring and keeping such managers.

PRACTICAL INSIGHT 13-2

Companies in Europe Seeking Executives
Who Can Cross Borders in a Single Bound

When Vittorio Levi decided to leave the warmth of Italy for a job in Sweden, everyone told him he was crazy. Scandinavians may dream of working in a Mediterranean climate, but Italians aren't supposed to be willing to go north. Nonetheless, Mr. Levi says he made the right choice when he joined Oy Nokia's Stockholm-based computer division, where he became president early last year.

Expatriate executives are no novelty, of course. As more companies try to compete globally, more executives are crossing borders—not just as a brief detour but as a critical, and sometimes inevitable, stage in their careers. That trend is particularly pronounced in Europe, where plans for a unified market after 1992 are spurring companies to reorganize.

Responsibilities are rapidly shifting from national to regional or pan-European units. At the same time, companies want to stay in touch with local tastes. So they need managers who can think big while understanding local nuances.

Mastering that tricky mix often means hiring what some companies call Euromanagers: people skilled at dealing with a variety of cultures and at bringing a diverse team together. And that means hiring and promoting more foreigners.

"You need as much cultural mix and diversity and experience as possible ... if you are running a global company," says Bob Poots, personnel director for the European division of London-based Imperial Chemical Industries PLC. ICI's executive ranks were predominantly British 20 years ago; now, only 74 of the company's top 150 executives worldwide are British.

That sort of change isn't easy to effect. The problem, headhunters and personnel managers say, is that Europe has a shortage of good senior executives who are willing to move. Tax and pension hassles, family ties, and simple chauvinism keep many top managers in their own back yards.

"It's easy to say 'Euromanager,'" notes Brian F. Bergin, president of the European division of Colgate-Palmolive Co. "In fact, [hiring them] is an extremely difficult task. But it's happening." To help realign its management, Colgate appointed a Pan-European human resources director, Peter Dessau, a Dane who moved to Brussels in 1989. His job is to encourage mobility among managers in the U.S. company's European units.

Colgate quizzed all of its top European managers about what kind of executive works best in an international setting. Among the main attributes, Mr. Dessau says, is flexibility in managing. "You don't always go by the book," he says.

ICI's Mr. Poots says he looks for people who are good at getting along with colleagues at home. "That skill travels remarkably well," he says. Any problems an executive has in dealing with colleagues, he figures, will be magnified in a foreign setting, where much more effort is needed to build understanding and trust.

Unilever Group, the Anglo-Dutch food and soap giant, shies away from bossy executives. "We tend to look for people who can work in teams and understand the value of cooperation and consensus," says Floris Maljers, chairman of Unilever NV, the group's Dutch arm.

Some recruiters want candidates who have learned at least one foreign language besides English. Even if the foreign language won't be needed much in a particular job, having learned it "shows you are willing to dive into someone else's culture," says Marc Swaels, a Brussels-based partner for Korn/Ferry International, a U.S. executive search firm.

Not surprisingly, many companies are above all looking for executives who have already succeeded in running at least one big operation outside their home countries.

Once the right kind of executive is found, companies wanting to move managers across borders must overcome differences in pay scales, pensions, and tax systems. In time, the European Community is expected to bring greater harmony in these areas, but for now the costs of solving such problems make some companies hold transfers to a minimum.

Even if the red tape can be cut, many European executives—especially senior ones with families—are reluctant to live abroad. British managers are often willing to leave their children in distant boarding schools, but Continental Europeans tend to want the family close together.

Another barrier to the free flow of executives is prejudice. Especially among older executives, history weighs heavily. Asked why his company wasn't moving into the German market, the chief of a Dutch retailer replied without hesitation, "Because we [in the company] don't like Germans."

To overcome these obstacles, companies are trying to be more flexible in managing people. Nokia Data, for instance, made it possible for the Italian Mr. Levi to keep his main residence in Turin. The company provides him with a small apartment in Stockholm and flies him home to Italy for weekends about twice a month.

Mr. Levi says such benefits have helped him make a smooth transition. At age 52, he is older than most executives in their first senior position abroad. Though he doesn't expect to spend the rest of his career in Stockholm, he says his international job gives him a better understanding of Europe's political and economic transformation. "In a time of great change," he says, "you get a closer view if you are in a position like this than if you stay home in Italy with your friends."

Companies also try to identify potential Euromanagers at an early stage. ICI has long recruited heavily from British universities; now it is trying harder to attract Continental students. A new program offered 20 university students two-month internships last summer at an ICI site outside their home country.

Rainer Goldammer, personnel chief for the European division of Minnesota Mining & Manufacturing Co., asks the company's local operating units for lists of young managers who might do well internationally. The company would like to send more young managers abroad for experience, but relocation and other expenses mean such managers cost about twice as much as local hires, Mr. Goldammer says.

An alternative is to give young managers international experience without moving them out of their home country. Both 3M and Colgate put managers on project teams with colleagues in other countries. "It's a way of seeing the light," says Colgate's Mr. Dessau. "You find out that you don't need to stay in the boundaries you're used to."

Honeywell Europe, a Brussels-based unit of Honeywell Inc., encourages managers to relocate by clearly showing them how such international experience could lead to promotions later on. Jean Pierre Rosso, a Frenchman who heads Honeywell Europe, says the company persuaded a reluctant Frenchman to take a post in Hong Kong by telling him that the next step would be a top job back in France. In general, it helps if foreign executives feel they have a chance to rise to the top. In Honeywell's European division, 12 of the top 13 jobs are held by non-Americans. Mr. Rosso, a Frenchman who in 1987 became the first non-American to head Honeywell Europe, says he hopes a European executive eventually will sit on the board of Honeywell in the U.S. Unilever has six nationalities on its board, but most companies' executive directors come almost

PRACTICAL INSIGHT 13-2 *(continued)*

exclusively from the home country. A boss's natural inclination, says Korn/Ferry's Mr. Swaels, is to surround himself with people from a similar background, speaking the same language. But Mr. Swaels and others say it will be vital for global companies to build up "an international culture" at the very top. Partly because true Euromanagers are in short supply, some European companies turn to Americans or other non-Europeans who have worked for U.S.-based multinationals. U.S. companies sometimes have an edge in Europe because—whether through naivete or foresight—they have always tended to view Europe more as one big market than as a series of small nations. Colgate's top executive in Europe, Mr. Bergin, is Australian. The top finance man is Argentine.

At 3M, more Americans are filling top jobs in Europe these days. But Mr. Goldammer, a German who moved to Brussels a year ago, says the next generation of European managers will be more internationally minded and mobile. That would let 3M send more Americans back home.

Source: Bob Hagerty, "Companies in Europe Seeking Executives Who Can Cross Borders in a Single Bound," *The Wall Street Journal*, January 25, 1991, pp. B1, B8. Reprinted by permission of The Wall Street Journal, © 1991 Dow Jones & Company, Inc. All Rights Reserved Worldwide.

Foreign Managers at Headquarters in Home Countries

More recently, foreign nationals have also come to occupy managerial jobs in the headquarters of U.S. and European multinational companies. Exhibit 13-1 gives a sample of foreign-born executives in top management positions in American companies. There are a host of other foreign-born managers that hold senior positions in companies, the list of which would be far too long to include here.

There are several reasons for the appearance of foreign-born managers in executive positions in international companies:

1. The realization by international companies that first-rate people are by far the most important resource that a company can have, and therefore only by recruiting the best people—regardless of their nationality, country of birth, or religion—can a company enhance its competitive position in the industry. And the best people may not be those from the home country alone.

2. The enlightened policies of companies that call for the promotion from within of the most qualified persons for positions open in regional or global headquarters. Hence, executives who have demonstrated excellence at the subsidiary level or at regional headquarters get promoted to positions at higher organizational levels.

3. The horizontal and vertical acquisitions and mergers between companies from different countries cause managers from the companies involved to migrate across national borders. For example, the president of an acquired company may end up as the senior vice president in the acquiring company.

4. The globalization of companies and industries has made many international companies dependent upon the success of their international business operations. Companies will therefore promote to key positions at the parent company level those managers who have done especially well in the company's major foreign markets.

EXHIBIT 13-1
Foreign-Born Managers in Top Management Positions

Country of Origin	Name	Position & Company
Britain	Alex Trotman	President, *Ford Motor Company*
Scotland	Anthony O'Reilly	President, *H. J. Heinz & Co.*
Switzerland	Friz Ammann	President, Chief Executive Officer, *Esprit de Corp.*
Germany	Eckhard Pfeiffer	President, Chief Executive Officer, *Compaq Computer*
Germany	Heinz Schimmelbusch	Chief Executive Officer, *Safeguard International Group, division of Safeguard Scientifics, Inc.*
India	Rajat Gupta	Managing Director, *McKinsey & Company*
France	Samir Gibra	President, *Goodyear Tire & Rubber Company*

Because of these reasons, we shall see far more foreign-born managers in top management positions in international companies in the years ahead.

CRITERIA FOR SELECTING MANAGERS FOR FOREIGN ASSIGNMENTS

One of the most important factors in determining the success of a foreign operation—be it a branch or a fully integrated manufacturing subsidiary—is the quality of the home country managers sent abroad to manage it. This is particularly true during the start-up phase of the foreign operation.

The problem facing multinational companies is finding a manager who can readily adapt to the demands of a foreign assignment. There do not exist as yet valid and reliable screening devices to identify, with certainty, managers who will succeed in a foreign assignment. What we do have is a set of criteria that a manager should be able to meet before he or she can even be considered for an assignment in a foreign country. Both home country and third-country managers are expatriates from their homelands. Therefore, the criteria we do have should apply in the selection of candidates for either of these two groups.

What are the ideal characteristics of an international manager? Following is one opinion on the subject.

> Ideally, it seems, he [or she] should have the stamina of an Olympic swimmer, the mental agility of an Einstein, the conversational skill of a professor of languages, the detachment of a judge, the tact of a diplomat, and the perseverance of an Egyptian

pyramid builder.... And if he is going to measure up to the demands of living and working in a foreign country he should also have a feeling for culture; his moral judgements should not be too rigid; he should be able to merge with the local environment with chameleon-like ease; and he should show no signs of prejudice.[12]

Of course, that is an idealized profile of what an international manager should be. There are, however, several more realistic traits or characteristics that most personnel executives would agree a candidate must possess if he or she is to succeed in an assignment abroad. Having some or most of these characteristics does not ensure success, but the lack of them vastly increases the chances of failure. The following paragraphs discuss some of these desirable traits.

Technical Ability

Obviously the candidate must have the technical knowledge and skills to do the job. Even though he or she may have each of the other attributes, if the candidate does not know what he or she is doing, there will be problems.

Managerial Skills

The candidate must know what it takes to be an effective manager. He or she must have knowledge of the art and science of management and the ability to put them into practice. A good indicator of a candidate's managerial ability is his or her past record as a manager. Someone who has not been an effective manager in the home setting is not likely to be successful abroad.

Cultural Empathy

All authorities agree that high on the list of desirable traits is cultural empathy, referring to "an awareness of and a willingness to probe for the reasons people of another culture behave the way they do."[13] It is critical for success abroad that the candidate be sensitive to cultural differences and similarities between his or her own country and the host country. "He must have a personal philosophy that accepts value differences in other people and the ability to understand the inner logic and rationale of other people's way of life. He must be tolerant towards foreign cultural patterns and avoid judging others by his own values and criteria."[14] If one has cultural empathy, he or she will demonstrate "an openness to experience, a willingness to respond realistically to relevant cues; a lack of dogmatism and a capacity for responding to the world, flexibly and dynamically."[15] Cultural empathy is undoubtedly a very desirable trait, even though it is difficult to identify in a candidate.

Adaptability and Flexibility

The ability to adapt to new circumstances and situations, and to respond flexibly to different and often strange ideas and viewpoints, is a characteristic found in successful international managers. The following are some specific types of adaptability and flexibility—listed originally in an American Management Association's research study—of which an international manager should be capable.

1. A high degree of ability to integrate with other people, with other cultures, and with other types of business operations.
2. Adaptability to change; being able to sense developments in the host country; recognizing differences, being able to evaluate them; and being able to qualitatively and quantitatively express the factors affecting the operations with which he or she is entrusted.

3. Ability to solve problems within different frameworks and from different perspectives.

4. Sensitivity to the fine print of differences in culture, politics, religion, and ethics, in addition to industrial differences.

5. Flexibility in managing operations on a continuous basis, despite lack of assistance and gaps in information rationale.[16]

All of the preceding items imply that there is a close association between cultural empathy and a manager's capacity to be adaptable and flexible. The candidate who lacks cultural empathy will find it extremely difficult to be adaptable and flexible in a foreign environment.

Diplomatic Skills

An international manager must be skilled in dealing with others. He or she must be able to represent the parent company in a foreign country as its ambassador, and be effective in advocating the parent company's point of view to foreign businesspersons, government bureaucrats, and political leaders. The manager should be a skilled negotiator, particularly in obtaining the most favorable treatment possible for the foreign subsidiary from the host country's government. Diplomatic skills are particularly important in all countries where the manager has to interact often with politicians and government officials, but they are especially crucial in the developing nations of Asia, Africa, and Latin America, where the role of the government in managing the business sector is quite significant.

Language Aptitude

The ability to learn a foreign language quickly can be quite an asset for an international executive. It is possible that the foreign assignment may be in a country where one can get by with English. This is true of all countries that were once British colonies, such as India, Kenya, Uganda, Guyana, Singapore, and Malaysia. However, the assignment may be to a country where English is not understood, in which case an aptitude for foreign languages could be of tremendous benefit.

The importance of foreign language competency in international business is stressed by Michael H. Armacost, who, as the U.S. Ambassador to Japan, observed that a linguistic barrier is by far the most stubborn obstacle to a smoother economic relationship between the United States and Japan (see Exhibit 13-2).

Personal Motives

A candidate for an international assignment should have positive reasons for seeking it. Many persons apply for a foreign assignment because they believe that the higher salaries paid to international managers will make them rich quickly. A candidate who has money as a primary motive is not likely to be effective abroad unless he or she also has the other attributes discussed before.

The candidate's history is a good indicator of his or her interest in foreign countries and cultures and of his or her preparation for a foreign assignment. Has he or she studied foreign languages, taken courses in international business, spent some years in the Peace Corps, or travelled or lived abroad for extended time periods?

Emotional Stability and Maturity

The emotional stability of a candidate has a direct bearing on that person's ability to survive in another culture. An emotionally stable person is one who is not subject to wide mood swings.

EXHIBIT 13-2
Failing in Our Language Requirements

Failing in Our Language Requirements

Sustaining our global leadership and preserving the health of our economy will require more Americans who are knowledgeable about internal conditions, more skilled in foreign languages, more familiar with foreign markets and business practices, and more capable of functioning abroad with professional skill and cultural sensitivity.

In my work in Tokyo, I observe trade barriers. But the linguistic barrier is, in many respects, the most formidable obstacle to a smoother economic relationship. . . . We are still one of the few nations where a student can graduate from a top-flight college without achieving proficiency in a second language.

Michael H. Armacost, U.S. Ambassador to Japan, commencement exercises,
College of Wooster, Wooster, Ohio, May 13

Source: Philadelphia Inquirer, May 20, 1991, p. 11A.

He or she does not get overly elated when good things happen, nor lapse into a depression when things do not go well. A good candidate maintains emotional equilibrium at all times, and is therefore able to cope constructively with adversity and to function daily in various kinds of situations without being thrown off balance.

Emotional stability is a corollary of emotional maturity. The less judgmental a person is in his or her relationships with others, the more understanding he or she is of others and their perspectives. The emotionally mature person is not likely to consider his or her way of doing things or behaving as the best way. An emotionally mature person is most likely to be emotionally stable as well.

Adaptability of Family

The ability of a manager to be effective in a foreign subsidiary depends to a large extent upon how happy the manager's spouse and children are in the foreign environment. It is not always easy for a manager's family to feel comfortable in a country where so many things are different from those at home. For example, a family from the United States placed in Sri Lanka will find that the people look different, talk a strange language, eat spicy food, and dress differently. Even the trees and shrubs, animals, birds, and insects are strange. To be transported to such an environment can be quite unsettling. The family might well get homesick for people at home and for familiar surroundings. An unhappy family takes its toll on the effectiveness of a manager at work, as illustrated in the following account.

"Some years ago, we chose a promising young man for a post in Nigeria. We were sure he was suited for the job. But the man had a family—two small children and a wife who had never been west of Pittsburgh. When they arrived in Nigeria that young wife from Montclair discovered how big insects are in Lagos. Three weeks later we brought the family home at a cost of almost $15,000."[17]

Here is another example to illustrate the problem that non-adaptability of the family can create for a company:

"Several years ago a U.S. engineering company ran into trouble while working on a steel mill in Italy. The crisis stemmed neither from inexperienced Italian personnel nor from volatile Italian politics but from the inability of an American executive's wife to adapt to Italy. Frustrated by language, schooling, and shopping problems, she complained incessantly to other company wives, who began to feel that they, too, suffered hardships and started complaining to their husbands. Morale got so bad that the company missed deadlines and, eventually, replaced almost every American on the job."[18]

What these examples imply is that no matter how gifted, competent, and suited a manager may be to work in a foreign country, that person's effectiveness as a manager will depend on the degree to which his or her family, and especially the spouse, adjusts to the foreign country's environment. A manager cannot perform at the peak of his or her abilities if his or her family is unhappy and yearning to go back home.

The preceding criteria are all important in selecting a manager for a foreign assignment. But what criteria do companies actually use in their selection process? A study by Rosalie Tung classified overseas managerial assignments into four categories:

1. The chief executive officer, who is responsible for the entire foreign operation.
2. The functional head, who is assigned the job of establishing functional departments in a foreign subsidiary.
3. The troubleshooter, who analyzes and solves specific operational problems.
4. The operative.

Tung was interested in finding out whether the criteria used for selecting foreign personnel were contingent on the nature of the job they were expected to perform, the duration of stay in a foreign country, and the degree of contact with the local culture that the job entailed. For instance, the chief executive officer would normally have greater contact with the local community and a longer length of stay abroad than would a troubleshooter.

Tung found that U.S. multinational corporations consider the most important criteria for the selection of a chief executive officer of a foreign subsidiary to be communication skills, managerial talent, maturity, emotional stability, and adaptability to new environmental settings. For the category of functional head, the most important criteria were maturity, emotional stability, and technical knowledge of the business, along with the same criteria that would be required for the same job at home. Technical knowledge of the business, initiative, and creativity were the criteria most important in the selection of a troubleshooter. And in the selection of an operative, the criteria considered to be most important were maturity, emotional stability, and respect for the laws and people of the host country.[19]

SELECTION METHODS FOR FOREIGN ASSIGNMENTS

Once company executives agree on the attributes that a candidate must possess as prerequisites for a foreign assignment, the next step is determining who among the available candidates has these attributes. Selection methods that companies use include (1) examination of past performance, (2) a battery of tests, and (3) extensive interviews.

It is generally accepted that past performance is not a sure indicator of future managerial success abroad. However, because of the very different circumstances in which a manager has to work in a foreign country, most executives do examine the work history of a candidate. The purpose of looking into a candidate's past performance is to weed out those who are clearly not suited for greater responsibilities, on the assumption that those who have not done well at home are not likely to succeed abroad.

Some companies like to use a battery of tests to determine a candidate's technical ability and psychological suitability. They seek to determine how a candidate measures up on the various desirable attributes discussed earlier, such as adaptability, emotional stability and maturity, and so on. However, not all companies are convinced that tests are useful as screening devices, so some choose to use them but do not rely heavily on them, and others do not use them at all.

There is widespread agreement that extensive interviews of candidates and their wives or husbands by senior executives are by far the best method available for obtaining necessary information in the selection process. In-depth interviews are conducted with the candidate to determine suitability for an assignment. The kinds of questions for which answers are sought are as follows:

1. Why does the candidate want to be considered for a foreign assignment?
2. How keen is he or she about getting a posting abroad?
3. Does the candidate have a realistic perspective of the opportunities, problems, and risks involved in living and working abroad?
4. Is there evidence that the candidate is self-reliant, adaptable, and able to work independently?
5. What evidence is there that the candidate can learn foreign languages quickly?
6. Has he or she made career moves in the United States successfully?
7. Does the candidate's family have any medical problems?
8. How many children does he or she have and how old are they? Will the children move or stay back home?
9. How enthusiastic is each member of the family about staying abroad?

These questions are just a few of the many that executives may ask in trying to determine how qualified a candidate is for a foreign posting.

Recognizing the importance of assessing the ability of executives and their families to adjust to life abroad, a growing number of companies are adopting a technique called adaptability screening.[20] The program is conducted either by a professional psychologist or psychiatrist on the company's staff or by a personnel director trained in the technique. Two factors are generally measured during the screening: the family's success in handling transfers in the United States, and its reactions to discussions of stresses that the transfer abroad and life in a particular foreign country may cause. The interviewer tries to alert the couple to personal issues involved in a transfer. For instance, the couple may have an aging, widowed, or ailing parent or close relative whom they may have to leave behind; they are told they may feel guilty and anxious. Or, family members might have strong bonds to their church or civic organizations. Such strong bonds could cause stresses after the family is physically separated from people and activities that are important to them. The frustrations of adjusting to a strange culture and learning to communicate in a new language are also highlighted during the interview.

The objective of adaptability screening is to make the family aware of the different types of potential stresses and crises that can arise in a transfer abroad, and to prevent a failure abroad by giving the family a chance to say no to the transfer before it takes place. A failed foreign assignment costs a company hundreds of thousands of dollars. It is estimated that U.S. companies lose between $2 billion and $2.5 billion a year from failed foreign assignments.[21] A housing allowance and tuition for children's private school can raise the average cost of maintaining an American executive in Europe to two to three times the base salary. A three-year stint abroad for an executive and his family costs General Motors, on average, $750,000 to $1 million.[22] Hence, it is far more cost effective to prevent a bad transfer than it is to send family members abroad only to have them request a transfer back home again. In addition to alerting the family, the screening interview also permits the interviewer to assess the family's suitability for a stint overseas. There have been times when a family wants to go abroad but the interviewer does not recommend a transfer.

PREPARING MANAGERS FOR FOREIGN ASSIGNMENTS

Once a manager is selected for a foreign assignment, it is in the best interests of the company to ensure that this person and his or her family are prepared to handle the foreign assignment as effectively as possible. This goal may be met by having the family group attend a well-planned predeparture training program. Such a training program has two principal objectives: (1) to make it easier for the manager to assume his or her responsibilities and be effective on the job in the foreign environment as soon as possible, and (2) to facilitate the adaptation of the manager and his or her family to the foreign culture with as few problems as possible. The best program will probably have two phases. The executive alone should be involved in the first phase of the program, and both the executive and his or her family should be included in phase two.

For the Manager

Phase one of the program, which is just for the executive, should include study and discussion of the following elements: characteristics of the economy, political structure, political stability, and legal environment of the host country. It should include the following:

- The relationship between the subsidiary and the rest of the company. The extent to which the subsidiary's operations are interlocked with the operations of other subsidiaries and of the parent company.
- The economic and political aspirations of the host country as reflected in the government's policies, and what it expects of the subsidiary in areas such as creation of more jobs, exports, development of local resources, and so on.
- Management practices peculiar to the host country (for example, the practice of permanent employment and consensual decision making, both of which are typical of Japanese management).
- A comprehensive job description that specifies the authority, responsibilities, duties, and tasks of a manager's position in the foreign subsidiary.
- The overall objectives and goals a manager is expected to achieve.

For the Manager and Family

Phase two of the program, which includes the executive and family, should focus on helping the participants to adapt to the foreign environment as effectively and quickly as possible. To achieve this goal, the program should at least have the following elements: (1) language training, (2) area study, and (3) cross-cultural training.

Language Training Language training is a must for the entire family. It gives them a start in becoming acclimated to their new country. The goal of language training is to provide the family with an elementary knowledge of vocabulary so that they can communicate with others on arrival in the host country. Simple things, such as ordering a meal in a restaurant, asking for directions, or reading street signs can be quite bewildering. Even a few hours of instruction prior to departure—as little as twenty to thirty hours—can make a tremendous difference, and will provide the family with the very basic vocabulary required to get started.[23]

Area Study This element of training includes an intensive study of the host country's culture, politics, geography, climate, food, currency, and attitude toward foreigners. The family may be given books to read on this subject. Lectures by area experts, accompanied by film presentations, have been useful because they give participants the opportunity to ask experts questions about specific areas of concern.

Cross-Cultural Training This training has as its purpose the preparation of executives and family to interact and communicate effectively in other cultures. Individuals learn how to work with people who think, behave, and perceive things differently, and who hold different beliefs and values. There are four basic models of cross-cultural training:[24]

Intellectual Model: This training model consists of lectures and readings about the host country. The premise of this model is that factual knowledge about another culture should prepare an executive for living or working in that culture.

Area Simulation Model: This is a program tailored to the specific culture in which the executive and his or her family will be immersed. Attempts are made to create a variety of situations that the participants are likely to face in the foreign culture. The premise is that exposure to these situations will teach the family how to function in the new culture.

Self-Awareness Model: Programs using this model are based on the premise that understanding oneself and the motivations for one's own behavior is critical to understanding other persons, particularly those of another culture. Sensitivity training is the main ingredient of this method.

Cultural Awareness Model: This training technique assumes that for an individual to function successfully in another culture, he or she must first learn universal principles of behavior that exist across cultures. The program attempts to make participants aware of the influence of culture on an individual, and of how participants differ from the peoples of other countries because of cultural differences. The focus of the program is on improving participants' ability to recognize cultural influences in personal values, behaviors, and cognitions. This ability should enhance a person's skill at diagnosing difficulties in intercultural communication, and lower his or her inclination to make judgments when confronted with behavior that appears strange.

There are many different methods of cross-cultural training, such as the Cultural Assimilator or the Contrast-American Method of Cross-Cultural Training. It is beyond the scope of this chapter to discuss these techniques in detail, but we can say that, regardless of the type of method used, the objectives of all cross-cultural training programs are similar.

1. They encourage more astute observations in new situations, as well as greater sensitivity toward people who are culturally different.

2. They foster greater understanding in dealing with representatives of microcultures within one's own country.

3. They improve employee and customer relations by creating an awareness of cultural differences and their influence on behavior.

4. They develop more cosmopolitan organizational representatives who not only understand the concept of culture, but can apply this knowledge to interpersonal relations and organizational culture.

5. They increase managerial effectiveness in international operations, especially with regard to cross-cultural control systems, negotiations, decision making, customer relations, and other vital administrative processes.

6. They improve cross-cultural skills of employees on overseas assignments, or representatives of microcultures in our own country.

7. They reduce culture shock when on foreign deployment, and enhance the intercultural experience for employees.

8. They apply the behavioral sciences to international business and management.

9. They increase job effectiveness through training in human behavior, particularly in the area of managing cultural differences.

10. They improve employee skills as professional intercultural communicators.[25]

Cross-cultural training programs may be conducted by professionals who understand cross-cultural education and challenges. Such professionals may include psychologists, cultural anthropologists, and communications specialists, as well as human resources development specialists, trainers, and facilitators. Host country nationals, third-country nationals experienced in the particular culture, and local professors with relevant expertise can all be drafted to assist in such a program. There are management consulting organizations, universities, and agencies that specialize in cross-cultural education who may also be called upon for assistance. A few observations are called for on training programs designed to prepare managers for foreign assignments.

Framework for Designing a Predeparture Training Program

An international company that has operations in a variety of countries and which has a constant stream of managers being sent abroad on assignments is faced with the question of whether the cultural dimension in the predeparture training program should be equally emphasized for all foreign assignments or whether such programs ought to be tailored to the special needs of each foreign assignment. Specifically, how rigorous should the predeparture training program be on the **cultural dimension**? Figure 13-1 illustrates the salient features of a framework to make this determination.

There are four dimensions incorporated in the predeparture training program planning framework:

1. The people dimension: The degree of interaction with people to effectively perform the job—with colleagues at the workplace as well as off-the-job with the local population. This interaction can range from high to low.

2. The cultural dimension: How similar or dissimilar is the culture of the host country from that of the manager's home country? The similarities between the two cultures can range from high to low.

3. The training focus: This refers to the focus of the predeparture training program—whether it ought to be on improving the technical aspects of the job in the foreign location, or on enhancing the effectiveness of interpersonal interactions required with the colleagues at work as well as with people off-the-job.

FIGURE 13-1
The Emphasis on Cross-Cultural Training in a Predeparture Training Program

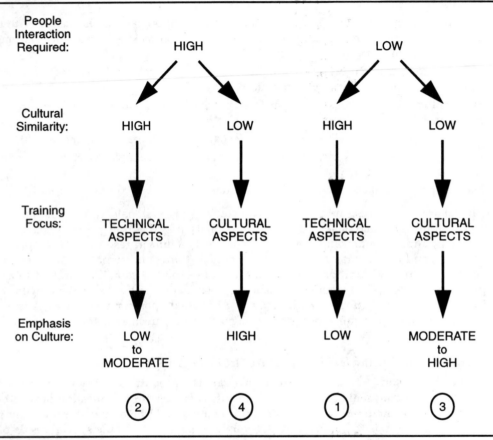

4. Program emphasis: The emphasis placed in the training program on the cultural dimension. The emphasis on the cultural dimension in the training program can be high, medium, or low. A high emphasis includes the use in the program of a wide array of cross-cultural training techniques, whereas a low emphasis might include only area study. If a foreign assignment involves a great deal of people-to-people interaction and if great differences exist between the home and host cultures, the manager should be subjected to as many cross-cultural training programs as possible, in addition to language training and area studies. However, area study may be sufficient if contact with the culture is low (e.g., the troubleshooter) and minimal cultural differences exist between the home and host countries (e.g., the United States and Canada). Between these two extremes there exist situations involving varying degrees of cultural differences between the home and host countries.

In applying these concepts in each of the four situations in Figure 13-1, the emphasis (high, medium, low) placed on the cultural dimension in the predeparture training program will vary based upon the following: (1) how much interaction with the people of the other culture is required to effectively perform the job, and (2) the extent to which the manager's home and host cultures are similar. The hypothesized emphasis on cross-cultural training is indicated in the flow chart with the least emphasis in situation 1, and the greatest emphasis in situation 4.

Cross-Cultural Training Programs in Companies

The number of cross-cultural training programs is growing in American companies. "AT&T's expatriate program is one of the most elaborate. Five years ago the telecommunications giant had no defined policy on prepping expatriates. Today, in addition to cultural and language courses, executives chosen for overseas assignments develop career plans with their superiors to spell out what skills will be enhanced abroad. More important, the plan offers possible ways those talents might be used when the executives return to the U.S."[26] A survey of 200 corporate clients by Berlitz International found that they needed cultural orientation more than its foreign language training. A senior vice president of personnel at Reynolds Metals Company says that "American businesses are dumb if they don't use cross-cultural training." Reynolds Metal's expatriate burnout fell to almost zero after the company began using cross-cultural training in the late 1970s. General Motors, despite massive cost cutting in the late 1980s and early 1990s, still spends nearly $500,000 a year on cross-cultural training for about 150 Americans and their families that live abroad. General Motors' expatriate failure rate of less than 1 percent compares very favorably with a 25 percent failure rate at companies that do not have adequate cross-cultural training programs.[27] *Practical Insight 13-3* gives several examples of cross-cultural training approaches used by several companies such as Procter & Gamble, Johnson Wax, Eastman Kodak, and Intel. The approaches can be grouped into three strategy categories: (1) centralized training, (2) decentralized training, and (3) combination training.

PRACTICAL INSIGHT 13-3
Cross-Cultural Training in Action

Within the last fifteen years, the world has become diversified and complex in the global arena. Multinational corporations operate and own subsidiaries and joint ventures all over the world. From foreign subsidiaries in the United States to the Asian and Eastern blocs opening up to worldwide trade, global competition has become a battleground for competitive success. To help achieve a competitive edge, global training has become an important ingredient for corporations seeking global success. So, how do multinational companies prepare their employees to achieve corporate goals throughout the world? Several training strategies are used by multinational corporations to achieve global success. In the following, we will look at several different training strategies used by successful global companies. The examples of centralized and decentralized approaches to training will also show how different training strategies provide global success.

Centralized Training Strategy

Johnson Wax Johnson Wax uses a centralized training strategy in which the corporate director of training develops and at times trains all of its subsidiaries around the world. To help the corporate trainer, there are human resource directors based in regions worldwide who have a good sense of cultural sensitivity and advise the corporate trainer on training needs. The corporate trainer also works with the general manager of a subsidiary for training agenda input.

Since Johnson Wax prefers a strong corporate culture, it doesn't normally change its training courses to fit a particular culture. However, at times it becomes necessary to adapt to cultural differences. For example, teamwork is imbued in Brazilian culture, so introducing a teamwork training course would be insulting and a waste of time. In China, setting objectives and performance appraisals seem worthless as the Chinese belief in destiny far outweighs the concept of self-development. Since this concept is an integral part of the corporate philosophy, it is integrated at a very slow pace. To achieve success, Johnson Wax feels that performance appraisals allow a management succession plan to work on a worldwide basis.

Decentralized Training Strategy

Eastman Kodak Eastman Kodak Company has a different strategy in global training as it uses a decentralized/customized approach along with help from corporate. Each region and major plant is responsible for training its employees. Therefore, all of the training organizations are self-sufficient. For example, corporate provides a five-segmented program called Internal Business Operations that focuses on cross-cultural awareness and skills. This program is geared toward managers and exempt employees who are just beginning to deal with foreign operations and customers. The chemicals group of the company provides a five-day program on cross-cultural training in dealing with the Asia/Pacific region. A lot of commitment has been put into this program as all fifty managers have attended it. Also, study trips taken to these countries focus on strategic issues.

Corporate-sponsored training is provided in several ways. Two- or three-day management conferences on globalization are offered along with forums on Japan that are followed by study trips. These conferences and forums are based on work/action, not lecture or case studies. Kodak also holds two management programs in a foreign location for every one program held in the United States. Kodak feels this gives them a competitive advantage in relation to international politics and economic developments. For example, Kodak held a program in Brussels in 1992 where the emphasis was on the formation of the EEC and what issues and opportunities emerged. Also, these programs entail both corporate and regional strategies along with global strategy.

Finally, Kodak believes that there are two important factors in their training success. Firstly, a sensitive needs analysis is done upfront because Kodak finds most employees are turned off by too much too soon. The second factor is that Kodak stresses that global learning is a progressive journey, not one-time training.

Procter & Gamble Procter & Gamble's training strategy consists of a decentralized approach in which each site has its own local training staff. The standard training curriculum is used worldwide, but each site adapts the courses to its needs. Although this training strategy is labor-intensive and time-consuming, Procter & Gamble developed a three-pronged approach to multicultural training for a major technology transfer to Japan. First of all, U.S. employees learned the Japanese language and vice versa. Second, employees received cross-cultural training in both the United States and Japan. Third, all of the employees received training in the company culture so they would all have a common base. This type of training strategy was a significant factor in the success of this technology transfer to Japan.

Procter & Gamble feels that the best training is done when it is run by each location. This way the company can react faster to local country conditions and implement the necessary changes efficiently.

Combination Training Strategy

Intel Corporation   Intel Corporation, a high-technology company, uses a combination of centralized and decentralized training. A training department along with a local country training manager is located in each major site. A worldwide intercultural training program is used in which external consultants and in-house, home-culture employees are used within each country. This training strategy consists of five areas: intercultural awareness, muticultural integration, culture-specific training, training for international assignments, and intact-team training.

With intercultural awareness, Intel educates its employees on cross-cultural training, which it considers as a building bloc of all of its global training. The reason Intel believes in cross-cultural training as the foundation of all global training is the fact that the company has a high cultural diversity among its manufacturing and engineering employees worldwide. Employees are taught how culture influences meetings and procedures, how to be culturally aware and sensitive, and how to know when to seek additional cultural-specific help or information. Intel believes a successful manager needs to have a global mentality and intercultural skills.

With multicultural integration, Intel trains foreign-born employees in communication skills and career development. In culture-specific training, employees learn how to work and do business in different cultures by analyzing their own culture and bridging the gap.

Training for international assignments gives the employee language training and country-specific orientations.

Finally, intact-team training incorporates intercultural perspectives when building teams. This is especially critical when Intel forms a joint venture with a foreign company. For example, a group of Japanese engineers came to the United States for training. A consultant was used for translating and helped the Japanese engineers learn English. The consultant also acted as an interpreter in meetings and was available in family emergencies. This type of support was a major factor in the efficiency of the work team of Japanese engineers. By following this training strategy, Intel believes its employees are flexible and can implement changes as needed, especially with unanticipated business ventures.

3M   3M takes the best attributes from centralized and decentralized training strategies to form a combination training strategy. Each subsidiary is responsible for its own training in which it develops and teaches its own curriculum. Each subsidiary also asks for help from corporate with training connected with a new product developed in the United States or with the use of standardized courses available from corporate which the subsidiary intends to adapt to local country conditions. 3M believes in making its foreign employees familiar with its corporate culture. To this end, the company frequently brings foreign employees to its home office. For example, 3M places a large emphasis on bringing its Chinese workers from its subsidiary in Shanghai to its home office in St. Paul, Minnesota. 3M feels that giving the employees a feel for the corporate culture and work ethics attracts the best workers who can then become role models for the other employees.

3M is also developing training programs in other parts of the world. A management development course was prepared in Europe which includes the participation of top executives from

PRACTICAL INSIGHT 13-3 *(continued)*

the United States. 3M continues to see this trend in Asia and Latin America as it feels that knowledge is everywhere, not just limited to the United States.

IBM IBM also uses a combination training strategy. Training is organized into five geographic units across the world. These five units act as coordination hubs. Each regional unit has an education director who is responsible for supplying and implementing training in each country. All training is done locally within each country and each has its own trainers. IBM has a very high commitment toward training as it has as few as five trainers in each country to two thousand in the United States.

While the training is done from a decentralized approach, most of the training courses are developed in the United States. The reasons for this are that most of the training content is tied to new products and most of the development of new products is done in the United States. This centralized strategy of training content is also based on the fact that seventy-five percent of the material may not be altered. The other twenty-five percent, IBM believes, may be customized in each country. For example, a new product for the banking system might need to be tailored to the local needs and conditions in different countries because their banking systems differ.

Out of all the previous companies mentioned, IBM has the biggest training operation worldwide. The company has dedicated a large amount of resources, time, and money to its training strategy. With trainers in 132 countries, it shows that global training is an important strategy in their global success.

Written by Janice Weiss, MBA student at Temple University. *Sources:* John Engen, "Training Chinese Workers," *Training*, September 1994, pp. 79-83; Beverley Gerber, "A Global Approach to Training," *Training*, September 1989, pp. 42-47; Sylvia Odenwald, "A Guide for Global Training," *Training & Development*, July 1993, pp. 23-31.

MANAGING DUAL-CAREER PERSONNEL

The phenomenon of dual careers is building rapidly. The number of dual-career couples has grown from 52 percent of all couples in 1980 to 59 percent in 1992. A survey of 127 U.S. and foreign multinational businesses conducted in May 1992 by Windham International and the National Foreign Trade Council has shown that about 41 percent of employees transferred abroad have spouses who worked before relocating.[28]

The dual-career expatriate couple issue has become a major concern for global companies that require, or sometimes insist, that experience in working in foreign cultures is a required qualification for promotion to senior positions. Commuter marriages, while not uncommon within the U.S., now sometimes span the globe as married men and women with careers of their own become less accepting of the idea that they ought to give up their careers for their spouses.

Global companies must have sound policies to ensure that a fast-track, bright male or female manager does not leave the company because of the hazards of separation from his or her spouse incident to an assignment abroad. Here are some policy suggestions:

1. Make the pangs of separation more bearable by paying for frequent visitation trips. One trip every two months is not unreasonable.

2. Give a very generous allowance for long-distance phone calls. A phone conversation can do wonders to remove loneliness.

3. Try to find a job for the spouse within the company in the foreign location if the spouse is willing to quit his or her job at home in order to be with his or her married partner. The U.S. State Department has the practice of finding jobs for spouses of U.S. foreign service personnel in U.S embassies and consulates abroad.

4. Network in the foreign location with other global companies for spousal jobs. For example, the Hong Kong subsidiary of a company like Procter & Gamble might be in a position to hire the spouse of an expatriate Colgate-Palmolive manager working in Hong Kong.

The stresses and strains of working in different countries and cultures can be brutal for dual-career couples. Therefore, global companies must realize that in order to retain competent managers, they must do everything within their grasp to enable dual-career couples to effectively cope with their difficulties and problems. *Practical Insight 13-4* gives examples of four dual-career families in which both spouses have independent careers.

PRACTICAL INSIGHT 13-4
Married But Worlds Apart

Michael and Judy Casper hoped to be together for their 25th wedding anniversary. They had planned a romantic three-week vacation in Alaska. But, alas, the Company called. Michael spent the anniversary watching a rented videotape. He could not get away from his new job as general manager of Gulf Bank in Kuwait City. Judy lives 7,700 miles away in Houston, Texas. She had been following Michael around the world for 17 years. Now she has a job of her own, her first for which she gets paid. Judy owns a successful home-interior shop. She celebrated the anniversary dining in an Italian restaurant with her three college-age children.

Ed and Rebecca Rolfes both had jobs in Brussels, Belgium, until Ed was sent packing for Chicago by his company. Rebecca is a researcher with the Conference Board in Brussels, Ed is an export manager with Navistar International Corporation. Rebecca stayed back in Brussels for 18 months with their teen-age daughter while Ed spent every other month in Brussels for a year. Rebecca claims that although staying in Brussels has helped her career it has not done their marriage any good.

Ingrid Ma works in Taipei, Taiwan. She is the first U.S. female manager sent abroad by Stride Rite Corporation. She runs the company's Taiwan operations. She left behind her husband and two daughters. Her husband Hansan is a top toy designer for Tonka Corporation's Parker Brothers division in Beverly, Massachusetts. Stride Rite pays for her personal calls and agreed to fly her home three times a year and fly her husband to Taipei four times a year. This enabled the couple to spend their 25th anniversary together in their Marblehead, Massachusetts, home.

Elizabeth McElroy is a marketing manager with Ameritech Corp. She has been transferred to Warsaw, Poland. Husband Robert runs a light fixture distributorship in Chicago. Ameritech pays for the couple to visit each other three times a year provided they fly coach. Robert is not very happy with his "commuter marriage." He complains that he is used to having her around in their home, and that he finds weekends especially difficult. He thinks that Ameritech could have done much more for them such as giving them trips to visit each other at least once every two months.

Source: Adapted from Joann S. Lubin, "Spouses Find Themselves Worlds Apart As Global Commuter Marriages Increase," *The Wall Street Journal*, August 19, 1992, pp. B1 and B5.

Until now we have been looking at the strategies an international company can use to improve the chances of a manager's success in a foreign assignment. But executives at the parent company cannot sit back and assume that, having prepared the manager for the foreign posting, they have done their part and now it is up to the manager to perform. The manager abroad may experience many anxieties that are not related to the environment in the foreign country, but that emanate from his or her being physically and emotionally separated from the parent company. Such anxieties can have a detrimental impact on job performance.

There are things that executives in the parent company can do—some before the manager's departure, and some during his or her tenure abroad—to help alleviate those anxieties. We shall examine this subject in the following section.

REPATRIATING THE INTERNATIONAL MANAGER

A problem that has become of increasing concern to both managers abroad and their companies is the reentry of managers into their home country organizations. Most expatriates take foreign assignments for several years, under the assumption that they eventually will return to their home company, either to headquarters or to a subsidiary in the home country. More often than not, the move back home is a source of potential anxiety for a manager.

What are the reasons for the anxiety about returning home? Among the foremost reasons is the fear that the company has not planned adequately for the manager's return. Perhaps he or she will be placed temporarily—which may mean months—in a mediocre or makeshift job.[29] There is also anxiety because an extended foreign stay may have caused the manager a loss of visibility in, and isolation from, the parent company—factors which may have an adverse effect upon the manager's career and upward mobility in the organization. The expatriate manager is anxious that, despite access to the formal power structure he or she had from the foreign post, a manager abroad still loses contact with the informal power structure within the company.[30] Managers have apprehension, too, that they may miss opportunities for advancement at home, and that peers will be promoted ahead of them. Another source of anxiety is the possibility of failure in a foreign assignment and its impact upon a once-promising career. If a manager fails at his or her foreign assignment, he or she is usually penalized indirectly by the company's attitude, which expresses disfavor with such failures. This attitude is exemplified in the following comment by the director of employee relations of Dow Chemical, U.S.A.: "If a person flunks out overseas ... we bring him home. . . . He's penalized indirectly because the odds are that if he flunked out over there, he's in trouble over here. But we bring him back and, generally, he has a tough row to hoe."[31] This attitude is neither fair nor logical, considering that the problems, both work-related and personal, and the environment of an expatriate manager are very different, and usually more difficult, than those facing his or her domestic counterpart.

Getting used to working under organizational constraints may be hard for some expatriates when they come back home. Abroad, the manager had a great deal more autonomy. Physical distance from the parent company permitted the manager to function independently and to demonstrate what he or she could accomplish without much corporate assistance. When the manager returns home, even if it means coming back to a bigger job in the organizational hierarchy, he or she still must operate as a member of an organization that constrains the freedom to act. In other words, "One minute he is Patton roaring across the desert . . . and the next he is on Eisenhower's staff where the moves must be made an inch at a time."[32]

A sense of loss of status may also be experienced by the executive upon coming home. Abroad, especially for a local general manager or senior executive, a manager was probably a very prominent member in the local community. Back home he or she is apt to be just another executive.

An expatriate manager may have to incur financial burdens when he or she returns. For instance, the returning manager may find that he or she no longer can afford to buy a home similar to the one sold a few years before. In addition, the abundant benefits and perquisites received as an inducement to accept the foreign post are eliminated upon an executive's return. Even if promoted, the returning manager may in essence be taking a pay cut.

What can companies do to ease the reentry of expatriate managers? Some companies, such as Westinghouse Electric, Dow Chemical, Union Carbide, Honeywell, and Minnesota Mining and Manufacturing, use repatriation agreements—written guarantees that a manager will not be kept abroad longer than two to five years and that, upon return, he or she will be placed in a job that is mutually acceptable. The written agreement does not promise the expatriate any promotion or specific salary increase upon return. However, it may state that the manager may be given a job equal to, if not better than, the one he had abroad. Such repatriation agreements could be of great value in alleviating the career-related anxieties of expatriate managers.[33]

Another strategy to ease repatriation is to make senior executives serve as sponsors of managers abroad. It is the responsibility of a sponsor to monitor the performance, compensation, and career paths of expatriate managers who are under his or her wing, and to plan for their return. Sponsors begin scouting anywhere from six months to a year prior to an expatriate's return for a suitable position that he or she can come back to.[34] Union Carbide, IBM, and 3M are companies that make use of such sponsors, but there are others as well.[35] Dow Chemical has a cadre of ten full-time counselors who act as "godfathers" of expatriates. Once a year they travel abroad to meet each of the foreign-based managers to explore and understand the manager's career goals and how any changes in such goals could be accommodated. The counselors also act as advocates for the managers back home to ensure that they are given due consideration for any promotional opportunities that may occur during their foreign stay.[36] Sponsors and counselors are helpful in keeping the expatriate manager in touch with developments at home, and they help to ease the career-oriented concerns of expatriates.

Other methods of keeping the expatriate manager plugged into the informal power structure include corporate management meetings around the world, regularly scheduled meetings at the headquarters, and combining home leave with an extended stay at the headquarters to work on specific problems or projects.[37]

To lessen the financial difficulties caused by inflation in the housing market, companies such as Aluminum Company of America and Union Carbide have established programs to rent or otherwise maintain an expatriate's home while he or she is away. Union Carbide pays real estate and legal fees to help most of its international executives rent their homes. Such a program can erase the problem an executive would otherwise face on returning home—finding that a home similar to the one he or she used to live in has become unaffordable!

But by far the most important thing that companies can do to alleviate the "out of sight, out of mind" syndrome among international managers is to design and implement a staffing policy that encourages managers to seek foreign assignments. Such a policy would make a foreign assignment a stop on the road to higher managerial ranks, and therefore a much sought-after plum. Such a policy is in place at most forward-looking companies and in such companies there is no lack of applicants for foreign assignments. "How many arms do we have to twist? Not many," says Nan Sheppard, manager of global resources at GE Medical Systems. "We have far more candidates than we have jobs offshore." Even executives who were formerly reluctant to accept foreign assignments for fear of disrupting family lives and spouses' careers feel they cannot risk turning down a foreign tour.[38]

THE HOST COUNTRY NATIONAL

It is not uncommon for host country governments to put restrictions on the employment of foreign nationals. Such restrictions reflect a desire to ensure full employment among their own workforce. These restrictions may appear to be unnecessary and inconvenient to the multinational corporation that wants to utilize the best human resources available, but the multinational corporation must realize that, just as they are seeking to maximize the return on their investment, so is the host government. As a result of these requirements, it is becoming increasingly common for local nationals to rise to top executive positions.

Advantages of Host Country Managers

A local manager does, in fact, have an advantage over an expatriate. Cultural differences may be difficult to overcome for the expatriate, but a local manager is very familiar with the local environment, businesspeople, and government officials. In the area of public relations, a local manager can be extremely helpful. Knowledge of local customs is essential for minimizing the inevitable bureaucratic red tape. In Latin America and Asia it is not uncommon for local officials to refuse to conduct business with anyone other than a local national of managerial status.[39]

A local manager helps to minimize any bad feelings a foreign government may have toward a multinational operation. A company having a responsible attitude toward the local community should alleviate many of the fears the local government might have. A company with a policy of training local nationals to assume greater responsibility within the corporation would be received enthusiastically, and should have good relations with the local community.

Recruitment and Selection

Problems are often encountered by multinational corporations seeking to recruit and select local nationals for positions within the corporation. Local customs and educational opportunities, particularly in underdeveloped countries, often produce individuals deficient in aptitudes traditionally regarded by Western management as essential to top management performance. Economic growth concepts and the role of capital, profits, savings, and investment are often misunderstood and unacceptable to those raised in developing countries. Consequently, the likelihood of finding suitable managerial candidates is reduced. This situation is not often a difficulty to the same degree in developed or industrialized countries.

Under the best of circumstances, finding acceptable local managers is a difficult and time-consuming assignment. There are four basic sources to choose from: the present workforce, local and foreign university graduates, government agencies, and local businesses. The first and most obvious place to look within an operating subsidiary is to the present workforce. Someone from the non-management ranks or a lower supervisory position may be prepared to assume greater responsibility.

Until the subsidiary is established, the executive search goes into the local business community. Local managers may feel that working for a foreign-owned organization poses certain threats; hence salary, fringe benefits, working conditions, and advancement opportunities must be comparable to or better than those offered by other local firms. When strong nationalistic feelings are part of a culture, a local manager is viewed as a bit of an economic traitor. This is especially true when the firm is in competition with a national company. Conditions must be attractive enough to make the adjustment worthwhile.

Finding the right person for a specific job in a foreign subsidiary is not easy. Few local managers have the experience or training desired by the multinational. In addition, local managers are not as accustomed to changing jobs frequently as are managers in the United States. An effective selection interview must be tailored to the local culture. For instance, in many countries, questions regarding a person's family, hobbies, parents, or religious convictions are often considered unacceptable.[40] In general, these areas are private and not subject to questioning by a stranger. An effective interview must probe, instead, into the candidate's motivations, ambitions, communication abilities, and management style. The multinational home management must also keep in mind that it is extremely difficult, if not impossible, to terminate an employee in most developing countries, where an employee is practically guaranteed a job for life.[41] Strong unions and government regulations restrict a company's actions when an employee proves unsuited for a given job.

Finally, the success of a local manager is necessary for the long-run success of the foreign subsidiary, for it is ultimately the local manager who will replace the managers from the home country and third countries.

INTERNATIONAL STAFFING PHILOSOPHIES

The international staffing practices of a company are influenced significantly by the attitude of top management executives at headquarters toward doing business around the world, and particularly, toward foreign executives in headquarters and subsidiaries. As we discussed in Chapter 9, Howard Perlmutter identified three primary attitudes among international executives that can be inferred from examining the managerial practices of companies that have substantial foreign operations: ethnocentric, polycentric, and geocentric.[42]

A multinational company of any country may exhibit ethnocentric, polycentric, or geocentric attitudes. In an ethnocentric corporation, the prevailing attitude is that home country attitudes, management style, knowledge, evaluation criteria, and managers are superior to anything the host country might have to offer. Consequently, top management executives at headquarters and at all subsidiaries are from the home country exclusively. A polycentric corporation treats each of its subsidiaries as distinct national entities. There is a conscious belief that only host country managers can ever really understand the culture and behavior of the host country market; therefore, a foreign subsidiary should be managed by local people. However, no local manager can ever hope to be promoted to a position at headquarters, which is staffed exclusively with home country people.

The third attitude, which is still rarely observed today among multinational corporations, is geocentrism. It is based on a policy of searching for management candidates on a global basis.

A geocentric philosophy of staffing must be accompanied by a worldwide, integrated business . . philosophy to be successful. Thus, the selection and training of management at the international level must take place without regard to the managers' nationalities. Management potential from anywhere in the world can be employed to the advantage of the multinational company as a whole and wherever it is necessary, at headquarters as well as in the subsidiaries.

It is true that geocentrism is limited in some countries by legal and political factors. Despite this fact, it is very important for a company operating as a true multinational entity to have a personnel policy that is also multinational. In view of the demands on a multinational company's management, it is necessary to have an internationally employable "fire brigade." Moreover, because the environment of a multinational company is truly global, the result of multinational recruiting should be a cadre of top management at headquarters, one that is not only internationally oriented but also composed of nationals of various countries.[43]

The feasibility of implementing a geocentric policy is based on the following five related assumptions.

1. Highly competent employees are available not only at headquarters, but also in the subsidiaries.
2. International experience is a condition for success in top positions.
3. Managers with high potential and ambition for promotion are constantly ready to be transferred from one country to another.
4. Competent and mobile managers have an open disposition and high adaptability to different conditions in their various assignments.
5. Those not blessed initially with an open disposition and high adaptability can acquire these qualities as their experience abroad accumulates.[44]

These five assumptions hold true in varying degrees, depending on a company's particular circumstances. In most cases, international firms with a truly global outlook realize the need to combine different nationalities in managing their operations. However, despite these beliefs and the desire to become geocentric, a large number of companies are still a long way from internationalizing their staff.

There is still a strong emotional attachment to an enterprise's original country, reflecting the attitude that the quality of management and the cohesion of an organization require at least a certain proportion of experienced people from the home country.[45] Nevertheless, the goal of a company's international staffing policy should be a corporate pool of experienced international executives who are available for assignment wherever their skills are needed. In other words, to operate as a truly geocentric company, a multinational firm must have geocentric managers.

INTERNATIONAL EXECUTIVE COMPENSATION

If there is one area of multinational personnel policy that can be designated the most complex, it has to be the area of compensation. The problems to date defy a simple solution and cause much intraorganizational resentment. The basic compensation strategy of international companies is to pay a base salary and apply to it the base differentials determined by the country of location of the affiliate. Problems arise in determining the base salary, the type and amount of the differentials, and the countries to which they apply. The following discussion covers some standard approaches to compensation developed by multinational companies; some methods of determining the salaries of home, host, and third-country nationals; and a review of various differentials.

Evolution of Compensation Systems

The development of multinational compensation systems in effect today has been quite haphazard. The American businessperson has been working abroad since this country began. In the early days, a manager received the same salary abroad that would have been received at home; there was no compensation for additional expenses. This policy fell apart when oil companies began sending employees to the Middle East, where they were often obliged to live and work in primitive conditions. Consequently, companies had a difficult time convincing employees to accept such positions. The idea of premium pay was then developed, and other companies followed the lead. In those early days of premium pay, there was no set percentage allowed for foreign service; rather, the embarking employee negotiated the amount of the premium. Understandably, the resultant variation in pay for one company's employees working in the same country caused some discontent. The policy eventually evolved into a standard percentage for premium pay anywhere abroad. Finally, it became a premium designed to maintain the expatriate's "real" salary in a particular foreign country.[46]

Today, expatriate compensation can roughly be categorized into three standard approaches. The first approach is based on the headquarters pay scale plus affiliate differentials. The base salary of the home country national is determined by the salary for that job at headquarters. With many companies now using the balance sheet method of determining differentials, an affiliate differential can be a positive addition to an expatriate's salary, or it can be a negative allowance to account for any extra benefits associated with the particular foreign assignment. Under this system, host country nationals are entitled neither to the base salary nor to the differentials allotted to home country nationals; rather, their salaries are based on local salary standards. Third-country nationals pose a problem, however. The company may treat them as either host country nationals or home country nationals; in either case, inequities are possible. This system is undoubtedly the most ethnocentric of the three.[47]

The citizenship salary system solves the problem of what to do about the third-country national. An executive's regular salary is based on the standard for his country of citizenship or native residence. An appropriate affiliate differential is then added, based on comparative factors between the executive's native country and his host country. This system works well as long as expatriates with similar positions do not come from countries with different salary scales. As affiliate staffing becomes more internationalized, it has become harder to avoid this problem. Consequently, the inequities arising from different salary scales for the same position do not go unnoticed.[48]

The global compensation system is a move toward a more geocentric personnel policy, although it too has its constraints. Under this system, the same job has the same base salary, regardless of country. Affiliate differentials are then added to the base. Differentials are determined by affiliate location and job or rank, but are unrelated to the home country of the expatriate. The resultant system allows for no unexplained inequities among employees performing the same job in the same subsidiary. A prerequisite for this type of compensation scale is a global system of job classification. The task of measuring comparable job elements across cultural boundaries is awesome, and no company has completely succeeded in this respect. Nevertheless, efforts are being made in this direction, and a global salary structure seems surely to be the system of the future.[49]

Dealing with Dissatisfaction

Until a global salary system becomes a reality, most multinational companies are operating under one of the first two compensation systems. Under these systems, the most troublesome problem has been the host country national's salary. In the past, the remuneration of local nationals has been ruled by local salary levels. This practice stems from the multinational companies' fear of raising the salary standards for the entire area, thereby raising the affiliate's costs of operation. The pressure to utilize more native managers, as well as local statutory limitations on expatriate employment, have increased the demand for capable host country nationals. Increased competition among companies with subsidiaries in the same country has led to a gradual upgrading of local managers' salaries.

One company has divided its employees into two classifications. If a local employee meets certain established performance standards, he or she is shifted from local management status to the international executive corps. His or her pay is then adjusted to the new, higher salary scale of the other international executives, including Americans. The promoted local manager, in turn, agrees to be available for transfer to any other country where his or her services may be needed.

Another approach is to shift all local managers above a certain level to the headquarters scale. Under this system, junior and lower middle management personnel may remain on a local salary standard, while upper level management is moved to a higher standard.

A third approach is to use management by objectives to determine local salaries. While this system does not necessarily eliminate the difference between local and expatriate salaries, it does provide a more rational explanation for the difference. Overall, however, international firms are moving toward a narrowing of the salary gap between the host country national and the expatriate.[50]

As the number of third-country nationals in multinational companies increases, their compensation levels approach those of the home country expatriates.[51] One of the problems peculiar to third-country nationals, however, is defining them. The most common definition is "one who works outside his home country for a company based in still another country."[52] But is a Frenchman working for a Spanish-based company in Geneva or an Argentine working for a U.S.-based firm in Santiago really an expatriate, third-country national? And why do most U.S.-based companies consider Canadian nationals working abroad as U.S. expatriates and not third-country nationals?[53] Some countries are using cultural zones rather than nations to define third-country nationals. For example, western Europe may be one zone, Africa another, and so on.[54] Other companies use a combination of geographic and language zones. Thus, an employee remains a local national (not a third-country national) unless he or she moves to a different geographic zone and a different language zone as well.[55]

Salary Differentials

The final section of this discussion on compensation is a brief review of the different types of salary differentials. It is not meant to be an exhaustive examination of each area, but simply an introduction to their different components and some of their problems.

Overseas Premium (OP) This differential is usually paid as a percentage of the executive's base salary. There are a number of reasons companies still use the OP, but three basic rationalizations emerge: (1) the executive is being compensated for the various emotional, cultural, and physical adjustments he or she will have to make; (2) the executive is being given an incentive to accept a foreign assignment; and (3) the company must offer an OP because its competitors are offering one.[56] Some sources feel that the OP is practical since it indicates to the employee that the company realizes the inconvenience he or she is undergoing. The company avoids the administrative costs of analyzing and pricing each inconvenience separately. The alternative would be to increase the base salary, distort the firm's salary structure, and increase the costs of pension and other salary-based expenditures.[57]

Many industrial relations specialists assert that paying the same flat percentage of base salary to the executive going from Peoria to the deserts of Saudi Arabia as that paid to the executive going from New York to Paris is preposterous, and a number of companies have considered eliminating or modifying their OP. One suggested modification is the reduction of the OP over time. Another is that the percentage should be based on the degree of contrast between the home country environment and host country environment.[58]

Reimbursement for Payments into Host Country Welfare Plans Most developed countries require workers to contribute to some type of state welfare plan, whether it be a pension plan, a medical plan, or an unemployment plan. Since the expatriate is almost always making payments concurrently to a pension fund in the United States, and because any benefits accruing to him or her abroad will probably not be claimed, companies often leave local payment to the expatriate, and compensate for it in the cost-of-living allowance. This situation occurs particularly when local tax regulations would treat the company's contribution to the host country program on behalf of an individual as a taxable fringe benefit. In the case of company pension plans, some companies "forgive" the employee's contributions while overseas. Where mandatory state medical plans exist, a company may reimburse the employee only for those expenses that are not provided free by the state.[59]

Housing Allowance A housing allowance is provided by companies to permit executives to maintain living accommodations comparable to what they had at home, and to house them in a fashion comparable to their foreign peers. Housing can be very expensive in some countries. A house in Tokyo rents for between $10,000 and $15,000 a month. Some companies simply pay the difference (or a portion of the difference) between normal housing costs at home and the cost of housing in the foreign country. The problem with this method is determining the cost of normal domestic housing. Another common approach is to require the employee to pay up to a certain percentage of his or her salary for housing, and make the company responsible for the difference. In these types of plans, the company may set a ceiling on the amount it will contribute in order to discourage excessively lavish choices of housing by the manager living abroad.[60]

Cost-of-Living (COL) Allowance This differential is probably the most controversial of the differentials. Critics claim that good international managers choose to experience the novel conditions of a foreign lifestyle, and that their families will eventually adjust their consumption patterns and tastes to the foreign environment. By this reasoning, a COL allowance is not needed, or can at least be decreased over time.

Proponents of the COL allowance counter that an expatriate has the right to live in a foreign country as he does at home. In addition, maintaining a familiar lifestyle may be essential to a family's satisfaction with a foreign assignment. The biggest problem here is determining cost-of-living indexes. The most easily available resource is the U.S. State Department's index, but it is often out of date and contains cultural biases. Many companies develop their own indexes or turn to a private research firm for one.[61]

Education and Perquisites This allowance includes schooling for children, club memberships, home leave, and other amenities. Education is probably the most commonly provided expense, and the policy is usually uniform among companies. The company attempts to provide the means whereby an expatriate can educate his or her children in their mother tongue up to the level required for university entrance in their home country, and at a cost to him or her no greater than it would have been at home. Implementation of this policy, particularly regarding transportation and the determination of an acceptable school, varies according to the parent country and local facilities.

Clubs are an essential feature of business life in some countries, and fees can be expensive. Some firms provide nothing for club membership; others pay the entrance fee but not the dues. Very few pay all membership fees.

Home leave also varies among companies, but the most common policy is to grant thirty days home leave after eleven or twelve months abroad. The class of travel allowed is usually determined by the amount of time spent in the air (e.g., first class for a flight exceeding ten hours, tourist for a shorter journey).[62]

Income Taxes Taxes can be an extremely complex area of international compensation. In some countries, only locally paid compensation is taxable, but in most, worldwide compensation is taxable. U.S.-based companies tend to prefer tax equalization plans in which the company withholds from the employee his U.S. tax liability and pays his local taxes. British companies, on the other hand, vary their policy depending on the affiliate country. The tax equalization policy presents the danger of paying multiple taxes; that is, in many countries a tax paid by a company on behalf of an employee is also taxable. It has been suggested that a company with operations in many countries would be better off adopting a tax equalization policy. It would gain in some countries, while losing in others. But if the company operates in only a few countries, it would be best to leave local taxes to the employee and adjust other local allowances accordingly.[63]

Fluctuations in Exchange Rates The fluctuations in exchange rates between parent and host countries are provided for by the inclusion of a currency cushion in the overseas premium—if the fluctuations are minor. Major currency changes are dealt with through special allowances. To avoid unnecessary problems and costs, local price reviews are sometimes delayed for six months after a major change; third-country nationals are paid in home country currency; a proportion of the expatriate's salary is retained in his or her home country; and any special allowance is reduced over time.[64]

In conclusion, a good compensation program must meet the needs of two groups: the corporation and its employees. "A multinational company that needs to widen its horizons to get the best managers regardless of citizenship must structure a salary plan equitable enough to compensate all managers fairly, and attractive enough to draw the top managers it needs."[65]

COMPENSATING THE HOST COUNTRY NATIONAL

In general, U.S. corporations have not offered local nationals compensation packages that are equal to those offered to home and third-country expatriates. Local nationals are typically compensated in accordance with local standards. In other words, the total compensation package of the local manager often amounts to as little as one-half or even one-third of that of an expatriate manager with identical credentials doing essentially the same job.

In order to attract and retain high-quality local managers, multinational companies must ensure that a total compensation package is not only internally equitable but also externally competitive. The various components of the package must consider local conditions, such as the tax structure; cultural variables, such as status symbols; and governmentally legislated social welfare schemes, such as health insurance and pension plans. Consideration of such factors, which vary from country to country, would enable the company to design a compensation package for a local manager that is most beneficial to him or her in terms of specific local conditions.

GLOBAL STOCK OPTION PLANS[66]

The design of an international company's compensation system—some elements of which were previously discussed—has a critical impact on the organization's ability to achieve its strategic goals. For this reason, the reward system's philosophy and objectives must reinforce and reflect the organization's culture, external environment, and business strategy.

The nature of a compensation plan can influence an employee's motivation level, the organization's operating costs, and the quality of people that it attracts.

Stock option plans are long-term incentive programs designed for employees at all levels of a company—although some companies do limit their availability only to middle and upper management personnel. It is believed that employees who are paid partly with company stock have a higher interest in the long-term profitability of the company. A stock option gives an employee the right to buy stock during a certain period of time (usually ten years) at a set price. That price usually is the market value of the share on the day that the stock option was offered. If the price rises above that level, the employee can exercise the option to buy the stock and immediately resell it for a risk-free gain. However, in order for the firm to gain from the employees thinking like shareholders and owners, companies hope, but do not require, that managers will hold on to their company's shares as long as they remain with the firm. Stock option plans have been very successful in the United States and most companies have adopted them as a means of getting a long-term commitment by employees to the company. However, the question for many international companies is whether this form of incentive makes sense in other countries and cultures?

In the following we shall address the problems that many international companies are facing in their attempts to introduce global stock option programs in different countries around the world.

Legal Hurdles

Gillette, a Boston-based razor maker, has 33,000 employees of which 77 percent are scattered in 52 countries outside the U.S. This January, the company introduced its global stock option program, and after a long examination the company decided to offer the program in only seven countries. In Belgium, for example, employees could not participate in the program because the stock conflicted with the Belgian government-imposed wage controls aimed at curbing inflation. In Brazil and China, on the other hand, Gillette could not implement the plan because foreign exchange rules do not allow workers to buy stocks on the New York Stock Exchange. In India, employees were excluded because the government does not allow Indian citizens to buy or own foreign stock. The difficulties Gillette has faced in these countries are examples of the legal hurdles that international companies can face abroad in offering stock options.

R.R. Donnelley & Sons went with the global stock option plan granting options for 100 shares to each of its 22,500 employees at home, and 1,500 employees in Barbados, Britain, Ireland, and Singapore. The company excluded its employees in the Netherlands because they would be taxed immediately, and in Mexico because the company was worried that it would be legally obligated to continue the award in the future, even though it planned a one-time grant.

PepsiCo, one of the pioneers of the program, started a "share power" program in 1989 to cover its employees in 47 countries, and passed most of the legal hurdles in many countries. Still, in the eastern European countries, employees could not participate in the program because of regulatory issues. The list of companies trying to implement global stock programs is long, and includes Procter & Gamble, Merck & Co., and National Semiconductor Corp.

Benefits and compensation consultants say that companies, despite the legal hurdles, can get around the regulations through other alternatives. For instance, they can tailor the stock's holding period to local tax laws or set up trusts in countries with favorable tax laws such as Luxembourg. The problems that are difficult to handle result from cultural differences among the countries.

The following table includes a sampling of countries and the problems that an international company might face in implementing a stock option plan.

Country	Problem Areas
Belgium	May conflict with government-imposed wage freeze.
Brazil	Foreign exchange controls prohibit out-of-country stock investment.
Britain	Labor unions can get in the way.
Eastern Europe	Bureaucrats make the task very difficult.
Germany	Prefer deutsche marks over dollars, when dollar is weak.
Israel	Foreign exchange control laws.
Mexico	Labor laws can force a one-time stock grant into an annual event.
Netherlands	Employees will not appreciate a hefty taxbill up front.
Philippines	Requires government approval and worker education, both of which may be time-consuming.

Cultural Clashes

The basic principle behind the stock option plan is ownership. An employee is encouraged to become an owner in the company and thus to share the benefits and the risks as well. U.S. employees view the program as a treasured benefit, and become motivated to improve their performance in order to increase the profits. However, employees in other countries have a different perception of the stock option programs because of a different economic reality, or a different perception of risk and ownership.

Switzerland and the Netherlands have very fiscally conservative cultures. Workers in these countries believe that savings should not go into risky venues such as stocks. They prefer savings accounts and other less risky investments. Employees in other European countries believe that the U.S. dollar is not the right currency for investment because of the continuous fluctuation of its value. For example, Buck Consultants, Inc. found that Germans feel more comfortable investing their savings in deutsche marks. The consultants believe that the job of the U.S. multinational is to convince employees not to worry about currency fluctuations, and instead to focus on investing in the company's good management around the world. However, this is not an easy task due to cultural differences.

Another aspect is the make up of the workforce in different countries. In many countries, workers have low disposable incomes and they cannot afford the risk associated with stocks. In Mexico, for instance, workers prefer to put their money under the mattress or purchase a taxicab medallion rather than purchase stocks.

Culture can affect the implementation of a stock option program in yet another way. For instance, William M. Mercer, an international human resources consulting firm in New York, describes a company that tried to introduce a stock option plan for workers at a Middle Eastern plant. Local managers said that a plan that included everybody would spell disaster in a country dominated by a caste system. Offering the same level of benefits to all employees is not culturally acceptable in many Middle Eastern cultures because of the psychological and social distance between workers and management.

In some countries, the idea of a stock option plan is strange to even the well-educated workers. Arthur Anderson & Co. tells of a U.S. company explaining a generous global stock option package to workers at its Asian subsidiary, until it realized that the employees had never heard of a stock option nor did they know what it was. In many of the former socialist countries, people do not understand the concept of ownership through stock. They do not have confidence that they can own a small amount of equity in a large foreign company, because in the past they did not own any private property.

For these reasons, international companies must think about where, when, and how to offer stock option plans. There is the concern that lower-level workers would cash in their options and never hold company stock, which would contradict the main objective of the plan to increase productivity through a sense of long-term ownership in the company by employees at all levels. Therefore, companies such as Gillette and National Semiconductor have offered stock purchase plans that resemble the U.S. company retirement plans known as 401(K) plans. These stock purchase plans, although not retirement plans, include payroll deductions and company contributions, but the only investment vehicle is the company's own stock. The employees cannot withdraw the money before retirement without being penalized.

To sum up, a stock option plan is a long-term incentive program aimed at motivating employees to maximize the future growth and profitability of the company, and at retaining and attracting outstanding employees from an outside labor market. The underlying belief of this compensation strategy is that the sense of ownership in the company will motivate employees to increase productivity. As U.S. multinationals expand their global operations, the need for integrating their global operations to achieve better efficiencies is becoming greater than ever. Companies are continuously looking for strategies to achieve this goal. A stock option plan is an excellent motivational vehicle to improve management performance and employees' productivity through a long-term relationship. By globalizing a compensation program such as a stock option plan, companies can realize the benefits of economies of scale and learning. They can reduce the costs associated with creating different compensation systems for different countries. In addition, the widespread use of telecommunication networks among subsidiaries is making it easy for employees around the globe to know what their colleagues in the U.S. have in their compensation package. Therefore, a global plan certainly contributes to the reduction in the sense of inequity among employees.

However, as is the case with other activities of international companies, stock option plans face legal as well as cultural barriers that must be overcome. It seems that cultural barriers are more difficult to handle; therefore companies should invest time and money to learn about cultural differences and demographics and to come up with suitable solutions that will accomplish the objectives of the plan. For legal barriers, companies can work out an alternative that is compatible with legal systems of the different countries.

COMPARATIVE EXECUTIVE LIFESTYLES IN THE UNITED STATES, JAPAN, GERMANY, AND GREAT BRITAIN

Many differences exist in the lifestyles of executives in the major world economies such as the United States, Japan, Germany, and Great Britain. Differences exist with respect to salaries and benefits, taxation, housing, food and clothing, medical care, and education. By far the most affluent lifestyle an upper-middle manager (earning between $75,000 and $150,000 per year) can attain is found not in Paris, Tokyo, London, New York, or Los Angeles, but in cities like Omaha, Atlanta, and Seattle—far from large and costly coastal cities. Some of these major differences will be discussed in the following sections.

Income

Although U.S. executive salaries are not the highest among their European or Japanese counterparts, differences in taxation and purchasing power afford them the maximum return on their dollar. As a result, American managers have more of everything—larger houses and property, more cars, appliances, electronic devices, and so on. Europeans in particular are penalized by high sales taxes (up to 15 percent in some countries) and protectionism (agricultural subsidies and import restrictions) that significantly diminish purchasing power for goods and services. The Japanese pay only 3 percent in sales taxes, but their cost of living is high due to extreme protectionism. To make up for lower disposable incomes, Europeans and the Japanese enhance compensation packages with generous, company-provided perquisites, such as company cars.

Pensions and Other Benefits

When it comes to pensions, most Europeans are given more generous plans than are Americans. In addition, American managers are more likely to be fired than are their counterparts anywhere else in the world. They are also more likely to change jobs, making their future financial security less certain than that of Japanese executives who are "employees for life" in their organizations.

Vacation time also varies among different countries. Europeans in general take four to six weeks vacation each year, while Americans average three weeks, and some managers feel guilty about taking any time off at all. In Japan leisure time is frowned upon, and managers often do not use all of their vacation time.

Health Care

Executives in the United States spend about as much on health care as do their foreign counterparts. The British, however, have the best system, and executives there can take advantage of the features of both the National Health Service and private plans.

Housing

Except in cities like New York, Los Angeles, Washington, D.C., and other places where real estate values and rents are excessive, Americans have by far the best advantage in housing. Americans can purchase much more square footage and land than is possible for their European and Japanese counterparts. In Germany, for example, zoning restrictions favor farming over construction, and city codes impose strict requirements on building materials and insulation. As a result, many Germans cannot afford a detached house, so, like the British, they live in row houses having much less space. The Japanese are in the worst position with respect to housing. In Tokyo, for example, the smallest detached home located within an hour's distance of the city cannot be purchased for less than $500,000. Middle managers who are fortunate enough to own homes either inherited them or bought them many years ago. To help ease their employees' housing burdens and to help them save money, Japanese corporations provide inexpensive, subsidized housing for their young managers. When employees are ready to purchase their own homes, the companies also help them with subsidized mortgages.

Education

Despite American executives' affluence, they are the only ones of their foreign counterparts who are daunted by the prospect of financing their children's education. Nowhere else in the world is this burden as heavy, although it does vary from country to country. In Germany, the government pays for tuition, as almost all colleges and high schools are state-sponsored. In Great Britain, where the public school system is not favored, private elementary and secondary schools present a financial burden for families concerned with the quality of their children's education. In Japan, education is less costly than in the United States but not nearly as inexpensive as in Germany. Executives tend to send their children to private high schools and colleges, but costs for this education are heavily subsidized by the government.

While the components that contribute to lifestyle vary from country to country, and although tastes differ dramatically, the United States still appears to offer executives the greatest amount of economic diversity and the widest variety of choices.[67]

Our discussion in this chapter has centered on the selection, training, and compensation of international managers, particularly on the special problems associated with assignment to a foreign affiliate. Such a foreign assignment is often a major step in the international manager's career, and the degree to which he is successful in that assignment will greatly influence his subsequent career progression. This leads us to the next chapter, in which we address the evaluation and control of foreign affiliates, and how their performance is assessed by the company's home office.

SUMMARY

International companies have three main sources from which they can draw their pool of international managers—the home country, the host country, and a third country. Home country nationals are the citizens of the country in which the headquarters of the company is located. Nationals of the country in which the foreign affiliate is situated are the host country nationals. Nationals of a country that is neither the home nor host country are third-country nationals. For instance, an Italian working in the French subsidiary of an American company would be classified as a third-country national. A fourth source, that of the "immigrant expatriate," has also begun to gain in importance in recent years.

Multinational companies have a tendency to staff the key positions in their foreign affiliates with home country nationals. Third-country nationals are also used frequently, but most companies prefer to use nationals of advanced countries in this capacity. Most multinationals use host country nationals in middle- and lower-level positions in subsidiaries that are located in developing countries. In more advanced countries, they employ host country nationals to a far greater extent at all levels of management. This is probably because more qualified personnel are available in advanced countries than in developing countries.

Recently, foreign nationals have been named to managerial positions in the headquarters of U.S. and European multinational corporations. However, this is still a rare occurrence.

Most personnel executives would agree that a candidate for a foreign assignment must possess a few key characteristics if he or she is to be successful abroad. Having these features does not ensure success, but not having them greatly increases the probability of failure. These characteristics are technical ability, managerial skills, cultural empathy, adaptability and flexibility, diplomatic skills, language aptitude, positive motives, emotional stability and maturity, and a family capable of living in a foreign country. Selection methods used by companies to determine which candidates have these attributes include an examination of each candidate's past performance, a battery of tests, and extensive interviews of the candidate and spouse.

The selected candidate should undergo a well-planned predeparture program, the purpose of which is to make a manager capable of assuming his or her new job abroad quickly and effectively. Such a program also facilitates a manager's and his or her family's adaptation to a foreign culture. We introduced a framework for developing a cross-cultural training program, based on four dimensions that characterize the foreign assignment, and looked at how several major international firms have tailored their own training programs.

The problem of personnel with dual-careers, wherein both spouses work and have independent careers, has gained considerable importance in global companies. Global companies must develop and implement policies that facilitate dual-career personnel retention because many fast-track managers belong to dual-career families. Increasingly, the human assets of a company are becoming one of the most critical ingredients for its competitive success, and therefore it is incumbent upon companies to develop effective personnel policies and programs to prevent the turnover of their best managers. Companies should also have effective programs to facilitate the reentry of the expatriate manager into the home country organization at the completion of a foreign assignment.

Companies exhibit ethnocentric, polycentric, or geocentric staffing philosophies. Companies that have an ethnocentric staffing philosophy staff their foreign affiliates almost exclusively with home country nationals. Host country nationals are employed predominantly by those companies that have a polycentric philosophy. Companies with a geocentric staffing philosophy adopt the strategy of selecting and placing the right candidate in the right job, anywhere in the world, regardless of the nationality of the candidate.

Probably the most complex aspect of international staffing is international executive compensation. The basic compensation strategy of international companies is to pay a base salary and apply to it base differentials contingent on the country of location of the affiliate. An additional means of executive compensation that is seeing increasing use is the global stock option plan. Such plans generally benefit both the participants and the company, but their widespread use is hampered by various legal and cultural constraints in different countries.

QUESTIONS FOR THOUGHT AND DISCUSSION

1. Describe the three sources of managers. Explain the reason for the increasing role in foreign assignments played by the "immigrant expatriate."

2. "Changes in international staffing policies tend to coincide with predictable stages of internationalization of multinational corporations." Discuss why this is so.

3. Does the nature of the job and the length of stay abroad influence the criteria for selection of candidates for a foreign assignment? What are the traits that an international manager should possess if he or she were to be appointed chief executive of a foreign affiliate?

4. Why is the preparation of a manager and his or her family for a foreign assignment just as important as the selection of the right candidate? What should be the objective and essential features of a predeparture training program?

5. Suggest policies that global companies should implement to ensure that fast-track managers, when given a foreign assignment, do not leave the company because of dual-career problems.

6. Explain the differences between centralized, decentralized, and combination training strategies.

7. "Planning to bring an executive back home after a foreign assignment is as important as planning to send him or her abroad." Discuss this statement.

8. Discuss the salient differences between an ethnocentric, polycentric, and geocentric staffing policy.

9. Explain the assumptions underlying an effective geocentric staffing policy.

10. How would you approach the problem of determining an equitable compensation package for an American and an Egyptian who have been assigned to work on similar jobs in the Japanese subsidiary of an American multinational company?

11. Discuss the various reasons why stock option plans are not effective in many countries and cultures.

12. Compare and contrast the executive lifestyles in the United States, Japan, Germany, and Great Britain in terms of income, pensions, vacation time, health care, housing, and education.

MINI-CASE
Geno's Burgers

Vik Harris is a marketing manager for Geno's Burgers, a fast-food chain whose principal competitors are McDonald's and Burger King. Vik has been with Geno's for the past 15 years. Vik is married and has two children, John, who is 6 years old, and Viveca, who is 15. His wife Anniina is an accountant with a CPA. She works for a major accounting firm in the Philadelphia area. Between the two of them Vik and Anniina can garner an income of $175,000. Vik has been asked by Geno's President Robert Wisniewski to be the managing director of Geno's franchises in India. India has one of the biggest markets for fast foods and consumer products, and Geno's wants to have a fast start in that market.

Although Vik is open to the idea of taking on the challenge of spearheading the drive into the Indian market, he is also concerned about his future prospects in the company. Moreover, he has heard that life in India can be exciting, but also quite difficult for someone who has never lived outside the United States. He is also concerned about how his wife will receive the transfer. His children are quite young. How will they adjust to the strange surroundings in India?

Vik has received the following memo from Tracey Corte, the vice president of human resources.

TO:	Vik Harris
	Marketing Manager
FROM:	Tracey Corte
	V.P. Human Resources
SUBJECT:	India preview

Vik:

The following should give you a brief introduction to what one should expect to find in India. We shall get you more information very shortly. I have asked the Indian Tourist Bureau in New York for whatever material they can put their hands on as soon as possible. Let's get together for lunch next Monday or Tuesday.

I look forward to hearing from you.

Best wishes,

(signed)
Tracey

Factors Affecting the Indian Way of Doing Business: An Overview

Differences between American and Indian culture affect how management decisions are made, how consensus is reached between American and Indian business partners, and how employees are expected to interact with one another.

One of the major cultural differences is that Indians behave more formally than Americans at the workplace, and in general keep a power distance between each other. An Indian executive would demand his or her subordinates to call him or her by Sir or Madam. It would be very rare to come across a boss and subordinates calling each other by first names.

The Indian society is male dominated. Women may not always be treated equally. This might especially create problems for female executives and subordinates. Public display of affection between the sexes is considered taboo.

Indians are quite individualistic. They work better as individuals than in teams. They say that "one Indian is better than two Japanese, but two Indians are worse than two Japanese!"

Indians usually tend to centralize control and authority. Bosses are in the habit of giving specific instructions to their subordinates, who follow them without challenging or questioning. The hesitation to delegate to others may come from the strong survival instincts of Indians, who have been subject to invasions from outside powers in the olden days.

Indians have an "elastic" view of time. Delays do not, therefore, have the same meaning to them as to an American or Westerner. At the same time, their lack of seriousness in keeping the appointments should not be taken as a lack of interest. For instance, two Americans will say "we should get together sometime," thereby setting a low priority to the meeting. The Indian who says "come over and see me sometime" means just that. It does not necessarily mean that he is attaching a low priority to the meeting. He would probably say it even if it happens to be an urgent matter. Also, there is a vast difference between dealing with a government business as opposed to a private business. Time has a very low priority in government business offices. However, many private offices are very punctual.

There is a lot of similarity between how space is perceived in the Indian and American corporate world. The size of the office will be directly proportional to the manager's rank.

In India, it is considered improper to discuss business in the home or at social occasions. One never invites a business acquaintance to his or her home for the purpose of furthering business aims. That would be a violation of sacred hospitality rules.

Americans usually think in terms of material things. "Money talks," says the American who goes on talking the language of money abroad. He is of the belief that money talks the same language all over the world. In India, this would not necessarily work. Indians attach a great amount of importance to family connections and to friendships, as opposed to material things. A company may not award a contract to another party just because it happens to be a low cost and high-quality option. A person who has good personal connections, through family or friends, has a better chance of winning a contract. The existence of bureaucracy, red tape in the administrative machinery, and a huge poverty-stricken population takes its toll. Bribery has become an inherent part of the work culture. To get things moving one has to be ready to pay bribes to low-level and sometimes to high-level officers. In such a situation, an American expatriate in India may find it very hard to justify such an expense to American headquarters.

In India a friend's role is to "sense" another friend's need and to do something about it. The idea of reciprocity as we know it is unheard of. An American expatriate in India will have a difficult time if he attempts to follow American friendship patterns. He gains nothing by extending himself on behalf of others, least of all gratitude, because the Indian assumes that what he does for others he does for the good of his own psyche. He will find it impossible to make friends quickly and is unlikely to allow sufficient time for friendships to ripen. He will also note that as he gets to know people better, they may become more critical of him, a fact that he finds hard to take. What he does not know is that one sign of friendship in India is speaking out one's mind.

There might be difficulties in communicating with store owners and neighbors. Although English is the official business language in India, less than 7 percent of the population speaks it. The transportation facilities in India are not very adequate. Dangerous road conditions and pollution may make it hard for American expatriates and their families to lead normal, healthy lives.

Although India is going through the process of economic liberalization, its political system is not fully cooperative to this change. There are old, bureaucratic ideologies still in conflict with each other. A considerable amount of political risk still exists. Recent elections held in India have added to this risk, as the political party which favored and introduced the whole process of liberalization is no longer as powerful. The political party in power has yet to fully demonstrate its attitude towards foreign investment. This might further complicate the matters facing American companies, especially if the present ruling party does not continue along the path of more liberalization of the economy.

Poor infrastructure, intense poverty, and a low standard of living may depress and discourage an expatriate and his or her family. For instance, limited telephone lines make communications through faxes and telephone calls inefficient, leading to high levels of frustration and stress. Lack of cleanliness, in general, overcrowded and bad roads, and an overloaded public transportation system might depress the family further.

Spouses will actually have tougher responsibilities, because they will be dealing with the real culture. This involves such difficulties as learning how and where to purchase groceries, and how to communicate with store owners, teachers, and neighbors. They would be the ones to figure out how to navigate the public transportation system.

Almost 80 percent of India's 850 million people are Hindus, 10 percent are Muslims, and the rest are either Christians, Jews, Buddhists, Sikhs, or Jains. Religious beliefs prohibit Hindus and Muslims from eating beef and pork, respectively.

The educational system in India is based upon the British system of education. However, it is tailored to the Indian scene. For instance, students learn Indian history with very little attention paid to historical developments in other parts of the world. However, the math curriculum is supposed to be among the very best.

Source: This mini-case was written by Arvind V. Phatak in collaboration with M. S. Adarkar, a student from India in the MBA program at Temple University. Copyright © 1997 by Arvind V. Phatak.

Discussion Questions for Mini-Case

1. What additional information should Vik Harris seek from the company's human resources department?

2. Discuss the various issues that Vik Harris should be concerned about regarding the transfer to India.

3. Suggest the types of financial and nonfinancial incentives that Geno's could offer to Vik to induce him to accept the India transfer. Address each concern of Vik, his spouse, and his family, which could be a deterrent to his accepting the assignment in India.

4. Using the framework discussed in the chapter, can you suggest the nature of an optimal predeparture training program for Vik Harris?

Notes

1 Patrick Oster, David Woodruff, Neil Gross, Sunita Wadekar Bhargava, and Elizabeth Lesley, "The Fast Track Leads Overseas," *Business Week*, November 1, 1993, pp. 64-68.

2 Edwin L. Miller and Joseph L. C. Cheng, "A Closer Look at the Decision to Accept an Overseas Position," *Management International Review*, Vol. 18, 1978, pp. 25-27.

3 Rosalie L. Tung, "U.S. Multinationals: A Study of Their Selection and Training Procedures for Overseas Assignments," *Academy of Management Proceedings*, 1979, p. 298.

4 Ibid.

5 R. L. Desatnick and M. L. Bennett, *Human Resource Management in the Multinational Company*, Nichols Publishing Co., New York, 1977, pp. 233-234.

6 Sanford Rose, "The Rewarding Strategies of Multinationalism," *Fortune*, September 15, 1968, p. 180.

7 Ibid.

8 Ibid.

9 Cecil G. Howard, "The Multinational Corporation: Impact on Nativization," *Personnel*, January-February 1972, p. 42.

10 Tung, p. 298.

11 Joseph LaPalombara and Stephen Black, *Multinational Corporations and National Elites: A Study of Tensions*, The Conference Board, New York, 1976, p. 57.

12 Jean E. Heller, "Criteria for Selecting an International Manager," *Personnel*, Vol. 57, May-June 1980, p. 48.

13 Ibid.

14 Arvind V. Phatak, *Managing Multinational Corporations*, Praeger Publishers, New York, 1974, p. 194.

15 William Voris, " Considerations in Staffing for Overseas Management Needs," *Personnel Journal*, June 1975, p. 354.

16 Heller, p. 49.

17 Robert C. Maddox, "Solving the Overseas Personnel Problem," *Personnel Journal*, Vol. 44, No. 2, February 1965, p. 93.

18 "Gauging a Family's Suitability for a Stint Overseas," *Business Week*, April 16, 1979, p. 127.

19 Tung, pp. 298-299.

20 "Gauging a Family's Suitability," pp. 127-130.

21 Joann S. Lubin, "Companies Use Cross-Cultural Training To Help Their Employees Adjust Abroad," *The Wall Street Journal*, August 4, 1992, p. B1.

22 Oster et al, pp. 64-68.

23 Alison R. Lanier, "Selecting and Preparing Personnel for Overseas Transfers," *Personnel Journal*, Vol. 58, March 1979, pp. 162-163.

24 Philip R. Harris and Robert T. Moran, *Managing Cultural Differences*, Gulf Publishing Co., Houston, 1979, p. 149.

25 Ibid., pp. 128-129. Reprinted by permission.

26 Oster et al, pp. 64-68.

27 Lubin, p. B1.

28 Joann S. Lubin, "Spouses Find Themselves Worlds Apart as Global Commuter Marriages Increase," *The Wall Street Journal*, August 19, 1992, p. B1.

29 Rosalie L. Tung, "Selection and Training of Personnel for Overseas Assignments," *Columbia Journal of World Business*, Spring 1981, p. 74.

30 John S. McClenahan, "The Overseas Manager: Not Actually a World Away," *Industry Week*, November 1, 1976, p. 53.

31 Ibid.

32 Lee Smith, "The Hazards of Coming Home," *Dun's Review*, October 1975, p. 72.

33 Joann S. Lubin, "Managing Your Career," *The Wall Street Journal*, August 25, 1993, p. B1.

34 "How to Ease Re-entry after Overseas Duty," *Business Week*, June 11, 1979, p. 82.

35 Lubin, "Managing Your Career," p. B1.

36 Ibid., p. 84.

37 McClenahan, p. 53.

38 Oster et al, pp. 64-68.

39 Desatnick and Bennet, p. 168.

40 Paul E. Illman, *Developing Overseas Managers—And Managers Overseas*, AMACOM, New York, 1980, p. 178.

41 Ibid., p. 176.

42 Howard V. Perlmutter, "The Tortous Evolution of the Multinational Corporation," *Columbia Journal of World Business*, Vol. 3, No. 1, January-February 1969, pp. 11-14.

43 W. A. Borrman, "The Problem of Expatriate Personnel and Their Selection in International Enterprises," *Management International Review*, Vol. 8, No. 4-5, 1968, pp. 37-38.

44 Yoram Zeira and Ehud Harari, "Genuine Multinational Staffing Policy Expectations and Realities," *Academy of Management Journal*, Vol. 20, No. 2, 1977, p. 328.

45 Borrman, p. 40.

46 Graef S. Crystal, *Compensating U.S. Expatriates Abroad: An AMA Management Briefing*, American Management Association, New York, 1972, pp. 1-3.

47 E. J. Kolde, *The Multinational Company*, Lexington Books, Lexington, Mass., 1974, pp. 176-178.

48 Ibid., pp. 178-179.

49 Ibid., pp. 179-180.

50 Ibid., pp. 180-181.

51 *Compensating International Executives*, Business International Corporation, New York, 1970, p. 33.

52 Ibid.

53 Ibid.

54 Crystal, p. 44.

55 Ibid.

56 Ibid., p. 9.

57 David Young, "Fair Compensation for Expatriates," *Harvard Business Review*, Vol. 51, No. 4, July-August 1973, p. 119.

58 Ibid., pp. 119-120.

59 Ibid., pp. 120-121.

60 *Compensating International Executives*, pp. 23-25.

61 Crystal, pp. 18-19.

62 Young, pp. 123-145.

63 Ibid.

64 Ibid.

65 Crystal, p. 10.

66 This section written by Bill Roberts, graduate student in Business at Temple University, based on material contained in: Tara Parker-Pope, "Culture Clash: Do U.S.-Style Stock Compensation Plans Make Sense in Other Countries? *The Wall Street Journal*, April 12, 1995, p. R7.

67 Shawn Tully, "Where People Live Best," *Fortune*, March 11, 1991, pp. 44-54.

Further Reading

Black, Stewart J., and Hal B. Gregersen, "The Other Half of the Picture: Antecedents of Spouse Cross-Cultural Adjustment," *Journal of International Business Studies*, Vol. 22, No. 3, Third Quarter, 1991, pp. 461-477.

Borrman, W. A., "The Problem of Expatriate Personnel and Their Selection in International Enterprises," *Management International Review*, No. 4-5, 1968.

Boyacigiller, Nakiye, "The Role of Expatriates in the Management of Interdependence, Complexity, and Risk in Multinational Corporations," *Journal of International Business Studies*, Vol. 21, No. 3, Third Quarter, 1990, pp. 357-381.

Compensating International Executives, Business International Corporation, New York, 1970.

Crystal, Graef S., *Compensating U.S. Expatriates Abroad: An AMA Management Briefing*, American Management Association, New York, 1972.

Desatnick, R. L., and M. L. Bennett, *Human Resource Management in the Multinational Company*, Nichols, New York, 1977.

Domsch, M., and B. Lichtenberger, "Managing the Global Manager: Pre-Departure Training and Development for German Expatriates in China and Brazil," *Journal of Management Development*, Vol. 10, No. 7, 1991, pp. 41-52.

Dowling, Peter J., Randall S. Schuler, and Denice E. Welch, *International Dimensions of Human Resource Management*, Wadsworth Publishing Company, Belmont, California, 1994.

Feldman, Daniel C., and Holly B. Tompson, "Entry Shock, Culture Shock: Socializing the New Breed of Global Managers," *Human Resource Management*, Vol. 31, No. 4, Winter 1992, pp. 345-362.

Franko, Lawrence G., "Who Manages Multinational Enterprises?" *Columbia Journal of World Business*, Vol. 8, No. 2, Summer 1973.

Harris, Philip R., and Robert T. Moran, *Managing Cultural Differences*, Gulf Publishing Co., Houston, 1979.

Heller, Jean E., "Criteria for Selecting an International Manager," *Personnel*, Vol. 57, May-June 1980.

Howard, Cecil G., "The Multinational Corporation: Impact on Nativization," *Personnel*, January-February 1972.

Illman, Paul E., *Developing Overseas Managers—And Managers Overseas*, AMACOM, New York, 1980.

Lanier, Alison R., "Selecting and Preparing Personnel for Overseas Transfers," *Personnel Journal*, March 1979.

LaPalombara, Joseph, and Stephen Blank, *Multinational Corporations and National Elites: A Study of Tensions*, The Conference Board, New York, 1976.

Maddox, Robert C., "Solving the Overseas Personnel Problem," *Personnel Journal*, June 1975.

McClenahan, John S., "The Overseas Manager: Not Actually a World Away," *Industry Week*, November 1, 1976.

Miller, Edwin L., and Joseph L. C. Cheng, "A Closer Look at the Decision to Accept an Overseas Position," *Management International Review*, Vol. 18, 1978.

Moskowitz, Daniel B., "How to Cut It Overseas," *International Business*, Vol. 5, No. 10, October 1992, pp. 76, 78.

Perlmutter, Howard V., "The Fortuitous Evolution of the Multinational Corporation," *Columbia Journal of World Business*, January-February 1969.

Phatak, Arvind V., *Managing Multinational Corporations*, Praeger Publishers, New York, 1974.

Rose, Stanford, "The Rewarding Strategies of Multinationalism," *Fortune*, September 15, 1968.

Smith, Lee, "The Hazards of Coming Home," *Dun's Review*, October 1975.

Tung, Rosalie L., "U.S. Multinationals: A Study of Their Selection and Training Procedures for Overseas Assignments," *Academy of Management Proceedings*, 1979.

——"Selection and Training of Personnel for Overseas Assignments," *Columbia Journal of World Business*, Winter 1981.

Voris, William, "Considerations in Staffing for Overseas Management Needs," *Personnel Journal*, June 1975.

Young, David, "Fair Compensation for Expatriates," *Harvard Business Review*, July-August 1973.

Zeria, Yoram, and Ehud Harari, "Genuine Multinational Staffing Policy: Expectations and Realities," *Academy of Management Journal*, Vol. 20, No. 2, 1977.

CHAPTER FOURTEEN

The Control Process in an International Context

LEARNING OBJECTIVES

After completing this chapter, you will be able to:

- Describe the four main elements in the managerial control process.
- Discuss problems of control that are particular to international companies.
- Explain the differences between direct and indirect controls and give examples of each.
- Define transfer pricing and discuss the implications of transfer pricing policy for measuring performance in the international company.
- Describe the key attributes of an effective international control system.
- Discuss three categories of parent-subsidiary relationships and the strategic control mechanisms appropriate to each.

An international company derives its strength from being able to recognize and capitalize on opportunities anywhere in the world, and from its capacity to respond to global threats to its business operations in a timely fashion. On the basis of an evaluation of global opportunities and threats, and of a company's strengths and weaknesses, top management executives of a multinational at the parent company level formulate corporate strategy for the whole company. The objectives of a multinational company serve as the umbrella under which the objectives of divisions and subsidiaries are developed. There is a considerable amount of give and take between the parent company, divisions, and subsidiaries before the divisional and subsidiary objectives are finally agreed to by executives at all three levels.

The objective of managerial control is to ensure that plans are implemented correctly. In this chapter, the focus will be on the parent company's managerial control over its foreign subsidiaries. We shall examine first the salient features of the managerial control process. Then, because multinational companies experience problems controlling their far-flung operations, we shall look at those problems and their causes. The chapter next includes a review of the typical characteristics of control systems used by international companies, then concludes with some suggestions for improving the international control process.

THE MANAGERIAL CONTROL PROCESS

Managerial control is a process directed toward ensuring that operations and personnel adhere to parent company plans. A control system is essential because the future is uncertain. Assumptions about the internal and external environment that were at one time the basis of a forecast may prove invalid, strategies may not be applicable, and budgets and programs may not be effective. Managerial control is a process that evaluates performance and takes corrective action when performance differs significantly from the company's plans. With managerial control, any deviations from forecasts, objectives, or plans can be detected early and corrected with minimum difficulty.

Managerial control involves several management skills: planning, coordinating, communicating, processing and evaluating information, and influencing people.

There are four main elements in the managerial control process:[1]

1. The setting of standards.
2. The development of devices or techniques to monitor the performance of an individual or an organizational system.
3. The comparison of performance measures obtained from monitoring devices to the company's plans in order to determine if current performance is sufficiently close to what was planned.
4. The employment of effectuating or action devices that can be used to correct significant deviations in performance.

There is a close relationship between managerial control and planning. Managerial control depends on the objectives set forth in tactical plans, which in turn are derived from the strategic plans of the organization. Tactical plans are for the short-term contributions of each functional area to the strategic plans, goals, and objectives.

Setting the Standards

The first step in the control process is the setting of standards. These standards are derived from the objectives defined in the planning process. Without a definition of objectives, there can be no formulation of standards.

After standards are formulated, a hierarchy of degrees of importance needs to be established. However, it would be inefficient and unrealistic to set specific standards for every organizational activity. Instead, management should continuously monitor the performance of activities in key areas, or those it considers to be essential. Whatever is not considered essential to the attainment of a company's objectives could be controlled by "exception," whereby monitoring is periodic and on a sample basis.[2] In key areas, standards need to be as concrete and as specific as possible, while taking into consideration the fact that some key areas, such as management development, cannot be expressed in specific and concrete terms.[3]

Monitoring Performance

Once standards have been established, the next step is the development of techniques to monitor and accurately describe performance. Budgets, managerial audits, and financial statements are the main measuring devices used to assess the performance of organizational systems. A *budget* is a "detailed listing of the resources or money assigned to a particular project or unit."[4] Here, standards of performance are translated into dollar amounts for each item in the budget. However, the dynamic, changing character of a business environment necessitates some flexibility with budgets.

There are several methods for making budgets flexible without eventually losing managerial control, such as the adoption of supplemental budgets, alternative budgets, and variable expense budgets. Supplemental budgets are used with budgets that establish limits on expenditures, such as for plant expansion, capital improvements, and so on. If a capital expenditure budget proves to be too low because of inaccurate costing in the planning stage, a supplemental budget can be prepared and added to the original budget.[5]

Alternative budgeting is another form of controlled budgeting. A budget is usually prepared on the basis of an organization's assessment of the most probable future conditions. However, if there is a real possibility that, for example, future sales may be lower (or higher), alternative budgets are prepared based on the implications of specific lower or higher sales figures.

A third type of budgeting is the variable expense budget found mostly in manufacturing organizations. Variable expense budgets are devised to ensure proper coordination of activities as changes take place in sales of manufactured goods. These budgets are "schedules of costs of production that tell managers what levels of critical activities actually should be established as changes occur in sales and output volume."[6]

All these budgetary techniques require accurate and timely communication. Variable expense budgets, in particular, depend on accurate and prompt reports from production and sales.

Another typical control mechanism of organizational systems is financial statements, particularly the income statement—which details the sources of revenues and expenses for a given year—the profit and loss statement, balance sheets, and so on.

Comparing Performance to Plan

The third step in the managerial control process is comparing the performance measures obtained from the different monitoring devices to the company's objectives, and evaluating whether current performance is sufficiently close to the company's original plan. Management must decide how much variation between standard and actual performance is tolerable, and what "sufficiently close" means for the organization.

Changes in the external environment may affect the limits of possible performance, which in turn may necessitate a change in the performance standards. Once the limits of the performance are altered, management must decide how the standards of measurement should be altered. Naturally, when the external environment does not deviate from the forecast, the task of managerial control is simply to evaluate whether performance is within acceptable limits.

Another aspect of the evaluation phase of the control process is related to feedback and feedforward controls. With feedback controls, the focus is on information about events that have already occurred, such as production and actual sales. This information is compared with a standard of performance in order to make necessary corrections for the future. For example, feedback control is typically used to monitor the productivity and performance of a factory worker against a preset production rate.

Feedforward controls are different in that the deviations from standards are anticipated or predicted before they occur. When those conditions do occur, certain actions are scheduled to take place in anticipation of the outcome of the first occurrence. For example, when sales volume reaches a predetermined level, management is automatically obliged to increase the level of inventory. This action is taken to prevent inventories from running out, a situation that would otherwise occur as the result of the first occurrence—the sales increase. "Feedback control cures problems: feedforward control prevents them."[7] Companies use both types of controls, although feedback is more common because it is less complicated and requires less forecasting.

From this discussion, it is apparent that accurate communication and a pervasive managerial information system are essential in management control. Management cannot appraise, compare, or correct performance without the proper reporting of appropriate and meaningful information.

Correcting the Deviations

The fourth step in the control process is correcting significant deviations from the standards. For this step, effectuating or action devices must be employed. The application of action devices requires many management skills such as decision making, persuading, effective communication, and so on. When a subsystem of an organization needs help, the corrective action might be to use different budgeting techniques, or to impose control mechanisms on costs, expenses, and so on. When the deviation concerns organizational personnel, the action devices can be either positive (promotions, salary increases, increased responsibility, and special privileges) or negative (reprimands, withdrawal of privileges, demotions, salary reductions, and termination of employment).[8]

It is essential to recognize the overriding human dimension in the managerial control process. The steps or elements in the control process are not automatic, but are activated by management. Monitoring, comparing, and action devices depend on human intervention. The necessary communication is between people. The effectiveness of the control system depends on the acceptance of the system as necessary, legitimate, and appropriate by the members of the organization. This human dimension is most significant in the managerial process in a multinational company.

PROBLEMS OF CONTROL IN AN INTERNATIONAL COMPANY

Control and the problems associated with it are far more complex in a multinational company than in one that is purely domestic because the multinational operates in more than one cultural, economic, political, and legal environment. Let us examine a few of the most important international variables having a major negative impact on the flow of information between headquarters and subsidiaries. These variables, in turn, influence the effectiveness of the international company's control system.

Despite the sophistication and speed of contemporary communication systems, the geographic distance between a parent company and a foreign affiliate continues to cause communication distortion. Differences in language between the parent company and its foreign affiliates are also responsible for distortions in communication. Language barriers caused by language differences involve both the content and the meaning of messages. Many ideas and concepts are not easily translatable from one language to another. Because of geographic distances, there is little face-to-face communication and the messages of nonverbal communication are lost. Problems are also caused by misunderstanding the communication habits of people in other cultures. Managers of different cultures may interact, and yet block out important messages because the manner in which the message is presented may mean something different in the sending and receiving cultures. For example, a manager may make a wrong judgment about a subordinate's performance because he or she is unaware of culturally different communication habits. As an illustration, consider that the aborigines in Australia exhibit attention by listening intently with their faces and bodies turned away from the speaker, and with no eye contact.[9] This behavior could easily be misread by a member of a different culture—one who is accustomed to associate body posture and eye contact with attention. Cultural distance is as significant as geographic distance in creating communication distortions. Lack of understanding and acceptance of the cultural values of a group may impair a manager's ability to evaluate information accurately, to judge performance fairly, and to make valid decisions about performance. This failure could create problems in an international company in the area of employee performance appraisal.

In some cultures one does not make criticism bluntly, but discusses critical areas in an oblique fashion. And in the Mexican culture, responsibility is viewed as being tied to fate. It is therefore deeply offensive to a Mexican to be told that he or she is personally responsible for some failure.[10] In contrast, the American style of managerial control fixes responsibilities for achieving certain organizational goals on specific members in the organization. Other control mechanisms are also affected by cultural differences. The detailed reporting required by some "tight" managerial control systems is not acceptable to some cultures. Also, the degree of harmony valued in a culture may make the accurate reporting of problems difficult.[11]

For example, in the Japanese culture, maintaining group cohesiveness is considered to be far more important than reporting a problem to a superior who would place blame on the group or an individual within the group. It is therefore not unusual for Japanese supervisors not to report a problem to upper management, in the hope that it can be resolved at the group level.

Communication distortion between the parent company and a foreign affiliate may occur because of the differing frames of reference of these two organizational units. The parent company may perceive each foreign affiliate as just one of many, and therefore may have a tendency to view each affiliate's problems in light of the company's entire global network of operations. However, foreign affiliate heads may view the problems of their own operations as being very important to them and their affiliates. Both the parent company and the affiliate heads may try to communicate their feelings and views to each other without much success because each could be communicating from a different frame of reference.

CHARACTERISTICS OF CONTROL SYSTEMS IN INTERNATIONAL COMPANIES

Multinational companies use a variety of control systems to monitor and change the performance of their foreign subsidiaries. Some of these controls are direct controls, whereas others can be categorized as indirect.

Direct Controls

Direct controls include the use of such devices as periodic meetings, visits by home country executives to foreign affiliates, and the staffing of foreign affiliates by home country nationals. Controls can be exercised by holding management meetings to discuss the performance of foreign affiliates.

Some companies, such as International Telephone and Telegraph Corporation, hold monthly management meetings at their headquarters in New York at which each ITT manager of every profit-and-loss division, however small, is in attendance. The meeting is presided over by the chief executive officer of the company, and reports submitted by each ITT unit head from around the world are discussed. Each report contains all facts concerning the performance of the unit, such as financial analyses of sales, profits, return on investment, and virtually every other measurement used in business. The report is also expected to contain a description of every existing and potential problem affecting the operation. A description of the problem, however, is not enough. The report must also explain how and why the problem arose and how the executive in charge of the unit plans to solve it. Other multinational companies also resort to meetings, similar to ITT's, for controlling their foreign affiliates. The focus of such meetings is on direct, face-to-face communication and direct feedback.

Visits by top executives from corporate headquarters to each foreign affiliate also serve as control devices. It is not unusual for the chief executive officer and a group of top headquarters executives to spend several days each month sitting across the table from subsidiary and regional managers. Such visits are held so that problems, such as competition problems, performance problems, or others, can be dealt with face to face.

The international staffing practices of some multinational companies are also aimed at ensuring adequate control over foreign affiliates. The practice adopted by many companies of staffing the top management slot of a foreign subsidiary with a manager from the home country is for this purpose. Whether the reason is a lack of trust of foreign nationals, or a belief that home country nationals are better managers and are more knowledgeable about the company's overall philosophies, policies, and strategies than are managers of foreign nationality, putting a home country national in charge of a foreign subsidiary is supposed to provide the subsidiary with the type and kind of management that the parent company wants. The idea is that the better a foreign subsidiary is managed, the fewer performance deviations from planned performance, and therefore the fewer problems associated with controlling its operations.

The organizational structure of the company is yet another control mechanism. In Chapter 12, we examined the various types of organizational structures that multinational companies have used to coordinate and control their global operations. No two companies have the same organizational structure because companies need different types of information flows in order to control their far-flung operations. For example, the creation of regional management units in a product division structure reflects an attempt by companies to shorten the distance between headquarters and the foreign affiliates, thereby promoting better control over foreign operations.

Indirect Controls

The preceding paragraphs dealt with direct controls. Companies also use indirect controls to control foreign subsidiaries. These include various reports, similar to those required by ITT from each foreign unit head, that each foreign subsidiary is expected to submit to top management detailing its performance during a certain period. Other forms of indirect controls include a whole range of budgetary and financial controls that are imposed through budgets, and various types of financial statements such as a balance sheet, profit-and-loss statement, cash budget, and an exhaustive set of financial ratios depicting the financial health of the subsidiary.

Three different sets of financial statements are usually required from subsidiaries to meet different needs. The first set of statements is prepared to meet the national accounting standards and procedures prescribed by law and other professional organizations in the host country. Use of national accounting standards also facilitates management's evaluation of a subsidiary's performance against its local competitors.

The second set of financial statements is prepared to comply with the accounting principles and standards required by the home country. For this compliance, accounts have to be restated and modified according to the home country's requirements. Only after these adjustments are made can financial statements of subsidiaries be deemed adequate for consolidation with those of the parent company, and for comparison with the relative performance of several subsidiaries.

A subsidiary prepares a third set of statements to meet the financial consolidation requirements of the home country. For consolidation, financial statements denominated in the host country's currency need to be translated into the currency of the home country. In this way, financial statements have a common basis of valuation. International Accounting Standard No. 3, adopted in the United States, requires a foreign subsidiary's financial statements to be consolidated line by line with those of the parent company. Subsidiaries are defined as entities over which the parent exercises control by ownership, majority equity capital, or control of the board. Although the parent is not required to consolidate the financial statements of its foreign associates with its own accounts, under the equity method it is required to record them. This method requires the value of an investment to be increased or decreased in the parent company's books in order to recognize the parent's share of profit or loss after the acquisition. A foreign associate is defined as a company over which the parent exercises significant influence by holding at least 20 percent of its voting power.

Any other corporate equity holdings are required to be recorded at cost in the balance sheet of a parent company. However, the dividends received from these investments are recorded in the parent company's income statement. Presently, FAS-52 requires U.S. multinationals to translate all assets and liabilities of a foreign subsidiary into dollar amounts at the current rate of exchange. Under this method, all assets and liabilities are first restated at their current price levels, then translated in the parent's book at current exchange rates.

Most companies use returns on investment and profits as the dominant criteria for an evaluation of the performance of a foreign affiliate. A study conducted by Robins and Stobaugh of 150 companies with foreign operations showed that 95 percent judge their foreign subsidiaries on precisely the same basis as domestic subsidiaries and, almost without exception, they use a form of return on investment (ROI) as their main measure of performance.[12] However, the reported profits of a foreign subsidiary and its ROI may not, and very rarely do, reflect its true performance. What follows is a discussion of why this is the case.

MEASURES OF PERFORMANCE: REPORTED PROFITS AND ROI

There are many decisions made above the subsidiary level at the parent company or regional headquarters that affect the operations of a subsidiary. Take, for example, the manipulation by the parent company or regional headquarters of the transfer prices of raw materials, components, or products in intracompany transactions. A higher-than-arm's-length price might be charged on exports made by a subsidiary located in a low income tax country to a subsidiary located in a country that has high income tax rates. Other things being equal, this maneuver would result in lower profits for the importing subsidiary, lowering its taxes, and higher profits for the exporting subsidiary. However, the important point is that the difference in tax rates could result in maximizing overall corporate profits.

It is alleged that the United States government is losing each year between $20 and $30 billion in unpaid taxes by foreign corporations doing business in the United States. It is further alleged by the U.S. Internal Revenue Service (IRS) that foreign companies are able to evade paying U.S. taxes by manipulating the prices charged for goods and services to their U.S. subsidiaries. Officials in the IRS also charge that U.S. multinationals could easily account for $5 billion in unpaid taxes as a result of transfer pricing strategies that minimize the total tax burden on the corporation.[13]

Practical Insight 14-1 gives examples of how companies like Toyota, Yamaha, and Westinghouse Electric have used transfer pricing to minimize their U.S. federal tax burden.

PRACTICAL INSIGHT 14-1
The Corporate Shell Game: How Multinational Firms Use 'Transfer Pricing' to Evade at Least $20 Billion in U.S. Taxes

Abuses in pricing across borders—"transfer pricing," in corporate jargon—are illegal, if they can be proved. Corporations dealing with their own subsidiaries are required to set prices at "arm's length," just as they would for unrelated customers. And there's no question that abuses can be enormous. In its biggest known victory, the IRS made its case that Japan's Toyota had been systematically overcharging its U.S. subsidiary for years on most of the cars, trucks, and parts sold in the United States. What would have been profits from the United States had wafted back to Japan. Toyota denied improprieties but agreed to a reported $1 billion settlement, paid in part with tax rebates from the government of Japan.

Some abuses are blatant. One foreign manufacturer, for instance, sold TV sets to its U.S. subsidiary for $250 each, but charged an unrelated company just $150. Most cases are nowhere near as clear. What if the set sold outside has a slight change in the casing? Which subsidiary gets charged for shipping and insurance? In one current case, the IRS says Japan's Yamaha forced Yamaha Motor Corp., U.S.A., to overstock motorcycles and all-terrain vehicles in the early '80s, and then made the subsidiary pay for discounts and promotions to unload the excess inventory. The result, says the tax agency, was that Yamaha Motor U.S.A. paid only $5,272 in corporate tax to Washington over four years. Proper accounting would have shown a profit of $500 million and taxes of $127 million, the agency says. But Yamaha argues that the IRS case ignores the colossal reality of the 1982 recession, which caught the company just as unprepared as its U.S. competitors. The U.S. Tax Court is mulling the case.

American-based multinationals have also been accused of squirreling profits away. Tax agents find it easier to monitor their books, since they're all in this country and follow SEC standards; as Wheeler explains it, "It's the difference between examining the head and several arms of an octopus, rather than just one tentacle." Even so, he thinks the U.S. multinationals could easily account for an additional $5 billion in lost taxes on profits dubiously allocated to tax havens. Wheeler and Richard Weber say they've found one case that is suggestive: Westinghouse Electric managed to book 27 percent of its 1986 domestic profit in Puerto Rico, where its final sales are tiny.

THE CORPORATE SHELL GAME

Germany	*Ireland*	*United States*
An item is manufactured at a cost of $80. It is then sold to an Irish subsidiary for $80.	The subsidiary turns around and resells the item at $150 to a U.S. subsidiary, earning a $70 profit.	The U.S. subsidiary sells the item at cost, for $150. No profit is earned. The Irish subsidiary then lends money to the U.S. company for future expansion.
Tax Rate: 48% **Tax Paid: $0**	**Tax Rate: 4%** **Tax Paid: $2.80**	**Tax Rate: 34%** **Tax Paid: $0**

CHAPTER FOURTEEN

PRACTICAL INSIGHT 14-1 *(continued)*

To spur the Puerto Rican economy, Washington has set the corporate tax rate there at zero. (Westinghouse says the accounting is proper, since its "highest-profit products are made in Puerto Rico.")

Source: Larry Martz and Rich Thomas, "The Corporate Shell Game: How Multinational Firms Use 'Transfer Pricing' to Evade at Least $20 Billion in U.S. Taxes," *Newsweek*, April 15, 1991, pp. 48-49. © 1991, Newsweek, Inc. All rights reserved. Reprinted by permission.

Transfer prices are manipulated upward or downward depending on whether the parent company wishes to inject cash into or remove cash from a subsidiary. Prices placed by a subsidiary on imports from a related subsidiary are raised if the multinational company wishes to move funds from the receiver to the seller, but they are lowered if the objective is to keep funds in the importing subsidiary. Similarly, prices on exports from a subsidiary to a related subsidiary are raised if the multinational company wishes to move funds from the importer to the exporter. Multinational companies have been known to use transfer pricing for moving excess cash from subsidiaries located in countries with weak currencies to countries with strong currencies in order to protect the value of their current assets. Transfer prices are also manipulated in order to give a better credit rating to a foreign subsidiary. Showing that a subsidiary has a good record of earnings makes it easier for it to borrow money in local money markets.

These are some of the ways in which transfer prices are used advantageously by multinational companies. However, transfer prices can create serious internal management control problems, because the manipulation of transfer prices forces the subsidiaries it affects to show profits that are allocated to them rather than actually earned by them. Hence, allocated profits reported by subsidiaries should not be used to measure their performance, because they do not reflect the real performance of the subsidiaries being monitored.

It is possible that a foreign country could have severe inflation for months or years without any devaluation of its currency. This situation could help a subsidiary in that country to earn high profits, but they would rightly be attributable to the high inflation rate rather than good management. On the other hand, when devaluation of the local currency vis-à-vis the U.S. dollar occurs within a given accounting period, the subsidiary, although well managed and profitable in terms of the local currency, may show a loss when its income statement is translated into U.S. dollars. This situation could result in a faulty evaluation of the subsidiary's management. What further complicates this problem is that, although inflation and deflation generally tend to be approximately equal in magnitude in the long run, they are rarely exactly equal within a given period of time. More often than not, devaluations are inadequate to compensate for domestic inflation.

The profitability criterion may have to be modified for a subsidiary that is located in a country where the government lets it be known that it expects the subsidiary to make positive contributions to the nation's economy. This requirement may compel the subsidiary to engage in activities that may not contribute to its short-run profitability, such as a maximum use of locally produced components (even though they may not meet quality requirements) and a no-layoff policy for the local labor force.

There are many companywide logistical decisions that are actually made above the subsidiary level but that affect the subsidiary's profitability for better or worse. For example, executives at the parent company level might decide to serve third markets that were previously served by subsidiary A, by exports from subsidiary B. This turn of events would adversely affect the sales volume and consequently the profits of subsidiary A. It would therefore be erroneous to assume that the reported profits of subsidiary A and subsidiary B reflect the performance of their respective managements without taking into consideration the impact on the subsidiaries' operations of the parent company's decision to shift exports to third markets from subsidiary A to subsidiary B.

DESIGNING AN EFFECTIVE INTERNATIONAL CONTROL SYSTEM

An effective control system cannot rely upon reported profits and ROI as the dominant measures of performance of a foreign subsidiary, because the corporate headquarters of the company, rather than the subsidiary manager, makes most of the major decisions affecting the profitability of the subsidiary. To obtain a more accurate picture of a subsidiary's performance one must be certain to eliminate extraneous factors—results, positive or negative, caused by decisions made above the subsidiary level, or results due to environmental variables, such as unprecedented fluctuations in the price of raw materials (for example, the unexpected sharp increase in the price of petroleum in 1974), or results due to government actions over which subsidiary management could not exercise any control. Thus, a subsidiary manager should be held accountable only for results that were caused by actions that he or she could initiate, without external interference, and by decisions that he or she could make unilaterally. The profit-and-loss statement or the ROI of a subsidiary should be adjusted to reflect its actual performance, taking into account the above-mentioned factors. It is quite conceivable, under such a system, for subsidiary managers to be rated quite favorably in spite of their having a poor profit-and-loss statement. The opposite is also possible; a manager who shows huge profits may still be judged a poor manager if his or her performance warrants such a judgment.

In addition to financial measures, an assessment should also use nonfinancial measures of performance, such as market share, productivity, relations with the host country government, public image, employee morale, union relations, community involvement, and so on. Most companies do take into account some nonfinancial factors. However, it might be advisable to formalize the process, with scorecard ratings for all subsidiaries based on the same broad range of variables. Finally, the level of performance expected from a foreign subsidiary in the following year should consider the characteristics of its environment and how it is likely to change from the current year. Thus, an environment that was generally favorable one year might be expected to change for the worse the following year, and the level of performance expected should be appropriately lowered as well. Not doing so could lead to unhealthy pressure on the subsidiary manager, perhaps inducing him or her to make decisions about maintenance expenditures or service to customers or the funding of process improvements that are detrimental in the long run to both the subsidiary and the company as a whole.

The control procedures and techniques to be used should be understandable and acceptable to the subsidiary heads concerned, and the subsidiary heads should actively participate in formulating them. Each subsidiary should be given realistic objectives that take into account its internal and external environment. The control system should detect and report deviations from subsidiary plans as soon as, or before, they occur. This information should then be made available to higher management and to the subsidiary head. The control system should not be allowed to stagnate, but should be revised and improved as changes in the subsidiary's environment require. Top management must tie compensation to results actually achieved, and outstanding performance must be tangibly rewarded.

Strategic Intent and Subsidiary Control

The strategic intent of the parent company in establishing a foreign subsidiary is often forgotten when the parent evaluates the performance of all subsidiaries. The evaluation process that is based upon financial considerations alone does not account for the variety of strategic considerations that may have come into play in the original decision to establish a foreign subsidiary.

For example, if General Motors decides to establish an assembly operation in China to take advantage of that country's cheap labor, then a company such as Ford may follow suit primarily to stay even with one of its chief competitors. The risk of a rival exploiting a low labor-cost country to gain a superior long-run competitive advantage would be too big for Ford to take. There might be other strategic considerations in establishing foreign subsidiaries. For instance, international companies may establish fully integrated subsidiaries in key foreign markets in response to political pressures imposed by host country governments to do so. Japanese car manufacturers have established such operations in Europe and in North America, largely to alleviate the political fallout from the huge trade deficits that Europe and the United States have had with Japan over the last several years—although the high value of the Japanese yen, which makes exports from Japan very difficult, is also a key factor in setting up manufacturing and assembly operations outside of Japan. Subsidiaries may be established in key foreign markets to serve as bases for launching counterattacks against competitors. For instance, a company that is attacked in the U.K. by a Japanese competitor may launch strikes against the "aggressor" in Japan, or in a third-country market like the United States where the Japanese company may have a strategic market position to protect. Several international companies have established such "launching pads"—subsidiaries for launching retaliatory strikes—in North America, Europe, the Pacific Basin, and Japan. The subsidiaries are placed in these areas because they represent big markets with the most growth potential, and in which most international companies have operations.

In each of the previous examples, the financial calculations of ROI alone might not provide the justification for the establishment of a foreign subsidiary. However, strategic considerations provide the necessary motives for setting up the foreign operation. Therefore, when it comes to evaluating the performance of foreign subsidiaries, parent company executives ought to consider the original strategic intent in establishing each subsidiary, and measure its performance in terms of the extent to which it has served its strategic intent. When strategic considerations of the types discussed are involved, ROI or profitability should not be used in a subsidiary's performance evaluation.

PARENT-SUBSIDIARY RELATIONSHIPS AND STRATEGIC CONTROL MECHANISMS

The network of subsidiaries in an international company is characterized by three types of relationships between each subsidiary and the parent company: dependent, independent and interdependent. A *dependent* subsidiary is one that is unable to generate strategic resources—such as technology, capital, management, and access to markets—independently of the parent company and must therefore obtain such resources from the parent company, or from other subsidiaries after prior approval of the parent company. At the other extreme is the *independent* subsidiary that can generate all the required strategic resources on its own. Between the two extreme positions is the *interdependent* subsidiary-parent relationship in which the parent and the subsidiary are able to generate some, but not all, of the required strategic resources. As such, in the interdependent relationship each side is dependent upon the other for some strategic resources that it cannot generate by itself.

Example of a dependent subsidiary: A subsidiary whose only role is to operate in the home market of a competitor and to launch strategic counterattacks locally against the competitor. The subsidiary is dependent upon the parent company for the financial resources needed to stay in business. The strategic intent of the parent company in establishing the subsidiary was mainly to keep an eye on the competitor and to gather information on the competitor's strategic moves. The dependent subsidiary cannot survive for long without the strategic resources provided by the parent.

Example of an independent subsidiary: A subsidiary in a country that has substantial restrictions on international trade that prevents the subsidiary from establishing production, marketing, financial, product, or service linkages with the parent and other sister subsidiaries. As such, the subsidiary is self-sufficient in the strategic resources required to implement its mission in the host country.

Example of an interdependent subsidiary: The subsidiary serves as a cash cow to the parent company. In return the parent provides the subsidiary with the state-of-the-art technology to maintain the subsidiary's competitive advantage in the host country. Neither the parent nor the subsidiary can do without the strategic resource that each provides to the other.

Prahalad and Doz have identified two principal methods by which a parent company can exercise *strategic control*, which they define as "the extent of influence that a head office has over a subsidiary concerning decisions that affect subsidiary strategy."[14] The two methods they identify are (1) *substantive control*: restricting the flow of strategic resources; and (2) *organizational context*: a blending of organizational structure, measurement and reward systems, career planning, and a common organizational culture, which would create the type of relationship between the parent and the subsidiary that would facilitate the continued influence of the former over the latter.[15]

Rewarding subsidiary managers for implementing strategies that support the global strategies of the international company, or making the position of subsidiary manager a "stop" on the way to higher level positions in the company, are examples of organizational contexts that would strengthen the parent's ability to exercise strategic control.

Substantive controls can be effective in influencing the strategy of dependent subsidiaries. Subsidiaries that are independent cannot be controlled with substantive controls alone because of their self-sufficiency from the parent company. In this case, the organizational context is most effective in compensating for the erosion of the parent's capacity to exercise strategic control. As the ability to use substantive control diminishes, the dependence of the parent company on organizational context to influence strategy of subsidiaries increases.[16]

The parent company will need a balance of both substantive control and the effective use of organizational context to control the strategies of subsidiaries with whom it is in an interdependent relationship. We shall call the joint use of both methods *combination strategic control*. Reliance solely upon either substantive control or organizational context would cause loss of strategic control.

Exhibit 14-1 illustrates the connection between dependent, independent, and interdependent parent-subsidiary relationships and the type of strategic control adopted by the parent.

Throughout our discussion of the issue of control in the international firm, we have emphasized that an effective control system must be able to differentiate between performance attributable

EXHIBIT 14-1
Parent-Subsidiary Relationship and Strategic Control Mechanisms

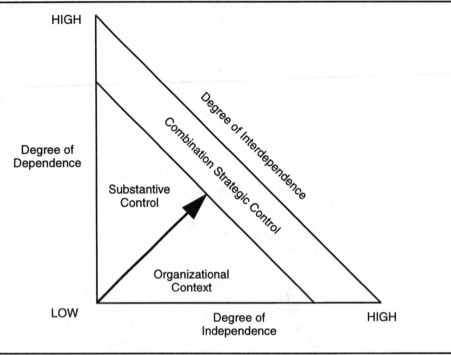

to the managers at the subsidiary and performance that was due to factors or decisions beyond the subsidiary's control. We have also shown that the effectiveness of different control mechanisms for a given subsidiary depends to a large extent on the nature of the relationship between that subsidiary and the parent company. Designing a realistic and effective control system is essential to the sustained success of the international firm, just as much as are the issues of structure and staffing that we discussed in earlier chapters.

Up to this point, we have covered a variety of the key dimensions of managing in the global environment. In the final chapter of the book, we will address a topic that has special importance for international companies by taking an in-depth look at the role and influence of ethical considerations for international managers.

SUMMARY

In this chapter we looked at the managerial control process in an international context. The focus was on the problems and characteristics of control systems adopted by multinational companies in order to manage their foreign subsidiaries, with emphasis on ways to improve the process.

Managerial control is the process of ensuring that actual performance is equal to planned performance. The purpose of control is to facilitate the implementation of plans by continuously monitoring the performance of the people responsible for carrying them out.

There are four principal elements in the control process: (1) establishing standards against which performance is to be measured, (2) developing devices or techniques to monitor individual or organizational performance, (3) comparing actual performance with planned performance, and (4) taking corrective action to eliminate significant deviations of performance from plans.

The process of control and the problems associated with it are far more complex in an international company than in its purely domestic counterpart because of the multiple cultural, economic, political, and legal environments in which its subsidiaries operate. Several divisive factors, such as geographic distance, language barriers, cultural distance, and differing frames of reference between the parent company and foreign subsidiary managers are responsible for distortion in the information that is required for control purposes.

International companies use several forms of monitoring devices to control their foreign subsidiaries. Among the direct controls commonly used are periodic meetings at headquarters between subsidiary and regional heads and corporate executives, visits by corporate executives to foreign affiliates, the staffing of subsidiaries with home country nationals, and the organizational structure. Indirect controls include such devices as periodic reports from subsidiaries detailing their performance for a given period, a range of financial controls such as budgetary control and financial statements, and financial ratios that depict the financial health of an operating unit.

Most companies use profits and return-on-investment figures as the two dominant criteria to evaluate the performance of subsidiaries. However, these measures may not accurately reflect the real performance level of a subsidiary because corporate or regional managers, not the subsidiary manager, make many significant decisions that affect the subsidiary's performance. Also, there may well be forces in the subsidiary's environment that the subsidiary manager cannot control, but that significantly affect, favorably or unfavorably, the subsidiary's performance. In other cases, the subsidiary may have been established or directed to fulfill a specific strategic intent of the parent, such as a "launching pad" for confronting a strong competitor, that is not necessarily intended to be profitable in its own right. Therefore, the profit-and-loss statement or the ROI of a foreign subsidiary should be adjusted to reflect its actual performance by removing from consideration positive or negative results that were due to forces or factors beyond the control of the subsidiary manager.

Nonfinancial measures, such as market share and productivity, should be used in conjunction with the financial measures. The performance level expected from a subsidiary should change from year to year depending on the characteristics of the environment in which it will have to operate from one year to the next.

The choice of strategic controls on a subsidiary will also depend on whether the subsidiary is highly dependent on the parent, highly independent from the parent, or whether there is a high degree of interdependence between the two. Substantive controls and control by means of organizational context can be balanced as appropriate to each relationship.

QUESTIONS FOR THOUGHT AND DISCUSSION

1. Why is the control process more difficult to implement in a multinational company as opposed to a purely domestic company? Discuss factors that influence the effectiveness of a multinational company's control system.

2. What are direct and indirect controls? Give examples.

3. Explain why the reported profits of a foreign affiliate may not be a good measure of its true performance.

4. What are the essential features of a sound international control system?

5. Explain how strategic intent and profitability may conflict for the subsidiary of an international firm. Give a specific example.

6. How does organizational context serve as a control mechanism? What combination strategic control do you think would be most effective for an independent subsidiary? For an interdependent subsidiary? Explain.

MINI-CASE
Computerlinks, Inc.

Computerlinks is an international company with gross sales revenue of $250 million a year. Foreign sales of laptop and notebook computers, the company's main line of business, account for 55 percent of total sales and 70 percent of net profits. Foreign affiliates are located in six countries—Mexico, France, England, Spain, India, and Japan. Affiliates in England and France are wholly owned subsidiaries. Those in Mexico, India, and Japan are joint ventures with leading domestic companies in which Computerlinks Inc. owns majority stakes in excess of 51 percent.

The affiliates in France and England were established in the early 1960s in anticipation of the unification of the markets of western Europe into a unified common market. Most businessmen, politicians, and economists expected the European Union (EU) to flourish and to enrich all member countries. In anticipation of this prospect, companies from North America and Japan were making huge direct investments mainly in England, France, Holland, and Germany. The Japanese subsidiary was set up in 1975 primarily to keep an eye on the Japanese competitors and as a window to Japanese technology. The Spanish subsidiary was established in 1987 following Spain's entry in the EU. Labor being cheaper in Spain than in other European countries was also a reason for establishing the Spanish operation. The Mexican subsidiary was established in 1993 following the creation of NAFTA primarily to take advantage of cheap labor and secondarily to exploit the growing Mexican market. The subsidiary in India was established in 1993 to capitalize on the liberalization of the economy by the Indian government, which enabled foreign companies to satisfy the huge appetite of the Indian middle class for computer technology and products. Skilled and unskilled labor is also very cheap in India.

The English and French affiliates imported components made in the Spanish subsidiary for assembly in plants in Manchester and Montpellier, respectively. The English affiliate specialized in laptops, and the French affiliate in notebooks. Laptops assembled in England and notebooks imported from the French affiliate were primarily targeted by the English affiliate to the domestic English market and to markets in Scotland, Ireland, Norway, Sweden, Finland, and Denmark. Notebooks assembled in France and laptops imported from England were marketed by the French affiliate in France, as well as in the rest of Europe. The English and French affiliates exported laptops and notebooks respectively to the Spanish affiliate, which were then sold by it in the domestic market.

Components imported from the Mexican subsidiary and some from the Spanish subsidiary were assembled in San Jose, California. Laptops and notebook computers assembled in the United States were marketed in the home market and exported to Canada, Mexico, and markets in Central and South America. The Indian subsidiary bought 40 percent of components sourced from indigenous suppliers, of which there were many, and the rest were imported from the Spanish subsidiary. Almost 80 percent of laptops and notebooks made by the Indian affiliate were sold in the Indian market, and the rest were exported to the neighboring countries of Sri Lanka, Nepal, and Bangladesh. The long-term plan of Computerlinks was to make the Indian affiliate the principal source of its products for exports to South Asia and the Middle East.

The markets in Mexico and India were booming, growing at the rapid pace of 10 to 15 percent during the past five years; the Spanish market at a steady pace of 6 percent during the same period; and those in France, England, and Japan at the rate of 2 to 3 percent per annum. The European market as a whole has been growing at 4 percent per annum. The company's home market in the United States is growing at a steady clip of 7 percent a year. Growth rates are expected to remain the same in these markets in the foreseeable future.

During the past five years annual inflation was pegged at the average rate of 50 percent in Mexico; 20 percent in Spain; 8 percent in France, Japan, and India; and 5 percent in England. Annual inflation during the same period stayed at 2.5 percent in the United States. The Mexican peso and the Spanish peseta have been devaluing steadily against the U.S. dollar at an average rate of 25 percent per year for the past five years. The exchange rates of the British pound, the French franc, and the Indian rupee have been floating in world currency markets and have held their value firmly against the U.S. dollar. The Japanese yen has been appreciating rapidly in value, from a rate of $1=350 yen in July 1975 to $1=81 yen in June 1995.

Competition in laptops and notebooks has been intensifying in the U.S. and European markets. Every major portable computer company in the world is engaged in the European market, with no single company holding more than a 20 percent market share in the U.S. and 10 percent in Europe. IBM and Fujitsu hold dominant market shares of 35 percent each in the highly competitive Japanese market.

Computerlinks has a policy of setting prices of products and components in intra-affiliate trade at levels designed to maximize companywide profits after taxes. In the past it has often shifted the sourcing of components and products from one affiliate to another to take advantage of exchange rate fluctuations.

John Volkmar, president of Computerlinks, is reviewing recommendations for salary raises and bonuses for each domestic and foreign affiliate manager submitted by Devin Gabriel, director of Human Resources. The reports include an assessment of the performance of each affiliate against a set of uniform financial criteria such as after-tax profits, return on assets, and return on equity. The results showed that the Spanish, U.S., and Japanese operations ranked lowest on these criteria, the English and French fell somewhere in the middle, and the Mexican and Indian affiliates showed the best results. John Volkmar is puzzled by the report. "How can I justify to the Spanish, American, and Japanese subsidiary heads that they do not deserve as big a bonus and salary increase as the others?" he asked of himself. "Surely there must be a better way of making a more valid evaluation of each of these foreign affiliates?" he asked Devin Gabriel.

Source: This mini-case written by Arvind V. Phatak. Copyright © 1997.

Discussion Questions for Mini-Case

1. Is there anything wrong with the approach of Devin Gabriel to evaluate the performance of Computerlink's foreign and domestic affiliates? Explain why.

2. If you do not agree with the method used by Devin Gabriel, recommend one that you believe would give a true picture of each affiliate's performance.

Notes

1 Martin J. Gannon, *Management: An Organizational Perspective*, Little, Brown and Co., Boston, 1977, p. 140.
2 Peter F. Drucker, *An Introductory View of Management*, Harper & Row, New York, 1977, p. 424.
3 George A. Steiner, *Strategic Planning*, The Free Press, New York, 1979, p. 268.
4 Gannon, p. 143.
5 Steiner, p. 220.
6 Ibid., p. 221.
7 Gannon, p. 141.
8 Ibid., p. 157.
9 David Clutterbuck, "Breaking Through the Cultural Barriers," *International Management*, December 1980, p. 41.
10 Ibid.
11 Arvind V. Phatak, *Managing Multinational Corporations*, Praeger Publishers, New York, 1974, p. 225.
12 Sydney M. Robbins and Robert B. Stobaugh, "The Bent Measuring Stick for Foreign Subsidiaries," *Harvard Business Review*, Vol. 51, No. 5, September-October 1973, p. 82.
13 Larry Martz and Rich Thomas, "The Corporate Shell Game: How Multinational Firms Use 'Transfer Pricing' to Evade at Least $20 Billion in U.S. Taxes," *Newsweek*, April 15, 1991, pp. 48-49.
14 C. K. Prahalad and Yves I. Doz, "An Approach to Strategic Control in MNCs," *Sloan Management Review*, Summer 1981, pp. 5-13.
15 Ibid., p. 8.
16 Ibid.

Further Reading

Clutterbuck, David, "Breaking Through the Cultural Barriers," *International Management*, December 1980.

Daniel, Shirley J., and Wolf D. Reitsperger, "Management Control Systems for J.I.T.: An Empirical Comparison of Japan and the US," *Journal of International Business Studies*, Vol. 22, No. 4, Fourth Quarter 1991, pp. 603-617.

Denali, Jacquelyn, "Keeping Growth Under Control," *Nation's Business*, Vol. 81, No. 7, July 1993, pp. 31-32.

Drucker, Peter F., *An Introductory View of Management*, Harper & Row, New York, 1977.

Gannon, Martin J., *Management: An Organizational Perspective*, Little, Brown and Co., Boston, 1977.

Geringer, Michael J., and Colette A. Frayne, "Human Resource Management and International Joint Venture Control: A Parent Company Perspective," *Management International Review*, Vol. 30, 1990, pp. 103-120.

Phatak, Arvind V., *Managing Multinational Corporations*, Praeger Publishers, New York, 1974.

Robbins, Sydney M., and Robert B. Stobaugh, "The Bent Measuring Stick for Foreign Subsidiaries," *Harvard Business Review*, September-October 1973.

Steiner, George, *Strategic Planning*, The Free Press, New York, 1979.

Ethics in International Business

LEARNING OBJECTIVES

After completing this chapter, you will be able to:

- Define business ethics and describe their four underlying moral philosophies.
- Identify several international accords that address business ethics and ethical codes of conduct for international companies and list five prominent issues on which they provide guidance.
- Discuss the issues of bribery and corruption and their role in the international business arena.
- Describe the antibribery provisions of the U.S. Foreign Corrupt Practices Act of 1977 and their impact on American-owned international companies.
- Explain how a company can effectively integrate ethics and business conduct among its managers and employees.

BUSINESS ETHICS DEFINED

Ethics has been defined as "inquiry into the nature and grounds of morality where the term morality is taken to mean moral judgements, standards, and rules of conduct."[1] It is a system of principles, a guide to human behavior, that helps to distinguish between good and bad or between right and wrong. Business ethics "is the moral thinking and analysis by corporate decision makers and other members regarding the motives and consequences of their decisions and actions."[2]

International managers are confronted with a variety of decisions that create ethical dilemmas for the decision makers. The following are illustrative of some real-life ethical dilemmas faced by companies.

Situation 1: Should a company continue to market in a foreign country, where it is legal, a product that is banned in the home country because it is harmful? Companies in advanced countries are continuing to sell products in foreign countries that are illegal at home but legal abroad. For instance, several pesticides, such as Velsicol, Phosvel, and 2, 4-D (which contains dioxin), are being sold directly or indirectly in other countries even though they have been banned in the United States. There is a strong link between the chemicals in the pesticides and cancer. The manufacturers of these pesticides argue that the benefits of using the pesticides to increase crop yields in poor countries with severe food shortages far outweigh the health risk associated with their use. The profit motive is also involved in this issue. For example, American Vanguard Corporation, who was banned from selling the pesticide DBCP directly to American companies, continues to export it to other nations. American Vanguard claimed that it would have gone bankrupt had it not sold DBCP in other countries.[3]

Situation 2:   Cigarette smoking has been generally accepted as harmful to human health in most advanced countries. Scientific studies have proven that cigarette smoke causes cancer and that it is associated with the onset of heart disease. Laws in the United States require that product labeling on cigarette packets warn customers of the harmful side effects of smoking. Cigarette smoking has been banned in offices and restaurants in the State of New York. Almost all companies and government offices have a ban on smoking in the workplace. Still, smoking is big business in other countries, especially in eastern Europe and Asia where little has been done to make the public aware that smoking is harmful to health. Cigarette company giants such as Philip Morris, RJR Nabisco, American Brands, and Rothmans International have targeted these world regions as the growth markets for cigarette sales to compensate for the mature home markets. The sales volume abroad of companies like Philip Morris is larger than at home. The ethical issue here is whether tobacco companies should target young men and women in other countries as potential long-term customers of a product when it is a generally accepted fact that cigarette smoking is addictive and harmful.

Situation 3:   The search for enhanced efficiencies and lower costs has induced international companies to transfer labor-intensive operations to countries that offer cheap labor. Companies have also resorted to buying products made by contract manufacturers in foreign countries. It has been documented by international human rights groups that in many cases the foreign contract manufacturers use child labor to make the goods. Chinese companies have used prison labor. The ethical question that arises in such cases is as follows: Is it ethical for companies to sell products made by children or forced prison labor?

Situation 4:   A foreign government official informs the vice president of marketing of a French aerospace company that the minister of defense will approve the purchase of aircraft from the aerospace company, worth several hundred million francs if the selling price is hiked by 15 percent. He is also told to deposit the 15 percent increase in a numbered Swiss bank account. Failure to comply with this request, he is told, would cause the purchase order to be cancelled and possibly given to a competing firm from another country. French law prohibits bribery in France but does not prohibit bribery of foreign officials abroad. If he refuses to give the bribe, the company would not get the order for the aircraft, and several hundred jobs at home would be lost. What should the vice president of marketing do?

The four situations presented are but illustrative of the innumerable ethical dilemmas faced by international managers almost daily. Unquestionably, managers could use frameworks that could serve as benchmarks in identifying ethical problems and for arriving at ethically sound solutions. To that end we draw upon the field of philosophy and offer four types of moral philosophies to better understand the basis of ethical dilemmas faced by managers.

MORAL PHILOSOPHIES OF RELEVANCE TO BUSINESS ETHICS

A moral philosophy is "the set of principles or rules that people use to decide what is right or wrong."[4] Moral philosophies help explain why a person believes that a certain choice among alternatives is ethically right or wrong. Managers fall back on their personal principles, values, and belief system to evaluate the "good" or "bad" and "right" or "wrong" aspects that are at the core of each alternative course of action available in decision making. Managers and businesspersons are guided by moral philosophies when confronted with ethical and moral dilemmas as they formulate their strategies and action plans, but they do not all use the same moral philosophy. Some managers, for example, may view producing a product at the lowest cost to be of foremost importance, and may therefore choose to locate the production plant in a country that offers the cheapest labor, even though the minimum health and safety standards that must be legally observed in production plants in that country are such that they would be considered below acceptable standards, and therefore illegal, in the home country. Other managers may believe that making profits at the expense of the health and safety of workers, in spite of it being legal in the host country, is unethical and immoral, and hence may decide to provide working conditions that are both healthy and safe for workers, even at the expense of higher production costs and lower profits for the company. Some managers may believe that giving bribes to obtain business is unethical, whereas other managers may think that it is not wrong to obtain business through bribes to politicians if it helps preserve jobs in the company.

There are several moral philosophies in the literature on the subject. Studying each one is beyond the scope of this book. Therefore we shall limit our discussion to only those that are most relevant to the study of business ethics. We shall introduce four moral philosophies that have evolved during the twentieth century and which serve as the principal foundations for the field of normative ethics: teleology, deontology, theory of justice, and cultural relativism.

Teleology

According to the moral philosophy called *teleology*, an action or behavior is acceptable or right if it is responsible for producing the desired outcomes; for example, a promotion at work, a bigger market share for a product or service, realization of self-interest, or utility. Teleological philosophies are often referred to as *consequentialism* by moral philosophers because of the emphasis placed by such philosophies on evaluating the morality of an action mainly by examining its consequences.

The two key teleological precepts that serve as guides for managerial decision making are (1) egoism and (2) utilitarianism.

Egoism evaluates how right or acceptable a behavior is depending upon its consequences on the person. The egoists profess that self-interest should be the primary determinant of a person's behavior. Self-interest may be different for different individuals. It may mean the acquisition of wealth, fame, power, a good family life, leisure, or prestige. When faced with the prospect of having to choose among a set of alternatives, an egoist will probably choose one that maximizes his or her personal self-interest. A more calculative form of egoism does indeed consider the interests of others if in so doing the egoist's own self-interests are advanced. For example, a manager may promote community development projects not because of some deep-seated altruistic motive, but because projects that benefit the community surrounding the company ultimately bring the manager personal prestige and elevate his or her standing within the company.

Utilitarianism, like egoism, holds that actions should be judged by their consequences; however, unlike egoists, utilitarians claim that behaviors that are moral produce the greatest good for the greatest number of people.[5] Utilitarians believe that a moral decision is one that creates the greatest total *utility*, i.e., the greatest benefit for each and every person affected by a decision. A utilitarian would be inclined to make an analysis of the costs versus the benefits, of each alternative course of action to those affected by the decision, and to choose the one alternative that results in the greatest utility.

Selecting a decision that not only considers the interests, but also maximizes the utility, of all individuals and groups that are affected by the decision can be very difficult and perhaps impossible. A utilitarian can take a shortcut and reduce the complexity of utilitarian decision making by simply obeying the rules of behavior prescribed by a preferred ideological system. Some utilitarian philosophers, called "rule utilitarians," have argued that general rules should be followed to decide what action is best.[6] They believe that there are certain principles or rules that when observed in one's behavior result in the greatest utility. Decision making that is based on the foundation of rules or principles reduces the complexity of utilitarian decision making and erases the need to examine each particular situation. For example, some religious ideologies prescribe behavioral norms which, if followed, are supposed to improve the human condition, e.g., the Koran preaches that it is immoral to crave for excess profit. Guided by this principle, a Moslem utilitarian businessperson will make various business decisions, none of which, in his eyes, exploit the workers, suppliers, or customers.

There are those who believe that bribery is bad for everyone. They theorize that bribery distorts the efficient allocation of resources by market forces and therefore everyone suffers because of the misallocation of resources. For example, a company whose product is far superior than those of its competitors may not get the business if a government official is bribed to buy it from someone else. In this instance, the taxpayers are the losers, as their taxes have been misused to buy an inferior product. A rule utilitarian would refuse to bribe an official, even if that meant the loss of workers' jobs, but would firmly stick to the rule: "No bribes!"

Other utilitarian philosophers called "act utilitarians" profess that whether an individual action is right or wrong should be evaluated based upon its ability to create the greatest utility for the greatest number of people and that rules such as "bribery is bad" should serve only as guidelines in decision making. Act utilitarians would agree that bribery is wrong, and not because bribery is inherently wrong, but because the total utility decreases when bribery places self-interest ahead of societal interests. Act utilitarians would argue that it would be quite acceptable to offer a bribe in order to obtain business if the alternative is to lose hundreds of jobs in the factory, which in turn would adversely affect the welfare of the surrounding community.

Deontology: The Theory of Rights

The deontological (from the Greek word *deontos* meaning binding, necessity) approach is "an ethical theory holding that acting from a sense of duty rather than concern for consequences is the basis for establishing our moral obligation."[7] Unlike utilitarians, dentologists argue that certain acts or behaviors must never be permitted even though they might maximize utility. The German philosopher Immanuel Kant (1724-1804) was the main proponent of deontology. He believed that "some acts are right, and some acts are wrong, quite independent of their consequences. He professed that it is irrelevant in determining our moral obligation whether an action makes us happy, or whether it contributes to human pleasure. We do that which is right because it is the right thing to do. No other consideration is relevant to our moral deliberation."[8]

Deontology also refers to "moral philosophies that focus on the rights of individuals and on the intentions associated with a particular behavior, rather than on its consequences."[9] Deontologists believe that "human beings have certain fundamental rights that should be respected in all decisions."[10] The following are the fundamental rights, several of which have been incorporated into the American Constitutional Bill of Rights, that deontologists say should never be violated.

1. *The right of free consent:* Every human being in an organization has the right to be treated only as he or she freely consents to be treated.

2. *The right to free speech:* Every person has the right to truthfully criticize the behavior and actions of others so long as the criticism does not violate the rights of other persons.

3. *The right to privacy:* Individuals have the right to keep from public scrutiny information about their private lives which they are not legally obliged to make public.

4. *The right to freedom of conscience:* No one should be forced to carry out any order or to engage in any act that violates his or her moral or religious norms.

5. *The right to due process:* Every human being has the right to a fair and impartial hearing when he or she believes that his or her rights are being violated.

Making decisions based upon deontological principles is much easier than with the utilitarian theory. One need only "do the right thing" and not interfere with the rights of others who might be affected by one's decisions. Thus, a manager who is faced with the question of whether or not to sell a product that is illegal in the home country because of its cancer-causing properties, but which is not illegal in a poor, developing country, might choose not to sell it because her conscience tells her that to do otherwise would be wrong.

Theory of Justice

There are three fundamental guidelines that the theory of justice provides to managers in decision making: be equitable, be fair, and be impartial. The behavioral prescriptions of the justice theory are captured in the following principles.

1. Do not treat individuals differently based upon arbitrary characteristics. Those who are similar in relevant attributes should be treated similarly, and those who are different in the relevant attributes should be treated differently in proportion to the differences between them.

2. Attributes and positions of individuals that are the basis for differential treatment must be justifiably connected to the goals and tasks at hand.

3. Rules must be clearly stated and promulgated, administered fairly, and consistently and fairly enforced. Those who do not obey the rules because of ignorance or those who are forced to break them under duress should not be punished.

4. Do not hold individuals responsible for matters over which they have no control.[11]

Although not as difficult to apply as the utilitarian theory, justice theory demands that justifiable attributes be determined upon which differential treatment of people may be based. Furthermore, this theory also requires the determination of facts to ensure the fair administration of rules and to hold individuals accountable for their actions.

Cultural Relativism

Cultural relativism asserts that "words such as 'right,' 'wrong,' 'justice,' and 'injustice,' derive their meaning and truth value from the attitudes of a given culture."[12] Thus, to the cultural relativist, ethical standards are culture-specific, and one should not be surprised to find that an act that is considered quite ethical in one culture may be looked upon with disdain in another. For instance, usury is forbidden by the Koran because it is considered unethical and immoral, and therefore Muslims must refrain from collecting interest on loans. This belief is not shared by Christians and Jews. Relativists would argue that businesspersons in fundamentalist Islamic countries such as Saudi Arabia and Iran ought to conform to the ethical and moral norms of those cultures when conducting business in those countries. Any other strategy might prove disastrous.

The Hindu religion considers the consumption of beef to be both unethical and immoral. Companies in the food industry must therefore respect this precept if they want to succeed in India, and not attempt to mix beef with non-beef ingredients and pass off the products as non-beef products, even though there might be foolproof ways to conceal the true identity of the ingredients.

The motto of the cultural relativists might be summed up as "when in Rome, do as the Romans do, ethically."

INCORPORATING ETHICS INTO INTERNATIONAL BUSINESS DECISIONS

Each of the moral philosophies discussed cannot by themselves take care of issues of concern in the other philosophies. Utilitarianism, for instance, seeks decisions that produce the greatest good for the greatest number of people; however, a decision that brings forth this outcome may very well result in the abridgment of the rights of some people. By the same token, a decision that respects the rights of all persons affected may at the same time prove to be ineffective in optimizing the benefits for the people involved. And decisions that may appear to be equitable, fair, and impartial in one culture may have the opposite effect in another culture. One way to resolve such problems resulting from a focus on one particular philosophy is to combine all four philosophical approaches into one unifying, eclectic, decision-making framework. With this in mind, we have incorporated all four moral philosophies in a decision tree, presented in Figure 15-1.

Philosophers urge us to resort to ethical reasoning to ensure that moral decisions are made by moral managers. Nevertheless, there is the danger that the different philosophies of ethical reasoning may lead to different behaviors in similar circumstances.

Moreover, because of cultural differences, what is considered "right" and "good" in one culture may be actually taken as "wrong" and "bad" in another culture. Therefore, managers in two different cultures, adhering to the same ethical philosophy (utilitarianism, theory of rights, or theory of justice), may choose behavioral patterns that are at the opposite ends of a spectrum. For example, managers in India and the United States may interpret differently the following principle of the theory of justice.

Attributes and positions of individuals that are the basis for differential treatment must be justifiably connected to the goals and tasks at hand.

Indian manager: " I must hire persons who belong to my caste because it is the right thing to do. The cohesiveness and morale of the group is the key for the success of my company."

American manager: " I must hire the best person for the job regardless of his or her class, race, religion, or national origin."

In this illustration, both managers are right in their judgment. In India it is an accepted fact that generally, if not always, persons from the same caste are given preference in hiring, whereas such a practice would be considered ethically unacceptable and illegal in America. What this means is that moral philosophies provide the *criteria* for making ethical decisions, however, it is the manager who must reach into his system of *values and beliefs* and make the judgment call as to what makes an action ethical or unethical. But as Clarence C. Walton points out, the potential problem with this reality is that "one theory may be used as a foil against another, thus permitting the decision maker to employ whichever weapon best suits his or her purposes at the time."[13]

FIGURE 15-1

A Decision Tree Incorporating Ethics in International Business Decision Making

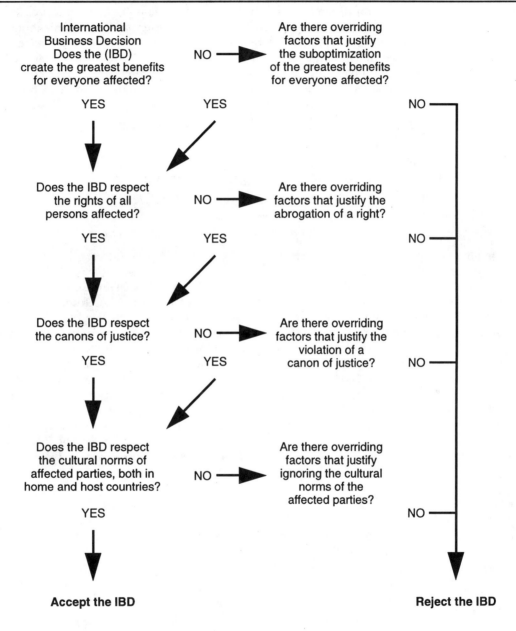

Source: Adapted from Gerald F. Cavanagh, Dennis J. Moberg, and Manuel Valasquez, "The Ethics of Organizational Politics," *Academy of Management Review*, Vol. 6, No. 3, 1981, p. 368.

INTERNATIONAL ETHICAL CODES OF CONDUCT FOR INTERNATIONAL COMPANIES

The fact that there are cultural differences that make it difficult to determine ethical conduct in various countries of the world has not deterred countries and international organizations from promulgating codes of ethical conduct for international companies. Since 1948 we have seen a proliferation of intergovernmental treaties, conventions, agreements, accords, compacts, and declarations that have been intended to prescribe principles governing the activities of governments, groups, international companies, and individuals. The six most prominent accords of relevance to the activities of international companies are as follows:

1. The United Nations Universal Declaration of Human Rights [UDHR] (1948)
2. The European Convention on Human Rights [ECHR] (1950)
3. The Helsinki Final Act [Helsinki] (1975)
4. The OECD Guidelines for Multinational Enterprises [OECD] (1976)
5. The International Labor Office Tripartite Declaration of Principles Concerning Multinational Enterprises and Social Policy [ILO] (1977)
6. The United Nations Code of Conduct on Transnational Corporations [TNC Code]

A thorough reading of these accords provides a set of explicit normative guidelines for the behavior of international companies in countries in which they operate. "It is generally accepted that business organizations tend to favor utilitarian reasoning in decision making and policy setting. An appropriate function of international codes of conduct, therefore, is to provide (international companies) with a basis for deontological reasoning."[14] The fact that several countries would agree on international codes of conduct signifies the need to recognize that, in spite of cultural differences in the world's community of nations, there are plenty of areas in which a "common ground" exists among the nation-states. Codes of conduct are particularly relevant in a discussion of ethics in business for they are seen as an alternative means to constitute an international *moral* authority by agreements among governments and to provide guidelines for multinational business activities.[15]

We present an inventory of code-of-conduct principles in the form of explicitly normative guidelines for the policies, decisions, and operations of multinational corporations (MNCs). The principles serve as normative anchors for the conduct of business operations, as well as fundamental obligations and responsibilities regarding basic human rights.

Employment Practices and Policies[16]

- MNCs should not contravene the manpower policies of host nations. (ILO)
- MNCs should respect the right of employees to join trade unions and to bargain collectively. (ILO; OECD; UDHR)
- MNCs should develop nondiscriminatory employment policies and promote equal job opportunities. (ILO; OECD; UDHR)
- MNCs should provide equal pay for equal work. (ILO; UDHR)
- MNCs should give advance notice of changes in operations, especially plant closings, and mitigate the adverse effects of these changes. (ILO; OECD)
- MNCs should provide favorable work conditions, limited working hours, holidays with pay, and protection against unemployment. (UDHR)

- MNCs should promote job stability and job security, avoiding arbitrary dismissals and providing severance pay for those unemployed. (ILO; UDHR)
- MNCs should respect local host country job standards and upgrade the local labor force through training. (ILO; OECD)
- MNCs should adopt adequate health and safety standards for employees and grant them the right to know about job-related health hazards. (ILO)
- MNCs should, minimally, pay basic living wages to employees. (ILO; UDHR)
- MNCs operations should benefit lower-income groups of the host nation. (ILO)
- MNCs should balance job opportunities, work conditions, job training, and living conditions among migrant workers and host country nationals. (Helsinki)

Consumer Protection

- MNCs should respect host country laws and policies regarding the protection of consumers. (OECD; TNC Code)
- MNCs should safeguard the health and safety of consumers by various disclosures, safe packaging, proper labeling, and accurate advertising. (TNC Code)

Environmental Protection

- MNCs should respect host country laws, goals, and priorities concerning protection of the environment. (OECD; TNC Code; Helsinki)
- MNCs should preserve ecological balance, protect the environment, adopt preventive measures to avoid environmental harm, and rehabilitate environments damaged by operations. (OECD; TNC Code; Helsinki)
- MNCs should disclose likely environmental harms and minimize risks of accidents that could cause environmental damage. (OECD; TNC Code)
- MNCs should promote the development of international environmental standards. (TNC Code; Helsinki)
- MNCs should control specific operations that contribute to pollution of air, water, and soils. (Helsinki)
- MNCs should develop and use technology that can monitor, protect, and enhance the environment. (OECD; Helsinki)

Political Payments and Involvement

- MNCs should not pay bribes nor make improper payments to public officials. (OECD; TNC Code)
- MNCs should avoid improper or illegal involvement or interference in the internal politics of host countries. (OECD; TNC Code)
- MNCs should not interfere in intergovernmental relations. (TNC Code)

Basic Human Rights and Fundamental Freedoms

- MNCs should respect the rights of all persons to life, liberty, security of person, and privacy. (UDHR; ECHR; Helsinki; ILO; TNC Code)

- MNCs should respect the rights of all persons to equal protection of the law, work, choice of job, just and favorable work conditions, and protection against unemployment and discrimination. (UDHR; Helsinki; ILO; TNC Code)

- MNCs should respect all persons' freedom of thought, conscience, religion, opinion and expression, communication, peaceful assembly and association, and movement and residence within each state. (UDHR; ECHR; Helsinki; ILO; TNC Code)

- MNCs should promote a standard of living to support the health and well-being of workers and their families. (UDHR; Helsinki; ILO; TNC Code)

- MNCs should promote special care and assistance to motherhood and childhood. (UDHR; Helsinki; ILO; TNC Code)

These guidelines should be viewed as a collective whole since they do not all exist in each of the six conventions. It was the clear intent of the international bodies that formulated the codes of conduct that they be taken seriously and that they be enforced in the policies and operations of international companies.

THE ISSUE OF BRIBERY AND CORRUPTION

Of all the issues of ethics confronting international managers, that of bribery and corruption has been most troublesome and pervasive. Bribery may be defined as the payment voluntarily offered for the purpose of inducing a public official to do or to omit to do something in violation of his or her lawful duty, or to exercise official discretion in favor of the payor's request for a contract, concession, or privilege on some basis other than merit. The greed of politicians and political parties has created systems of corruption and graft that one encounters to some degree in almost every country of the world. The phenomenon of bribery exists in rich industrialized countries as well as poor and underdeveloped countries, in democracies as well as dictatorships, in capitalist and socialist economies. Business firms are required, and sometimes forced, to bribe government officials merely to perform what to an objective observer would look like ordinary business activities.

The following example from Italy is illustrative of the nature and problem of bribery in many countries of the world.

> Over the last year, virtually every major Italian political party and many of the country's most prestigious companies have been tarred by a bottomless, tangled-as-spaghetti scandal that swallowed trillions of taxpayer lira—billions of dollars.
>
> For decades, the (political) parties were routinely and generously financed by illegal kickbacks for public contracts and boosted by jobs-for-votes deals. In some regions of Sicily, there is no end to forest rangers on public payrolls, but hardly any trees.
>
> Payoffs, called *targenti*, were standard operating procedure at virtually every level in virtually every city. Last week the jailed president of the state's ENI energy company told magistrates in Milan how he had been obliged to pay a 4 billion lira ($2.5 million) kickback to the Socialist Party so that ENI engineering company would get the contract to build turbines for a power plant being built by ENEL, the state electricity authority.[17]

Italy is certainly not alone in its problems of bribery and corruption. The following item from *The Economist* describes the situation in France.

"France is certainly one of the countries with the highest rate of public honesty," said Pierre Joxe, a former interior minister and now head of France's public accounts body, the Cours des Comptes. Really? One ex-minister is in jail. Another has been forced to resign. At least five more are under investigation in connection with corruption cases. Twenty-nine members or ex-members of parliament have been charged or already convicted. Dozens of prominent businessmen (some put the figure at over 100) face prosecution, and hundreds of lesser-known politicians, businessmen, and functionaries are under investigation . . . . Many maintain that it has become impossible to win a public contract or obtain planning permission without the payment of a kickback to the local mayor or party boss . . .

Until 1988, the only legal sources of income for political parties were membership dues, levies on members of parliament, and donations from individuals. There was no public funding of political parties and business contributions were forbidden. This obliged all parties to look to "unofficial" forms of fund-raising.

One of the most popular methods was to set up phoney consultancy services to help firms win public contracts in return for hefty "commissions." Companies were also asked to pay inflated sums of money for advertising in party or municipal newspapers. . . . . But the system began to be exploited by individuals to line their own pockets. Payments came in various forms: cash; cut-rate home improvements; free flats; foreign trips; swimming pools; works of art.

As a result, two laws on political party financing were passed in 1988 and 1990. They provided for some public funding of parties, allowed business contributions up to FF500,000 ($98,000) per party per year, and set limits on campaign spending. But they failed to stop the abuse.[18]

Practical Insight 15-1 illustrates bribery in Nigeria, which is considered by international businesspersons to be among the worst countries in the world with regards to this particular issue.

PRACTICAL INSIGHT 15-1
In Nigeria, the Payoff for Takeoff:
Bribery at Airport Is Rite of Passage

LAGOS, Nigeria— "Welcome to Nigeria," the customs agent at Murtala Muhammed Airport says, smiling as he greets an arriving passenger. Then comes the punch line: "What have you brought for me?"

Africa has long been associated with air travel hardships. Overbooked flights crowd to bursting with passengers and outsized carry-on baggage. Long delays are often spent in unventilated departure lounges that feel like steam baths.

But even for longtime travelers on the continent, including Nigerians, few experiences are considered as reliably unpleasant as passing through this huge aluminum structure whose bustle bordering on chaos and nonstop hassles make it a fitting introduction to the freewheeling country it serves.

PRACTICAL INSIGHT 15-1 *(continued)*

For those leaving Nigeria, there is the experience of wading through the tossing sea of would-be passengers and their families, whose peak hours turn the sprawling departure concourse into something resembling a pitched camp.

For those arriving there is that dangerous roulette game of finding a taxi driver who will not rob you en route to town, as frequently happens. For both, there are the officials who seem to take working at the airport as a once-in-a-lifetime chance to amass a fortune by hitting travelers with everything from innocent-sounding requests for money to outright extortion.

"It doesn't matter where you are coming from, when you fly into Nigeria, about half an hour before landing, anyone who knows this place begins to tense up with stress," said one Nigerian businessman.

He said that in his travels through the airport he had been arrested without charge, had his passport seized inexplicably, lost baggage, and been pressed by airport officials for bribes countless times.

"The beauty of flying out of Nigeria is that once you get on the plane, you can relax," he said.

For some, even this axiom does not seem to hold.

Forced against his protests to place a sophisticated camera into an airport X-ray machine recently, one American businessman was bluntly told to hurry on his way so as not to miss his flight as the officer operating the inspection equipment handed him a cheap model, saying: "All I know is a camera went in and a camera came out."

Angering this country's military government, the United States Department of Transportation has banned direct flights between the United States and Nigeria for the last 14 months because of what American officials say are security and safety problems.

Department of Transportation officials will no longer comment on the matter, but it has been reported in the Nigerian press that Murtala Muhammed Airport is in discussions with an American firm that would be hired to address Washington's concerns.

Diplomats in Lagos who have often had to rescue travelers from the clutches of airport officials and scam artists say they have abundant evidence that the two often work together.

"We have had to put people up in what amounts to safe houses to protect them from the police coming after them to prevent them from backing out of bogus business deals that they were lured to Nigeria to consummate," said one diplomat.

Source: Howard W. French, *The New York Times*, December 18, 1994, p. 4. Copyright © 1994 by The New York Times Company. Reprinted by permission.

Bribery and corruption may take more subtle forms in industrialized countries such as the United States. *Practical Insight 15-2* makes this point by illustrating the activities of America's prestigious Speaker of the House of Representatives, Newt Gingrich. By no means is Mr. Gingrich the only Congressperson involved in such potentially questionable activities. The point being made here is that bribery and corruption is certainly not a strictly non-American phenomenon, but is also prevalent at levels of government in the United States—national, state, local, township, and district.

PRACTICAL INSIGHT 15-2
Gingrich, Critic of 'Business as Usual,'
Helps Out Special Interests Like 'Any Member of Congress'

LITTLE ST. SIMONS ISLAND, Ga.—Last Thanksgiving weekend, House Speaker-to-be Newt Gingrich headed off with his wife, Marianne, to visit this idyllic, private resort off Georgia's coast, which ordinarily charges as much as $500 a day.

On an island offering seven miles of beach, horseback riding, and three gourmet meals a day, Mr. Gingrich had much to be thankful for. So too did his host, Michael Berolzheimer, a California timber executive whose family owns the unspoiled, 10,000-acre isle.

Three months earlier, Mr. Gingrich had written a letter to the U.S. International Trade Commission at the request of Mr. Berolzheimer's company, P&M Cedar Products Inc., and an affiliated group. Although Mr. Gingrich is an avowed free trader, his letter urged the commission to impose anti-dumping duties against pencil makers in Thailand and China. A group of U.S. pencil makers had petitioned for the trade protection, and P&M supported the effort because it is a major supplier of pencil wood. The petition was filed shortly before Thanksgiving 1993, when the Gingriches spent their first weekend on the island as Mr. Berolzheimer's guests.

"I am writing to make you aware of my support for this petition," Mr. Gingrich wrote.

Late last year, the ITC decided to permit anti-dumping tariffs on most pencils from China, but not from Thailand.

Speaker Gingrich came to power promising to change the "business as usual" culture of Washington. The special interest favor bank was to be closed. He railed against the Democratic majority for being subservient to special interest groups, ineffective and unethical in its behavior.

But a review of Mr. Gingrich's communications with the executive branch over the years, obtained through the Freedom of Information Act, shows that he has used his position, in a series of noteworthy intercessions, to help his own friends with special connections.

Some of his own associates acknowledge privately that the fine lines that separate personal pursuits, political efforts, and governmental actions appear to blur at times in Mr. Gingrich's quest for a new political order.

Former Minnesota Republican Rep. Vin Weber says Mr. Gingrich long has defined himself as a "national congressman, and he almost performed his constituent service in a national way. I have never known there to be anything venal about his approach . . . but now he's speaker, and he has to worry about appearances."

Mr. Gingrich declined to comment in detail for this story. "The basis for any of his (official actions) is the merit of the idea, not who's giving him the idea," says Gingrich spokesman Tony Blankley. All of his actions "are consistent with his political philosophy," including advocating trade sanctions. "This story or others like it could be written on any member of Congress" because Mr. Gingrich's actions represent "the standard appropriate pattern for congressmen and senators in our form of government."

The House Ethics Committee is reviewing a host of complaints against Mr. Gingrich, including some alleged conflicts of interests involving contributors to the congressman's multimillion-dollar fund-raising operations, known collectively as Newt, Inc.

In each of several cases disclosed in recent months, Mr. Gingrich has denied any connections between his official actions and contributions or other favors. Yet the timing in some additional cases that have now come to light suggests at least extraordinary coincidences.

Letter to the SEC

On April 29, 1994, for example, the Georgia Power Co. made a $7,500 tax-deductible donation to the Progress and Freedom Foundation to help finance Mr. Gingrich's nationally televised college course. Ten days later, he wrote the Securities and Exchange Commission on behalf of Georgia Power's parent, Southern Co., which had grown impatient with the agency ten months after filing an application to form a wireless communications subsidiary. "I would, therefore, urge the Commission to act expeditiously, whether favorably or unfavorably," Mr. Gingrich wrote SEC Chairman Arthur Levitt. (The SEC approved the application late last year.) Southern Co. spokesman David Mould says the letter was routine and similar to ones sent on its behalf by other lawmakers.

In another case, on Sept. 25, 1989, Southdown Inc. of Houston gave $10,000 to Gopac, Mr. Gingrich's political action committee. A day later, cement makers from Arizona, Florida, New Mexico, and Texas petitioned the ITC and the Commerce Department for anti-dumping tariffs against Mexican competitors.

A month later, Mr. Gingrich, who had been elected GOP whip earlier that year, was one of 35 House members who signed a letter to the ITC on behalf of the U.S. cement makers. The letter urged "a complete and thorough investigation" of the petitioner's complaint. Mr. Gingrich was the only signatory who wasn't from one of the four states or with a petitioner's headquarters in his state. Eventually, the U.S. cement makers, after having failed in five previous tries, won the fight, and the Bush administration imposed high tariffs on imported cement, causing U.S. prices to rise.

Source: Phil Kuntz, *The Wall Street Journal*, April 3, 1995, p. A16. Reprinted by permission of The Wall Street Journal, © 1995 Dow Jones & Company, Inc. All Rights Reserved Worldwide.

International business managers will face the problem of bribery and corruption in most places in this world. The bribe goes by different names in different countries. It is called *la mordida* in Mexico; *dash* in South Africa; *baksheesh* for a tip or gratuity in India, Pakistan, and in the Middle East; *schimengeld* for grease money in Germany; and *bustarella*, a little envelope, in Italy.

Many businesspeople believe that bribes are a necessary cost of doing business in certain countries. A unit of Teledyne Inc. has admitted to paying $3.2 million in illicit commissions between 1986 and 1990 to sell aerospace equipment to the Taiwanese military. Litton Industries is also accused by the U.S. government of surreptitiously funneling millions of dollars to a middleman for obtaining business abroad. And General Electric is being accused by an engineer in the company who discovered that the company had paid hundreds of thousands of dollars to win a $124.7 million contract with the Egyptian government for a sophisticated radar system.[19] Such abuses by American companies were supposed to have ended with the passage of the 1977 Foreign Corrupt Practices Act (FCPA) [the FCPA will be covered later in this chapter], "however, it appears that after a few early high-profile prosecutions, federal watchdogs shifted their efforts elsewhere."[20] By no means are American companies the only ones involved in making questionable payments. There is enough evidence to suggest that Japanese, German, and French companies are heavily involved in the bribery of foreign officials to obtain business worth millions and sometimes billions of dollars.

Why Payoffs?

Why do companies feel obliged to pay huge sums of money to generate business abroad, and why do people in host countries accept such payments? The reasons that induce international companies to offer questionable payments abroad and the host country factors responsible for bribes are presented in Table 15-1.

Types of Payoffs

Bribery takes different forms and bribes are made in a variety of ways in different parts of the world. Table 15-2 depicts four categories of bribes.

The Foreign Corrupt Practices Act of 1977: Antibribery Provisions[21]

Earlier in this chapter, a reference was made to the 1977 Foreign Corrupt Practices Act (FCPA). The FCPA specifically permits certain types of payments, called facilitating payments, whereas it prohibits other types of payments that could be categorized as bribes. We shall examine the antibribery provisions of the FCPA in some detail since an understanding of this legislation is crucial for international companies in order to stay clear of making illegal payments.

U.S. firms seeking to do business in foreign markets must be familiar with the FCPA. In general, the FCPA prohibits American companies from making corrupt payments to foreign officials for the purpose of obtaining or keeping business. The Department of Justice is the chief enforcement agency, with a coordinating role played by the Securities and Exchange Commission (SEC).

Background   Investigations by the SEC in the mid-1970s revealed that over 400 U.S. companies admitted making questionable or illegal payments in excess of $300 million to foreign government officials, politicians, and political parties. The abuses ran the gamut from bribery of high foreign officials in order to secure some type of favorable action by a foreign government to facilitating

TABLE 15-1
Factors Responsible for Bribes

Home Country Factors
- Competitors are giving bribes to obtain business.
- The pressure for higher levels of performance by top management and shareholders.
- This is an accepted practice in the host country. Cannot expect to get any business without conforming.
- Tax laws of the country encourage bribery. Bribes can be written off as a business expense in Germany (not in the U.S.).

Host Country Factors
- Government control over business activities. Permits and licenses from government officials required to conduct normal business functions.
- Government officials are poorly paid, use bribes to supplement salary.
- Bureaucratic delays can be costly for business (e.g., clear products through customs on time to meet delivery schedules).
- Pressure from politicians to make contributions to political parties or favorite political organizations or causes.

TABLE 15-2
Major Types of Bribes

Facilitating Payments

Disbursement of small amounts of cash or kind as tips or gifts to minor government officials to expedite clearance of shipments, documents, or other routine transactions. Example: "In India not a single tile can move if the clerk's palm is not greased. Distribution of *bustarella* (an envelope containing a small amount of money) in Italy to make things move in an inefficient and chaotic social system."

Middlemen Commissions

Appointment of in-between people as middlemen (agents and consultants) to facilitate sales in a non-routine manner, and payment of excessive allowances and commissions to them that are not commensurate with the normal commercial services they perform. Often, the middlemen may request that part or all of their commission be deposited in a U.S. bank or a bank in a third country. Example: Northrup Corporation's payment of $30 million in fees to overseas agents and consultants, some of which was used for payoffs to government officials to secure favorable decisions on government procurement of aircraft and military hardware.

Political Contributions

Contributions which can take the form of extortion since they are in violation of local law and custom. Also payments which, while not illegal, are specifically made with the intent of winning favors directly or indirectly. Example: Gulf Oil Corporation's payments of $3 million in 1971 to South Korea's Democratic Republican Party under intimidation and threat.

Cash Disbursements

Cash payments made to important people through slush funds or in some other way, usually in a third country (e.g., deposit in a Swiss bank) for different reasons such as to obtain a tax break or sales contract or to get preferential treatment over a competitor. Example: Payment of $2.5 million, via Swiss bank accounts, to Honduran officials by United Brands Company for the reduction of the export tax on bananas.

Source: Subash C. Jain, "What Happened to the Marketing Man when His International Promotion Pay-Offs Became Bribes?" in Peter J. LaPlaca, ed., *The New Role of the Marketing Professional*, American Marketing Association, 1977 Business proceedings, series # 40, p. 140. Reprinted by permission.

payments that allegedly were made to ensure that government functionaries discharged certain ministerial or clerical duties. Congress enacted the FCPA to bring a halt to the bribery of foreign officials and to restore public confidence in the integrity of the American business system. The antibribery provisions of the FCPA make it unlawful for a U.S. person to make a corrupt payment to a foreign official for the purpose of obtaining or retaining business for or with, or directing business to, any person.

The FCPA also requires issuers of securities to meet its accounting standards. These accounting standards, which were designed to operate in tandem with the antibribery provisions of the FCPA, require corporations covered by the provisions to maintain books and records that accurately and fairly reflect the transactions of the corporation and to design an adequate system of internal accounting controls.

Basic Provisions Prohibiting Foreign Corrupt Payments The FCPA makes it unlawful to bribe foreign government officials to obtain or retain business. The antibribery provisions apply both to certain issuers of registered securities and issuers required to file periodic reports with the SEC (referred to as "issuers") and to others (referred to as "domestic concerns"). A "domestic concern" is defined to mean any individual who is a citizen, national, or resident of the United States, or any corporation, partnership, association, joint-stock company, business trust, unincorporated organization, or sole proprietorship which has its principal place of business in the United States, or which is organized under the laws of a State of the United States, or a territory, possession, or commonwealth of the United States.

The FCPA's antibribery provisions extend to two types of behavior. The basic prohibition is against making bribes directly; a second prohibition covers the responsibility of a domestic concern and its officials for bribes paid by intermediaries.

The FCPA's basic antibribery prohibition makes it unlawful for a firm (as well as any officer, director, employee, or agent of the firm or any stockholder acting on behalf of the firm) to offer, pay, promise to pay (or even to authorize the payment of money, or anything of value, or to authorize any such promise) to any foreign official for the purpose of obtaining or retaining business for or with, or directing business to, any person. (A similar prohibition applies with respect to payments to a foreign political party or official of a political party or candidate for foreign political office.)

Payment by Intermediaries It is also unlawful to make a payment to any person, while knowing that all or a portion of the payment will be offered, given, or promised, directly or indirectly, to any foreign official (or foreign political party, candidate, or official) for the purposes of assisting the firm in obtaining or retaining business. "Knowing" includes the concepts of "conscious disregard" or "willful blindness."

Enforcement The Department of Justice is responsible for all criminal enforcement and for civil enforcement of the antibribery provisions with respect to domestic concerns. The SEC is responsible for civil enforcement of the antibribery provisions with respect to issuers.

Antibribery Provisions—Elements of an Offense
(1) Basic Prohibition With respect to the basic prohibition, there are five elements which must be met to constitute a violation of the Act:

A. Who—The FCPA applies to any individual firm, officer, director, employee, or agent of the firm and any stockholder acting on behalf of the firm. Individuals and firms may also be penalized if they order, authorize, or assist someone else to violate the antibribery provisions or if they conspire to violate those provisions. A foreign-incorporated subsidiary of a U.S. firm will not be subject to the FCPA, but its U.S. parent may be liable if it authorizes, directs, or participates in the activity in question. Individuals employed by or acting on behalf of such foreign-incorporated subsidiaries may, however, be subject to the antibribery provisions if they are persons within the definition of "domestic concern." In addition, U.S. nationals employed by foreign-incorporated subsidiaries are subject to the antibribery provisions of the FCPA.

B. Corrupt intent—The person making or authorizing the payment must have a corrupt intent, and the payment must be intended to induce the recipient to misuse his official position in order wrongfully to direct business to the payor. One should note that the FCPA does not require that a corrupt act succeed in its purpose. The offer or promise of a corrupt payment can constitute a violation of the statute. The FCPA prohibits the corrupt use of the mails or of interstate commerce in furtherance of a payment to influence any act or decision of a foreign official in his or her official capacity or to induce the official to do or omit to do any act in violation of his or her lawful duty, or to induce a foreign official to use his or her influence improperly to affect or influence any act or decision.

C. Payment—The FCPA prohibits paying, offering, promising to pay (or authorizing to pay or offer) money or anything of value.

D. Recipient—The prohibition extends only to corrupt payments to a foreign official, a foreign political party or party official, or any candidate for foreign political office. A "foreign official" means any officer or employee of a foreign government or any department or agency, or any person acting in an official capacity. One should consider utilizing the Department of Justice's Foreign Corrupt Practices Act Opinion Procedure for particular questions as to the definition of a "foreign official," such as whether a member of a royal family, a member of a legislative body, or an official of a state-owned business enterprise would be considered a "foreign official."

Prior to the amendment of the FCPA in 1988, the term "foreign official" did not include any employee of a foreign government or agency whose duties were essentially ministerial or clerical. Determining whether a given employee's duties were "essentially ministerial or clerical" was a source of ambiguity, and it was not clear whether the Act prohibited certain "grease" payments, such as those for expediting shipments through customs, placing a transatlantic telephone call, securing required permits, or obtaining adequate police protection. Accordingly, recent changes in the FCPA focus on the purpose of the payment, instead of the particular duties of the official receiving the payment, offer, or promise of payment, and there are exceptions to the antibribery provision for "facilitating payments for routine governmental action" (see below).

E. Business Purpose Test—The FCPA prohibits payment made in order to assist the firm in obtaining, or retaining business for or with, or directing business to, any person. It should be noted that the business to be obtained or retained does not need to be with a foreign government or foreign government instrumentality.

Third Party Payments Generally—The FCPA prohibits corrupt payments through intermediaries. It is unlawful to make corrupt use of the mails or of interstate commerce in furtherance of a payment to a third party, while knowing that all or a portion of the payment will go directly or indirectly to a foreign official. The term "knowing" includes conscious disregard and deliberate ignorance. The elements of an offense are essentially the same as described previously, except that in this case the "recipient" is the intermediary who is making the payment to the requisite "foreign official."

Permissible Payments and Affirmative Defenses As amended in 1988, the FCPA now provides an explicit exception to the bribery prohibition for "facilitating payments" for "routine governmental action" and provides affirmative defenses which can be used to defend against alleged violations of the FCPA.

Exception for Facilitating Payments for Routine Governmental Actions There is an exception to the antibribery prohibition for facilitating or expediting performance of "routine governmental action." The statute lists the following examples: obtaining permits, licenses, or other official documents; processing governmental papers, such as visas and work orders; providing police protection, mail pick-up and delivery; providing phone service, power and water supply, loading and unloading cargo, or protecting perishable products; and scheduling inspections associated with contract performance or transit of goods across country.

"Routine governmental action" does not include any decision by a foreign official to award new business or to continue business with a particular party.

Affirmative Defenses   A person charged with a violation of the FCPA's antibribery provisions may assert as a defense that the payment was lawful under the written laws of a foreign country or that the money was spent as part of demonstrating a product or performing a contractual obligation.

Whether a payment was lawful under the written laws of a foreign country may be difficult to determine.   Moreover, because these defenses are "affirmative defenses," the defendant would be required to show in the first instance that the payment met these requirements.   The prosecution would not bear the burden of demonstrating in the first instance that the payments did not constitute this type of payment.

Sanctions Against Bribery   The following criminal penalties may be imposed for violations of the FCPA's antibribery provisions: firms are subject to a fine of up to $2 million; officers, directors, and stockholders are subject to a fine of up to $100,000 and imprisonment for up to five years; employees and agents are subject to a fine of up to $100,000 and imprisonment for up to five years.   One should also be aware that fines imposed on individuals may not be paid by the firm.

There can be civil penalties as well.   The Attorney General or the SEC, as appropriate, may bring a civil action for a fine of up to $10,000 against any firm as well as any officer, director, employee, or agent of a firm, or stockholder acting on behalf of the firm, who violates the antibribery provisions.   In addition, in an SEC enforcement action, the court may impose an additional fine.   The specified dollar amount may vary depending upon the egregiousness of the violation ranging from $5,000 to $50,000 for a person, and from $100,000 to $500,000 for a firm.

The Destructive Costs of Bribery and Corruption

Bribery, when used as the primary weapon to obtain business, has several dysfunctional consequences. First, a company that has the best product or service, or the best value at a given price, may not get the business. The business may go to that company which has given the biggest bribe to the government official who has the discretionary authority to decide which company may sell its products in the local market. In such a situation, the consumers are the real losers because their money does not fetch the best products or services that could have been available absent the bribes. Second, if bribes are used to sell capital equipment such as a factory or military hardware to the government, the taxpayer's money is being misallocated if government officials choose an inferior piece of equipment over one which may clearly be the better choice. Third, the incentive to compete on the basis of quality, price, and service is destroyed when these factors are rendered irrelevant by decisions influenced by factors such as bribery and corruption.

Thus, bribery can cause the misallocation of a country's resources as resources do not get allocated, because of the intervention of bribes, to where they can be best put to use based on a purely objective set of criteria such as price, quality, and service. The economic costs of corruption can be quite significant. For instance, underreporting of income taxes in exchange for a bribe could reduce income tax revenues by up to 50 percent, and overinvoicing by government officials for public works and capital goods could raise the prices of goods and services by as much as 100 percent. Ultimately it is the country's consumers that bear the burden of these increased costs due to corruption.

Critics of the FCPA have alleged that it places American companies at a competitive disadvantage because the law applies only to American businesses; competitors from European nations and Japan do not have a comparable law that puts similar prohibitions on their use of improper payments to key foreign officials. The tax laws in some countries might actually encourage the giving of bribes to obtain business. For instance, Germany permits resident corporations to deduct foreign bribes, known as "sonderspesen" or "special expenses," from corporate taxes.[22]

While there is increasing discussion among European governments to enact some sort of antibribery legislation, to date no country other than the United States has a law like the FCPA. Therefore, if companies from the United States, Japan, and Germany were bidding on a project to build power plants in India, the Japanese and German firms could use financial inducements in their efforts to get the contract, but it would be illegal for American firms to do so. The evidence most cited to support the "competitive disadvantage" argument is found in the results of a series of opinion surveys of executives. However, research conducted by Richman[23] and Graham[24] refute the perception of business leaders that the FCPA has hurt the competitive position of American industry.

Critics of the FCPA also argue that the law exports the values of the culture of one country—namely the United States—to countries that do not share similar values. They claim that bribery is a perfectly acceptable practice in most countries and that "while in Rome, do as the Romans do." However, the fact remains that probably every country has laws that prohibit domestic bribery. Hence, companies that bribe local officials in foreign countries would be breaking local laws against giving bribes to corrupt officials and bureaucrats. But, local laws against giving or accepting bribes are not strictly enforced, which leaves open the opportunities for companies to engage in behavior that corrupts local officials in host countries.

So what can companies do to ensure that employees do not engage in giving improper payments in order to obtain business abroad? Most companies have addressed this issue, in conjunction with a host of other ethical and moral dilemmas that employees face all over the world, in "company ethics programs." We shall take up this topic next.

WHAT COMPANIES CAN DO TO INTEGRATE ETHICS AND BUSINESS CONDUCT

The issue of business ethics has attracted the attention of companies worldwide and several companies have incorporated ethics training as part of the general orientation of all employees. The following are recommendations to integrate ethics into business conduct.

Top management must be committed to the company's ethics program. Top management involvement is essential. At Chemical Bank, for example, some 250 vice presidents took part in a two-day seminar on corporate values that began with an appearance by the Bank's chairman.

A written company code that clearly communicates management's expectations must be developed. The code must be explicit in stating management's intent, e.g., "The law is the floor. Ethical business conduct should normally exist at a level well above the minimum required law" (from *A Code of Worldwide Business Conduct*, Caterpillar Tractor Company). Extensive interviews with managers at different levels of the organization, in various subsidiaries at home and abroad, may be conducted before and after the ethics code is drafted to ensure that the code is comprehensive in its coverage of the variety of ethical dilemmas that managers are most likely to encounter. For example, to develop the company's ethical guidelines, Levi Strauss & Company formed a working group of 15 employees from a broad section of the company. The working group spent nine months in developing the guidelines, during which time it researched the views of various key stakeholder groups—vendors, contractors, plant managers, merchandisers, sewing machine operators, contract production staff, shareholders, and others.[25] The Code of Business Conduct of Rohm and Haas Company as it pertains to gifts and entertainment and the FCPA is presented in Exhibit 15-1.

EXHIBIT 15-1

Rohm and Haas Company: Political Payments, and Gifts and Entertainment

The Company

Rohm and Haas Company is an ethical company which complies with applicable laws. This Code of Business Conduct applies to all directors, officers, and employees of the Company, its subsidiaries and controlled affiliates.

Political Payments

(a) We encourage participation in the political process, and we recognize that participation is primarily a matter for individual involvement.

(b) Any payment of corporate funds to any political party, candidate, or campaign may be made only if permitted under applicable law and approved in advance by the General Counsel. U.S. laws generally prohibit payments of corporate funds to any U.S. political party, candidate, or campaign.

Gifts and Entertainment

(a) Gifts of cash or property may not be offered or made to any officer or employee of a customer or supplier or any government official or employee unless the gift is (1) nominal in value, (2) approved in advance by the appropriate Regional Director, Business Group Executive, or Corporate Staff Division Manager, and (3) legal. In most countries it is illegal for corporations to make gifts to government officials or employees; any gift to a government official or employee must be approved in advance by the General Counsel as well as the appropriate Regional Director, Business Group Executive, or Corporate Staff Division Manager.

(b) Employees of the Company should decline or turn over to the Company gifts of more than nominal value or cash from persons or companies that do (or may expect to do) business with Rohm and Haas.

(c) Business entertainment (whether we do the entertaining or are entertained) must have a legitimate business purpose, may not be excessive, and must be legal. Business entertainment of government officials or employees is illegal or regulated in most countries; therefore, the propriety of such entertaining should be reviewed in advance with the General Counsel or his delegates.

Translation

Translations of the Code will be prepared in French, German, Italian, Portuguese, Spanish, and Japanese. Other translations will be prepared if necessary to ensure that recipients of the Code are able to understand it fully. The General or Resident Manager in each country will be responsible for translations.

Dissemination

(a) A copy of the Code in the appropriate language will be given to all employees of the Company (including employees of domestic and foreign subsidiaries and controlled affiliates). New employees will be given a copy of the Code at the time of their employment.

(b) The Regional or Staff Division Personnel Directors are responsible for dissemination of the Code.

Compliance

(a) All salaried employees of the Company (its subsidiaries and controlled affiliates) will be asked to certify annually in writing their compliance with the Code substantially as follows (with such exceptions as may be noted therein):

EXHIBIT 15-2 *(continued)*

"I have reviewed and understand the Code of Business Conduct. I hereby confirm that (1) I have complied with the Code during the preceding year, and (2) each recipient of the Code who reports to me has certified in writing his or her compliance with the Code."

(b) The Regional and Business Directors will be responsible for obtaining certifications not later than February 1 with respect to the preceding year.

Source: Rohm and Haas, *Code of Business Conduct*, January 1994, pp. 1 & 3. Reprinted by permission.

Provide an organizational identity to the ethics program. Most companies would agree that there should be strong organizational support for a company's ethics program. The best way to ensure that ethics is not downplayed is to establish a high-level ethics committee at the board of directors level and an ethics committee at different organizational levels. For example, McDonnell Douglas has a Board of Directors Ethics Committee, an internal corporate committee led by a senior executive, a committee at each division (component company) level reporting to the highest level, and, further down the line, an ombudsman who is a senior manager available to counsel employees who wish to have private and confidential advice.

In a similar vein, international companies could establish ethics committees at different organizational levels, starting with the top management levels of the parent company, and within the various divisions and subsidiaries of the company at home and abroad. The Boeing Company, a leading aircraft manufacturer, has "ethics advisors" in subsidiaries and a corporate office for employees to report infractions.[26]

A formal program must be in place to implement the ethics code. Every employee must be made to go through a formal training program that teaches and indoctrinates employees the ethical code of the company. Case studies and role playing that highlight ethical dilemmas faced by international managers have proved to be very useful in encouraging participants to look at the operating principles in the company code for guidance. For instance, Levi Strauss & Company held training sessions for 100 in-country managers who would have to enforce the company's ethical global sourcing guidelines in the plants of the company's 700 contract manufacturers worldwide. The training included case studies and exercises in decision making. Following this training the managers made presentations on the guidelines to the contractors, performed on-site audits, and worked with the contractors to make the necessary improvements.[27]

Companies often require employees to make a signed statement that they have read, understood, and agree to comply with the company's ethics code.

Training in ethics is done by the line managers, not consultants. The line manager is the "role model" of ethical behavior for his or her subordinates. Each line manager must be cognizant of his or her own responsibilities in creating a culture of ethical norms that will be strictly adhered to. A line manager who deviates from the ethics code at crunch time will send the signal to subordinates that "the code is just a bunch of words that don't matter." The company's chief executive is the supreme line manager and, therefore, ethical guidelines of what is acceptable and what isn't and why are established by the messages sent by his or her own behaviors and actions over time.

Strict enforcement of codes is essential. Those who violate the company code ought to be punished. Chemical Bank has fired employees for violation of the company's code of ethics even when there are no violations of the law. Xerox Corporation has dismissed employees not only for taking bribes but also for minor manipulation of records and petty cheating on expense accounts.[28]

Actions speak louder than words. It is not what a company code or what a company's top management and line managers say but what they actually do in their decisions and actions on behalf of the company that counts. Companies such as Federated Department Stores, Liz Claiborne, and Spiegel have pledged to stop their business activities in Burma because of human-rights concerns in that country, while others such as Unocal have decided to continue their involvement in Burma, giving as justification for their continued involvement the influence that they and other like-minded companies believe would have on changing the policies of the government of Burma. (Please read *Practical Insight 15-3.*)

PRACTICAL INSIGHT 15-3
U.S. Companies Back Out of Burma, Citing Human-Rights Concerns, Graft

A number of U.S. companies are backing out from their recent forays into Burma, partly because of pressure from human-rights groups and partly because doing business in the corrupt, junta-run country just isn't worth the trouble.

Yesterday, Macy's said it would stop making clothing in Burma within 90 days because of a "lack of infrastructure" as well as corruption in the country.

The retailer, a unit of Federated Department Stores Inc., is the latest U.S. multinational to withdraw from the Southeast Asian nation, where the ruling military regime has been accused of widespread human-rights violations since it overturned a democratic election in 1990 that would have handed political power to civilians.

Burma, which was renamed Myanmar by its military rulers in 1989, is "fast becoming the South Africa of the '90s," said Simon Billenness, an analyst at Franklin Research & Development Corp.

Only in the past few years has the long-isolated nation, with a population of about 43.5 million, even tried to woo foreign business. And it was beginning to have some success, albeit limited, mainly because of its low wages.

'Become an Embarrassment'
However, in recent months, Liz Claiborne Inc. and Spiegel Inc.'s Eddie Bauer have pledged to stop importing apparel from Burma. Earlier this month, Starbucks Corp., the specialty-coffee company, asked that a new cold coffee drink it is creating not be bottled or distributed in Burma by PepsiCo Inc., which does business in Burma and is Starbuck's partner in the coffee-drink effort.

In withdrawing from Burma, the companies have acknowledged the human-rights concerns. "The consumer pressure is beginning to have an effect," says Thomas Lansner, a member of the Free Burma Action Group in New York. "Even if there's good business to be done in Burma, it has become an embarrassment for them to make money there."

For its part, Macy's wasn't embarrassed—just disappointed because it was "impossible to make money there," a spokeswoman said. The company added that Burma's corruption "makes normal operations impossible."

Macy's had been contracting out private-label men's clothing in Burma for about 15 months. It thought the three factories it was using were private, but they turned out to be partly owned by the military government.

PRACTICAL INSIGHT 15-3 *(continued)*

Unocal Is 'Committed'

Not all multinationals find Burma inhospitable. Unocal Corp., which has paid the Burmese government at least $10 million so far for rights to develop offshore gas fields, said it is "absolutely committed to this project." A spokesman added that Unocal thinks its involvement in Burma "will bring sustainable long-term benefits to (the) people of Myanmar."

Critics argue that such investment only nourishes the military junta. Burma's elected government-in-exile has called for economic sanctions against the country.

But some investment advocates think private corporations actually may have more sway over such regimes than international bodies or other governments.

"These companies can really press for change . . . because the country needs them and their investment," says Deborah Leipziger, director of international programs for the Council on Economic Priorities.

Source: G. Pascal Zachary, *The Wall Street Journal*, April 13, 1995, p. A10. Reprinted by permission of The Wall Street Journal, © 1995 Dow Jones & Company, Inc. All rights reserved worldwide.

Child labor and its abuses are of great concern to most people of conscience; however, few companies have made any attempts to eliminate use of child labor in the production process. The following item, which appeared in *The Philadelphia Inquirer*, illustrates the cruelties of child labor in developing countries.

Lahore, Pakistan: Demanding an end to child labor, thousands of children and other protesters marched through Lahore yesterday to commemorate the killing this month of young activist Iqbal Masih.

About one-third of the 3,000 marchers were children, many of them workers in carpet-weaving factories and other industries that routinely employ child laborers for as low as one rupee, or about 3 cents a day. The march, which led to the governor's office in Punjab Province, was organized by the Bonded Labor Liberation Front, a private group trying to end the widespread practice of child labor in Pakistan.

The group two years ago rescued Iqbal, who was then 10 and had already spent six years working in carpet-weaving factories. Iqbal, who achieved international recognition for his activism, was gunned down April 17 in his village of Muridke, 22 miles northwest of Lahore. Eshan Ullah Khan, head of the Bonded Labor Liberation Front, alleges that Iqbal was killed by people in the carpet industry who were angry at his campaign against child labor.[29]

Few companies have taken steps to eliminate the abuses of child labor. Most give the argument that competition forces the company to use child labor. Others argue that the company itself does not employ child labor, its contractors do, and therefore there is not much that the company can do to control the employment of workers that it does not hire directly. A fine example is provided by Levi Strauss & Company of how a company indeed can prohibit the use of child labor by manufacturing contractors linked with the company.

Levi Strauss has operations in many countries and diverse cultures. Robert D. Hass, Chairman and CEO of the company, says: "we must take special care in selecting our contractors and those countries where our goods are produced in order to ensure that our products are made in a manner that is consistent with our values and reputation. In early 1992, we developed a set of global sourcing guidelines that established standards our contractors must meet to ensure that their practices are compatible with our values. For instance, our guidelines ban the use of child labor and prison labor."[30] The Company rules stipulate that working hours cannot exceed 60 hours a week, with at least one day off in seven, and wages must, at a minimum, comply with local law and prevailing local practice. The Company accepts the fact that at times there are issues that are beyond the control of the local contractor, and therefore the Company has a list of country-selection criteria. For instance, the Company refuses to source in countries where conditions such as human-rights violations run counter to the values of the company and would adversely affect the Company's global brand image. The Company's phased withdrawal from China was reflective of its concern for human-rights concerns in that country. Another example of the application of this principle is in the way the company handled the problem of two of its manufacturing contractors in Bangladesh and one in Turkey who employes underage workers. This was a clear violation of Levi Strauss' guidelines against the use of child labor. The company could have (1) instructed the contractors to fire the children, knowing that this action would have caused severe hardships on the children's families, many of whom depended on the earnings of the children as their only source of income; or (2) continued to employ the children, ignoring the company's position against the use of child labor. None of these two options was acceptable to the company, and therefore a third win-win solution was found and implemented. The company worked out an arrangement with the contractors which called for the contractors to pay the children their salaries and benefits while they went to school on the factory site (the children did not work during this time), and Levi Strauss paid for books, tuition, and uniforms. The children will be offered full-time jobs in the plant when they reach working age. At times the contractors passed on to Levi Strauss in the form of higher unit prices the costs of adhering to these company standards. In other cases the company has forgone cheaper sources of production due to unsatisfactory working conditions or concerns about the country of origin.[31]

We end this chapter with these words of Robert D. Hass:

There is a growing body of research evidence from respected groups that shows a positive correlation between citizenship and financial performance. These studies underscore that companies driven by values and a sense of purpose that extends beyond just making money outperform those that focus only on short-term profits. The former have higher sales, sustain higher profits, and have stocks that outperform the market.

These findings mirror our experiences. Our values-driven approach has helped us:

- identify contractors who really want to work for Levi Strauss;
- gain customer and consumer loyalty because they feel good about having us as a business partner or about purchasing our products;
- attract and retain the best employees;
- improve the morale and trust of employees because the company's values closely mirror their own personal values;
- initiate business in established and emerging markets because government and community leaders have a better sense of what we stand for and what to expect from us; and
- maintain credibility during times of unplanned events or crisis.

The conclusion is clear: There are important commercial benefits to be gained from managing your business in a responsible way that best serves the enterprise's long-term interests. The opposite is also clear: There are dangers of not doing so.[32]

SUMMARY

Business ethics concern the consideration of moral issues in corporate decision making and actions. International managers may be confronted with a variety of ethical dilemmas, usually due to differences among different markets or nations in what constitutes legal or acceptable practice.

Beliefs about what constitutes moral or ethical business behavior commonly stem from one of four underlying moral philosophies: teleology, which evaluates decisions based on their consequences; deontology, based on the inviolability of certain rights; the theory of justice, grounded in fairness; and cultural relativism, which recognizes that different cultures have fundamentally different concepts about right and wrong. An eclectic framework incorporating aspects of all four may provide a useful decision tool.

There are several prominent international accords that address ethical behavior by international companies. One or more of these provide specific guidance with respect to employment practices and policies, consumer and environmental protection issues, political payments and involvement, and basic human rights and fundamental freedoms. While the accords are not legally binding with force of law, they display the clear intent of the international community to foster ethical conduct.

Bribery and corruption is the most troublesome and pervasive ethical issue confronting international managers, common to industrialized and developing countries alike. The line between proper and improper behavior is not always clearly drawn and, in many cases, making a payoff may appear obligatory if the international company wishes to continue to do business. Laws and practices differ widely in different countries.

For U.S. companies, the Foreign Corrupt Practices Act of 1977 (FCPA) is specific in prohibiting bribes of money, gifts, or other considerations by U.S. companies to foreign parties. The only exceptions are for certain facilitating payments for routine governmental action such as customs clearance or obtaining licenses, visas, police protection, etc. The United States is the only nation with a law similar to the FCPA, a fact that some believe is a disadvantage to American international firms with respect to competitors from other countries.

A growing number of international companies have adopted comprehensive ethics programs involving ethics training and, often, a published code of conduct for all company personnel. An effective integration of the company's ethics program and the business behavior of the company's people depends on top management, and the entire organization, demonstrating that they are serious about the program on an ongoing basis. Training, enforcement, and leadership by example are essential to success.

QUESTIONS FOR THOUGHT AND DISCUSSION

1. Which of the four moral philosophies described in the chapter do you feel offers the best framework for evaluating ethical behavior by international companies? Why do you think so? Can you think of any "loopholes" in the theory you selected—i.e., whereby an act you would consider clearly unethical could be justified under the theory? Discuss.

2. In the text, we discussed five areas of interest to international companies that are covered by specific guidelines for ethical behavior from international accords. Find an article in the current business press that reports negatively on a company's behavior with respect to one of these five areas. What repercussions does the company face as a result of its actions? In your opinion, are they justified? Why do you suppose the company's decision makers acted as they did? Are "right" and "wrong" clearly defined in this situation? Discuss.

3. We stated in the text that the United States is currently the only nation with a law such as the Foreign Corrupt Practices Act governing its international companies. Based on the information provided in the text, do you feel that the FCPA creates a disadvantage for U.S. firms against their competitors from other countries? Why? If your answer was yes, do you consider this disadvantage to be fair or unfair? Discuss.

4. Different companies exhibit differing degrees of formality in their corporate ethical policies and programs, but all incorporate the seven recommendations contained in the chapter to some extent. In your opinion, which of the seven is most critical to the success of a company's program? Why? Would your answer be the same for all firms in all industries? If not, what factors might determine the most essential recommendation for a given firm?

MINI-CASE
Situational Ethics

You are taking part in an ethics training program given by your company for all international managers. The following seven situations are given to you for analysis.[33] How would you handle each situation? Would it make a difference if you were an employee of a German company?

Situation 1. The best lawyer in a foreign town is the London-educated son of the Minister of Commerce. Should he be prevented from accepting clients who need permits from the Ministry? Should a U.S. corporation be prevented from retaining him? Would it make any difference if he were a consultant or agent instead of a lawyer? The opportunities for abuse here are undeniable but not inevitable.

Situation 2. A U.S. corporation is asked by the Provincial Governor to contribute to the local Health and Welfare Fund, his favorite charity. Is this the obligation of a public-spirited company or an opportunity for covert graft?

Situation 3. A U.S. corporation, already doing substantial business in a foreign country, wishes to invest in one of its local suppliers. The Prime Minister is the latter's principal stockholder. Would it make any difference if it were another U.S. company in which they would be investors together?

Situation 4. A U.S. corporation's valuable inventory abroad is stored in a remote warehouse. The nearest police are willing to act as after-hours guards if they are paid by the corporation for their overtime services. Must a less effective and more expensive alternative be found?

Situation 5. A U.S. corporation wishes to form a joint venture with a local firm owned by a member of the ruling family (not unusual or considered unethical in small countries with small elites). But see Situation 1.

Situation 6. A U.S. corporation, seeking to locate its plant in an impoverished land, invites the Minister of Environmental Affairs to fly to the United States at its expense for a tour of its domestic installations, reportedly to demonstrate that its proposed plant will not pollute the local air and water. At what point does its hospitality become excessive, and should this expensive trip be more permissible than contributing the cash equivalent thereof?

Situation 7. A U.S. corporation is informed that the government permit for which it was bidding has already been issued to a local corporation of unknown ownership who is willing to sell it to the U.S. bidder at the bid price. If no extra payment is thus involved, does the additional step render the transaction improper?

Notes

1 Paul W. Taylor, *Principles of Ethics: An Introduction to Ethics*, 2nd ed., Dickenson, Encino, Calif., 1975, p. 1.

2 Sita C. Amba-Rao, " Multinational Corporate Social Responsibility, Ethics, Interactions, and Third World Governments: An Agenda for the 1990s," *Journal of Business Ethics*, Vol. 12, 1993, p. 553.

3 Davis Weir and Mark Schapiro, *Circle of Poison*, Institute for Food and Development Policy, San Francisco, 1981, p. 22.

4 O. C. Ferrell and John Fraedrich, *Business Ethics: Ethical Decision Making and Cases*, 2nd ed., Houghton Mifflin Company, Boston, 1994, p. 60.

5 J. S. Mill, *Utilitarianism*, Bobbs-Merrill, Indianapolis, 1957, (1863).

6 Richard Brandt, *Ethical Theory*, Prentice-Hall, Inc., Englewood Cliffs, N.J., 1959, pp. 253-254.

7 Donald M. Borchert and David Stewart, *Exploring Ethics*, Macmillan Publishing Company, New York, 1986, p. 199.

8 Ibid.

9 Ferrell and Fraedrich, p. 57.

10 Gerald F. Cavanagh, Dennis J. Moberg, and Manuel Velasquez, "The Ethics of Organizational Politics," *Academy of Management Review*, Vol. 6, No. 3, 1981, p. 366.

11 Adapted from Cavanagh, Moberg, and Velasquez, "The Ethics of Organizational Politics," p. 366.

12 Thomas Donaldson, *The Ethics of International Business*, Oxford University Press, New York, 1989, p. 14.

13 Clarence C. Walton, *The Moral Manager*, Ballinger Publishing Company, Cambridge, Mass., 1988, p. 110.

14 Kathleen A. Getz, "International Codes of Conduct: An Analysis of Ethical Reasoning," *Journal of Business Ethics*, Vol. 9, 1990, p. 571.

15 Getz, p. 569.

16 The material on codes of conduct for MNCs is quoted from William C. Frederick, "The Moral Authority of Transnational Corporate Codes," *Journal of Business Ethics*, Vol. 10, 1992, pp. 166-167.

17 William D. Montalbano, "A Challenge to Italy's Status Quo," *The Philadelphia Inquirer*, March 21, 1993, pp. E1 and E4.

18 "Hands up all those hit by sleaze," *The Economist*, October 29, 1994, pp. 55-56.

19 Andy Pasztor and Bruce Ingersoll, "Buying Business: Some Weapons Makers are Said to Continue Illicit Foreign Outlays," *The Wall Street Journal*, November 5, 1993, pp. A1 and A5; Douglas Pasternak, "Selling Hardware Overseas," *U.S. News and World Report*, November 15, 1993, p. 64.

20 Pasztor and Ingersoll, p. A5.

21 Arthur Aronoff, "Antibribery Provisions of the Foreign Corrupt Practices Act," National Trade Data Bank, June 26, 1992.

22 Jerry Landauer, "Proposed treaty against business bribes gets poor reception overseas, U.S. finds," *The Wall Street Journal*, February 28, 1977, p. 28.

23 Barry M. Richman, "Can We Prevent Questionable Foreign Payments?" *Business Horizons*, June 1979, pp. 14-19.

24 John L. Graham, "The Foreign Corrupt Practices Act," *Journal of International Business Studies*, Winter 1984, pp. 107-121.

25 Robert D. Hass, "Ethics in the Trenches," *Across the Board*, May 1994, pp. 12-13.

26 John A. Byrne, "Businesses are Signing Up for Ethics 101," *Business Week*, February 15, 1988, pp. 56-57.

27 Hass, pp. 12-13.

28 Byrne, pp. 56-57.

29 "Thousands in Pakistan call for end to child labor," *The Philadelphia Inquirer*, April 26, 1995, p. A8.

30 Hass, pp. 12-13.

31 Ibid.

32 Ibid.

33 Adapted from Theodore C. Sorensen, "Improper Payments Abroad: Perspectives and Proposals," *Foreign Affairs*, Vol. 54, No. 4, July 1976, pp. 719-733.

Cases

IKEA CONQUERS THE WORLD

For managers, the only thing harder than rescuing a failing business is reinventing a successful one. Nobody knows this principle better than retailers who venture overseas. As store chains strike out beyond their home markets, they often have to change the formula that had previously guaranteed success. This happens to many types of businesses, but retailers are particularly close to customers. They must move especially fast to adapt to local peculiarities. The trick is to do so without destroying the very thing that made them successful in the first place.

As the world's most competitive retail market, the United States has a well-deserved reputation as a graveyard for foreign retailers and especially for Europe's non-food retailers. Even Britain's Marks and Spencer has struggled to make a success of its acquisition of Brooks Brothers. Four years ago it looked as if IKEA might suffer a similar fate.

Today, however, this Swedish firm is going from success to success in America. Its secret seems to be a classic example of the difficult art of "change management": IKEA has draped itself in the stars-and-stripes by adapting but not destroying its original formula. Meanwhile, its experience in America has persuaded it to remix its recipe elsewhere.

IN THE BEGINNING, HUBRIS

It is not hard to see why IKEA was initially so confident about America. In the decade following the opening of its first non-Scandinavian outlet in Switzerland in 1973, the furnishing chain's vast out-of-town warehouse stores decked out in Sweden's blue and yellow colors had marched triumphantly across much of western Europe.

Its formula was based on reinventing the furniture retailing business. Traditionally, selling furniture was a fragmented affair, shared between department stores and small, family-owned shops. All sold expensive products for delivery up to two months after a customer's order.

IKEA's approach trims costs to a minimum while still offering service. It starts with a global sourcing network, which now stretches to 2,300 suppliers in 67 countries. An IKEA supplier gains long-term contracts and receives technical advice and leased equipment. In return, IKEA demands an exclusive contract and low prices. IKEA'S designers work closely with suppliers to build savings into products from the outset.

IKEA displays its enormous range of more than 10,000 products in cheap out-of-town stores. It sells most of its furniture as knocked-down kits for customers to take home and assemble themselves. The firm reaps huge economies of scale from the size of each store and the big production runs made possible by selling the same furniture all around the world.

This allows the firm to match rivals on quality while undercutting them by up to 30 percent on price. An IKEA store, with its free day nursery and Scandinavian cafe, is supposed to be a "complete shopping destination" for value-conscious, car-borne consumers. In the *Harvard Business Review* last year Richard Norman and Rafael Ramirez gushed that IKEA had forced both customers and suppliers to think about value in a new way "in which customers are also suppliers (of time, labour, information, and transportation), suppliers are also customers (of IKEA's business and technical services), and IKEA itself is not so much a retailer as the central star in a constellation of services."

432

AMERICANS THINK BIGGER

Why, then, did this successful and apparently flexible system hit problems in America? In 1985, IKEA opened a 15,700 square meter (169,000 sq. ft.) warehouse store outside Philadelphia. At first, with the dollar at around SKr8.6, it was quite easy to make money, says Anders Moberg, IKEA's chief executive. Six more shops (five on the East Coast and one in Los Angeles) followed in as many years.

But things had started to go wrong. By 1989 the American operation looked to be in deep trouble. In each new European country it entered, the company had normally broken into profit after two or three years with its third or fourth store. In America it was still losing money. And this could not be blamed wholly on a slowdown in the economy and a weak furniture market.

Many people visited the stores, looked at the furniture, and left empty-handed. Customers complained of long queues and constant non-availability of stock. Imitators were benefiting from the marketing effort IKEA had made in introducing Americans to Scandinavian design. Worst of all, since it was still making many of its products in Sweden, IKEA's cherished reputation for low-cost furniture was threatened as the dollar's value dropped to SKr5.8 by 1991.

Another retailer might at that point have sought a dignified exit. IKEA says it never considered that option. "If you're going to be the world's best furnishing company you have to show you can succeed in America, because there's so much to learn here," says Goran Carstedt, who took over North American operations four years ago.

Its perseverance has paid off. IKEA'S American operation is finally booming. Since 1990 sales have tripled, to $480m in the year to August, and the company says it at last made a profit 18 months ago. In December 1991 IKEA purchased Stor, an imitator with four shops in the Los Angeles area. In October it opened its 13th American store, a franchised outlet in Seattle. Two more are under development.

USE YOUR EYES

To achieve this IKEA had to revise several of its central tenets. The most basic was that it could sell the same product in the same way in Houston as it could in Helsingborg. IKEA took this approach to such extremes that its advertising deliberately stressed not only its clean Scandinavian design, but its blue-and-yellow Swedishness.

IKEA had cheerfully broken several of the rules of international retailing: enter a market only after exhaustive study; cater for local tastes as much as possible; gain local expertise through acquisition, joint ventures, or franchising. "We don't spend much money or time on studies. We use our eyes and go out and look, and say it will probably do quite well here. Then we may adapt, but quite often we stick to our opinions," says Mr. Moberg.

This iconoclasm had paid off in Europe, but it helped to get the firm into trouble in America. In 1989 and 1990 Mr. Moberg himself spent much time in the American stores, talking to customers. "We were behaving like all Europeans, as exporters, which meant we were not really in the country," he says. "It took us time to learn this."

Unapologetically European products jarred with American tastes and sometimes physiques. Swedish beds were narrow and measured in centimeters. IKEA did not sell the matching bedroom suites that Americans liked. Its kitchen cupboards were too narrow for the large dinner plates needed for pizza. Its glasses were too small for a nation that piles them high with ice: Mr. Carstedt noticed that Americans were buying the firm's flower vases as glasses.

So IKEA's managers decided to adapt. The firm now sells king and queen-sized beds, in inches, as part of complete suites. After noticing that customers were inspecting IKEA's bedroom chests and then walking away without buying, Mr. Carstedt worked out that because Americans use them to store sweaters in, they wanted the drawers in the chests to be an inch or two deeper. Sales of the chests immediately increased by 30 to 40 percent. In all, IKEA has redesigned around a fifth of its product range in America; its kitchen units are next on the list.

The firm has changed its American operations in other ways, too. "When we went in, we hadn't planned a clear strategy of how to supply the American market at low cost," Mr. Moberg admits. That meant, for example, that it was shipping sofas from Europe, adding to costs and problems of stock availability.

Now, 45 percent of the furniture in the American stores is produced locally, up from 15 percent four years ago. This has helped the firm to cut prices in its American stores for three years running. And because Americans hate queuing, the firm has installed new cash registers that speed throughput by 20 percent and has altered store layout. It offers a more generous returns policy than in Europe, and a next-day delivery service.

SOUL SEARCHING

Successful though the outcome has been, IKEA's American experience posed wider questions for the whole firm's future. Could it adapt its retailing concept to local peculiarities without compromising the Swedish identity at the heart of its marketing and brand image? Could it continue to control costs if it was forced to dilute the uniformity of its product range? And as the firm's operations became ever more global, could IKEA retain the intimate corporate culture that was an important part of its success?

In many ways, IKEA is still seeking answers. The search became urgent when, hard on the heels of its American difficulties overall, sales growth slackened thanks to slower than expected growth in eastern Europe and recessions in Sweden and Germany, IKEA's two largest markets. The firm reacted with intense soul searching. In 1992-93, it opened only six new stores, compared with 16 the previous year.

One problem was that IKEA had become lax about costs. *Sweden Business*, a newsletter, estimates that costs excluding the purchase of goods climbed from 30 percent of sales in the late 1980s to 37.5 percent by the fiscal year 1991-92. Mr. Moberg is still trying to return them to 30 percent. This involves cutting the amount of time it takes to develop new products and, over three years, trimming 10 percent of the workforce at the firm's Swedish product development and purchasing center.

Another problem imposed by growth was the management of an increasingly complex global supply chain, one that led to glitches in quality control and stock availability. The firm has begun random checks on goods as soon as it receives them; it has also taken equity stakes in some eastern European suppliers to help improve quality.

In making these adjustments, IKEA could draw on an egalitarian culture forged by its founder, Ingvar Kamprad (who remains the chairman of its supervisory board despite having just admitted to a youthful flirtation with a Nazi group, saying that he "bitterly regretted it"). Fast decision making is helped by a management structure that is as ruthlessly flat as the firm's knocked-down furniture kits, with only four layers separating Mr. Moberg from the checkout or warehouse worker. Even senior managers must share secretaries and travel economy class.

The firm describes itself as a learning and problem-solving organization that trusts the intuition of its staff. Insiders are much exercised about how this problem-solving culture can thrive beyond its Swedish roots. In recent years, Mr. Kamprad has held annual seminars for managers on the firm's corporate culture. Experience with globalization has forced managers to adapt in three important ways in order to maintain the firm's antibureaucratic culture.

The first change involved giving more autonomy to Mr. Carstedt than his European counterparts enjoy. "You can't steer America from Europe," says Mr. Moberg. The second decision was characteristically unconventional: in 1992 IKEA abolished internal budgets. "We realized that our business planning system was getting too heavy; we can use the time saved for doing other things better," Mr. Moberg says. Now each region must merely keep within a fixed ratio of costs to turnover.

Lastly, to encourage IKEA to stay lean in the absence of stock market pressures—the firm remains private, with ownership vested in a Dutch charitable foundation—Mr. Kamprad has created internal competition: in 1992 he bought Habitat's British and French stores (which are separately managed), and he has split off franchise rights into Inter IKEA Systems. Although IKEA itself has first refusal over new markets, the idea is that it must show it can do a better job than franchisees would.

AND YOUR LESSON TODAY

IKEA's contortions should frighten all would-be globalists. They show how even an adaptable system based on what Mr. Moberg calls "permanent evolution" could not prevent teething troubles in a major market. But unlike many foreign venturers, IKEA started with the advantages of being both unconventional and rich. As Vanessa Cohen, a retailing consultant at Coopers & Lybrand, points out, IKEA did comply with at least one of the rules of international retailing: its strong balance sheet in Europe enabled it to absorb its initial American losses.

So far the results of IKEA's reorganization are encouraging. At 8.35 billion guilders ($4.5 billion), its sales for the year to August grew by 6 percent. IKEA does not reveal its profits, but outsiders estimate its 1993 net profit margin at 6 to 7 percent, a creditable figure given recession in core European markets. The firm claims that in the year to August, 116 million customers—equivalent to 2 percent of the world's population visited its 108 wholly owned stores, spread across 18 countries (another 15 stores, mainly in the Middle East, Hong Kong, and Spain, are franchised).

On November 4th IKEA announced that it plans to move into China, where it will open up to ten stores in the "foreseeable future." In making this move, the firm is sticking to its tradition of jumping into big new markets feet first, as it did in America. IKEA's managers stress that its American experience showed that it is easier to make changes to the product range once critical volume has been achieved.

But IKEA also takes to China other lessons from America. It has already set up the bones of a supply network in the country. Above all, the firm is tilting towards a more decentralized system of managing. In America, the result is that IKEA's Swedish identity is evolving into "a new alloy," according to Mr. Carstedt. "It's still blue and yellow, but mixing in the stars and stripes." Expect a red star to join IKEA's multi-coloured galaxy.

Source: "Furnishing the World," *The Economist*, November 19, 1994, pp. 101-102. Copyright © 1994 The Economist Newspaper, Ltd. Reprinted by permission. All rights reserved.

Discussion Questions

1. Discuss the strategy of IKEA that has changed the traditional furniture retailing business in Europe.

2. Explain the IKEA system in which customers are also suppliers and suppliers are also customers that has made the company the central star in a constellation of services.

3. Discuss the nature of IKEA's relationships with its worldwide network of suppliers that allows it to match rivals on quality while undercutting them by up to 30 percent on price.

4. Why did the IKEA business system that was so successful in Europe hit problems in America?

5. What changes did IKEA make in its American operations?

6. What lessons can one learn from IKEA's experience in America?

7. How can a global company maintain its global identity and at the same time adapt to local peculiarities? Has IKEA shown that it is possible to have both?

ENRON DEVELOPMENT CORPORATION

On August 3, 1995, Rebecca Mark, chairman and CEO of Enron Development Corporation (EDC), hurried to the airport to catch a flight from Houston to Bombay. Earlier that day she had received word from India that EDC's $2.8 billion Dabhol power plant project in India had been canceled. Given the political situation in the state of Maharashtra, the cancellation was not completely unexpected. However, if the decision could not be reversed, EDC's potential financial losses were significant. More importantly, EDC was counting on Dabhol as a beachhead that would lead to further projects in India. India's power-generating capacity was forecast to triple in the next 15 years. The cancellation of the Dabhol project could seriously undermine EDC's participation in this massive development.

ENRON CORPORATION

Houston-based Enron Corporation (Enron), formed in 1985 in a merger between InterNorth, Inc. and Houston Natural Gas Corp., was a leading firm in the worldwide energy industries. The firm's new slogan was "Creating Energy Solutions Worldwide" and its stated vision was to become "The World's Leading Energy Company—creating innovative and efficient energy solutions for growing economies and a better environment worldwide."

Enron was the largest natural gas company in the United States and operated the largest gas pipeline system in the world outside of Gazprom in Russia. The firm was involved in developing more natural gas-fired independent power plants than any other company in the world. Enron owned and operated energy facilities in 15 countries and had projects underway in 15 additional countries. In 1994, the firm had revenues of $9 billion and an operating profit of $944 million. Enron's international operations had earnings before interest and taxes of $148 million in 1994, an increase of 12 percent over the previous year. International operations represented 15 percent of the company's total sales and operating income. Table 1 provides a financial summary for Enron.

Enron had five operating divisions:

- Enron Operations Corp. was responsible for U.S. interstate natural gas pipelines; operated the company's worldwide physical assets (except those owned by Enron Oil & Gas); and provided engineering, construction, and operating services expertise across all business lines.

TABLE 1
Enron Financial Summary

(Dollars in Millions, Except per Share Amounts)	Year Ended December 31,				
	1994	1993	1992	1991	1990
Revenues	$8,894	$7,986	$6,415	$5,698	$5,460
Income Before Interest, Minority Interest and Income Taxes	$944.4	$797.7	$767.2	$715.3	$662.1
Income Before Extraordinary Items	$453.4	$332.5	$328.8	$232.1	$202.2
Earnings per Common Share	$1.70	$1.46	$1.21	$0.98	$0.86
Total Assets	$11,966	$11,504	$10,312	$10,070	$9,849
Return on Shareholders' Equity	16.5%	15.0%	14.9%	12.4%	11.2%
NYSE Price Range					
High	$34 5/8	$37	$25	$19 1/8	$15 5/8
Low	$27	$22 1/8	$15 1/4	$12 3/8	$12 1/2
Close December 31	$30 1/2	$29	$23 3/16	$17 1/2	$13 5/8

- Enron Capital & Trade Resources Corp. conducted the majority of the firm's worldwide marketing activities for natural gas, liquids, and electric power and was responsible for U.S. power development.

- Enron Oil & Gas was involved in exploration and production activities in natural gas and crude oil.

- Enron Global Power & Pipelines owned and operated natural gas pipelines in emerging market countries. Enron Corporation held a 52 percent ownership interest in Enron Global Power & Pipelines.

- Enron Development Corporation (EDC) was involved in the development of international energy infrastructure projects such as power plants, pipelines, fuel transportation, and natural gas processing plants.

Enron Development Corporation

EDC's focus was on natural gas projects. The firm had an international reputation as a reliable provider of turnkey natural gas projects on a timely basis. All of EDC's projects were project-financed and had long-term contracts with pricing agreements reached in advance. Revenues were tied to the U.S. dollar, and the host government or an outside agency held responsibility for currency conversions.

EDC's projects spanned the globe. On Hainan Island in China, EDC was constructing a $135 million, 150-megawatt (MW) power plant. This independent power plant was the first developed by a U.S. company in China. After completion by late 1995, Enron would be the operator and fuel manager. In the Dominican Republic, EDC was completing the first phase of a 185-MW power plant. This project had a 20-year power purchase agreement with the government. In Columbia, EDC was constructing a 357-mile natural gas pipeline for the state-owned oil company. Other projects in active development included a 478-MW gas-fired power plant in Turkey; a 1120-mile natural gas pipeline from Bolivia to Sao Paulo, Brazil; a 500-MW gas-fired power plant in Java, Indonesia; and a $4 billion liquefied natural gas processing plant in Qatar.

There was a close relationship between EDC and Enron Global Power & Pipelines (EPP). The parent firm had granted EPP a preferential right to acquire all of EDC's ownership interests in completed power and gas projects outside the United States. The projects under construction in which EPP had preferential rights included the firm's interest in the Dominican Republic power project, the Hainan Island power project, the Columbia pipeline, and the first and second phases of the 2,015-MW Dabhol project in India.

MARKET REFORM IN INDIA

India gained its independence in 1947. From that time until the mid-1980s, the government pursued an economic policy of self-sufficiency. This policy was often referred to as *swadeshi*, a Hindi word meaning indigenous products or made in India. The term was first used by Mahatma Gandhi during the independence movement to encourage people to buy native goods and break the British economic stranglehold on India. To many Indians, *swadeshi* evoked images of patriotism and Indian sovereignty.

After decades of socialist-oriented/statist industrial policy focused on achieving self-sufficiency, India was financially strapped and bureaucratically bloated. High tariffs kept out imports and official government policy discouraged foreign investment. In the 1970s, Coca-Cola and IBM were among the multinational firms that pulled out of India. During the period 1985 to 1990, foreign investment in India averaged only $250 million annually.

Efforts to reform the Indian economy began after the 1991 federal elections. The Indian government was on the verge of bankruptcy and foreign exchange reserves were sufficient for only three months of imports. After considerable prodding by the IMF and Finance Minister Manmohan Singh, Prime Minister Rao introduced free market reforms in July 1991. Singh urged that India follow the free market models of South Korea and Taiwan in achieving rapid economic development. India's economic liberalization plan moved the economy away from its traditionally protectionist policies toward actively encouraging foreign participation in the economy. As part of the plan, the Prime Minister's office set up a special "fast track" Foreign Investment Promotion Board to provide speedy approval for foreign investment proposals. In October 1991, the government of India opened the power industry to private sector foreign direct investment. In February 1992, the Indian government allowed the rupee to become partially convertible. In 1994, India ratified the World Trade Organization agreement on intellectual property laws.

The economic reform program had a powerful effect. By 1995, the Indian economy was growing at an annual rate of more than 8 percent. Exports were up by 27 percent over the previous year in the April-June quarter. The country had more than $20 billion in foreign reserves, up from $13.5 billion in 1994 and only $1 billion in 1991. Food stocks were at an all time high and inflation was under 10 percent. Tariffs, while still high and ranging from 30 to 65 percent, were only about one fifth what they were before liberalization. By some estimates, the government's policies had produced up to $100 billion in new entrepreneurial projects in India since 1992. In January 1995, a delegation of U.S. executives accompanied U.S. Commerce Secretary Ron Brown on a visit to India. During the trip, Brown was asked if the CEOs from the energy sector had expressed any fears about doing business in India. Brown replied "if they had any [fears] before they came, they certainly have been dissipated by this visit."[1]

Despite these efforts to encourage market reform and economic development, many hurdles remained. In 1995, foreign direct investment in India was only $1.3 billion, as compared to $33.7 billion in China. About 40 percent of the industrial economy remained government-owned. Perhaps the greatest impediment to both rapid growth and attracting foreign investment was the lack of infrastructure that met international standards. In particular, India suffered from a substantial electricity shortage.

DEMAND FOR ELECTRICITY

The Indian population was starved for electricity. It was estimated that many of India's industries were able to operate at only half their capacity because of a lack of electric power. Frequent power outages were taken for granted. In New Delhi, the government-owned power company imposed rotating one to two hour blackouts periodically during the summer, when demand for electricity peaked and temperatures were often as high as 115 degrees. More remote areas had no power at all. India's current annual electrical generating capacity was about 80,000 MWs. Demand was expected to nearly triple by 2007[2], as Table 2 shows.

Virtually all of India's power was generated and managed by state-owned electricity boards (SEBs). It was widely acknowledged that these boards suffered from chronic managerial, financial and operational problems.[3] As much as a quarter of the electricity generated was stolen. Government-run power plants typically operated at about 50 percent capacity. In comparison, the private power plants run by Tata Steel, an Indian company, operated at around 85 percent capacity.

Indian power rates were among the lowest in the world. Farmers paid less than 15 percent of the cost of electricity generated by new thermal power plants. In several states, small farmers paid nothing for electricity. Although the SEBs had been trying to raise rates, this had proved to be very difficult. In 1994, in the state of Gujarat, the opposition government encouraged farmers to blockade roads and bum government property after rural power rates were increased. The government was forced to back down and lower the amount of the increase.

Because of these problems and because all levels of government were so short of funds, the central government decided to turn to the private sector. The Electricity Act was amended in October 1991 to make this possible. However, the response from the private sector was poor, so the act was amended again in March 1992 to provide further incentives, including a 16 percent rate of return to investors. In comparison, the Chinese government in 1994 announced a 12 percent rate of return cap on private power projects.

TABLE 2
Power Demand Projections (as of March 1995)

Current capacity	78,900 MWs
Estimated growth rate of demand to 2007	approximately 9% per year
Total requirements by 2007	220,000 MWs
Likely rate of addition to 2007	3,000 MWs per year
Total capacity by 2007	115,000 MWs
Likely shortfall in 2007	107,000 MWs
Additional investment needed	5 trillion rupees ($160 billion U.S.)

Still, potential investors remained skeptical of the central government's commitment to reform and were doubtful of the SEBs' ability to pay for privately generated power. The government took one more step. In May 1992, a delegation of Indian central government officials visited the United States and the United Kingdom to make a pitch for foreign investment in the power sector. The delegation included then power secretary S. Rajagopal, finance secretary K. Geethakrishan, and cabinet secretary Naresh Chandra. The visits were a major success. Many independent power producers (IPPS) immediately sent executives to India. By July 1995, more than 130 Memorandums of Understanding (MoUs) had been signed by the government of India with IPPS. Twenty-three of the 41 pending electricity projects bid on by non-Indian companies were led by American firms.

THE DABHOL PROJECT

In turning to the private sector for power plant development, the Indian Government decided to give the first few private sector projects the status of pioneer projects; later these projects became known as "fast track" projects (of which eight such projects were eventually signed). For the fast track projects, the central government decided not to follow the standard public tendering process. Instead, it would negotiate with IPPs for individual projects. The rationale was that the government was not in a strong negotiating position and therefore the financial risk to the IPPs had to be reduced to entice them to invest in India. At a press conference, power secretary S. Rajagopal said the first few projects "would not be allowed to fail."

EDC's Rebecca Mark met with the Indian delegation when it visited Houston. In June 1992, Mark and several other EDC managers, at the Indian government's invitation, visited India to investigate power plant development opportunities. Within days, Enron had identified a potential site for a gas-fired power plant on the western coast of India in the port town of Dabhol, 180 miles south of Bombay in the state of Maharashtra. Maharashtra was India's richest state and the center of Indian industrialization. The huge port city of Bombay was the capital and the headquarters of most of India's major companies, including Air India and Tata Enterprises, the largest Indian industrial conglomerate. Firms based in Bombay generated about 35 percent of India's GNP.

EDC, acting on the government's assurances that there would not be any tendering on the first few fast track projects, submitted a proposal to build a 2,015-MW gas-fired power plant. The proposed project would be the largest plant EDC had ever built, the largest of its kind in the world, and, at $2.8 billion, the largest foreign investment in India. The liquefied natural gas needed to fuel the Indian power plant would be imported from a plant EDC was constructing in Qatar. The proposal was very favorably received by both the central government and officials in the Maharashtra state government. The Maharashtra State Electricity Board (MSEB) had long wanted to build a gas-fired plant to reduce its dependence on coal and oil. Other countries with limited petroleum reserves, such as Japan and Korea, had followed a similar strategy and built coastal gas-fired power plants.

EDC was the first IPP to formally submit a proposal. Later in June 1992, EDC signed an MoU with the MSEB. A new company called Dabhol Power Company was formed. Enron held 80 percent of the equity in Dabhol and its two partners, General Electric and International Generation Co., each held 10 percent. International Generation was a joint venture between Bechtel Enterprises Inc. (Bechtel) and San Francisco-based Pacific Gas & Electric, formed in early 1995 to build and operate power plants outside the United States. General Electric was contracted to supply the gas turbines and Bechtel would be the general contractor. Exhibit 1 lists the various individuals involved with the Dabhol project and Exhibit 2 shows the timing of the various events.

ENRON DEVELOPMENT CORPORATION

EXHIBIT 1
Individuals Involved in the Dabhol Project

Lal Krishna Advani	President of the Federal BJP Party
Manohar Joshi	Chief Minister of Maharashtra, deputy leader of Shiv Sena
Kenneth Lay	CEO of Enron Corporation
Rebecca Mark	Chairman and CEO of EDC
Gopinath Munde	Deputy Chief Minister of Maharashtra with direct responsibility for the state energy ministry, BJP party member
Ajit Nimbalkar	Chairman and Managing Director of Maharashtra State Electricity Board
Sharad Pawar	Former Chief Minister of Maharashtra, voted out of office March, 1995; known as the Maratha strongman
P.V. Narasimha Rao	Prime Minister of India
N.K.P. Salve	Federal Power Minister
Manmohan Singh	Federal Finance Minister, architect of free market reforms and economic advisor to PM Rao
Robert Sutton	EDC Managing Director
Balashaheb "Bal" Thackeray	Leader of Shiv Sena

EXHIBIT 2
Timing of Events Associated with the Dabhol Project

October 1991	Government of India invites private sector participation in the power sector
May 1992	Indian delegation visits U.K. and U.S.; EDC invited to India by government of India
June 1992	Maharashtra State Electricity Board signs MoU with EDC
February 1993	Foreign Investment Promotion Board (FIPB) grants approval
March 1993	Power Purchase Agreement negotiations start
November 1993	Central Electricity Authority clears Dabhol project
February 1994	Government of Maharashtra signs counter guarantee
September 1994	Government of India signs counter guarantee
March 1995	Dabhol financing completed
March 1995	Maharashtra State election results announced
April 1995	Construction begins; government of Maharashtra orders a review; Munde Committee set up to investigate Dabhol Project
August 1995	Project canceled by government of Maharashtra

Following the signing of the MoU, EDC began a complex negotiation process for proposal approval, followed by more negotiations on the actual financial details. Officially, no power project could be developed without technical and economic clearance from the Central Electricity

Authority. Typically, this process could take many months, or possibly years. The Foreign Investment Promotion Board (FIPB) was the central government's vehicle for a speedy approval process. The FIPB asked the Central Electricity Authority to give initial clearance to the Dabhol project without the detailed information normally required. However, final clearance would still be necessary at a later date.

In November 1992, EDC made a detailed presentation at a meeting chaired by the central government's finance secretary* and attended by various other senior government officials, including the chairman of the MSEB. From this meeting came a recommendation to the FIPB to approve the project. In turn, the Central Power Ministry, acting on the advice of the FIPB, asked the Central Electricity Authority to expedite the approval process. The Central Electricity Authority gave an in-principle (not final) clearance to proceed with the project since the Ministry of Finance had found the project satisfactory.

In March 1993, with the necessary government approvals largely in place, EDC was in a position to negotiate the financial structure of the deal. The most critical element was a Power Purchasing Agreement (PPA) with the MSEB. The PPA was the contract under which EDC, as the owner of the power plant, would supply power to the MSEB electric grid. Over the next year or so, Rebecca Mark visited India 36 times. Ajit Nimbalkar, chairman and managing director of MSEB, described the negotiations:

> This is the first project of this kind that we are doing. MSEB did not have any experience in dealing with international power developers. It was a complicated exercise, for the money involved is large, and so the negotiations took a long time.[4]

MSEB turned to the World Bank for advice in the negotiations. The World Bank offered to fund a team of international consultants. The MSEB chose Freshfields, a British law firm, and the British office of the German Westdeuche Landesbank Girozentale as consultants in the PPA negotiations.

In addition to negotiating the project financial structure and gaining state and central government approvals, EDC had to obtain dozens of other government approvals, some of which dated back to British colonial times. For example, to get permission to use explosives on the construction site, EDC had to visit the western Indian town of Nagpur, where British Imperial forces once stored munitions.[5]

In November 1993, the Central Electricity Authority officially cleared the Dabhol project. In December 1993, the MSEB signed the Dabhol PPA. The state government of Maharashtra signed a financial, or counter, guarantee in February 1994, and the central government signed a counter guarantee in September 1994. The central government counter guarantee, which was to become very controversial, was signed with EDC before the government's guarantee policy was announced publicly.

STRUCTURE OF THE DABHOL PROJECT

Although the original plans were for a 2,015-MW project, the Maharashtra government decided to break the project into two phases. Phase I would be a 695-MW plant using distillate fuel instead of natural gas and Phase II would be a 1,320-MW gas-fired plant. The capital cost for Phase I

---

* The finance secretary was the senior civil servant in the finance department and reported directly to the Finance Minister.

would be $920 million, with an estimated turnkey construction cost of $527 million.[6] The second phase would cost about $1.9 billion.

Dabhol was broken into two phases because EDC had been unable to finalize its gas contracts and because the government had become concerned about the mounting criticism of the project. The shift from gas to distillate was done because distillate, a fuel indigenous to India, could be sourced from local refineries, helping deflect the criticism that gas imports would be a persistent drain on India's foreign exchange. Furthermore, using distillate instead of gas eliminated the need to build a port facility for Phase I.

The capital cost for Phase I included some costs for infrastructure items that would normally have been provided by the state, such as a pipeline. If these costs were deducted from the total capital cost, the cost per MW was comparable with the other fast track power plant projects. However, Dabhol was the only project that had been finalized. The other projects were still going through planning and approval stages.

The Indian government generally followed what was known as a fixed rate of return model. Investors were assured a 16 percent rate of return on net worth for a plant load factor of up to 68.5 percent. Beyond 68.5 percent, the rate of return on equity would increase by a maximum of 0.70 percent for each I percent rise in the plant load factor. Net worth was based on the total costs of building the power plant. The main objection against this model was that it provided no incentive to minimize the capital costs of investment.

The Dabhol project used a different model. A tariff of Rs2.40 ($1 equaled about 36 rupees) per unit (kilowatt/hour) of electricity was established. The tariff consisted of a capacity charge Rs1.20 based on the capital cost of the plant and an energy charge of Rs1.20 for the price of fuel. By using a fixed tariff, the problems of a cost-plus system were eliminated and consumers would not be affected by increases in the capital cost of the project. For EDC and its partners, there was an incentive to become more efficient to improve shareholder returns. Based on the capital costs per MW, Dabhol was comparable to other proposed projects in India. As to the tariff of Rs2.40, other fast track power projects had similar tariffs, as did several recently approved public sector projects. Several existing public sector plants were selling power in the Rs2.15 range (although the average tariff for state electricity boards in India was Rs1.20). Enron's estimated internal rate of return on the project after adjusting for inflation was 19 percent. Dabhol was granted a five-year tax holiday.

Nevertheless, because there was no competitive bidding on the Dabhol project, critics argued that the Rs2.40 per unit was too high and that the company would be making huge profits. Kirit Parekh, director of the Indira Gandhi Institute of Development and Research, was an ardent critic:

> In the United States, power generated from gas-based plants is sold to utilities at 3-4 cents at the busbar while Enron is charging 7 cents. It is a rip-off. The China Power Company, which is setting up a 2000 MW power plant in Hong Kong, and which will go on stream in 1996, is doing so at 15 percent less capital than Enron.[7]

Further criticism was directed at the company's lack of competitive bidding for its principle equipment supplier, General Electric, and its construction partner, Bechtel. Although General Electric and EDC had worked closely in the past, some critics suggested that foreign equipment suppliers were favored over Indian suppliers. EDC countered with the argument that it had awarded more than 60 contracts worth more than $100 (Rs360 crore) million to Indian companies.

EDC was also subject to criticism because of its plan to import gas for Phase II from its gas processing plant in Qatar. When completed, this plant would be owned by a joint venture between Enron Oil & Gas and the Qatar government. Although Enron vigorously denied it, critics suggested that Enron would make excessive profits through transfer pricing and charging arbitrary prices for the fuel. From EDC's perspective, taking responsibility for fuel supply was a means of reducing its risk, since the contract specified penalties when the plant was not able to generate electricity. Fuel supply failure would not constitute sufficient grounds for being unable to generate electricity.

The federal counter guarantees also came in for criticism. A World Bank report questioned the counter guarantee arrangement because in its opinion, it was nothing more than a loan made by the federal government on behalf of the MSEB if it cannot cover its payments to Enron. EDC's Sutton countered:

> It is only after the government of India decided as a policy to give counter guarantees that we also decided to ask. It would have been impossible to raise money from international bankers at competitive rates without the guarantee when others are approaching the same bankers with guarantees in their pockets.[8]

THE POLITICAL SITUATION IN INDIA

India's political process was based on a parliamentary system. At the national, or Central level as it was referred to in India, the Congress (I) party formed the government and its leader, P.V. Narasimha Rao, was Prime Minister. The Congress (I) Party was the descendant of the Indian National Congress, which was formed in 1855 and became the major vehicle of Indian nationalism. From 1947 to 1989, some form of the Congress Party ruled India in an unbroken string of governments. Indira Gandhi, who had been Prime Minister since 1964, founded the Congress (I) Party after her defeat in the 1977 election. In 1980, Indira Gandhi and the Congress (I) party regained power. After Indira Gandhi was assassinated in 1984, her son Rajiv became Prime Minister. In the 1989 election, Congress (I) lost and turned power over to a minority Janata Dal government. During the 1991 election campaign, Rajiv Gandhi was assassinated and P.V. Narasimha Rao became the Congress (I) party leader. Congress (I) regained power in a minority government and although Rao was not considered to be a strong leader by opponents or supporters, he had proven to be surprisingly resilient. The next election was scheduled for May 1996. Predictions in August 1995 were that three parties, Congress (I), Left Front, and BJP, would each get about 150 of the 543 available seats in the Lok Sabha (House of the People).

The official opposition party was the Bharatiya Janata Party (BJP). In English, this translated to the Indian People's Party. The BJP platform emphasized support for traditional Hindu goals and values, making the party less secular than the Congress (I) Party. Many of its members belonged to the urban lower middle class and distrusted the free market reforms and modern cultural values. The BJP believed it could build support among the business community that sought decentralization and deregulation but resented intervention on the part of foreign multinationals. The BJP was considered to be the front party for a Hindu fundamentalist movement led by Rajendra Singh, known as Rashtriya Swayamsevak Sangh (RSS; translation: National Volunteers Core). The RSS supported economic nationalism and promoted anti-Muslim, anti-feminist, and anti-English language views. In 1990, the RSS formed the Swadeshi Jagaran Manch, or National Awakening Forum, to promote economic nationalism. The Forum deemed the marketing of Western consumer goods frivolous and wasteful ("India needs computer chips, not potato chips"). According to the Forum's Bombay representative, "Soft drinks and instant cereals do not serve the mass of Indian people. We are not pleased with the way [Coke and Pepsi] are demolishing their rivals."[9]

The Maharashtra Election

The political parties at the state level mirrored those at the central level, although the Congress (I) was less dominant. In two states, West Bengal and Kerala, politics had long been dominated by the Communist party. The BJP was particularly strong in the industrial, heavily populated, and largely Hindu northern states. Decision making was decentralized in India and many of the states had a substantial amount of power and autonomy. For example, the World Bank had secured an agreement to lend directly to individual states.

On February 12, 1995, a state election was held in Maharashtra. Results were to be announced about four weeks later because the chief election commissioner in Maharashtra had a policy of delinking voting from the counting of votes. The incumbent Congress (I) Party and an alliance between the BJP and Shiv Sena Parties were the primary contestants. State elections were normally held every five years. In the previous election in 1990, the Congress (I) party had formed a majority government under Chief Minister Sharad Pawar. Pawar was confident of retaining power in the 1995 election.

The BJP Party was closely aligned with the national BJP Party. Shiv Sena was a Maharashtra-based party with the stated objective of protecting the economic interests and identity of Maharashtrians and safeguarding the interests of all Hindus. The official leader of Shiv Sena was Manohar Joshi, but he had limited power and openly admitted that the real authority was Bal Thackeray (sometimes referred to as Mr. Remote Control for his ability to control the party from an unofficial capacity). Thackeray was a newspaper cartoonist before he become a right-wing activist. A talented organizer and rousing orator, he set up the Shiv Sena Party in the mid-1960s to appeal to poor Hindus who resented the influence of foreigners and non-Maharashtrians, particularly those from South India. Thackeray was prone to provocative and somewhat threatening statements. He wanted to change the name of India to Hindustan, and during the Maharashtra election he talked about chasing non-Maharashtrians out of the state.

The Dabhol power project was a major campaign issue leading up to the election. Election Commission norms in India prohibited a state government from making decisions on vital matters in the run-up to an election. However, the BJP and Shiv Sena did not make this an issue in February. Had they done so, the Election Commission might have ordered the state government to defer the decision on Dabhol.

The BJP/Shiv Sena election campaign rhetoric left little doubts as to their sentiments—one of their slogans was "Throw Enron into the Arabian Sea." The BJP platform promoted economic nationalism and sovereignty and denounced the Dabhol project. The BJP attempted to isolate Chief Minister Pawar as the only defender of Enron. The Dabhol project was described as a typical case of bad government—the failure of the ruling party to stand up to pressure from multinationals, corruption, and compromising on economic sovereignty. The BJP had always been opposed to the project for various reasons: the social and environmental aspects, alleged bribes, the project's cost, and the lack of competitive bidding. The BJP/Shiv Sena campaign strategy painted the Congress (I) Party as anti-poor, corrupt, and partial to foreign firms. This platform evidently appealed to Maharashtrians. On March 13 the election results were announced. The BJP/Shiv Sena coalition won 138 of 288 seats and, with the help of several independent members, formed the new government. The Shiv Sena's Manohar Joshi became the new Chief Minister.

Not long after the election, Enron CEO Kenneth Lay noted, "If something happens now to slow down or damage our power project, it would send extremely negative signals to other foreign investors."[10] Other firms with power projects underway or in planning included the Swiss firm ABB, the U.S. firms AES Corp. and CMS Energy, and Hong Kong's Consolidated Electric Power Asia.

CONSTRUCTION BEGINS

On March 2, 1995, EDC completed the financing for Phase I of the Dabhol project. Phase I financing would come from the following sources:

- a 12-bank syndication led by the Bank of America and ABN-Amro (loans of $150 million)
- U.S. Export-Import Bank ($300 million; arranged by GE and Bechtel)
- Overseas Private Investment Corp. ($298 million)
- Industrial Development Bank of India ($98 million)

Construction was soon underway. But the new state government in Maharashtra, in keeping with its campaign promises, decided to put the project under review.

THE MUNDE COMMITTEE

The Munde Committee was formed by the Maharashtrian state government to review the process and details of the Dabhol project. The committee had two members from the BJP and two from the Shiv Sena. The chairman of the committee was deputy chief minister and state BJP president Gopinath Munde, a known critic of Dabhol. An open invitation to individuals to appear before the committee was followed up by letters to the MSEB and Dabhol Power Company. The committee was scheduled to submit its report by July 1.

Over the next few months, the committee held more than a dozen meetings and visited the site of the power plant. The committee was assisted by five state government departments: energy, finance, industries, planning, and law. All requests for appearances before the committee were granted. Among those making depositions were environmental groups, energy economists, a former managing director of the Bombay Suburban Electric Supply Company, representatives of other IPPS, and representatives of the IPP Association. The Industrial Development Bank of India (a prime lender to the project), representatives from the former state government, and the Congress (I) party did not appear before the committee.

During the committee hearings, the BJP continued its public opposition to Dabhol. The issue of irregularities—a euphemism for bribes—was raised. According to a senior BJP official:

> Though it is impossible to ascertain if kickbacks were paid to [former Maharashtra chief minister] Anwar, even if we can obtain circumstantial evidence it is enough. The project has been padded up and if the review committee can establish that, it is sufficient to cancel the project.[11]

Allegations of bribery were vigorously denied by EDC. Joseph Sutton, EDC's managing director in India, had told delegates at India Power '95, a conference on the power sector held in New Delhi in March, "during the three years we have been here, we have never been asked for, nor have we paid, any bribes."[12]

On June 11, the RSS (the Hindu fundamentalist group) issued a directive to the BJP that it would like the party to honor its commitment to the *swadeshi* movement. The economic advisor to the Central BJP Party, Jay Dubashi, said:

> We think canceling this project will send the right signals. It will demonstrate that we are not chumps who can be taken for a ride. Enron probably never imagined that Sharad Pawar [former Maharashtra Chief minister] would go out of power. They thought he would see the deal through.[13]

Pramod Mahajan, the BJP's All-India secretary, was also fervently against Dabhol, stating that "we will go to court if necessary and decide in the long-term interest of the country."[14] Mahajan also ruled out paying penalties to EDC if the project were scrapped.

Meanwhile, EDC officials were shuttling back and forth between New Delhi and Bombay, trying to convince the press and the government, of the viability of the Dabhol project. At one point, the U.S. ambassador to India, Frank Wisner, met with BJP president, L. K. Advani. Advani refused to meet Enron officials. The issue was even discussed during U.S. Treasury Secretary Robert Rubin's visit to India in April. According to the Assistant Secretary of the Treasury, "we pushed for resolution of the issue."[15] In May 1995, the U.S. Department of Energy warned that failure to honor the contract would jeopardize most, if not all, other private projects proposed for international financing in India. Maharashtra had attracted more than $1 billion of U.S. investment and more than half of all foreign direct investment projects in India were in this state. Furthermore, more than 25 percent of all foreign direct investment in India was from the United States.

In the meantime, Bechtel had not stopped construction. A spokesman for Bechtel said the company can't afford to have its 1,300 workers idled during a month-long review. "We have to meet a schedule; we have to provide power according to the power purchase agreement."[16]

CANCELLATION OF THE DABHOL PROJECT

The Munde Committee report was submitted to the Maharashtra government on July 15, 1995. Prior to the release of the report, N.K.P. Salve, India's power minister stressed that the "Enron contract can be canceled only if there is a legal basis for doing so, not for any arbitrary or political reason."[17] On August 2, the Indian Supreme Court dismissed a petition by a former Maharashtra legislator challenging the Dabhol project on the grounds of secrecy.

On August 3, Chief Minister Joshi (who had visited the United States in the previous month to attract investment to India) announced to the Maharashtra legislature that the cabinet unanimously agreed to suspend Phase I of the project and scrap Phase II. The following are excerpts from Chief Minister Joshi's lengthy statement in the Assembly:

> The Enron project in the form conceived and contracted for is not in the best interests of the state. . . . Being conscious of the deception and distortion in the Enron-MSEB deal which have caused grave losses, the sub-committee is clear that the project must not be allowed to proceed. The sub-committee whole-heartedly recommends that the Enron-MSEB contract should be canceled forthwith. . . . Considering the grave issues involved in the matter and the disturbing facts and circumstances that have emerged pointing to extra-commercial considerations and probable corruption and illegal motives at work in the whole affair, immediate action must be initiated under the penal and anti-corruption laws by police.
>
> The wrong choice of LNG [liquefied natural gas] as fuel and huge inflation in capital costs, along with unprecedented favours shown to Enron in different ways, including in the fuel procurement [had all resulted in an] unreasonable fuel cost to the consumers . . . . The documentary evidence obtained by the committee shows beyond any reasonable doubt that the capital cost of Enron Plant was inflated and jacked up by a huge margin. The committee believes that the extent of the inflation may be as high as $700 million. Being gas-based, this project should have been cheaper than coal-based ones, but in reality it turns out to be the other way about.

Cases

> I am convinced that Enron, Bechtel, and GE will sell off at least 50 percent of their equity for the recovery of their expenditures on the project plus profits and the government would be a helpless spectator. The government should have sought some part of this for itself. . . . This contract is anti-Maharashtra. It is devoid of any self respect; it is one that mortgages the brains of the State which, if accepted, would be a betrayal of the people. This contract is no contract at all and if by repudiating it, there is some financial burden, the State will accept it to preserve the well-being of Maharashtra.[18]

Other grounds were given for cancellation: there had been no competitive bidding; EDC held secret negotiations and used unfair means to win its contract; there was potential environmental damage to a region that was relatively unpolluted; the guaranteed return was well above the norm; and concerns about the $20 million earmarked by EDC for education and project development. The BJP government charged that concessions granted to EDC would cause the state of Maharashtra to lose more than $3.3 billion in the future. The committee was also outraged that loose ends in the Dabhol project were being tied up by the Maharashtra government as late as February 25, almost two weeks after the state election. In effect, the contract had been made effective by an administration that had already been rejected by voters.

When the decision was announced, Prime Minister Rao was on a trade and investment promotion trip to Malaysia. He indicated that the economic liberalization policies initiated by his government would not be affected by this decision. Sharad Pawar, the chief minister of Maharashtra at the time the original agreement was signed with Enron, criticized the BJP's decision to cancel the Dabhol power project:

> If the government of Maharashtra was serious about the industrialization of Maharashtra and its power requirements for industrialization and agriculture, they definitely would have appointed an expert group who understands the requirement of power, about overall projection, about investment which is coming in the fields of industry and agriculture, legal sides; but this particular angle is totally missing here and that is why I am not so surprised for this type of decision which has been taken by the government of Maharashtra.[19]

On the day after the government's cancellation announcement, the *Saamna* newspaper, known as the voice of the nationalist Shiv Sena Party, published a headline that read, "Enron Finally Dumped into the Arabian Sea." Later that week, *The Economic Times* in Bombay reported that local villagers celebrated the fall of Enron (see Exhibit 3).

EDC'S NEXT STEPS

About 2,600 people were working on the Dabhol power project and it was nearly one-third complete. More than $300 million had been invested in the project and estimated costs per day if the project were shut down would be $200,000 to $250,000. Cancellation of Phase II was less critical because EDC had not yet secured financing commitments for this portion of the project.

A few days before the Munde Committee report was made public and anticipating a cancellation recommendation, Rebecca Mark had offered publicly to renegotiate the deal. She told the media that the company would try to meet the concerns of the MSEB. On August 3, EDC announced that while it was aware of the reported announcement in the Maharashtra Assembly on the suspension of Dabhol, the company had received no official notice to that effect. The statement, issued in Houston, said:

448

EXHIBIT 3

Excerpts from *The Economic Times*, Bombay, August 7, 1995

Villagers Celebrate 'Fall' of Enron

The 'Fall' of Enron was celebrated with victory marches, much noise of slogans, firecrackers and dancing outside the gates of the Dabhol Power Project and in the neighboring villages of Guhagar, Veldur, Anjanvel and Katalwadi on Sunday.

The march was led by local BJP MLA, the boyish Mr. Vinay Natu, whose father, a former MLA, is said to have originally brought the Enron project to its present site. The younger Natu denies this and says it is Enron propaganda to defame his father.

Much action was expected at the project site by the accompanying police escort. If nothing else, the celebrators were expected to pull down the Dabhol Power Company signboards on the gates of the high fence. They had earlier trailered this in Guhagar when women pulled down a DPG signpost indicating way to the site and trampled it with fury.

Instead, the processionists danced, threw gulai in the air, and burst long strings of firecrackers before moving on to the next gate. Behind the wire fences at the site stood the tense security staff of the project; in the distance on higher ground could be seen site engineers observing the proceedings through binoculars.

Lining the fence inside were hundreds of construction workers who came to see the show. These workers too come from the neighboring villages, including those where the celebrations were being held. And even among the processionists were many who on other days worked inside the fence area on pay much higher than anything they can get in their villages. The paradox of benefiting by the Enron project as well as protesting against it has been the most striking aspect of the controversy.

The local Congress leader, 'Mama' Vaidya, was most unimpressed by the show or the opposition to the project. "This backward area needs the project," he said. As to any Congress efforts in the area to muster support for the project or economic development of the area, Mr. Vaidya said there was infighting in the party and coordinated action was not possible.

At DPC itself work goes on. There's worry on the faces of engineers, but they are determined to go on until they are told by their bosses to stop. No such order has been served yet.

> [EDC] remains available for discussions with the government on any concerns it may have. . . . [EDC] has very strong legal defenses available to it under the project contracts and fully intends to pursue these if necessary. The DPC [Dabhol Power Company] and the project sponsors would like to reiterate that they have acted in full compliance with Indian and U.S. laws.[20]

Source: This case was written by Professor Andrew Inkpen of Thunderbird and Professor Arvind V. Phatak of Temple University, with research assistance from Katherine Johnston, for the sole purpose of providing material for class discussion. It is not intended to illustrate either effective or ineffective handling of a managerial situation. Any reproduction, in any form, of the material in this case is prohibited unless permission is obtained from the copyright holder. Copyright © 1996 Thunderbird, The American Graduate School of International Management.

Discussion Questions

1. Why has the situation occurred? Should EDC have predicted that the Dabhol project would be canceled?

2. Assume that there will be a meeting involving (1) Rebecca Mark and Robert Sutton, (2) Gopinath Munde, Deputy Chief Minister of Maharashtra with direct responsibility for the State Energy Ministry, and (3) Ajit Nimbalkar, Chairman and Managing Director of Maharashtra State Energy Board. What will be the positions of the three parties?

3. What should Rebecca Mark do?

Notes

1 N. Chandra Mohan, "New Beginnings," *Business India,* January 30-February 12, 1995, p. 135.

2 "India: 3rd Quarter Report," *The Economist Intelligence Unit,* 1995, p. 22.

3 Michael Schuman, "India Has a Voracious Need for Electricity: U.S. Companies Have a Clear Inside Track," *Forbes,* April 24, 1995, pp 162-163.

4 Bodhisatva Ganguli & Tushar Pania, "The Anatomy of a Controversial Deal," *Business India,* April 24-May 7, 1995, p. 57.

5 Marcus W. Brauchli, "A Gandhi Legacy: Clash Over Power Plant Reflects Fight in India For Its Economic Soul," *The Wall Street Journal,* April 27, 1995, p. A6.

6 Ganguli & Pania, p. 59.

7 Ganguli & Pania, p. 58.

8 Ganguli & Pania, p. 56.

9 "India Power Down: A Major Blow to Rao's Reform Drive," *Asia Week,* August 18, 1995.

10 Emily MacFarquhar, "A Volatile Democracy," *U.S. News and World Report,* March 27, 1995, p. 37.

11 Ganguli & Pania, p. 56.

12 Ganguli & Pania, p. 55.

13 Ganguli & Pania, p. 55.

14 Ganguli & Pania, p. 55.

15 Ganguli & Pania, p. 55.

16 *San Francisco Business Times,* May 5, 1995 Sec: 1, p. 1.

17 "Foreign Investment in India: The Enron Disease," *The Economist,* July 29, 1995, p. 48.

18 "Indian State Axes $2.8 BN Dabhol Power Project," International Gas Report, *The Financial Times,* August 4, 1995; Mahesh Vijapurkar, "Enron Deal Scrapped, Ongoing Work Halted," *The Hindu,* August 4, 1995, p. 1.

19 All-India Doordarshan Television, August 3, 1995.

20 Vijapurkar, p. 1.

A TALE OF TWO JOINT VENTURES

JOINT VENTURE #1
THE CORNING-VITRO DIVORCE

Monterrey, Mexico—Seldom do either marriages or business alliances develop without crises. Still, when Corning and the giant Mexican glass manufacturer Vitro made a cross-border alliance two and a half years ago, it seemed a blessed union.

"Vitro and Corning share a customer-oriented philosophy and remarkably similar corporate cultures"—that was the enthusiastic toast offered at the time by Julio Escamez, a Vitro executive.

Both companies had long histories of successful joint ventures, both were globally oriented, and both had founding families still at their centers.

In February, however, Corning handed back Vitro's $130 million dowry and called off the joint venture. "The cultures didn't match," said Francisco Chevez, an analyst with Smith Barney Shearson in New York. "It was a marriage made in hell."

The 25-month union was hurt by constant cultural clashes. Corning managers were sometimes left waiting for important decisions about marketing and sales because in the Mexican culture only top managers could make them and at Vitro those people were busy with other matters. Vitro's sales approach was less aggressive, the remnant of years in a closed economy, and this sometimes clashed with the pragmatic approach Corning had developed over decades of competition.

To varying degrees, such cultural issues have plagued many mergers and alliances with their roots in the North American Free Trade Agreement. "Mexico initially appears to be the United States except that people speak Spanish," said Harley Shaiken, a labor economist who often works in Mexico. "That's just not the case, which everyone finds out in the short term rather than the long term."

The trade pact may have created false expectations about how much like the United States Mexico has become. In discussing cultural differences, it's difficult not to slip into stereotypes about "mañana" Mexicans who move at a slower pace. But what the gap separating the two business cultures really amounts to is a different approach to work, reflected in everything from scheduling to decision making to etiquette.

When Banc One of Columbus, Ohio, was contracted to assist Bancomer, one of Mexico's largest banks, in setting up a consumer credit card operation, it found that cultural differences made working difficult because simple things like scheduling meetings became ballets of clashing customs. The Americans were used to eating lunch at their desks, but in Mexico City, bankers go out, often for hours, for leisurely meals. The solution: full lunch in the company dining rooms.

There was also a problem with schedules because Mexicans, with their long lunches, typically have a much longer workday, starting at 9 and often lasting until 9 at night. So Bancomer executives wanted to hold 7:30 p.m. meetings, and even then were often late, but Banc One advisers wanted to be home by that time. The solution: meetings could be held into the evening, but a piggy bank was placed on the center of the table and anyone arriving late had to pay a few pesos per minute. In the Corning venture, the Mexicans sometimes saw the Americans as too direct, while Vitro managers, in their dogged pursuit of politeness, sometimes seemed to the Americans unwilling to acknowledge problems and faults. The Mexicans sometimes thought Corning moved too fast; the Americans felt Vitro was too slow.

But it wasn't just cultural differences that undid the alliance. Added complications came from a strong peso, increased overseas competition, and a rethinking of marketing strategies by both companies. But the cultural disparities hurt the companies' ability to react to a fast-changing market, and in the end led both sides to throw in the towel.

Corning and Vitro continue to market each other's products and are reluctant to rehash their squabbles. But the abrupt end of the alliance still has them trying to figure out exactly what went wrong.

"We've reflected on this a lot ourselves," said John W. Loose, chairman of the Corning Consumer Products Company, the successor to Corning-Vitro in the United States.

Corning is most often associated with oven-ready glassware but has diversified into fiber optics, environmental products, and laboratory services. Vitro, Mexico's largest industrial group, makes dozens of products, including beer bottles, automobile windshields, and, in a joint venture with Whirlpool, washing machines.

Although both are aggressive global concerns, their cultural differences are sometimes quite obvious. Take their headquarters. Corning's offices in upstate New York are in a modern glass-enclosed building, while Vitro's headquarters in Monterrey, often thought of as Mexico's Pittsburgh, are in a replica of a 16th-century convent, with artwork, arched ceilings, and antique reproductions.

Another difference quite obvious from the beginning was the manner of making decisions and the time it took to make them. Vitro and other Mexican businesses are much more hierarchical, with loyalty to fathers and patrons somehow carried over to the modern corporation. As a matter of either loyalty or tradition, decisions are often left either to a member of the controlling family or to top executives, while middle-level managers are often not asked their opinions.

"If we were looking at a distribution decision or a customer decision," said Mr. Loose, "we typically would have a group of people in a room, they would do an assessment, figure alternatives, and make a decision; and I as chief executive would never know about it. My experience on the Mexican side is that someone in the organization would have a solution in mind, but then the decision had to be kicked up a few levels."

Even the way they have responded to the failure of the venture shows how different the cultures sometimes are. Americans are normally willing to discuss what went wrong and learn from it, while Mexicans are often reluctant to criticize anyone, especially a partner, preferring simply to focus on the fact that the marketing arrangement between the companies continues in spite of the breakup. In interviews, Vitro executives expressed dismay that Mr. Loose had spoken so openly. "It is unfortunate that he made those comments," one Vitro executive said in private.

The president of Vitro, Eduardo Martens, denied that corporate cultures in Mexico and the United States differ any more than the cultures of any two corporations. But in an interview last year, before his comments could be taken as being in any way critical of Corning, he said, "Business in Mexico is done on a consensus basis, very genteel and sometimes slow by U.S. standards."

Richard N. Sinkin, a corporate consultant said cultural differences generally are "the No. 1 problem for doing business in Mexico." Though that may be an exaggeration, it underscores the difficulty of transferring a culture across the border. His own experience, he said, bears that out. He is bilingual and often works in Mexico, but has found that it isn't always easy to get paid because the Mexican view of contracts differs markedly from the one commonly held in the United States.

In Mexico, the terms of a contract "are kind of ideal things that you strive to achieve," he said, "while in the U.S. they are law."

In general, corporate style is more formal in Mexico than in the United States. Titles are common, and nearly everyone is "licenciado," which loosely refers to having any professional training. Forgetting the honorific can be seen as a serious insult.

While executives in Mexico can expect the unquestioned loyalty of employees, outsiders are often viewed with mistrust. Horace E. Scherer, director general of Hobart Dayton Mexicana, the Mexican subsidiary of Hobart Corporation, said his salespeople must often make four trips to complete one transaction because of that lack of trust. To sell the company's scales and other equipment, a salesperson starts with a visit to the client's top official. If a sale is made, a representative of the company itself must deliver the goods because the customer won't accept delivery from DHL or some other service. If all the papers are in order on delivery, the company representative is told to come back on an appointed day to present an invoice, in person, and if the invoice is accepted an appointment is made to return to receive payment.

Source: Anthony DePalma, "A Corning-Vitro Joint Venture Was a Case Study in Clashing Styles," *The New York Times*, June 26, 1994, p. F5. Copyright © 1994 by The New York Times Co. Reprinted by permission.

JOINT VENTURE #2
THE VOLVO-RENAULT MARRIAGE

The most successful alliances result from the union of two companies that share a common business vision and have complementary resources and skills. Take the case of Volvo of Sweden and Renault of France. "Volvo understood long ago that in order to compete in the worldwide automotive market, it had to recognize economies of scale that were just not possible when you are a very limited niche manufacturer," says Rick Dowden, president and CEO of Volvo North America. Volvo manufactures 400,000 cars a year in an industry where major competitors manufacture millions, so in order to remain competitive Volvo sought a partner.

In searching for its partner, Volvo had several criteria in mind: to ally itself with a company that understood its business, offered complementarity, and was not so large that it would swallow up Volvo and dominate the relationship. Having previously been involved in a successful project to jointly produce engines with Renault, Volvo felt comfortable with the company. The product lines and marketing strengths also were complementary, according to Dowden. Essentially, both Volvo and Renault are in the same business—the manufacture of cars, trucks, and buses. Renault is strong in small cars and diesel engine technology, and Volvo is strong in larger cars and gasoline technology. And, geographically, Volvo is strong in northern Europe and North America, whereas Renault is relatively weak in North America, but strong in southern Europe and Latin America.

Aside from strategic fit of the two companies, there was a great deal of chemistry between the top executives. Volvo Chairman Pehr Gyllenhammar and Renault's then-Chairman Raymond Levy were very close in their philosophy about what kind of products they wanted, how they wanted to market them, and how they wanted their companies to be viewed in the marketplace, according to Dowden. "These were two people who knew and respected each other and had common goals and aspirations for their companies," he says. "If the people don't work together, I don't care how much the numbers seem to work, you won't get that (spirit) of cooperation."

In order to facilitate the alliance between Renault and Volvo, working groups were set up to examine the elements of the industrial system, such as product design and procurement, as well as the manufacture of components for cars, trucks, and buses, to determine if an alliance would benefit both Renault and Volvo in terms of competitiveness and long-term profitability. The groups came up with some projections that were appealing to both parties. In February 1990, the Volvo-Renault alliance was officially announced.

The alliance with Renault covers every aspect of Volvo's business and is viewed as a permanent arrangement. "There are no provisions in our agreement for dissolving this relationship. It is intended to be a marriage," says Dowden.

Furthermore, each company bought a significant percentage of each other's stock. "They created such an economic interdependence that people couldn't succeed in their own part of the business without assuring that the partner succeeded," Dowden adds. "This (alliance) is not just a couple of people from Renault and a couple of people from Volvo who have lunch once in a while. This is a company that has to produce on a bottom line of its own."

Cases

Bringing together two companies from not only different countries but also different corporate cultures potentially could cause some problems. In the Volvo-Renault alliance, however, there have been no major clashes. "Volvo is an increasingly decentralized company and Renault has remained a very centralized company. But by setting up these joint (workgroups) to administer different parts of the industrial system, we have found a very good way to bridge (gaps) because it forces a certain amount of decentralization and compromise between them," Dowden explains.

And for now, Volvo doesn't expect to enter into any major alliances of the same size and scope as the one with Renault any time soon, even though the company will continue to pursue joint ventures.

Source: Julie Cohen Mason, "The Marriage of Volvo and Renault," *Management Review*, May 1993, p. 12. Copyright © 1993 by the American Management Association. Reprinted by permission.

Discussion Questions

1. Explain the reasons for the failure of the Corning-Vitro joint venture and the apparent success of the Volvo-Renault alliance.

2. (a) Identify the variety of dimensions that differentiate the organizational cultures of Corning and Vitro and (b) explain each of the dimensions that you identified.

3. Why did cultural differences not cause problems in the Volvo-Renault alliance?

4. What did managers in the Volvo-Renault alliance do to make the marriage compatible for both partners?

5. What lessons can one learn from the Corning-Vitro case and the Volvo-Renault case?

PIZZA HUT MOSCOW

"Pizzastroika" was the term coined to commemorate the September 1990 opening of the two Pizza Hut restaurants in Moscow. The opening was the culmination of five years of negotiation, planning, and training involving Pepsico and its joint-venture partner Mosrestoranservise, the restaurant-operating division of the city of Moscow.

In May 1991, after nine months of operation, the Pizza Hut restaurants were averaging 20,000 customers each week. One of the restaurants was capable of producing 5,000 pizzas each day and had the distinction of being the largest pizza kitchen in the world. Lines of people were always waiting to gain entrance, and although many problems had arisen, the joint venture had generated more sales than anyone had predicted.

Andy Rafalat, regional director of Pizza Hut's operations in eastern Europe and the Soviet Union, had managed the Moscow venture from its inception. Rafalat, 39, was faced in May 1991 with difficult decision. During initial negotiations with the city of Moscow, Pizza Hut had agreed to transfer management of the joint venture over to the Russians eventually. Were the Russians prepared to take the helm?

HISTORY OF PIZZA HUT

On June 15, 1958, Dan and Frank Carney, two college students from Wichita, Kansas, opened the first Pizza Hut restaurant. It was a sterling success. By the following February, the Carney brothers had opened two more restaurants and had begun to develop plans for the first franchised outlet. The chain grew rapidly: 43 restaurants opened by 1963, and 296 by 1968. Pizza Hut went public in 1969 and in 1977 was acquired by Pepsico, Inc. In 1971 Pizza Hut had become the largest restaurant chain in the world in both sales and number of restaurants. Sales reached $1 billion in 1981 and $13 billion in 1988. In 1990 Pizza Hut, still headquartered in Wichita, had over 7,000 units and 125,000 employees worldwide.

Pizza Hut restaurants usually displayed a distinctive freestanding design and characteristic red roof. Until 1985 all Pizza Hut restaurants were full-service, eat-in/carryout, family-style operations seating about 60 to 90 customers and normally open from 11 a.m. to midnight. In 1985 Pizza Hut began opening delivery-only units to meet rising competition from such pizza delivery restaurants as Domino's.[1]

HISTORY OF RUSSIAN JOINT VENTURES

In January 1987, the Presidium of the U.S.S.R. Supreme Soviet authorized the establishment of joint ventures between Western companies and Soviet entities such as factories and government organizations. President Mikhail Gorbachev envisioned that this joint cooperation would satisfy Soviet requirements for certain industrial products, raw materials, and foodstuffs; attract foreign technology, management experience, material, and financial resources; and develop the export base of the country.[2]

When the law was first introduced, a foreign partner was entitled to a maximum of 49 percent ownership in a venture.[3] The decree required that all joint ventures be self-supporting and established a two-year tax holiday, after which profits would be taxed at 30 percent. No limitations existed on the number of partners or composition of the joint venture's capital structure. Foreign companies were not allowed to "repatriate" their profits, that is, they could not convert ruble earnings into hard currency. Therefore, Western partners often attempted to formulate strategies through which the joint ventures would generate more hard currency than they used.

HISTORY OF THE PIZZA HUT JOINT VENTURE

During 1987, Anatoly Dobrynin, then Soviet Ambassador to the United States, and Donald Kendall, the chairman of Pepsico, discussed the possibility of opening a Pizza Hut in Moscow. Pepsico had been doing business in the Soviet Union since 1972, when it signed an agreement to provide Pepsi-Cola concentrate in exchange for Stolichnaya vodka. Dobrynin and Kendall, believing that the time was right for introducing a restaurant business, decided that the Pizza Hut operation would be a component of a $3 billion commercial countertrade pact between Pepsico and the Soviet Union.

The pact involved the creation of 26 new Pepsi plants in the Soviet Union; Pepsico retained exclusive rights to the sale of Russian vodka in the United States. The deal also included the construction by the Soviets of ten commercial shipping vessels that would be sold or leased. Foreign-exchange credits generated for the Soviets from the sale and lease of the ships would be partly used as investment in the Pizza Hut restaurants.[4] Kendall commented at the signing of the deal:

> This latest agreement further strengthens a highly successful and long-standing trade relationship between Pepsico and the Soviet Union. Equally important, as trade between nations expands, so does the level of understanding and cooperation among those nations'

citizens. This agreement reflects increasingly closer ties between the U.S., the Soviet Union, and other Western interests, and the expressed optimism for a shared future. It expands even further the positive collaborations which can help bring the two superpowers and their people closer towards the universally shared goal of world peace.[5]

Altruism and improved relations were not the only reasons for the trade agreement. Business rationale was also strong. The Pizza Hut joint venture was viewed by some as a symbolic "toe in the water" for both Pizza Hut and Western businesses planning to start joint ventures. Recent political changes suggested that the East European market would soon open to capitalist operations. Eastern Europe was the largest untapped base of consumers in the world and according to Rafalat the thinking at the time was that Pepsico's experience with both Soviet consumers and long-standing relations with an East European government would provide the company with considerable leverage and a strong "calling card" in this emerging market.[6]

The decision to begin U.S.S.R. operations in Moscow was a reasoned one. Moscow, with a resident population of 9 million, was one of the largest cities in the world.

Pizza Hut would be a 49 percent partner in the joint venture and was required by the terms of the pact to source the majority of its food requirements locally, to engage in the transfer of both financial and technological expertise, and to train a Russian management team for eventual on-site management. The technology transfer included management and distribution training and training on the state-of-the-art equipment to be used in the restaurant.

Many business analysts believed that the joint venture had symbolic importance to the future of business in the Soviet Union. Kendall waxed philosophic: "We are not, however, just bringing pizza to Moscow. Nor are we just helping to satisfy the local Soviet appetite for consumer goods. We're helping to meet the changing needs of the Soviet economy."[7]

CULTURE CLASH

Managing this joint venture was not an easy task. Many times the problem was just getting each side to understand what the other wanted. Many of the Pizza Hut team's preconceived notions about doing business didn't apply. Rafalat commented:

> Don Kendall gets the request and passes it down on our side. We can't be sure it is always passed down on the Russian side. The first people we met here were construction people. They simply wanted to build a pretty restaurant. We said, our job is not about buildings, it's about a system of management. It all dragged on and on, and after 18 months we were told there was no real interest in developing Pizza Huts at all. They had no concept of the difference between a small Vietnamese restaurateur and a multinational chain. We had to work out a book of rules. That took time. The words we were using had totally different meaning to these guys.[8]

This communication problem was the largest barrier in the early days. Interpreters seemed unable to help. For instance, the Soviet staff protested operations running 365 days a year. They believed, given a need to close for "hygiene days," that it was impossible. Pizza Hut had to explain the concept of cleaning as a part of routine, daily business operations.

During these times, Mosrestoranservise provided as much assistance as it could. Assistance was limited, however, because of the difficulties and changing environment in Moscow at the time.

CONSTRUCTION OF THE RESTAURANTS

Senior Pizza Hut managers wanted to have two restaurants in Moscow located in high-traffic areas. They finally signed contracts to build restaurants at 12 Gorky Street, near Pushkin Park and only minutes from the Kremlin, and at 17 Kutozovsky Prospekt, one of Moscow's busiest streets. Taylor Woodrow International was chosen to manage the construction of the Pizza Hut restaurants using design and construction standards similar to those found in the West.

Taylor Woodrow, based in England, assembled an international team to construct the restaurants. Some 100 laborers including skilled craftsmen from Britain, Italy, Sweden, Portugal, Poland, and Russia worked at the two sites. In the demonstration of how to accomplish individual tasks, the spoken and written word often took second place to sign language. The work encountered supply problems, as Taylor Woodrow divisional director, Ian Greenwood, pointed out: "We had no local builders' merchants on hand, even for basic things like nuts and bolts, so we had to import just about everything in the way of tools and equipment—even down to screwdrivers." As a result, costs of production were three to four times higher than they would have been in western Europe.[9]

FINDING AND CREATING SUPPLY SOURCES

Pizza Hut managers soon found that the establishment of internal supply sources would be a significant challenge. Although McDonald's had created an entire food-production facility to supply its restaurant, Pizza Hut decided to source 70 percent of all supplies from existing local suppliers within the Soviet Union (see Exhibit 1), in order to help them improve their quality and standards. Rafalat believed that this approach would ensure the long-term viability of the operation and provide benefits to the growing class of Soviet entrepreneurs. "We are not food producers," he explained. "Our expertise is in restaurants. Where possible, we're happy to share know-how and technology that enables the Soviets to make what we need, sell it to us at a profit, and also meet local market needs."

EXHIBIT 1
Weekly Food Requirements Purchased Locally

French bread	8,000	loaves
Garlic puree	320	lbs
Flour	8,800	lbs
Mushrooms	680	lbs
Onions	6,640	lbs
Tomatoes	5,000	lbs
Cucumber	5,000	lbs
Carrots	5,000	lbs
White cabbage	2,600	lbs
Beetroot	5,000	lbs
Pickles	5,000	lbs
Ice cream	2,000	lbs
Pepsi syrup	264	gallons
Beer	1,000	bottles

At the same time, however, Rafalat realized that Moscow's long and extreme winters would make internal sourcing especially challenging. The city often experienced shortages during the winter months and some Muscovites were known to survive entirely on pickled vegetables. Moreover, Rafalat could not expect to purchase supplies from the warmer, southern republics of the country, which were refusing to send supplies to Moscow because of the escalating political and ethnic tensions.

Pizza Hut faced other supply problems. Cheese, one of the main components of pizza, was common in the Soviet Union, but not mozzarella cheese, which was unavailable. Rafalat visited numerous cheese-processing plants around the country but with little success:

> We couldn't find anybody even interested in supplying us. Finally, we found one in Motensk, 300 kilometres from Moscow, somebody who had been touched by Western thinking. He was happy to give it a try. We would provide the equipment and expertise, he would make the cheese.

Pizza Hut flew the Russian to England to see how the cheese was made and brought cheese-making experts to his plant to provide training on the modern process and equipment. Nevertheless, the mozzarella produced was unacceptable, because the domestic milk did not contain enough butterfat. Cheese had to be imported until a sufficient number of cows could be raised on a strict diet of Western grain.

The search for a supplier for meat toppings also met with no success. Both quality and reliability were missing from every meat plant Rafalat visited. Finally, Pizza Hut's Swedish meat supplier agreed to set up its own joint venture with a partner in Moscow and guaranteed that Pizza Hut would receive the lion's share of its output. Unfortunately, the plant would not be ready for at least another year, so another key ingredient had to be imported.

Pizza Hut also needed to find a way to transport supplies to the restaurants. Because refrigerated trucks were virtually nonexistent in the Soviet Union, Pizza Hut had no choice but to import two trucks to form its own distribution system. The trucks were painted with the distinctive Pizza Hut logo so that they might also serve as a traveling advertisement for the joint venture.[10]

MARKET RESEARCH

In many ways, the Moscow restaurants were an experiment. Because of the novelty value of the Pizza Hut product, typical marketing research methods and tools were useless for establishing market size and taste preferences. Pizza Hut managers observed, however, as McDonald's opened a restaurant in the city's Pushkin Square in January, customers in the thousands lining up to taste Western-style fast food. They believed the same novelty value would play a strong role in bringing Russians into Pizza Hut restaurants. Pizza, however, was not an unknown food in the Soviet Union; it had been served by Italian and Canadian joint-venture restaurants. It was even prepared by some Russians at home. In addition, a traveling pizza truck offered customers individual slices of pizza. These pizza foods were of varying quality and taste; thus the Soviet consumer had come to view products termed pizza as having a varying quality.

Pizza Hut scheduled bake-offs to allow Muscovites to sample and compare its product with others. The company received rave reviews. Rafalat believed the Soviet consumers were easily able to discern quality and would communicate their findings quickly through word of mouth.

Pizza Hut would also be different because it would offer both fast- and full-service meals. Rafalat thought that a dinner at Pizza Hut could be viewed as a trip to an expensive restaurant, while McDonald's would still offer only fast food. Rafalat wanted to combine speed with service and offer Soviet consumers something entirely new: quick table service geared for the entire family. "The market is not consumer driven at all," Rafalat said. ". . . there is a real lack of consumer choice. Pizza Hut will immediately be ranked as a four- or five-star restaurant in the city."

Pizza Hut decided to offer a menu comparable to that found in Western Pizza Huts—with Pepsi soft drinks, a newly brewed Soviet bottled beer, and wines from Hungary and the Soviet Union. They also developed a "Moscow Pizza" with a salmon-based topping designed to fit with the fish-heavy Soviet diet (see Exhibit 2).

PRICING, THE RUBLE, AND HARD CURRENCY

The restaurants would also differ from other Moscow restaurants in that customers would be able to purchase pizza in either rubles or hard currency. The Gorky Street restaurant would have a walk-up window for ruble customers and a full-service restaurant for hard-currency customers. The restaurant at 17 Kutozovsky Prospekt would actually be two separate full-service restaurants. Both ruble and hard-currency customers would receive full service, but they would never interact with each other.

Rafalat had attempted to determine who would visit each type of restaurant based on customers' incomes. The average monthly income for a Soviet citizen at the time was 250 rubles. Recently, however, a burgeoning middle class of entrepreneurs had found a higher standard of living than the government employees. Rafalat believed that this middle class enjoyed an average monthly salary of approximately 2,000 rubles. He hoped to serve these entrepreneurs in the ruble restaurants. He also thought that Westerners and black marketeers would visit the hard-currency restaurant. His initial estimates were that the foreign customers would be 40 percent Americans and 30 percent Japanese with Germans, Australians, and British making up the balance.

Ongoing changes in the currency exchange rate complicated pricing decisions for the restaurants. At the time the joint venture was being negotiated, the official government rate was 1.6 dollars per ruble, although most people believed that the ruble was worth far less. It was against the law for Soviets to hold hard currency, which over the years had led to the creation of a black market. In the late 1980s, many Soviets were illegally purchasing hard currency on the black market at a rate of approximately 10 rubles per dollar. By the time the Pizza Hut restaurants were ready to open, Soviet President Gorbachev had acknowledged that the ruble had been artificially propped up and he had introduced a mixed exchange rate. He set an official rate of 2 rubles per dollar and a tourist rate of 6 rubles per dollar. At the same time, however, because the poor quality of Soviet goods had been recognized around the world, the black market rate had fallen to nearly 30 rubles per dollar.[11] This trend suggested that the Soviet government still had a long way to go before reaching an equilibrium between its fixed exchange rate and the free market rate established by the black market.

After studying these fluctuations in the exchange rate and attempting to set reasonable prices for the restaurants' food, Rafalat decided that the restaurants would offer identical menus but that the prices would differ. Prices in the ruble restaurants would be roughly comparable to those found in some of the better full-service Soviet restaurants. Prices in the hard-currency restaurants would be similar to those found in Pizza Hut restaurants in the United States. For instance, a large pepperoni pizza in the ruble restaurant would cost 18.20 rubles, while it would cost $6.90 in a hard-currency establishment. At the tourist exchange rate in September 1990 (6 rubles per dollar), an American student would pay more than twice as much money to eat in the hard-currency restaurant as he/she would pay to eat in one of the ruble restaurants.

EXHIBIT 2
Full-Service Menu

Welcome to Pizza Hut

Home of the Pan Pizza

Here at Pizza Hut every pizza is made fresh to order using only the finest ingredients. Baking your pizza may take a little time, so while you wait why not try some garlic bread or salad. Our waiters and waitresses are here to help so please ask if you require any assistance.

Garlic Bread

Garlic bread is the ideal complement to your pizza or on its own as a starter.

Garlic Bread freshly toasted slices of bread, covered with garlic butter.

Garlic Bread Supreme
Garlic Bread with melted Mozzarella cheese on top, a special treat.

Garlic Bread (4 pieces)	3.00
Garlic Bread Supreme (4 pieces)	4.00

Salad Bar

We have a salad bar where you can choose your own salad from the fresh selection available. All you have to do is ask for a salad. Your waiter or waitress will then give you a salad bowl. You simply choose your own salad at the salad bar. This price is for one visit to the salad bar only.   4.00

Pan Pizza

At Pizza Hut we offer a choice of pizza to suit everybody's taste. All our pizzas are made from dough prepared daily in each restaurant and covered in a delicious tomato sauce and two layers of mozzarella cheese.

All of Pizza Hut's pizzas are baked fresh to order.

Our world famous **Pan Pizza** is light and fluffy inside with a crisp crust and baked in its own pan to a delicious golden brown. We also have our **Thin'n Crispy™** pizza, prepared and baked to perfection with a thin and crispy crust.

Specialty Pizzas

There are nine different specialty pizzas to choose from in three different sizes. The choice is yours.

You can order a pizza for one person or share between a few people.

Our pizzas come in 3 sizes:

	Small	Medium	Large	
	ideal for one person	*perfect for two to share*	*for three or four people to share*	
	Small	Medium	Large
Margherita			
Special tomato sauce and cheese	5.00	8.00	11.00
Pepperoni			
Pepperoni, mushroom	6.00	10.00	14.00
Hawaiian			
Ham, pineapple	7.00	11.00	14.00
Vegetarian			
Onion, green pepper, mushroom	7.00	12.00	15.00
European			
Ham, beef topping, mushroom	7.00	12.00	15.00
Moskva Seafood			
Moskva fish selection, onion	7.00	12.00	17.00
Meat Treat			
Beef topping, pork topping, onion	8.00	13.00	17.00
Supreme			
Pepperoni, beef, pork topping, mushroom, onion, green pepper	8.00	14.00	18.00
Super Supreme			
Pepperoni, ham, spicy pork, pork topping, beef, mushroom, onion, black olives, green pepper	10.00	16.00	22.00

Beverages

Ideal with your pizza - Choose a refreshing drink from our wide selection of beverages.

	Small (330ml)	Pitcher
Minerals		
Pepsi	2.00	6.00
Diet Pepsi	2.00	6.00
Fiesta or Tanlets	2.00	6.00
Beer		
Local Beer	3.00	
Imported Beer	4.00	

	Local	Imported
Wine	12.00	16.00
Red or White Wine by the bottle	12.00	16.00
by the glass	3.00	

Hot Drinks	
Tea	1.00
Coffee	2.00

Desserts

The best way to finish your meal is with one of our desserts.

Ice Cream	
Chocolate or vanilla	3.00
Apple Pie	
A slice of traditional apple pie, made with chunks of apple, specially prepared pastry and served with ice cream	4.00

Takeaway Service

With Pizza Hut you can enjoy great pizzas at home with our Takeaway Service.

All you have to do is place your order at the Takeaway counter in the hard-currency Pizza Hut restaurant, **Kutozovsky Prospekt, 17.**

Then just pick up your pizza when it's ready and take it away!

The prices on the menu are for US Dollars, payment can also be made in Pounds Sterling, Deutschmarks, or Finnish Marks.
We also accept the following credit cards: American Express, Diners Club, Mastercard, Visa, and J.C.B.

Why then would an American choose to pay in dollars? The answer was simple: Pizza Hut planned to maintain a standing line of at least 30 minutes in front of the full-service ruble restaurant. Therefore, foreigners would be paying extra for the quick service. (The long line was also intended to serve as a testament to the value of the Pizza Hut product.) The mixed-pricing decision was key to Rafalat's strategy: Pizza Hut would gain a source of hard currency, which was important because foreign companies could not repatriate ruble profits, and be able to hedge the extreme exchange-rate risk.

HUMAN RESOURCES

The requirement that the management of the joint venture would eventually be 100 percent Soviet made the hiring of management personnel a critical task. "Our experience is that, to make joint ventures work, you have to give the local management team the responsibility for running the business," Rafalat said. "I will be called the deputy general manager. I will be like the coach, training the people around me, not taking an active part in the business."[12] This Pizza Hut strategy differed widely from that of the McDonald's joint venture.

In addition to the legal requirement, another rationale for emphasizing Soviet management of the joint venture was the sometimes contradictory Soviet view of Westerners, particularly Americans. Westerners were loved because of the economic and technical assistance they could provide but hated because of the elite status their knowledge and finances afforded them.

Rafalat decided that the best way to find managers was to visit restaurants in Moscow. At one particular establishment, he noted that the staff smiled (a rarity in Moscow) and that the interior was clean. When Rafalat and representatives from Mosrestoranservise spoke with the manager, Alexander H. Antoniadi, they found that he also knew his sales and profit figures. Highly impressed, they offered him the job of general director of the Pizza Hut restaurants. He accepted.

Antoniadi, 46, had managed five different restaurants in the Moscow system, including one full-service restaurant, two fast-food restaurants, and a bakery. Born in Georgia and of Greek descent, he was one of few Soviets who had visited the West. He considered his exposure to Western management practices and service levels a significant factor in his past (and potential future) success. "You can't compare Western and Soviet restaurants," Antoniadi said. "You [Westerners] are used to taste, quality, and far higher worker discipline. Moscow restaurants employ people who are not used to Western service standards."

After Antoniadi was named general director, Pizza Hut still needed two on-site managers for the restaurants. They approached Alexander Youdin and Boris Paiken, both 36, who ran a Georgian-style fast-food cafe called the Pancake, after its famous main dish, a joint venture. Both were known for their commitment to quality and their democratic form of management. Initially, Paiken resisted leaving his joint venture, because he believed Pizza Hut would not allow Soviets to manage the operations. He called them "stables," meaning that he thought Russians, like livestock, would provide little more than physical assistance. After lengthy discussions with Pizza Hut managers, however, he joined the team.

Pizza Hut also needed a financial specialist. Olga Ignatova, 27, was a former member of the Moscow Finance and Planning Department. Rafalat and members of the Pizza Hut team were so impressed with her work during the initial phases of the joint venture that they offered her the opportunity to come aboard as a member of the staff.

Valery Ginsberg, who held a doctorate in steel and alloys from the Moscow Institute, was hired as director of technical services. Ginsberg had initially been hired by Taylor Woodrow

International during the construction phase. His knowledge and exacting work ethic earned him an offer to join the management of the joint venture.

The entire management staff was flown out of the country to train in a Pizza Hut restaurant in the United Kingdom. The goal was to establish an understanding of the Pizza Hut philosophy, not necessarily standard procedures. "We wanted people to understand both systems," Rafalat said.

> We told them to take a look at the U.K. system, and then decide how it could best work in Moscow. Taking people out for training meant they come back totally different people. Telling them the same thing here had no meaning. It was only when they went to London and saw our restaurants working that the penny really dropped.

HIRING AND TRAINING STAFF

In hiring staff for the joint venture, Pizza Hut found it had an extremely strong group of applicants from which to choose. In an attempt to hire 300 kitchen and wait staff, Rafalat placed an advertisement in the Moscow Communist Youth daily newspaper. The text of the advertisement read:

> Joint Soviet-American venture invites you to test yourself in a new job. You will gain great experience in the Pizza Hut system of restaurants, developed in 55 countries. We invite young people, 18-25 years old, who are ready to work with enthusiasm. If you meet our needs, we will be glad to speak with you.

The small advertisement elicited 3,500 responses. The applicant pool was the most qualified one Pizza Hut management had ever encountered.

The two basic requirements were that applicants speak at least one foreign language and have some experience working in restaurant joint ventures. Many applicants had college degrees, while some had masters and doctorates. Another characteristic Pizza Hut deemed important in hiring was that an applicant have as little experience as possible working in government-owned establishments. Rafalat believed that individuals became accustomed to a low-productivity work ethic in typical Soviet enterprises because, in general, such enterprises were characterized by lax discipline and almost total job security.

Many of the applicants were former staff of the McDonald's joint venture. Two reasons were cited for their leaving McDonald's: (1) they viewed Pizza Hut's full-service restaurant as being a prestige environment in which to work and (2) McDonald's management had hired so many to staff their restaurant that individuals were actually referred to by numbers, not by their names.

Three hundred people were eventually hired to staff the two restaurants, three times the number for a Western Pizza Hut with comparable output. Rafalat believed that the oversize staff was necessary because of the expected low productivity and unique Soviet employment laws that gave workers two days on, two days off. "As for finding the right people, we had to turn our personnel rules upside down," Rafalat said. "All the good English speakers are academics, so that was no good. Instead, we chose people who were as near to street-wise as possible."

The staff that was eventually hired could only be termed eclectic. For instance, the 16 cashiers all had banking diplomas, many of the members of the wait staff were young mothers with little or no academic training, and some of the kitchen staff held doctorates in engineering. Although many employees were extremely academically advanced, their experience with Western service levels and productivity standards was limited.

A staff of trainers from Britain, Australia, Belgium, Canada, Egypt, and the United States flew into Moscow two months prior to the openings. Their goal was to establish an understanding of and commitment to service unseen in the Soviet Union at that time. One of the ways Pizza Hut attempted to create that understanding was to establish standards of performance relative to each person's job. These standards involved both actual job activities and general workplace attitudes and demeanor.

Rafalat believed that an understanding among workers of a "democratic" work environment would also be needed. "Unfortunately, a part of the Soviet mentality is to maintain the minimum of your potential. This is a consequence of the autocratic management system. Many think that you can forget about standards." For this reason, he created the first standards incentive program in the Soviet Union. The system was unique in that employees were given full incentive payments to start, but amounts were debited as employees failed to meet standards. For example, each worker contracted to work 173 hours per month and would receive a salary of 600 rubles. If an individual were tardy or failed to show up for work, an established amount of his or her monthly salary would be subtracted. If a waitperson failed to smile or deliver food on time, she or he would have an amount subtracted from salary.

Waiting tables presented unique problems and required equally unique solutions. Waiters and waitresses in Pizza Huts would be allowed to receive tips, although tipping was an unfamiliar practice to Soviet consumers. Customers would have to be educated about both the practice of tipping and the amounts appropriate to various service levels.

The restaurants were to have two separate wait staffs. The ruble restaurant was viewed as the training department for waitpersons; the more experienced and efficient staff would work in the hard-currency restaurant. Because holding hard currency was illegal for Soviet citizens, tips received by waiters/waitresses in the hard-currency restaurants would be held by management in an account. The staff would be given a catalogue (covering many goods that could not be found in the Soviet Union) from which they could then choose items. Management would use funds from their accounts to purchase the goods on the staff's behalf.

OPENING

Despite the many hurdles faced by Rafalat and the joint venture, the two restaurants opened as scheduled in September 1990. The opening was as much an event as any international summit. VIP's from Pepsico and Pizza Hut, Soviet and United States government officials, and the international press were all on hand. Kendal, U.S. Secretary of Commerce Peter Mosbacher, and former Soviet Ambassador to the United States Anatoly Dobrynin all sat down with Rafalat to sample the first pizzas to come from one of the world's largest pizza kitchens. (The capacity was twice that of a normal Pizza Hut restaurant.) The training team serenaded the trainees with a song specially written for the occasion.[13] (See Exhibit 3.)

Lines of customers formed on the first regular business day, but they were not as long as those seen during the launch of the McDonald's restaurant. About 100 people waited for the doors to open that morning. Some expressed a desire to be among the first in the Soviet Union to try Pizza Hut. Others gave more pragmatic reasons: "I ate pizza recently in New York, and I wanted to have a taste," said one young woman. "I came today because in a few months it's likely to be like McDonald's, where some of the ingredients, like tomatoes and lettuce, are always missing."[14]

EXHIBIT 3
Serenade for the New Trainees

With a song in their hearts

The training team launched their trainees into action with a specially devised song, set to the melody of 'Those Were The Days'. . .

Once upon a time there were two brothers
Frank and Daniel Carney were their names
They lived in Wichita which is in Kansas
And they started up the biggest pizza chain

They named it Pizza Hut
They named it Pizza Hut
It grew and grew all over this great land
It grew so wide and far
Into the USSR
At Pizza Hut you know you've got it made

The training team was captained by a Belgian
She sent for reinforcement global wide
From around the world the Training Team were comin'
With an assistant called Ivan by her side

They came from Canada and America
Egyptians too were not left out of the crew
There were some Brits and Welsh
They needed someone else
So they threw in an Aussie too

Now all of you take heed to what we tell you
The future of success is in your hands
So remember all the things that we have taught you
And you'll make the greatest pizzas in the land

You all are Pizza Hut
You all are Pizza Hut
The way you smile
They'll come from near and far
You've all worked very hard
You're held in high regard
You are the pride of the USSR!

THE FIRST SEVERAL MONTHS OF OPERATION

As business continued, Rafalat, Antoniadi, and the management staff found that the skill most necessary in managing operations was flexibility. The only thing they could count on was the unanticipated:

> Only a few days after opening, the regional government temporarily closed both restaurants ostensibly for not having a sanitation permit. In reality, however, the closures resulted from a power struggle between the radical Moscow City Council and the conservative District Council. The incident left Rafalat wondering what the country's worsening political situation would mean for two restaurants and for any expansion plans. But one thing he knew for sure: He would need to cover his bases with all levels of the Soviet government; federal, republic, and local.[15]

Another problem that presented itself not long after the opening was an increase in the prices of supplies. The Soviet government raised prices on basic foodstuffs by an average 300 percent. Soviet wages rose, but only by about 20 percent, making Pizza Hut prices less accessible to ruble customers. This problem was compounded by Pizza Hut's decision to raise prices by 40 percent to make up for the increased cost of supplies.

On the positive side, Pizza Hut found new sources for supplies. When supplies from the government were unavailable, black marketeers proved to be quite ingenious at locating new sources. The Soviet government had recently allowed private farmers to grow and sell excess crops. Once, during the middle of the winter, a private farmer showed up at one of the restaurants' back door with a truck full of tomatoes. Whenever Pizza Hut used these sources, however, the prices were considerably higher than government goods.

Employee turnover was low in the Pizza Hut restaurants relative to other joint ventures such as McDonald's. "Low" in the Soviet Union, however, still meant hiring one new person each day. If that rate continued, the entire staff would turn over in a year's time. The turnover made ongoing training a necessity and resulted in sizable lost productivity. Moreover, the ongoing training did not yield the same results as seen with the original staff. New employees did not have the same level of respect for standards or the same level of enthusiasm regarding working at Pizza Hut. Thus, overall quality and service levels began to fall.

The establishment of a team ethic among employees was one of the goals of the managers but employees believed that their management had made little progress toward this end. "McDonald's does team building," a kitchen staff member said. "They took all of their employees on a cruise. They also took them to dinner and they gave them a Christmas and New Year's party. They have a soccer team that is composed of former Olympic athletes; we do too. Perhaps our management could arrange a game in one of the Moscow city stadiums."

Moreover, other factors began to cause tension between the ruble and hard-currency staffs. Different service requirements and the greater level of gratuity compensation in the hard-currency restaurant created resentment among the ruble staff. Staff turnover in the hard-currency restaurant was also slow, which opened up few slots for the many ruble waitpersons wanting to move up. On the other hand, while the hard-currency waiters and waitresses were receiving larger tips, the catalogue from which they could order goods was strangely absent. They began to wonder when they would be able to make use of the tips they were saving in their accounts. One waitress said, "I get a receipt for the tips that I turn in. I have these receipts, but I still haven't been able to use them. The catalogue? I have no idea when it will arrive or what is in it."

The standards incentive program created by Rafalat had been successful in rewarding workers who maintained standards but it did not penalize those who did substandard work, nor did it award exceptional service. Compensation could not fall below a floor of 300 rubles. Because this salary level provided an income that was greater than that of the average Soviet, many found little reason to maintain standards. Absenteeism, particularly among the kitchen staff, became a daily problem. Employees who worked overtime to cover absenteeism received no benefit from their additional work.

Not only did many employees work overtime, but they also were often required to do jobs that they were not hired to perform. They became proficient at all functions within the kitchen operation, but again, they received no incentive for their contributions. Employees who maintained standards felt cheated not only by their peers but also by a management staff that did not recognize their efforts.

Even without absenteeism, the shift arrangement created stress for many employees. Employees were scheduled 12 hours a day, 2 days on, 2 days off. Soviet managers believe this schedule was necessary to give employees time to stand in line for food and other supplies. The employees, on the other hand, believed they would prefer a Western-style 8-hour, 5-day schedule. Schedules were a source of frequent discussion, and the policy had been changed at least four times since the restaurants opened. Rafalat had been told by Soviet managers that the employees voted on the scheduling policy. Employees said that management simply handed it down.

The long hours caused problems in the personal lives of the wait staff. Some 80 percent of the wait staff were married, and 60 percent had children. The long hours caused many to feel that they were being negligent regarding their parental responsibilities. Furthermore, many did

Cases

not complete their shifts until after midnight, which prevented them from leaving in time to use Moscow's subways. Many had to use taxis, which were quite expensive. Commutes were long, and some employees traveled as much as 90 minutes one-way each day.

Communication between management and staff was limited. Many employees believed that, when they voiced their concerns, these opinions were not welcomed and fell on deaf ears. "There is a difference between words and deeds," a cook said. "They never take our claims seriously. In fact, we don't even know if they receive them. If you can substantiate your suggestions, then and only then can things change." Another said:

> Many people would like to see a union. However, it is very difficult to organize one. This is because of the philosophy in this country. Unions that support a specific group of workers really don't exist. The government controlled our working conditions until now. They were supposed to act in our interest. Many feel that, if they voice their complaints, they could lose their jobs. They are not happy about voicing their complaints.

Despite their expressed dissatisfaction, most staff believed that they would suggest seeking employment at Pizza Hut to others. One waitress summed up the feelings of the staff: "The work here is much more exciting and pays much better than anything you might be doing while working for the state, though it has not proven to be what we dreamed capitalism would be like."

CONCLUSION

Andy Rafalat smiled and looked from the dining room at the line of customers reaching around the block. His "toe in the water" was being called a success. It had exceeded expectations in sales and profitability.

Rafalat knew there were critical problems: employee turnover was high, quality was diminishing, and employee discontent was rising. Soon the Russian managers would take over total management of the operation. Would they be able to turn around the growing problems? What could he do to better prepare them for the management transfer?

On a different level of worry were the rumors of growing discontent with the Gorbachev government. If Gorbachev's reform policies fell out of favor, what would be the result for the Pizza Hut joint venture?

Source: This case was prepared by Gregory B. Fairchild, MBA 92 and Bonnie K. Matosich, MBA 92 under the supervision of Elliott N. Weiss, Associate Professor of Business Administration. Copyright © 1992 by the University of Virginia Darden School Foundation, Charlottesville, VA. All rights reserved. Rev. 4/93.

Discussion Questions

1. How has the cultural context in Moscow affected Pizza Hut's creation of its service-delivery system?
2. What expectations did the different parties involved—PepsiCo, Mosrestoranservise, new Pizza Hut workers, the customers, the suppliers—have? What impact do these have on the success of Pizza Hut in Moscow?
3. What has Pizza Hut done well in its Moscow restaurants? What should have been done differently?

466

4. How would you address the issues facing Andy Rafalat in May 1991? Is the Russian management staff prepared to take over day-to-day management of the venture?

Notes

1 Patrick J. Kaufmann, *Pizza Hut, Inc.,* Harvard Business School case, 1987.
2 Jeffrey M. Hertzfeld, "Joint Ventures: Saving the Soviets from Perestroika," *Harvard Business Review,* January-February 1991, p. 85.
3 In 1991, there was no ceiling on foreign ownership of joint ventures—in effect, joint enterprises could be 99 percent foreign-owned. In addition, President Gorbachev authorized the establishment of 100 percent foreign-owned companies in the Soviet Union.
4 "Pepsi will be Bartered for Ships and Vodka in Deal with the Soviets," *The New York Times,* April 9, 1990, p. A1.
5 "Pepsico Signs Largest-Ever Commercial Trade Pact with the Soviet Union," *PR Newswire,* April 9, 1990.
6 Geneive Abdo, "Pizza Hut Opens its First Restaurants in Moscow," *Reuters,* September 11, 1990.
7 Pizza Hut News release, *Pizza Hut Opens First Two Restaurants in Moscow,* September 11, 1990.
8 Quentirb Peel, "Pizza Hut Gives Food for Thought to Soviets," *Financial Times,* September 21, 1990, p. 18.
9 "Taylor Woodrow Creates a Slice of Western Living for Muscovites," *Origin Universal News Services Limited,* September 10, 1990.
10 Abdo, *Reuters,* September 11, 1990.
11 "Soviet Banks to Set Market Rate for 'Tourist Ruble,'" *Reuters,* November 29, 1991.
12 Peel, *Financial Times,* September 21, 1990.
13 "Pizzastroika," Pizza Hut Newsround, November 1990, p. 1-4 (from p. 3-35). Coincidentally, the Moscow restaurants were opened the day after an opening in Beijing. The Beijing opening was viewed as one of the first steps in renewing Western business interests in China following the Tiananmen Square protests and subsequent supporters of democracy crackdown.
14 Ibid.
15 "Wanna Make a Deal in Moscow?" *Fortune,* October 22, 1990, p. 13.

WIL-MOR TECHNOLOGIES, INC.

In February 1991, David McNeil, CEO of Wilson Industries Inc. (Wilson), was meeting with Ron Berks, the president of Wilson's North American Automotive Division. "Ron, the situation with the Wil-Mor joint venture (JV) does not seem to be improving," said McNeil. "After three years it is still losing money. What's going on down there?" Berks, a JV board member and the Wilson executive who initiated the JV formation, realized there was a problem but was not sure what to do. Not only were the JV managers not concerned, they were talking about expansion. Wilson's Japanese JV partner did not even want to discuss profitability; all they seemed to care about was lowering costs and keeping the JV's largest customer happy. McNeil emphasized that something had to be done, adding, "When we formed this venture you predicted it would reach breakeven by the second year of operation. We are not even close to that after three years."

WILSON INDUSTRIES INC.

Wilson, a Detroit-based company founded in 1923, was a manufacturer of plastic and metal parts for the automotive and appliance industries. Total sales in 1990 were $360 million, of which $210 million came from the North American Automotive Division. The Automotive Division produced plastic parts such as wheel trim covers, bumper reinforcements, plastic trim, and battery trays. Ford and Chrysler accounted for 80 percent of Wilson's sales with the remainder going to General Motors. For several years, the Automotive Division's sales had remained flat and profits had been decreasing.

In recent years, Wilson had taken steps to internationalize its automotive operations. In 1983, exports began to Germany and a small plant was purchased in England. Besides Wil-Mor, a JV was launched in 1988 to distribute Wilson products in Australia.

THE AUTOMOBILE INDUSTRY

The North American automobile industry changed dramatically in the 1980s. The primary impetus for much of the change was the emergence of the Japanese producers as leading competitors. In 1981, there were no Japanese assembly plants in North America. By 1990, there were nine Japanese-operated assembly plants in the United States and three in Canada. These plants produced 1.8 million cars in 1990, more than 20 percent of total North American production. By the end of 1990, the Japanese assembly plants, referred to as transplants, had combined capacity in place or had announced plans to make 2.3 million vehicles per year. Transplant production, plus imports from all countries, accounted for more than 40 percent of the units sold in North America. With the growth in transplant capacity, some industry observers were projecting that North American automobile capacity could exceed demand by three million units or more during the 1990s.

The three largest Japanese companies, Honda, Nissan, and Toyota, were being referred to as the "other Big 3." They were becoming full-fledged North American producers capable of designing, engineering, and assembling vehicles entirely in North America. Toyota, for example, had an objective of 75 percent North American content in its cars by 1992. Nissan was in the process of completing a modern engineering center near Detroit that would have employment of 600 by 1992. Honda was sourcing about 75 percent of its parts and components in North America and 25 to 30 percent of its tooling and equipment. In 1990, Honda, for the first time, sold more cars in North America built domestically than imported from Japan.

Automotive Suppliers

The typical car is made up of more than 10,000 parts. In the initial years of the automobile industry, carmakers tried to produce as many parts in-house as possible. By the 1950s, outsourcing of parts from independent suppliers had become commonplace. Suppliers were given blueprints and asked to bid on parts contracts. The lowest bidder generally was awarded the contract, usually for one year. In the 1980s, the world's automobile companies were all using outsourcing to some degree. General Motors was the most integrated company with 70 percent of its parts made in-house. Saab, on the other hand, made only 25 percent of its own parts.

In the 1980s, the North American companies increased their outsourcing and made substantial cuts in the number of suppliers they dealt with. The customer-supplier relationship began to shift to a structure based on tiers of suppliers. The first-tier suppliers dealt directly with the vehicle manufacturers and, increasingly, participated jointly in the design of new systems and parts. The first-tier suppliers coordinated the operations of many smaller second-tier suppliers who, in turn, worked with their own sub-suppliers. The advantage of this multilayer approach, used by the Japanese producers for many years, was that the automakers could deal with a limited number of companies and work closely with them in design and engineering.

Besides the move toward outsourcing and multitiered supplier arrangements, several other trends characterized the supplier industry. One, automakers were pushing their suppliers toward just-in-time delivery systems and increased investment in design and engineering capabilities. Two, mergers were becoming prevalent in the supplier sector, largely because of the heavy demands for research and development, new equipment, and employee training. Three, suppliers were moving away from their traditional focus on home markets toward foreign investment. For example, more than 300 Japan-based supplier firms had operations in North America, most of which had arrived in 1987-88.

The arrival of the transplant automakers was the major reason Japanese suppliers were locating in North America. However, many of these suppliers were making inroads into the domestic automakers as well. The implications were clear: like the situation with automaking capacity, excess capacity at the supplier level was becoming a reality. The overcapacity and competition from foreign-based component suppliers were creating increasingly difficult conditions for North American automotive suppliers. One senior manager in a U.S. component supplier stated:

> The next five years are going to be horrible. With the new Japanese companies coming in, with peripheral capacity, and with component integration and the car companies all chasing the same market . . . a lot of suppliers are going to fall out.[1]

The Transplants

By the mid-1980s, with the traditional North American market eroding, many suppliers, including Wilson, saw a potentially lucrative market in supplying the transplants. The transplants were committed to North American content and were rapidly building up their manufacturing capacity. Unfortunately, becoming a supplier to a transplant firm was proving to be very difficult for many North American-based firms. North American companies were often unfamiliar with the rigors of Japanese just-in-time inventory systems and demands for flexible production. A further problem frustrating the efforts of North American suppliers was that unlike their North American competitors, the Japanese automakers rarely changed suppliers. For example, Toyota's supplier base had remained virtually unchanged since the 1950s. Many of the Japanese suppliers were partially owned by the automakers and, as part of a keiretsu, had a relationship that was much stronger than a North American supplier relationship. The president of Nissan's U.S. operations explained:

> Nissan's mix of U.S. suppliers and Japanese suppliers is not likely to change much. Given our philosophy, once you become our supplier you're our supplier forever on that part, unless you mess up so bad we can't fix you.[2]

The Japanese firms put much more emphasis on trust and cooperation in the supplier relationship. As one supplier executive commented:

> The North American supplier relationship is often adversarial. The supplier usually works with the blueprint provided by the automaker. You manufacture according to the blueprint and if the part doesn't fit, "you tell your customer to stuff it." With Honda our

relationship is supportive as long as we deliver the product. And the blueprint is only the starting point. The part must fit the car; if it doesn't Honda will say, "What can we do together to make it fit?" If you ship 150 bad parts to General Motors, they will tell you that you have a problem and you better fix it fast. Honda may say you have a problem but they will also say, "How can we help you fix it?" The Japanese customer will not use its power to threaten or harass the supplier. Once the marriage is formed they will try to make it work.

In North America, the threat that supplier contracts could be canceled or moved in-house had created a system in which, according to some observers, neither party fully trusted the other. By contrast, the Japanese approach was based on long-term relationships, mutual discussion, and bargaining. While suppliers were expected to decrease prices over the term of the contract, joint activities between supplier and automaker were critical to the relationship. According to one study, "The [Japanese] system replaces a vicious circle of mistrust with a virtuous circle of cooperation."[3]

Of course, the Japanese automakers could, and did, fire their suppliers. When it became obvious that a supplier could no longer meet the exacting quality standards or improve on cost and quality, the Japanese customer was as likely to look for a new supplier as an American customer. The difference was that the Japanese automaker would expend more effort in assisting the supplier than was typical in the North American context. In addition, the Japanese companies usually kept their suppliers better informed about their performance relative to other suppliers.

THE JV FORMATION

In 1983, Ron Berks was convinced that the transplant share of the North American market would continue to grow. He began to explore the possibility of becoming a supplier to the transplant firms. He made several trips to Japan and initiated discussions with Honda America in Ohio. However, after several years of fruitless efforts, he became convinced that access to the Japanese transplants was virtually closed to North American companies that did not have an established relationship with a Japanese firm.

In the meantime, the Japanese presence in the automobile industry continued to grow. The transplant automakers were encouraging their Japanese suppliers to build plants in North America in order to maintain established customer relationships and also because of political pressure, increased domestic content was a priority. While some of the larger suppliers already had operations in North America, most did not. Trepidation about starting a new facility in North America and pressure from the Japanese automakers to involve local firms in the supply chain encouraged many Japanese suppliers to form JVs with American partners.

In late 1985, Berks first considered the feasibility of forming a JV. An obvious choice for a JV partner was Morota Manufacturing Company Ltd. (Morota). For several years Wilson had been involved in a licensing agreement with Morota. Morota, founded in 1950, was a manufacturer of small electric motors for products such as sewing machines and small appliances and also produced various plastic components for the automobile industry. Morota had sales of $320 million in 1990 with $180 million to the automobile industry. About 70 percent of the automobile sales were to Toyota with the remainder going to Nissan, Honda, and Mitsubishi. Toyota owned 10 percent of the shares in Morota. Except for a JV in Korea, Morota had limited international experience.

Berks knew that Morota wanted a plant in North America. In early 1986, he contacted the president of Morota and set up a meeting in Japan for July. Berks learned at the meeting that

Morota was being encouraged by Toyota to form a JV in North America. He also learned that Morota was "internationally naive and probably scared to death to come to the U.S. They were particularly worried about dealing with an American workforce." At the meeting, the two firms agreed to work toward forming a JV.

The JV Agreement

JV discussions between Wilson and Morota started in late 1986 and six months later a JV agreement was signed. The JV was named Wil-Mor Technologies, Inc. (Wil-Mor). Initially, Berks had hoped that Wilson would have about 70 percent ownership. However, although the Morota executives would not say so explicitly, Berks sensed that there would be problems with Toyota if Wilson had a majority position. Berks therefore agreed to 50/50 ownership. The JV agreement specified that Wilson would be responsible for locating a plant site and managing the workforce. Morota would be responsible for the equipment acquisitions and installation. Morota would provide initial engineering support and help train the workforce, both in Japan and the U.S. Morota would also work with Toyota to ensure that the JV had contracts when the JV became operational.

The JV president would be nominated by Morota and the general manager would be nominated by Wilson. These two managers would be responsible for the JV start-up. The JV board would include three executives from each firm. From Wilson, there would be Berks, an Automotive Division vice president, and the JV general manager. Morota's representatives would include Morota's president, its executive vice president, and the JV president.

Berks was very enthusiastic about the JV's potential. After the JV announcement in early 1987, his opinion was that the joint venture was a very important strategic move for Wilson. The JV was seen as an extension of Wilson's existing operation that would help increase market share and provide access to a growing segment of the market. The JV would also help Wilson learn from its Japanese partner. There was even some thought that in a few years, the JV would be able to export parts back to Japan.

Startup

Berks thought that an experienced American manager should be general manager. He selected 58-year-old Dan Johnson, a Wilson employee for 30 years and most recently a plant manager. The president, Akio Sakiya, was 55 years old and had spent his entire career with Morota. Although an engineer by training, he was vice president of finance prior to becoming the JV president.

Johnson was given the task of selecting the plant site. He chose Elizabethtown, Kentucky, a small town south of Louisville and close to the new Toyota plant in Georgetown. The initial investment in the JV was $18.2 million. Each partner contributed $3 million; the other $12.2 million was borrowed by the JV and guaranteed by the partners.

The JV plant was based on the manufacturing system used by Morota. Most of the equipment in the plant was Japanese. Morota put together a Japanese team of engineers and technical specialists. This team was responsible for installing the equipment, getting the process started, and training the workforce. The workforce was hired by Johnson and Sakiya. Their emphasis was on young people with little or no manufacturing experience (from Morota's perspective, "no bad habits"). Both partners wanted to keep the JV union-free.

The JV began operations in early 1988 with contracts from NUMMI, the JV between General Motors and Toyota, and Toyota's new Georgetown plant which would open later in the year. All contracts were for plastic trim parts, identical to parts made in Japan by Morota and very similar to parts made by Wilson for their Big 3 customers. The initial start-up was done very slowly and for some months there was only enough work for about two to three days a week. The start-up, slower than Wilson would have liked, was based on Morota's attitude of "training before operating."

JV Management

Besides the president and general manager, JV management came from both partners. Wilson provided the operations manager, human resource manager, controller, and a marketing manager. None of these managers had any Japanese language capability or experience with the transplants. Morota provided the engineering manager, the quality manager, and a marketing manager (see Exhibit 1 for an organization chart). None of these managers had any prior international experience and, except for the marketing manager, had only limited English language skills. The

EXHIBIT 1
Wil-Mor Technologies, Inc. Organization Chart

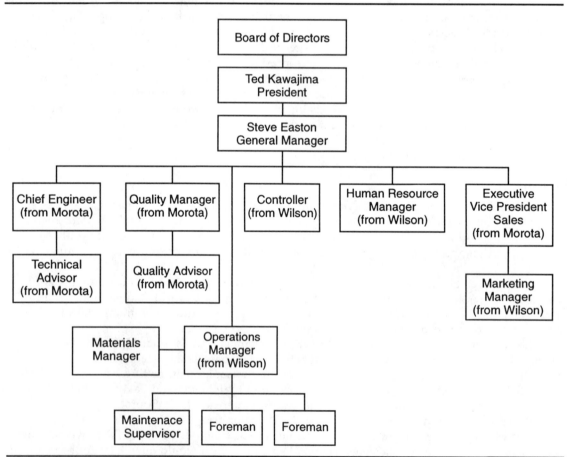

Japanese managers, including the president, had three- to five-year visas. At the end of the visa terms these managers would be rotated back to the Japanese parent. The American managers were in the JV for an indefinite period. The partners hoped that, eventually, the Japanese managers could be replaced by American managers promoted from within the JV.

The JV did not begin smoothly. The Japanese managers insisted on complete technical responsibility. Johnson, the general manager, was not allowed to assist in the technical setup. This caused several problems because the Japanese were unfamiliar with many of the basic aspects of establishing a new plant, especially one in North America. The Japanese insisted on running the operation their way. They used a Japanese approach in selecting suppliers. Johnson estimated he could have saved the JV about $250,000 a year if a North American approach had been used to select suppliers. However, the Japanese insisted that, if possible, suppliers should be selected not just on the basis of price but because they had established themselves as capable suppliers to Wilson or Morota.

When the JV started, the Japanese managers were initially skeptical about the ability of an American workforce to produce a quality product. They wondered: Can they run the machines properly? Do they know what a good product is? The Japanese managers drove the workers very hard at the outset. Several times Sakiya became furious with what he saw on the shop floor and berated the workers in Japanese.

Johnson became convinced that the Japanese managers were deliberately excluding him from the management process. The Japanese managers would regularly hold meetings and exclude the Americans. When meetings were held with both Americans and Japanese present, they would last for hours because of the necessity to translate from English to Japanese. In addition, the Japanese managers corresponded daily by fax with their head office in Japan and would meet socially in the evenings and on weekends. The inevitable result was two distinct management "camps": the Americans and the Japanese.

By March 1989, it was obvious to Ron Berks that there were serious management problems in the JV. Although the contracts with Toyota seemed to be working out well, the plant was still running at far less than capacity. Very few decisions in the JV were "joint" because the Americans and Japanese rarely talked to each other. The American managers were looking after areas such as materials sourcing, human resources, accounting, and finance. The Japanese managers concentrated on product design, quality, pricing, and sales.

Berks discussed the situation with Morota's president. They decided to replace the JV president and the general manager. The new general manager, Steve Easton, was 46 and a former plant manager who had recently been working at Wilson headquarters in an international development position. The new president was 51-year-old Ted Kawajima, an engineer with several years of international experience and an excellent command of English.

The New Management Team

The new management team got off to a much better start than the previous one. Both Easton and Kawajima were avid golfers. They began playing golf together regularly and involved several of the other managers. Gradually, the tension between the American and Japanese "camps" began to ease. Although the regular faxing between the JV and Japan continued, meetings of Japanese managers became less frequent.

The JV was also successful in winning new contracts with Toyota and was quoting on some work for Mazda and Ford. Through the NUMMI relationship, initial contacts were established with General Motors. At first, General Motors was reluctant to deal with Wil-Mor. Because

Morota was partially owned by Toyota, there was a belief that buying from the JV was, in effect, subsidizing the competition. However, that belief was slowly disappearing as more and more Japanese suppliers became established in North America. By early 1990, Wil-Mor had successfully bid on several General Motors contracts. The JV customer mix was now about 80 percent Toyota, 10 percent General Motors, and 10 percent NUMMI. The JV was actively seeking new customers and was encouraged by Toyota to do so.

Annual sales in the JV were now close to $30 million. Employment had reached 300 and the plant was close to capacity. Although the JV was still losing money, Easton and Kawajima were considering a possible expansion.

Head Office Concerns

Ron Berks was pleased by the improved managerial situation in the JV but was troubled by a financial situation that did not seem to be improving. He knew at the outset that it would take a few years for the JV to become profitable. However, based on Morota's estimates, he thought that the JV could at least be at breakeven by the end of 1989 and making a profit by 1990. In early 1991 the JV was still losing about $100,000 a month.

Even more troubling was the fact that at the most recent JV board meeting in November 1990, the Morota executives did not seem concerned that the JV was losing money. In fact, they seemed pleased that the losses were not greater. At the board meeting, when Berks questioned the JV's performance, Kawajima replied that the JV was meeting expectations and was exceeding Toyota's quality standards. He went on to say that the JV still had to get its costs down and had some way to go before quality was at a level consistent with that in Morota's Japan plants. When Berks angrily asked how many years it would be before there was a profit, Kawajima replied:

> Profit is obviously important but to achieve profitability there has to be a satisfied base of customers. We have achieved a good record with Toyota and now we are trying to build a relationship with General Motors. I think that we are in a very strong position.

Berks left the board meeting without a clear understanding of the Japanese expectations about profits in the JV. They seemed concerned only about the quality of the product and not about making money.

Easton's Perspective

Steve Easton knew that Berks, his boss, was concerned about the JV performance. He explained:

> There is an unresolvable conflict in the relationship between the partners. Morota is willing to lose money in the JV for as long as it takes to build up market share and quality in North America. Right now, their primary focus is on customer service and product improvement, not profit. They intend to be in this market for the long term and they know that Toyota plans to increase its North American capacity. Morota is determined to make money in North America but is willing to be patient. They believe that if there is a quality product and low costs, profit will take care of itself. They cannot answer the question about when the JV will be profitable because it is not consistent with their philosophy. Their approach is that prices are not the issue; costs must be improved first.
>
> When the JV was formed, the partners thought that they were in sync about prices and profit margins that might be expected. Clearly, that was an incorrect assumption.

Wilson wanted to make a quick buck; they were skeptical of making long-term investments. They saw the JV as a way to make some money. They expected a profit in two or three years. Morota expected the JV to lose money for about five or six years. However, they never communicated this to Wilson and no business plan was prepared.

Easton suspected that part of the problem was that Berks did not do his homework when the JV was formed. He commented:

The JV was started on blind faith. Each partner had some expectations about the other which have not been met. Wilson expected faster production and higher efficiency. The only thing certain at the outset was that Toyota would be a customer. Berks expected that a share of Toyota's business would be great to have and that it would be profitable. Unfortunately, nobody in Wilson had any idea of the potential profitability of supplying the transplants.

The reality is that we are unable to get the same kind of profit margins with Toyota as we can with the Big 3. We make more money on the parts we sell to GM than on the parts we sell to Toyota. A lot of suppliers are starting to say that transplant business is not good business because the prices are too low.

Easton also sensed that there was some resentment in Wilson toward the JV and an unwillingness to acknowledge openly that the JV provided an excellent learning opportunity:

I have given other Wilson managers an open invitation to visit the JV and see what we are doing. There has been some response to my invitations but there seems to be some resentment toward us. When I attend corporate meetings at Wilson, I show people what we are doing and it is clear that the JV is outperforming the other Wilson plants on a quality basis. In terms of reject rates, we beat Wilson by 10 times. Wilson talks about quality but we do it. I don't like to brag about our success in the JV but what I would like to see is an interest by the other Wilson managers in finding out why the JV is able to do so well.

The JV and the relationship with Toyota have put Wilson in a position to start questioning their capabilities. Berks would like to have Toyota as a customer so he invited Toyota purchasing managers to visit the Wilson plants. Toyota reported back to Wilson and the report was scathing. Berks's attitude was "these guys are just unreasonable."

Berks has acknowledged that some changes at Wilson may be necessary but he has avoided the serious questions. The reality is that Wilson would have to cross a lot of hurdles to get any Toyota business. However, the senior management at Wilson don't know that and would be surprised to find out. They have not addressed it and it is not a priority because of their existing business. My own belief is that Wilson has not grasped what world class manufacturing is.

On the relationship between the partners, Easton commented:

Kawajima and the Morota executives realize that Berks is not pleased with the JV performance. However, they view their relationship with Wilson from a long-term perspective. They intend to succeed in North America and assume that Wilson thinks the same way. Should Wilson express some desire to end the JV, Kawajima and the other Morota executives would be shocked and take it as a serious affront. From their perspective, strengthening the relationship between the partners is critical to the success of the JV.

THE CURRENT SITUATION

The meeting with David McNeil left Berks in a difficult position. Berks was aware that at Wilson headquarters there was growing opposition to the JV because it was not making money. Some managers were even starting to question Morota's capabilities, arguing that if they can't make money when they have a new plant and a guaranteed customer, how can we ever hope to learn anything from them?

McNeil wanted to see a JV return on investment at least as high as the other Wilson plants but Berks did not know when that would happen. At a meeting with Easton the previous week, Easton had assured him that Wil-Mor had the potential to be a leading supplier to both the transplants and the Big 3. Easton had also said that an expansion would soon be necessary. Berks knew that McNeil would never approve further capital investment until the JV started showing a profit. However, Easton argued that without expanding, the JV would lose market share and would probably take even longer to become profitable.

Ron Berks wondered what should be done about the JV. Maybe Wilson should cut its losses and get out of the JV. Or, perhaps, it would be better if Wilson lowered its ownership interest to about 20 percent. That would reduce Wilson's share of the losses and would allow Wilson to maintain its relationship with Morota. Whatever the decision, Berks knew that McNeil was expecting something to be done very soon.

Source: This case was prepared by Professor Andrew C. Inkpen of Thunderbird, the American Graduate School of International Management. Copyright © 1991 Western Business School, The University of Western Ontario. Reproduced with permission of Western Business School. Reproduction of this material in any form is prohibited unless permission is obtained from the copyright holder.

Discussion Questions

1. Why was the JV formed? Consider this from both partners' perspectives.

2. What are the major problems in the relationship between Wilson and Morota?

3. As Ron Berks, what action would you take?

4. How do you think Morota, the Japanese partner, will respond to your decision?

5. As Steve Easton, how would you respond to Berk's concerns? What action would you recommend?

Notes

1 *Ward's Auto World*, No. 7, 1989, p. 37.
2 *Ward's Auto World*, February 1991, p. 29.
3 James P. Womack, Daniel T. Jones, and Daniel Roos, *The Machine that Changed the World*, Rawson Associates, New York, 1990, p. 150.

THE MCA-MATSUSHITA SAGA

It all started with the best of intentions and high hopes. After all, it was a marriage of reason where the complementarity of the partners' strengths seemed to bode well for a bright future.

In the late 1980s, Matsushita, a Japanese manufacturer of electronic goods, was looking to acquire a company in the entertainment industry with the objective of diversifying its operations and benefitting from synergies that could possibly result in merging the two types of businesses.

A consultant hired by the Japanese company identified MCA as the best acquisition target. MCA, a glamorous Hollywood company that owned Universal Pictures, Universal Studios theme parks in Hollywood and Orlando, and broadcasting and music labels, needed to merge with a wealthy parent that could sustain its growth. The union of the two companies was sealed with the $6.1 billion acquisition of MCA by Matsushita in 1990.

Seldom, however, have two partners been so different. Matsushita's eighty-year conservative tradition favored slow and careful decision making and an emphasis on decision making by consensus. The American company, in contrast, was characterized by a fast-paced corporate environment, where senior managers often made decisions quickly and acted upon them immediately.

Matsushita's executives reportedly spoke little or no English, and seldom visited the United States. As a result, contacts with the American managers were limited. Consequently, suspicions and mutual mistrust between the partners contributed to the weakening of the partnership. Thus, when the first serious clash erupted, it was far from a "lovers' quarrel."

MCA's 81-year-old chairman and chief executive, Lew R. Wasserman, and its 59-year-old president and chief operating officer, Sidney J. Sheinberg, had made the long journey to Japan in September 1994 to promote and defend a proposal to invest in an American television broadcast network. The two men had been at the helm of the Hollywood company for decades and commanded great respect and influence in the entertainment industry.

In Osaka, the two senior executives were appalled by the welcome they received. Matsushita's president, Yoichi Morishita, came two hours late to the meeting. In the meantime, lower-level executives had told the Americans that Matsushita would not consider their proposal. The Japanese company had already quashed other MCA plans, including a proposal to build a Universal Studios theme park in Japan and a proposed $600 million acquisition of Virgin Records.

The outspoken Mr. Sheinberg was so exasperated and angered that he reportedly told the president of Matsushita: "Mr. Morishita, you are going to go down in history as the man who lost billions of dollars for your company."

The bad feelings continued to linger long after the return of the two executives to the United States. Mr. Sheinberg told a *New York Times* reporter, "It is very distressing, I did not feel that we had been treated as adults. I felt that we had been treated as children. Our people were totally demoralized. . . "

Although more circumspect in expressing his emotions, the patrician Mr. Wasserman was also deeply insulted by the behavior of Matsushita's executives. After the Osaka episode, the two men began insisting on increased autonomy for their company. They even presented a proposal to repurchase control of MCA.

The Japanese executives, reared in a culture that shuns confrontation, abhors defiance, and values respect of superiors and maintenance of harmony, even if only in appearance, were dismayed by the behavior of their American subordinates.

Faced with a blunt Mr. Sheinberg, who didn't hesitate to write scathing letters and, at one tense meeting, even yelled at his Japanese bosses, Matsushita's executives were, in the words of one insider, "just running left and right from the attacks of MCA people."

The foray into the glitzy world of Hollywood had clearly proved to be a fiasco for the staid, buttoned-down electronic hardware managers at Matsushita. For all the talk about building synergies between consumer electronic products and the entertainment industry, there was really little which linked movie making and selling TV sets and VCRs.

When they abruptly turned down MCA's latest investment proposal, the Japanese were concerned with recessionary signs in their own country which had made it inopportune to finance "sideline projects," in the words of a Matsushita executive; and imperative to remain with the core business in electronics.

In addition, the emergence of new technologies that had put the world of entertainment in a flux made the Japanese feel unsure of the future of the network television business.

Finally, Matsushita's executives apparently feared an anti-Japanese backlash, similar to the wave of negative media coverage that followed the acquisition of Columbia Pictures by Sony.

In any event, the rejection of the proposal had much wider and deeper consequences than anticipated: it was "the straw that broke the camel's back," in that once the Americans' hostility toward their bosses erupted in the open, it did not subside. Their public insubordination made relations that were already difficult, almost impossible to manage.

The divorce had become inevitable, and it came to be in April 1995, when Matsushita announced that it would sell an 80 percent stake in its Hollywood subsidiary to Seagram Corporation for $5.7 billion. Thus ended Matsushita's four-year elusive search for synergies in its attempt to create a "multimedia" business comprising electronics hardware and entertainment software.

Although the sale price was much lower than expected and the Japanese company would face a huge currency loss should it decide to repatriate the proceeds from the sale (the yen had appreciated by 60 percent between 1990 and mid-1995), Matsushita can now focus on its profitable electronics goods business.

MCA's new parent, Seagram Corporation, under the helm of 39-year-old Edgar Bronfman, Jr., has been operating a long-term shift in focus that is judged harshly by many investors. Analysts have been accusing the young Mr. Bronfman, who took the reins of Seagram from his father only last year, of being "star-struck" and guilty of "monumental stupidity" in substituting the MCA shares for the tried-and-true DuPont (Seagram held a 24 percent stake in DuPont).

Many commentators point out that success in the entertainment industry is widely unpredictable.

Nevertheless, more than one senior executive has been seduced by the glitz and glamour of Hollywood. Witness the travails of Melvin Simon, the shopping-mall magnate, whose foray into the movie-making business produced a few hits and a great number of duds, and, all told, suffered almost $40 million in losses, between 1977 and 1984.

"People overpay for studios because they are overwhelmed by the glamour and want to hobnob with the movie stars and go to the Oscars. And they all think it's a better business than it really is," says Harold Vogel, a securities analyst at Cowen & Co., in New York.

Mr. Bronfman, a sometime songwriter who had tried his hand at movie producing with limited success prior to joining the family business, contends that he has "a great knowledge" of the entertainment business. His enthusiasm for the MCA acquisition is not shared by many Seagram's stockholders whose skepticism is reflected in a plunge in the value of the beverage company's stock.

Others, however, believe that the dip is temporary and comparable to the beating Coca-Cola Co. shares took when Coke acquired Columbia Pictures in 1982.

Although profits in the movie industry may be elusive, MCA's Universal Studios had two relatively good years with the success of "Jurassic Park" and "Schindler's List." However, costly disappointments, such as "Junior" and "Waterworld," have weighted down the profitability of MCA's movie production business, while its television business is suffering from a dearth of hits.

Seagram seems poised to make the necessary changes to improve the lackluster results posted by MCA. Mr. Bronfman strongly believes that growth and profit potential are much greater in the entertainment industry compared to chemicals or Seagram's basic beverage business.

Seagram's young senior executive confides, "I can tell you, MCA now has a committed, passionate partner in Seagram. We are intent on helping MCA to grow and there are any number of strategic alliances and opportunities that we can and should be discussing in the months ahead."

At long last, MCA's chairman, Lew R. Wasserman, and its ebullient president, Sidney J. Sheinberg, seem to have found the parent company that they were so eagerly seeking to finance their company's growth. The Bronfmans, on the other hand, were reportedly going out of their way to treat the two entertainment business veterans most cordially. Mr. Wasserman could be offered a board seat at Seagram and remain at MCA as chairman emeritus.

The younger Mr. Bronfman pointedly expressed his "respect and admiration" for the two MCA executives, although he also said that he had not yet had time to focus on "issues of management."

Mr. Sheinberg's ties to the producer and director Steven Spielberg is highly valued by Seagram's senior management. Mr. Spielberg, who left MCA to form his own company, DreamWorks, has maintained close ties with the MCA senior executives. The latter are thus regarded as crucial to a potentially lucrative distribution deal for DreamWorks' movies, records, and other products.

Seagram must make several important decisions about MCA: urgent measures are needed to revive the poorly performing television production unit; the fate of a new theme park plans overseas must be decided, and MCA's plans to develop a 415-acre property at its Universal City, California, headquarters have to be evaluated.

Whatever the outcome on these issues, there seems to be one certainty: the days of incessant sparring and confrontations with a tight fisted parent company are over.

Source: This case was prepared by Farid Sadrieh, doctoral student at Temple University, from the following sources: G. Fabrikant and A. Pollack, "MCA's Impatience with Wary Parent," *The New York Times*, November 4, 1994, p. D1; L. Landro, "Ego and Inexperience Among Studio Buyers Add Up to Big Losses," *The Wall Street Journal*, April 10, 1995, p. A1; S. Hwang, "Seagram Holders Assail MCA Accord," *The Wall Street Journal*, April 10, 1995, p. C1; D. Hamilton, "Red-Faced Matsushita Gets Back to Basics," *The Wall Street Journal*, April 10, 1995, p. A17. Copyright © 1997 by Arvind V. Phatak.

Discussion Questions

1. Identify and explain the principal reasons for the failure of the Matsushita-MCA venture. Would these reasons apply to the future success or failure of the MCA-Seagram venture?

2. Differentiate between the effects of national culture and corporate culture in the Matsushita and MCA relationship. To what extent do you think corporate culture is influenced by national culture?

3. "You can't own any business like this with such a unique culture, without being alongside it. Do what I did. Come out here," says media mogul Rupert Murdoch from the California headquarters of the Fox network, where he moved in 1992 from Australia. How comfortable would Matsushita managers have been in following this advice?

4. What would you recommend to Seagram regarding MCA's plans to develop property, build theme parks overseas, or invest in a television network? How about other possible investment projects? Justify your answers and clearly explain and articulate your reasoning.

THE RISE AND FALL OF ELI BLACK

On February 3, 1975, Eli Black, president, chairman, and chief executive officer of United Brands, arose early in the morning. He dressed in a familiar uniform—blue suit and conservative, patterned tie—then went into the living room and filled his large, satchel-like briefcase to capacity with heavy books chosen at random from the shelves.

A little before 8:00 a.m., he was driven by his chauffeur from his apartment at 900 Park Avenue to the Pan Am Building. He went to his office on the 44th floor, removed his hat and coat, and bolted both doors to his office. Using his briefcase, Black smashed a hole in the sealed, quarter-inch-thick, tempered plate-glass window of his office. He removed pieces of glass until the hole was almost three-by-four feet. Then he plunged to his death carrying his briefcase.

No suicide note was found. Friends and business associates attributed the suicide to the pressure of operating the company during a money-losing year (Exhibit 1). They said Black was working 16- to 18-hour days over the weeks before the suicide, and he was becoming "severely depressed because of tension." Bernard Fischman, a family friend, said, "Deep down he was always measuring himself on a different scorecard from the other fellow. He felt deeply his responsibilities to his shareholders, but he also believed that business was a human operation."

Black's business associates were surprised by his suicide; they felt that the worst period for the company was over. Edward Gelsthorpe, the executive vice-president, said, "The great tragedy of Eli Black's death at this time is that under his leadership the company was on its way to overcoming several crises. We were convinced the traumatic period was behind us." Gelsthorpe also said that there were no additional business problems or personal financial problems that could have contributed to Black's depression.

ELI BLACK

Eli Black was a descendant of ten generations of rabbis and scholars. He graduated magna cum laude from Yeshiva University in 1940. As an ordained rabbi, he served a small congregation in Woodmere, Long Island. Black was a trustee of Lincoln Center, the American Jewish Committee, the Federation of Jewish Philanthropies, the Jewish Guild for the Blind, the Jewish Museum, and Babson College. He was also a member of the board of *Saturday Review* and a member of the Business Committee for the Arts.

At his funeral, Black was eulogized by Dr. Samuel Belkin, president of Yeshiva University, and Rabbi Leonard Rosenfeld, a friend for 35 years. Dr. Belkin remembered Black as a brilliant student, a scholar, and a practical man. He described him as a person who "tried to integrate the world of scholars, the world of high morals, and the world of practical affairs." Rabbi Rosenfeld described his friend ". . . as a fiscal giant who remained a rabbi, searching for God all his life." Rosenfeld asked the question, "How many persons pushed Eli to a desperate option—how many contributed to his untimely tragedy—and who called on Eli to choose the wrong door?"

EXHIBIT 1
United Brands Company Summary of Operations
(000s)

	Year Ended December 31,		
	1975	*1974*	*1973*
Net sales	$2,186,525	$2,020,526	$1,841,738
Operating costs and expenses	2,126,013	2,018,436	1,787,126
Operating income	60,512	2,090	54,612
Interest and amortization of debt expense	(34,468)	(37,080)	(29,585)
Interest income and other income and expenses, net	2,372	2,488	7,952
Income (loss) from continuing operations before items shown below	28,416	(32,502)	32,979
Unusual or infrequently occurring items	(1,048)	(26,808)	—
Income (loss) from continuing operations before income taxes	27,368	(59,310)	32,979
Estimated U.S. and foreign income taxes	(17,300)	(12,000)	(15,250)
Income (loss) from continuing operations	10,068	(71,310)	17,729
Income from discontinued operations	—	13,768	741
Gains on disposal of discontinued operations		10,704	7,238
Income (loss) before extraordinary items	10,068	(46,838)	25,708
Extraordinary items	700	3,231	(345)
Net income (loss)	$ 10,768	$ (43,607)	$ 25,363
Average number of primary shares outstanding (000s)	10,779	10,775	11,193

Source: 10-K, United Brands Company, 1975.

Eli Black's death triggered the revelation of a scandal that has since been called "Bananagate." The Securities and Exchange Commission (SEC) began an investigation of the company, as it routinely does after the suicide of a top corporate executive. On April 8, 1975, the company, after inquiries from *The Wall Street Journal*, issued a press release indicating that it had made a payment of $1.25 million to an official of the Republic of Honduras. On April 9, the SEC commenced action against United Brands in the United States District Court. The complaint filed by the SEC alleged that United Brands had violated the Securities and Exchange Act of 1934 and SEC rules by bribing foreign officials. The bribery itself was not illegal; the violation was that the company had not reported the bribe in annual reports or letters to the shareholders.[a] According to the SEC complaint, United Brands agreed to pay $2.5 million to high government officials of the Republic of Honduras in exchange for favorable governmental action with respect to the export-tax problem. In September 1974, United Brands had deposited $1.25 million in the Swiss bank accounts of the Honduran official. The company agreed to pay an additional $1.25 million during 1975. The money was corporate funds obtained from foreign subsidiaries; the books and records were falsified to disguise the payments.

An additional charge of the SEC was that "cash payments approximating $750,000 were made to officials of a foreign government in Europe in connection with the securing of favorable business opportunities." The complaint did not identify the country, but it was subsequently identified as Italy. Apparently this was how Chiquita bananas, despite Italian import quotas, had remained the most popular brand in Italy.

Additional suits were filed by shareholders, including Jean and Jesse Meer, Henry Neugarten, and The Walsh Agency, Inc. On September 5, 1975, the shareholders' suits filed in U.S. District Court for the Southern District of New York were consolidated into one suit. This action alleged derivative, class, and individual claims. The derivative claim alleged that the bribes were in violation of the law and damaged the company; the class claims alleged that shareholders who purchased the stock during the period over which bribes were paid had purchased the stock at inflated prices; and the individual claims alleged that proxy statements were false and misleading.

Other events following the April 8 press release included the United States Attorney for the Southern District of New York instituted a grand jury investigation of the charges in the SEC complaint, the Subcommittee on Multinational Corporations of the United States Foreign Relations Committee began requesting information from the company, and the Honduran government created a special investigating committee.

UNITED BRANDS

Eli Black made United Brands what it was in 1974. Black became involved with the company that was to become United Brands while he worked for American Securities Corporation. In his position as head of the business-and-industry section, he handled the financing for a $5 million producer of paper caps for milk bottles, American Seal-Kap Corporation. In 1953 he was asked to become a director of the company, and in 1954 he was hired as chairman and chief executive.

Black expanded American Seal-Kap through extension of Seal-Kap's line of paper products and by acquiring such companies as the Chicago Railway Equipment Company. By 1957 sales were $32 million. Black found additional growth difficult, however; therefore, he began a complete review of every division and every product line. By 1966 some divisions were completely gone, including the entire packaging company and the Chicago Railway Equipment Company. Black was left with $10 million in cash acquired by selling these divisions, a division that made lock

---

a Bribes are accepted practice in many countries. They are called "baksheesh" in the Middle East, "dash" in Africa, "squeeze money" in Asia, and "mordita" in South America. Bribes are a way of life in these countries; officials are frequently paid minimal wages under the assumption that the wages will be supplemented with bribes. Telephone operators must be paid to secure overseas lines in Zaire, and traffic cops must be tipped to make a left-hand turn in Southeast Asia. In fact, prior to a 1958 ruling, bribes were a tax-deductible expense in the United States if the foreign government demanded or acquiesced in the payment.

washers for the railroad and automotive industries, a small iron foundry, and more than half the stock in NRM Corporation, a maker of manufacturing equipment for the rubber and plastic industries. Even the name of the company was new; it was no longer American Seal-Kap, but AMK, the company's stock exchange symbol.

With the $10 million in his pocket, Black went shopping for acquisitions. A reasonable expectation would have been to double AMK's earnings by the purchase of a company with earnings of $1 million to $2 million a year. Black, however, decided on a more ambitious course. He purchased a company 20 times the size of AMK, John Morrell and Company. Two years later, he purchased another industry giant, United Fruit.

By 1974 AMK had become United Brands, one of the Fortune 500. United Brands had sales of over $2 billion and employed 50,000 people (see Exhibit 1 for 1973-75 corporate financial data). The company was divided into three basic parts: John Morrell and Company, United Fruit (or the Agrimark Group), and Diversified Operations. Sales and contributions to operating income for these divisions are shown in Exhibits 2 and 3.

John Morrell and Company

In 1967 AMK's annual sales increased from $39,000,000 to $840,700,000. This increase gave AMK its place among the Fortune 500 (Number 101). It was the greatest increase in sales for any company in 1967. The growth came about through one deal—the pooling-of-interest merger with John Morrell and Company, the fourth largest meatpacker in the United States. Alone, AMK had earnings of $1,872,000; with Morrell, it had earnings of $7,434,000. On a per-share basis, Eli Black had increased his company's earnings 109 percent from 1966.

History When Black went looking for a company where improved management could increase earnings, he found it in Morrell. Meatpackers as an industry had done little to bring their business methods up to date, and Morrell was no exception. It had very poor organization methods and systems; it owned 20 meat-processing plants and slaughterhouses, which were operated as 20 separate businesses with no central controls.

EXHIBIT 2

United Brands Company Net Sales
(000s)

	1975	1974	1973
Bananas & Related Products	$ 657,087	$ 549,440	$ 449,971
Meat Packing & Related Products	1,329,011	1,288,996	1,258,415
Diversified Group			
Food Processing & Food Services	123,677	103,525	67,624
Agriculture & Floriculture	53,205	51,003	48,426
Other	23,545	27,562	17,302
Total Sales	$ 2,186,525	$2,020,526	$1,841,738

Source: 10-K, United Brands Company, 1975.

EXHIBIT 3

United Brands Company Contribution to Operating Income
(000s)

	1975	1974	1973
Bananas & Related Products	$45,396	$(7,523)	$26,323
Meat Packing & Related Products	11,467	3,576	23,687
Diversified Group			
Food Processing & Food Service	4,809	1,576	4,900
Agriculture & Floriculture	562	2,450	2,011
Other	3,128	5,349	1,143
Corporate overhead	(4,850)	(3,527)	(3,452)
Operating income	$60,512	$ 1,901	$54,612

Source: 10-K, United Brands Company, 1975.

Despite a recent slump in earnings (Morrell earned only $.55 per share or $695,000 in 1966) and the lack of a centralized control system, Morrell had been a good takeover candidate: there were only 1,250,000 shares of common stock outstanding, book value was $42 per share, long-term debt was just under $14 million, and the stock was selling for about $22 per share.

In the spring of 1966, Black arranged an introduction to W. W. McCallum, Morrell's president through Price Waterhouse. Over lunch, Black told McCallum of his interest in Morrell; however, he assured him that AMK would not move secretly. Over the next few months, the two men met several times. By fall of 1966, AMK had purchased $3 million in shares, less than 10 percent of the company, with McCallum's blessing. At that point, Black began to meet with company executives and tour some of Morrell's plants. In November 1966, AMK made a public tender offer for 200,000 shares of Morrell stock at $2.50 above the market price of $25. Almost one-half of the outstanding stock was offered, but to avoid going into debt, AMK purchased only 300,000 shares. This move gave AMK one-third of the outstanding shares.

By 1967 Black had engineered a merger agreement through an exchange of common and convertible preferred. (Morrell's stock was at $44 and AMK's had risen from $12 in 1966 to $50 in 1967.) AMK emerged a winner.

Operations In 1974 Morrell's primary business was still the slaughtering and packaging of meat from hogs, cattle, and lamb, which it distributed fresh, frozen, and processed throughout the United States. In 1974 Morrell sold 2.4 billion pounds of meat and meat by-products. Products were marketed under names such as Morrell Pride, Tom Sawyer, Green Tree, Hunter, and Broadcast. A secondary line of business was the distribution of animal feed under the Golden Sun name. A total of 9,500 employees worked for the Morrell division.

From 1967 to 1974, Morell had sporadic profits, despite increasing sales (Exhibits 2 and 3). In an effort to increase profitability, a number of fiscal measures were attempted, but despite these efforts, Morrell contributed to the heavy losses of 1974. A total of $11 million was lost in the cattle feedlot that had been started in 1973. The market price of the cattle declined below Morrell's costs. Additional problems were the increased cost of fuel, fertilizer, packaging, feed, grain, and other raw materials. These increased costs were not recovered by higher prices because of the general state of the economy.

United Fruit

On September 4, 1968, the New York Stock Exchange ticker recorded a trade of 733,200 shares of United Fruit's stock at $56, $4 above the market price. It was the third largest block of shares ever traded on the Exchange, in both dollars and numbers of shares. The buyer—AMK. The same day, AMK purchased 7,100 shares of stock on the open market, which gave it more than 9 percent of the stock outstanding in United Fruit. By buying less than 10 percent, Black avoided becoming an insider according to SEC regulations. Thus he did not have to report his trade, and he was not prohibited from taking short-term gains. This move protected Black in case he was unable to buy the rest of the company.

Black had purchased the shares of United Fruit hurriedly. United Fruit had no funded debt and a rumored $100 million in cash. Thus it was an attractive takeover possibility. Because rumors existed that other companies were interested, Black acted before talking to John Fox, president of United Fruit. When Fox learned about his newest shareholder, his immediate response was that the conservative Boston Company was not interested. Black waited, stating that he would not make his tender offer public without the support of United Fruit's management.

On September 5, 1968, executives from Zapata Norness, Inc., came to Boston to make an offer for United Fruit. Zapata's offer was not very different from the AMK offer, but Zapata insisted on a majority on the board of directors, while AMK asked for only minority representation.

Fox began to seek other buyers. Dillingham Corporation, a contractor and real estate developer, and Textron, a New England conglomerate, made offers. Both companies withdrew their offers, however, when their shareholders responded negatively.

Fox finally realized that either Zapata or AMK would gain control. He dismissed Zapata's offer as "not in the best interests of the shareholders." When AMK finally made its tender offer, more than 80 percent of the shares were tendered. AMK got United Fruit and over $250,000 in intangible goodwill for the balance sheet.[b]

History The United Fruit Company was born in 1899. It developed in the years after the Civil War when New England ship captains were searching for something to replace the slave cargoes they had lost. One captain, Lorenzo Dow Baker, sailed into Port Morant, Jamaica, in June of 1870 for a load of bamboo. While he was docked, he was approached by a local man with some green bananas. Baker paid the man 15¢ a bunch; 11 days later, he sold the bananas for 10 to 15 times as much. By the 1880s, Baker had a new schooner and was carrying 10,000 stems of bananas from Jamaica to Boston in about a week and a half. In 1885 he formed the Boston Fruit Company. By the end of the next decade, Lorenzo had 11 ships that flew the company flag; he called them the Great White Fleet. (The color was a necessity; it reflected the sun and kept the cargo cooler so that it lasted longer.)

At about the same time, Minor C. Keith was building railroads in Costa Rica. His most notable achievement was the 25 miles of track between Port Limon and San Jose; 5,000 men died, however,

---

b Black acquired United Fruit prior to the date APB Opinion 17 took effect. If AMK had purchased the company after November 1970, it would have been required to write off the goodwill over a 40-year period. Note that when AMK acquired Morrell, it paid less than net asset value, and it did write off $641,000 a year from 1966 to 1976 in negative goodwill.

building the railway. Minor Keith's major problem once the railway was finished was finding people to ride it. To pay back the loan for the construction of the railway, Keith was forced to plant bananas within a short distance from the track. By 1883 he owned three banana companies. In 1899 he incurred a debt of $1.5 million and was forced to sell his shares to the Boston Fruit Company. Thus the United Fruit Company was born.

By 1929 United Fruit was the personification of the Ugly American. It was reported that striking plantation workers in the "banana republic" were often brutalized, as were seamen and dockworkers—anyone who tried to disrupt the marketing timetable. The company was called "el pulpo," the octopus, because it had tentacles in everything, including the selection of the governments. Unfriendly foreign heads were removed with a phone call. A former ambassador to a Central American republic told an interviewer, "If I was away, General . . . would call The Company to pass on Government appointments. He didn't want trouble. I tell you, it wasn't easy to find talent in that place then to satisfy The Company."

The bitterness against the company remained for many years, as evidenced by the poem of Nobel laureate Pablo Neruda:

THE UNITED FRUIT COMPANY

It rechristened its territories
As the "banana republic"
And over the sleeping dead
Over the restless heroes
Who brought about the greatness,
The liberty and the flags
It established a comic opera:
Established the independencies,
Presented crown of Caesar,
Unsheathed envy, attracted
The dictatorship of the flies.

United Fruit appeared to learn from history, however. By 1972 the company had won acceptance and even goodwill in Central America. In Honduras, for example, it maintained wage rates far above those of other Honduran workers. Company pickers averaged $95 a month, while the average agricultural worker received only $12 a month. The salaries exceeded even those of secretaries and clerks, who averaged $30 a month.

Workers received fringe benefits in addition to good salaries. The company supplied free housing and electricity to all of its workers. These houses had indoor plumbing, tile baths, and a plot of land large enough for a garden. The cost to United Fruit was $1.5 million a year. If workers did not want to live in company housing, the company had a program to build houses for workers. The houses cost $3,600 to build but were sold to workers for $1,800.

The company also had a policy favoring the hiring and promoting of locals into supervisory positions. In Honduras, for example, although the residential manager was North American, in 1972 most of his principal aides were Honduran. In total, of the 325 employees at the supervisory level, only 5 were North American.

Health care and a free education were also available. The company financed a system of hospitals and clinics for all workers in Central America. It paid the entire cost of a school system with 210 teachers. Scholarships were available for those with the ability to finish high school and college.

Eli Black apparently wanted to change this paternalistic operation. A key United Brands executive said,

> Mr. Black was not impressed by the fact that our workers there were the best paid, housed, and schooled. He was appalled by the whole operation. One solution we were advancing was the turning over of the plantations to the small farmer from whom we could buy the fruit. That was getting us out of the welfare business all over the area.

A more cynical observer stated that the reason the company managers planned to use this approach was that they thought it would be easier than dealing with the government. He stated, "... it is always costlier to deal with a government than a farmer who must move his crop within a very short time."

Operations In 1974 United Fruit, now known as the Agrimark Group of United Brands, was still engaged in the production and sale of bananas. Bananas were grown on land owned by the company or were purchased from local growers from Panama, Honduras, Costa Rica, Guatemala, Ecuador, Colombia, and the Philippines. Bananas were then transported to the United States, Canada, Europe, or Japan on one of the 40 refrigerated vessels owned by the company (see Exhibits 4 and 5 for markets). Independent wholesalers purchased the bananas and resold them to retail food stores. United Brands bananas were sold with the trademarks Fyffes, Chiquita, or Amigo.

Most of United Brands' employees worked in the Agrimark division: 34,000 of the total 50,000. Of these, 28,000 worked in agriculture. United Brands' assets were also concentrated in these operations, as evidenced by the high percentage of assets located within Latin America (see Exhibit 6).

The operations in Latin America were subject to agreements of the governments of the countries that governed the manner and rate at which United Fruit was taxed. The agreements also provided exemptions from certain customs duties on items imported for use in operations. United Brands recognized that its assets were in a vulnerable position and susceptible to adverse political developments, including nationalization. Expropriation, however, seemed unlikely, because the countries did not have the ships or the marketing organizations needed to bring the

EXHIBIT 4

Percentage of Dollar Sales of United Brands Bananas (net of import duties)

	1974	1973	1972	1971	1970
U.S. & Canada	38	40	49	49	50
Europe	52	52	46	45	43
Japan	10	8	5	6	7

Source: 10-K, United Brands Company, 1975.

EXHIBIT 5

Number of 40-Pound Boxes Shipped by United Brands
(000s)

Destination	1974	1973	1972
U.S. & Canada	39,414	36,408	45,758
Europe	43,290	44,290	46,754
Japan	6,213	5,492	5,831
	88,917	86,190	98,343

Source: 10-K, United Brands Company, 1975.

EXHIBIT 6

United Brands Company Net Assets
(000s)

	1974
Outside U.S.	
Latin America	$253,629
Europe	79,178
Other	17,133
U.S.	121,607
	$471,547

Source: 10-K, United Brands Company, 1975.

highly perishable bananas to market.[c] In addition, the basic agreements did not expire for some years: 1986 in Panama, 1988 in Costa Rica, and 1995 in Honduras.

The banana operations were also susceptible to natural disasters, including disease and tropical weather conditions. United Fruit, however, had been successful in combating the problem of disease. The company had become famous for its Gros Michel banana, or Big Mike. It was a large, tough-skinned banana that could be easily transported. The banana was, however, easily ravaged by a blight called Panama disease. In 1942 a breed of bananas called Cavendish Valery was found in a botanical garden in Saigon. These bananas were resistant to the dread Panama disease, so United Fruit converted its banana acreage from Gros Michel to Valery. These

---

c The commercial life of a banana, from tree to table, was six weeks.

plants also had the advantage of being shorter, thus less exposed to wind damage, than the Gros Michel variety. The major problem was that Valery bananas were easily bruised, which resulted in a change in how the bananas were shipped. Gros Michel bananas were shipped on the stem and loaded in bulk; Valery bananas were packed and shipped in 40-pound boxes.

Despite the move to a shorter banana plant, the Valery plants were still subject to destruction by tropical windstorms. In 1969 and 1970, the company suffered significantly from hurricanes and floods in Honduras and Panama. In 1973 a tropical windstorm resulted in a loss of $8.3 million. Then in 1974, Hurricane Fifi destroyed 70 percent of the banana crop in Honduras. The company's loss was $19.5 million; $15 million was written off for the lost crops.

By the early 1970s, the banana business had become extremely competitive. After World War II, United Fruit Company dominated domestic banana sales with more than 80 percent of the market; however, the demand for United Fruit's bananas depended on the supply of other fresh fruit as well as the supply of other importers' bananas. By 1974 the competition had made significant inroads in United Fruit's market, particularly because between 1969 and 1970, United Fruit had been forced to decrease shipments as a result of the hurricane and flood damage. By 1974 United Brands had only a 37 percent share of all the bananas sold in the United States and Canada. Of the 12 other importers in 1974, the major competitors were Castle & Cooke, Inc., with a 41 percent share of the North American market, and Delmonte, with a 16 percent share.

Despite the increased costs of transporting bananas by 1974, the market was sufficiently competitive for the price of bananas to have changed very little in 20 years. In the United States, the average retail price was 16.4¢ per pound in 1952, 16.5¢ in 1973, and 18.4¢ in 1974. Meanwhile, costs had risen significantly. By 1975 wholesalers were willing to pay $5.20 for a 40-pound box of bananas. It cost United Fruit approximately $3.50 to deliver the box from Panama: the purchase price in Panama was 4.75¢ per pound of bananas; the freight for the box was $1.25; and it cost 35¢ to unload the box. (These figures do not include any export tax.)

Diversified Group

The diversified group of United Brands employed 6,500 people in 1974. It was involved in food and food processing, agriculture and floriculture, telecommunications, and plastic manufacturing.

When Black acquired United Brands he gained a number of food and food-processing companies. Fox, the president of United Fruit, had purchased them in his drive to make United Fruit a more diversified company that was less dependent on one product. Included in the original group was A & W International (franchiser of family restaurants), Baskin-Robbins, Inc. (franchiser of ice cream stores), J. Hungerford Smith (syrups and toppings), and Clemente Jacques & Cie (processed foods). The Compania Numar group was also considered part of food processing. This unit purchased palm oil from United Fruit and produced cooking oil, salad oil, and margarine for sale in Central America. (By 1974 United Fruit's financial situation was such that it was forced to sell its 83 percent interest in Baskin-Robbins to J. Lyons & Co., Ltd.)

The agriculture and floriculture part of United Brands was Inter Harvest, Inc. and United Brands Floriculture. Inter Harvest was a grower and marketer of lettuce, celery, and other produce grown on 25,000 acres of land leased in California and Arizona. In the early 1970s, this portion of the company experienced significant difficulties with labor problems and low prices in the lettuce market. United Brands Floriculture imported flowering and foliage plants from Honduras to the United States. These plants were sold with other garden-supply items.

In addition to the food-processing operations, United Fruit had a radiotelegraph-telephone company, TRT Telecommunications Corporation, when it was acquired by Black.

Petrochemicals constituted the last significant operation owned by United Brands. The company produced certain banana-related items, including pressure-sensitive labels and polyethylene bagging. The unit also produced plastic pipes and a line of houseware and office items. Black, in an effort to expand this line, had purchased Foster-Grant Co., Inc., a prized possession. In 1974, however, he was forced to sell the company's 62 percent interest in Foster Grant to cover the company's losses and to generate some working capital. J. E. Goldman, one of United Brands' directors, said, "It was Eli's last, very brilliant coup."

THE BRIBE

Seven South American countries formed the Union de Paises Exportadores de Banano: Guatemala, Honduras, Nicaragua, Costa Rica, Panama, Ecuador, and Colombia. The countries met in Panama in 1974 to discuss a uniform tax of $1.00 to $2.00 per box. Ecuador, Nicaragua, and Guatemala decided not to impose a tax; Costa Rica provided for a tax of $.25; Panama provided for a tax of $1.00; Honduras settled on a tax of $.50; Columbia increased its "reintegrow" by $.40.

The total impact of the taxes was severe; however, the most significant aspect was that it put United Brands at a severe competitive disadvantage. The bulk of Delmonte's bananas came from Guatemala, while Castle & Cooke obtained their bananas from Costa Rica, Ecuador, and Nicaragua. Neither company obtained bananas in Panama or Honduras, where the tax was the greatest.

Company officials spent much of the spring and summer of 1974 trying to negotiate a reduction in the tax. John A. Taylor, senior vice-president of the Agrimark group, said that in May of 1974 he and Black met with General Oswaldo Lopez Arellano, president of Honduras. During the discussion Black suggested that, if the tax were reduced, there would be several hundred thousand in it for Lopez. Lopez dismissed the idea.

On August 8, Harvey Johnson, vice-president of the United Fruit group, received a telephone call from Abraham Bennaton Ramos, Honduran Minister of economics, and on August 10, they met in Miami. Bennaton said that the tax could be reduced for $5 million. Johnson checked with Black; the proposal was refused.

On August 14, Bennaton told Johnson that he would accept $2.5 million paid in two installments. The first installment would be paid after the banana export tax was reduced to $.25 per box, and the second installment would be paid after the renewal of the Tela Concession in April 1975.[d] Johnson called Black; after discussing the offer, Black called Taylor and instructed him to authorize Johnson to make the payment. Taylor asked Black if the payment would violate U.S. law, and Black replied that he was informed that it would not.

Bennaton was informed that the company agreed to his offer. He scheduled a meeting on August 19; on the second day of the negotiations, the tax was reduced to $.25 per box.

On September 3, Taylor arranged the deposit of $1.25 million in a Swiss account opened for Bennaton. A million of the money was charged to one European subsidiary, and $250,000 was withdrawn from another European subsidiary as an intercompany debit. Taylor left it to the officers of the European subsidiaries to determine how the payments would be shown on the

---

d In 1912 the Honduran government had granted the company rights to a tract of land, including the right to build a railroad, a port facility, and a telegraph system, as well as freedom from taxes and import duties on certain imports.

books. The payments were recorded as commissions for the procurement of bananas. (Although the payments were inaccurately recorded, they were properly treated for tax purposes.)

On September 6, 1974, Black sent a letter to the company's shareholders stating,

> Since I last wrote to you on August 8th, there have been several rapidly changing developments in the "banana tax situation" which have made it impossible for me to write sooner to give you an accurate status report. However, since that time, the situation has become more defined and I feel I should report to you again on these very important matters affecting our Company.
>
> Some days ago, the Company reached an understanding with the Government of Honduras, under which the tax situation in that country was settled on the basis of the Company paying a tax of $.25 per box, with yearly escalations beginning in 1975, which may depend, in part, on the banana market at the relevant times. There are other terms involved in the settlement but the significant item is that the tax for the balance of this year was fixed at $.25 per box.

The letter did not mention the $1.25 million; neither did the 10-K Form of September 10, 1974.

A number of officers and directors of the company learned about the payment during the next few months. Black told M. Robert Gallop, senior vice-president and general counsel as well as a member of the board of directors, some time in August that he had resolved the Honduran tax problem but that it had cost money. Gallop assumed the money had already been paid, and he did not inquire further.

Black told Maurice Kaplan, a member of the board of directors and chairman of the board's Finance Committee, in September. Apparently Black did not discuss the recipient or the mechanics of the payment. Kaplan assumed that Black was satisfied as to the propriety of the action.

Donald R. Meltzer, vice-president for administration and finance, discussed the payment and the method of accounting in the company's books with Taylor and Black in August 1974. Meltzer informed Controller James F. Powers of the substance of this discussion in September. About the same time, he informed company Treasurer Patrick Brangwynne that a special cash payment had been made in Europe. Brangwynne was told that he did not need to know anything about the payments and that he should not pressure the subsidiaries for a cash remittance.

Edward Gelsthorpe joined the company on September 3, 1974, as vice-president of marketing. Within one month, he was promoted to executive vice-president and chief operating officer, and by November he was a member of the board of directors. In October 1974, Taylor told him about the bribe, because Gelsthorpe was his immediate superior.

On November 5, Gelsthorpe, Meltzer, and Powers explained the facts of the Honduran payment to Gallop and Kaplan. During January, Gelsthorpe mentioned the Honduran payment to George Gardner, Jr., Georges F. Doriot, and Jay Welles—all members of the board of directors. (During subsequent investigation, only Gardner remembered the conversation.)

On January 10 at the board of directors meeting, Gardner asked Black whether the company had made any unusual deals or payments in foreign countries. Black referred the question to Taylor, who indicated that there was a situation that Black was aware of in Honduras. Black replied that any unusual payment must have been made prior to 1970. None of the directors who knew about the payment contradicted Black.

Meltzer and Powers, with Gelsthorpe's approval, told Arthur Siegel, a partner in Price-Waterhouse, United Brands' accountants, about the payment. Fearing dismissal, they asked him

Cases

not to tell anyone about it. Siegel agreed to wait to see if the company's regular audit revealed the payment.

On February 6, the board of directors met to deal with the problem created by Black's death. At that time, Gelsthorpe informed them about the payment. After the board meeting, Gelsthorpe discussed the payment with two Price-Waterhouse partners, who questioned whether or not the payments should have been disclosed under federal securities law.

On February 20, 1975, the company retained the law firm of Covington and Burling to advise them on whether these payments had to be disclosed.

Source: This case was prepared from public sources by Monica S. Krieger under the supervision of Henry W. Tulloch, Executive Director of the Olsson Center for Applied Ethics, as a basis for class discussion. Copyright © 1985 by the Darden Graduate Business School Foundation, Charlottesville, Virginia. Rev. 7/90

Discussion Questions

1. What could Eli Black have done differently when confronted with the banana-tax problem?

2. Following his decision to provide the "bribe money," what should he have done differently, if anything?

3. Develop a stakeholder framework and identify who was best served by Eli Black's decision to bribe.

4. What are the ethical/moral issues involved in Eli Black's suicide? Whose interests were best served? Is suicide ever an appropriate moral act?

Endnotes

CHAPTER 1

1   John D. Daniels and Lee H. Radebaugh, *International Business: Environment and Operations*, 6th. ed., Addison-Wesley, Reading, Mass, 1992, p. 8.

2   Donald A. Ball and Wendell H. McCulloch, Jr., *International Business: Introduction and Essentials*, 4th. ed., BPI/Irwin Homewood, Illinois, 1990, p. 17.

3   Betty Jane Punett and David A. Ricks, *International Business*, (Boston: PWS/Kent Publishing Company, 1992), p. 7.

4   "The Business Week Global 1000," *Business Week*, July 10, 1995, p. 62.

5   United Nations Conference on Trade and Development, *World Investment Report 1994*, New York: United Nations, 1994, pp. 5-8.

6   Ibid., p. 131.

7   John H. Dunning, "Changes in the level and structure of international production: the last one hundred years," in Mark Casson (ed.), *The Growth of International Business*, Allen and Irwin, London, 1983, pp. 84-139.

8   United Nations Conference on Trade and Development, *World Investment Report 1994*, New York: United Nations, 1994, p. 131.

9   Ibid., p. 9.

10 Martin Kenney and Richard Florida, "How the Japanese Industry is Rebuilding the Rust Belt," *Technology Review*, February-March 1991, p. 28.

11 Dinah Lee, Jonathan Levine, and Peter Coy, "ATT Slowly Gets Its Global Wires Uncrossed," *Business Week*, February 11, 1991, p. 82.

12 Daniel Pearl, "Federal Express Finds Its pioneering Formula Falls Flat Overseas," *The Wall Street Journal*, April 15, 1991, p. A8.

13 William J. Holstein, Stanley Reed, Jonathan Kapstein, Todd Vogel, and Joseph Weber, "The Stateless Corporation," *Business Week*, May 14, 1990, p. 99.

14 Ibid., p. 100.

15 Paul Magnusson, Stephen Baker, David Beach, Gail DeGeorge, and William C. Symonda, "The Mexico Pact: Worth the Price?" *Business Week*, May 27, 1991, pp. 33-34.

16 Kevin McDermott, "Border Crossing Ahead," *D & B Reports*, January-February 1991, p. 24.

17 Sumantra Ghoshal, "Global Strategy: An Organizing Framework," *Strategic Management Journal*, Vol. 8, 1987, pp. 425-440.

18 Ibid., p. 427.

19 Michael Zielenziger, "India's star rises in technology race," *San Jose Mercury News*, July 4, 1995, pp. 1A & 22A.

20 Paul Blustein, "Hewlett-Packard's Role in Asia Marks the Growth Area for U.S.," *Philadelphia Inquirer*, November 26, 1993, p. C4.

21 From an advertisement placed by Ranbaxy Laboratories Limited in *India Abroad*, May 5, 1995, p. 11.

CHAPTER 2

1   United Nations Conference on Trade and Development, *World Investment Report 1994*, United Nations, New York, 1994, p. 13 and table II.10, p. 59.

493

Endnotes

2   Ibid., Table I.6, p. 17.

3   Ibid., Table I.8, p. 19.

4   Pete Engardio, Rob Hof, Elizabeth Malkin, Neil Gross, and Karen Lowry Miller, "High Tech Jobs all over the World," *Business Week,* 21st Century Capitalism, Special 1994 Bonus Issue, November 18, 1994, pp. 112-119.

5   Ibid.

6   Ibid.

7   United Nations Conference on Trade and Development, *World Investment Report 1994,* United Nations, New York, 1994, p. 5.

8   *Business Week,* "The Business Week 1000," July 10, 1995, p. 62.

9   Ibid., p. 62.

10   "Japanese Banking: The Big One," *The Economist,* April 1, 1995, p. 61.

11   Christopher Farell, "The Triple Revolution," *Business Week*, Special 1994 Bonus Issue, November 18, 1994, p. 17.

12   Ibid.

13   "Selling the State," *The Economist,* August 21, 1993.

14   Rahul Jacob, "India is Open for Business," *Fortune,* November 16, 1992, p. 128.

15   Rahul Jacob, "The Big Rise: Middle Classes Explode Around the Globe, Bringing New Markets and Prosperity," *Fortune,* May 30, 1994, pp. 74-90.

16   Ibid.

17   Bill Saporito, "Where the Global Action Is," *Fortune,* Autumn/Winter 1993, pp. 63-65.

18   Ibid.

19   Rahul Jacob, "The Big Rise: Middle Classes Explode Around the Globe, Bringing New Markets and Prosperity," *Fortune,* May 30, 1994, p. 78.

20   Gene Bylinsky, "The Digital Factory," *Fortune,* November 14, 1994, pp. 92-107.

21   Kelly Holland, Paula Dwyer, and Gail Edmondson, "Technobanking Takes Off," *Business Week,* 21st Century Capitalism, Special 1994 Bonus Issue, November 18, 1994, pp. 52-53.

22   Paula Dwyer, Pete Engardio, Zachary Schiller, and Stanley Reed, "Tearing Up Today's Organization Chart," *Business Week*, 21st Century Capitalism, Special 1994 Bonus Issue, November 18, 1994, p. 83.

23   Catherine Arnst, "The Networked Corporation," *Business Week,* June 26, 1995, pp. 86-89.

24   "The Global Economy," *The Economist,* October 1, 1994, p. 3.

25   Ibid.

26   Laurence Zuckerman, "Defying Gravity: Trade will make most Asian nations soar in 1994," *The Wall Street Journal Classroom Edition,* February 1994, pp. 12-13.

27   Kathleen Madigan, "In Fast-Growing Asia, Japan is Leaving the U.S. in the Dust," *Business Week,* September 12, 1994, p. 26.

28   David E. Sanger, "More Growth Predicted for New Markets," *The New York Times,* November 4, 1994, p. D1.

CHAPTER 3

1   See the classic study by Jacob Viner, *The Customs Union Issue,* Carnegie Endowment for International Peace, New York, 1950.

2   "The Trouble with Regionalism", *The Economist,* June 27, 1992, p. 79.

3   Ibid.

4   Jagdish Bhagwati, "Negotiating Trade Blocs," *India Today,* July 15, 1993, p. 65.

5   "GATT: The Eleventh Hour," *The Economist*, December 4, 1993, pp. 23-24.

6   *Economic Report of the President, February 1994*, United States Government Printing Office, Washington, D.C., 1994, p. 233.

7   "A Guide to GATT," *The Economist*, December 4, 1993, p. 25.

8   "Finally GATT May Fly," *Business Week*, December 20, 1993, p. 36.

9   *Survey of Current Business*, U.S. Department of Commerce, June 1994, p. 74.

10 Geri Smith, "Free Trade Isn't Coming Cheap," *Business Week*, December 6, 1993, pp. 58-59.

11 Ibid.

12 *Business Week*, November 22, 1993, p. 42.

13 Charles Goldsmith and James Pressley, "European Unity Boosts Export Prospects," *The Wall Street Journal*, July 25, 1994, p. B5A.

14 Ibid.

15 Ibid.

16 "European Union: Wishful Thinking," *The Economist*, September 24, 1994, pp. 84-85.

17 Ibid, p. 84.

18 "European Union: Back to the Drawing Board," *The Economist*, September 10, 1994, pp. 21-23; also Bill Javetski and Patrick Oster, "Europe: Unification for the Favored Few," *Business Week*, September 19, 1994, p. 54.

19 "Trade Roundup: A Roundup of Important Trade News in the Americas," *U.S./Latin Trade*, July 1994, p. 12.

20 Ibid.

21 Chile and Bolivia announced on June 25, 1996 their decision to join MERCUSOR making it a free-trade bloc encompassing nearly 210 million people and a combined gross national product of $907 billion.

22 *The Wall Street Journal*, September 22, 1994, p. A4.

23 *Defining a Pacific Community: A Report of the Carnegie Endowment Study Group*, Carnegie Endowment for International Peace, Washington, D.C., 1994, p. 15.

24 Bernard Wysocki, Jr., "In Asia, the Japanese Hope to 'Coordinate' what Nations Produce," *The Wall Street Journal*, August 20, 1990, pp. A1-A2.

CHAPTER 4

1   William D. Coplin, *The Functions of International Law*, Rand McNally Company, Chicago, 1966, pp. 8-9.

2   Ibid., pp. 3-4.

3   Faye Rice, "How Copycats Steal Billions," *Fortune*, April 22, 1991, pp. 157-164.

4   "Beijings Blatant Piracy Could Slash Its U.S. Trade," *Business Week*, April 22, 1991, p. 46.

5   Edward A. Gargan, "U.S. May Thwart China's Trade Goal," *The New York Times*, July 24, 1994, p. 14; Patrick E. Tyler, "China Pressing to Join Trade Club," *The New York Times*, November 14, 1994, p. D1.

6   Thomas L. Friedman, "China Faces U.S. Sanctions in Electronic Copyright Piracy," *The New York Times*, July 1, 1994, p. D2.

7   Patrick E. Tyler, "China Pressing to Join Trade Club," *The New York Times*, November 14, 1994, p. D2.

8   Thomas L. Friedman, "China Faces U.S. Sanctions in Electronic Copyright Piracy," *The New York Times*, July 1, 1994, p. D2.

9   Jessica M. Bailey and James Sood, "The Effect of Religious Affiliation on Consumer Behavior: A Preliminary Investigation," *Journal of Managerial Issues*, Vol. 5, No. 3, Fall 1993, p. 333.

10 Mushtaq Luqmani, Zahir A. Quaraeshi, and Linda Delene, "Marketing in Islamic Countries: A Viewpoint," *MSU Business Topics*, Summer 1980,

11 "Banking Behind the Veil," *The Economist*, April 4, 1992, p. 76.

12 Luiz Moutinho and M. Hisham Jabr, "Perspective on the Role of Marketing in Islamic Banking," *Journal of International Consumer Marketing*, Vol. 2, No. 3, 1990, pp. 29-47; Geraldine Brooks, "'Riddle of Riyadj' Islamic Law Thrives Amid Modernity," *The Wall Street Journal*, November 9, 1989, p. A1.

13 "Islamic Banking Rules Spell More Paperwork but the Same Result," *Business Asia*, March 11, 1991, p. 81.

14 Michael Litka, *International Dimensions of the Legal Environment of Business*, Second Edition, PWS-KENT Publishing Company, Boston, 1991, p. 214.

CHAPTER 5

1 John Plamenatz, *Ideology*, Praeger Publishers, New York, 1970, p. 15.

2 Roy C. Macridis, *Contemporary Political Ideologies, 5th ed.*, Harper-Collins Publishers, Inc., New York, 1992, p. 2.

3 Plamenatz, p. 2.

4 For more on the concepts of consensus and legitimacy please read Roy C. Macridis and Bernard E. Brown, (Eds.), *Comparative Politics: Notes and Readings, 3rd. ed.*, The Dorsey Press, Homewood, Ill., 1968, pp. 107-114.

5 Joan Edelman Spero, *The Politics of International Economic Relations*, 4th ed., St. Martin's Press, New York, 1990, p. 9.

6 Ibid., p. 4.

7 Elaine Kurtenbach, "Beijing cuts McDonald's deal short," *The Philadelphia Inquirer*, November 27, 1994, p. A1.

8 Ted Gurr, "A Causal Model of Civil Strife: A Comparative Model Using New Analysis," *The American Political Science Review*, Vol. 62, No. 4, December 1968, p. 1104.

9 Ibid., pp. 1105-1106.

10 Ibid., p. 1105.

11 Ibid., p. 1106.

12 Ibid.

CHAPTER 6

1 For an excellent documentation of incidents illustrating such blunders, see David Ricks, Marilyn C. Fu, and Jeffrey S. Arpan, *International Business Blunders*, Grid, Inc., Columbus, Ohio, 1974.

2 See, for example, Harlan Cleveland, Gerard J. Mangone, and John Clarke Adams, *The Overseas Americans*, McGraw-Hill Book Co., New York, 1960; John D. Montgomery, "Crossing the Culture Bars: An Approach to the Training of American Technicians for Overseas Assignments," World Politics, Vol. 13, No. 4, July 1961, 544-560; George M. Foster, *Traditional Cultures, and the impact of technological change*, Harper and Brothers, New York, 1962; John Fayerweather, *The Executive Overseas*, Syracuse University Press, Syracuse, 1959; and Conrad M. Arensberg and Anther H. Niehoff, *Introducing Social Change: A Manual for Americans Overseas*, Aldine Publishing Co., Chicago, 1964.

3 Don Adams, "The Monkey and the Fish: Cultural Pitfalls of an Educational Advisor," *International Development Review*, Vol. 2, No. 2, 1969, p. 22.

4 Melville J. Herskovits, *Man and His Works*, Alfred A. Knopf, New York, 1952, p. 17.

5   Clyde Kluckhohn, "The Study of Culture," in Daniel Lerner and Harold Laswell (eds.) *The Policy Sciences,* Stanford University Press, Stanford, 1951, p. 86.

6   David Dressler and Donald Carns, *Sociology, The Study of Human Interaction*, Alfred A. Knopf, New York, 1969, pp. 56-59.

7   Ibid., p. 60.

8   John L. Graham and Yoshihiro Sano, *Smart Bargaining: Doing Business with the Japanese*, Ballinger Publishing Co., Cambridge, Mass., 1989, p. 18.

9   Edward T. Hall, "The Silent Language in Overseas Business," *Harvard Business Review,* May-June 1960, p. 138.

10 Adapted from Elaine Sciolino, "Christopher Confers with Saudi King on Aid and Arms," *The New York Times,* March 13, 1995, p. A7.

11 Thomas R. Batten, *Communities and Their Development*, Oxford University Press, New York, 1957, pp. 10-11. Reprinted by permission.

12 Edward T. Hall and William Foote Whyte, "Intercultural Communication: A Guide to Men of Action," *Human Organization*, Vol. 19, No. 1, Spring 1960, p. 9. Reproduced from *Human Organization* by permission of the Society for Applied Anthropology.

13 Ibid., pp. 8-9.

14 *Business Week*, March 7, 1988, p. 28.

15 Daniel Pearl, "Federal Express Finds Its Pioneering Formula Falls Flat Overseas," *The Wall Street Journal*, April 15, 1991, p. A8.

16 Thomas F. O'Boyle, "Bridgestone Discovers Purchase of U.S. Firms Creates Big Problems," *The Wall Street Journal*, April 1, 1991, p. A1.

17 Geert Hofstede, *Culture's Consequences: International Differences in Work-Related Values*, Sage Publications, Beverly Hills, 1980; Geert Hofstede, "Motivation, Leadership, and Organizations: Do American Theories Apply Abroad?" *Organizational Dynamics*, Summer 1980, pp. 42-63.

18 Geert Hofstede and Michael Harris Bond, "The Confucius Connection: From Cultural Roots to Economic Growth," *Organizational Dynamics*, Vol. 16, No. 4, Spring 1988, pp. 4-21.

19 Richard H. Franke, Geert Hofstede, and Michael H. Bond, "Cultural Roots of Economic Performance," *Strategic Management Journal*, Vol. 12, 1991, p. 167.

20 Hofstede and Bond, pp. 16-17.

21 Franke, Hofstede, and Bond, pp. 165-173.

22 Herskovits, p. 17.

23 Clyde Haberman, "Jerusalem Journal, Dishing Up Lunch for A Land That Isn't All Kosher," *The New York Times,* April 16, 1992, p. A4.

CHAPTER 7

1   Jack Sawyer and Harold Guetzkow, "Bargaining and Negotiation in International Relations," in Herbert C. Kelman, (ed.), *International Behavior: A Social-Psychological Analysis*, Holt, Rinehart and Winston, New York, 1965, p. 466.

2   Jeswald W. Salacuse, "Making Deals in Strange Places: A Beginner's Guide to International Business Negotiations," *Negotiation Journal*, January 1988, pp. 5-13, reprinted in Roy L. Lewicki, Joseph A. Litterer, David M. Saunders, and John W. Minton, *Negotiation: Readings, Exercises, and Cases*, Richard D. Irwin, Burr Ridge, Illinois, 1995, pp. 521-529.

3   Some concepts for this section have been borrowed from Jeswald W. Salacuse, "Making Deals in Strange Places: A Beginner's Guide to International Business Negotiations," *Negotiation Journal*, January 1988, pp. 5-13.

4 Craig Torres, "Mexico's Woes Accelerate as Peso Falls Further," *The Wall Street Journal*, December 28, 1994, p. A3.

5 Tim Carrington, "U.S. Visit by India's Prime Minister Was Reminder of Hard Balancing Act," *The Wall Street Journal*, May 23, 1994, p. A10.

6 Ibid.

7 John J. Curran, "China's Investment Boom," *Fortune*, March 7, 1994, p. 117.

8 Ibid., p. 118.

9 Martin Crutsinger, "Clinton-Murayama downplay trade gap," *The Philadelphia Inquirer*, January 12, 1995, p. A3.

10 Mary Parker Follet, "Constructive Conflict," in H.C. Metcalf and L. Urwick, (Eds.), *Dynamic Administration: The Collected Papers of Mary Parker Follet*, Harper, New York, 1940.

11 The eight categories are adapted from Dean Allen Foster, *Bargaining Across Borders*, McGraw-Hill, Inc., New York, 1992, pp. 272-293; however, the ideas are derived from this source as well as from the author's own viewpoints.

12 Dean Allen Foster, *Bargaining Across Borders*, McGraw-Hill, Inc., New York, 1992, p. 272.

13 Ibid., pp. 287-288.

14 Ibid., p. 289.

15 Ibid., p. 292.

16 For a comprehensive and detailed treatment of the negotiating characteristics and patterns of different countries, the reader is referred to Frank L. Acuff, *How to Negotiate Anything with Anyone Anywhere Around the World*, AMACOM, New York, 1993; or to Dean Allen Foster, *Bargaining Across Borders: How to Negotiate Business Successfully Anywhere in the World*, McGraw-Hill, New York, 1992.

17 Rosalie L. Tung, "Handshakes Across the Sea: Cross-Cultural Negotiating for Business Success," *Organizational Dynamics*, 19:3, Winter, 1991, pp. 20-30.

18 Frank L. Acuff, *How to Negotiate Anything with Anyone Anywhere Around the World*, AMACOM, New York, 1993.

CHAPTER 8

1. Russell A. Ackoff, *A Concept of Corporate Planning*, Wiley Interscience, New York, 1970, p. 1.

2. Ibid., p. 4.

3. George Steiner, *Top Management Planning*, Macmillan, New York, 1969, p. 6.

4. Ibid.

5. M. Y. Yoshino, "International Business: What Is the Best Strategy?" *Business Quarterly*, Fall 1966, p. 47.

6. Arvind V. Phatak, *Managing Multinational Corporations*, Praeger Publishers, New York, 1974, p. 162.

CHAPTER 9

1 K.S. Nayar, "A Showcase for Information Technology," *India Abroad*, May 5, 1995, p. 30.

2 Doron P. Levin, "'Flexible' Plant for Fast-Changing Chrysler," *The New York Times*, September 9, 1994, p. 37; Alex Taylor III, "The Auto Industry Meets The New Economy," *Fortune*, September 5, 1994, pp. 56 and 58.

3 Kendall Roth and David Ricks, "Goal Configuration in a Global Industry Context," *Strategic Management Journal*, Vol. 15, 1994, pp. 103-120; George S. Yip, "Global Strategy in a World of Nations?" *Sloan Management Review*, Fall 1989, pp. 29-40.

4 Roth and Ricks, pp. 103-120.

5   Howard V. Perlmutter, "The Tortuous Evolution of the Multinational Corporation," *Columbia Journal of World Business*, Vol. 3, No. 1, January-February 1969, pp. 9-18.

6   Patrick Oster and John Rossant, "Call It Worldpool," *Business Week,* November 28, 1994, p. 98.

7   Ibid., p. 99.

8   Op. cit.

CHAPTER 10

1   Claire Poole, "Pepsico's Newest Generation," *Forbes*, February 18, 1991, p. 88.

2   *Business Week*, March 7, 1988, p. 55.

3   Sanjeev Agarwal and Sridhar Ramaswami, "Choice of Foreign Market Entry Mode: Impact of Ownership, Location, and Internalization Factors," *Journal of International Business Studies*, Vol. 23, No. 1, 1992, pp. 1-27.

4   Charles W. Hill, Peter Hwang, and Chan W. Kim, "An Eclectic Theory of the Choice of International Entry Mode," *Strategic Management Journal,* Vol. 11, 1990, pp. 117-128.

5   Ibid.

6   Ibid.

7   Agarwal and Ramaswami, pp. 1-27.

8   Krishna M. Erramilli, "The Experience Factor in Foreign Market Entry Behavior of Service Firms," *Journal of International Business Studies*, Vol. 22, No. 3, 1991, pp. 479-501.

9   Bruce Kogut and Harbir Singh, "Entering United States by Joint Venture: Competitive Rivalry and Industry Structure," in Farok Contractor and Peter Lorange, (Eds.), *Cooperative Strategies in International Business,* Lexington Books, Lexington, MA, 1988, pp. 241-251.

10   Gary Hamel and C. K. Prahalad, "Do You Really Have a Global Strategy," *Harvard Business Review,* July-August, 1985, pp. 139-148.

11   Hill, Hwang, and Kim, pp. 117-128.

12   Oliver E. Williamson, *Markets and Hierarchies: An Analysis of Antitrust Implications*, Free Press, New York, 1975; David J. Teece, "The Multinational Enterprise: Market Failure and Market Power Considerations," *Sloan Management Review*, September 1981, pp. 3-17.

13   Kogut and Singh, pp. 241-251.

14   Agarwal and Ramaswami, pp. 1-27.

15   Chan W. Kim and Peter Hwang, "Global Strategy and Multinationals' Entry Mode Choice," *Journal of International Business Studies*, Vol. 23, No. 1, 1992, pp. 29-53.

16   Agarwal and Ramaswami, pp. 1-27.

17   Bruce Kogut and Harbir Singh, "The Effect of National Culture on the Choice of Entry Mode," *Journal of International Business Studies*, Fall, 1988a, Vol. 19, No. 3, pp. 411-432.

18   Krishna M. Erramilli and C.P. Rao, "Choice of Market Entry Modes by Service Firms: Role of Market Knowledge," *Management International Review*, Vol. 30, 1990, p. i2.

19   Agarwal and Ramaswami, pp. 1-27.

20   Hubert Gatignon and Erin Anderson, "The Multinational Corporation's Degree of Control Over Foreign Subsidiaries: An Empirical Test of a Transaction Cost Explanation," *Journal of Law Economics and Organization*, Vol. iv, No. 2, 1988, pp. 305-336.

21   Agarwal and Ramaswami, pp. 1-27.

22   Kim and Hwang, pp. 29-53.

23   Gatignon and Anderson, pp. 305-336.

24   Gatignon and Anderson, pp. 305-336, and Kogut and Singh, *Effect of National Culture*, pp. 411-432.

25 Richard N. Osborn and Christopher C. Baughn, "Forms of Inter-Organizational Governance for Multinational Alliances," *Academy of Management Journal*, Vol. 33, No. 3, 1990, pp. 503-519.

26 Hamel and Prahalad, pp. 139-148.

27 Kim and Hwang, pp. 29-53.

28 Ibid., pp. 29-53.

29 John H. Dunning and Alan M. Rugman, "The Influence of Hymer's Dissertation on the Theory of Foreign Direct Investment," *AEA Papers and Proceedings*, May 1985.

30 Ibid.

31 Stephen H. Hymer, *The International Operations of National Firms: A Study of Direct Foreign Investment*, MIT Press, Cambridge, 1976 [1960].

32 Williamson.

33 Kogut and Singh, *The Effect of National Culture*, pp. 411-432.

34 Williamson.

35 John H. Dunning, "The Eclectic Paradigm of International Production: A Restatement and Some Possible Extensions," *Journal of International Business Studies*, Spring 1988, pp. 1-31.

36 Paul W. Beamish and John C. Banks, "Equity Joint Ventures and the Theory of the Multinational Enterprise," *Journal of International Business Studies*, Summer 1987, pp. 1-16.

37 Jean-Francois Hennart, "A Transaction Costs Theory of Equity Joint Ventures," *Strategic Management Journal*, Vol. 9, 1988, pp. 361-374.

38 Erin Anderson and Hubert Gatignon, "Modes of Foreign Entry: A Transaction Cost Analysis and Propositions," *Journal of International Business Studies*, Fall 1986, pp. 1-26.

39 Erramilli, pp. 479-501.

40 Gatignon and Anderson, pp. 411-432.

41 Agarwal and Ramaswami, pp. 1-27.

42 Kogut and Singh, "The Effect of National Culture on the Choice of Entry Mode," *Journal of International Business Studies*, Vol. 19, No. 3, pp. 411-432.

43 Hamel and Prahalad, pp. 139-148.

44 Hill, Hwang, and Kim, pp. 117-128.

45 Kim and Hwang, pp. 29-53.

CHAPTER 11

1 Udayan Gupta, "Sony Adopts Strategy to Broaden Ties with Small Firms," *The Wall Street Journal*, February 28, 1991, p. B2.

2 Stuart M. Dambrot, "Foreign Alliances that Make Sense," *Electronic Business*, September 3, 1990, p. 68.

3 Stephen D. Moore, "Volvo Contract on Joint Facility Appears Near," *The Wall Street Journal*, April 26, 1991, p. A12.

4 Michael J. McCarthy, "Coke, Nestle Get Together Over Coffee," *The Wall Street Journal*, November 30, 1990, p. B1.

5 Carole A. Shifrin, "Delta Travelers To Reach Heathrow On Virgin," *Aviation Week and Space Technology*, May 23, 1994, p. 28.

6 Richard Gibson, "Cereal Venture Is Planning Honey of a Battle in Europe," *The Wall Street Journal*, November 14, 1990, pp. B1 and B8.

7 Julia Flynn, Catherine Arnst, and Gail Edmondson, "Who'll be the First Global Company," *Business Week*, March 27, 1995, p. 117.

8 Ibid.

9 Douglas Lavin, "Sprint's Venture With Germany, France, Takes Step Forward Amid Many Delays," *The Wall Street Journal*, May 31, 1995, p. A12.

10 David P. Hamilton, "Nippon Telegraph & Telephone to Align With AT&T for Long-Distance Service," *The Wall Street Journal*, March 1, 1995, p. B2.

11 Jeremy Main, "Making Global Alliance Work," *Fortune*, December 17, 1990, p. 124.

12 Michael Selwyn, "Making Marriages of Convenience," *Asian Business*, January 1991, p. 26.

13 Jordan D. Lewis, "Competitive Alliances Redefine Companies," *Management Review*, April 1991, p. 14.

14 Jonathan B. Levine and Gail E. Schares, "IBM Europe Starts Swinging Back," *Business Week*, May 6, 1991, pp. 52-53.

15 Susan Carey, "Airline Ties Boost Revenue, GAO Says, But Transportation Agency Is Criticized," *The Wall Street Journal*, May 5, 1995, p. B4B.

16 Ibid.

17 Main, p. 124.

18 Gary Hamel, Yves L. Doz, and C. K. Prahalad, "Collaborate with Your Competitors and Win," *Harvard Business Review*, January-February 1989, p. 134.

19 Main, pp. 121-122.

20 Yumiko Ono, "Borden's Breakup with Meiji Milk Shows How a Japanese Partnership Can Curdle," *The Wall Street Journal*, February 2, 1991, p. B7.

21 For an excellent expose of the concept of core competence, see C. K. Prahalad and Gary Hamel, "The Core Competence of the Corporation," *Harvard Business Review*, May-June 1990, pp. 79-91.

22 Craig M. Watson, "Counter-Competition Abroad to Protect Home Markets," *Harvard Business Review*, January-February 1992, pp. 40-42.

23 Gary Hamel and C. K. Prahalad, "Do You Really Have a Global Strategy," *Harvard Business Review*, July-August 1985, pp. 139-148.

24 "The Revenge of Big Yellow," *The Economist*, November 10, 1990, pp. 77-78.

25 Maria Shao, Robert Neff, and Jeffrey Ryser, "For Levi's, A Flattering Fit Overseas," *Business Week*, November 5, 1990, pp. 76-77.

26 Nicholas Valery, "Consumer Electronics Survey," *The Economist*, April 13, 1991, p. 17.

27 "The Goal Is Genuine Internationalism," *Business Week*, July 16, 1990, p. 80.

28 David Woodruff, "A Little Machine that Won't Shred a Sari," *Business Week*, June 3, 1991, p. 100.

29 Amy Borrus, "Japan Streaks Ahead in East Asia," *Business Week*, May 7, 1990, p. 55.

CHAPTER 12

1 Raymond Vernon and Louis T. Wells, Jr., *Manager in the International Economy*, 3rd ed., Prentice-Hall, Englewood Cliffs, N.J., 1976, p. 31.

2 Michael G. Duerr and John M. Roach, *Organization and Control of International Operations*, The Conference Board, New York, 1973, p. 5.

3 Stanley Davis, "Basic Structures of Multinational Corporations," in Stanley Davis, Ed., *Managing and Organizing Multinational Corporations*, Pergamon Press, New York, 1979, p. 202.

4 Gilbert H. Clee and Wilbur M. Sachjan, "Organizing a Worldwide Business," *Harvard Business Review*, Vol. 42, No. 6, November-December 1964, p. 60.

5 Business International, *Organizing the Worldwide Corporation*, Research Report No. 69-4, Business International, New York, 1970, p. 9.

6 John M. Stopford and Louis T. Wells, Jr., *Managing the Multinational Enterprise*, Basic Books, New York, 1972, p. 51.

7   Stanley M. Davis, "Trends in the Organization of Multinational Corporations," *Columbia Journal of World Business,* Summer 1976, p. 60.

8   Peter J. Dowling, Randall S. Schuler, and Denice E. Welch, *International Dimensons of Human Resource Management,* Wadsworth Publishing Company, Belmont, California, 1994, p. 27.

9   Davis, "Basic Structures," p. 203.

10 Ibid., p. 205.

11 Arvind V. Phatak, *Managing Multinational Corporations,* Praeger Publishers, New York, 1974, p. 183.

12 Duerr and Roach, p. 12.

13 Ibid., p. 10.

14 Davis, "Trends in the Organization," p. 66.

15 Stopford and Wells, p. 87.

16 Stanley M. Davis and Paul R. Lawrence, "Problems of Matrix Organizations," *Harvard Business Review,* May-June 1978, p. 4.

17 Peter Drucker, *Management: Tasks, Responsibilities, Practices,* Harper & Row, New York, 1974, p. 598.

18 Bruce Caldwell, "Industrious IBM?" *Informationweek,* May 23, 1994, p. 15; Ira Sager, "Big Blue Wants the World to Know Who's Boss," *Business Week,* September 26, 1994, p. 78.

19 ". . . and Other Ways to Peel the Onion," *The Economist,* January 7, 1995, p. 52.

CHAPTER 13

1   Patrick Oster, David Woodruff, Neil Gross, Sunita Wadekar Bhargava, and Elizabeth Lesley, "The Fast Track Leads Overseas," *Business Week,* November 1, 1993, pp. 64-68.

2   Edwin L. Miller and Joseph L. C. Cheng, "A Closer Look at the Decision to Accept an Overseas Position," *Management International Review,* Vol. 18, 1978, pp. 25-27.

3   Rosalie L. Tung, "U.S. Multinationals: A Study of Their Selection and Training Procedures for Overseas Assignments," *Academy of Management Proceedings,* 1979, p. 298.

4   Ibid.

5   R. L. Desatnick and M. L. Bennett, *Human Resource Management in the Multinational Company,* Nichols Publishing Co., New York, 1977, pp. 233-234.

6   Sanford Rose, "The Rewarding Strategies of Multinationalism," *Fortune,* September 15, 1968, p. 180.

7   Ibid.

8   Ibid.

9   Cecil G. Howard, "The Multinational Corporation: Impact on Nativization," *Personnel,* January-February 1972, p. 42.

10 Tung, p. 298.

11 Joseph LaPalombara and Stephen Black, *Multinational Corporations and National Elites: A Study of Tensions,* The Conference Board, New York, 1976, p. 57.

12 Jean E. Heller, "Criteria for Selecting an International Manager," *Personnel,* Vol. 57, May-June 1980, p. 48.

13 Ibid.

14 Arvind V. Phatak, *Managing Multinational Corporations,* Praeger Publishers, New York, 1974, p. 194.

15 William Voris, " Considerations in Staffing for Overseas Management Needs," *Personnel Journal,* June 1975, p. 354.

16 Heller, p. 49.

17 Robert C. Maddox, "Solving the Overseas Personnel Problem," *Personnel Journal,* Vol. 44, No. 2, February 1965, p. 93.

18 "Gauging a Family's Suitability for a Stint Overseas," *Business Week,* April 16, 1979, p. 127.

19 Tung, pp. 298-299.

20 "Gauging a Family's Suitability," pp. 127-130.

21 Joann S. Lubin, "Companies Use Cross-Cultural Training To Help Their Employees Adjust Abroad," *The Wall Street Journal,* August 4, 1992, p. B1.

22 Oster et al, pp. 64-68.

23 Alison R. Lanier, "Selecting and Preparing Personnel for Overseas Transfers," *Personnel Journal,* Vol. 58, March 1979, pp. 162-163.

24 Philip R. Harris and Robert T. Moran, *Managing Cultural Differences,* Gulf Publishing Co., Houston, 1979, p. 149.

25 Ibid., pp. 128-129. Reprinted by permission.

26 Oster et al, pp. 64-68.

27 Lubin, p. B1.

28 Joann S. Lubin, "Spouses Find Themselves Worlds Apart as Global Commuter Marriages Increase," *The Wall Street Journal,* August 19, 1992, p. B1.

29 Rosalie L. Tung, "Selection and Training of Personnel for Overseas Assignments," *Columbia Journal of World Business,* Spring 1981, p. 74.

30 John S. McClenahan, "The Overseas Manager: Not Actually a World Away," *Industry Week,* November 1, 1976, p. 53.

31 Ibid.

32 Lee Smith, "The Hazards of Coming Home," *Dun's Review,* October 1975, p. 72.

33 Joann S. Lubin, "Managing Your Career," *The Wall Street Journal,* August 25, 1993, p. B1.

34 "How to Ease Re-entry after Overseas Duty," *Business Week,* June 11, 1979, p. 82.

35 Lubin, "Managing Your Career," p. B1.

36 Ibid., p. 84.

37 McClenahan, p. 53.

38 Oster et al, pp. 64-68.

39 Desatnick and Bennet, p. 168.

40 Paul E. Illman, *Developing Overseas Managers—And Managers Overseas,* AMACOM, New York, 1980, p. 178.

41 Ibid., p. 176.

42 Howard V. Perlmutter, "The Tortous Evolution of the Multinational Corporation," *Columbia Journal of World Business,* Vol. 3, No. 1, January-February 1969, pp. 11-14.

43 W. A. Borrman, "The Problem of Expatriate Personnel and Their Selection in International Enterprises," *Management International Review,* Vol. 8, No. 4-5, 1968, pp. 37-38.

44 Yoram Zeira and Ehud Harari, "Genuine Multinational Staffing Policy Expectations and Realities," *Academy of Management Journal,* Vol. 20, No. 2, 1977, p. 328.

45 Borrman, p. 40.

46 Graef S. Crystal, *Compensating U.S. Expatriates Abroad: An AMA Management Briefing,* American Management Association, New York, 1972, pp. 1-3.

47 E. J. Kolde, *The Multinational Company,* Lexington Books, Lexington, Mass., 1974, pp. 176-178.

48 Ibid., pp. 178-179.

49 Ibid., pp. 179-180.

50 Ibid., pp. 180-181.

51 *Compensating International Executives,* Business International Corporation, New York, 1970, p. 33.

52 Ibid.

53 Ibid.

54 Crystal, p. 44.

55 Ibid.

56 Ibid., p. 9.

57 David Young, "Fair Compensation for Expatriates," *Harvard Business Review*, Vol. 51, No. 4, July-August 1973, p. 119.

58 Ibid., pp. 119-120.

59 Ibid., pp. 120-121.

60 *Compensating International Executives*, pp. 23-25.

61 Crystal, pp. 18-19.

62 Young, pp. 123-145.

63 Ibid.

64 Ibid.

65 Crystal, p. 10.

66 This section written by Bill Roberts, graduate student in Business at Temple University, based on material contained in: Tara Parker-Pope, "Culture Clash: Do U.S.-Style Stock Compensation Plans Make Sense in Other Countries? *The Wall Street Journal*, April 12, 1995, p. R7.

67 Shawn Tully, "Where People Live Best," *Fortune*, March 11, 1991, pp. 44-54.

CHAPTER 14

1 Martin J. Gannon, *Management: An Organizational Perspective*, Little, Brown and Co., Boston, 1977, p. 140.

2 Peter F. Drucker, *An Introductory View of Management*, Harper & Row, New York, 1977, p. 424.

3 George A. Steiner, *Strategic Planning*, The Free Press, New York, 1979, p. 268.

4 Gannon, p. 143.

5 Steiner, p. 220.

6 Ibid., p. 221.

7 Gannon, p. 141.

8 Ibid., p. 157.

9 David Clutterbuck, "Breaking Through the Cultural Barriers," *International Management*, December 1980, p. 41.

10 Ibid.

11 Arvind V. Phatak, *Managing Multinational Corporations*, Praeger Publishers, New York, 1974, p. 225.

12 Sydney M. Robbins and Robert B. Stobaugh, "The Bent Measuring Stick for Foreign Subsidiaries," *Harvard Business Review*, Vol. 51, No. 5, September-October 1973, p. 82.

13 Larry Martz and Rich Thomas, "The Corporate Shell Game: How Multinational Firms Use 'Transfer Pricing' to Evade at Least $20 Billion in U.S. Taxes," *Newsweek*, April 15, 1991, pp. 48-49.

14 C. K. Prahalad and Yves I. Doz, "An Approach to Strategic Control in MNCs," *Sloan Management Review*, Summer 1981, pp. 5-13.

15 Ibid., p. 8.

16 Ibid.

CHAPTER 15

1 Paul W. Taylor, *Principles of Ethics: An Introduction to Ethics*, 2nd ed., Dickenson, Encino, Calif., 1975, p. 1.

2   Sita C. Amba-Rao, " Multinational Corporate Social Responsibility, Ethics, Interactions, and Third World Governments: An Agenda for the 1990s," *Journal of Business Ethics*, Vol. 12, 1993, p. 553.

3   Davis Weir and Mark Schapiro, *Circle of Poison*, Institute for Food and Development Policy, San Francisco, 1981, p. 22.

4   O. C. Ferrell and John Fraedrich, *Business Ethics: Ethical Decision Making and Cases*, 2nd ed., Houghton Mifflin Company, Boston, 1994, p. 60.

5   J. S. Mill, *Utilitarianism*, Bobbs-Merrill, Indianapolis, 1957, (1863).

6   Richard Brandt, *Ethical Theory*, Prentice-Hall, Inc., Englewood Cliffs, N.J., 1959, pp. 253-254.

7   Donald M. Borchert and David Stewart, *Exploring Ethics*, Macmillan Publishing Company, New York, 1986, p. 199.

8   Ibid.

9   Ferrell and Fraedrich, p. 57.

10 Gerald F. Cavanagh, Dennis J. Moberg, and Manuel Velasquez, "The Ethics of Organizational Politics," *Academy of Management Review*, Vol. 6, No. 3, 1981, p. 366.

11 Adapted from Cavanagh, Moberg, and Velasquez, "The Ethics of Organizational Politics," p. 366.

12 Thomas Donaldson, *The Ethics of International Business*, Oxford University Press, New York, 1989, p. 14.

13 Clarence C. Walton, *The Moral Manager*, Ballinger Publishing Company, Cambridge, Mass., 1988, p. 110.

14 Kathleen A. Getz, "International Codes of Conduct: An Analysis of Ethical Reasoning," *Journal of Business Ethics*, Vol. 9, 1990, p. 571.

15 Getz, p. 569.

16 The material on codes of conduct for MNCs is quoted from William C. Frederick, "The Moral Authority of Transnational Corporate Codes," *Journal of Business Ethics*, Vol. 10, 1992, pp. 166-167.

17 William D. Montalbano, "A Challenge to Italy's Status Quo," *The Philadelphia Inquirer*, March 21, 1993, pp. E1 and E4.

18 "Hands up all those hit by sleaze," *The Economist*, October 29, 1994, pp. 55-56.

19 Andy Pasztor and Bruce Ingersoll, "Buying Business: Some Weapons Makers are Said to Continue Illicit Foreign Outlays," *The Wall Street Journal*, November 5, 1993, pp. A1 and A5; Douglas Pasternak, "Selling Hardware Overseas," *U.S. News and World Report*, November 15, 1993, p. 64.

20 Pasztor and Ingersoll, p. A5.

21 Arthur Aronoff, "Antibribery Provisions of the Foreign Corrupt Practices Act," National Trade Data Bank, June 26, 1992.

22 Jerry Landauer, "Proposed treaty against business bribes gets poor reception overseas, U.S. finds," *The Wall Street Journal*, February 28, 1977, p. 28.

23 Barry M. Richman, "Can We Prevent Questionable Foreign Payments?" *Business Horizons*, June 1979, pp. 14-19.

24 John L. Graham, "The Foreign Corrupt Practices Act," *Journal of International Business Studies*, Winter 1984, pp. 107-121.

25 Robert D. Hass, "Ethics in the Trenches," *Across the Board*, May 1994, pp. 12-13.

26 John A. Byrne, "Businesses are Signing Up for Ethics 101," *Business Week*, February 15, 1988, pp. 56-57.

27 Hass, pp. 12-13.

28 Byrne, pp. 56-57.

29 "Thousands in Pakistan call for end to child labor," *The Philadelphia Inquirer*, April 26, 1995, p. A8.

30 Hass, pp. 12-13.

31 Ibid.

32 Ibid.

33 Adapted from Theodore C. Sorensen, "Improper Payments Abroad: Perspectives and Proposals," *Foreign Affairs*, Vol. 54, No. 4, July 1976, pp. 719-733.

Further Readings

Ackoff, Russell A., *A Concept of Corporate Planning*, Wiley & Sons, New York, 1970.

Adams, Dan, "The Monkey and the Fish: Cultural Pitfalls of an Educational Advisor," *International Development Review*, No. 2, 1969.

Arensberg, Conrad M., and Arthur H. Neihoff, *Introducing Social Change: A Manual for Americans Overseas*, Aldine Publishing Co., Chicago, 1964.

Babbar, Sunil, and Arun Rai., "Competitive Intelligence for International Business," *Long Range Planning*, Vol. 26, No. 3, June 1993, pp. 103-113.

Batten, Thomas R., *Communities and Their Development*, Oxford University Press, New York, 1957.

Bible, Geoffrey C., "Global Competition: Getting Ahead, Staying Ahead," *Executive Speeches*, Vol. 7, No. 2, October/November 1992, pp. 1-6.

Black, Stewart J., and Hal B. Gregersen, "The Other Half of the Picture: Antecedents of Spouse Cross-Cultural Adjustment," *Journal of International Business Studies*, Vol. 22, No. 3, Third Quarter, 1991, pp. 461-477.

Borrman, W. A., "The Problem of Expatriate Personnel and Their Selection in International Enterprises," *Management International Review*, No. 4-5, 1968.

Boyacigiller, Nakiye, "The Role of Expatriates in the Management of Interdependence, Complexity, and Risk in Multinational Corporations," *Journal of International Business Studies*, Vol. 21, No. 3, Third Quarter, 1990, pp. 357-381.

Clee, Gilvert H., and Wilbur M. Sachtjan, "Organizing a Worldwide Business," *Harvard Business Review*, Vol. 42, No. 6, November-December 1964.

Cleveland, Harlan, Gerard J. Mangone, and John C. Adams, *The Overseas Americans*, McGraw-Hill, New York, 1960.

Clutterbuck, David, "Breaking Through the Cultural Barriers," *International Management*, December 1980.

Compensating International Executives, Business International Corporation, New York, 1970.

Crystal, Graef S., *Compensating U.S. Expatriates Abroad: An AMA Management Briefing*, American Management Association, New York, 1972.

Daniel, Shirley J., and Wolf D. Reitsperger, "Management Control Systems for J.I.T.: An Empirical Comparison of Japan and the US," *Journal of International Business Studies*, Vol. 22, No. 4, Fourth Quarter 1991, pp. 603-617.

Daniels, John D., and Lee H. Radebaugh, *International Business: Environments and Operations*, 5th ed., Addison-Wesley, Reading, Mass., 1989.

Davidson, William H., *Global Strategic Management*, John Wiley & Sons, New York, 1982.

Davis, Stanley M., "Trends in the Organization of Multinational Corporations," *Columbia Journal of World Business*, Summer 1976.

——*Managing and Organizing Multinational Corporations*, Pergamon Press, New York, 1979.

Davis, Stanley M., and Paul R. Lawrence, "Problems of Matrix Organizations," *Harvard Business Review*, May-June 1978.

Denali, Jacquelyn, "Keeping Growth Under Control," *Nation's Business*, Vol. 81, No. 7, July 1993, pp. 31-32.

Desatnick, R. L., and M. L. Bennett, *Human Resource Management in the Multinational Company*, Nichols, New York, 1977.

Domsch, M., and B. Lichtenberger, "Managing the Global Manager: Pre-Departure Training and Development for German Expatriates in China and Brazil," *Journal of Management Development*, Vol. 10, No. 7, 1991, pp. 41-52.

Dowling, Peter J., Randall S. Schuler, Denice E. Welch, *International Dimensions of Human Resource Management*, Wadsworth Publishing Company, Belmont, California, 1994.

Dressler, David, and Donald Carns, *Sociology, The Study of Human Interactions*, Alfred A. Knopf, New York, 1969.

Drucker, Peter, *Management: Tasks, Responsibilities, Practices*, Harper & Row, New York, 1974.

Drucker, Peter F., *An Introductory View of Management*, Harper & Row, New York, 1977.

Duerr, Michael G., and John M. Roach, *Organization and Control of International Operations*, The Conference Board, New York, 1973.

Erdmann, Peter B., "When Businesses Cross International Borders: Strategic Alliances and Their Alternatives," *Columbia Journal of World Business*, Vol. 28, No. 2, Summer 1993, pp. 107-108.

Farmer, Richard N., and Barry B. Richman, *International Business: An Operational Theory*, Richard D. Irwin, Homewood, Ill., 1966.

Fayerweather, John, *The Executive Overseas*, Syracuse University Press, Syracuse, 1959.

Feldman, Daniel C., and Holly B. Tompson, "Entry Shock, Culture Shock: Socializing the New Breed of Global Managers," *Human Resource Management*, Vol. 31, No. 4, Winter 1992, pp. 345-362.

Foster, George M., *Traditional Cultures, and the impact of technological change*, Harper & Brothers, New York, 1962.

Francis, June N.P., "When in Rome? The Effects of Cultural Adaptation on Intercultural Business Negotiations," *Journal of International Business Studies*, Vol. 22, No. 3, Third Quarter 1991, pp. 403-428.

Franko, Lawrence G., "Who Manages Multinational Enterprises?" *Columbia Journal of World Business*, Vol. 8, No. 2, Summer 1973.

Gannon, Martin J., *Management: An Organizational Perspective*, Little, Brown and Co., Boston, 1977.

Geringer, Michael J., and Colette A. Frayne, "Human Resource Management and International Joint Venture Control: A Parent Company Perspective," *Management International Review*, Vol. 30, 1990, pp. 103-120.

Glover, M. Katherine, "Do's & Taboos: Cultural Aspects of International Business," *Business America*, Vol. 111, No. 15, Aug. 13, 1990, pp. 2-6.

Goggin, William C., "How the Multidimensional Structure Works at Dow Corning," *Harvard Business Review*, January-February 1974.

Hall, Edward T., "The Silent Language in Overseas Business," *Harvard Business Review*, May-June 1960.

——*The Silent Language*, Anchor Press Doubleday, Anchor Books Edition, Garden City, N.Y., 1973.

Hall, Edward T., and William F. Whyte, "Intercultural Communication: A Guide to Men of Action," *Human Organization*, Vol. 19, No. I, Spring 1960.

Hamel, Gary, and C. K. Prahalad, "Do You Really Have a Global Strategy?" *Harvard Business Review*, July-August 1985, pp. 139-148.

——"Strategic Intent," *Harvard Business Review*, May-June 1989, pp. 63-76.

Hamel, Gary, Yves L. Doz, and C. K. Prahalad, "Collaborate with Your Competitors and Win," *Harvard Business Review*, January-February 1989, pp. 133-139.

Harrell, Gilbert D., and Richard O. Kiefer, "Multinational Strategic Market Portfolios," *MSU Business Topics*, Winter 1981, pp. 5-15.

Harris, Philip R., and Robert T. Moran, *Managing Cultural Differences*, Gulf Publishing Co., Houston, 1979.

——*Managing Cultural Differences*, 2nd ed., Gulf Publishing Company, Houston, Texas, 1987.

Heller, Jean E., "Criteria for Selecting an International Manager," *Personnel*, Vol. 57, May-June 1980.

Herskovits, Melville J., *Man and His Works*, Alfred A. Knopf, New York, 1954.

Howard, Cecil G., "The Multinational Corporation: Impact on Nativization," *Personnel*, January-February 1972.

Illman, Paul E., *Developing Overseas Managers—And Managers Overseas*, AMACOM, New York, 1980.

Further Reading

Kobrin, Stephen, "An Empirical Analysis of the Determinants of Global Integration," *Strategic Management Journal*, 1991, pp. 12, 17-31.

Kogut, Bruce, "Designing Global Strategies: Comparative and Competitive Value-Added Chains," *Sloan Management Review*, Summer 1985, pp. 15-28.

——"Designing Global Strategies: Profiting from Operational Flexibility," *Sloan Management Review*, Fall 1985, pp. 27-38.

Kogut, Bruce and Nalin Kulatilaka, "Operating Flexibility, Global Manufacturing, and the Option Value of a Multinational Network," *Management Science*, 40(1), 1994, pp. 123-139.

Lanier, Alison R., "Selecting and Preparing Personnel for Overseas Transfers," *Personnel Journal*, March 1979.

LaPalombara, Joseph, and Stephen Blank, *Multinational Corporations and National Elites: A Study of Tensions*, The Conference Board, New York, 1976.

——*Multinational Corporations in Comparative Perspective*, The Conference Board, New York, 1977.

Lei, David, and John W. Slocum, Jr., Global Strategy, Competence-Building and Strategic Alliances, *California Management Review*, Vol. 35, (1), Fall 1992, pp. 81-97.

Lerner, Daniel, and Harold D. Lasswell, eds., *The Policy Sciences*, Stanford University Press, Stanford, 1951.

Luqmani, Mushtaq, Zahir A. Quraeshi, and Linda Delene, "Marketing in Islamic Countries: A Viewpoint," *MSU Business Topics*, Summer 1980.

Maddox, Robert C., "Solving the Overseas Personnel Problem," *Personnel Journal*, June 1975.

Maruyama, Magoroh, "Lessons from Japanese Management Failures in Foreign Countries," *Human Systems Management*, Vol. 11, No. 1, 1992, pp. 41-48.

McClenahan, John S., "The Overseas Manager: Not Actually a World Away," *Industry Week*, November 1, 1976.

Miller, Edwin L., and Joseph L. C. Cheng, "A Closer Look at the Decision to Accept an Overseas Position," *Management International Review*, Vol. 18, 1978.

Montgomery, John D., "Crossing the Culture Bars: An Approach to the Training of American Technicians for Overseas Assignments," *World Politics*, Vol. 13, No. 4, July 1961.

Moskowitz, Daniel B., "How to Cut It Overseas," *International Business*, Vol. 5, No. 10, October 1992, pp. 76, 78.

Ohmae, Kenichi, "The Global Logic of Strategic Alliances," *Harvard Business Review*, March-April 1989, pp. 143-154.

Organizing the Worldwide Corporation, Research Report No. 69-4. Business International, New York, 1970.

Perlmutter, Howard V., "The Fortuitous Evolution of the Multinational Corporation," *Columbia Journal of World Business*, January-February 1969.

Phatak, Arvind V., *Evolution of World Enterprises*, American Management Association, New York, 1971.

——*Managing Multinational Corporations*, Praeger Publishers, New York, 1974.

Robbins, Sydney M., and Robert B. Stobaugh, "The Bent Measuring Stick for Foreign Subsidiaries," *Harvard Business Review*, September-October 1973.

Rose, Stanford, "The Rewarding Strategies of Multinationalism," *Fortune*, September 15, 1968.

Ricks, David, Marilyn Y. C. Fu, and Jeffrey S. Arpan, *International Business Blunders*, Grid, Inc., Columbus, Ohio, 1974.

Schwendiman, John S., *Strategic and Long-Range Planning for the Multinational Corporation*, Praeger Publishers, New York, 1973.

Shanks, David C., "Strategic Planning for Global Competition," *Journal of Business Strategy*, Winter 1985, pp. 80-89.

Simon, Jeffrey D., "A Theoretical Perspective on Political Risk," *Journal of International Business Studies*, Winter 1984, pp. 123-143.

Smith, Lee, "The Hazards of Coming Home," *Dun's Review*, October 1975.

"Stages of Global Development," *Chief Executive*, Jan/Feb 1993, pp. 6-9.

Steiner, George A., *Top Management Planning*, Macmillan, New York, 1969.

Steiner, George, *Strategic Planning*, The Free Press, New York, 1979.

Stopford, John M., and Louis T. Wells, Jr., *Managing the Multinational Enterprise,* Basic Books, New York, 1972.

Sugiura, Hideo, "How Honda Localizes Its Global Strategy," *Sloan Management Review*, Fall 1990, pp. 77-82.

Terpstra, Vern, *The Cultural Environment of International Business*, South-Western Publishing Company, Cincinnati, Ohio, 1978.

Townsend, Anthony N., Scott K. Dow, and Steven E. Markham, "An Examination of Country and Culture-Based Differences in Compensation Practice," *Journal of International Business Studies*, Vol. 21, No. 4, Fourth Quarter 1990, pp. 667-678.

Tung, Rosalie L., "U.S. Multinationals: A Study of Their Selection and Training Procedures for Overseas Assignments," *Academy of Management Proceedings*, 1979.

——"Selection and Training of Personnel for Overseas Assignments," *Columbia Journal of World Business*, Winter 1981.

Turpin, Dominique, "Strategic Alliances with Japanese Firms: Myths and Realities," *Long Range Planning*, Vol. 26, No. 4, August 1993, pp. 11-15.

Ueno, Susumu, and Sekaran Uma, "The Influence of Culture on Budget Control Practices in the U.S.A. and Japan: An Empirical Study," *Journal of International Business Studies*, Vol. 23, No. 4, Fourth Quarter 1992, pp. 659-674.

UNCTAD, *World Investment Report, 1993, Transnational Corporations and Integrated International Production*, United Nations, New York, 1993.

Vernon, Raymond, and Louis T. Wells, Jr., *Manager in the International Economy*, 4th ed., Prentice-Hall, Englewood Cliffs, N.J., 1981.

Vincent, Edgar, "Developing Managers for an International Business," *Journal of Management Development*, Vol. 7, No. 6, 1988, pp. 14-20.

Voris, William, "Considerations in Staffing for Overseas Management Needs," *Personnel Journal*, June 1975.

Walle, A.H., "International Business and Raging Tigers: Operationalizing the Global Paradigm," *Management Decision*, Vol. 30, No. 2, 1992, pp. 35-39.

Walters, Kenneth D., and R. Jose Monsen, "State-Owned Business Abroad; New Competitive Threat," *Harvard Business Review*, March-April 1979, pp. 160-170.

Weigand, Robert E., "International Trade Without Money," *Harvard Business Review*, November-December, 1977.

Yoshino, M. Y., "International Business: What Is the Best Strategy?" *Business Quarterly*, Fall 1966.

Young, David, "Fair Compensation for Expatriates," *Harvard Business Review*, July-August 1973.

Zeria, Yoram, and Ehud Harari, "Genuine Multinational Staffing Policy: Expectations and Realities," *Academy of Management Journal*, Vol. 20, No. 2, 1977.

Index